MIMOLOGICS

Mimologics

(*Mimologiques: Voyage en Cratylie*)

Gérard Genette

Translated by Thaïs E. Morgan

With a Foreword by

Gerald Prince

University of Nebraska

Lincoln & London

1995

© Éditions du Seuil, 1976.
© 1994 by the University of Nebraska Press.
All rights reserved.
Manufactured in the United States of America.
The paper in this book meets the minimum require-
ments of American National Standard for
Information Sciences — Permanence of Paper for
Printed Library Materials, ANSI Z39.48-1984.
Library of Congress Cataloging in Publication Data
Genette, Gérard, 1930–
[Mimologiques. English]
Mimologics-Mimologiques: voyage en Cratylie
Gérard Genette: translated by Thaïs E. Morgan:
with a foreword by Gerald Prince.   p.   cm.
Includes bibliographical references and index.
ISBN 0-8032-2129-0. — ISBN 0-8032-7044-5 (pbk.)
1. Language and languages. I. Morgan, Thaïs E.
II. Title III. Mimologiques.
P106.G42513 1995 400–dc20
94-28679 CIP

THIS TRANSLATION
IS DEDICATED TO
BOB SCHOLES

Contents

Foreword   ix

Publisher's Preface   xiii

Translator's Preface   xv

Invitation to a Voyage in Cratylusland, Thaïs E. Morgan xxi

MIMOLOGICS

Introduction   3

Chapter 1   Eponymy of the Name   7

Chapter 2   *De ratione verborum*   29

Chapter 3   *Soni rerum indices*   37

Chapter 4   Hermogenes, the Master of Words   43

Chapter 5   Mimographisms   53

Chapter 6   Painting and Derivation   65

Chapter 7   Generalized Hieroglyphics   91

Chapter 8   Onomatopoetics   115

Chapter 9   White Bonnet/Bonnet White   143

Chapter 10   Internal Inflection   179

Chapter 11   Desert Languages   189

Chapter 12   Failing Natural Languages   201

Chapter 13   The Age of Names   249

Chapter 14   The Stakes of Writing   261

Chapter 15   *Signe: Singe*   277

Chapter 16   Taking Sides with Words   297

Chapter 17   The Genre and Gender of Reverie   301

Chapter 18   Mimophony Restricted   309

Notes   337

Index   431

Foreword

For over thirty years Gérard Genette has been associated with literary structuralism. *Figures* (1966) established his reputation as a critic and theorist. Comprising eighteen essays written between 1959 and 1965, it evinces his range (from Sponde and Saint-Amant to Proust, Borges, and Barthes), his acuity (I must mention at least "Silences de Flaubert," "Vertige fixé" on Robbe-Grillet, "Structuralisme et critique littéraire," "Figures"), his view of poetics as being to literature what linguistics is to language, and his wonderful sense of figure — Genette defines the figural as "the tiny but vertiginous space that opens up between... two languages in the same language." Articles such as "Frontières du récit," in the famous issue of *Communications* (number 8) on the structural analysis of narrative, and "Vraisemblance et motivation," in another celebrated issue (number 11) of the same journal, as well as *Figures II* (1969) — which reprints both pieces together with important essays on Proust, rhetoric, poetics, and the space of literature — confirmed his distinction. In 1970 Genette, Cixous, and Todorov founded *Poétique*, the finest journal in French (and perhaps in any language) devoted to poetics. Two years later Genette published *Figures III*, which contained the classic "Discours du récit" (*Narrative Discourse*) and made him narratologically preeminent. The following two decades saw the publication of *Mimologiques* (1976), on Plato's *Cratylus* and a tradition that believes in essential links between words and things; *Introduction à l'architexte* (1979), on generic theory; *Palimpsestes* (1982), on hypertextuality, or the set of relations connecting two texts, one of which results from the transformation of the other; *Nouveau discours du récit* (1983), which refines and develops some of the arguments advanced in *Narrative Discourse; Seuils* (1987), an investigation of paratextuality, of the links between texts and their paratexts (titles, subtitles, epigraphs, prefaces, book jackets, and so on); and, most recently, *Fiction et diction* (1991), on the conditions for literariness.

Whereas *Narrative Discourse*, say, is a (narratologist's) household title, *Mimologiques* has been perhaps the least known of Genette's works in the Anglophonic world. I will not examine the possible causes of this neglect, which should come to an end now that we have Thaïs Morgan's fine translation. Nor will I discuss the many reasons for deploring that neglect; Morgan's introduction is more than suggestive in this respect. Instead, I want to indicate some of the connections between *Mimologiques* and Genette's other works and I want to stress certain aspects of it that exemplify his enterprise and his manner.

A privileged theme of structuralist criticism is language, and an important subtheme is the relation between linguistic units and objects in the world. *Mimologics* not only provides a structuration of that subtheme, a set of reference points organizing its potential illustrations; it also encourages the study of its manifestation in any (literary) text. Besides, Genette's work on the Cratylian tradition is not limited to this book. He himself notes that chapter 13 ("L'Âge des noms") constitutes a revised version of part of an essay in *Figures II* on Proust and indirect language. At least two other essays in the same collection — "Le jour, la nuit" and "Langage poétique, poétique du langage" — raise mimologic questions. *Figures* too evidences an interest in mimology and forms of the linguistic imagination (see "Proust palimpseste" or "Bonheur de Mallarmé?") and the same interest resurfaces in *Palimpsestes,* for example, and in the final chapter of *Fiction et diction,* on the nature of style and signification. More generally, Genette's project as a poetician is the mapping of spaces constituting literature as a kind of space: between signifier and signifier or signified and signified, two words with the same meaning or two meanings of the same word (*Figures, Figures II*); or between two narrations of the same sequence of events (*Figures III, Nouveau discours du récit*), between genre and text (*Introduction à l'architexte*), between one work and another (*Palimpsestes*), one text and its paratext (*Seuils*), factual and fictional narratives, true assertions and fictive statements, language and style (*Fiction et diction*). *Mimologics* surveys the (unbridgeable) space between verbal signs and nonverbal referents.

Adopting a roughly chronological order, Genette's book constitutes more a typology than a history of the Western mimological imagination. It is not that, for him, history does not exist or matter; certain moments in mimology — for instance, the end of the eighteenth century — clearly have the weight of irreversibility. But structuralist-inspired historical science tries to describe and account for systematic transformations rather than linear successions, and it views the establishment and comparison of synchronisms as essential to the understanding of these transformations. Genette isolates the structure of motifs governing the *Cratylus,* and with the support of a series of texts from different periods — including our own — he discusses (possible) rearrangements of these motifs and of their variants. In other words, he primarily characterizes the genre "mimology" while providing an overall view of its diachronic deployment as well as a set of synchronic tableaux indispensable to further historical exploration.

Though Genette's account is indisputably rich, he points out that it is not exhaustive and that mimology may go through new and unpredictable developments. *Mimologics* thus represents the open structuralism he has consistently practiced. In fact, Genette's whole enterprise can be viewed as antithetic to the theoretical project of mimology, which not only shows a powerful attraction to closure and certainty but also favors substance over structure, analogy and not homology, the concrete instead of the abstract, "natural" significations rather than cultural constructs, brazen engagement (for one sound, one language, one race, one gender) as opposed to cautious neutrality.

Genette's undeniable interest in the generic and the structural does not, however, entail a neglect of individual texts and specific objects. Throughout his career he has tactfully combined (global) poetics and (local) criticism. *Figures* underlines their complementarity; *Narrative Discourse* is a classic of narratology as well as a treat for students of Proust's *Recherche;* and *Mimologics* lays bare the general laws presiding over Cratylian speculation at the same time that it sheds light on the functioning of singular works. As Genette himself once suggested, he believes that "God is *between* the details." But he also makes the details fascinating.

Indeed, if Genette does not show much enthusiasm for mimological arguments and proofs—with their "inevitable platitude and pointless redundancy" —he is sensitive to the aesthetic dimension of mimology, its literariness, its poetry. As a true poetician (and master of rhetoric) Genette has a passion for naming and for naming well. His terminological finds are famous: homodiegetic/heterodiegetic, peritext/paratext, archtextuality/hypertextuality/metatextuality. With *Mimologics* he runs the gamut from geomimology to faunologic, and not surprisingly, his linguistic appetite leads him to try the Cratylian game. Besides, poetics explores the virtual as well as the real. In *Nouveau discours du récit,* for example, Genette envisions the possibility of a meta- and homodiegetic narrative with external focalization, and in *Palimpsestes* he offers a number of (potential) parodies and pastiches. No wonder he engages in mimological reverie.

It is perhaps above all this ability to mix the ludic with the serious, theory with practice, science with poetry, that makes *Mimologics* such a captivating text and Genette the best poetician of our time.

GERALD PRINCE

Publisher's Preface

The gargantuan labor that produced *Mimologiques* in French required similar effort to translate. A large and erudite book about language demands a translation keenly attuned to rhythms, inflections, nuances, and etymological echoes. Equal to that demand, Professor Thaïs Morgan devoted years of her life to this translation. In the midst of her work, Professor Morgan became seriously ill, but still summoned time and strength to see the book through to completion. For her relentless effort, the University of Nebraska Press would like to express its lasting gratitude.

Translator's Preface

"Do you know Languages? What's the French for fiddle-de-dee?"
"Fiddle-de-dee's not English," Alice replied gravely.
"Who ever said it was?" said the Red Queen.
— Lewis Carroll, *Through the Looking-Glass*

As Genette's own introductory remarks suggest, the tone of *Mimologics* is (to borrow his later description of the Cratylian tradition itself) "ludic but always basically serious." Bearing in mind the need for clarity, I have tried to render in this English translation the scholarly seriousness as well as the witty playfulness that characterizes Genette's style in French.

Beginning with what Genette calls the first chart of sound symbolism in the mimological tradition, which appears in Plato's *Cratylus*, I have tried whenever possible to find English equivalents for the mimological habit of matching the sounds of language with the things they are imagined to evoke. This has drawn me willy-nilly into Cratylusland itself, and many a time I have had to fight the temptation to engage in word/sound plays in addition to those already invented by the mimologists or by Genette.

Especially challenging to the translator are the onomatopoetic word formations that constitute a mainstay of the mimological tradition and, hence, Genette's analysis of it. Charles Nodier's theory of onomatopoeia and the origin of language in chapter 8, for example, led me on many a wild goose chase through a forest of words that sound wonderfully like things we encounter every day. Likewise, chapter 18 is veritable Old MacDonald's Farm of bellows, chirps, and heehaws. Despite the serious scientific intent of early twentieth-century research on the sound laws of language, a certain playfulness — if not ludicrousness — insinuates itself into all mimological proceedings.

Throughout, I have tried to capture the Platonic principle of *phōnē mimēsis*. As a result, I ask the expert reader to understand, my translation choices sometimes involve not the primary lexical sense of words but peripheral ones. Indeed, translating Genette's book has led me to some interesting (mimological?) discoveries about the hidden resources of language. Idiomatic phrases that recur as favorite examples in Cratylist arguments, whether made in Greek, Latin, or French, often involve the entire human body. A case in point is the French phrase *patati patata:* one must conjure up a dramatic situation in which a native speaker of French gives a disparaging shrug, tilts the head, turns down the mouth, and rotates the hand — all at once. Imaging this body language helps one understand the phrase, which I have rendered in English as "blah-blah-blah."

By way of inviting the reader to play along with the mimologists whom Genette discusses, I provide the French equivalents of onomatopoeias, puns, homonyms, and so on throughout the book. In many cases, though, such as Nodier's mimological theories (chapter 8) and Michel Leiris's ludic glosses (chapter 15), the Anglophone reader needs to keep in mind that the mother tongue of these authors is French, so that most of their examples of sound-word-thing equivalences come from the phonetic and semantic system of that language.

In order to make Genette's historical and theoretical study of mimologism as accessible as possible, I have added many Translator's Notes throughout my translation of the author's own notes, but a few key terms and phrases that recur in *Mimologics* should be mentioned at the outset. One of the most important of these is *parti pris,* a running theme in Genette's analysis of the mimological tradition and its debates. Sometimes I have translated this as "bias," but I often retain the French idiom to remind the reader of its fuller sense: a preconceived idea or a deliberate decision to side with one view against another.

Another leitmotif, beginning with Plato's *Cratylus,* is the pair of terms *la justesse des noms* ("the correctness of words") and *le mot juste* ("the correct word"); several Translator's Notes to chapters 1 and 12 attempt an explanation of their complex resonance. The two terms are further linked to the important idea of *defaut,* as in Stéphane Mallarmé's famous phrase *la défaut des langues,* rendered "the failing of natural languages" or "the defect of natural languages" — which also serves as the title of Genette's chapter 12. The project of secondary Cratylism espoused by most of the philosophers, linguists, and literary writers mentioned in *Mimologics* is to "correct" the "defect" of proper and ordinary names (nouns) by inventing alternative, supposedly better — because more mimetic, more motivated, less arbitrary — sound symbolism, alphabets, writing systems, and so on.

It has usually seemed best to translate the technical term *vocable* straightforwardly by the English "vocable" instead of substituting various periphrases such as "word unit" or "verbal unit." In a few passages, however, *vocable* is quite precisely a synonym for "word," and there I have rendered it that way. Similarly, I have consistently translated the French term *onomatopée* as "onomatopoeia," despite the slight awkwardness to the English ear when it is used in plural form. The rough equivalents "onomatopoetic formation," "onomatopoetic word," "onomatopoetic instance," varying widely by context, seemed equally awkward, if not more so.

Sometimes, I have preferred one translation over another in order to capture not the primary dictionary sense of a word but its specific meaning in the context of a certain mimologist's work. An example is my rendition of *noter* ("to record, transcribe") as "to note, notate" because of the analogy in Antoine Court de Gébelin's theory between musical notes and words, between musical keys and linguistic ones, and between the notation system in music and the writing system in French. Another example is *figurer*, which I have translated as "to represent figuratively" (rather than merely "to represent") in order to bring out the visual sense of the term in Charles de Brosses's theory of language (chapter 6) and the writings of his heirs. In a few cases I use two English equivalents for one French word because it carries two senses that are equally important to understanding Genette's argument. The most important of these is *nom* (in chapter 1 and thereafter): "name and noun."

Unless otherwise indicated by reference to an English edition, all translation from the French is my own. Specialist readers will find large portions of works by de Brosses (chapter 6), Gébelin (chapter 7), Nodier (chapter 8), and several French Enlightenment rhetoricians (chapter 9) rendered into English here for the first time.

For the translation of specialized terms from linguistics and language-oriented critical theories, I have consulted the following sources: Oswald Ducrot and Tzvetan Todorov, *Encyclopedic Dictionary of the Sciences of Language* (1972), translated by Catherine Porter (Baltimore: Johns Hopkins University Press, 1979); and A. J. Greimas and J. Courtés, *Semiotics and Language: An Analytical Dictionary* (1979), translated by Larry Crist, Daniel Patte, et al. (Bloomington: Indiana University Press, 1982).

A note on the English version I have used of Ferdinand de Saussure: *Course in General Linguistics*, translated and annotated by Roy Harris (London: Duckworth, 1983). Roy Harris is a well-known British scholar who has worked extensively on the history of theories of language. I find his translation of Saussure's *Cours de linguistique générale* more sensitive to crucial distinctions between terms and concepts than the other English versions currently available.

Where Genette quotes from texts originally published in English, I have restored the original whenever possible; occasionally the unavailability of the original forced me to retranslate or paraphrase Genette's French renderings of such passages. When he quotes from French works available in English translation, I have sometimes slightly reworded the standard English version to suit the context of Genette's argument and also to preserve consistency in the present translation (all such instances are signaled in the notes). Further, in order to preserve continuity of argument and tone in the framework of Genette's thinking, I have thought it best to (re)translate passages from the works of several modern French writers — Paul Claudel (chapter 14), Michel Leiris (chapter 15), Francis Ponge (chapter 16), Gaston Bachelard (chapter 17), and various early twentieth-century French linguists (chapter 18) — though in so doing I consulted the available English versions of their books, as indicated in the notes. Where Genette quotes from works in a language other than English or French, however, I have mostly avoided rephrasing; again, the exceptions (in chapters 1 and 12) are noted.

Every effort has been made to check the accuracy of quotations and bibliographical references. I have silently corrected inaccuracies and lacunae in both, insofar as the resources available to me would permit. Where Genette uses abbreviated titles in either the text or his footnotes, I have provided both full titles and subtitles and as much publication information as possible. The notes that correspond to Genette's footnotes cite current or standard English translations of foreign-language works; additionally, for the reader's convenience I have provided translations of the main titles and important section or chapter titles from as-yet-untranslated French works mentioned in the text. Elsewhere, I have added source notes — in order to include many more page numbers, for example, than the author has supplied; all such additions appear in braces. Where Genette quotes freely from Latin and French works written before 1800, however — above all, in chapter 9 — I have perforce adopted his system of giving only occasional citations for long passages of text.

For the most part, I have also retained Genette's text placement of note numbers, even though his practice sometimes runs counter to American publishing practice. Space breaks, too, are Genette's. Occasionally, however, I have taken the liberty of dividing his lengthiest paragraphs and sentences.

Finally, a word about parentheses, brackets, and braces. In his text and commentary notes Genette often uses parentheses to clarify or to comment briefly on an immediately preceding point in his argument; he also uses square brackets to insert clarificatory words or remarks into a quotation. All these have been retained. In contrast, whatever appears in braces is the translator's insertion. English words in braces directly after titles or phrases in a foreign language are my translations of those elements; Greek, Latin, German, or French words in braces directly after an English word or phrase represent what was said in the original text in question, whether Genette's or another author's, and signal key terms or concepts. I also use braces when an essential foreign-language term already in parentheses in the text requires a translation.

Ⓢ This translation of Gérard Genette's *Mimologiques: Voyage en Cratylie* would not have been possible without the support of many scholars and several institutions.

First, I thank the American Council of Learned Societies for a twelve-month Grant-in-Aid beginning in the fall of 1987. This funded the initial research and the services of a superb editor (about whom more below). I also thank my home institution, Arizona State University, for a Faculty Mini-Grant in 1988.

Preparing Genette's book for an English-speaking audience has been both a personal odyssey and a group effort. I thank the following scholars in classics, medieval studies, modern languages and literatures, rhetoric, philosophy, and religious studies who took time from their own work to read and comment on various chapters: Yopie Prins (Oberlin College), chapter 1; Robert Bjork (Arizona State University), chapter 2; Jonathan Bennett (Syracuse University) and Peter Remnant (University of British Columbia), chapter 4; Julia Douthwaite (Purdue University), chapter 7; David Gorman (Northern Illinois University), chapters 3, 5, 8, and 10; Deborah Losse (Arizona State University), chapter 6, 12, and 17; Keith Miller (Arizona State University), chapter 9; Richard Martin (Arizona State University), chapter 11; Tatiana Greene (Emerita, Barnard College), chapter 14; Anne Liebold (Arizona State University), chapter 15; Judith Radke (Arizona State University), chapter 16; and Hélène Ossipov (Arizona State University), chapter 18.

For the greater part of this project I had the good fortune of working with a resourceful bibliographer, Susan Fischman, who was then a graduate student at Brown University and is now a professor of comparative literature. Susan performed feats nothing short of heroic in the labyrinth of references and cross-references presented by Genette's original French version. Equally admirable was the bibliographic assistance provided in the final stages by Michelle Bloom, then also in comparative literature at Brown University. Additionally, I thank Rachel Rue, a classicist, who helped me with the Greek language that is pivotal to Genette's argument in chapter 1.

Above all, I thank my most constant traveling companion during the years of voyaging through Cratylusland: Jennifer Gage. Acting as editor of my translation, Jennifer also became my guide and teacher at every step of the way. Without her experienced translator's advice and friendly support, I would have faltered countless times — though any lapses in the final English text are mine.

Finally, I wish to thank Gerald Prince for his eagle-eyed reading of this book before it went to press.

THAÏS E. MORGAN

Invitation to a Voyage
in Cratylusland

> "There is something to see [*voir*]
> in *voyage*." — Francis Ponge

 Gérard Genette's book *Mimologiques* bears an intriguing subtitle: *Voyage en Cratylie*, which can be translated *Voyage in the Kingdom of Cratylus* or, more playfully, *Voyage in Cratylusland*. This subtitle has many literary resonances; above all, it evokes a heterogeneous collection of eighteenth-century narratives called "voyages," written by speculative scientists, utopians, satirists, and philosophers, as well as by travelers in the real world. Typically, the narrator voyages to a fantastic land where he learns many new ideas and makes revealing comparisons between that alternative world and life back home. It is this genre that Genette has in mind when he issues an invitation to his readers to voyage with him in Cratylusland, which is populated by an entire tradition of Western thinkers concerned with the relationship between words and things.

Do the sounds, shapes, and patterns of language imitate the world? Genette's *Mimologics* explores a wide range of answers to this fundamental question, beginning with Plato's philosophical dialogue *Cratylus* and reaching to modern linguistics during the first half of the twentieth century. Cratylusland, then, is the place where the most important activity is debating different views about if and how words are related to things. Determining language's connection to the phenomenal world is an important enterprise because it bears upon the extent and accuracy of our knowledge about that world. At the same time, thinkers tend to use their imaginations quite freely when they discuss language, inventing clever — and sometimes ridiculous — explanations of how words imitate things.

Arguments quoted here from Genette's *Mimologics* appear in double quotation marks without a note number. Primary materials quoted by Genette in the course of *Mimologics* appear in single within double quotation marks, along with the number of the chapter in which he uses them and cites their sources. Material quoted solely for this essay appears in double quotation marks with a note number, and the sources are given in the notes following the essay.

As Genette's book shows, this fancifulness brings together in Cratylusland the otherwise separate domains of philosophy, science, and literature—often in unexpected ways.

The following six short essays provide historical and contemporary contexts for the major topics discussed in *Mimologics*. First, "The Name Game; Or, Everyone Can Play" examines the issues raised by Plato's *Cratylus,* along with some modern and postmodern avatars of the mimological tradition that grows out of this seminal text. Second, "The Canine Letter and Other Capers" traces the various mimologies suggested by the letter *r* by way of providing an overview of Genette's main arguments. Third, "Orange/Orangutan/Origin of Language" describes diverse speculations on language origin and onomatopoeia, or words that seem to sound like things. Fourth, "'Looks like a...': Seeing Things in Words" surveys various claims that the shapes of letters and words, and the visual patterns made by sentences, are keys to the meaning of language. Fifth, "The *Parti Pris* of Linguistics: Demotivating versus Remotivating the Sign" focuses on twentieth-century linguistics and ongoing debates about the nature of language. Finally, "The Infinite Voyage: Cratylusland Past, Present, and Future" considers the serious, satirical, and ludic aspects of mimology in well-known works of philosophy and literature.

The Name Game; or, Everyone Can Play

> "Of course they answer to their names?" the Gnat remarked carelessly.
> "I never knew them to do it."
> "What's the use of their having names," the Gnat said, "if they won't answer to them?"
> "No use to *them,*" said Alice; "but it's useful to the people that name them, I suppose. If not, why do things have names at all?"
> —Lewis Carroll, *Through the Looking-Glass*

℗ *Mimologics* is a book about our continual fascination with language. In his introductory remarks, Genette defines *mimologism* as the belief and the determination to prove that there must be "a relation of reflective analogy (imitation) between 'word' and 'thing' that motivates, or justifies, the existence and the choice of the former." Mimologism is not limited to any one historical period, field of study, or genre of writing. The wish to make words resemble things in a variety of ways—by sound, by shape, and even by smell and taste—has repeatedly manifested itself in the works of philosophers, theologians, rhetoricians, grammarians, philologists, poets, novelists, and linguists. All are enchanted by language; all participate in *mimologics,* or "reveries on words."[1]

When Shakespeare's Juliet asks, "What's in a name?" she is posing the Cratylian question par excellence: do words represent the world? The most influential treatment of this topic is Plato's dialogue *Cratylus,* to which Genette devotes his first chapter. This classic text has been and continues to be the focus of much discussion as commentators have tried to tease out Plato's own theory of language from the three-way conversation among the titular character Cratylus, his friend Hermogenes, and the philosopher Socrates.[2] Cratylus speaks for a realist position, maintaining that proper and common nouns (in Greek, *onoma, -ata*) are names that must directly represent persons or things. From this naturalist perspective, if a name fails to designate its referent correctly, then it is not a name at all. On the other side, Hermogenes speaks for a nominalist position, claiming that whatever each speaker decides to call a person or a thing must be its correct name. According to this conventionalist view of language, all names are correct not because they refer to the world accurately (Cratylus's criterion) but because they have been given by an individual and used by custom within a certain community.[3]

Plato's *Cratylus* inquires into the epistemological basis of language: is a name or noun "'correct'" because it refers to a universal truth, or because it has gained social acceptance, or because an individual decides to use it in a particular way? Significantly, Cratylus begins the dialogue by challenging the correctness of his interlocutor's proper name: *Hermogenes* ("'of the race of Hermes' [god of wealth]") is a false description of his friend, who is actually a poor man. Hermogenes retorts that the names Athenians give to their newly acquired slaves are considered correct, regardless of what names the slaves may have borne previously.

Enter Socrates, who demonstrates the pitfalls first in Hermogenes' and then in Cratylus's arguments. As Genette explains, rather than offer a synthesis of their views, Socrates adopts "an original position," one that may or may not be equivalent to Plato's. In order to determine the correctness of names, Socrates proposes two kinds of investigations, which Genette terms "eponymy" and "mimophony." In both cases, the *Cratylus* sets an important precedent by focusing attention exclusively on the name or noun: whether treated as a definition of the thing to which it refers (in eponymy) or analyzed into its constituent sounds and letters (in mimophony), the isolated name or noun is assumed to afford direct access to knowledge about the world. The idea that nouns are names for things is perhaps the most salient feature of the Cratylian tradition.

Genette draws an important distinction between etymology as employed by nineteenth-century philologists (see his chapter 10) and Socrates' practice of eponymy in Plato's *Cratylus*. Whereas etymology aims to trace words back to their historical origins according to the laws of filiation, eponymy allows for imaginative free play. Socrates — and a host of mimologists after him — analyzes words by adding, deleting, and/or substituting letters or syllables according to nonce rules of phonetic similarity and punning. As a result, Socrates' eponymies initiate a potentially endless language game, limited only by the player's ingenuity. From a philosophical perspective, therefore, the eponymy of proper names and common nouns cannot guarantee any true knowledge of things. Indeed, observes the contemporary philosopher Umberto Eco, not only linguistic but all types of signs place us in an epistemological quandary: "A sign is everything which can be taken as significantly substituting for something else. This something else does not necessarily have to exist. ... Thus ... [signs are] *everything which can be used in order to lie.*"[4] In this context, Plato's *Cratylus* may be understood as a treatise on the problem of language as a kind of lying. Words suggest an infinite variety of imaginary connections to things, yet the more we enjoy the name game, the further we find ourselves from the ideal of truth.

Socrates' witty eponymies, then, lead to philosophical aporia. At this point in the dialogue, he shifts ground and resorts to a different method, that of mimophony. In contrast to eponymy, which consists of analyzing words in contemporary usage, mimophony establishes direct links between the basic elements (*stoicheia*) out of which words are made and the basic elements of physical phenomena. Of special importance in mimophony are the very first words (*prōta onomata*), whose letters have presumably retained the closest ties to their referents. According to Genette, the table of elementary sound symbolism that Socrates constructs here is the first of many in the Western tradition of mimologism.

Yet as Socrates elaborates the idea that the basic sounds of language imitate things, it becomes clear that mimophony redoubles rather than resolves the problem of attaining true knowledge of the world by means of words. Another question arises: is Socrates pursuing truth in earnest, or is he just joking? For Genette, Plato's *Cratylus* both inaugurates and epitomizes the tension between the serious and the ludic modes of discourse which characterizes the genre of mimologics. He concludes that Plato's text has "a seriousness excluding neither sophism nor a sense of play."

Ultimately, the *Cratylus* leaves us torn between philosophical doubts about language and the sheer fun of playing with words. In the last section Socrates offers a mischievous hypothesis: what if the inventor of language was a divine onomaturge who made a mistake? What if he misassigned some names to things to which they did not properly (either by eponymy or by mimophony) correspond? Neither Cratylus nor Hermogenes is happy with this idea, for despite their opposing viewpoints they both fundamentally believe that all names are correct. Having raised many questions about language's epistemological status,

Socrates settles upon a wisely ambiguous position that Genette dubs "*secondary Cratylism (or mimologism).*" Although he would prefer that names and nouns correctly and directly designate things, Socrates acknowledges that eponymy proves only that names indirectly represent the world through other names to which they can be connected by analysis. Likewise, the mimetic capacity of letters and sounds, or mimophony, is at best only partial. Yet Socrates' theory of the originary mistake of the divine onomaturge presupposes that a greater truth of words does exist somewhere (in the realm of ideal Forms?). As a secondary mimologist, then, Socrates "*appeals against* language as it is to language as it might be, and consequently *should* be."

A constant in the Cratylian tradition after Plato, secondary mimologism generates controversies and efforts to reform language that extend into the twentieth century. In chapter 4, Genette provides a useful chart of the major positions taken on the question of the relationship between words and things in the mimological tradition. He points out that if Cratylus represents "absolute mimologism" (language should be, can be, and is mimetic), and if Socrates represents "secondary mimologism" (language should be, sometimes can be, but is not always mimetic), then Hermogenes' stance cannot be said to represent conventionalism, because it falls somewhere between these two. Rather, the best example of "absolute conventionalism" is the work of the modern linguist Ferdinand de Saussure (language should not be, cannot be, and is not mimetic). In turn, Socrates' secondary mimologism finds its clearest reversal in the philosophy of Gottfried Wilhelm Leibniz, who stands for "secondary conventionalism" (language should not be mimetic but it often is, so an artificial language must be invented as a surer means of access to true universals).

Yet even Saussure, the founder of structural linguistics, who introduced the notion of the "arbitrariness" of the sign or its relative freedom from ties to the phenomenal world, also enthusiastically engaged in mimologics. Intrigued by what he called "anagrams" and "paragrams," Saussure filled many notebooks with eponymic analyses of Vedic and Homeric verses and inscriptions, discovering the names of ancient gods and heroes mysteriously concealed in letters and sounds.[5] Saussure the conventionalist was therefore at heart a secondary mimologist in the manner of Socrates in Plato's *Cratylus*.

The line between the philosopher and the poet is similarly a fine one in the work of the contemporary writer Michel Leiris. As with Socrates, so with Leiris: the reader must constantly wonder, is he in earnest or in jest?[6] In chapter 15 Genette brings out several affinities between Leiris's *biffures* and "glosses" and Socrates' methods of eponymy and mimophony. For example, Socrates' discovery of the definition of man in the Greek word for "man" (*anthrōpos = anathrōn ha opōpe*, "he who looks up at what he has seen" is matched—if not outdone—by Leiris's discovery of the familiar scene of the animals surrounding the Christ-child's manger in the French name for "Bethlehem": *Bethléem* = *haleine de bêtes*, "the good warmth of the powerful breath of the beasts in the stable." In Plato's and Leiris's texts, proper names and nouns are "motivated," or given meaning, not directly by reference to things but indirectly by relay to letters and sounds belonging to still other words. This name game is both serious and spurious at the same time: it does produce new knowledge, but how reliable is that knowledge in the real world outside of Cratylusland? Thus, when Leiris defines the word "morphine" as *mort fine* (a fine death), we cannot be sure whether he is just fooling around or calling attention to something more grave.

In the chart of typical mimological doctrines at the end of chapter 4, Genette leaves one row blank. Does this imply that there is a line of thinking that somehow escapes the recurrent opposition between mimologism and conventionalism in debates over language? Every reader will have her or his own candidate for this spot; my choice would be Jacques Derrida, whose use in *Glas* of eponymy and mimophony in both philosophical and ludic ways recalls but also challenges that of Socrates in Plato's *Cratylus*.[7] "Of the remain(s), after all, there are always, overlapping each other, two functions": so begins Derrida's *Glas*, which elsewhere alludes directly to *Cratylus* and several of the "remains" of its divided legacy, including Saussure's *Course in General Linguistics*.[8] The *découpage* of language—the separation of the always already interdependent functions of referring to the phenomenal world and creating an alternative world—is visually represented in *Glas* by the two columns of texts by and about Hegel and Genet on each page (a conventionalist and a mimologist, or two mimologists?). Today, we continue to debate the same kinds of issues about language that agitated generations of thinkers before us: "Departed then are ... the archeologists, philosophers, hermeneuts, semioticians, semanticians, psychoanalysts, rhetoricians, poeticians, even perhaps all those readers who still believe, in literature or anything else."[9]

For Derrida as for Plato, the critical question remains: "What is the name of a thing?" Like Socrates, Derrida ironically undoes the "great stake" of philosophical and literary discourses, both of which perform the "transformation of [the] proper name, [treated as a] *rebus*, into the name of things."[10] Derrida reconsiders the entire mimological enterprise. One of the running columns in *Glas* is devoted to the modern writer Jean Genet, whom Derrida sees as an exemplary "Cratylean nomothete" because he "institutes ... himself in his own proper signature."[11] In other words, by writing and then signing his texts, the criminal author Genet both properly returns to the law (*nomos*) and gives it the lie by using an improper, borrowed and invented, name whose eponymy is *genêt*, "horse-broom" (a wildflower). Moreover, as a renegade nomothete, Genet flies from the law (*voler*, to fly) and steals its authority away by playing with names (*voler*, to steal). Likewise, Derrida is both escaping the Platonic laws of philosophy and stealing Plato's thunder by using eponymy and mimophony to uncover a surprising range of things in the name "Genet." [12]

"What does the *glas* of the proper name signify?" Derrida asks at one point.[13] Not coincidentally, the consonantal cluster *gl-* appears in the original table of sound symbolism in Plato's *Cratylus*. There, Socrates asserts that *gl-* stands for all things that are "'glutinous,'" "'sweet,'" and "'gummy.'" He also claims that *gl-* imitates its own articulation as a speech sound: "'The gliding of the tongue is stopped by the sound of the *g*.'" As the nomothetic inventor of "grammatology," which depends upon a "'picto-ideo-phonographic'... style" of composition called *Écriture* ("Writing"), Derrida is fully alert to the mimological vitality of the *g* in the alphabet (the Greek word for this letter is *gamma*) and to the signification of the *g* in *gramma* (Greek, written letter).[14] In effect, *Glas* reveals that the phonomimetic capacities of *gl-* are limitless. For example, besides the wild horse-broom (*genêt*), Derrida discovers in the proper name "Genet" a more delicate flower, the *gladiolus;* this *gl-* word, in turn, yields up the correct name (however improper) for a part of Genet's own body: the *glans*, which is intimately connected to his homosexuality as well as to his writing. Built upon "association," Derrida tells the reader, the name game of eponymy "is a sort of gluing" that "not only takes hold in the signifying paste" or the physical qualities of words but "also sticks ... to the sense" so that sound and meaning seem to cohere in every case—the first rule of mimophony.[15] Yet what, finally, "remain(s)" of the *Cratylus* in *Glas?* Is Derrida deconstructing or reconstructing Plato's philosophical project? "Remain(s) — to be known." [16]

The Canine Letter and Other Capers

> "There's the tree in the middle," said the Rose. ...
> "But what could it do, if any danger came?" asked Alice.
> "It could bark," said the Rose.
> "It says 'Bough-wough!'" cried a Daisy.
> — Lewis Carroll, *Through the Looking-Glass*

Ⓖ The letter *r* (especially when pronounced as a rolled "r") is the *canina litera,* or canine letter, in mimological tradition. During its interesting history in Western thought, *r* has stood for a dog's bark, a man's anger, and the course of a river, among other things. By following the history of mimologics attached to the letter *r,* one can become acquainted with the main categories and subcategories used in Genette's book.

The first recorded mimology on the letter *r* occurs in Plato's *Cratylus* (see Genette's chapter 1), where Socrates reasons that since the Greek *r* appears in words such as *rhein* (to flow), its function must be to designate dynamic movement in general. The connection between an alphabetic letter and the things to which familiar words starting with that letter refer is a persistent motif in the mimological tradition. Socrates also claims that each letter in the alphabet conforms both to its actual articulation during speech and to its natural referent(s). Notice how this doubles the mimetic potential of language: r = the motion of the tongue on the palate when this letter is pronounced + the motion of certain physical phenomena, such as rivers and wheels. This argument, too, reappears in the work of many mimologists.

The Roman satirist Persius, whose work was widely read during the Middle Ages, describes speech expressive of anger in terms of the "canine letter": "'Sonat hic de nare canina litera'" (The canine letter reverberates from one side of the nose around here). Citing this authoritative source (see chapter 3), Geoffroy Tory in his sixteenth-century rhetoric observes that when dogs put on a "'menacing look'" and bare their teeth just before a fight, they seem "'to pronounce the r.'" Similarly, when a man is "'angry, or jibing'" he utters "'harsh, injurious [words], full of strident letters, which are the letters rr repeated and harshly pronounced.'" For both these mimologists, the dramatic scenario evoked by the r seems to prove that language is directly tied to the world: as mad dogs bark and snarl, so do angry people when they talk.

This line of reasoning was quite acceptable to the seventeenth-century philosopher and grammarian John Wallis (see chapter 3). Wallis argues that words can be analyzed into monosyllabic clusters, each of which refers to a thing: hence his main principle, *soni rerum indices* (words are indexical signs for things). In combination with hard consonants, for example, r indicates "violent motion: br stands for a "'generally loud splitting apart,'" while cr is "'something broken up, generally with a crash ... caved in or twisted.'" Clearly, Wallis's own native language, English, has biased his mimologism here: br from the word "break" and cr from the word "crash." A similar pattern of inference can be found in the *Brevis designatio* by Leibniz (see chapter 4), who asserts that the letter r designates rapid motion, as in the Latin word *cursus;* this is exactly what Plato's Socrates says about the Greek letter r (as in *rhein*).

Whereas Plato, Wallis, and Leibniz are interested in *mimophony,* or the ways in which the sounds of speech imitate things, several influential eighteenth-century thinkers focus instead on *mimography,* or the ways in which written letters imitate things. Furthermore, Genette explains, mimography itself falls into two types: *ideomimography* and *phonomimography* (see chapter 5). Although theoretically separate, these subcategories often merge in practice. Take, for instance, the work of Rowland Jones (discussed in chapter 5), who aimed to reconstruct the original universal language. Embodied in the monosyllables of the word "crocodile," Jones believed, is not only the animal to which this word refers but also its habitat. In "'ac-ir-oc-o-dil,'" just imagine that the letter r represents flowing water, the rapid movement of the animal itself, the crocodile's notorious irrritability, and its hypocritical character (as in "crocodile tears").

Another mimologist who was struck by the mimetic potential of the letter *r* is Charles de Brosses (see chapter 6). A general grammarian of the Enlightenment, he envisioned a complex web of close analogies between nature and language. Based on a postulate of resemblance, de Brosses's theory of language makes the sound of human speech, the shape of the articulatory apparatus, and the shape of written letters correspond in an "'organic'" whole. Letters are "'figures'" that represent the mouth and throat in the act of pronounciation as well as the things to which language refers. In a chart of sound symbolism reminiscent of the one in the *Cratylus,* de Brosses classifies *r* as the most "'harsh'" articulation; its function is to "'paint'" rough exterior surfaces. His proof consists of words beginning with the letter *r* in two classical and two modern languages: for example, the French words *rude* (rough) and *racler* (to scrape), and the German word *rheein,* which recurs in the names of torrential rivers (the Rhine, the Rhone, the Garonne).

De Brosses's mimologism is highly intertexual; it is built upon an array of previous arguments about the relationship between words and things from the Cratylian tradition. An interesting example may be seen in his explanation of why the letters *r* and *n* are related: as the sign of negation or negativity, *n* implies *r,* the sign of anger. This association owes partly to de Brosses's own imagination and partly to that of previous mimologists, such as Persius (speakers roll their *r*'s when they are scornful or irate) and Geoffroy Tory (an angry man sounds like a barking dog). One of the central lessons of Genette's *Mimologics,* then, is that there is nothing new under the intertextual sun that illuminates the Western history of ideas.

In the later eighteenth century, inspired by de Brosses, Antoine Court de Gébelin formulates a master table of the "'primeval'" alphabet, which he deems to have been entirely "'hieroglyphic'" (see chapter 7). According to Gébelin, the letter *r* originated in the nose. At the very beginning, he says, its sound was represented by a pictogram showing a human nose; next, the pictogram was schematized into a simpler figure, an ideogram consisting of two lines set at an angle to evoke a nose; finally, this nasal ideogram used to sign the letter *r* was assimilated into ancient alphabets, including Phoenician, Hebrew, and Chinese. On such evidence, Gébelin concludes that each letter of the Roman alphabet used in Europe can be infallibly traced back to a thing-picture and hence to the natural world itself. However, as Genette shows, Gébelin's "hypercratylian" belief in universal mimesis is not based on a direct relationship between words and things but, like all mimological projects, draws freely upon eponymy, mimophony, and mimography — each of which is an intertextual practice — in order to reconnect language with nature.

xxix

Genette adapts two of his leading terms, "mimologism" and "mimologics," from the early nineteenth-century linguist Charles Nodier (see chapter 9). A "secondary mimologist" who finds that language is not perfectly mimetic and resolves to make it so, Nodier proposes a reformed alphabet consisting of "'organic'" letters that stand in for real things. For the rolled *r*, Nodier imagines the noise made by physical bodies moving in space—a recurrent motif in the Cratylian tradition. As well, like de Brosses, Nodier asserts that the external motion denoted by *r* corresponds to the internal motion of the articulatory apparatus when this letter is pronounced. For Nodier, the superiority of the "phonomimetic" alphabet is corroborated by the phenomenon of onomatopoeia, which he considers to be the most natural, hence the original, form of speech. His separate study of onomatopoeia abounds with delightful mimologies. The word *brouter* (to graze) is said to imitate the noise herbivores make "'in breaking off plants at the root and tearing them up with their teeth.'" Recalling Wallis's fanciful associations with the consonantal cluster *cr*, Nodier thinks that the rolling *r* in the word *écraser* (to crush) signifies a gradual, steady "'breaking apart,'" such as "'the crack of chalk bursting apart and being pulverized underfoot.'"

During the nineteenth century, however, the Cratylian tradition is seriously challenged by the positivist comparatists (see chapter 10). The mimological desire for words that are like things therefore turns away from the study of language and reinvests itself in literature, especially poetry (see chapter 12). The work of Stéphane Mallarmé exemplifies the ambiguous status of mimologism in modern poetics. Like Plato's Socrates, Mallarmé wishes for a total mimetic "correctness" of words, but—also like Socrates—he recognizes that language is a deeply flawed representational medium. Seeking a compromise, he locates his impossible ideal in a language other than his own: English. In this "linguistic utopia," an initial *r* in a word always stands for "'raising, removal, richness, rending, radicalness.'" Mimetically as well as metaphysically, *r* is the "'articulation par excellence.'" Yet unlike many mimologists before him, Mallarmé stops short of claiming that letters physically represent things in a one-to-one correspondence. Instead, he places the task of restoring the link between things and words in the hands of the poet. Only poetry can "'compensate'" for the "'failing in natural languages'" by using art to resurrect the true nature of words.

The modernist writer Paul Claudel undertakes a comparable mission to return the truth of things to words, this time under the inspiration of the divine Word (see chapter 14). In particular, Claudel is fascinated by the shape of language, or the signifier: for him, each letter of the alphabet represents an object, creature, or event, while a whole word furnishes an ideogrammatic picture of its referent. Believing that all letters are a "'sort of dynamic *pattern* or *central power source*,'" Claudel sees the *r* as "'a siphon or sometimes... a hook'"—a tool that can be used to repair and tune up the machine of language. Elsewhere, he discovers a funny but poignant story in the French word RÊVE (dream): "'The circumflex [^] is a butterfly. A hunter armed with a net extends his leg in pursuit of this elusive sliver of a creature [R]. With a ladder [E] ... he attempts to entrap it. He reaches his arms out toward it [V]. ... In vain, for only the ladder [E] remains.'"

Although metaphysical and epistemological questions about language continue to be of concern, modernist and postmodernist mimology displays an increasing interest in the ludic aspect of writing, or the "game" (*jeu*). Genette distinguishes between the kind of secondary mimologism underpinning the Cratylian tradition from Wallis to Mallarmé, which offers various "fictitious" examples of words that directly imitate things in the serious attempt to prove that language embodies the world, and a more recent kind of secondary mimologism offering "factitious" verbal inventions that humorously expose the provisionality of language as a means of conveying truth. For instance, in Michel Leiris's mimological "'glossary,'" *r* has become a complex intertextual sign that both reveres and mocks the wisdom of the Bible (see chapter 15). Deriving the proper name "Caïn" from the word "canine" through sound symbolism, Leiris also uses eponymy to forge a semantic link between the story of Cain and the canine letter: you can predict that someone so named would brutally kill his brother from the way the French pronunciation "Caïn" rhymes with *canine*, which itself rhymes with *babines* (jaws). Another postmodern writer, Francis Ponge, engages in a "mimo(typo)graphy" that is ludic to the point of being antimimetic (see chapter 16).[17] Are we to believe, for example, that the double rolling *r* in the word *verre* (glass) causes the liquid in the glass to vibrate? Well, maybe: Socrates does say in the *Cratylus* that the divine onomaturge designed the *r* specially to represent motion.

Despite the widespread rejection of mimologism in the study of language after Saussure, the canine letter still capers about in the imagination of Roman Jakobson, a structuralist poetician and psycholinguist (see chapters 12 and 18). In his famous essay "Linguistics and Poetics" Jakobson puts forward his theory of generalized "'parallelism,'" or the systematic similarities on phonetic, morphological, grammatical, and semantic levels that occur whenever an utterance is governed by the "'poetic function'" of language. The poetic function may become dominant in everyday conversation, as in the following example: "A girl used to talk about 'the horrible Harry.' 'Why horrible?' 'Because I hate him.' 'But why not *dreadful, terrible, frightful, disgusting?*' 'I don't know why, but *horrible* fits him better.'"[18] According to Jakobson, besides the poetic alliteration in "*horrible Harry*," this nickname is motivated by the emotive context: "horrible Harry" expresses the girl's intense dislike of the person she is referring to. In making this analysis, though, the linguist has unwittingly entered Cratylusland, for who but a mimologist would have recognized the snarl of the canine letter in this girl's utterance? As Genette wryly observes of Jakobson's role in perpetuating the Cratylian tradition: "*Scratch Hermogenes and you (re)discover Cratylus.*"

Mimologism animates later twentieth-century linguistics, too. In articles published during the 1980s, Ivan Fonagy elaborates a theory of "oral mimesis." All sorts of "speech sounds are expressive," including paralinguistic phenomena such as "vocal style" and "intonation," and intralinguistic ones such as semantic transfer or "metaphor." Specifically, Fonagy reports that he has experimentally established that "anger is expressed in French as well as in Hungarian" by "fast, spasmodic tongue movements" and by "withdrawal of the mandible, retraction of the lower incisors [and] biting of the upper incisors on the lower lip."[19] These details strikingly resemble those in de Brosses's descriptions of articulatory mimesis some two hundred years earlier.[20] Fonagy measures the articulatory apparatus during pronunciation of the letter r in order to prove his hypothesis that r = anger — a leitmotiv of the Cratylian tradition. Carried away by his imagination into Cratylusland, Fonagy creates a new genre, sociobiological mimology: "The vigorously erected rolling tongue [in pronouncing r] may represent the erected (menacing) finger or the erected penis. ... The loss of the rolled r ... seems to be related to castration fear."[21]

The canine letter acquires the significance of a return of the repressed in Derrida's *Glas*. Derrida portrays the writer Jean Genet as a rebellious, post-Saussurean mimologist: "Genet would then rejoin this powerful, occulted tradition that was long preparing its coup ... while hiding its work from itself, anagrammatizing proper names, anamorphizing signatures and all that follows."[22] Derrida alludes to the anagrams and paragrams of Saussure, who privately indulged in mimologically motivated reveries while publicly proclaiming the arbitrariness of the sign. The "powerful, occulted tradition" making a comeback in twentieth-century thought would be Cratylism itself. If Genet uses mimologism as an insurrectionary weapon, then so does Derrida. Challenging the arguments of Plato and Saussure, among others, about the relationship between words and things, Derrida sustains a serio-ludic practice of eponymy, mimophony, mimotypography, and other forms of mimologism throughout *Glas*. For instance, as if vindicating Wallis's mimological explanation of *cr* as the sign for violent movement, Derrida sums up Genet's life and work in the words *cracher* (to spit) and *écrire* (to write). Spit is associated with sperm viscerally and visually, while the act of writing for Genet is connected by mimophony and eponymy to both of these, as well as to the feeling of disgust (*écoeurement*): "'*je m'écoulais*'" (I was discharging sperm), "'*j'écrivais*'" (I was writing), '*je m'écrivais*' (I was writing myself) in '*tant d'écoeurement*' (so much disgust)."[23]

Elsewhere, Derrida has deconstructed the concept of an origin of language in which speech preceded writing, and he restates this view in *Glas*: "There is no sign, no tongue, no name, and above all no 'primitive word' in the Cratylian sense."[24] Yet the *cr,* functioning precisely like a "primitive word," motivates several of the main arguments in *Glas.* Genet's anger against God, the law, women, and his own homosexuality, Derrida suggests, is expressed in his texts by the obsessively repeated string *cracher-écrire-écoeurement.* At the same time, we can hear Derrida's own i*rr*itation with the philosophical tradition (largely Platonic) resonating in the rolling *r*'s.

Genette finds that Leiris's work epitomizes the new Cratylism, defiantly anti-philosophical and anticommunicational, ludic and individualistic (see chapter 15). To underscore this point, Genette parodies Leiris in his turn by glossing the title of Plato's *Cratylus* with an ironic, mimophonic pun: "*Cratyle, il crache son style*" (Ever a Cratylus, he spits out his style). By the same critical mimologic, Derrida's *Glas* can be seen as a postmodern gloss on the West's philosophical and literary traditions. In the *cr* of the parodic [s]-*tyle* which Derrida spits out in *Glas,* the canine letter's bark can still be heard across the centuries.

Orange/Orangutan/Origin of Language

> "We called him Tortoise because he taught us," said the
> Mock Turtle. — Lewis Carroll, *Alice in Wonderland*

ⓢ The origin of language is a persistent issue in the mimological tradition. Numerous theories have been forwarded, but often, as Genette explains, their basic assumptions overlap despite differences in emphasis. The seemingly endless conversation on the subject crosses historical periods and national borders as well as disciplines and fields of study. Consequently, speculation about the origin of language has generated a complex intertextual discourse in which each successive thinker holds dialogues with authors past and present.

A major goal of mimologism is to establish an absolute continuity or *chain* between things in the world and the units of human speech.[25] In the *Cratylus,* Socrates constructs a chain that links proper names and common nouns to their referents, first through eponymy and then through sound symbolism. In one example, since the body (*sōma*) can be understood as the outward sign (*sēma*) of the inner soul, the body can also be said to be the tomb (*sēma*) of the soul, inasmuch as it serves as its safeguard (*sōzema*). This series of associations appears to prove that the elements of the chain *body-sign-tomb-safe* are connected in their essence (*ousia*) and that the words merely reflect this real relation. Thus, the divine onomaturge must have been right in his creation of names: language is "'correct.'" However, as Genette indicates, many of Socrates' eponymies are ironic and do not in fact anchor words in things; on the contrary, they juggle phonetic and semantic units at will, proving instead that the knowledge obtainable through language is purely intralinguistic. The chain between words and things has therefore always already been broken in the founding text of Cratylism.

The question of the origin of language preoccupied late Latin and medieval grammarians and theologians. For Saint Augustine (see chapter 2), God's Word (*Logos*) enters human history through Adam's naming of the beasts in Eden. The genesis of human language is thus seen as coterminous with Genesis, forming an unbroken chain between man and God. After the Fall, the originary language is transmitted to Adam's descendants, albeit — especially after the Tower of Babel — in a degraded form. Writing within this theological context, Pope Innocent III asserts that the birth of speech echoes the birth of man (and woman, too): "For the newly born male says 'Ah,' the female 'E.' All are born of Eve saying 'E' or 'Ah.' ... Either syllable is the interjection of one in pain."[26] As this example shows, etymology, used in conjunction with eponymy, becomes an accepted way of establishing divine and natural truth in the Middle Ages. The Christian metaphor of the Chain of Being leading from God all the way down to the beasts, or from divine *Logos* to human language, comes to replace the Socratic ironies about the gap between words and things. Subsequently, Genette observes, the *Cratylus* is taken "without nuances" as the source text for a long line of "upholders of [the] doctrine [of mimologism], and often its adversaries" as well. "Like any posterity, this one is misunderstanding, betrayal, diversion from the origin."

Augustine's influential theory of language plays a crucial role in the Cratylian tradition by giving a mimologistic reading to Plato's *Cratylus*. In general, Augustine's work partakes of what R. Howard Bloch calls the "profound resistance to breaking entirely with the wish for continuity between language and matter[,] along with a radical denial of the practical consequences of such a rupture," which characterizes medieval Christian thought.[27] In particular, Augustine's revisionist interpretation of the *Cratylus* (a title he never cites) depends on the principle of resemblance, above all *similtudo* (analogy), as the means of determining relationships between words and things. Since he cannot prove that the sounds of speech imitate the material world directly, Augustine proposes what Genette calls a "tropological semantics": a rhetoric based on the principle of indirect imitation, or similarity. The very kind of intralinguistic relations between words that Socrates invented in his eponymies and then rejected as false are taken as evidential by Augustine and his heirs.

Equally important to the future of the mimological tradition, according to Genette, is Augustine's psychological approach to language. In *Theories of the Symbol*, Tzvetan Todorov notes that Augustine's definition of the word is "double" because it posits "first, the relation between sign and thing (this is the framework of designation and signification), second, the relation between speaker and hearer (this is the framework of communication)." Already in the first type of relation, however, "things participate in signs as signifiers, not as referents," for there is only one true referent: God. In this way, Augustine's theory of signification also gets around the vexed quarrel between Cratylists and Hermogenists: "We no longer depend upon empirical contingency to distinguish among signs ... but upon a difference in structure" within signs themselves — a displacement from relations between things and words to one between words and words, which will recur much later in Saussurean linguistics.[28]

Nevertheless, the origin of language remains a hotly debated topic. If Adam's naming of the beasts in Eden seems to confirm the Cratylist position, the appearance of many different tongues after Babel suggests a disastrous break in the Chain of Being. "As the seventeenth century opens," therefore, says Russell Fraser, "the forging of an exact correspondence between names and things becomes a matter of impatient concern."[29] Of the several mimological projects undertaken in the 1600s, Wallis's theory that the basic sounds of the English language correspond directly to things, *soni rerum indices,* is typical (see chapter 3). Wallis holds that an unbroken chain leads from the sonority of each letter, which stands for a certain class of natural phenomena, up to whole words. By the 1700s various plans to reform the supposed imperfections of natural languages, thereby restoring the linkage between words and things presumed to have existed at the origin of language, take center stage. This tendency toward secondary mimologism is epitomized by de Brosses's theory of the multiple analogies that conjoin the units of speech, the articulatory apparatus, " 'organic' " orthography, and the natural world (see chapter 6).

In investigations made during the Enlightenment, according to Todorov, "original language is conceived in terms of increasing proximity between the sign and what it designates, or ... in terms of the referent's presence in the sign."[30] Étienne Condillac, de Brosses, and Gébelin all hope to rediscover in current languages (considered complex, abstract, and decadent) the primal words that embody things, thereby reaching back to the human mind as it was in its first, purely natural state. These three thinkers exemplify the three major views of the origin of language that emerged in the 1700s: the " 'language of action' " (Condillac's theory of indexical gestures); word " 'painting' " (de Brosses's theory of imitative speech sounds); and " 'hieroglyphics' " (Gébelin's theory of iconic writing systems).

In "An Essay on the Origin of Human Knowledge," Condillac maintains that gestures are the original signs because they form an integral part of what they represent. At its source, language would be both natural or spontaneous and constructed or conventional. The "language of action" or gesture at once embodies and expresses man's basic needs, hence his "understanding." From this initial stage, Condillac reasons, man's needs would generate, in succession, "speech, declamation, arbitrary marks for words or things, music, poetry, eloquence, writing, and the different characters of language."[31] Cratylian in spirit, Condillac's theory makes the act of nomination—focused on the one-to-one correspondence of the noun with the thing it names—the key to the origin of language. Condillac's ideas presuppose strong continuity in the development of language and mind, or a chain paradigm. In this regard, Condillac operates within what the historian Michel Foucault calls the "Classical episteme": that is, the belief in a vast system of resemblances uniting humanity, nature, and language.[32]

Condillac's influential theory of a primitive "language of action" effects a compromise between Cratylism (words are motivated by a direct relation to nature) and Hermogenism (words are chosen by individuals and used by social convention). The notion that words come to supplement gestures and eventually supersede them, however, poses its own problems.[33] In *The Archeology of the Frivolous*, Derrida deconstructs the secondness or supplementary status of metaphysics in relation to language and that of language in relation to the truth of nature, as presented in Condillac's philosophy. Rather than securing the traditional Chain of Being, the "general principle of analogy" in Condillac "gives rise to an ambiguous axiology."[34] According to Condillac, if "the first expressions of the language of action are given by nature" based on man's needs, then "analogy forms the others and extends this language, which little by little becomes suited to representing our ideas."[35] But as Derrida shows, analogy itself is tropological, imaginary, and divorced from nature. A paradox is produced: as language progresses in complexity and becomes more capable of expressing our ideas, language falls away from its own origin as a sign-thing or signifying gesture. This means that the progress of language entails its increasing arbitrariness, what Condillac calls its "artificiality," yet such secondariness must have already defined language at its origin, since emotional cries and spontaneous gestures do not count as signs or language until they have become conventionalized: that is, detachable from immediate physical situations and usable for social "commerce."[36] Thus, Derrida concludes, "the *proper*, the *property* of the sign is the system of the arbitrary" and the entire enterprise of philosophy—which, since Plato's *Cratylus*, has consisted of reasoning about reality through language—is "frivolous" because it tries to cover over with figures and tropes the "congenital breach" between words and things.[37]

Nodier, although he belongs to the first half of the nineteenth century, carries on several ideas from the Enlightenment. Above all, he is determined to justify the Cratylian thesis of the continuity between language and nature. For him, the present diversity of languages signifies not a fall or decadence but the richness and flexibility of each language as it responds intimately to the geography, climate, and temperament of its speakers. This idea, which Genette dubs "geomimology," can also be found in de Brosses, Gébelin, and Jean-Jacques

Rousseau, among others, and persists among nineteenth-century comparatists such as Ernest Renan (see chapters 10–11) as well as among Romantics such as René Chateaubriand and Victor Hugo (see chapter 18). "'Quite naturally,'" says Nodier (see chapter 8), "'the languages of the Orient and of the South generally would have been limpid, euphonic and harmonious, as if they had received the impress of the transparency of their sky, and had been married through a marvelous concord to the sounds that emanate from the palm trees swayed by the wind, to the trembling of the savannahs that bow down and lift up the forehead of their undulating harvests.'" Predictably, Nodier imagines the languages of the North as exactly opposite: they "'show the effects of the energy and the austerity of a harsh climate. In their raw and clashing vocabularies they merge with the cry of the cracking fir trees, with the rumbling rush of crumbling rocks, and with the downward crash of the falling cataracts.'"

Nodier builds another part of his theory on a story which by his time had become a stock motif in the Cratylian tradition. In order to discover the origin of language, King Psamtik I of Egypt ordered two children to be reared in the desert among goats, without human contact. When they were brought back to his court, the children uttered the word *bekos*, which means "bread" in Phrygian. To Psamtik, this experiment proved that Phrygian must be the mother of all languages. Nodier, however, uses this story to support his hypothesis that language originated in the human imitation of animal sounds. He declares that the wise king's experiment validates "'the universal opinion of lexicologists, who have always related the invention of our first consonant {b} to the *bique* (nanny-goat) or the *brebis* (ewe).'" This circular argument — that language must have started as an imitation of animal vocalizations because the conventional sounds assigned to a given animal by one's own language are present in familiar words in that language — is an instance of what Genette terms "faunologic." In Cratylusland, all animals sound like themselves only when they speak our own language.

Through an ambitious comparison between the development of language in the child and the stages of language in human history, Nodier seeks to establish the necessary, natural order in which each vowel and consonant emerged over time. His reverie on the origin of *b* is a wonderful example of how alliteration, onomatopoeia, and faunologic can overdetermine the study of language: "'The *bambino*, the babe-in-arms, the brat has discovered the three labials: he broods, he pouts, he mopes; he babbles, blabbers, prattles, blathers, bleats, blabs, bawls, broods, smacks his lips; he grumbles over a bauble, a bagatelle, a piece of rubbish ... a bonbon, a booboo.'" The primacy of *b* can also be proved, Nodier adds, by eponymy. Just look at the many proper names starting with this letter in the Bible: the earliest society "'has a fortress raised against God, called *Babel*, a capital city called *Biblos*, a king called *Bel* or *Belus*, a false god called *Baal*, and even a mystagogue who makes animals talk and who is called *Balaam*.'"

Nodier's inexhaustible mimological imagination generates many delightful entries for his dictionary of onomatopoetic words in the French language. For example, the *ha-ha:* a phonetic imitation (in Nodier's own terminology, a "'mimologism'") of an "'exclamation of surprise, and by extension, the name of a barrier or ditch that appears unexpectedly and wrenches this exclamation from the travelers.'" Or *catacombes* (catacombs): a "'picturesque sequence of sounds for rendering the ringing of the casket, gradually rolling down on the sharp angles of the stones and suddenly coming to a halt in the middle of the tombs.'" Although Nodier's explanations of these words as direct imitations of things may be convincing, they are also highly intertextual: that is, dependent not on things but on other mimologists' words about words. This intertextual chain can be detected if one compares Nodier's "'onomatopoetic'" for *catacombes* to Socrates' eponymy for *sōma-sēma* in Plato's *Cratylus.* Just as Socrates sees the body (*sōma*) as the tomb (*sēma*) of the soul, so Nodier hears the clattering of the casket on the crypt stairs in *catacombe* (*tombe:* tomb). Along similar lines, Derrida's grammatological play on *tomber* (to fall) encapsulates the life and death of Jean Genet, who fell out of grace with God, fell foul of the law, and fell for a series of guys.[38]

In the 1860s, Max Müller derided what he dubbed "the *Bow-wow* theory and the *Pooh-pooh* theory," which assigned the origin of language to onomatopoeia and interjections, respectively.[39] During the same period the authoritative Société de Linguistique banned all further research into this question of language origin.[40] John Lyons fairly sums up the prevailing attitude since then: "Most linguists would say that the question is unanswerable and … totally irrelevant to the construction of a general theory of the structure of language and the description of particular languages."[41] Despite these strictures, the quest for the origin of language retains its fascination for a variety of scholars and researchers today.

Pursued through scientific methods in the laboratory rather than through eponymy, etymology, and other kinds of verbal ingenuity, the topic lingers in the fields of psycho- and neurolinguistics. Consider, for example, the debate between "interactionists" (such as Jerome Bruner) and "innatists" (such as Noam Chomsky).[42] In brief, the interactionists, after John Locke and Condillac, emphasize the importance of the immediate physical and social environments to a child's progress in learning language. In this view, early language consists of names for things and depends on the use of gesturing (pointing to the thing spoken about) in the company of other people. The innatists, preferring Chomsky's theory that a "Language Acquisition Device" exists in the human brain, maintain that even if a child were never taught language by adults, he or she would invent it.[43] In this controversy, the position of Cratylus is taken by the interactionists (language originally refers directly to things), while that of Hermogenes is filled by the innatists (language is a matter of individual creation and collective use).

Another manifestation of the enduring interest in the origin of language is the recurrence of stories about "wild children." Even when conducted within a scientific framework, observations on such children tend to confirm the Cratylian desire that language be directly tied to the world. An eighteenth-century French case made famous by François Truffaut's film *The Wild Child* (1969) is that of "Victor," also known as the "wild boy of Aveyron."[44] Because he learns basic words by pointing to and handling the things to which they refer, "Victor" seems proof that when people were in a state of nature, language was a nomenclature. The power of the mimological imagination over the methods of science can also be seen in a recent case of a "wild child" named "Genie."[45] Kept in extreme isolation by her parents, "Genie" presented the perfect subject for experimentation regarding the origin of language in the individual, but the results have not led to consensus. While Cratylist interactionists read the data obtained to show that language is primarily learned through contact with the environment, Hermogenist innatists interpret the same data as evidence that language is an internally (neurologically) governed sign system.

Mimology plays a large part in the field of glossogenetics, which combines socio- and neurobiology with linguistics in the attempt to determine how and when language originated. According to Gordon Hewes, "human language began with a few gestures, perhaps with a simple deixis or ostension, as it seems to begin in human infants." Reminiscent of Condillac's theory of a primitive "language of action," Hewes's "glottogenetic scenario" posits that the earliest hominids used "vocal signs [that] were motivated, rather than arbitrary.... Some may have been onomatopoetic."[46] Hewes's idea of originary "'mouth-gestures,'" like Fonagy's idea of "oral gesturing," recalls de Brosses's theory of articulatory mimesis, in which written letters reflect the shape of the mouth pronouncing them.[47]

Children are curious about how language began, too. *The Cow That Went OINK*, a picture- and storybook by Bernard Most, playfully suggests that language originated in zoomorphic onomatopoeia.[48] In this story, the cow that went OINK is ostracized by the other cows on the farm because she fails to speak what is presumably the natural language of all cows: MOO. But "one day she heard a friendly MOO" uttered by a pig who, like the cow, is ostracized by his species for not speaking in natural pig language: OINK. So the oinking cow and the mooing pig teach each other: at the end of the story, the cow has learned how to say "MOO OINK," while the pig can say "OINK MOO," and everybody is happy. Ultimately, Most is suggesting, onomatopoeia may be conventional, but perhaps the conventions themselves come from nature — or is it the other way around?

"Looks like a…": Seeing Things in Words

> "My *name* is Alice. …"
> "It's a stupid name enough!" Humpty Dumpty inter-
> rupted impatiently. "What does it mean?"
> "*Must* a name mean something?"
> "Of course it must," Humpty Dumpty said with a short
> laugh; "*my* name means the shape I am. … With a name
> like yours, you might be any shape, almost."
> — Lewis Carroll, *Through the Looking-Glass*

⑨ Whereas some mimologists think of the relationship between language and the natural world as a chain linking the sounds of speech to the sounds of things, other mimologists argue that our writing systems provide a visual representation or picture (French *tableau*) of the things around us. When language is seen as a picture, the emphasis lies upon mimography (imitative writing) rather than upon mimophony (imitative speech). Far from being mutually exclusive, however, these two principles often reinforce each other.

The iconicity of writing is a recurrent idea in the mimological tradition. Briefly, an icon may be defined as any sign that resembles its referent in some way.[49] The theory that writing originated in pictures has always had a strong appeal.[50] Beginning with "pictography" or the "rebus principle," in which schematic visual representations conveyed the things referred to, writing is widely thought to have progressed through an ideogrammatic stage, in which ideas themselves were represented pictorially, toward a phonetic system or alphabet in which "the sign became independent of [the] original referent (and eventually of [its] external shape) and could be combined productively in a conventional system," or language (*langage*) as Saussure specifies it.[51]

A central topic in speculation on the origin of writing in pictures is the Egyptian hieroglyphic. According to ancient Egyptian myth, the words of the creator god Thoth were magically transformed into real objects at the moment he uttered them. This story implies that the meaning of Egyptian hieroglyphics (pictograms) should be sought in the visual identity between language and the world.[52] The eighteenth-century English philologist Rowland Jones sees in hieroglyphics a means of realizing the ideal of a universal language made up of written signs that are wholly transparent to their natural referents (see Genette's chapter 5). In *Hieroglyphic* and other treatises, Jones argues that the "ideomimographic" form of Celtic letters proves that they remain closest to the origin of language in pictures. For instance, the shape of the letter *O* represents the infinity of space and time: a circle. *O* also depicts the sun: hence (by semantic association) light. Its opposite is the terrestrial letter *A*, whose medial bar represents the limits set on earthly in contrast to heavenly life. By decomposing words into letters and letters into elementary graphemes in this manner, Jones believes that he can reconstruct the original "'hieroglyphic.'" Jones is important in the history of mimologism because he transforms the principle of mimophony (first announced in Plato's *Cratylus*) into the principle of mimography.

The notion of language as a system of hieroglyphics achieved general currency during the eighteenth and nineteenth centuries. In *American Hieroglyphics*, John Irwin details the impact on American thought of ideas from the French Enlightenment: "For the writers of the American Renaissance, the hieroglyphics [of Egypt] and the question of man's origin are implicit in one another; if you start with one, sooner or later you will be led to the other."[53] Ralph Waldo Emerson's comments in *Nature* are typical: "As we go back in history, language becomes more picturesque. ... if we could trace them to their sources, we should find in all languages, the names which stand for things."[54] In *Walden*, Henry David Thoreau sees so many similarities between "the multiplicity of natural forms" and "the language of convention" that he equates words with hieroglyphics and hieroglyphics with things themselves. The close examination of a dry leaf evokes a complicated mimological reverie: "*Internally* ... it is a moist thick *lobe*, a word especially applicable to the liver and lungs and *leaves* of fat; ... *externally*, a dry thin *leaf*, even as the *f* and *v* are a pressed and dried *b*. The radicals of lobe are *lb*, the soft mass of the *b* (single lobed, or *B*, double lobed), with the liquid *l* behind it pressing forward."[55] Here, etymology (that is, eponymy: lobe-leaf), mimophony (*l* in leaf and lobe), and mimography (the things seen in the shapes of the lower-case *b* and the capital *B*) lend Thoreau's vision of nature the universality and timelessness of divinely inspired truth.

Nonetheless, the fascination with hieroglyphics in the mimological tradition betrays an anxiety about the ultimate reliability of language as a means of finding truth. Only if language can be shown to be anchored in things can the Cratylist be sure of its veracity. This epistemological problem fuels the debate between Cratylus and Hermogenes in Plato's dialogue, and between all their heirs on either side thereafter. Whereas Augustine sees the Fall as the cause of the disruption of the pristine continuity between God's Word and human language, Enlightenment philosophers consider language as fallen primarily in relation to Nature. A variety of attempts are therefore made to "reform" the writing system in order to return it to its presumably original state in which each word names a thing. Such reforms exemplify "secondary mimologism": the view that language should be and could be mimetic but sadly is not and therefore must be artificially (re)made to be so.

The influential de Brosses thinks that language has lost touch with nature — hence, truth — through the process of "derivation" and "abuses" in usage (see chapter 6). Establishing that language can and should be a *tableau* or picture of things is the main goal of his work. He defines both speech and writing as *peinture* (painting); the former imitates nature by means of sounds, the latter by means of letters. Everything is connected by "'resemblance'" or analogy, which, in turn, guarantees the truth of language. Thus, when we speak, each vocal organ "'takes on, as nearly as it can, the form {*la figure*} of the very object it wants to depict with the voice: it produces a hollow sound if the object is hollow, or a harsh one if the object is rough.'" Likewise, in our writing system, the shape (*la figure*) of each letter of the alphabet should correspond as accurately as possible to the object depicted by the word.

In de Brosses's opinion, language has become "'decadent'" over time, necessitating a reform of writing. He proposes to replace our merely "'verbal'" alphabetic writing system with a "'real'" writing system modeled on hieroglyphics. The new letters will take the shape of the vocal organs during the act of pronunciation (see the charts at the end of chapter 6). Through this systematic combination of mimophony and mimography, de Brosses seeks to "compensate for and neutralize" the defects of language by returning words to the truth of painting (*la vérité de peinture*) — the form of representation he considers closest to nature itself.

Whereas Socrates and de Brosses are "disappointed" Cratylists who find that language in actual usage falls far short of their ideal, Genette characterizes Gébelin as a "happy mimologist" because he is so utterly certain of the correctness of language in its current state (see chapter 7). Gébelin complicates de Brosses's metaphor of language as painting by adding to it an analogy between language and music. For Gébelin, the "'harmony'" of nature is reflected by the "'harmony'" of speech, which picturesquely "'paints'" the place where its native speakers live. Gébelin's "geomimology" anticipates the reveries about language and place in nineteenth-century mimologists such as Nodier and Renan. Like de Brosses, Gébelin uses the resources of both mimophony and mimography in developing his theory of writing as doubly iconic or "'hieroglyphic.'" As a "picto-ideogram," each written letter provides "'the painting of an object'" for the eye; and as an "ideophone," it represents the object for the ear (see the charts at the end of chapter 7). Although they have a "gratifying circularity," concludes Genette, Gébelin's "generalized hieroglyphics" tend to collapse the difference between sign and referent, word and thing. The result, as Socrates already had warned in Plato's *Cratylus*, is "'nonsense.'"

The ethnocentric assumption that an authentic writing system must be phonetically based runs through many of the texts Genette discusses in *Mimologics*, beginning with Plato.[56] In several eighteenth- and nineteenth-century mimologists, an overvaluation of alphabetic writing as the most sophisticated kind entails a primitivist nostalgia for iconic writing as being closer to nature. A subtopic of this ethnocentric mimologic is the equation of advanced languages with the use of both vowels and consonants, as in Indo-European alphabets. Ernest Renan's studies of the "Semitic" languages of the Middle East are a case in point (see Genette's chapter 11). In Renan, the "Cratylian desire" for a picture-language travels to the Orient, generating a series of geomimological reveries whose racism is only thinly veiled by the scientific discourse of comparative linguistics.[57] Renan sees the homelands, the minds, and even the physiognomies of Jews and Arabs reflected in the supposedly inferior structure of their languages. He imagines that these primarily consonantal Semitic languages match the desert—dry, hard, monotonous. For him, the "'consonantal skeleton'" of Hebrew and Arabic writing systems corresponds to the familiar icon of the Bedouin—a tall, lean figure standing by his camel—which appears throughout nineteenth-century European Orientalist painting. On the metaphysical level, too, the sounds and the letters of Hebrew and Arabic convey to Renan the severity and the sterility of the monotheistic beliefs of Judaism and Islam.

The Western mimological imagination has been powerfully attracted not only to the Egyptian hieroglyph but also to the Chinese ideogram.[58] Hieroglyphics and ideograms evoke the Orient (Near and Far East, respectively) as what Genette terms a "linguistic utopia," a Cratylian land where words really do embody things. The literary writer probably best known to Anglo-American readers for his interest in Chinese ideograms is Ezra Pound. By featuring them in the *Cantos,* he tries to put into practice the mimological theories of two contemporaries: Ernest Fenollosa, author of *The Chinese Written Character as a Medium for Poetry* (1936), and Alan Upward, author of *The New Word.* Fenollosa maintains that the shapes of certain Chinese characters stand for the shapes of real things. Ideograms, Pound himself avers, are true icons because they picture "the energy of process in nature."[59] This doctrine of the thingness of language is supported by Upward's etymologies (mostly eponymies based on mimophony, like those of Socrates in the *Cratylus*) and by his persuasive mimographical reveries: "What is the sign of Change? ... I find that I have drawn a Spring."[60] Ultimately, though, like Renan's vision of an Arab in Arabic, Pound's idea that only Chinese ideograms capture the full presence of things depends on an Orientalist projection of the writing system of the Other. In fact, the ideogram is no less a conventional sign than the alphabetic letter: "The appearance of a necessary or motivated link between a picture and what it represents" says Steven Winspur, "can exist only *within* an arbitrary or coded system of meaning. ... the 'natural' motivation between a pictogram [or an ideogram] and the scene it depicts ... is not natural at all but rather a fictional *ideal.*"[61]

Claudel, like Pound, gives a central place to iconicity in his poetics, but unlike Pound, who imports Chinese ideograms wholesale into his poetry, Claudel uses them as a point of departure for the invention of "Occidental ideograms" (see chapter 14). Moreover, the hieroglyph and the ideogram seem interchangeable for Claudel, who seeks above all a system of graphemes that can satisfy his mimological imagination: "'Is it so absurd to believe that the alphabet is the abbreviated form and the vestige of all the acts, all the gestures, all the attitudes and consequently all the feelings of humanity in the bosom of the creation that surrounds it?'" In effect, Claudel grafts what he takes to be the purely iconic principle of the Chinese ideogram onto the phonetic alphabet. He sees in loco-motive, for example, "'a drawing made to order for children. First, in its length, the word is an image of the animal. L is the smoke, o the wheels and the boiler, m the pistons, and t the marker of its speed ... in the manner of a telegraph post, or else a connecting rod; v is the control gear, i the whistle, e the coupling device, and the underlining is the rail!'"

Defiantly, Claudel tosses his Occidental ideograms in the face of modern lin-guists who deny what poets have always known: namely, that the sound of language *is* perfectly adapted to the sense of the words (mimophony) and that words *do* look like the things they refer to (mimography). "'Are we to believe that between the phonic act and the written sign, between the expression and the thing expressed ... the relationship is purely formal and arbitrary? – or on the contrary, that all words are made up of an unconscious collaboration of eye and voice with the object?'" But if the shape of a word is directly motivated by the thing it refers to, how can one word, such as *toît* (roof) stand for all the different things Claudel claims it does? At first, he sees in it the "'complete representa-tion of a house, not even missing the two chimneys: O is the wife and I is the husband, characterized by their basic differences: care and force; the dot of the i is the smoke of the hearth or, if you prefer, the spirit shut away behind doors and the private life of the home.'" Soon after, he sees instead an egg or a mouth in the lower-case o. Several years later, the "'two bars'" across the T's indicate the crossbeams over the walls of the house, while the O has become the family's dining table, and the I is the fireplace with the smoke drifting up out of it.

Genette appreciates the delicate balance between "facticiousness" and "fic-titiousness" which Claudel is trying to strike. Wishing to discover the truth naturally present in existing languages rather than to forge a patently artificial language, Claudel engages in serious play (*jeu*) with, on, and about language in his poetics. Consequently, what Genette calls "the stakes of writing" for Claudel are high: this Catholic poet, in order to remain close to nature, hence to God, must ceaselessly engage in the act of nomination, "'in the act of creating ... like a painter on a canvas.'" In this sense, seeing things in words is for Claudel an act of worship. "The main point," says Jean-Claude Coquet of him, "is not to search for a formal representation of the world in language, but to rediscover in oneself, despite the various types of writing systems and the changes in the story, the trace ... of ... universal history: 'One only learns the secret of things by creating them.'" [62]

A strong vein of Cratylism runs through much devotional literature, especially poetry, written in Catholic and Protestant contexts. One example known to every student of the *Norton Anthology of English Literature* is George Herbert's "The Altar," a sixteenth-century lyric in which the words are typographically arranged to suggest the shape of an altar. In Marshall McLuhan's terms, "the medium is the message" here. Theoretically speaking, "The Altar" exemplifies the use of mimological typography, or *mimo(typo)graphy*, in order to guarantee the truth of written language. By making words, letters, and their spacing into a holistic icon of his topic, the devotional writer both praises and reincarnates the Word of God.[63]

The Cratylian dream of language as a picture of the whole world was carried forward into modern poetics by the French Symbolists. Arthur Rimbaud's famous poem "Voyelles" (Vowels), for instance, assigns very specific chromatic, tactile, and aural properties to the letters *A, E, I, O,* and *U* (see chapter 18, in which Genette also discusses the chromatic alphabet created by Victor Hugo). Mimophony and mimotypography converge in Rimbaud's poem. Thus, *O* both sounds like and looks like a "suprême Clarion plein des strideurs étranges" (supreme Clarion full of strange stridor): besides the phonetic effect of the *o* in "Clarion," imagine the round shape of the end of the musical instrument itself.[64] Although widely thought to be an avant-gardist poetic device, this Symbolist mimologic is part of the Cratylian tradition. Rimbaud's "supreme Clarion" in which the *O* evokes eternity recalls Rowland Jones's claim that the letter *O* stands for the circle of the cosmos.

Any attempt to return writing to its supposedly original function as an immediate picture of things is fraught with contradictions. Wendy Steiner's study of modernist poetry analyzes the work of "concrete poets" such as Augustos de Campos and Eugen Gomringer, who try to transform poems into things by foregrounding the physical palpability of the sign. Through making the visual layout of a text serve as the main signifier for its own semantic content or message — sometimes substituting icons for words, sometimes displaying words and pictures side by side — the concrete poets challenge the supremacy of the alphabetic writing system. "It is important to keep in mind, however," Steiner remarks, "that the poetic exploitation of typography in and of itself does not create concreteness."[65]

Mallarmé, a Symbolist whom the concrete poets claim as a forerunner, struggled with precisely this problem (see chapter 12). As Genette explains, Mallarmé's secondary mimologism does not involve miming things themselves through words. Rather, his poetics is designed to "'compensate for the failings of natural languages'" by embedding words in the absolute systematicity of verse, which corrects them by ordering them according to exact semiotic rules. The rigor of verse, Mallarmé hopes, will at last overcome the damage that

xlv

historical change, individual whim, and other events of "'chance'" (*le hasard*) have done to language. For Mallarmé, the deleterious linguistic effects of chance are epitomized by the "'perverse couple'" *jour/nuit*, in which the phonetic sequence is just the reverse of what semantic logic would require because -*ou* is a dark sound, while -*ui* is a light sound. Perhaps the best-known example of experimental mimotypography in poetry, Mallarmé's "Un Coup de dés n'abolira jamais le hasard" (A throw of the dice will never abolish chance), aims at fulfilling the Cratylian desire for a perfect language. Thus, Genette argues, Mallarmé's final purpose is not merely to achieve "graphic mimologism" but to "absolutely transcend the linguistic given, bestowing ... a *purer* meaning on the words of the tribe."

Is Mallarmé a mimologist then, or not? According to Derrida in "The Double Session," much of Mallarmé's poetry and prose seeks a way out of or around mimesis, which has dominated literature in the West since Plato.[66] Mallarmé emphasizes the "nothingness" that underlies mimesis, which is always an imitation of something else and hence nothing in itself, by itself, for itself. Both writing and painting — and, even more so, the metaphor of writing as *peinture* — are complicit in the fraud that is mimesis.[67] In order to counteract this entrenched misrecognition of the status and function of writing, says Derrida, Mallarmé engages in a "practice of spacing" (*espacement*) that upsets the traditional adequation between words and things — the ground of truth.[68] Instead, Mallarmé locates truth within the ongoing process of writing. "Why should we perform the miracle," Mallarmé asks in *Crise de vers*, "by which a natural object is almost made to disappear beneath the magic waving wand of the written word, if not to divorce the object from the direct and the palpable, and so to conjure up the pure idea?"[69]

Genette and Derrida agree that Mallarmé avoids simply rejecting the heritage of mimesis from Western philosophy and literature. More ambitiously, he mines the problematics of representation from the inside. Derrida's term for this iconoclastic enterprise is the *hymen*, or the spacing(s)-between, through which Mallarmé approaches the oppositional pairs of concepts that have long organized our thinking about the relation of language to the world: word-thing, word-picture, sound-letter, voice-writing, and so on.[70] The idea of writing as a picture (*tableau*) of things, for instance, is critically redirected in Mallarmé's poetics: "'Peindre, non la chose, mais l'effet qu'elle produit'" (To paint not the thing but the effect it produces). Derrida admires the way Mallarmé's use of language always hovers "in-between" reference, meaning, and the ironic nullification of both. Finally, Mallarmé's Cratylism — if that is the correct name for his attitude to language — presents us with a "hymen" between imitation as truth and imitation as game (*jeu*).[71]

Troubled by the "'crisis in literature'" (*crise de vers*) that Mallarmé's exposure of the fallacies of mimesis inaugurated, Paul Valéry redefines poetic language as an "'algebra,'" thereby siding with the Hermogenists against the Cratylists. But, as Genette shows, Valéry remains a Cratylist at heart (see chapter 12). In identifying the superiority of poetry over prose with the special "'poetic state'" that the former creates in the reader, Valéry reveals that he still thinks of poetry as a representational system—specifically, for the emotions. Moreover, in describing poetry as a "'musicalized'" version of the world, and in analogizing poetry with dance, Valéry slips back into thinking about language in terms of a picture (*tableau*). He even writes a mimological prose poem entitled "Alphabet" about how we can see, hear, and touch the essence of things through letters.[72] Thus, Genette concludes, Valéry's poetics is deeply aporetic: his extreme nominalism leads him back willy-nilly to extreme realism.[73] The road to Cratylusland is often traveled by Hermogenes.

The ludic mimologism that characterizes much of modern and especially postmodern literature can be understood in the light of this persistent tension within the Cratylian tradition. Can one ever be sure that words either do or do not refer to things? James Joyce's practice of mimotypography in *Finnegans Wake* epitomizes this ambivalence, for it simultaneously proves and disproves Cratylism: as Jean-Michel Rabaté observes, iconicity "permeates not only the visual strategies, but also the aural devices, while it is at the same time grounded on the disjuncture of seeing and hearing."[74] Comparable to Mallarmé's "Coup de dés," Joyce's text self-deconstructs by exposing the nullity of the very mimophony and mimography it uses to produce its most persuasive mimetic and aesthetic effects.

Johann Georg Wachter, a traditional mimologist, takes very seriously the premise that words imitate things; he believes that all letters whatsoever can be reduced to two original iconic signs, $\oplus$ and $\otimes$ (see chapter 5). By contrast, Joyce uses such sigla to construct what Rabaté calls a "deliberately baffling iconic system" made up of "the interaction of particular languages—as many as possible, ... even those he cannot read or understand such as Chinese and Japanese." Joyce's aim, unlike that of the seventeenth- and eighteenth-century philosophers, is not to achieve transparency for the sign but rather to multiply the sonorous and semantic effects generated by the reader's own efforts to make sense of a largely opaque sign: "The iconicity of the text cannot therefore be reduced to a 'mimetic' principle" because of the commotion caused by mimotypography itself. Indeed, "the various emblematic, archetypal, stereotypical, and graphological devices through which 'soundsense' and 'sensesound' are made kin" in Joyce's *Wake* herald Derrida's deconstructive grammatology in *Glas*.[75]

The gambit of making words look like things motivates the mimotypographical constructions of Francis Ponge (see chapter 16). In a well-known manifesto Ponge refuses to choose between mimologist and conventionalist views of language: "'TAKING SIDES WITH THINGS *equals* TAKING ACCOUNT OF WORDS.'" Ponge's work deliberately blurs the eternal Cratylian question—which came first, the thing or the word?—by going back and forth between the two. Ponge may share Claudel's fascination with the ideogram, but he may also sympathize with Mallarmé's distrust of the "'failings of natural language.'" Commenting on the postmodern crisis in language, Ponge expresses concern with today's increasingly mediated and abstract literature. Part of his purpose in writing, therefore, is to show us all the things that are in words, lest we forget them. Look carefully at *gymnaste* (gymnast): see the man's goatee and moustache, and the creased leotard he wears? And there is "'a resting bird in profile'" in *oiseau* (bird). Elsewhere, adopting the perspective of secondary mimologism, Ponge complains about mismatches between words and things and sets about correcting language so that it will better reflect reality.[76] Thus, although pleased to find that *oiseau* "'contains *all the vowels*,'" he remarks that "'instead of the S, as its only consonant, I would have preferred the ... V of the breast-bone, the V of the outspread wings, the V of *avis* {Latin, bird}—OIVEAU.'"

Are all these mimologists kidding or are they serious? And which side are they on, that of things or that of words? (Is there ultimately a difference?)

The Parti Pris *of Linguistics: Demotivating versus Remotivating the Sign*

> "When *I* use a word," Humpty Dumpty said,
> in a rather scornful tone, "it means just what I
> choose it to mean. ...."
> "The question is," said Alice, "whether you *can*
> make words mean so many different things."
> —Lewis Carroll, *Through the Looking-Glass*

℗ One of Genette's many insights concerns the historical and axiological inseparability of philosophy, linguistics, and poetics. Nowhere is their overlap more evident than in the continuing controversy over the motivation versus the arbitrariness of language. Several of the questions raised in the *Cratylus* about the relation of language to knowledge and truth reappear as issues in modern linguistics and poetics, where they are complicated rather than resolved and passed on to postmodern literary theory. Three topics have been central to the "quest for the essence of language" in the West during the twentieth century: sound symbolism, diagrammatism, and tropology.[77]

The idea that the sounds of spoken words are connected to the persons or things to which the words refer makes its debut, according to Genette, in Plato's *Cratylus*. Yet it is important to remember that Socrates turns to mimophony as an expedient only when the method of eponymy has failed to prove beyond a

xlviii

doubt that names and nouns are "'correct'": that is, accurate and true representatives of their referents. "'It will,'" admits Socrates, "'seem ridiculous that things are made manifest through imitation in letters and syllables; nevertheless it cannot be otherwise. For there is no better theory upon which we can base the truth [alētheia] of... names.'" Even in this foundational text, then, sound symbolism has the equivocal status of wishful thinking: Socrates would prefer that words imitate things directly, and since eponymy can establish only indirect (that is, semantic) links between language and the world, he resorts to arguing that the constituent units of words — letters and syllables — are motivated by the natural phenomena they are assigned to represent.

The Cratylian tradition as it has developed since Augustine does not find the least bit ridiculous the idea that the sounds of letters, syllables, and whole words have a mimetic relation to things. On the contrary, mimophony has long been a staple of the philosophy of language, rhetoric, and poetics. Sound symbolism also holds an important place, albeit an embattled one, within modern linguistics. The founder of structural linguistics, Ferdinand de Saussure, dismissed the phenomenon of onomatopoeia as irrelevant to the concerns of the new study of language: "Such words are never organic elements of a linguistic system."[78] Saussure may be reacting against the hyperbolic Cratylism of his immediate predecessors (such as Nodier's "'onomatopoetics'"); moreover, when he declared the sign to be "arbitrary," he was issuing a challenge to the entire Cratylian tradition. Yet Saussure himself, as his posthumously published notebooks reveal, was not a pure conventionalist.

The theory of what Genette calls "restricted mimophony" in modern linguistics (see chapter 18) can be understood as a sort of compromise position between the claims of Cratylus and those of Hermogenes. Like Socrates in Plato's dialogue, modern linguists such as Maxime Chastaing, literary critics such as René Etiemble, and cultural anthropologists such as Edward Sapir *wish* that language were directly tied to the world, so they interpret optimistically and generalize rather freely from any evidence for mimophony they find. Indeed, dozens of statistical studies on the correlations between the use of vowels and the size, shape, color, and gender of persons or things to which vocalic clusters refer were carried out by linguists and stylisticians during the 1930s, 1940s, and 1950s. These experiments lend the authority of science to mimology: the quantitative data gathered seem to prove that words, or at least the sounds of speech, do correspond to things — in one way or another. And that is just the problem: because scientific methods ultimately yield only *relative* conclusions, most modern mimologists are forced to admit that the correspondence between intra- and extralinguistic domains is at best weak, at worst illusory — in short, "restricted."

Overall, says Genette, the formation of linguistics as a discipline has involved a constant tug-of-war between resolute Hermogenists and equally determined

Cratylists, or between Saussurean conventionalists who would demotivate language and intuitive mimologists who would remotivate language in relation to material and emotional realities. Specifically, "while [Otto] Jespersen and his heirs were working hard to establish the objective existence of a phonic symbolism [e.g., onomatopoeia] on the basis of experiments, an event took place in the field of linguistic science ... that can be described as a *rupture between the phonic* (or the graphic, or any other material support of the functioning of language system) *and the linguistic.*" The study of the sounds and shapes of words, or mimophony and mimography, which hitherto constituted the mainstay of Cratylism is now relegated to phonetics, a subfield within linguistics. Linguistics proper has come to be defined, after the manner of Saussure, as having to do with the structures of language (*langage*) and their systematic coherence. Emphasis falls on the necessary arbitrariness of all components of language whatsoever.

Nonetheless, Genette observes, this disciplinary *parti pris* — the postulate of the arbitrariness of the sign, which is tantamount to "the *professional ideology* of the linguist" — has not succeeded in excluding the practice of mimologism. Far from it. In fact, as Jakobson's influential work attests, secondary mimologism can sit quite comfortably alongside the most rigorous structuralism in linguistics or in poetics or in literary theory. Thus, as Genette shows, Jakobson's interest in "'parallelism'" among the structural levels of language — phonetic, morphological, semantic, syntactic — leads him to postulate a principle of resemblance operative in language generally (see chapter 12).[79] Under the "'poetic function,'" which, Jakobson maintains, is present in all uses of language but dominates aesthetic discourse, every aspect of language has the potential to become (re)motivated.[80] In this way, he relegitimizes the question of sound symbolism, including onomatopoeia and chromatism, for linguistic investigation: "Phonic oppositions not only play a ... conventionally distinctive role with regard to grammatical entities of languages endowed with a specific meaning ... [but] also possess their own direct yet latent significance."[81] Describing it in cautiously formal terms, Jakobson also revives another favorite Cratylian motif, "colored audition" or synaesthesia: "The relations linking the distinctive oppositions of language and the systematics of colors in particular seem to open ... promising avenues for common research among physicists, anthropologists, psychologists, art historians, and linguists, provided that these comparisons are founded on a consistent relativism."[82]

Perhaps the most extensive of Jakobson's remotivations of language takes the form of diagrammatism. Most of the mimologists Genette discusses are concerned with "imagistic" iconicity in language: that is, a close similarity between a word and its referent. By contrast, diagrammatic iconicity is defined by Max Nänny as "an arrangement of [words], none of which necessarily resembles its

1

referent, but whose relationships to each other mirror the relationships of their referents."[83] Because it claims an indirect resemblance between language and the experiential world, one mediated by structural "homologies" and "parallels," diagrammatism is more acceptable within the framework of a Saussurean linguistics than the kinds of direct resemblance between words and things sought by mimologists before the twentieth century. Julius Caesar's famous *veni, vidi, vici* (I came, I saw, I conquered), says Jakobson, provides a syntactical representation or diagram of the order of historical events: "The symmetry of three disyllabic verbs with an identical initial consonant and identical final vowel added splendor to [his] laconic victory message."[84] As another example, Jakobson locates in a political slogan both phonetic and syntactic diagrams of how the voter feels about the candidate: "Both cola of the trisyllabic formula 'I like Ike' rhyme ... and the second of the two rhyming words is fully included in the first one ... /layk/-/ayk/, a paronomastic image of a feeling which totally envelops its object."[85]

As Genette indicates, Jakobson's diagrammatism has many venerable forerunners in the annals of Cratylism. A central point of contention in the long Quarrel between the Ancients and the Moderns during the 1600s and 1700s was the correct order or *rectus ordo* that all languages should follow in their syntax (see chapter 9). The most "natural" (the most strictly mimetic) order of words was thought to be the key to determining the most logical and also the universal linguistic representation: *rectus ordo = naturalis ordo*.[86] During this same era, in the wake of John Locke's powerful arguments for the conventionality of language, Cratylian desire moved from the search for one-to-one correspondences between words and things to the exploration of mimeticism at the level of syntactical and discursive "arrangement." In an important sense, then, Jakobson's structural diagrammatism is a recent avatar of the theory of the *naturalis ordo*. Compare, for instance, his iconic interpretation of the slogan "I like Ike" with the following analysis by Denis Diderot of the "'hieroglyphic beauties'" in Virgil's account of the death of Euryalus (*Aeneid* 433–37): "'the image of spurting blood, *it cruor*' (... '*it* is analogous both to the spurt of blood and to the small movement of the drops of water on the leaves of a flower'); 'and that image of the head of a dying man falling back on his shoulder, *cervix collapsa recumbit.*'"

A subtler type of Cratylism, diagrammatism exerts an almost irresistible appeal. Since the 1970s, interest in syntactic and discursive iconism, intertwined with sound symbolism, has recurred in linguistics. For instance, Roger Wescott's work draws upon ethology, neurolinguistics, and glossogenetics to argue that our original language(s) employed mimophony and iconic syntax. The Cratylian desire for words to resemble things shapes his central hypothesis: "Iconicity is a relative rather than an absolute characteristic of any communication system, language included. As regards iconism, then, the only realistic question we can ask about a given form is not 'Is it iconic?' but rather 'How iconic is it?' " [87] David Armstrong offers a sociobiological explanation for linguistic iconicity. Language possesses a "duality of patterning" (gesture : word :: motivated : arbitrary) as a result of evolution: "Language has, perforce, remained grounded in the world of experience, and it has employed a complex set of 'iconic' devices in order to do so." [88] Finally, Marge Landsberg has made numerous contributions to the theory of iconicity or "the imitation of nonlinguistic reality" that occurs on morphological, phonological, and syntactic levels of language. Acknowledging Jakobson as an important model for her work, Landsberg polemicizes against those linguists who, like Hermogenes and his modern heir Saussure, "still vehemently and rather caustically" deny "the existence of iconic elements" in language.[89]

Besides sound symbolism and diagrammatism, a third site of recurrent controversy between Cratylists and Hermogenists over the centuries is the status of tropes. Do metaphor and metonymy connect language and our experience of the world? Or are these master tropes just one more example of the power of language to create an illusion of reality? According to Genette, the mimological tradition strictly speaking begins not with Plato, whose *Cratylus* ends on a note of uncertainty regarding the truth of language: eponymy fails to prove that all words are mimetic, and sound symbolism proves only that speech may have mimetic potential. The tradition begins rather with Augustine (see chapter 2), who is determined to establish indubitably that words embody things: would the Christian Creator have created a language that is any less than perfectly mimetic? His effort produces a strong misreading of Plato's legacy by valorizing a universal principle of resemblance achieved through a "tropological semantics." By refocusing attention on the links inside and between the words in metaphor, metonymy, and synecdoche (signifier-signified and sign-sign relations), Augustine manages to construct a "fragile" but persuasive "camouflage" that hides the gap between words and things left open by Plato's text.

Within the overarching Cratylian quest from Augustine's time through the nineteenth century, however, a split emerges between partisans of metaphor as the one true link between words and things and the proponents of metonymy for that honor. In his first three books (*Figures I, II, III*) Genette discusses a range of issues bearing upon rhetorical theory and literary interpretation. These separate studies furnish an important background to his project in *Mimologics* (see especially chapters 9, 12, 13, and 18).[90] Noting that "the modern idea of rhetoric" is founded on the very "*division* of the tropes," Genette argues in an essay titled "Rhetoric Restrained" that the reduction of the tropological field to the oppositional pair metaphor/metonymy pushes theoreticians in the 1700s and after decisively toward "figures with a stronger semantic tenor ... and, among these, preferably ... figures of a 'sensory' semanticism." The widespread understanding of all kinds of linguistic figures in terms of a relation of similarity (metaphor) was a triumph for "a kind of eternal Cratylism." At the same time, the main criterion for high achievement in literature, or the aesthetic use of language, becomes how closely it captures the "physical or sensory": that is, its mimetic "'correctness.'"[91]

In both "Rhetoric Restrained" and *Mimologics,* Genette emphasizes the importance of Jakobson's influence on the development of modern rhetoric and literary theory. The "valorization of the analogical" that pervades Jakobson's work in phonology, psycholinguistics, and poetics is characteristic of Russian Formalism, whence it travels into French Structuralism. What Jakobson calls the "metaphorical pole" of language also governs Anglo-American philosophy of language and criticism before 1960; see the work, for instance, of I. A. Richards.[92] In short, the history of modern rhetoric may be seen as a prolonged effort to remotivate language by concentrating on how words represent the "figures" of things.

Several pieces in Genette's *Figures* examine the ways in which individual writers approach the Cratylian problematic underlying modern rhetoric. In *Mimologics* (chapter 13), Genette returns to his earlier discussion of the poetics of the proper name in Proust's novels. As Roland Barthes observes in "Proust and Names," *Remembrance of Things Past* undertakes a thorough (re)motivation of language by applying sound symbolism and metaphor to the names of persons and places familiar to the narrator in the story.[93] What further interests Genette about Proust's novels is their tension between the Cratylian desire to see all relationships in terms of metaphorical resemblances and the potentially disruptive mode of metonymy. For Proust's fictional hero Marcel, as for Cratylus, etymology (actually, eponymy) and sound symbolism irrefutably prove that "the *essence of things* lies in the *hidden meaning* of their names." Everything is connected in a seamless web of experience and truth. But, Genette reminds us, the narrator of Proust's fiction keeps an ironic distance from his character's naive mimologism, much in the way that Socrates avoids taking sides with Cratylus at the very end of Plato's dialogue. Thus, *Remembrance of Things Past* "offers simultaneously a very faithful account of mimological reverie and a critique ... of this form of imagination."

At the core of mimologism in Proust and the many other authors discussed in *Mimologics* is "the *referential illusion*" or "the belief in an identity between the signified (the 'image') and the referent." This idea usually entails another: "the belief in a natural relation between the signified and the signifier, or what could be ... termed the *semantic illusion.*" Two major philosophers of the twentieth century who succumbed to both these mimological illusions, Genette says, are Jean-Paul Sartre and Gaston Bachelard (see chapters 12 and 17). Sartre reorients the familiar opposition words versus things into the contrast things-that-are-signs versus things-in-and-of-themselves, and upon this distinction he grafts another: "*'signification'*" (assigned to an object by convention) versus "*'meaning'*" (the natural property of a given object). Notably, Sartre locates "'meaning'" in literature: like a real thing, the word in a literary text has meaning because it evinces "'the participation of a present reality within its being, in the being of other realities ... and by degrees in the universe.'"

Sartre's theory of the word seems a departure from the Cratylian line inasmuch as it depends on either a relation of part to whole (synecdoche) or a relation of effect to cause (metonymy) instead of a relation of resemblance (metaphor). For example, Sartre regards a historical artifact as having meaning because it is an index or "*'vestige'*" of the past. Similarly, he interprets the poetry of Jean Genet as an attempt to "'transform the signification of ... words into meaning,'" thereby restoring words to the world of phenomena in revolt against the conventionality of language. But as Genette demonstrates, Sartre ultimately reinstates the old notion of "poetic language defined as mimesis." Like Diderot's reading of Virgil, Sartre's interpretation of Genet is based on the rule of metaphor, under which words and things are made euphorically interchangeable. Thus, in a poetic phrase from Genet, *moissoneur des souffles coupés* (reaper of gasping breaths), Sartre feels that "'the ... meanings spread through each other and coexist'": breaths = flowers = wind = life and/or death.

Bachelard's imagination is also governed by metaphor or the Cratylian desire to equate words and things. A philosopher of science turned literary critic, Bachelard well illustrates Genette's contention that mimology pervades thinking and writing about language across the disciplines. Setting out to perform a psychoanalysis of empirical methods in physical science, Bachelard gradually succumbs to the spell of the sounds of words and their secret meanings. In his *Water and Dreams* the "material imagination" and the "imagination of matter" coincide: while we imagine the meaning of things, things themselves may be exercising their own imagination, projecting their aura over us, especially if we are poets.[94]

Once Bachelard enters Cratylusland, there is no return. As Genette points out, Bachelard's mimologism consists of "*justifying* the gender of a noun through a relation of conformity between that gender and the sexual identity metaphorically given to the object named." He dwells appreciatively on the "'softness'" (*douceur*) and the "'unhurriedness'" (*lenteur*) of feminine endings in the French language. In his daydreams on the semantic universe of water (*l'eau*, fem.), he discovers the very essence of femininity. He imagines the natural world to be divided between water and fire, earth and air, as between femininity and masculinity: *l'eau* (fem.): *le feu* :: *la terre* : *l'air* (masc.). But these musings are wholly metaphorical, inspired by the material world but not finally actually in it. Along with Sartre, then, Bachelard gives himself over to the twin pleasures of the "referential illusion" and "the semantic illusion." For Bachelard as perhaps for all Cratylists, mimological reverie affords "a return to originary intimacy: that is, to the security of sameness, ... a refusal of and flight from difference, a desire or nostalgia for the reassuring and blissful ... identity between word and thing, language and world, which is projected onto verbal reality."

The Infinite Voyage: Cratylusland Past, Present, and Future

> "But I don't want to go among mad people," Alice remarked.
> "Oh, you can't help that," said the Cat: "we're all mad here. I'm mad. You're mad."
> "But how do you know I'm mad?" said Alice.
> "You must be," said the Cat, "or you wouldn't have come here."
> — Lewis Carroll, *Alice in Wonderland*

🖉 What do philosophers of language, etymologists, grammarians, rhetoricians, philologists, glossogeneticists, phonologists, and psycholinguists have in common with poets, novelists, satirists, travel and science fiction writers? They are all fascinated by the same kinds of questions about language: where does language come from? do words embody things? can the study of languages lead us to universal truths about humanity, the natural world, and beyond? Genette's *Mimologics* takes us on a voyage through centuries of the Western imagination as it puzzles over, pulls apart, and plays with speech sounds, the shapes of letters, and the thingness of words. The familiar division between serious philosophical and scientific inquiry on one side and ludic literary and creative production on the other side does not hold in Cratylusland. What the Cheshire Cat says to Alice applies to all the mimologists Genette discusses: each of them, in his own way, is slightly "mad" when it comes to language.

Genette's interest in mimologics grows out of his work in the field of narratology, or the structural study of narrative, during the 1960s and 1970s.[95] In the 1980s Genette turns his attention to the task of formalizing the great variety of what he terms "hypertextual" discourse. In three related books—*Introduction à l'architexte, Palimpsestes,* and *Seuils*—he lays out the parameters of the vast transhistorical and interdisciplinary system of textual relations that organizes literature in the West.[96] According to Genette, "intertextuality" is just one of the kinds of "transtextuality" by which a given text "transcends" its own location in literary history through its multiple links with other texts.[97] Genette's theory

lv

of transtextuality provides a key to his aims in this book, for mimologics is a highly complex discourse that draws upon a plethora of textual materials from all corners of culture.

At the same time, *Mimologics* is a contribution to the field of intellectual history, the history of ideas. Organized chronologically, the book offers both a synchronic sampling of "the typology of the genre" of mimologics and a diachronic tracing of "the main lines of its history." Genette sees the entire mimological tradition contained *in nuce* in the issues raised by one foundational "hypotext": Plato's *Cratylus*. Tracking the development of the main ideas about language across several eras is no simple matter, however. One of Genette's central arguments is that a reductive, linear approach to the history of ideas must give way to a "transformational" approach that is informed by structural principles yet remains responsive to axiological shifts as well as to the quirks of individual biography. As he states elsewhere: "I persist in thinking that absolute relativism is a shibboleth, that historicism kills History, and that the study of transformations entails the examination of, hence a taking into account of, continuities." [98]

Above all, Genette considers mimologics to be a genre, identifiable through certain recurrent features. From Plato's *Cratylus* to Jakobson's "Quest for the Essence of Language," the genre typically takes the form of a voyage—already suggested in the *Cratylus:* at the end, Socrates refrains from taking sides with Cratylus, instead wishing him "'a good trip in the company of (or maybe under the *escort* of) Hermogenes.'" Genette comments: "A long voyage begins, enlivened by brilliant arguments, ever new, ever the same." The Cratylian itinerary may be oriented either toward the past, as in philosophical and paleolinguistic reconstructions of the origin of language; toward the present, as in universal grammars and satires on scholarly research into language; or toward the future, as in programs for reforming language and the invented languages of science fiction. In practice, the genre of mimologics is infinitely flexible, which partly accounts for its popularity. [99]

Genette finds that hypertextual discourses such as mimologics tend to appear in three major "modes": the "serious," the "satiric," and the "ludic." [100] The serious voyage into Cratylusland is exemplified by de Brosses's use of etymology to "enable a methodical reconstruction of the geographical movements of peoples through history." [101] Aiming to construct a comprehensive "'archeology'" and a "'universal vocabulary,'" de Brosses imagines that the sounds and shapes of words recapture primal languages based on vocal imitations of the phenomenal world. In the context of eighteenth-century knowledge, his geomimology is neither intended nor taken as mere whimsy; it is a serious investigation into the nature and history of humankind.

By contrast, Jonathan Swift's *Gulliver's Travels* exemplifies the satirical voyage into Cratylusland. Among the many targets of Swift's wit are the philosophers and grammarians of the 1600s and early 1700s.[102] Their ambitious mimological enterprises are reduced to absurdity, as in the following scene: "[The Professor] then led me to the Frame, about the Sides whereof all his Pupils stood in Ranks.... The Superficies was composed of several Bits of Wood... all linked together by slender Wires. These Bits of Wood were covered... with Papers... and on these Papers were written all the Words of their Language in their several Moods, Tenses, and Declensions, but without any Order." By collecting "several Volumes in large Folio" of "broken Sentences" made up of the odd bits and pieces of words spewed out by this contraption, the Professor (Wallis? Wachter? Rowland Jones?) hopes to discover the key to all languages, "to give the World a compleat Body of all Arts and Sciences."[103]

Swift's fictional Laputa satirizes the very first principle of Cratylism. In the School of Languages, Gulliver meets three Professors sitting "in Consultation upon improving that of their own Country." Devoted mimologists all, they believe that "in Reality, all things imaginable are but Nouns" (Cratylus's idea of language as a nomenclature). To prevent the "Diminution" of thought as well as health, which they believe is caused by using language, the Professors propose "a Scheme for entirely abolishing all Words whatsoever": people are urged to express themselves not indirectly by words but directly by things, "which hath only this Inconvenience attending it; that if a Man's Business be very great, and of various Kinds, he must be obliged... to carry a greater Bundle of *Things* upon his Back."[104]

Exemplifying the third, or ludic, mode of mimologics is Jorge Luis Borges's short story "Funes, the Memorious." Like the Laputan Professors in Swift's satire, Funes spends all his time studying the relation between words and things. In his view, Locke rightly "postulated... an impossible idiom in which each object, each stone, each bird and branch had an individual name," and Funes is determined to achieve this project of secondary Cratylism himself. But, the narrator comments, the "task" of remembering all the particulars of the world, without relying on words to organize them into categories, "was interminable and... useless." In the world of Funes, even to think about something becomes undesirable, for to cogitate "is to forget a difference, to generalize, to abstract." Thus, Borges's Funes represents a ludic transformation of the central premise of Cratylism. In this surreal, "overly replete" Cratylusland, we would not think or even dream about language; there would be "nothing but details, almost contiguous details," and we would all expire "of a pulmonary congestion" brought on by what Sartre once called the "nausea" of existing among/as things.[105]

The serious, satirical, and ludic modes of mimologism often overlap, as Swift's and Borges's texts illustrate. Combining all three modes are Lewis Carroll's *Alice in Wonderland* and *Through the Looking-Glass*. As my six epigraphs for the sections of this essay indicate, Carroll's work addresses in a playful form many of

lvii

the questions about language raised in a more serious way in Genette's *Mimologics*. The scholarly qualities of his work notwithstanding, Genette also recognizes the pleasure of mimologics — the sheer fun of playing with words, which no formal discussion can quite capture. In his conclusion he observes: "In twenty centuries of 'reasonable theorizing,' Hermogenes has produced nothing truly seductive," whereas "Cratylus leaves us with a series of picturesque, amusing, sometimes troubling works."

In this same spirit, Genette pauses here and there to chuckle at the ludicrous lucubrations of the authors he studies, and he cannot resist joining in the fun. In chapter 15 (on Leiris) he makes up a mimologic gloss on a pivotal word used in his own theory: Cratylism, he suggests, is "a verbal hallucination caused by excessive imbibing of bad wine. For the victim, 'everything doubles, and he cannot tell which are the names and which are the things' (Plato *Cratylus* 432d)." Ironically, this make-believe definition is etymologically correct, since in Latin (from the Greek) the word *cratera* means a large bowl used for mixing wine with water. Furthermore, by referring to a specific passage in Plato concerning the paradoxical copresence of similarity and difference in representation, Genette reminds us that Cratylism, or the belief that language should, can, and does imitate things, has been the primary subject of his book.

Reader, welcome to Cratylusland. *Bon voyage!*

NOTES

1. Gaston Bachelard's theory of "reveries on words" draws upon phenomenology and psychology as keys to how language shapes our existence; see Genette's chapter 17. The terms "mimologics" and "mimologism" were first used by Charles Nodier to explain how onomatopoetic words are created; see chapter 9.

2. See, e.g., the bibliography of articles and books provided by Michael D. Palmer in *Names, References, and Correctness in Plato's Cratylus*, American University Studies, ser. 5: Philosophy, vol. 55 (New York: Peter Lang, 1989).

3. On the logical structure of the *Cratylus* and the connection between the correctness of names and truth, see Mary Margaret MacKenzie, "Putting the *Cratylus* in Its Place," *Classical Quarterly* 36.1 (1986): pp. 124–50.

4. Umberto Eco, *A Theory of Semiotics* (Bloomington: Indiana University Press, 1979), p. 7 (original emphasis).

5. Saussure's notebooks are extensively cited and discussed in Jean Starobinski, *Words upon Words: The Anagrams of Ferdinand de Saussure*, trans. Olivia Emmet (New Haven: Yale University Press, 1979); for an example of a Saussurian anagram that is comparable to Socratic eponymy, see the treatment of the name "Scipio" (pp. 16–17).

6. Reviewing Michel Leiris's *Langage tangage: ou Ce que les mots me disent*, John Sturrock comments that "Leiris can no longer quite believe" in the techniques of

eponymy and phonetic substitution on which his writing still relies. "Seriously in the 1920s and 30s," when Leiris participated in the Surrealist movement, "and nostalgically now, he plays the cratylist, deriving the sense of a word from its sound" ("Nostalgic Cratylism," *Times Literary Supplement*, 4 October 1985, p.1092).

7. Derrida's *Glas* was published by Seuil (Paris) in 1974, just two years before Genette's *Mimologiques*.

8. Jacques Derrida, *Glas*, trans. John P. Leavey, Jr., and Richard Rand (Lincoln: University of Nebraska Press, 1986), p.1 (citations hereafter refer to this edition).

9. Ibid., p.41.

10. Ibid., p.5.

11. Ibid., p.11.

12. See "Sounding the Unconscious" by Gregory L. Ulmer, an essay on the Genet column of Derrida's *Glas*, in *Glassary*, ed. John P. Leavey, Jr. (Lincoln: University of Nebraska Press, 1987), pp.23–128.

13. Derrida, *Glas*, p.20.

14. Gregory L. Ulmer, *Applied Grammatology: Post(e)-Pedagogy from Jacques Derrida to Joseph Beuys* (Baltimore: Johns Hopkins University Press, 1985), p. xi. Ulmer's first chapter, "Grammatology," is helpful to our understanding of Derrida's work in relation to the kinds of questions raised by Plato's *Cratylus*.

15. Derrida, *Glas*, pp.142, 149.

16. Ibid., p.37.

17. Michel Aquien argues that what Genette calls "primary cratylism," as epitomized by Cratylus in Plato's dialogue, also describes the poetics of Saint-John Perse. See "*Saint-John Perse et le Cratylisme*," *L'Information littéraire* 39.2 (1987): 62–67.

18. Roman Jakobson, "Linguistics and Poetics," in *Style in Language*, ed. Thomas A. Sebeok (Cambridge, Mass.: MIT Press, 1960), p.357.

19. Ivan Fonagy, "Preconceptual Thinking in Language (An Essay in Linguistic Paleontology)" in *Glossogenetics: The Origin and Evolution of Language*, ed. Eric de Grolier (New York: Harwood Academic Publishers, 1983), pp.329–331.

20. Fonagy's diagram of the articulatory mechanism (ibid., p.349) pictures the buccal cavity at the center of two concentric circles which are intersected by six vectors. Positioned on these circles are twelve olfactory, tactile, temporal, and spatial qualities which, he claims, are expressed by distinct configurations of the buccal cavity in the process of phonation. This schema is the visual equivalent of Charles de Brosses's descriptions of articulatory mimesis in *Traité de la formation mécanique des langues* (1765).

21. Fonagy, "Preconceptual Thinking," p.333.

22. Derrida, *Glas*, p.41.

23. Ibid., p.43.

24. Ibid., p.235. For Derrida's deconstruction of the concept of an origin of language, see his chapter on Jean-Jacques Rousseau in *Of Grammatology*, trans. Gayatri C. Spivak (Baltimore: Johns Hopkins University Press, 1967), pt.2, chap.3, pp.165–268.

25. On the chain as a major paradigm underlying eighteenth-century language theo-

lvix

ries, see Julie Andresen, "Linguistic Metaphors in Charles de Brosses's *Traité* of 1765 and the History of Linguistics," *Linguistica Investigationes* 5.1 (1981): 1–24.

26. Quoted in John M. Fyler, "Saint Augustine, Genesis, and the Origin of Language," in *Saint Augustine and His Influence in the Middle Ages*, ed. Edward B. King and Jacqueline T. Schaefer (Sewanee, Tenn.: Press of the University of the South, 1988), p.74.

27. R. Howard Bloch, *Etymologies and Genealogies: A Literary Anthropology of the French Middle Ages* (Chicago: University of Chicago Press, 1983), p.46.

28. Tzvetan Todorov, *Theories of the Symbol*, trans. Catherine Porter (Oxford: Basil Blackwood, 1982), pp.36, 40–41, 51.

29. Russell Fraser, *The Language of Adam: On the Limits and Systems of Discourse* (New York: Columbia University Press, 1977), p.13. See also A. O. Lovejoy, *The Great Chain of Being* (Cambridge, Mass.: Harvard University Press, 1936).

30. Todorov, *Theories of the Symbol*, p.236.

31. Quoted in Jacques Derrida, *The Archeology of the Frivolous: Reading Condillac*, trans. John P. Leavey, Jr. (Lincoln: University of Nebraska Press, 1987), p.109.

32. On the position of language in the "Classical episteme," with attention to Condillac, de Brosses, and Gébelin, see "Speaking," chap.4 in Michel Foucault, *The Order of Things: An Archaeology of the Human Sciences* (New York: Vintage Books, 1970), pp.78–124. Foucault emphasizes the centrality of the *name:* "One might say that it is the Name that organizes all Classical discourse; to speak or to write is not to say things or to express oneself, it is not a matter of playing with language, it is to make one's way towards the sovereign act of nomination, to move, through language, towards the place where things and words are conjoined in their common essence, and which makes it possible to give them a name" (pp.116–17).

33. Quoting Condillac's definition of natural languages as a "supplement" to the original "language of action," Herman Parret concludes that, despite his intention to uphold the principle of *"continuity"* in language, "the Condillacian project could not be anything but an illusory metaphor of *identity"*—that is, an attempt to realize the Cratylian dream of a language in which words correspond exactly to things ("Idéologie et sémiologie chez Locke et Condillac: La Question de l'autonomie du langage devant la pensée," in *Ut Videam: Contributions to the Understanding of Linguistics*, ed. Werner Abraham (Lisse: Peter de Ridder Press, 1975), p.237 (my translation).

34. Derrida, *Archeology of the Frivolous*, p.81.

35. Quoted in ibid., p.82.

36. Quoted in ibid., p.112.

37. Ibid., pp.112, 118.

38. The fall (*tomber*) of structural linguistics is effected as well, as symbolized by Derrida's "grammatological reading" of the vocable *glas*, one of the examples of onomatopoeia (which Saussure believes is a very limited phenomenon) used in Saussure's *Course in General Linguistics*. See Derrida, *Glas*, esp. pp.90–95.

39. Friedrich Max Müller, *Lectures on the Science of Language* (London: Longman, Green, & Roberts, 1862), p.365.

40. See James H. Stam, *Inquiries into the Origin of Language: The Fate of a Question*, Studies in Language, ed. Noam Chomsky and Morris Halle (New York: Harper & Row, 1976), pt.3.

41. John Lyons, *Semantics* (Cambridge: Cambridge University Press, 1977), 1:85.

42. Talbot J. Taylor, in "Linguistic Origins: Bruner and Condillac on Learning How to Talk," *Language and Communication* 4.3 (1984): 209-24, views Jerome Bruner's 1983 book, *Child Talk*, as an attempt to compromise between interactionism and innatism that leans strongly toward the former. Taylor discusses the relationship between Condillac's and Bruner's ideas about the origin and acquisition of language, respectively.

43. Hans Aarsleff documents the affinities between Chomsky's theories and ideas about language among Descartes, Locke, Condillac, and the general grammarians of the Enlightenment, in "The History of Linguistics and Professor Chomsky," in *From Locke to Saussure: Essays on the Study of Language and Intellectual History* (Minneapolis: University of Minnesota Press, 1982), pp.101-19. Chomsky's Cratylian view of language as naturally innate is contrasted with Saussure's view of language as an arbitrary system of conventions in the context of Plato's *Cratylus* as well as contemporary literary theories in Joseph F. Graham, *Onomatopoetics: Theory of Language and Literature* (Cambridge: Cambridge University Press, 1992).

44. See Roger Shattuck, *The Forbidden Experiment: The Story of the Wild Boy of Aveyron* (New York: Farrar, Straus & Giroux, 1980).

45. Russ Rymer, "A Silent Childhood," *New Yorker*, April 13, 1992, pp.41-81, and April 20, 1992, pp.43-77. See also Rymer, *Genie: An Abused Child's Flight from Silence* (New York: Harper Collins, 1993).

46. Gordon W. Hewes, "The Invention of Phonemically Based Language," in *Glossogenetics: The Origin and Evolution of Language*, ed. Eric de Grolier (New York: Harwood, 1983), pp.144, 147.

47. See Ivan Fonagy, "Live Speech and Preverbal Communication," in *The Genesis of Language: A Different Judgment of Evidence*, ed. Marge E. Landsberg (New York: Mouton, 1988), pp.183-85.

48. Bernard Most, *The Cow That Went OINK* (New York: Harcourt Brace Jovanovich), 1990. See also the list of French "zoomorphic onomatopoetic words" provided by Nodier, cited in Henri de Vaulchier, *Charles Nodier et la lexicographie française: 1808–1844* (Nancy: Didier-Erudition, 1984), p.144.

49. The American philosopher C. S. Peirce is the source most frequently mentioned for the theory of iconicity. He distinguishes three kinds of signs on the basis of their relative degree of "similarity" to the referent. In decreasing order of naturality and increasing order of conventionality, these are the index, the icon, and the symbol. Eco, in his *Theory of Semiotics*, pp.191-217, criticizes the epistemological naiveté of the concept of iconicity: in other words, its mimologism.

50. See Wayne M. Senner, "Theories and Myths on the Origins of Writing: Historical Overview," in *The Origins of Writing*, ed. Wayne M. Senner (Lincoln: University of Nebraska Press, 1989), pp.1-26.

51. Quoted in ibid., p. 5; see also the comparative chart of pictographic writing systems on p. 6. Today, "petrograms," or rock paintings, and "petroglyphs," or rock carvings, are considered to be the earliest forms of iconic writing.

52. See Henry George Fischer, "The Origin of Egyptian Hieroglyphics" in Senner, *The Origins of Writing*, pp. 59–76.

53. John T. Irwin, *American Hieroglyphics: The Symbol of the Egyptian Hieroglyphics in the American Renaissance* (New Haven: Yale University Press, 1980), p. 61.

54. Quoted in ibid., pp. 12–13.

55. Quoted and analyzed in ibid., pp. 17–19. Michael West discusses the influence of Locke, Condillac, de Brosses, and Gébelin, among others, on nineteenth-century American ideas about language in "Thoreau and the Language Theories of the French Enlightenment," *English Literary History* 51.4 (1984): 747–70.

56. Senner points to one of many examples of the Eurocentricism implicit in the privileging of phonetically based writing systems: "Like Roger Bacon, the sixteenth-century Spanish missionary Diego de Landa ... tried to understand ... Mayan glyphs ... in alphabetical terms: 'I will set down here an alphabet of these letters since their difficulty does not allow anything more'" ("Theories and Myths," p. 17). Roy Harris concludes that the most influential modern theories on the origin of writing, including those of Leonard Bloomfield, I. J. Gelb, and David Diringer, are "unsatisfactory" because their typologies are built upon the assumption that phonetic script is superior to all others. Harris suggests that this bias is due to the long ascendancy of Aristotle's definition of writing as a representation of speech. See Harris, "The Evolutionary Fallacy," chap. 3 in *The Origin of Writing* (London: Duckworth, 1986). Derrida also refutes Aristotelian-Saussurean phonocentrism in *Of Grammatology*, pt. 1.

57. On Renan, see Edward Said, "Silvestre de Sacy and Ernest Renan: Rational Anthropology and Philological Laboratory," in *Orientalism* (New York: Random House, 1978), chap. 2, sec. 2, pp. 130–66.

58. See Senner, "Theories and Myths," p. 18; and David N. Keightley, "The Origins of Writing in China: Scripts and Cultural Contexts," in Senner, *The Origins of Writing*, pp. 171–202.

59. Quoted in Richard Godden, "Icons, Etymologies, Origins, and Monkey Puzzles in the Languages of Upward and Fenollosa," in *Ezra Pound: Tactics for Reading*, ed. Ian F. A. Bell (Totowa, N.J.: Barnes & Noble, 1982), p. 223.

60. Quoted in ibid., p. 225. See Ernest Franciso Fenollosa, *The Chinese Written Character as a Medium for Poetry*, ed. Ezra Pound (San Francisco: City Lights Books, 1936); and Allan Upward, *The New Word*, rev. ed. (London: Fifield, 1908).

61. Steven Winspur, "Poetry, Portrait, Poetrait," *Visible Language* 19.4 (1985): 429–30. In a polemical piece titled "Misreading the Ideogram: From Fenollosa to Derrida and McLuhan," Hwa Yol Jung points out "the fascination with Chinese grammatology of non-sinologists ... who are primarily interested in advancing their own theories of language and literature" (*Paideuma* 13.2 [1984]: 214).

62. Jean-Claude Coquet, "La Lettre et les idéogrammes occidentaux," *Poétique* 11 (1972): 404 (my translation).

63. Max Nänny surveys a variety of mimological texts that display visually evocative "juxtapository techniques" from the nineteenth and twentieth centuries in "Iconicity in Literature," *Word & Image* 2.3 (1986): 199–208. Other examples of the kind of mimotypography used in Herbert's poem include a *Mother Goose in Hieroglyphics* (mentioned in Irwin, *American Hieroglyphics*, p. 31) and Guillaume Apollinaire's *Le Bestiare*.

64. The poem, "Voyelles," with an English translation, can be found in *Rimbaud: Complete Works, Selected Letters*, trans. Wallace Fowlie (Chicago: University of Chicago Press, 1966), pp. 120–21.

65. Wendy Steiner, "*Res Poetica:* The Problematics of the Concrete Program," *New Literary History* 12.3 (1981): 529–545 (quotation, p. 537).

66. Derrida, "The Double Session," in *Dissemination,* trans. Barbara Johnson (Chicago: Chicago University Press, 1981), pp. 173–285.

67. Ibid., p. 188. Johnson's translation uses the word "collusion."

68. Ibid. On the adequation between words and things, see pp. 205–6.

69. Quoted in Steiner, "*Res Poetica,*" p. 537.

70. See Derrida, "Double Session," p. 212.

71. "These plays ... are anathema to any lexicological summation, any taxonomy of themes, any deciphering of meanings" (ibid., p. 277).

72. See James R. Lawler, "The 'Alphabet' of Paul Valéry," in *The Prose Poem in France: Theory and Practice,* ed. Mary Ann Caws and Hermine Riffaterre (New York: Columbia University Press, 1983), pp. 163–79.

73. Michel Jarrety characterizes Valéry as a "nominalist" in "Le Rhéteur, le sophiste et les idolâtres," *Littérature* 56 (1984): 23–41.

74. Jean-Michel Rabaté, " 'Alphybettyformed verbage': The Shape of Sounds and Letters in *Finnegans Wake*," *Word and Image* 2.3 (1986): 237.

75. Ibid., pp. 239, 243.

76. Judith E. Preckshot sees Ponge's mimotypographical poetics as "a turning back to a tradition of rhetorical discourse" — one steeped in mimology — rather than "a revolution" ("A Case of Entrapment: Francis Ponge's 'L'Araignée mise au mur,'" *Stanford French Review* 7.3 [1983]: 339).

77. "Quest for the Essence of Language" (1965) is an essay by Roman Jakobson; see *Selected Writings,* vol. 2, *Word and Language* (Paris: Mouton, 1971), pp. 345–59. This piece is consistently cited by that group of contemporary linguists who maintain that language imitates natural and social phenomena.

78. Ferdinand de Saussure, *Course in General Linguistics,* trans. Roy Harris (London: Duckworth, 1983), p. 69. For a comprehensive introduction to Saussure's work, see Jonathan Culler, *Ferdinand de Saussure* (New York: Penguin Books, 1976).

79. See Jakobson's extensive remarks on parallelism in *Dialogues,* with Krystyna Pomorska, trans. Christian Hubert (Cambridge, Mass.: MIT Press, 1983), pp. 99–109.

80. Jakobson's most important statement on poetic and aesthetic discourse is the essay "Linguistics and Poetics."

81. Jakobson and Pomorska, *Dialogues*, p. 55. See also Jakobson and Linda R. Waugh, "The Spell of Speech Sounds," in *The Sound Shape of Language* (Bloomington: Indiana University Press, 1979), chap. 4, pp. 177–222.

82. Jakobson and Pomorska, *Dialogues*, pp. 54–55. See also D. Barton Johnson, "The Role of Synesthesia in Jakobson's Theory of Language," *International Journal of Slavic Linguistics and Poetics* 25–26 (1982): 219–32.

83. Nänny ("Iconicity in Literature," p. 199) bases this definition on Peirce. Jakobson had made the same Peircean distinction in "Quest for the Essence of Language," p. 350: "In images the *signans* represents the 'simple qualities' of the *signatum*, whereas for diagrams the likeness between the *signans* and *signatum* exists 'only in respect to the relations of their parts.'" For a contemporary linguist's view of iconicity, see Lyons, *Semantics*, 1: 102–5. Todorov surveys "diagrammatic" and other theories of sound symbolism in "Le Sens des sons," *Poétique* 11 (1972): 446–62.

84. Jakobson repeats this example in "Linguistics and Poetics" (p. 358) and in "Quest for the Essence of Language" (p. 350).

85. Jakobson, "Linguistics and Poetics," p. 357. See also Linda R. Waugh, "The Poetic Function and the Nature of Language," in *Verbal Art, Verbal Sign, Verbal Time*, ed. Roman Jakobson with Krystyna Pomorska and Stephen Rudy (Minneapolis: University of Minnesota Press, 1985), pp. 143–68: "And, indeed, poetry is based to a large extent on *iconicity*—a factual similarity relation between *signans* and *signatum* ... —or on *artifice*—an imputed similarity relation between *signans* and *signatum*" (p. 157).

86. Foucault emphasizes the importance of "order" as the linchpin of the Classical episteme: "The ... world of resemblance finds itself dissociated and, as it were, split down the middle: on the one side, we shall find the signs that have become tools of analysis, marks of identity and difference, principles whereby things can be reduced to order, keys for a taxonomy; and, on the other, the empirical and murmuring resemblance of things, that unreacting similitude that lies beneath thought and furnishes the infinite raw material for divisions and distributions" (*The Order of Things*, pp. 57–58).

87. Jacob Bronowski, "Human and Animal Languages," in *To Honor Roman Jakobson* (The Hague: Mouton, 1967), 1: 377, quoted in Roger Williams Wescott, *Sound and Sense: Linguistic Essays on Phonosemic Subjects*, Edward Sapir Monograph Series in Language, Culture, and Cognition, no. 8 (Lake Bluff, Ill.: Jupiter Press, 1980), p. 15. (The essays in *Sound and Sense*, fairly representative of the range of Wescott's work, were published in the same year as number 3 of *Forum Linguisticum* 4.)

88. David F. Armstrong, "Iconicity, Arbitrariness, & Duality of Patterning in Signed and Spoken Language: Perspectives on Language Evolution," *Sign Language Studies* 38 (1983): 69.

89. Marge E. Landsberg, "Iconic Aspects of Language: The Imitation of Nonlinguistic Reality," *Quaderni di Semantica* 7.2 (1986): 322, 321. Landsberg is editor of *The Genesis of Language*, a collection of essays by diverse scholars who urge reconsideration of

the question of the origin of language in light of current science. See her own contribution, "On Linguistic Territoriality, Iconicity, and Language Evolution" (pp. 205–15):
"The most amazing and conspicuous fact that emerges from our data is the overt iconic
character of these phenomena" (p. 208). See also the focus on iconicity in the piece by
Fonagy, "Live Speech," in this same volume.

90. Eleven essays from Genette's series of books *Figures I, II,* and *III* have been translated by Alan Sheridan as *Figures of Literary Discourse* (Oxford: Basil Blackwell, 1982).

91. Genette, "Rhetoric Restrained," in *Figures of Literary Discourse,* pp. 106–7, 120,
110.

92. In "Rhetoric Restrained," pp. 111–13, Genette discusses I. A. Richards, *The Philosophy of Rhetoric,* and also examines Jakobson's theory of the "two poles" of language
(p. 107); see also chapter 12 of *Mimologics.*

93. Roland Barthes, "Proust and Names" (in *New Critical Essays,* trans. Richard
Howard [New York: Hill & Wang, 1980]), analyzes Proust's use of two types of motivation for words, "natural and cultural," in relation to the issues raised by Plato's *Cratylus.*

94. For a useful critique of some of the contradictions in Bachelard's phenomenology, especially as it bears upon his literary criticism, see Katrine Keuneman,
"L'Imagination matérielle chez Bachelard," *Poétique* 41 (1980): 128–36.

95. Genette, *Narrative Discourse: An Essay in Method,* trans. Jane E. Lewin (Ithaca,
N.Y.: Cornell University Press, 1980). See also Gerald Prince, *A Dictionary of Narratology* (Lincoln: University of Nebraska Press, 1987).

96. Genette's three studies on systematic textual relations — *Introduction à l'architexte*
(1979), *Palimpsestes: La littérature au second degré* (1982), and *Seuils* (1987) — were all
published in Paris by Editions du Seuil. The first has been translated as *The Architext:
An Introduction* by Jane E. Lewin (Berkeley: University of California Press, 1992).

97. "The text interests me (solely) in its aspect of *textual transcendence,* meaning everything that places it into relation, hidden or overt, with other texts. I call
that *transtextuality,* and I include in this term *intertextuality* strictly speaking, ... that
is, the literal presence ... of one text in another" (Genette, *Introduction à l'architexte,*
p. 87 [original emphases]; my translation). On Genette's *Palimpsestes* in the context of
other contemporary theories of textual relations, see Thaïs E. Morgan, "The Space of
Intertextuality," in *Intertextuality and Contemporary Fiction,* ed. Patrick O'Donnell and
Robert Con Davis (Baltimore: Johns Hopkins University Press, 1989), pp. 266–71.

98. Genette, *Introduction à l'architexte,* p. 84 (my translation). In her review essay on
Mimologiques, Stephanie Merrim draws attention to Genette's specific "mode of writing intellectual history 'intertextually'": "What emerges as the unsuspected nucleus of
the work" is a discussion of "language models, history and literary theory" ("Cratylus'
Kingdom," *Diacritics* 11 [1981]: 45, 48). Genette himself, rebutting an interpretation by
Nicolas Ruwet in a previous issue of *Poétique,* clarifies and underscores his position on
history in "*Cratylisme et persécution,*" *Poétique* 44 (1980): 515–18.

99. Marina Yaguello, *Lunatic Lovers of Language: Imaginary Languages and Their
Inventors,* trans. Catherine Slater (London: Athlone Press; Rutherford, N.J.: Fairleigh

Dickinson University Press, 1991), covers some of the same ground as Genette's *Mimologics* but focuses on utopian fiction, science fiction, and "unconscious productions (cases of glossolalia or xenoglossia)" (p. xv).

100. See the chart of modes and structural relations that constitute "hypertextual practices" in Genette's *Palimpsestes* (p. 37).

101. Quoted in William Pietz, "Geography, Etymology, and Taste: Charles de Brosses and the Restoration of History," *L'Esprit Créateur* 25.3 (1985): 93.

102. For a more detailed description of Swift's satire in relation to the language theories of his time, see Stam, *Inquiries into the Origin of Language*, pp. 55–61.

103. Jonathan Swift, *Gulliver's Travels: An Annotated Text with Critical Essays*, ed. Robert A. Greenberg (New York: Norton, 1961), p. 156.

104. Ibid., p. 158.

105. Jorge Luis Borges, "Funes, the Memorious," in *A Personal Anthology*, ed. and trans. Anthony Kerrigan (New York: Grove Press, 1967), pp. 42–43.

MIMOLOGICS

There is too much to lose in deciding that cultural history as a whole is insignificant, and that mankind has spent its time arguing about nothing and for nothing. Too much to lose by putting the dimension of the past behind us, and even more to lose at the foundation, in what we could learn about ourselves as thinking beings.... Each debate is both old and new; even when we deem it to belong to earlier times, it continues to circulate in us.

Judith Schlanger, *Penser la bouche pleine*

"The word *chien* {dog} does not bite": so a few experts and the wisdom of the ages assure us. Nor does *chien* bark, or even simply growl, for want of that *canine letter* {r}, for instance, which we will encounter again, and which would provide it with teeth. But nothing stops anyone from believing the contrary, and from pricking up his ears or guarding his rear. Or from looking for a more expressive term, in another language or in the same one: maybe *perro* {pooch} or *clébard* {mutt}. Or from summoning up, like a poet, some punishing epithet: *chiens dévorants* {dirty dogs}. Or from consoling himself elsewhere, in the softness of *chat* {cat}, the majesty of *éléphant,* the grace of *libellule* {dragonfly}. "At one time or another, we have all suffered through those unwinnable debates in which a lady, with copious interjections and anacoluthons, vows that the word *luna* is (or is not) more expressive than the word *moon.*"[1] Expressive words? "One day, we were talking (of this) in the presence of somebody who seemed enthusiastic about the examples that we pointed out and the commentary on them; suddenly he said: 'And the {English} word *table?* You know, it really does give the impression of a flat surface standing on four legs.'"[2] And outside such intellectual circles: "A German-Swiss peasant woman … asked why her French-speaking countrymen say *fromage:* "*Käse* ist doch viel natürlicher! {*Cheese* is just so much more natural!}."[3]

These three speakers share one common feature: not their sex—no, no—but rather a certain turn of thought or of imagination which assumes, rightly or wrongly, a relation of reflective analogy (imitation) between "word" and "thing" that *motivates,* or justifies, the existence and the choice of the former. More or less conforming to rhetorical tradition, and without stinting on terminology, let us call this type of relation between word and thing *mimology;* the delightful reverie this relation evokes, *mimologic;* and the linguistic fact in which this relation operates or is surmised to operate, and by metonymic extension the discourse presupposing this relation and the doctrine investing it, *mimologism.*

Such is the scope of this book. But obliging interlocutors like these are not met with every day, and for us these three mimologists are already just heroes in a story, neither more nor less "real" than some character in a dialogue by Plato—for example. For us, in fact, mimologist discourse comes down almost entirely to a set of texts, a corpus, perhaps better called a *genre,* whose founding text, the matrix and program for a whole tradition (including variants, lacunae, and interpolations), is precisely, as the reader has guessed, Plato's *Cratylus*—whence, in a deserved tribute, the term currently used today, *Cratylism.* As a synonym for *mimologism*—with its original or at least archetypal connotation—*Cratylism* will therefore also designate any manifestation of the doctrine and any utterance in which it shows up. A Cratylism—like an anglicism or a mannerism—is among other things an *imitation,* but in another sense; it is an utterance "in the style of Cratylus," even for those who do not know the initial text, but begin-

5

ning with this very text also, for it is not at all, of course, initial: Socrates' first discourse, speaking "for" Cratylus, is already a pastiche, if not a parody.

We will be consulting this "formidable dossier"[4] here, then, without any claim to exhaustiveness and, despite the roughly diachronic order, from a perspective that is less historical than typological, with each stop along the way representing less a stage than a state—a variant, a species of the genus or sample of the genre. This methodological *parti pris* will probably not prevent certain moments from imposing themselves with that weight of irreversibility which is the mark of History; even if it turns out (after all) that the theme contains virtually all its variations, these evidently cannot be presented in just any order. But (so) let's not anticipate—on the contrary.

Or, to put it more briefly and again parodically: one day, I got the idea of making a survey of the posterity of *Cratylus*. At first, I considered this text to be as unique as the phoenix of the rhetoricians. But no text is unique; by dint of frequent rereadings of *Cratylus*, I thought I recognized its voice, or at least an echo of it, in other texts from various periods. I call to mind a few of these here, in chronological order, and without overindulging in either commentary or apocryphal examples.

CHAPTER 1

Eponymy of the Name

 Everyone is familiar with the problem of the *Cratylus:* Socrates is placed between two opponents, one of whom (Hermogenes) holds out for the so-called
conventionalist thesis (*thesei*) according to which names result simply from a
convention and an agreement (*sunthēkē kai homologia*) among mankind, and
the other (Cratylus) for the so-called naturalist thesis (*physei*) according to
which each object has received a "correct denomination" that belongs to it
through a natural appropriateness.[1] Socrates seems, in the beginning, to support the second thesis against the first, then the first against the second. This
contradictory, or at the very least ambiguous, position was deliberately simplified by the classical tradition, which, disregarding the final reversal, decided the
entire dialogue in favor of its eponymous hero; and by the majority of modern commentators, who, being more eager to interpret the dialogue in terms of
"philosophical" polemics, have postulated that on the contrary the first part is
hardly more than a joke[2] in which Socrates caricatures the naturalist thesis by
pushing it to an extreme, and that the true signification of the *Cratylus* should
be sought in the second part, which takes aim through the naive disciple at the
master-teacher Heraclitus and his philosophy of flux.

Without taking sides on the issue as laid out above, I would like straightforwardly to read this dialogue—or, in point of fact, this double monologue by
Socrates—on the ground where it is explicitly situated, that of language,[3] and to
consider a priori both its parts as equally serious, of a seriousness clearly excluding neither sophism nor a sense of play. Perhaps it will then become apparent
that Socrates' two successive attitudes are not contradictory but complementary,
and that their occurrence side by side clears the way for an original position that
is not the same as either that of Cratylus or that of Hermogenes: a complex yet
rigorous and coherent position that would belong specifically to Socrates. And,
doubtless, to Plato, at least at the time when he wrote this dialogue.[4]

 The first gesture in the dynamics of the argument—the fastest and most
ruthless—consists of dismissing the conventionalist thesis, at least provisionally.
In order to achieve this, Socrates leads Hermogenes, in a rather sophistic way,
to overemphasize his position until it becomes literally untenable.[5]

7

Hermogenes' initial position, let us recall, defined the correctness of the name as being nothing but *a convention and an agreement*. It goes without saying that "correctness" {*orthotēs; justesse*} in this case can signify not a deep adequation of the word to the thing but merely an artificial correspondence accepted and recognized by everyone: "For I think no name belongs to any particular thing by nature, but only by the habit and custom (*nomō kai ethei*) of those who employ it and who established the usage."[6] It also goes without saying that the "convention" referred to can be only a social or, at the very minimum, an interindividual consensus. Anxious above all to show that, in his thesis as in Cratylus's, all names are correct — "For it seems to me that whatever name you give to a thing is its correct name"[7] — or, in this sense, that for him one convention is as good as another, Hermogenes resorts to a double-edged example: the name given by the master to his slave. It is no accident that the choice here is a proper name, since the attack has already been launched against the "correctness" of Cratylus, Socrates, and Hermogenes as names: we will return to this crucial point. "We give new names to our slaves, and the newly given name is no less correct than the one which was given before": this example may serve as an elementary or minimal form of linguistic convention, one that unites two individuals. And the unequal character of their relation, in the present case, should not invalidate this. Just the opposite: admittedly, the master names the slave "arbitrarily" (this is actually the word used) and without consulting him, but not, for all that, without his *agreement*. Whether he is satisfied or not with this denomination, the slave must certainly at the very least *recognize* it in order for it to function; that is to say, for example, he must come when called by this name and not do so upon hearing another name that he might perhaps like better. There is a forced agreement here, which does not presuppose any deep assent but which has the same effect as an acceptance or a consent. But isn't this exactly the meaning of *homologia*, and the truth of our linguistic constitution, as it is actually experienced by the "users" of a natural language which they adopt as it stands, without having been consulted on its makeup? The arbitrary naming of the slave is indeed, therefore, an apt illustration of the conventionalist thesis.

It is thanks to this illustration, however, that Socrates is going to trap Hermogenes in an impasse — that is, by exploiting the *individual* character of the master's decision, as if that decision, irrevocable though it may be, were the sole aspect of the situation: "Whatever name we decide to give each particular thing is its name?" — "Yes." — "Whether the giver be a private person or a city?" — "Yes."[8] Hérmogenes cannot say no, since Socrates is apparently merely summarizing his own previous line of argument. Thus, Socrates presses home his advantage: "Well then, suppose I give a name to something or other, designating, for instance, that which we now call 'man' as 'horse' and that which we now call 'horse' as 'man'; will the real name of the same thing be 'man' for

8

the public and 'horse' for me individually, and in the other case 'horse' for the public and 'man' for me individually? Is that your meaning?" — "Yes, that is my opinion."[9] Clearly, in this new example Socrates has simply "forgotten" the necessity for consensus, and Hermogenes has "forgotten" to remind him of it. So he finds himself decked out with a thesis that no longer has anything "conventionalist" about it, and according to which *everyone* can name every object at his own pleasure. To this now impracticable thesis, Socrates need only contrast his own in order to win Hermogenes' acquiescence, or at least his passive and somewhat contrite attention.

This expeditious elimination of the social dimension of language and its communicative function leaves face to face two terms of the linguistic relation which are henceforth privileged: the object to be named, and the naming subject. At the same time, linguistic activity is reduced to the function that unites these two terms, or the *act of naming {onomazein; nomination}*. With any third hypothesis excluded, this act can only result either from an individual caprice of the subject, or from typical properties of the object: "Then if a man speaks as he fancies he ought to speak, will he speak correctly, or will he succeed in speaking if he speaks in the way and with the instrument in which and with which it is natural for us to speak and for things to be spoken? ... Then in naming also ... we cannot follow our own will, but the way and the instrument which the nature of things prescribes must be employed, must they not?"[10]

From this point on we are led back to one of the favorite grounds of Socratic-Platonic dialectic, that of the fabricating activity of the craftsman: to name is to fabricate a name; the name is instrumental to the relation between man and thing; therefore, to name is to fabricate an instrument. This instrument can be effective only if it corresponds to the properties of the object, as the shuttle must correspond to the properties of the cloth to be woven, depending on whether one works with linen, wool, or some other material. The function of the instrument, or its relationship to the object to which it is applied, or ultimately the nature of that object, determines an ideal form which the fabricator of instruments must realize by "imposing" it on matter (wood for the shuttle, iron for the drill, and so on). If we transpose this process into the domain of language, the nature of an object determines the ideal form for the instrument that will serve to name it; let us call this form the ideal name, or the "idea of the name." Properly speaking, the act of naming, or the act of fabricating the name, will consist in *imposing {tithenai; imprimer}* this ideal form on linguistic matter, or on "sounds" and "syllables": "giv[ing] to each thing the proper form of the name, in whatsoever syllables," "keep[ing] in view the name which belongs by nature to each particular thing, and ... impos[ing] its form on the letters and syllables"[11] — herein lies the work of the fabricator of names.

Clearly, then, the *natural* and *necessary* character of the relation between the

9

name and the object does not, for all that, mean that naming is an easy act within everyone's reach. So, making a name is a piece of work, a *craft {technē; métier}*, and it requires a specialized artisan, like the carpenter for the shuttle or the blacksmith for the drill: "It is not for every man {*pas anēr; le premier venu*} ... to give names, but for him who may be called the name-maker {*onomatourgos*}."[12] But by naming (in his turn) the name-maker, we have merely hypostasized a function without specifying to whom it belongs, since name-making is not yet a (well) known and listed craft. Who, then, has the competence to make names? Here a secondary bit of sophism intervenes, and the conventionalist thesis will bear the full brunt of its argument: truth to tell, it is a simple play on the word *nomos*, which designates both usage and law. Hasn't Hermogenes declared from the beginning that the name is a matter of usage (*nomos*)? Now, isn't usage itself, or rather law (*nomos*), the business of the law-giver {*nomothetēs*}? Naming will thus also be the business of the law-giver. Now we have our artisan of words — but we have him at some distance, for he is not your everyday type of fellow. The name-maker is the law-giver: that is to say, the kind of artisan "who is of all the artisans among men the rarest." In other words, he is just the opposite of that "every man" (*pas anēr*) whom Mallarmé, on the same subject or nearly so, will call (in a literal translation of the Greek) "*Monsieur Tout-le-Monde*" {Mister Everyman}. This competence requirement is very firmly reiterated further on: "And Cratylus is right in saying that names belong to things by nature, and that not everyone is an artisan of names."[13] Clearly, without seeing anything paradoxical about their connection, this last phrase closely links two features that seem in conflict to us: the naturalness of the name and the necessity of a professional name-maker are linked, just as the rejection of "every man" naturally associates the "arbitrary" (conventional) sign with the mediocrity of the run-of-the-mill. It is because all words that are not *the* right word {le *mot juste*} *are interchangeable* (Hermogenes recognized this), and therefore each of them exactly equals any other one: whatever, within the reach of whomever. In contrast, the correct word, or the "natural name," is unique, hard to discover, even harder to "impose" on acoustic matter. This is why the name-maker is not the first person who happens along but indeed the last, that rare bird, nearly impossible to find, who is the competent law-giver. Yet he is not infallible, and we will encounter the not inconsiderable consequence further on.

We are quite far here from the folklorist concept of spontaneous creation that will (extensively) mark Romantic mimologism later: a "well-made" language is not a popular creation but rather the business of *specialists* — almost of the initiated. And Socrates pushes this spirit of specialization, for which Nietzsche will reproach him one day, so far that even the "user" of language, an anonymous and collective being par excellence, becomes doubled if not supplanted by that professional and qualified locutor who is to the name-maker what the musician is to the lyre-maker, or the pilot to the ship-builder, and naturally the weaver to the shuttle-maker: the dialectician, to whom falls, then, the essential task of directing (*epistatein*) and judging or verifying (*krinein*) the work of the name-maker. He is a sort of word-inspector, like inspectors of weights and measures elsewhere. Clearly, the (future) notion of "linguistic competence" here functions in a typically restrictive sense. If making words is a craft, utilizing them — in other words, speaking — is, ultimately, one also.

This last equivalence will probably appear farfetched: naming[14] is not the sum total of the language system, and Socrates takes good care to specify, on the contrary, that it is merely a "part": *tou legein morion to onomazein* {naming is a part of speaking}.[15] But it is evidently no accident that this part is constantly taken for the whole: for Socrates — and the defeat of Hermogenes is probably predicated on the acceptance of this point of departure[16] — naming is really the linguistic act par excellence, once naming has been defined as "an act that refers to things" and one that must be modeled on "the way and with the instrument in which and with which it is natural for us to speak and for things to be spoken." It is assumed that the act of relegating the social dimension of language, and thus its "pragmatic" function (in Morris's sense), must inevitably lead as well to downplaying its "syntactical" function — very broadly defined to include natural language as a system and the spoken word as a sequence and construction — and therefore to reducing language to its *semantic* function, understood as the exclusive relation between word and thing. If speaking is essentially *an act that refers to things* — a formula whose crucial character and weighty consequences can never be overemphasized, as Horn says[17] — then language necessarily becomes a collection of vocables whose entire function is limited by this atomization to a relationship between isolated designations: one word, one thing, one word, one thing, and so forth. This is exactly what Saussure will disdainfully call a "nomenclature."[18] Indeed, a "collection of vocables" is even saying too much; as its subtitle expressly indicates, the inquiry of the *Cratylus* bears not upon the whole lexicon but solely upon "names" or "nouns" (*onomata*), or substantives (and secondarily what we call adjectives), to the exclusion of verbs and grammatical words. This choice is neither justified nor even clarified, and this silence itself is probably significant: for it goes without saying, and thus it follows, that just as "the word" equals the language system itself, "the name" or "the noun" is in turn the verbal unit par excellence.[19] It will take several centuries for a motif to be articulated (perhaps not the same as the one occulted by the *Cratylus*): to wit, that only the noun designates a determinate, concretely assignable "object," with which it can maintain a natural (that is to say, mimetic) relation.

Of course, much could be said about the "concrete" character of the nominal referent, and it is not clear that *table* or *movement* is less abstract than *to eat* or *to run.* Ultimately, the only truly satisfying Cratylian object will be the proper

11

name—*Socrates, Cratylus, Hermogenes*—assuming that it applies quite exclusively to one single individual. Thus, Proust, contrasting common nouns and proper nouns, will call the former "words" and the latter "names" (for which he reserves the Cratylian speculations of his hero), as if "proper name" also signified *name, properly speaking {nom proprement dit}*. This final reduction is foreshadowed from the first page of the dialogue, since its kickoff is in fact a quarrel over the "appropriateness" of the names of Cratylus, Socrates, and Hermogenes, and since it is confirmed—but I would prefer to say that it is foreshadowed a second time—in that second kickoff which is the beginning of the investigation into Homeric namings.[20] Further on, we will see the signification carried by this privileged status, this exemplary function of the proper name, in a dialogue whose subtitle might be nicely translated—playing on an ambiguity of which it is plainly unaware—thus: *on the propriety of names {de la propriété des noms}*.[21]

⊚ Apparently, the Socratic-Cratylian thesis—*Socratylian*, then—is henceforth established, and all the rest of the first dialogue will be no more than a task of argumentation and illustration in which the "correctness of names" is demonstrated, primarily by means of "etymologies" and secondarily by speculations on sound symbolism. In fact, it seems to me, the function of this sequel (which, moreover, takes up three-fourths of the text) is much more important: it is not merely demonstrative but properly theoretical and, as such, essential to the definition of Platonic mimologism—I mean not the Cratylism of Cratylus but the Cratylism of the *Cratylus*.

For the moment, let us remember, this mimological thesis remains in its most rudimentary form, which is more or less contained in three words: *natural correctness of names {justesse naturelle des noms}*. Of what does this correctness consist? Of the faithfulness of the actual name, embodied in sounds and syllables, to the ideal name, or "natural" name. But this, of course, merely pushes the question down to the next level: of what, then, does the correctness of the natural name consist? On that point, we still have only an entirely provisional and very incomplete indication: the idea that the name is a tool, which must be adapted to the object to which it is applied.

Note that there are here the beginnings of a rather rare concept of linguistic motivation: to wit, motivation not by analogy (the word resembling the thing) but by instrumental adequation, and therefore by a sort of causalist contiguity— in short, by metonymy and not by metaphor, or, more accurately, by a metonymic relationship that may or may not be doubled by a metaphorical relation, depending on whether or not one assumes that the instrument must resemble "its" object, too. Moreover, these beginnings are deceptive, for further on we will see the instrumental relation entirely submerged by the mimetic relation, as if

12

the only possible adequation of the signifier or the signified lay in resemblance to the object.

The Socratic definition of "correctness" thus remains considerably open and somewhat indeterminate. It is now going to be made more specific through two apparently strongly opposed perspectives, one of which applies in principle to compound and later names (*hustata onomata*) and the other to simple names, considered to be the earliest ones (*prōta*). The first perspective is revealed in a series of what has been traditionally called "etymologies."

The use of this term is likely to create a good many misunderstandings, and it has not failed to do so. If one takes the term to mean the search for the true origin of a word, then it is clear, or at least it should be, that the "etymologies" in the *Cratylus* are not etymologies at all.[22] Let us remember that the term is absent from the dialogue as from Plato's entire work[23] — which is of course not sufficient proof. The historical "falseness" of the majority of these "etymologies" (120 out of 140, according to Méridier) does not tell us very much about their real function; obviously, then, a filiation made up on the spot today could have been accepted at face value in Plato's time, and we will see besides that Socrates could capitalize just as easily on "correct" filiations. In contrast, the presence of multiple "etymologies," like those for *psychē* {soul} or *Apollōn* {Apollo},[24] indicates quite plainly that Socrates does not intend to establish historical filiations here: the "overdetermination" that Todorov discusses is incompatible with the aim of etymology in its modern sense.[25] What, then, is the true function of Socrates' alleged "etymologies"? Before (and by way of) answering this question, it might be useful to look closely at what they consist of.

The majority of them are, properly speaking, *analyses* of words, the type of "syntagmatic analyses" (*dix-neuf = dix + neuf; cerisier = cerise + ier*) {nineteen = ten + nine; cherrytree = cherry + tree} that Saussure will make into indices of relative motivation.[26] A typical example: *alētheia* (truth) = *alē + theia* (divine wandering). Here,[27] the word is treated strictly as a compound whose analysis extracts the components in order to clarify its signification. Of course, cases of such pure compounding, without excess, gaps, or distortions, are very rare. But classified in the same category, despite their lesser purity, will be decompositions like *Dionysos = didous oinon* (giver of wine), *Pelōps = pelas opsis* (he who sees only what is near), *Agamemnōn = agastos epimonē* (admirable for remaining), *phronēsis* (wisdom) = *phoras noēsis* (perception of motion), and even *technē* (art) = *echonoē* (the possession of mind), whose "belabored" quality Socrates himself emphasizes, as Hermogenes says, by recognizing that in order to identify the components it is necessary "to remove the *t* and insert an *o* between the *ch* and the *n*, and between the *n* and the *e*."[28] For Socrates, the reason behind these deformations is primarily a sort of tasteless aestheticism that compels

13

speakers to embellish primitive words by removing or adding letters, until they become unrecognizable; the idea of a blind and involuntary phonetic evolution is as foreign to him as that of an anonymous and collective linguistic creation. These syntagmatic analyses are sometimes so extended that one hesitates to keep calling them that. Examples include *sōphrosynē* (self-restraint) = *sōtēria phronēseōs* (salvation of thought), or *anthrōpos* {man} = *anathrōn ha opōpe* (he who looks up at what he has seen), *aischron* (base) = *eaei ischon ton rhoun* (that which restrains the flow), or *Selēnē* = *selas aei neon te kai henon* (light that is always both new and old).[29] In effect, these expanded analyses constitute genuine glosses or, if one wishes, *paraphrases* in which the theme word, like the Saussurean hypogram, is opened out and anamorphosized, its elements disseminated and multiplied as if in a broken mirror. We will run across this practice much later on, and in a (theoretically) entirely different field.

The principle of analysis, which consists in discovering the interpretant inside the interpreted term, was here stretched to its utmost limits, but it was conserved. It was, so to speak, turned upside down into the sort of inverse derivation that accounts for the noun *hōrai* (seasons) by the fact that the seasons "divide (*horizein*) winters and summers and winds and the fruits of the earth"[30] — just as one could say that spring has that name because it is spring-like. Analysis has nothing more to do in motivations by paronymy such as the following: "*gynē* (woman) seems to me to be much the same as *gonē* (birth)"; "*boulē* (intention) denotes *bolē* (shooting)"; *hemera* (day) is explained by *himerō* (to long for), or — the most famous of all for other reasons — the etymology of *sōma* (the body).[31] This one is double, and even triple, but in a rather odd way. Let us bring the text to mind:

> Some say it {the body} is the *tomb* (*sēma* {*tombeau*}) of the soul, their notion being that the soul is buried in present life; and again, because by its means the soul gives any signs which it gives, it is for this reason also properly called *sign* {*signe*} (*sēma*). But I think it most likely that the Orphic poets gave this name, with the idea that the soul is undergoing punishment for something; they think it has the body as an enclosure to *keep it safe* {*garder*} (*sōzetai*, like a prison, and this is, as the name itself denotes, the *safe* {*geôle*} (*sōma*) for the soul, until the penalty is paid, and not even a letter needs to be changed.[32]

Evidently, *sōma* is first of all explained by *sēma*, but this explanation is itself "overdetermined"[33] and open to two interpretations, due to the polysemy of *sēma*: tomb and sign (in fact, of course, tomb because sign), two meanings that are both appropriate to the definition of the body; except for this peculiarity we have here, exactly as with *gynē-gonē* or *boulē-bolē*, a simple paronymy. The case of *sōma-sēma* is more subtle: apparently, it is a matter of motivation by homonymy, the borderline case of paronymy. As well, it should be added that *sōma* (safe) is (at least to my knowledge) a pure lexicographical fiction, whose function here is to embody, as it were, the "affinity" *sōma* (body)–*sozein* (safeguard) through an implicit analysis into *sōma* = *sōzēma*.[34]

Clearly, then, the Socratic "etymologies" consist of lexical manipulations that are quite diverse in method, which the most reductive description can boil down to just two classes: analysis and paronymy; and this structural duplicity is not unimportant, as we shall see. In contrast, all of them have one feature in common, whatever the means of analysis used — a common feature that sufficiently justifies their presence in a dialogue on the "correctness" of names: their role in *motivation*.

The use of this term here demands an explanation, or at least a distinction. Normally, when one talks about the motivation of the sign — whether, with Saussure, to deny it or, with Jespersen, to affirm it (even if partly) — one thinks of a direct relation between signifier and signified of the onomatopoetic type, as in *cocorico* {cock-a-doodle-doo} or *patatras* {crash!}. Quite obviously, there is nothing like this in the Socratic etymologies. But an indirect motivation can also be envisaged, of which Saussure's "relative motivations" (*dix-neuf, poir-ier* {pear-tree}) are only a special case. As has been previously remarked, this is of course merely a displacement of "arbitrariness," since if *dix-neuf* is "motivated" by its analysis into *dix* + *neuf*, its two components remain without natural relation to their respective signifieds; and the same could obviously be said about an analysis such as *alētheia* = *alē* + *theia*. Plato is not at all unaware of this difficulty, and we will see further on with what rigor, perhaps excessive (perhaps sophistic), Socrates poses the problem and, in the final instance, the requirement of a direct motivation of so-called "primitive" or elementary words.

But the deferral of this requirement ought not to lead us to underestimate the specific value of indirect motivation, "in its order" and according to the criteria proper to it. The question raised, let us not forget, is the "correctness of names," and it would certainly risk a betrayal of this notion to claim that it can be translated immediately in terms of a direct mimetic relation between signifier and signified. In order to grasp the true meaning of the question, one has to put it back on its own ground, into its original context: that of the first rejoinders in the dialogue, which deal with the names of Socrates, Cratylus, and Hermogenes. It then becomes apparent that its most accurate formulation is, in a more modest and informal wording, something like "Are names well chosen?" or, better, "What is a well-chosen name?" At the same time, or rather by the same token, it becomes clear that the original ground of the question and its *starting point* are the proper names; it is only by departing from the problematics of the *correct-*

ness (or *propriety*) *of proper names* that the general problematics of the (indirect) correctness of nouns can be understood, for the latter is merely an extension of, or rather an extrapolation from, the former.

🅰 Let us return, then, to that point of departure. A proper name, as is well known, theoretically has no "signification" but only a designative function. *Hermogenes* is an acoustic aggregate that designates or, rather, *serves to designate* the (supposedly unique) individual who "bears" this name. This function is universally accepted, and Cratylus himself, for example, knows full well who is meant when this name is uttered. But it is another thing to ask *why* Hermogenes is called *Hermogenes:* in other words (we will see the reason for this equivalence in a moment), to ask whether or not this name is really Hermogenes' "true name" — that is to say, whether it is well chosen (or well borne), whether it fits the personality of the one who bears it, as for example those of Socrates and Cratylus do. This is what Cratylus formally contests in the present instance: "Well, your name is not Hermogenes, even if all mankind call you so."[35] Moreover, he refuses to justify this objection, but Socrates does it for him (as he does everything else): "Perhaps he thinks that you want to make money and fail every time."[36] Hermogenes is poor; now analytically, his name signifies "of the race of Hermes (god of wealth)." Roughly transposed, we get: this poor man is called Mr. Rich; this name is therefore not *correct* (now for Cratylus, all names are correct; therefore, this one is not a name). In contrast, dropping this completely exceptional case of nonconformability, the name *Astyanax* fits the son of Hector, and that of *Dionysos* fits the god of wine, because analysis reveals that the former signifies "ruler of the city," and the latter, as previously mentioned, "giver of wine." In other words, in addition to its designative function, one can discover a true signification in the proper name as revealed by the "etymological" procedure; its correctness consists exactly of an agreement based on suitability between designation and signification (between the designated and the signified), the second acting as it were to reduplicate, reinforce, confirm the first — in a word, to *motivate and justify {motiver}* the proper name by giving it a *meaning*. I still do not know why Hermogenes is called *Hermogenes*, and I may never know, since this name does not fit him and thus is deprived of any *motive* or *ground {motif}* — motivation by antiphrasis not entering (yet) into the system. But I do know why Dionysos is called *Dionysos:* it is because this name fits him.

Of course, this kind of name is, par excellence, one *chosen* as such — that is, a *significant name* or *nickname:* in Greek, "eponym" (*epōnymon*). Whence the central concept of the *eponymy* of the name (*hē tou onomatos epōnymia*),[37] even though it appears only once in the text and hurriedly at that (and not at all in Méridier's translation, which unpardonably skips it). The eponymy of a person lies in the fact that he bears a significant name; the *eponymy of the name* lies in

its value as a nickname, in the agreement between its designation and its signification, in its indirect motivation. By extension, we will say that eponymy as a
"science" (like toponymy) is the study of this type of motivation. Thus, given a
proper name about which we already know *whom it designates*, it is the act of
wondering about its *meaning* besides, and recording — or imagining — the agreement of these two functions, which Jean Bollack calls "deictic" and "epideictic,"
respectively.[38] As Méridier's translation clearly states, this time, in regard to the
name of Zeus, it is the act of reading the name as a genuine "definition."[39] Now
we have hold of the term that was missing for several centuries, one that can be
substituted for the awkward term "etymologies," and we did not have to go far
to find it: *for, you see, the "etymologies" of the* Cratylus *were eponymies.*

As is well known, almost the entire opening series actually focuses on proper
names: names of Homeric heroes, names of gods. But what follows will focus
on natural phenomena and moral notions, and words such as *anthrōpos, psychē,
sōma* had already been slipped in among the names of gods. Consequently, if
the *question of eponymy* is born on the privileged ground of the proper name, it
gains all its value and importance only by being able to transpose, or transplant,
itself afterward to the more difficult, but more far-reaching and hence more significant, ground of "common" names or nouns.

More difficult, of course, because the common name or noun, when I apply
an eponymic study to it, is already quite officially provided with a signification.
Sōma signifies "the body," as everyone knows, and if you put it that way, everything has been said. I will not put it that way, then; just as I have treated proper
names as nicknames, I am going to treat this common noun (and all the others)
as a proper name by *suspending*, as it were, its signification, which I will treat as
a simple designation: *sōma* serves to designate the body. Fine, but on the other
hand, *what does* sōma *mean?* In order to find out, I apply an eponymical procedure to it: for example, the "etymology by affinity," *sōma-sēma.* Thus, I find
that *sōma,* which designates the body, means "sign" and "tomb"; and since the
body is both the sign and the tomb of the soul, I conclude that the noun *sōma*
is correct and felicitous as its designation, just as *Dionysos* is to designate the
god of wine. Or, equally well, I apply another etymology: *sōma* = **sōzēma,* and
since the body is also the prison of the soul, here is a word twice, nay, thrice well
chosen. From such a perspective, it is obvious that the "overdetermination" of
eponymy is not only acceptable but even welcome: if an "object" displays several
characteristic features, its name will be that much more correct as it "signifies"
the greatest number of these features. It is equally obvious that the historical
"truth" or "falsity" (in our view) of the proposed link in no way affects its eponymic efficacity. Today, everyone "knows" that *alētheia* is analyzable not into
"divine wandering" but into "un-veiling" (*a-lētheia*).[40] But everyone also knows
that this "true" etymology can *produce an eponymy* just as easily as the false one

can, and that it has done so; whatever the criterion, *alētheia* is a well-formed nickname.

The eponymic function of the Socratic "etymologies" justifies (for the moment) yet another feature, which is their necessarily *indirect* character. Eponymy serves to give a meaning to a name thought to be without one: that is to say, to find in it one or two hidden names, themselves hypothetically meaningful; or, in Proustian terms, to find the *names* hidden in the *words*. The imposition of meaning on a purely designative sign, or one treated as such, inevitably goes through the relay of another sign (itself treated as *significant*), which is *recognized* in the first one. To transform the designation *sōma:* "body" into a signification entails going through a chain of affinities, *sōma-sēma*-"tomb"-"body," thanks to which, by the necessary detour *sēma*-"tomb," I establish a relation of affinity (of correctness), until now impossible to discover, between *sōma* and "body."

Having reached this point, the analytical process is unavoidably stymied by a difficulty previously glimpsed in regard to relative motivation according to Saussure (that of the arbitrariness of component signs) but now formulated in a slightly different way. The use of the chain *sōma-sēma*-"tomb"-"body" is plainly a sophism or, more accurately, an evasive tactic in which the presence of the two affinities *sōma-sēma* and "tomb"-"body" — that is, the affinities between the two names on the one hand and between the two "things" on the other — has the effect of diverting attention from the central link, or the relation *sēma*-"tomb," whose significance or motivation, in short, "correctness," has hitherto not been proved by anything. This link in the chain is a pure illusion, in the technical sense of the term; the central void is concealed by the lateral plenitude; again, and always, an unbridgeable gulf separates signifiers from signifieds.

Once this weak point has been noticed, then, there remains the task of motivating (*justifying*) the relation *sēma*-"tomb" in its turn. This would probably not be very hard, and we have at hand everything needed to do it, since we know that *sēma* also signifies, precisely, the "sign," and nothing is simpler (and, in the present case, more "true") than interpreting the tomb as the sign (*monumentum*) of the dead person it shelters and thus establishing a new chain *sēma-sēma*-"sign"-"tomb." But here again a faulty link appears: it is the relation *sēma*-"sign" — the emblematic arbitrariness of the word *sign*. The task of justifying this in its turn then remains, and so on.

The point of all this is clear: the problem with eponymical motivation is its *infinite* facility. It is an easy procedure, with a touch of complacency, of course (for what, exactly, is a "tomb of the soul"?), but literally interminable. Every word is related to another, and so forth, until the inevitable return to the point of departure (since the lexicon itself is finite). The analytical process is laughably circular, as in bad dictionaries, and can be symbolized, not too unjustly, by an ultimate eponymy, apocryphal but to be expected — the chain *sēma-sōma-*

"body"-"sign," which can be interpreted in the following way: the word *sēma* (sign) is correct because the sign (*sēma*) is the body (*sōma*) of the meaning. After the shuttle we come to the spinning wheel.

Plato, as I have said, saw the trap. He also found the way out: the shift from indirect to direct motivation — that is, to sound symbolism.

For once, it is Hermogenes who raises the crucial objection. Rudely interrupting the series of eponymies (not without paying tribute to their "boldness"), he challenges Socrates to account for words previously used as mediators of motivation, such as *ion* (going), *rheon* (flowing), *doun* (binding).[41] At first, Socrates points out — only to reject it — an easy "expedient" that would consist in breaking off the eponymical circuit by forcing these words back down into the darkness of a barbarous origin of language, where all eponymy becomes impossible. In actual fact, this expedient is not only unworthy but ineffective, since it permits merely an interruption of the quest, not attainment of the goal. Such a procedure, therefore, is illegitimate:

> "We must play the game and investigate these questions vigorously. But let us bear in mind that if a person asks about the words by means of which names are formed, and again about those by means of which those words were formed, and keeps on doing this indefinitely, he who answers his question will at last give up, will he not?" — "Yes, I think so." — "Now at what point will he be right in giving up and stopping? Will it not be when he reaches the names which are the elements of the other sentences and names? For these, if they are the elements, can no longer rightly appear to be composed of other names. For instance, we said just now that *agathon* was composed of *agaston* and *thoon;* and perhaps we might say that *thoon* was composed of others, and those of still others. But if we ever get hold of one which is no longer composed of other names, we should be right in saying that we had at last reached an element, and that we must no longer refer to other names for its derivation." — "I think you are right." — "Are, then, these names about which you are now asking elements, and must we henceforth investigate their correctness by some other method?" — "Probably." — "Yes, probably, Hermogenes; at any rate, all the previous ones were traced back to these."[42]

And a few pages further on: "If anyone is … ignorant of the correctness of the earliest names, he cannot know about that of the latest, since they can be explained only by means of the earliest names, about which he is ignorant. No, it is clear that anyone who claims to have scientific knowledge {to be *technikon*} of names must be able first of all to explain the earliest names perfectly, or he can be sure that what he says about the later ones will be nonsense."[43]

The legitimate solution for Socrates, therefore, consists in positing that all the preceding eponymies — and all the innumerable ones they represent — lead us to elements (*stoicheia*) or earliest names (*prōta onomata*) that cannot be broken down and at which the eponymical movement thus comes to a halt of its own accord. This *thus* assumes that the movement in question consists strictly and exclusively of analytical procedures, and therein lies the (perhaps unconscious) sophism, for we have in fact seen that things do not work this way, and that as a result nothing prevents — and nothing exempts — one from recommencing the circuit, departing from *rheon* or from *doun,* as Socrates contemplates doing from *thoon* — and as he has already done from *theoi.*[44] But Hermogenes, as if bewitched by his interlocutor's demanding proclamations (we must play the game and investigate these questions vigorously, and so on — all banner headlines), will not make this objection, and it would be a little late to make it today. Hence, it will be understood that the "latest" words "all" refer back to the "earliest" ones, and that — as if the issue until now had been merely analysis — these primary words are definitely the *elements* of the language system: that is to say, the monemes "beyond" which only "syllables and letters" are found. In short, by the very play of eponymic "analysis," we are irresistibly (and very fortunately) expelled from the eponymic circuit and launched despite ourselves into a symbolics of an entirely different order, one finally capable of throwing a bridge between signifiers and signifieds — between "body" and *sōma* — between things and, no longer words, which is quite difficult, but *sounds.* The perhaps unsolvable question of the "correctness of names" is suddenly replaced by the perhaps easier question of the correctness of *sounds,* otherwise called *phonic mimesis:* "It will, I imagine, seem ridiculous that things are made manifest through imitation in letters and syllables; nevertheless, it cannot be otherwise, for there is no better theory upon which we can base the truth (*alētheia*) of the earliest names."[45]

⊕ Clearly, Socrates takes good care to mark out the *necessity* for the shift, as if this necessity could mitigate its abruptness. (As for its effectiveness, that is plainly not guaranteed at all: "we have nothing better." A little further on and also much further on, we will again encounter this problem, the most important of all.) He also specifies that the quality of "correctness," which is "to indicate the nature of each being," "must be found *to the same degree* in all names, the earliest as well as the later ones,"[46] as if this quantitative equality could, in its way, mitigate the qualitative difference between the methods. In spite of these precautions, a completely new problematics opens up here, one whose novelty Socrates unwittingly accentuates by forcibly introducing into his demonstration a detour via a nonlinguistic (and nonvocal) form of mimesis, imitation by gestures {*la mimique gestuelle*}: "If we had no voice or tongue, and wished to make things clear to one another, should we not try, as dumb people actually do, to make signs with our hands and head and person generally?"; "By bodily imitation only can the body ever express anything"; "And when we want to express ourselves, either with the voice, or tongue, or mouth, the expression is simply their imitation of that which we want to express?"; "Then a name is vocal imitation (*mimēma phōnē*) of that which the vocal imitator names or imitates?"[47] Verbal mimesis, therefore, is a sort of vocal transposition of the means proper to gestural mimesis: it is a *vocal imitation* {*mimique vocale*}, whose definition, and even whose description, demands a detour via imitation "properly speaking," as if the instrument of speech were out of its role or its register here, playing a score that is not strictly its own. This necessary problem and its necessary adaptation will have certain consequences for Socrates' final position in this debate: we will meet them in their place.

Perhaps these consequences will be all the more serious as Socrates does not refrain, from this point onward, from upping the ante somewhat by positing a supplementary requirement that "Hermogenes" himself has apparently not thought of. *Mimēma phōnē*, an already complex and paradoxical formula (which could also be translated by something like *image* or *vocal portrait*), does not satisfy him; it would apply equally well to the simple (vocal) imitation of the noise made by things, as among "people who imitate sheep and cocks and other animals."[48] Many others will be content, even delighted with this sort of imitation when it is labeled *onomatopoeia*.[49] But for Socrates, the noise made by things, like their color, is merely a superficial manifestation of their being. Speech should aim higher: to imitate not the vain appearance but the essence (*ousia*) of the object. On the other hand, the pure "vocal image," the imitation of a sound by the voice, would come under music instead of speech. In no sense is every vocal sound a word; it merits this title only if it fulfills a particular specification (one that prefigures in its way[50] the future distinction between phonetics and phonematics): among vocal sounds, the only ones that belong to speech are those that Socrates baptizes "letters and syllables" (*grammata te kai syllabai*). The use of the word "letter" where writing is not at all theoretically implied should not be misunderstood; we will see that Socrates is indeed thinking of articulated sounds, but that should not be surprising, either. The capacity for being designated by a letter is precisely (and especially in an alphabet as rigorous as ancient Greek) the most reliable empirical criterion for the phonematic quality of a sound or (for the time being) its belonging to natural language.[51] There is, therefore, a double requirement and a double restriction: on the side of the signified, the spoken word will imitate not just anything but solely the essence of each object; on the side of the signifier, it will imitate not through just any sound but solely through phonemes. The formula *vocal imitation* thus becomes *imitation of the essence of each object by means of letters and syllables*.[52] Such will be the Socratic definition of the "earliest name," or the simple noun, the ultimate limit of onomastic analysis.

But not the limit of semiotic analysis in general, since a shift from a semantics of verbal units to a semantics of the sounds of natural language is, in fact, entailed. Here we have, then, the first known (or at least preserved) attempt, in our cultural tradition, at charting phonetic symbolism.[53] To these elements (*stoicheia*) of sound must correspond as many elements of meaning, which will next be grouped or not, depending on whether complex or simple elements are to be named. This idea implicitly governs all this part of the text[54] and is probably intended by the following somewhat enigmatic sentence: "When we have made all these divisions (phonemically, among vowels, consonants or mutes), we must then divide well all the beings which ought to be given names, if there are any categories to which they can all be referred (as was the case with the letters), through which one can both see them in themselves and see whether or not there are any classes among them, as there are among the letters."[55] Apparently, the task would be merely to *classify* the signifieds in the same way as the phonic signifiers, but such a classification cannot do without a rudimentary analysis: extricating the features shared by all the "beings" naturally expressed by the vowels, the consonants, and so on. This path will not, in fact, really be followed, and the chart, incomplete besides, will not take any account of the phonetic classification outlined, which will thus remain without any semantic function.[56] Let us recall the main set of values proposed by this chart (I am keeping to the order, or disorder, of the text):

— *r*: motion. Examples: *rhein* (to flow), *rhoē* (current), etc. "He [the name-giver] expresses the action of them all chiefly by means of the letter *r;* for he observed, I suppose, that the tongue is least at rest and most agitated in pronouncing this letter."

— *i*: lightness and the ability to pass through all things. Examples: *ienai* (go), *hiesthai* (hasten).

— *ph, ps, s, z*: aspiration, blowing, agitation. Examples: *psychron* (shivering), *seiesthai* (shake). All of these phonemes actually include an "aspiration."

— *d, t*: binding (*desmos*), rest (*stasis*). In these articulations there is a "compression and pressure of the tongue."

— *l*: smooth (*leion*), to slip (*olisthanein*), sleek (*liparon*), gluey (*kollōdes*). "The tongue slips especially on the *l.*"

— *gl*: glutinous (*glischron*), sweet (*gluku*), gummy (*gloiōdes*). The gliding of the tongue in the *l* is stopped by the sound of the *g.*"

— *n*: inwardness: *endon* (inside), *entos* (within). The articulation of the *n* has an "internal" quality.

— *a* and *ē*, long vowels: size. {Examples:} *mega* (great), *mēkos* (length).

— *o*: roundness. Example: *gongylon* (round).

This chart occasions at least three critical remarks. First of all, despite the constant use of the word *gramma* {written letter}, the real subject throughout is exclusively phonemes, except maybe in the case of the *o*, whose semantic quality of rotundity is probably at least confirmed, if not determined, by the form of the grapheme: the opening of the mouth is, in effect, also "round" in the pronunciation of *u* or *ou*. Second, the announced "mixtures" or clusters of phonemes are here represented only by the single group *gl*. Finally and above all, the justification for the values proposed proceeds along two completely different paths, although these are constantly mingled in the text. One consists in showing the presence of the phoneme under consideration in words whose accepted signification includes the value assigned by Socrates to this phoneme (example: the presence of *t* in *stasis*). The other consists in showing the physical presence, so to speak, of this value in the acoustic effect and/or in the articulatory production of this phoneme (example: the value of the stop in the dental articulation). The first might be deemed an indirect proof and the second a direct proof, were it not for the fact that neither of the two is really convincing. The second is a sort of physical *explanation,* but everyone knows that explanations can be given for things that do not exist, like Fontenelle's tooth of gold. The first is a simple statistical presumption, whose demonstrative force has a numerical basis and, more precisely, the numerical superiority of the favorable over the unfavorable cases. The respective role of these two arguments in Socrates' demonstration deserves a closer look: all the interpretations, except for the *i* and the *o* (where it is implicit), rely on a physical justification, most often of the articulatory type. The statistical demonstration, on the other hand, is reduced to a few favorable examples — without the shadow of an excuse, as commentators have not failed to point out, for the absence of *r* (the phoneme of movement) in the word *kinēsis* (movement), a counterexample if there ever was one. Moreover, the rejection on principle of any statistical examination will be stated further on in another regard, and in terms that might perhaps be described as "ideological," in the course of the conversation with Cratylus: "Are we to count names like votes, and shall correctness rest with the majority? Are those to be the true names which are found to have that one of the two meanings which is expressed by the greater number?" — "That is not reasonable." — "No, not in the least, my friend." [57] In fact, this imbalance between the two types of argumentation seems to carry major significance, which we are going to encounter in a moment, and which is nothing less than the distinctive position of Socrates — of Plato? — in the debate between Cratylus and Hermogenes.

ⓔ As discussed earlier, the most widely accepted opinion among commentators on the *Cratylus* is that the second dialogue (where Socrates, abandoning

Hermogenes for being a little too easily confounded, returns to his antagonist) is a recantation pure and simple: Socrates (and with him, Plato) is seen as repudiating the Cratylian thesis that he had maintained to this point—a de facto abandonment accompanied only by a sort of theoretical regret: "There remains, then, simply the regret of having to abandon this highly promising theory."[58] Indeed, says Socrates, "I myself prefer the theory that names are, so far as is possible, like the things named; but really this attractive force of likeness is, as Hermogenes says, a poor thing, and we are compelled to employ in addition this commonplace expedient, convention, to establish the correctness of names. Probably language would be, within the bounds of possibility, most excellent when all its terms, or as many as possible, were based on likeness, that is to say, were appropriate, and most deficient under opposite conditions."[59] Note that such nostalgia, or such a *preference* for mimetic motivation—even if disappointed—already precludes assimilation of Socrates' "final" position with that of Hermogenes, who is perfectly happy with convention, not at all "vulgar" in his eyes—less vulgar, after all, than a banal resemblance. And since "Hermogenes" is also for us the *eponymous* hero of a tradition that ends with Saussure, it is worth recalling (anticipating) here the way, no less forceful, in which the *Course in General Linguistics* will express the opposite *parti pris:* "Signs which are entirely arbitrary convey better than others the ideal semiological process."[60]

So much for the indisputable regret of Socrates. But as for the "abandonment" itself, we need to look at that a little more closely. Socrates' arguments against the Cratylian thesis consist of one theoretical and two substantive objections. The theoretical objection is, as it were, hyperbolic and holds up only against the hyperbole of Cratylism itself, which maintains the absolute resemblance of word to thing. This is the well-known tirade against the perfect portrait that would be a veritable double of its model, and thus against a perfect mimology that would make language into a double for reality, "and no one could tell in any case which was the real thing and which was the name."[61] It goes without saying, I think, that such an argument, if it can nonplus Cratylus, does not hold up at all against the Socratic definition of the name as an "imitation of the essence of each thing through letters and syllables," a definition that excludes, as we have seen, any subjection to appearances. The imitation of the essence does not claim to be a "perfect" imitation; hence, it is not dismissed by this typically "philosophical" argument.[62]

The first substantive objection is the examination of the word *sklērotēs* (hardness), an example of a vocable that is badly compounded from the viewpoint of phonic values, since it contains an *l*, expressive of softness,[63] and whose signification Cratylus has to admit that he recognizes only "by custom" (*dia to ethos*)—that is, Socrates immediately adds, by convention. The second substantive objection is a series of words badly formed from the viewpoint this time,

24

of "etymological" analysis, especially if one adopts, as Cratylus does, Heraclitus's axiology of flux: thus, *epistēmē* (knowledge), something that makes our soul stand still (*histēsin*); or *amathia* (ignorance), something that on the contrary "goes with God" (*hama theou iontos*).[64] Besides, there is more irony than genuine controversy in this passage, which cannot operate both as a polemic against Heraclitus and an argument against Cratylus, since the vocables at issue can be "wrong" only if Heraclitus is right to valorize movement. For a disciple of Parmenides, these vocables would be irreproachable eponyms; the point, therefore, is above all to embarrass Cratylus by showing a contradiction between his linguistic theory and his philosophical values. It remains a fact that these contested vocables, like the very name Hermogenes, emblematically recalcitrant to eponymy in the beginning of the dialogue, come in the end to compromise indirect motivation, just as *sklērotēs* (and implicitly *kinēsis*) discredit direct motivation.

Socrates' position emerges loud and clear during this entire discussion: it consists in showing that words — at least certain words — *can* be poorly chosen or badly formed. Notice first of all that this allowance for inadequation is never attributed here, as it will so often be later on, to any historical erosion or decadence of natural language. For Socrates, on the contrary, malformation is typically originary and *congenital*, being unequivocally related to an *initial* error of the name-maker: "For if the giver of names erred *in the beginning* and *thenceforth* forced *all other* names into agreement with his own *initial* error, there is nothing strange about that. It is just so sometimes in geometrical diagrams; the *initial* error is small and unnoticed, but all the numerous deductions are wrong, though consistent."[65] This is a not insignificant point, for it rejects in advance the entire mythology connected with a golden age of language, with a perfect and originary natural language subsequently betrayed by history. For Socrates, the perfect natural language has never existed; badly formed words were always that way, not deformed over time. From the very beginning, the name-maker could have *made a mistake {se tromper}*.

In a sense, Socrates' attitude is more rigorous, more exacting than the majority of the theories that will feed the succeeding Cratylian tradition. But this relative austerity should not mislead us with regard to Socrates' position on the heart of the question. I would like to suggest that this position can be found already completely contained, or prefigured, in the very use of the expression "to make a mistake" (*sphallomai*). The name-maker could have made a mistake: but what does *to make a mistake {se tromper}* or, rather, *to be able to make a mistake {pouvoir se tromper}* signify, if not that it would also have been possible not to make a mistake, and that there is therefore a sort of *truth {vérité}* of the language system, in relation to which the error of the law-giver is defined (and to begin with, *produced*)? The *error {erreur}* of the law-giver — as we already know in a certain way — is an unacceptable hypothesis for Hermogenes and Cratylus alike. For Hermogenes, all names are correct because a convention is always right, even if it is modified from one day to the next by someone saying *oui* or *non* to it.[66] For Cratylus, all names are correct because language *can* imitate things and because the name-maker, in his superhuman infallibility, *could not* have made a mistake; inappropriate names (like that of Hermogenes) are simply not names.[67] Both Hermogenes and Cratylus, therefore, believe in the "correctness of names" but in quite different senses. As for Socrates, he does not believe in it, and in this sense he simply dismisses both opponents as equally unsatisfactory, with the particular philosophical lesson for the latter that a knowledge of things is based not on names but on things themselves.[68] But we must be more specific. Clearly, Socrates, like Cratylus, *prefers* mimetic motivation to convention; again like Cratylus, he believes in the *possibility* of the correctness of names — that is to say, in the *mimetic capacity of the elements* of the language system. This is definitively shown by the passage devoted to the expressive value of phonemes. But unlike Cratylus — it is on this point, and on this point alone, that Socrates parts ways with him regarding the subject of the debate — Socrates does not believe in the infallibility of the name-maker; or, if you like, he does not believe that phonic expressiveness inevitably presides over the constitution of the lexicon: that is (for him), over natural language. This explains his great reserve concerning statistical proof: the lexicon as constituted is often unfaithful to the semantic capacities of its constitutive sounds; *r* indicates movement and *l* softness, but *kinēsis* contains no *r* and *sklērotēs* contains an *l;* the name-maker did make a mistake. But once again this error presupposes, in the act of betrayal, a *truth of sounds* which natural language *betrays* — in both senses of the word: it reveals this truth and forsakes truth.

⑭ The "anti-Cratylism" of Socrates, then, is not Hermogenism, first because he shares in the *values* of Cratylism, and second because he thinks that the materials of language do contain what is needed to satisfy these values. Socrates, therefore, is in this double sense a disappointed Cratylist and, evidently, a *discontented* one. His quarrel with *sklērotēs* strikingly anticipates Mallarmé's quarrel with the "perverse" pairs *jour/nuit* {day/night}, *ombre/ténèbres* {shadow/ darkness} as being incapable of expressing their respective objects "by touch-keys corresponding to them in coloring or in rhythm, which exist in the instrument of the voice, throughout languages and sometimes in one." *Which exist...* Therein lies the Cratylian heart of that anti-Cratylism which criticizes natural language as it is but not as it might be or, rather, which *appeals against* language as it is to language as it might be and consequently *should* be.

I propose to baptize this attitude *secondary Cratylism* (or *secondary mimologism*), for the almost irresistible desire that its adherents feel to *correct* in one way or another that error of the law-giver which Mallarmé calls the "failing {*défaut*} in natural languages"—and thus to establish or reestablish in the language system, through some artifice, the state of nature that "primary" Cratylism—that of Cratylus—naively believes to be still or already established there. For his part, Socrates is rather disdainfully unaffected by this temptation, as he was unaffected by the mirage of origins, the myth of the lost linguistic paradise; or more accurately, he avoids it but not without acknowledging it (like Ulysses with the Sirens) and, so to speak, *programming* it for several centuries to come, as he does nearly all the rest—leaving Cratylus, as expected, to propose, *lectio facilior,* that naive and overly felicitous correction: *skrērotēs.* Socrates himself "proposes" nothing in order to "get out" of the dilemma, doubtless having his reasons, among which the strongest is perhaps that it is better, all things considered, to "stay with it"—to remain discontented.[69] To conclude, he prefers to wish Cratylus a good trip accompanied by (or maybe *escorted* by) Hermogenes: *propempsei de se kai Hermogenēs hode.* A long voyage begins, enlivened by brilliant arguments, ever new, ever the same. A long voyage: it is still going on, or nearly so. Socrates will not be there: he knows the way, as if he had already "made" the journey—in both senses. He is absent from the voyage, then, but present—and for good reason—at each stage, as we will now find out by (re)visiting a few of them.

CHAPTER 2

De ratione verborum

 Whether intentionally or not, then, the *Cratylus* did reveal a gap — indeed even pronounced a divorce — between the indirect ("etymological") motivation of derivative words and the direct (mimetic) motivation of the *prōta onomata* or, rather, actually the phonic elements alone. These two aspects of original Cratylism seem henceforth doomed to function separately, albeit in the same author and in the same text, and the difficulty, indeed the impossibility, of joining them will be one crux of Cratylian doctrine.

We see this quite clearly, for example, in the Latin grammarians such as Nigidius Figulus or Aelius Stilo, influenced by various classical philosophies (Pythagorean, Stoic,[1] sometimes Epicurean[2]) but all bound indirectly to the tradition opened up or authorized by Plato. On the one hand, there were speculations on the expressiveness of elementary sounds; on the other, a sort of etymological hermeneutics (whose practice, tapped by Christian exegesis, would persist throughout the Middle Ages, in Isidore of Seville and many others, for demonstrative purposes: *homo = humus; malum,* "apple" = *malum,* "evil," and so on).[3] After Plato, phonic aesthetics becomes widespread up through Dionysius of Halicarnassus, for whom *l* delights the ear, *r* irritates it, *s* is completely disagreeable, and the nasals *m* and *n* resonate like a horn.[4] Varro talks about sonorities as harsh (*trux, crux, trans*), smooth (*lana, luna*), stunted (*hic, hoc*), expansive (*facilitas*), stiff (*ignotus*) or pliable (*aedes*) and immediately connects these perceptible qualities to the signification of words (aptly) chosen as examples: *luna* is a heavenly body that glides along, *lana* a fabric that one slips into; *trux* signifies cruel, *crux* the cross, an instrument of torture; *trans* expresses the exertion of crossing over; *facilitas* expands with facility; *ignotus* evokes an obtuse ignorance, *aedes* "the ease and tranquility of home";[5] the demonstratives *hic* and *hoc* have the brevity of a gesture; *flumen,* too, nicely expresses the liquidity of the river, and *stillicidium* imitates the exquisite purling song of the drainpipe.

Among other examples, Nigidius, who according to Aulus Gellius holds out for the *physei* thesis in his *Commentarii grammatici,* illustrates this in a subtler way ("in eam rem multa argumenta dicit cur videri possint verba esse naturalia magis quam arbitraria {on this matter he gives many arguments why words can seem to be natural rather than arbitrary}"), by the following symbolic interpre-

29

tation of the personal pronouns, one that is still famous: "When we say *vos*, we make a movement with the mouth appropriate to the meaning of this word, for we slowly advance the tip of the lips and direct our breath toward those whom we are addressing. On the contrary, *nos* is pronounced without projecting the breath or advancing the lips, but by retracting them, as it were, toward the inside of the mouth. Likewise for *tu* as opposed to *ego*, *tibi* as opposed to *mihi*. Just as in affirming or denying we make a head movement that agrees with what we mean to say, so the pronunciation of such words involves a sort of natural gesture of mouth and breath."[6] Moreover, the same Aulus Gellius quotes, also from Nigidius, some etymologies of the Socratic type, such as *locuples* (rich) = *qui tenet pleraque loca* (he who possesses a large number of lands), *avarus* = *avidus aeris* (eager for money), *frater = fere alter* (almost an other self).[7] For Aelius Stilo, *vulpes* (fox) is *volipes* (that which flies on its feet); by antiphrasis, *caelum* (sky, seen by everyone) comes from *celare* (to hide), *lucus* (dark grove) from *lucere* (to shine), and *miles* (soldier) from *mollitia* (the easy life).[8] Finally, in Varro, among the numerous examples cited by Jean Collart, let us note *templum* (temple) from *tueri* (to contemplate), *hiems* (winter) from *hiatus* (opening of the mouth, because in winter the breath is visible), *canis* (dog) from *canere* (to sing), *fons* (fountain-head) from *fundere* (to pour out), *hordeum* (ogre) from *horridum* (bristling), *armenta* (livestock) from *arare* (to plow), *pratum* (meadow) from *paratum* (prepared, because it does not need to be tilled) or *rus* (countryside) from *rursum* (again, on account of the eternal return of the seasons). The relation between the expressive theory of the *primigenia verba* such as *crux*, and the etymology based on semantic parallels applied to these *derivata verba* remains unformulated and problematic, to say the least.

Such is no longer the case in a text that has nevertheless clearly been influenced by Varro, among others, and that presents itself as a simple overview of Stoic doctrine on the question: the sixth chapter, "*De origine verbi*" {On the Origin of Words}, of *De dialectica* {*On Dialectic*}, attributed to Saint Augustine.[9] The very notion of *origo verbi* or *verborum* (the origin of the word or of words) here takes on a scope wide enough to embrace the *primigenia* and the *derivata* at once. It is, however, presented with some reservations as to its utility (a study "more a matter of curiosity than of necessity," "whose prosecution would go on indefinitely") and its objectivity: "like the interpretation of dreams, it is a matter of each man's ingenuity."[10] (The comparison is not trivial and may not be irrelevant: every word, Valéry will say, is like a sort of "brief daydream" {*songe bref*}, and perhaps the attempt at motivation closes the gap between the arbitrariness of the sign and the caprices of the daydream in the same manner.) As proof, and in a rather sly wordplay on his own title — *origo verbi* being momentarily taken in the sense of "origin of the word *verbum*" — the author picks out a few conflicting etymologies such as *verberare aurem* (to reverberate on or strike the ear), *verberare aerem* (to reverberate in the air), *verum* (truth), and, more exhaustively, *verum boare* (to sound the truth). Let us recall that Socrates, on the contrary, saw no problem with proposing several glosses for the same word: the critical attitude of *On Dialectic* regarding these rival analyses therefore manifests a keener feeling for etymology as real filiation.

Having thus put himself on guard, or under cover, against the pitfalls and weaknesses of such a study, the author nonetheless takes upon himself the overview of a theory to which we can hardly gauge his own contribution but from which he does not at all appear, as we will see, to dissociate himself in principle and on essential points. Actually, the text reads as if this theory were merged with his own or could take its place, the overall argument being more or less as follows: if you want to know about the origin of words, I will tell you what the Stoics said.[11]

To start off with, Saint Augustine himself replies to one of his own objections to etymological research — the very one that compelled our attention in the reading of the first section of the *Cratylus,* the infinite recurrence of the "pursuit": "Because it would be easy to refute them by saying that this would be an infinite process, for by whichever words you interpret the origin of any one word, the origin of these words would in turn have to be sought, they {the Stoics} assert that you must search until you arrive at some similarity of the sound of the word to the thing." Apparently, this is Socrates' very reply when, having reached or believing he has reached the *prōta onomata* through analysis, he abruptly switches from indirect to direct motivation. But in fact the two outcomes are not at all identical. In Plato the shift to direct mimesis required a veritable leap from the plane of words, albeit the "first" ones, to that of elementary sounds, and once again we have here that abyss, so difficult to bridge, between the phonic level and the lexical level — a difficulty that compromised the entire theory and foreshadowed the final reversal. The shift reveals itself to be even more difficult on the way in than on the way out: the symbolics of sounds, a necessary but not sufficient hypothesis, does not guarantee the appropriateness of words and therefore that of natural language. Augustine, maybe without realizing it, escapes this difficulty by not leaving the lexical plane: the point of no recurrence in the method, which will become the hypothetical point of departure for the *origo verborum,* is not elementary sounds but always words — nonderivative ones, of course, and thus *primigenia,* but still not necessarily elementary like *ion* or *rheon.* The limits of recurrence, but not of analysis, are simply those words whose mimetic character is (taken to be) self-evident: onomatopoetic words (although Augustine does not use this term) such as *tinnitum* (tinkling), *hinnitum* (whinnying), *balatum* (bleating), *clangor* (clang), *stridor* (stridency): "You clearly see that these words sound like the things themselves which are signified by these words."[12] Here, then, is a first class of vocables whose mimesis

31

is established without apparent difficulty; the unnoticed, or disguised, difficulty lies entirely in the qualification "first," but we will return to this.

In a second moment, for objects without sound an analogical equivalence — later to be called "correspondence" or "synaesthesia" — is also established easily between, for example, their tactile quality, either softness or hardness, and the auditory quality of their names: "Since there are things which do not make sounds, in these touch is the basis for similarity (*similitudo*). If the things touch the sense smoothly or roughly, the smoothness or roughness of letters in like manner touches the hearing and thus has produced the names for them."[13] Thus, *lene,* soothing to the ear, will designate gentleness of touch; *asperitas,* harsh to the ear, its roughness; *voluptas,* pleasure; *crux,* cross; *mel,* honey; *vepres,* thorns, and so on. Here we no longer have the *direct* imitation of a noise by the sound of a word, but we do not yet have the *indirect* imitation that will characterize the next class: this second mimesis, which can just as well be seen as a variant of the first, could be labeled *oblique,* with both ensuring a *more or less direct* relation between signifier and signified, without the acknowledged interposition of another signifier and/or signified.

Such, then, is what "the Stoics" looked upon as the cradle (*cunabula*) of words, which consists of the "impression made on the senses by the things ... in harmony with the impression made on the senses by the sounds"[14] — this harmony characterizing at the same time onomatopoetic words properly speaking and what Maurice Grammont will call "expressive words." Direct or oblique, we have not yet left behind the resemblance between words and "things." In fact, however, it must be gotten beyond, apparently (although Augustine does not say why), and it is here that the shift is made to a new principle of motivation, which is the resemblance of things to each other: "Hinc ad ipsarum inter se rerum similtudinem processisse licentiam nominandi."[15] Let us take this to mean that the similarity between two things authorizes the derivation of the name for one from the name for the other: in this way, from *crux,* which resembles the cross through its unpleasant phonics, is derived *crus,* whose signifier (the leg or shinbone) no longer has anything unpleasant about it but resembles the wood of the cross through its length and its hardness. The semantic relation is very different, but the shared term of *similitudo* allows one to avoid the rupture; in switching from one similarity to another, one does not leave the analogical sphere: derivation by metaphor is still, in its way, a mimetic nomination. More precisely, it entails an analogical relation in the Aristotelian sense — that is to say, a proportional relation: *crus* is to *crux* as "leg" is to "cross." But since, unlike Socrates, Augustine has been careful to give himself an imitative (onomatopoetic) point of departure here, the etymological chain will nowhere show the weak link found in Plato between, for example, the word *sēma* and the thing "tomb." The chain corresponding to *sōma-sēma-*"tomb"-"body" here becomes *crus-crux-*"cross"- "leg," and the latter is unbreakable: *crus* sounds like *crux, crux* is painful like the cross, the cross is hard like a shinbone. The series of resemblances is continuous; at no point is the mimetic current interrupted. So, finally, there is indeed an *indirect analogical relation* between the word *crus* and the thing "shinbone."

The next class completely abandons the analogical relation, but it preserves a necessary relation (between the signifieds), now one of proximity (*vicinitas*), later to be called *coexistence* (Beauzée) or *contiguity* (Jakobson). This is derivation by metonymy: "Fishpond (*piscina*) is applied to baths, in which there are no fish and nothing like fish ... because they contain water, in which fish live."[16] In other words, we pass from *pisces* {fish} to *piscina* in the name of a relation of contiguity between water (in general) and fish.[17] There are other examples of metonymical derivation: from cause to effect, *potatio* (drinking) yields *puteus* (a well); from container to contained, *orbs* (circle) yields *urbs* (city); from contained to container, *hordeum* (barley) yields *horreum* (granary), even if it serves just as well to store wheat, keeping its name in that case through misuse or catachresis (*abusio*); from part to whole, *mucro* (sharp point) becomes the name for the entire sword (though this is no longer a derivation but rather a genuine trope, in this case a synecdoche; the slippage is typical, and we will come back to it).[18]

The last category is derivation through antiphrasis (*contrarium*), as in *lucus* from *lucere* (to shine [previously found in Stilo]), *bellum* (war) from *bellus* (handsome), or *foedus* (alliance) from *foedus* (dishonorable). Here, too, the motivation is produced by the relationship between the signifieds: a very variable relationship but always motivated, whether it is a matter of similarity, proximity, or contrariety. "How do I go beyond that? Whatever else is added, you will see that the origin of the word is contained either in the similarity of things and sounds, in the similarity of things themselves, in proximity, or in contrariety.[19] We cannot pursue the origin of a word beyond the similarity of sound, and at times we are unable to do even this. For an explanation can be sought for innumerable words for which there either is no origin {Latin *origo;* French *motivation*}, as I believe, or for which it is hidden, as the Stoics maintain."[20] Plainly, this conclusion[21] is very cautious, and it certainly does not authorize us to rank its author among the most intransigent defenders of the naturalist thesis. On the other hand, it seems to me to indicate *a contrario* his agreement with "the Stoics" on the remaining points — that is, the apparently essential point: not the determination of the quantitative relationship between the arbitrary and the motivated (as in Socrates, for whom a single faulty word discredited the whole system, whereas here the unmotivated vocables represent no more than an apparently secondary lacuna) but indeed the very definition and the general theory of motivation.

⑨ The most remarkable feature of this text is the way it maintains the principle of motivation, from one end to the other of the etymological chain, by coming up with the relation between signifieds at the moment when that between signifiers and signifieds begins to weaken, and by carefully handling the transition and the continuity — thanks to the shared notion of *similitudo* — before resigning itself to other types of necessary relations. In this way we slide, almost without noticing it, from direct (mimetic) motivation to indirect — "etymological," of course, but in an etymology rehabilitated by the very bold and apparently novel recourse to the categories of tropological semantics. These categories (similarity, proximity, contrariety) are themselves very new in the field of rhetoric, since no classification of tropes has appealed to them until now — neither in Aristotle, nor in Cicero, nor in Quintilian. Indeed, they probably come from Aristotle, but from his psychology of associations,[22] which thus finds in the theory of tropes an application that promises a bright future. It is even more remarkable to see them make their entrance here, for this text is not at all rhetorical in principle. The filiations with which it deals are not (except *mucro*, a revealing confusion) tropes properly speaking, since the question is not how "a word changes its meaning," but how one word derives from another. The associative process is the same, however, and it becomes apparent that these few pages of etymological theory are conducted according to a schema that will command the theory of tropes for several centuries (from Vossius to Fontanier) before commanding historical semantics (from Bréal to Ullmann) for a century. There is, therefore, a remarkable convergence of four legacies here: the theory of phonic expressiveness, etymology, the psychology of associations, and the rhetoric of tropes. This is a remarkable and partly ephemeral convergence, for if the two latter disciplines are henceforth hand in glove, the same will not always hold for the entire team: in certain authors, like President de Brosses, we will encounter a less optimistic view of derivation, and especially of the switch from mimetic *similitudo* to metaphorical *similitudo*. Nevertheless, one of the great avenues of mimological speculation has been opened.

This stroke of inspiration, which pulls etymological motivation toward the mimetic, is completed by another one that symmetrically pulls the mimetic toward the etymological. This is the confusion, perhaps unconscious, between a decreasing gradation of the forms of motivation (onomatopoeias, words derived by metaphor, metonymy, antiphrasis), and the appearance of a general filiation of word units, as if metaphors derived from onomatopoeias and expressive words, metonymies from metaphors, antiphrases from metonymies, and therefore as if onomatopoeias — which are still mimetic but already words — could be the *cunabula verborum,* root and seed (*stirpem atque adeo sementum*) of the entire lexicon or, more accurately, of the entire remaining lexicon.

Thus, the central problem of the *Cratylus* — the delicate jointure between direct and indirect motivations — reappears here, but displaced and at the same time almost erased. In Plato the etymological motivation of derivative words hung completely and explicitly on the mimetic motivation of the primary words, itself suspended in the last instance from the expressive value of the phonic elements. With the latter presumed established (and this is indeed Socrates' hypothesis), the whole edifice of linguistic motivation ought to be established at the same stroke. We know that, finally, nothing of the sort occurs and that Socrates attributes this failure quite simply to some initial error (just one would suffice) of the name-maker: "initial" meaning, of course, at the time of the formation of *prōta onomata* such as *ion* or *rheon*, although the error would be revealed only downstream, in the derivative *sklērotēs*. In Augustine we do find a case of complete filiation, *vitis-vincere-vis*, which leads back to a sort of mimetic root **v = vigor*, but this example remains an isolated one. The most typical "first" vocables here are complex onomatopoeias of the type *clangor, hinnitum, tinnitum*, or expressive words of the type *asperitas, crux, mel*, or *vepres*, for which is claimed a lineage as manifold as it is improbable. In the *Cratylus*, the weak link was definitely (recognized) between the mimetic phonemes and the *prōta onomata;*[23] henceforth, it shifts over to one between the mimologisms and the rest of the lexicon, and it makes this shift unnoticed, or at least unacknowledged: a fragile camouflage, but one that does at least permit Socrates' negative conclusion to be replaced by a *fairly positive* conclusion.

🕭 This curious text therefore represents, among other things, an important stage in the constitution and history of Cratylist doctrine, which is itself mythical. All the while protesting his distrust with regard to Stoic speculations, the author gives them perhaps the most synthetic and probably the cleverest overview — and incidentally, the only one surviving to us. In so doing, and whatever part sophistry may play, he successfully closes up, at least in appearance — that is, sufficiently for anyone disposed in advance to be convinced — the widest breaches in the Cratylian edifice and therefore refutes implicitly, or at least smooths over, the consequences that Socrates himself draws at the end of the dialogue. It is as if the role of this chapter, at least symbolically, were to erase the problematic character and disillusioned conclusion of the original text, without ever, exactly, referring to it. Henceforth, upholders of this doctrine, and often its adversaries,[24] will constantly take the *Cratylus* without nuances, and not without boldness, for a mimologist text. Like any posterity, this one is misunderstanding, betrayal, diversion from the origin. What speaks in the "strange silence" of *On Dialectic* is really already the forgetting of the *Cratylus* — a lapse in memory that founds and inaugurates the Cratylian tradition.

CHAPTER 3

Soni rerum indices

℗ The phrase *soni rerum indices* is barely translatable unless one forces the sense of the Latin word *index*. The subject is plainly the sounds of natural language, vowels and diphthongs, consonants and groups of consonants. *Index* is less strong than *imago* or *simulacrum:* it is a natural sign but not necessarily based on similarity; rather, it is an evidential sign or trace, like the print for the foot or smoke for fire. Let us hazard a translation something like *sounds as the marks of things {les sons marques des choses}.*

The phrase is the title in the margin of a section of chapter 14, "De etymologia," in *Grammatica linguae anglicanae {Grammar of the English language}* by John Wallis[1] — a few pages of mimological speculation, characterized by fine intensity and rare coherence, applied to the English language.

Wallis's inquiry focuses in succession on a list of initial consonantal groups, then on a (much shorter) list of final syllables. Here, summarized as briefly as possible and with most of the examples necessarily curtailed drastically, are the main points about the symbolic values he proposes.

In the initial position, the group *str* indicates[2] force or effort, as in *strong, strength, to strike, stroke, strife, to struggle, to stretch, straight, string, stream, strand, to strip, strange, to stride.*[3]

— *st* indicates a weaker force, "needed to hold on to what one has, rather than to acquire something": *to stand, to stop, to stamp, still, stone.*

— *thr* indicates a violent movement: *to throw, through.*

— *wr* shows obliquity or twisting: *wry, wrong, wreck,* and *wrist,* "which twists itself and everything else in all directions."

— *br* points to breach, violent and generally loud splitting apart: *to break, breech* ("because of the split"), *brook.*

— *cr* indicates "something broken up, generally with a crash, at the very least caved in or twisted." Actually, this family divides into three groups. The first one indicates rupture: *to crack; to crake,* augmentative, to crack with a continuous loud noise; *to crackle,* frequentative; *to cry; to crush,* "even noiselessly, because of the dark vowel"; *to crash,* with a brighter vowel; *creek,* "where through a fissure in the ground a stream or a river carves out a path toward the sea." The second group suggests curvature: *crook, to creep, cradle.* The third group indicates an intersection: *cross; crab,* "because of its transversal or backwards gait." It is as if the first ones came from the Latin *crepo,* the second ones from *curvo,* the third ones from *crux.* "But the canine letter *r*[4] suggests something uncouth and unpleasant, at least in the vocables that head up these families, and from which the others obviously derive."

— *shr* suggests a strong contraction: *to shrink; shrimp,* "a miniscule and as though shrunken fish"; *to shrive, shroud.* "Without *r,* the meaning is more subdued."

— *gr* "indicates something rough or hard, painful and completely unpleasant, either because of the roughening letter *r,* or because it seems to be taken from *gravis*": *to grate; to grind,* "as if this word came from *grate* and *wind*"; *to grip; greedy,* "as if it were formed from *grip* and *needy*"; *to grasp,* "as though formed from *grip* and *clasp.*"

— *sw* suggests an almost still agitation, or a slight lateral movement: *to sway, to swim, to swing, swift, sweet.*

— *sm* is very close to *sw: smooth, small;* but *smart* indicates a sharp pain.

— *cl* reflects adherence or retention: *to cleave, clay, to climb, close,* "almost all of which come from *claudo.*"

— *sp* indicates "a certain dispersion or expansion, preferably rapid, especially with the addition of an *r,* as if coming from *spargo* or *separo*": *to spread, to spit.*

— *sl* is a silent gliding, a nearly imperceptible movement: *to slide, sly, slow.*

— *sq, sk, scr* indicate a violent compression: *to squeeze, to screw.*

— the ending *-ash* (*crash, flash*) indicates "something bright and high-pitched. In contrast, *-ush* (*to crush, to blush*) indicates something dim and quiet. Both, however, indicate a rapid and sudden movement, but one that gradually breaks off, because of the continuous sound *sh.*"

— in *ing,* "the tinkling of the ending *-ng* and of the high-pitched vowel *i* indicate something like the prolongation of a tiny movement or of a vibration that ends by disappearing but without an abrupt breaking off": *ding, to swing;* whereas *-ink,* "which terminates in a completely silent consonant, indicates a sudden finish": *to clink, to think.* "If an *l* is added, as in *jingle, sprinkle, twinkle,* this indicates a frequent repetition of very faint movements: these are both frequentatives and diminutives." We find the same meaning, but with movements that are "less subtle because of the more striking vowel *a,* in *-angle*" (*to tangle, to mangle*).

— *umble,* with its "dark *u* indicates something dark and dull, and the piling up of consonants in *mbl* indicates something like a confused agglomerate (*to mumble, to stumble*)." The same meaning is found in *-amble* "but somewhat more acutely, because of the striking vowel *a*" (*to ramble, to scramble*). "Thus, the final *l,* like the *r,* especially after another consonant, generally indicates a fre-

38

quent repetition, particularly of faint movements, because these two consonants are produced by a vibration of the tongue. The proliferation of the consonants *ml* or *mbl* in a confused agglomerate indicates confusion or disorder." The ending *-imble* points to "something even more acute and subtle" than *-amble,* and the resonance of the word *nimble* "wonderfully imitates what it signifies. ... the acuity and the liveliness of the vowel and the voluble grouping of the consonants indicate celerity."

First of all, let us note that the lists of examples illustrating the values of the initial consonantal groups are presented as genuine etymological families. These groups are clustered, sometimes explicitly, around inductor words such as *strong, strand, throw, break, crash, shrink, sweet, smile, cling, slide, squeeze,* through which one can follow how the fundamental or original sense is propagated from derivation to derivation, although it gradually exhausts itself, without ever being completely lost. In this way, the two types of motivation that were so sharply separated in the *Cratylus* — the direct and the indirect[5] — are brought together anew, in accordance with Saint Augustine's principle and model. On the other hand, there is nothing like this in the lists of final syllables, for the obvious reason that the root lies wholly in the initial consonantal group. The endings merely provide secondary variations on the fundamental theme; they are, therefore, actually in the service of derivation: *stand, stay, stop,* and so on differ only in their final syllables, and a more complete chart of these values might have permitted an explanation of their semantic differences through the distinctive signification of the final *-and, -ay, -op,* and the like. Indeed, considering that for Wallis the authentic English word is almost always monosyllabic (we will return to this point), it is clear that an exhaustive list of initial consonantal groups and an equally exhaustive list of terminal groups would suffice to account for the entire original lexicon of the English language. Admittedly, we are wide of that mark, but such really is the potential scope of the project, since for Wallis the combination of initial + final group exhausts the structure of the English word. It would at least be possible, therefore, to take an inventory of the vocables whose initial and final clusters Wallis studied, for example, *str-ing, stu-mble, br-ing, cr-ash, sh-rink, sm-ash, spr-ing, scr-amble.* A few of these actually appear in his lists, several under both categories, and in at least three cases Wallis has not backed off from the test of a complete analysis. The first case is *smart:* "*a smart blow* properly signifies a blow that, from a silent movement at first, indicated by *sm,* comes to a head with acute violence, indicated by *ar,* and finishes up suddenly, indicated by *t.*" The second case is *sparkle,* in which "*sp* indicates dispersion, *ar* high-pitched crackling, *k* sudden interruption, *l* frequent repetition." The third case is *sprinkle,* identical to the preceding one except for *in,* which "indicates the fineness of scattered drops of water." Such endeavors (and, in the present instance, such successful ones) are quite rare in the Cratylian tradition. They introduce us to one of the most original and invaluable features of Wallis's speculation: an acute awareness of the syntagmatic structure of the word, and of the difference in value between the sounds according to their position in this chain.

For Wallis, then, the English word may be exhaustively described as an initial consonantal group that bears the fundamental meaning, and a final syllable composed of a vowel and a consonant or a consonantal group that lends the word its specific nuance: a substantial modality (light, thickness, weight, and so on) and a dynamic modality (sudden or progressive interruption, frequency, amplitude, and so on). This characteristic division has the obvious result of placing the vowel at the weakest semantic pole, forming almost a sort of secondary suffix with the final consonants: one of a number of examples, in Cratylusland, of the semantic valorization of the consonant. Next, one notices that no initial consonant appears on its own but is always in a group of two or three; no mention is made in the foregoing lists of words with a simple initial consonant, even those as typical as *top, catch, find*.[6] So, the groups of initial consonants seem at first to be indivisible, in meaning as well as in form, and the majority (*st, wr, sw, sm, sl, sp, cl, sq*) will in fact resist any decomposition. On the other hand, the consonants that appear both in the initial and the final position (*s, sh, g, k, b, l*) do not give rise to any attempt to reduce them to a common semantic value. Position is the determining factor, and it is as if there were not even a question of the same sounds. We must therefore proceed very cautiously in the course of our analysis in order to avoid betraying the intentions, or simply the intuitions, of Wallis by shifting from the molecular level, as it were, where he situates himself most naturally, to the level of phonic and semantic values.

Regarding the vowels, at least, the commutations performed by Wallis himself (*-ash/-ush, -ing/-ang, -umble/-amble/-imble*) allow us to extract with confidence a more or less clear scale of values but a highly restricted one, focused only on *u, a,* and *i*. Moreover, it must be specified (given the great variety of sounds marked by these three letters in English) that the scale includes for *u* only the sound [ʌ] (with an exception for the [u] in *push*); for *a*, the sound [ae]; and for *i*, the sound [i]. Within these limits, the system has solid coherence. To a phonic range of increasing "high pitch" corresponds a semantic range of increasing lightness, liveliness, and luminosity: *u* is low-pitched and subdued, indicating darkness and silence; *a* is more high-pitched and more precisely "brilliant," its values being brighter and livelier; *i*, even more high-pitched, indicates smaller or even tiny objects with the utmost liveliness. These equivalences are very widespread (keeping within the field of English, they will be found again, for example, in Jespersen and Sapir),[7] compelling recognition through a kind of immediate evidence.

The consonants, once again, are more difficult to isolate, but a certain number of specific values can be disengaged by subtraction. In the initial position, the comparison of *str* and *st* implicitly gives a dynamic value to *r* (already proposed by Plato) which quite agrees and perhaps merges with the explicit index for harshness attributed to *cr, shr,* and *gr:* the *r* is "rough" and "canine," for obvious articulatory reasons. It would be tempting to assign to *s* a value of slipperiness—which is found more or less equally in *sw, sm, sl*—but the meaning of *st* and of *sc* conflict with this; the presence of a continuant consonant behind the *s* is indispensable for producing this value. On the other hand (by subtracting the "violence" that belongs to *r* in *thr* and maybe in *shr*), one locates this value without too much trouble in the affricates *th* and *sh,* with an implicit confirmation for *sh* drawn from the ending *-ash/-ush.* In the final position, *g,* the resonant velar consonant, opposes its value of "prolonged vibration" to that of *k,* the unvoiced velar, which merges with the value of *t* (the unvoiced dental consonant), or the "sudden stop": the vibratory value thus seems to belong to voicing and the stop to unvoiced occlusion, whatever the articulatory position. The meaning "confusion," which is assigned to the groups *mbl* and *ndl,* plainly stems more from the cluttering together of three consonants than from their articulatory nature. In contrast, the frequentative value of *l* is linked to its pronunciation by a "vibration of the tongue."[8] Finally, let us note the opposing values of *k* ("dull" consonant = thickness) and *n* ("sharp" consonant = thinness), illustrated solely by the pair *thick/thin,* which is obviously suspect for its "suggestion through the meaning." But perhaps overly obvious suspicions are to be distrusted, too. In Wallis, physical motivation stands out instead for its relative cautiousness—restrained as it is by the importance of positional factors and nearly buried under the abundance of lexical illustrations that give this whole inquiry an almost inductive cast. Wallis moves from verbal material to the elementary values that he exploits to advantage, and no longer, as Socrates did, from the symbolic values to vocables which, judiciously selected, can (provisionally) confirm them. *Soni rerum indices* is, before and above everything, a speculation on a phenomenon believed to be exceptional and typically English: the expressive monosyllable.[9]

Indeed, we need to come back to this essential point, which is the exclusive valorization of the English language. As a Puritan and a resolute anti-Papist, Wallis advocated a return to the Anglo-Saxon sources of the language and a grammar independent of Latin categories—even though his book, in a paradox that recalls that of *De vulgari eloquentia* {Dante}, is written in Latin. Quite clearly, these pages from *Grammatica linguae anglicanae* are in keeping with an overall purpose of defense and illustration. Thus, among other merits ascribed to English is that of a very special aptitude for phonic mimeticism, at least in its "native" (*nativi*) words, those from the Anglo-Saxon base predating the Norman Conquest. It is solely (theoretically) in these words that Wallis locates a "great harmony (*consensus*) between the letters and the significations." The "letters" here are clearly the sounds; there is no trace of graphic motivation in Wallis. "Moreover," he immediately specifies, "the *sonorities* of these letters, sustained, shrill, thick, dull, soft, strong, bright, dark, strident, etc., often indicate analogous dispositions in the objects signified, and sometimes even several in one word, albeit monosyllabic."

The mimetic superiority of English is again asserted, and much more aggressively, in the conclusion:

In the same way, in *squeek, squeak, squele, squall, brawl, wrawl, yawl, spawl, screek, shreek, shrill, sharp, shriv'l, wrinkle, crack, crake, crick, creak, creek, croke, crash, clash, gnash, plash, huff, buff, crush, hush, tush, push, hisse, sisse, whist, soft, jarr, hurl, curl, whirl, buz, bustle, spindle, dwindle, twine, twist* [there we really have the canonical English vocables], and countless other words, one can observe a similar adequation of sound to sense; and that, in a manner truly so frequent that I know of no other natural language able to rival ours in this regard: in such a way that in a single word, often monosyllabic (as nearly all of ours are, if the inflection is removed), one designates expressively what other languages can only explain by means of compound or derivative words, or perhaps accompanied by a great many periphrases, and this not without difficulty, even when they do succeed. And definitely, the greatest part of our native vocables are indeed formed in this manner; and I have no doubt that there were quite a few more of this kind before the intrusion into our language of an enormous *fatras* {jumble} of French words condemned such a great number of our original vocables to exile and oblivion.

Such glorification of one's own language is not in the least exceptional in the Cratylian tradition, which implicitly practices it all the time, since the maternal tongue is generally taken to be a manifestation par excellence of the imitative capacities of the language system in general. But in Wallis, this exemplary value becomes so displaced as to reverse itself, since indigenous English is ultimately[10] presented as the *only* mimetic language—which obviously contradicts the Cratylian principle of the language system as natural, hence universal. This contradiction is all the more noticeable because it is apparently not accompanied, as we will see in other authors, by a mythical filiation between the idiom thus valorized and the originary, Adamic language before Babel. It is as if Wallis's fanatical Anglocentrism disdained such a common justification, an open door to God-knows-what shocking promiscuities. We will run across this question of the mimetic superiority of English again elsewhere. For the moment, let us simply raise our hats to Wallis as a rare case of *reserved* Cratylism, one that is deliberately protectionist and, in a word, insular.

CHAPTER 4

Hermogenes, the
Master of Words

⑨ Right in the middle of the classical age, the Platonic debate seems to reproduce itself with exemplary fidelity in an equally famous and nearly as fictive dialogue between "Philalethes" and "Theophilus," alias John Locke and Gottfried
Wilhelm Leibniz. Nevertheless, we will see that this is by no means a repetition
and, more precisely, that if Locke is indeed, after a few others, a new Hermogenes, Leibniz does not altogether reincarnate Cratylus, much less Socrates. But
let us not anticipate.

Hermogenes is not a talkative fellow. As it must, his (negative) profession of
faith here consists of a sentence in Locke, in the first paragraph of the second
chapter of the third book of *An Essay concerning Human Understanding,* repeated almost word for word by Leibniz in the corresponding chapter of *New
Essays on Human Understanding.*[1] "*Words* ... come to be made use of by Men,
as *the Signs of* their *Ideas;* not by any natural connexion, that there is between
particular articulate Sounds and certain *Ideas,* for then there would be but one
language amongst all Men; but by a voluntary Imposition, whereby such a Word
is made arbitrarily the Mark of such an *Idea.*"[2] The response from "Cratylus"
is more elaborate; it occupies the longest rejoinder not only in *New Essays*[3] but
also in other works, doubtless including a posthumous, undated fragment which
is probably already an outline of it and which is translated here from the Latin:

[*On the connection between words and things, or rather on the origin of natural languages.*] We cannot claim that there is an exact and well-determined
connection between words and things; however, signification is not purely
arbitrary, either. There simply must be some reason for having assigned
such and such a word to such and such a thing.

We cannot claim that signification springs from a merely arbitrary institution, unless in certain artificial languages, such as Chinese in Golius's
hypothesis, or in the languages forged by Dalgarno, Wilkins, and others.
As for the originary language of the first human beings, some think that it

43

springs from a divine imposition, others that it was invented by Adam, inspired by God, when according to tradition he gave names to the animals. But such a language must have died out entirely, or left behind only a few fragments in which the artifice is no longer recognizable.

Languages do have, however, a natural origin in the harmony between the sounds and the effects produced in the soul by the spectacle of things; and I am inclined to believe that this origin can be seen not only in the first natural language but still in the natural languages born later, in part from the first one, in part from the new usages acquired by mankind, scattered as it was over the surface of the globe. And to be sure, the imitation of nature is often unmistakable in onomatopoeia: thus, we say that frogs *croak* (*coaxatio*) or we express the command to be silent by *st,* rapid movement by *r* (*cursus*), laughter by *hahaha,* and the cry of pain by *ouaie* (*vae* {ow!}).[4]

Clearly, the first objection is purely "philosophical"; it is the determinist argument: *no effect without a cause.* No act of naming can be "purely arbitrary," because there must be a real reason why one particular word and not another was assigned to a particular object. Very obviously, this argument can hold good only against a hyperbolic version of the Hermogenist thesis, for which the choice of a noun can never be determined. But conventionalism, in Locke as elsewhere, denies only that this determination is to be sought in the nature of the object, which is another matter entirely. Likewise, it is never without reason that parents choose a particular first name for their unborn child, but this reason cannot be the child's physical appearance or character. The causalist argument, therefore, refutes only a clumsy or exaggerated interpretation — already — of the word *arbitrary.* So it is irrelevant to the debate. If it were relevant, the implicit line of reasoning (sophism) would inevitably be this: no act of naming can be without cause; therefore, all nominations have their cause in the nature of the object to be named. It follows, of course, that *no* natural language can be conventional, which is as far as could be from Leibniz's thinking, as the rest of the argument indeed shows.

The second, true rejoinder is actually a distinction that completely displaces the problem: the issue will no longer be whether "language" in general and in the absolute sense is conventional or motivated, but — it being implicitly granted that language can just as well (if not as easily, a point we will return to) be one or the other, and provisionally granted that certain natural languages are conventional and certain others motivated — which natural languages, or more precisely which sorts of natural languages, are conventional and which are motivated. Leibniz's answer is then rather patent: the only conventional languages, or more precisely the only *purely* conventional languages, are the "artificial" ones, the most recent example of which is found in the endeavors of George Dalgarno and John Wilkins.[5] As for languages that will later be called "natural"—that is, languages without a specific master of words, which happen to be, setting aside Chinese, the only ones actually spoken by nations on earth—they are all *at least partially* motivated by "the harmony between the sounds and the effects produced in the soul by the spectacle of things."

This way of posing—and of resolving—the problem seems to me entirely distinctive, and we will have to come back to it in order to appreciate all its consequences. But first we should examine more closely the arguments from fact which, according to Leibniz, support such a conclusion. Let us start with the special case of Chinese. This artificialist hypothesis reappears, without attribution, in the corresponding text of *New Essays:* "Perhaps there are some artificial languages which are wholly chosen and completely arbitrary, as that of China is believed to have been." And again, but once more attributed to Golius, in the *Brevis designatio* of 1710: "Artificial languages ... such as Chinese according to Golius's hypothesis, a not inconsiderable authority."[6] This, then, is the same formula as in the Latin fragment, only strengthened by a seal of approval. But the most specific mention occurs in *New Essays,* book 3, chapter 1, section 1: "So it was the opinion of Golius, the noted mathematician and great authority on languages, that their language {Chinese} is artificial—that is, it was invented all at once by some ingenious man in order to bring about verbal communication between the many different peoples occupying the great land we call China, although this language might by now be changed through long usage."[7]

This interpretation of Chinese, therefore, is not Leibniz's own. We find other echoes of it in the Orientalist Nicholas Fréret and in Baron de Montesquieu, and, in fact, it expresses a reaction not to the Chinese language but to Chinese writing, then perceived as a purely conventional and nonrepresentational ideography (this will not always be the case, as we shall see). The connection between convention and artifice is clearly pointed out by Montesquieu: "I would be inclined to believe that these characters were invented by a society of intellectuals who wanted to conceal their activity from the people. ... My reason for this is that the characters are by no means an image of the thing they represent."[8] As Madeleine David's study has rightly shown, in the classical age all thinking on nonphonetic writing systems (then considered as such) is marked by two antithetical valorizing or "prejudiced" myths: the ideogram as pure convention, and (from Athanasius Kircher to Barthélémy) the "hieroglyph" as pure mimesis.[9] This opposition is apparent in Leibniz himself: "I do not know what to say about the Egyptians' hieroglyphics, and I have difficulty believing that they are conformable to those of the Chinese. For it seems to me that the Egyptian characters are more popular and are very close to resembling tangible things, like animals and other creatures, and consequently are like allegories; whereas the Chinese characters are perhaps more philosophical and appear to be built

45

on more intellectual considerations, such as those that yield number, order and relations; thus, there are only detached lines that do not support any kind of resemblance to a given body."[10] Clearly, this description is not wholly exempt from valorizing connotations; this is a crucial characteristic, and I will return to it.[11]

A second factual given, and a demonstratively decisive one, is the originary natural language (*primigenia*). On this point, the Latin fragment {quoted above} is rather difficult to interpret. Apparently, Leibniz contents himself with describing the two traditional theses, that of direct divine institution (which is, after all, Locke's, among others), and—a variant nearer to the text of Genesis— that of a natural language created by Adam when he baptized the animals but in fact inspired by God. And then Leibniz seems to cast this originary natural language, divine or Adamic, back into the shadows of an antiquity that is forever lost. But if we do not want to make this double reference out to be a simple excursus without demonstrative purpose, clearly we have to situate and define these hypothetical languages in relation to the cardinal opposition between motivated-natural languages and conventional-artificial languages. For the hypothesis of divine institution, the very choice of the formula *ab instituto divino*, so close to the *ex instituto* which Leibniz usually uses to designate the conventional thesis,[12] indicates rather clearly that an "arbitrary" language is at issue. The *Brevis designatio* explicitly confirms this: "Such a language [like Wilkins's universal tongue or Golius's Chinese] would also have been the one that God, if he did so, taught to men."[13] In the Adamic hypothesis, it could be assumed that God inspires in his noblest creature a natural language of the same type, and nothing in Leibniz's text conflicts with this; indeed, on the contrary, the term for artifice (*artificium*) seems to apply to both.

But here, the *Brevis designatio* resolutely settles things in the opposite direction: "In natural languages that are born gradually, the words arise by chance from an analogy between the vocal sound and the feelings provoked by the perception of the thing; and I cannot believe that Adam went about his namings in any other way."[14] The language of divine institution would therefore have been conventional, and the Adamic tongue natural and mimetic. For Leibniz, the two variants of the Judaeo-Christian tradition in regard to the nature of language are therefore absolutely opposed to each other, and the choice between them becomes crucial, since in one case all human languages would come from a conventional origin, and in the other case from a motivated, and motivating, origin. The function of this double reference is hardly digressive, then, since once the two possible types of natural language are defined, it is finally a question of which one really describes human languages—except Chinese, of course. In principle, and according to the last sentence of this second paragraph, this crucial choice is also an impossible one, since the trace of this originary language is lost forever anyway. But in fact, the rest of the text—and the whole context

46

of Leibniz's theories on the history of natural languages—settles things in favor of the Adamic hypothesis interpreted in the style of Jacob Böhme[15]—that is, in naturalist terms. The divine hypothesis is finally rejected, and the Adamic one, a symbol of "natural" origin, definitively carries the day: with Chinese set apart, the natural languages actually spoken by men in fact do have "a natural origin in the harmony between the sounds and the effects produced in the soul by the spectacle of things." Or, to quote the most categorical (and the richest) formulation last of all, the one in the *Brevis designatio:* "Natural languages were not created by convention, not founded as if by decree; they were born out of a sort of natural tendency of men to harmonize sounds with the affections and the movements of the soul. I make exception for artificial languages, such as Wilkins's, and so on."[16]

That this "harmony" is composed, as usual, of a mimetic relation is amply proved by the several examples cited above, in which we again find the familiar categories of mimology: onomatopoeia (*coassement* {croaking}, and probably *st,* if one hears the abrupt stop *t* from a continuous hissing *s* here); exclamations or verbal imitations of "natural" cries (*haha, ouaïe*); oblique, indirect symbolism (the *r* expressing movement, as in the *Cratylus*). The text of *New Essays* contributes several details and supplementary illustrations here. The expression of movement is refined into *r* = *violent movement* and *l* = *gentle movement,* correspondences obviously linked to the difference in articulatory force between the two "liquids": "Thus we see that children and others who find the *r* too harsh and difficult to pronounce replace it with the letter *l*—and ask their palish pliest to play for them."[17] But above all, Leibniz no longer contents himself with noting down the evidence: that is, the expressive capacity of this articulatory opposition. He sees in it one of the active sources of the lexicon—at least in Indo-European natural languages.[18] The symbolic value of *r,* which was not discoverable in *kinēsis,* is invested in Greek *rhēo* (color); German *rinnen* {to flow}, *ruhren* {to move}, in *Rhin, Rhône, Ruhr, rauschen* {to roar}, *recken* {to stretch}; French *arracher* {to tear off}, and so on. The value of *l* appears in German *leben* {to live}, *lieben* {to love}, *lauffen* {to glide swiftly}; Latin *lentus* {slow}, *labi* {to glide}, and so on, and in the Latin and German diminutives. The *Brevis designatio* is even more detailed, placing two verbal schemas opposite each other, *r-k,* which express an abruptly interrupted movement: "By the very nature of its sonority, the canine letter indicates a violent movement, and the final *k* the obstacle that stops it," as in *Ruck* (shake) or *recken* (to stretch), "when suddenly, with great force and much noise one tightens a thread or some other thing, in such a way as not to break it but to stop the movement; a curved line is thus transformed into a straight line and stretched like the string of a musical instrument." If the shock nears the breaking point, under prolonged movement, *r-k* yields to *r-s* or *r-z,* as in *Riss* (rip) or *Ritz* (crack). "Such," Leibniz continues, "do the first origins of the lexicon reveal themselves to be, whenever one can trace far back to the root of an onomatopoeia."[19]

In all fairness, Leibniz's judgment is usually more prudent, or more moderate. We have previously read, for example: "Signification is not *purely* arbitrary, either"; or again, in *New Essays:* "There is *something* natural in the origin of words — something which reveals a relationship between things and the sounds and motions of the vocal organs." And regarding the expressive value of the *l* sound we read: "I cannot claim that this principle applies universally, however, since the lion, the lynx and the leopard are anything but gentle. But perhaps people seized upon another of their characteristics, namely their speed (*lauf*), which makes them feared or which compels flight, as if anyone who saw such an animal coming would shout to the others *Lauf!* (Run!); besides, various accidents and transformations have left most words greatly changed and far removed from their original pronunciation and signification."[20] And continuing on this point of the gradual erasure of motivation, *Brevis designatio:* "But most often, through the effect of time and numerous derivations, the original and innate (*veteres et nativae*) significations have been modified or obscured."[21] But it is just so characteristic of his attitude for Leibniz to say "natural languages are motivated" in one place, and "natural languages are *partially* motivated" in another place, and finally "natural languages were motivated at the origin, but over time this motivation was lost" in yet another place, without worrying about these nuances, or dissonances.

We recall that one ill-formed word was (nearly) enough to turn Socrates against the Cratylian hypothesis, and we will see how the weakening of vocal mimesis in the course of derivation will vex President de Brosses to the point of jettisoning it in search of another type of imitation. For Leibniz, as for the author of *On Dialectic*, to some degree, several gaps, many gaps, even more and more gaps do not compromise the general principle — or, rather, the exception proves the rule. Is this a typical manifestation of *optimism*? As well as, and doubtless a more accurate one, of another feeling or another attitude, which I would not want to label too hastily. The true "optimism" on this topic[22] belongs to Cratylus himself or, as we shall see, to Court de Gébelin, neither of whom wishes to acknowledge or to catch sight of any weak link in the system. As for Leibniz, he perceives and acknowledges many of its weak links, and this apparently matters little to him, as if he only wanted to draw attention to a few exceptions to the opposite system. But after all, is this not the case? Philalethes claims that there is *no* "natural connection" between words and things; Theophilus elegantly refutes him, simply showing that there sometimes are *a few* of them. In short, as anticipated, he is to this Hermogenes what Socrates was to Cratylus.

This formulation can seem both strained and insignificant, if one judges that Socrates himself is midway between Cratylus and Hermogenes, successively

48

demonstrating to each of them that there is something extravagant and partial about his theory. But we have seen that this is not really so, and that there is no symmetry between the first and the second movement of the dialogue, at least for the reason that Socrates refutes Cratylus without pleasure, and despite explicitly sharing his system of values: to wit, that "an imitation by likeness is preferable to just any means at hand." There is nothing like this in Leibniz; he contents himself with noting a few facts about "imitation by likeness" and interjecting them into Locke's conventionalism as pure matter of fact, without any valorization or even concern for the extensiveness of the phenomenon, which might be put down to a certain indifference.

Is it necessary to go further? We need at least to do something purposely postponed until now, which is to turn around to the other side, to the side of what Leibniz conceded at the very first to *pure convention*. This flip side, let us recall, is entirely occupied by the *artificial* languages, those "invented all at once by some ingenious man in order to bring about verbal communication between ... many different peoples." This definition, where "all at once" is opposed, from one text to another, to "gradually" (*paulatim*) for the genesis of natural languages, is here applied to Chinese but equally to the philosophical languages of Dalgarno, Wilkins, "and others," and hypothetically, moreover, to a language that would have been invented by God himself. Now it happens that none of these attributions is axiologically neutral. For the one concerning Chinese, I refer to the letter to Bouvet, cited above, in which the comparison with the "Egyptians' hieroglyphs" foregrounds a striking intellectual superiority. The divine institution is obviously flattering in itself; after all, nothing necessarily links it to conventionality, unless it is an implicit valorization. For Socrates, the superhuman work that required an infallible master of words was mimetic nomenclature; simple convention, on the contrary—labeled a "vulgar expedient" and defined as a capricious or fortuitous adoption of just any name for just any object—was within the reach of just anyone (*pas anēr*). For Leibniz, it is apparently the opposite: onomatopoeia was within the reach of the "popular" mind of the first men, but pure convention, a "philosophical" task, required a divine intelligence or at least that of an "ingenious man" yet to come, such as Dalgarno, Wilkins, *and others.*

It is time to bring up what everyone knows: that *aliique* {and others} is a modest formula through which Gottfried Wilhelm designates himself, who never ceased to dream about a universal language more philosophical still than that of his predecessors, a logical algebra whose nomenclature would rest upon a rigorous analysis of thought into a combinatory of simple ideas. The detail of these plans does not concern us directly here;[23] it suffices to notice that Leibniz includes himself, and legitimately, in the list of those masters of words, superhuman or not, who have forged or tried to forge a universal language, rigorously rational in the organization of its signifieds and purely conventional in the choice of its signifiers. These three properties do not mutually imply each other a priori, and we will encounter elsewhere at least an attempt at a language that is universal, rational, and *mimetic*.[24] Apparently, Leibniz never thought of this, dominated as he was by what Madeleine David calls the "criterion of the *superior value of the non-figurative sign.*"[25] Moreover, this "criterion" might be called, with reference to Saussure, the *semiological* (versus *symbolic*) *parti pris*. If the Cratylian debate is reduced to its ultimate core of valorization, this is the Hermogenist criterion par excellence — so much so that Hermogenes himself, in the *Cratylus*, nowhere explicitly satisfies it.

It is clear now, I hope, in what way Leibniz's position is symmetrical and inverse to that of Socrates: as Socrates was a Cratylist in principle (in value) and a Hermogenist in practice, so Leibniz is a mimologist in practice (since he recognizes and "demonstrates" the role of motivation in natural languages) and a conventionalist in principle, since he implicitly criticizes this role in other passages by seeking to forge, in his own words, a "purely arbitrary" language. If one agrees, as we have done, to baptize as *secondary mimologism* the attempt at artificial remotivation to which the Socratic conclusion (natural language ought to be and could be mimetic, but it is not) logically leads — even though Socrates himself evades it — then one can inversely describe as *secondary conventionalism* Leibniz's endeavor, which is in its own way an attempt at artificial demotivation: natural language would profit from being entirely arbitrary; it could be so, it is not so; therefore, we have to reform it in this direction or at least invent another language that might meet this need.

I do not intend to downplay the equally strained and mythical aspect of this overly neat symmetry, probably inspired by the demon of taxonomy and the rage for structural diagrams. I simply plead that the object of study lends itself to this and modestly dedicate to it this last attempt at systematization:

Say we agree to reduce the mimologist "doctrine" to these three previously stated propositions: (A) *language should be mimetic;* (B) *language can be mimetic;* (C) *language is mimetic.* We then observe, as is correct, that only Cratylus and his true disciples grant these three propositions. Socrates, and secondary mimologism in his wake, grants only the first two. Hermogenes grants neither the second nor (consequently) the third and comes to no conclusion on the first. But the absolute conventionalist, of which Saussure might provide, provisionally, the paradigm, grants none of these. Leibniz, to my knowledge the sole representative of secondary conventionalism[26] and the complete antithesis of Socrates, grants only the last two. One could think of a few other combinations still (excluding, obviously, all those — logically inadmissible — that would grant the third proposition without the second). One of these would deserve special attention, but I have some reasons for not mentioning it right away, leaving the task of deducing it to the impatient reader. Here, then, is the inevitable chart, where + signifies acceptance; −, rejection; ?, silence and perhaps indifference. I am deliberately leaving one row blank; maybe I will come back to it.

A	B	C	
+	+	+	Absolute mimologism (Cratylus)
+	+	-	Secondary mimologism (Socrates)
?	-	-	Hermogenes
-	-	-	Absolute conventionalism (Saussure?)
-	+	+	Secondary conventionalism (Leibniz)

CHAPTER 5

Mimographisms

⚘ From Plato to Leibniz, we have been able to observe a few modifications but no real displacement in the field of debate, whose active center has remained *mimēma phōnē*, imitation of meaning by vocal sounds. Now natural language does not materialize in speech only but in writing, too, and beside a phonic mimesis (or below it, or above it, depending; I will come back to this), can be dreamed — has been dreamed — a graphic mimesis: imitation by the concrete forms of writing. Imitation of what? Here a distinction ignored by phonic mimologism, in fact if not in theory, becomes vital: just as easily as speech, writing can be understood as an imitation of the objects it designates. As we have seen, this is more or less the idea of the Egyptian "hieroglyph" adopted in the neoclassical period. But a writing system that is called phonetic, like our own, can also be understood as an imitation of the sounds it notates, each letter (for example) being the visual analogue of a phoneme. In order to arrive at a more synthetic and more effective terminology, mimology in general can be divided into *mimophony* (this is the home territory of classical Cratylism) and *mimography*, which in its turn subdivides into *ideomimography* and *phonomimography*. Theoretically, these two varieties of mimography are completely heterogeneous and independent of each other. In practice, they can sometimes merge if the mimophonic principle is added to the mimographic principle. If writing imitates speech, which for its part imitates things, it necessarily follows that writing, even without trying to, will imitate things; and reciprocally, if speech and writing imitate things, each in its own way, they will inevitably imitate each other. We will encounter such effects of convergence again at the appropriate time. For the moment, let us be content with simpler, or more dissociated, situations. Among a few others, the neoclassical period offers us two rather pure, and nearly contemporaneous, mimographic systems: that of Johann Georg Wachter, which is a phonomimetic interpretation of our alphabet, and that of Rowland Jones, which is an ideomimetic vision of it.

⚘ The principle of phonomimography is clear, but it is not as simple as it may a priori appear, for the reason at least that the sounds of speech can be viewed either in their properly acoustic aspect or in their articulatory aspect. Thus, one

53

might imagine two types of mimetic alphabet: one would represent graphically the sounds of speech, without troubling about the conditions for their production by the vocal apparatus, and the other would imitate the form of this apparatus at the moment of utterance. An attempt of the first type for the notation of vowels will be encountered in President de Brosses, and much more recently a complete system of notation based on electronic transcription has been proposed.[1] But that gets us into the domain of artificial alphabets and thus into the mode of secondary mimographism. Graphical Cratylism properly speaking — that is, the mimetic interpretation of existing writing systems — seems to have turned much more readily toward articulatory phonomimesis.[2] This preference is quite understandable: the translation of acoustics into graphics is within the reach of laboratory machines more than of the unsophisticated imagination, and the known alphabets really lend themselves very poorly to an interpretation in this direction. On the other hand, between the form of certain letters and that, for example, of the mouth (of the lips) during the utterance of the corresponding sound, the comparison is rather easy, and there is at least one, well founded or not, that seems to go without saying and that has often been proposed: the obvious case of the O.

It is found, for example, in *Champ fleury* (1529), a treatise on typography by Geoffroy Tory: "The O must be pronounced with a breath and sound that come out of the rounded mouth, as the figure and drawing (of the letter) show"; or in the *De causis linguae latinae* (1559) by Julius Caesar Scaliger: "The figure comes from a representation of the circle of the mouth, whereas the I, which notates the shrillest sound, appears without either hump or belly."[3] It occurs again, as everyone knows, in the phonetics lesson of Molière's *Bourgeois Gentleman* (1670) — "The opening of the mouth makes exactly a small circle that represents an O"[4] — and implicitly in Bernard Lamy: "The entire mouth becomes rounded, and the lips form a circle, whereas in the pronunciation of an *I* {in French} they form ... a straight line."[5] Concerning the O, we have a genuine commonplace, which we will meet with again in Charles Nodier; the straight line of the I (apparently rotated by a quarter circle) is less obvious. But regarding the A,[6] we have something much more complex, again in *Champ fleury*, which paraphrases Galeotus Martius at this point: "*A ex duabus lineis constat, quae suo contactu angulum constituunt acutum, spiritum ab utraque parte palati emanantem indicant. Quae vero per transversum posita est, certam mensuram hiatus ostendit, quanto opus est in hujus elementi enunciatione.* That is to say, A is formed by two lines that touch one another at the tips and make a sharp angle. And for this reason they are the index for the voice coming out of the mouth between part of the palate and part of the upper cavity. Also, the line placed crossways shows the exact degree of hiation required to pronounce this vocalic letter A. Therefore, the crossways line of the above-mentioned A signifies that it must be pronounced with the mouth neither too open nor too closed."[7]

These are still only isolated mentions. More systematic is the attempt by Franciscus Mercurius, Baron Van Helmont, in his *Alphabeti vere naturalis hebraici brevissima delineatio.*[8] Each letter of the Hebrew "alphabet" is analyzed, with plates for illustration, as a drawing representing in profile the position of the tongue at the moment of utterance. Certain of these positions leave one perplexed, but this is probably to be blamed on the reader's incompetence.

Wachter's system is a more sober illustration, and (although it claims to be a genealogy of all writing systems) it relies essentially on the Latin alphabet. The main points are found in chapters 2 and 3 of *Naturae et scripturae concordia,*[9] whose redundant titles are perfectly explicit: "Primas literarum formas ab instrumentis loquendi desumptas esse," and "Primas literarum formas instrumentis suis similes fuisse." For Wachter, nature has provided not only the sounds of the vowels and consonants but also and simultaneously the form of their letters, which required "no invention, but a simple imitation": it is enough to study the form of the vocal organs. Any other research would be pointless and inefficacious besides, for in this primitive state of the human mind the signs of the writing system had to be as clear and mnemotechnical as possible, and nothing fulfills this condition as well as lifelike signs: *nam a similibus similium fit recordatio.*

First, let us consider the vowels, or rather the vowel, a "simple sound, emitted with open mouth, with the tongue remaining immobile in place; and this sound naturally derives its image (*effigiem*) from the round form of the open mouth — a form expressed by the sign O. And although there are five vowels, different and distinct in sound, it is certain that they are all akin and all produced by the same opening of the mouth, drawn more or less tight." These five vowels, therefore, are merely five secondary varieties of one single sound, exclusively characterized by the opening of the mouth and notated by an imitation of this opening. We will encounter this fundamental unity of the vowel elsewhere, focused here on the O (and not, as usual, on the A) for obvious graphical reasons. Moreover, it is likely, for Wachter, that the first people did not distinguish vocalic nuances: still today, "in the mouths of the common people, all the vowels are confused," and "not every people knows how to use all the vowels." The vowel letters besides O are thus recent, conventional in their distribution and very likely derived from this simple and fundamental form "either by means of a transversal support, whence the Coptic or Greek A, or by dividing the surface of the circle into fourths, whence the Greek and Latin E, I and V." That is to say, probably, that a figure like ⊕ or ⊗ yields the material for these various signs, which in this way are found to come indirectly from the mimetic form O without having themselves a relation by analogy with the sounds they notate. Apparently, for Wachter, the mimetic principle need only be present at the origin; even if it must later change or disappear, this initial action suffices to motivate the whole chain.

The consonantal system is more complex. It is subdivided into gutturals, linguals, dentals, labials, and nasals, each group being reducible, like that of the vowels, to an articulatory unit that provides its fundamental written figure.

The gutturals, whether they are expirated (*h*), aspirated (*ch*), or plosive (*k, c, q, g*), all come from a working of the throat; and their Latin letters (K, C, Q, G) all derive from the figure Q "which so well represents the entryway to the throat and the pathway for breathing, or the vocal cord." All the gutturals, that is, except H, which was formed "by fusing two conventional signs for breathing, the harsh breath 'and the gentle breath,'" and which is therefore arbitrary in its components but motivated through the act of using the signs for breathing in order to notate exhalation.

The "linguals" can result from three different articulatory movements, whence three fundamental figures: (1) simple contact of the tongue with the front of the palate is the sound *l*, and the figure <, whence are obviously derived the Greek Λ and (through rotation) the Latin L; (2) pushing the tongue on the upper teeth makes the sound *d* or *t* (usually called dental, or apico-dental), depending on the force of articulation, notated by the figure <, origin of the Greek Δ and the Latin T; (3) vibration of the tongue against the upper teeth, which produces "the uproar *r*, whose natural figure is a line with a twisted tip, ⤳," whence the Hebrew ר and the Greek P, and indirectly the Latin R.

The single "dental" is actually a sibilant, produced by "the tongue squeezing the breath on the teeth, which yields its figure, or, beyond dispute, ח." This is the visible form of a lower incisor; keeled over on its side and a bit warped by its fall, it generates the Greek Σ and then, through various softenings, the Latin S and C.

The labials are produced by a closing up of the lips: (1) complete closure by simple contact (*b, p* sounds), whence the figure representing two conjoined lips in profile, Ɜ, whence our B and P; (2) complete closure with compression (*m* sound), for which variant the same figure is turned around by a quarter circle, ⋏, whence of course our m, become the angular M under the chisel of inscription engravers; (3) with partial closure, letting the carefully guided breath pass through the aperture between the lips (*f* or *v* sound), the figure will represent two half-open lips, ⟨, propped up into K, whence, it seems, the Greek F (digamma) and our F.

Finally, the nasal (*n* sound) is an exhalation through the nose, whose natural figure is the external form of a nose seen fullface, Λ, whose inconvenient resemblance to the Greek lambda is passed over in silence; it produces by simple reversal the Greek ν and, by doubling, the Greek and Latin N.

Clearly, Wachter's system does not claim to establish a mimetic motivation for the minute details of all writing systems. He needs a mimetic origin for only a few basic figures, whose subsequent deformation is not enough to ruin the principle: a modest position that will not be found among certain of his heirs such as Court de Gébelin. But the main interest of this attempt lies precisely in the invention of those mother figures — *matres scripturae,* one might say — halfway between the articulatory schema and the graphic sign properly speaking, which introduce into the writing system a category unknown to all the existing alphabets, a generic index and (imaginary) trace of a genuine phonetic classification. *Mimēma phōnēs,* the written page begins to teem with little mouths opening or closing, with gullets, with upside-down noses, with pointed or curled-up tongues — more or less recognizable, always both open to view and hidden away in the thicket of letters. Paul Claudel will say that "writing possesses this mystery: it speaks."[10] There is no mystery here; on the contrary, there is the fantastic evidence of a spoken word lying down on the paper but still alive and ever murmuring. This hallucination — "phonocentric," if anything is — constitutes not only an advance in knowledge for Wachter but also a source of pleasure and an emancipation: the end of a tyranny, precisely the one exercised by the now dissipated "mystery" of writing or, if one wishes, the mystery of dissipated writing, since writing itself resolves into and becomes effaced by speech:

It is not always justified to ask — what is the use of this, what is it good for? — even if a new invention happened not to have any utility, except for pleasure. Indeed, just as no one asks for utility from paintings where art imitates nature, but, satisfied by the grace and the truth of the image, each devotes himself unreservedly to the pleasure of seeing; similarly, I do not know whether there is more injustice or more stupidity in looking in the graphic signs drawn from nature for a utility other than the pleasure born out of the feeling for harmony and, for lack of this utility, to despise an entire painting, however lifelike it may be. So severe a judge, who measures all things only by their utility, shouldn't he also, frowning, show contempt for all the treasures of Antiquity? In order to appease the rancor of my censors, who will call me an old abecedarian, I agree willingly that some truths are of so little importance that the lack of utility deprives them of any entitlement for attention. But the truth of natural writing is of a completely different order. Thanks to it, as a matter of fact, we now possess the explanation of letters — that is, of the first elements of human knowledge, which have been until now like magical or tyrannical signs, imposed on everyone and understood by no one: the explanation so often sought for but never found throughout the centuries. This discovery cannot fail to bring a new luster to the most distinguished studies and a new light to the most ancient letters. Such is the true grammar, invented before all grammars. To bring it to light is the true paleography, because after all, what is older than nature itself?

Rowland Jones's contribution is as long-winded, repetitive, and muddled as Wachter's is clear and to the point.[11] I will prune back this brushwood in order to get a paradigm of ideomimography out of it, without much consideration of its fine points, developments, and contradictions.

Jones is one of the many supporters of the Celtic thesis, in England as in France, who trace one or both of these two idioms back to the Celtic language, itself often affiliated with Hebrew or with a hypothetical communal primitive language. His overall aim is to demonstrate this thesis, and his goal is the *restoration* of this language, as one of his titles proclaims, or, as another proclaims, the *institution* of a *universal hieroglyphic language consisting of English letters and sounds*. These two projects are really one, since English, the "main Celtic dialect," is for Jones the most direct and most faithful heir of the primitive natural language. Two great themes of eighteenth-century linguistic thought — speculation on the origin of natural languages, and the project of a universal or "philosophical" language — converge here to the advantage of an actual idiom, considered to be both the most primeval and (therefore) the best qualified for universalization.

Considering also the peculiar frame and construction of the Celtic, its retention of the original characters, sounds, and manner of composition, and its independency of all other languages, there seems to be no room to doubt its being the first speech of mankind; unless some Asiatic or other language should appear to have the like perfection, which neither the learned Bochart[12] nor any other antiquary come to my knowledge have as yet been able to shew. ... whether the illustrating, defining, and fixing the ancient language, origin and antiquities of ... the primaeval Celtes ... will not ... aid the operations of the human understanding, and tend towards the advancement of learning in general, or at least to the restoration of first universal language. ... And of all those Celtic dialects, English seems to be the most apt to become a universal language, due to the simplicity of its construction, the abundance of its primitive locutions, and its close kinship with primitive languages. If certain vocables have been lost, one may be able to find them without leaving Great Britain. And if one follows the filiation of all the vocables to its origin, English will appear perhaps as the most important of the Celtic idioms, and far preferable to any of the others recently advanced as original by people who, without knowing Celtic themselves, pretend to teach us something of the origin of language. English enters the lists, alone against all! And, like Aaron's rod, it will only gulp down the others in mouthfuls. It will take the lead since that is the only means of imposing and forming a universal language.[13]

If Rowland Jones's aim were limited to this kind of co-optation of the old project of a philosophical language to the benefit of English, he would not directly concern us here. But Jones's universal language is not only a real and "natural" language (and not an artificial one like those of George Dalgarno and John Wilkins) but also, contrary to the constructs of his predecessors, a "hieroglyphic" language—that is, in the terms used at the time, mimetic.[14] "For such certainly ought to be the construction of a language proposed for universal assent; and such in my opinion is the English, whose vocables are hieroglyphic; and their meaning agreeing with the picturesque combination."[15] In this way, a network of equivalences is woven between English and Celtic, the originary language, the universal language, and the very principle of a natural mimetic language system. Thus, all of Jones's ventures can combine in a motivating interpretation of the elements of language:

If the original meaning of all the letters, particles, or parts of discourse were thus defined precisely, all languages could be restored to the primitive state of a universal language. From there, one could establish a lexicon giving the primitive roots in italics, followed by a comparative table with the vocables derived from diverse dialects, with their original, secondary, derived and accepted meanings, the why and the how of their deviation in regard to the original, a small number of simple grammatical rules of construction, and the actualizing particles to add to names in order to form verbs, according to the English manner. . . . Moreover, it would be useful to translate meritorious works into this universal language; and thus, allowing all other idioms to fall away, one will teach in the schools, in place of the doctrine of arbitrary sounds, the knowledge of things in the universal language of nature, the only one that has a natural connection with human understanding.

Clearly, this statement of intention theoretically concerns all levels and all forms of linguistic construction. In fact, and through a slippage that remains vague and perhaps unnoticed, Jones's interpretations are going to focus essentially on the elements of (Latin) alphabetic writing and their combination into "particles" or syllables. Unlike John Wallis, who was a true phonetician, capable of arguing about the phonic substance alone, Jones, having analyzed the words of language into elements which he calls, as do so many others, "letters," seems to entrap himself in this terminological confusion, and from that point on he stubbornly sticks to graphical analysis. The whole edifice of language will therefore rest on a symbolic reading of the alphabet, which we will summarily consider in itself.[16]

The letter O symbolizes the "indefinite circle of time and space," the world and, more specifically, the globe of the sun and, by derivation, movement, heat, and light. The I, with its dot {i} again representing the sun, is a line extended out virtually to the limits of vision: hence verticality, hence fire, hence anger. It is the self (*I*), the figure for a man standing upright "in his primitive state of innocence."[17] The A, which should be written as α, is a division of O as though enclosed by a stroke of the pen; it is the terrestrial element, whose materiality is opposed to the spiritual elevation of O.[18] E, which should be written as ε, is yet another division of O, but, left open, it represents the aquatic element, gushing and flowing water; it is the feminine letter, by opposition to the masculinity of A. The U, a double i without the dots resting on a C laid sideways, indicates an upward and infinite action (*up*). C, as half of O (motion), in effect symbolizes the effort of moving: hence action. B, or rather b, is the sum of c + I (a description that would better fit d, but Jones does not explain this anomaly), whence the upward action of being: life. D, to be written d, is the contrary or negation of b; g is a weak version of c, symbolizing slighter actions, like birth or growth, as its figure in the form of a sheaf or scythe, or also the genitals, indicates. L is composed of a vertical I to indicate length and a horizontal I to indicate width; it therefore symbolizes a wide expanse. M, or m, represents a contour of hills and valleys or waves in the sea, whence earth, sea, mountain, but also death. N is the diminutive or negative of M. P, another reversal of b, indicates an action directed downward and therefore all that is material and particular. T, which is an I without a dot and closed on top, designates the sky, the roof, and any kind of covering.

This list, in simplified form, exhausts Jones's chart of graphical symbolism.[19] Through its confusions, its doublings, and its lacunae, an attempt at arrangement nevertheless emerges: the vowels, or at least O, I, A, and E, divide among them the cosmic forces — without allocating the four traditional elements in systematic fashion, however, since I is fire, A is earth, but E means simultaneously air and water. The consonants (to which U can be added) derive mainly from the C (itself stemming from O) and as such designate essentially movements and various actions, except for L, M, N, and T, which represent spatial form. Thus, we are not far from a quite standard distribution on the phonic plane, one that we will run across again: vowels = elements + substances; consonants = forms + movements — an equivalence clearly suggested by a spontaneous interpretation of the act of vocalization, and one that surreptitiously falls back on writing, although the opposition has no relevance on the graphic plane, as the filiation here of O with C and C with U, and that of I with L and T, unintentionally shows.

Actually, one finds in Jones as in Wachter, despite their different aims, a system with several stages in which the mimetic power operates fully only in the basic forms (in this case, I and O, the straight line and the circle; we will encounter nearly the same elements in Claudel). The other forms, which derive from these morphologically through deformation or combination, are hardly symbolic except by delegation, as it were: the mimeticism of C refers back to that of O, that of U to the mimeticisms of C and I, and so forth, each time at the expense of an intellectual postulate (of the type: action is part of movement) that relays and hence weakens the initial symbolic evidence. Jones insists several times on the analytical character of his remarks: "the decomposition of languages and words, to their first principles."[20] This feature is indeed fundamental and of great importance for the definition of this variety of mimology. Graphical mimesis does not function here — as it will in Claudel, for example — at the immediate and common level of the vocable understood as a total ideogram or, in Charles Bally's apposite term, as a mimetic *monogram.* The word must be "decomposed" into letters, and quite often the letters themselves into those more elementary graphemes provided by the O and the I, in order to discover a mimetic power that definitely acts within the whole edifice of the writing system and the language, but resides and appears fully only in their "first principles": that is to say, both in their elements and at their origin. Plainly, this is the situation of the *Cratylus,* transposed into the writing system, but without the handy (and suspect) relay of indirect motivation by etymology.

In effect, Jones's construct develops, without any formal theoretical break and through simple combinatory addition, from elementary graphemes to individual letters, from letters to syllables, and finally from syllables to complex words. The most developed phase, repeated with diverse variants in each of his works, is that of syllables or "particles," most frequently presented in the formula *vowel + consonant,*[21] with each of these combinations (*ab, ac, ad,* and so on) carrying a complex signification that combines the simple values of the vowel and the consonant. We are not going to consider the entire range of this tedious and often obscure combinatory. By way of example, let us mention *ol,* an extension of the globe, whence Everything (*all, whole*); *ic,* the action of fire (Latin *ignis*); *ir,* a fiery emanation (*fire;* Latin *ira*); *al,* an expanse of earth, whence space, specified by reversal in *land; eb,* life and the swelling up of water, whence by specification *beer; ur,* "the boundless spirit of man, as he prepares to leap infinitely across eternity," whence the Latin *vir.*

The words cited in these few examples are very limited, generally monosyllabic vocables, and hence simple lexicalizations of the elementary "particles." The next level of integration obviously concerns complex words, which Jones considers to be fixed syntagms, or even genuine propositions. In these vocables, the concatenation of particles has led to numerous elisions of radical vowels, which the analyst must restore in order to find the original form and the motivation for the meaning. This supreme effort has left its traces in only one passage of *Hieroglyfics* from which I will extract these few examples: *blackish* is analyzed into *b-li-ack-ish*, "a thing without light"; *dread* into *id-ir-ad*, "at the fire"; *flow* into *af-il-ow*, "a spring of the rays of the sun"; *cold* into *ac-ol-id*, "to be without sun"; *grass* into *ag-ar-as*, "the action upon the ground"; *speak* into *si-pe-ak*, "the action of the sound part"; *star* into *sta-ir*, "the standing fires"; *property* into *pe-or-pe-er-ty*, "possession of the parts of land and water or of this globe."[22] I have saved the best for last, two animal names whose analysis does not want for charm: *snail*, which is read as *si-in-na-il*, or "it is without light"; and *crocodile*, alias *ac-ir-oc-o-di-il*, which obviously signifies "an angry, active, and (nevertheless) deceitful water animal." To his misfortune, that is what the elephant child in Rudyard Kipling's *Just So Stories*, who allowed himself to be taken in, did not know.

⑨ The principal merit of this enterprise, which should clearly be judged more by its intentions than by its results, is to link together, through graphism, the Cratylian dream of a mimetic interpretation of the real language system and the more modern project of an artificial "philosophical" language. In the present case, English is analyzed as a construct at once mimetic in its elements and rigorously combinatory in its organization and functioning. It is an *expressive combinatory* in which each word indicates by itself and completely naturally (and hence without any need for learning) the assembly of the simple properties that form the object designated. The "well-made language" of which Étienne Condillac speaks is totally merged here with the encyclopedic edifice of knowledge; the science of words merges with that of things. This synthesis has an optimism that is in tune with its time and that Socrates, we remember (but not Cratylus), rejected in advance. The distance between these two attitudes, definitely more crucial than the shift from phonics to graphics, is clearly marked by the difference previously pointed out between the "etymologies" of the *Cratylus* and the word analyses of *Hieroglyfics*. Socratic eponymy referred an opaque word back to one or several other words that were supposed to shed light on it but remained just as opaque themselves, awaiting an elementary symbolics whose connection with the etymological procedure remained problematic and uncertain. Saint Augustine's *On Dialectic* overcame this weak link by playing on the confusion between direct motivation (of the word by the thing) and tropological motivation (of the word by the relation between two things). Jones's etymologies, albeit very low in number, sufficiently illustrate a third and entirely different approach, in an entirely different situation: "to decompose" a word here is (mythically, of course) to open it up and lay it out in order to read, without relays, without weak links, without screens, as if in a mirror, the transparent play—I ought to say, the play showing through the transparency of the word—of its "first principles." For the first and to this extent for the last time, etymology presents itself not as a deceptive stopgap or a temporary palliative but, in conformity with its own *etymon,* as the truth of discourse and the discourse of truth, "knowledge of things in the universal language of nature." Through this somewhat unexpected success, *mimēma graphē* reveals itself to be one of the most fertile avenues for Cratylian dreaming. In case *mimēma phōnē* fails, a backup is guaranteed.[23]

CHAPTER 6

Painting and Derivation

 Traité de la formation mécanique des langues {Treatise on the mechanical formation of natural languages}, by the famous (in other respects) President Charles de Brosses, appeared in 1765.[1] Its subtitle, or rather its title, continues: *et des principes physiques de l'étymologie* {and the physical principles of etymology}. As for Socrates in the first part of the *Cratylus*, it is indeed etymology that carries the motivation of language. But whereas for Plato etymologies serve to prove the "appropriateness of names," for de Brosses on the contrary the demonstration of the mimetic nature of words serves the "art of etymology," to which their mimeticism lends a solid foundation. Here, etymology, as indicated by the literal sense of the word that designates it, is nothing other than the science and the study of the *truth of words*, or their mimetic virtue: "The first rule, the simplest one as indicated by nature in the formation of words, is that they be *true;* that is to say, that they represent the thing named as accurately as it is possible for the vocal instrument to do. The truth of words, just like that of ideas, lies in their conformity with things: so too the art of deriving words was called *etymology*, or *true discourse; etumos, verus; logos, sermo* (from *etos, verus, quod est* or from *eimi, sum*). There can be no doubt that the first names were fitted to the nature of the things they express; to think otherwise would be to believe mankind insane, for that would be to argue that their aim in speaking was not to communicate."[2]

Truth = representation = conformity (= resemblance) of words (and of ideas) to *things.* Words, or (*vel*) nouns: again we find that typically Cratylian shift, that almost imperceptible slippage from genus to species. De Brosses is not quite as neglectful of the "other parts of speech" as Plato is; he will make room for verbs in his list of onomatopoeias, but he clearly does not grant them the same degree of "appropriateness" as the nouns.[3] Never linked to a stable and determinate external "object," the verb designates an "abstraction" more conspicuously than does the noun; it therefore offers arbitrariness a greater foothold: "Arbitrariness is much more present in verbs than in nouns for physical substances, because the action expressed by the verb often comes more from the man than from the thing, and moreover because verbs, when considered only in themselves, can be

65

counted as abstract terms."[4] Linguistics is thus reduced here, more or less, to an *etymology of nouns.*

In fourth-century Greece, Plato, although he sometimes has recourse to barbarian idioms as a handy expedient when needed, could discuss the Greek language as if it were Language itself, or even the language of the gods; Greek was so preeminent over dialects reputed to be barely articulate stammerings that it could lay claim to universality by right. In the middle of the eighteenth century, despite Rivarol and Frederick II, it is difficult to grant such a monopoly to the French language — though as we will see, it does happen rather often that national prejudice finds a way of expressing itself in this or that detail of an argument. In principle, the object of investigation will therefore be "an original natural language ... common to the whole human race, which no people knows or practices in its primal simplicity; which all mankind nevertheless speaks, and which forms the primary basis of language for all countries."[5] In actual fact, this mother tongue, to the (slight) extent that it is not just simply decreed and deduced from a priori principles, will come from a comparison of "all known natural languages," which for President de Brosses more or less boil down to classical languages and modern European languages. We have here, then, something like a rough idea of what will be, in the next century, the Indo-European of comparative grammar but implicitly presented, if not as the primeval universal language,[6] at least as the natural language par excellence and one that can give us the most accurate idea of such.

This original natural language is described with three adjectives that I deliberately omitted from the foregoing quotation: "organic, physical, and necessary." It is hard to assign a specific meaning to each of these adjectives, which are nearly synonyms in de Brosses: natural language is *necessary* in that it is *physical,* imposed by nature and not arbitrarily instituted by man, and this necessity is *organic* in that it results from the constitution of the vocal organs. But determining the language system is really more complex in de Brosses than this formula makes it seem. The "choice of words" is dictated by not one but two causes: "One is the constitution of the vocal organs that can produce only certain sounds analogous to their structure; the other is the nature and property of the actual things which one wants to name. This forces us to employ sounds that depict the things in making names for them, by establishing between thing and word a relationship through which the word may excite an idea of the thing."[7] Clearly, for de Brosses the only relationship capable of exciting an idea of the thing is the relationship of resemblance, here designated — in a manner that seems not unimportant to me — by the verb *dépeindre* {depict}, which obviously connotes a pictorial, or graphic, notion of imitation.[8] Elsewhere he writes, even more explicitly, that the choice of the articulations necessary for the "fabrication of a word" is "physically determined by the nature and by the quality of the object

66

itself, so as to depict {*dépeindre*}, as much as possible, the object as it really is; without this, the word would not yield any idea of the object."[9] We will come across this pictorial theme again further on. Let us notice, too, the *evenly mimetic* character of the relation, obviously causal, that is established between the sound and the vocal organs, which can produce only sounds "analogous to their structure": thus the effect must *resemble* its cause, in a reduplication typical of the relation. Here as elsewhere, the metonymic linkage becomes overdetermined by a metaphoric relationship: like father, like son; like speech organ, like function.

This secret analogy (clearly reciprocal) between the sound and the vocal organ (as if one were to say that the sound of a flute resembles a flute and that of a piano, a piano) saves de Brosses's Cratylism, by something of a miracle, from the inevitable difficulty into which it was thrown by his principle of double determination, at once organic (relation of sound to vocal organ) and mimetic (relation of word to object). Language must "paint" {*peindre*} objects, but it *can* be only what the vocal organs make it; and this double necessity would not be without some conflict, or at the very least some trouble, if it did not turn out — or if de Brosses had not decided — that the vocal organ itself is analogous to the sound it produces and therefore (according to the principle *if a = b and b = c, then a = c*) analogous to the object imitated by that sound.

> The vocal organ takes on, as nearly as it can, the form {*figure*} of the very object it wants to depict with the voice: it produces a hollow sound if the object is hollow, or a harsh one if the object is rough; in such a way that the sound resulting from the form and from the natural movement of the vocal organ placed in this position becomes the name of the object; a name that resembles the object through the harsh or hollow noise which the chosen pronounciation conveys to the ear. To this end of naming, the voice tends to use that one of its organs whose own movement will best figuratively represent to the ear either the thing, or the quality or effect of the thing it wants to name. Nature leads the voice to use, for example, an organ whose movement is harsh in order to form the expression *racler* {to scrape}.

Or again: "If vocal sounds signify ideas representing real objects, this is because the vocal organ began by trying to take a shape {*se figurer lui-même*}, as nearly as it could, similar to the objects signified, in order to render the incorporeal sounds it molds as similar as possible to these objects in this way also."[10] The "vocal organ," which in fact is composed of several organs ("throat," palate, teeth, lips, and so on), all capable of changing place or shape, *chooses,* in order to imitate the object to be named, the one sub-organ best suited to that object, through its *form* and its *movement.* This organic imitation is indeed given as a means toward the end of phonic imitation ("*in order* to render in this way also"), but the effect of this strange "also," which proportionately diminishes the value of the final proposition, should be noted immediately—as if the "end" were in reality merely a secondary effect of the "means": the organ imitates the object, and *by this very process* (and as if secondarily) the sound produced by the organ imitates the object *also*. It is clear that, ultimately, linguistic mimesis might be able to do without the verbal sound, which is here merely a sort of epiphenomenon of the work completed by the vocal organ in order to "assume a figure similar" {*se figurer semblable*} to the object signified, or to take on its form: the analogical relationship connects the organ almost directly to the object; the language system is a kind of articulatory miming {*mimique*}, a highly marked specification of the Platonic *mimēma phōnē*. This linguistic utopia, which clearly is more asserted than reasoned out, begins to signal a characteristic feature of de Brosses's mimologism, which is, paradoxically, a relative devalorization of the properly acoustic phenomenon—let us say, of the voice itself—in favor of more visible or tangible elements (in his vocabulary, more representable {*figurable*}) of the verbal act; we will meet with this feature again, too. Here, at least in theory, the chain or continuity of mimesis, from the vocal organ to the sound and from the sound to the object, is maintained.

℘ De Brosses's phonetics is structured around a very strongly valorized and overdetermined opposition between vowels and consonants. The vowel is a pure vocal utterance; it is the *voice* in its pure state, or rather in its raw state, without any modification, it would seem, other than that of intensity. There is no inkling here of the modern phonetic distinctions between front and back vowels, closed and open vowels, and so on; there is a "full" voice that is no longer the O, as in Wachter, but the A, of which the other {French} vowels are merely weakening degrees in the following order: *è, é, i, o, ou, u*. The real modification of the voice is brought about by the consonantal articulations. The vocal instrument is like a flute in which the voice is only a neutral, continuous breath without its own quality (apart from intensity), which receives its phonic value from intonations fixed on various organic stops, the consonants: "There are therefore as many ways of modifying the sound and giving it, so to speak, a figure, as there are organs along the windpipe, and these are the only ways."[11] In other words, vowel and consonant are "like matter and form, substance and mode."[12]

But this musical comparison and this philosophical formula still do not reveal the true meaning of the opposition as de Brosses interprets it. Perhaps the reader has noticed in passing the word used to designate the modifying action of the consonantal articulation on the vocal matter or substance: this term—*figure*—is somewhat unexpected for us in this context.[13] It is used here in its visual sense, for all forms are of a plastic nature for de Brosses; consequently, the consonants, which give form to the voice by compressing it at this or that point or in this or that way, belong to the visual order just as the vowels, or the vowel, belong to the aural order: "The difference in the vowel affects the hearing more than the sight, and the difference in the consonant does the reverse." The vowel "falls more within the realm of hearing than that of sight. The consonant is merely the form of the sound, less perceptible to the hearing than the sound itself, and producing its effect more rapidly through the alphabetical figure: it falls within the realm of sight more than that of hearing." [14] This time, one notices the phrase "alphabetical figure," which serves to clarify and to motivate the visual nature of the consonants: this obviously means the letter. In fact, there is in de Brosses an entirely natural chain of equivalences between the consonantal *key,* the *form* it gives to the sound, and the alphabetical *figure* that records it. We can see this chain fully at work if we take up a sentence previously quoted, this time along with the one that follows it: "There are as many ways of modifying the sound and giving it, so to speak, a figure, as there are organs along the windpipe, and these are the only ways. These movements imprinted on the sound are what we call letters or consonants." *Figures, imprinted* movements, *letters:* whether intentional or not, the metaphorical convergence is striking. For de Brosses, consonants are the only genuine *letters,* and these two terms (just like that of *figure*) [15] are totally interchangeable in his mind. Of course, this equivalence is argued on the basis of "Oriental" languages — that is, in the present instance, Semitic languages: "Thus the Oriental ancients . . . neglected to mark the *voice,* which while reading they supplied at intervals between the genuine *letters* which are the *consonants.*" [16] Those languages that privilege consonants are therefore "languages for the eye," whereas ours are instead "languages for the ear." [17]

The valorization of consonants, then, is linked to a valorization of writing, which we will reencounter further on from another angle and in a more explicit formulation. For the etymologist this connection is invaluable because it authenticates and justifies the well-known linguistic "conservatism" of the written form, which thus becomes fidelity to the only essential part of the signifier. "Etymological language" speaks more to the eyes than to the ears: "The reason for this is that the image, being visual at its source, is as permanent as the voice, being aural at its source, is impermanent, and must as a result be less susceptible to changes in form. Thus, even though nothing can be recovered in the sound, everything can be recovered in the figure (= letter) with a little scrutiny. The sound consists of the vowel only, which is completely vague in all speakers. In contrast, the figure consists of the letter (= consonant) only, which, although variable, rarely becomes completely lost, hardly ever exceeding the limits of the vocal organ that is proper to it." [18] Parenthetically, I have to insert the modern terms here, but we should clearly preserve the full value of this slippage in meaning which makes the consonant-letter-figure, an unpronounced phoneme ("the sound consists of the vowel only"), into an always already (or still) graphic entity even in its vocal state.

For the etymologist, then, vocalic variations have almost no relevance. Two words formed from the same consonants with different vowels will be two variants of the same word; two natural languages that differ only in their vowels are only two dialects of the same tongue. "Wachter cleverly indicates in brief the nature of the difference between languages and dialects. 'Languages,' he says, 'differ among themselves through the consonants ... and dialects through the vowels.' That is so accurate and so clear that I have nothing to add to it." Except that de Brosses does come back to it a few pages further on while proposing to distinguish between natural languages whose words differ through the consonants, "for in that case they differ in essence," and those languages that differ only through the vowels, "for in that case they are no more than provinces of the same state, dialects of the same language."[19] It is the "figure," and it alone, that bears difference and (therefore) signification.

ⓝ The most immediate result of this *parti pris* is a huge disproportion between the fate meted out to vowels and to consonants in the chart of symbolic values assigned to the phonemes. The only noteworthy commentary concerning the vowels refers to the *a,* hailed as "the first and the simplest of the sounds," thus meriting its position in the alphabet, and also, according to a remark borrowed from Plutarch, the precedence that always places it (in French as well as in Greek, according to de Brosses) at the head in diphthongs: *ai, au, ae,* and not the reverse; *a* is the "full voice" — in fact, the fundamental vowel — of which all the others are merely weaker degrees. Ultimately, therefore, there is only one vowel, which opens the alphabet; the rest are consonants, acquired by the species as by the individual in the following "natural order": first the labial, then the dental, next the guttural, finally the lingual and the palatal. The order of the alphabet thus markedly conforms to the order of acquisition of the sounds, apart from the one error that consisted of placing the "guttural" (*c*) before the dental (*d*).[20] For de Brosses, this order of acquisition is amply illustrated by the fact that the first words pronounced by the child include only labial consonants and fully voiced vowels: *Maman* and *Papa,* of course. It is true that the Hurons, a people emblematic of the state of nature, as we know, are reputed to be without the use of the labial articulation. But this can only be a misunderstanding or an incomprehensible perversion: "A Huron child left to his own devices would form the labial letters naturally; and ... it is only through examples of the opposite custom ... of his nation that he could lose this natural habit."[21] A linguistic monster, already the product of culture.

As we saw above, for de Brosses, the significant values of the consonants result essentially from the imitative nature of their articulatory movement: "The lips *smack* {*battent*} or *hiss* {*sifflent*}; the throat *breathes in* {*aspire*}; the teeth *gnash* {*battent*}, the tongue *strikes* {*frappe*}; together, the tongue and palate *flow* {coulent}, rustle { frôlent} or hiss; the nose whistles {siffle}." [22] Following are a few symbolic assignments pointed out here and there in the Traité:

— t, the "firm" dental articulation, designates fixity (as in Plato), because the teeth are "the most immobile of the ... vocal organs." [23]

— c or k, the letters of the "throat," "the hollowest and most cavernous of the six organs," designates the hollow or cavity.

— n, "the most liquid of all the letters characterizes that which acts on liquid: No {Latin, I swim}, Naus, Navis {Latin, ship}, Navigium {Latin, vessel}, Nephos, Nubes {Latin, cloud}, Nuage {cloud}, etc." [24]

— r, the most "harsh" of all the articulations, serves to paint "the rough external of things." "No proof other than words of this type is needed: rude {rough}, âcre {acrid}, ... roc {rock}, rompre {to rupture}, racler {to scrape}, irriter {to irritate}, etc." The same inflection determines "the name of things that travel with a quick and rather forceful motion. Rapide {rapid}, ravir {to ravish}, rota, rheda, rouler {to roll}, racler {to rasp}, rainure {groove}, raie {ray}. It is also often used for the names of torrential rivers: rheein, Rhine, Rhone, Eridanus, Garonne, Rha (the Volga) ... etc." [25]

— s, which de Brosses persistently defines as a nasal consonant, "is by its construction suitable for painting hissing and whistling noises. Examples: sibilare {Latin, to hiss, whistle}, siffler {to hiss, whistle}, souffler {to blow}. In these words the vocal organ itself performs the action signified by pushing air out through the two nasal tubes [sic] and from the mouth simultaneously, with the two nasal and labial letters." [26] Moreover, s, the nasal consonant, like the "nasal voicing" {in French} in (for example, in-croyable, in-fidèle), expresses negation or the "idea of privation": thus, in Italian, s-fortunato, s-naturale, and so on. This encounter between the values of the vowel and the consonant is surely neither fortuitous nor conventional, "for there is no resemblance between the nasal vowel in and the nasal consonant s. This is not, therefore, the result of an intentional or reasoned choice, but the outcome of a secret analogy, resulting from the physical mechanics of the body." [27] There is, then, a definite fit, but this time an inexplicable one (a "secret analogy"), between the nasal and negation. The nose is the nay-saying organ {Le nez est l'organe du non}.

— "gaping things are painted by the letter of the throat (g), such as gouffre {abyss}, golfe {gulf}, or even better by the aspirating letter, as in hiatus"; h, a "deep guttural aspiration, serves to paint something that is open to the depths." [28]

Moving from simple consonants to consonantal groups, we note that:

— st expresses "firmness and fixity" even more clearly than the simple dental." Examples: the interjection st!, "which we use in order to get someone to stay in a state of immobility," and words like stare {Latin, to stand}, stabilité {stability}, *stirps* {Latin, stem}, *stellae* {Latin, stars}, *structure, estat* {Old French, state}, *stone,* etc."[29]

— *sc* designates "hollowness and excavation": *scutum* {Latin, shield}, *secare* {Latin, to cut}, *écu* {shield}, *écuelle* {bowl}, *sculpture.*[30]

— *fl* is "liquidity, categorized as fluid, whether fiery or aquatic or aerial: *flamme* {flame}, *fluo* {Latin, to flow}, *flatus* {Latin, blast}, *flabellum* {Latin, small fan}, *floccus* {Latin, flock of wool}, *flocon* {fleck}, *flot* {flood}, *souffle* {breath}, *soufflet* {bellows}, *flambeau* {torch}, *flûte, flageolet* {musical instruments}, etc." The same articulation is also applied to "that which, by its mobility, can have a relationship to elementary liquids: *fly, flight, flèche* {arrow}, *vol* {glide}, *viste, pli* {fold}, *flexible, flagro* {Latin, I burn with passion}, *flagellum* {Latin, whip}, *fléau* {flail}, *flotte* {fleet}, *flos* {Latin, flower}, *phyllon, feuille* {leaf}, *soufflet* {slap}, etc."[31]

— *fr* combines roughness and bursting out: *frangere* {Latin, to shatter}, *frustra* {Latin, in vain}, *briser* {to break}, *brèche* {breach}.[32]

— *sr* is equivalent to movement and toughness (*sreien, sragen*); *str* combines movement, fixity and toughness, as in *stringere* {Latin, to draw tight}, *strangulare* {Latin, to strangle}.[33]

— *sm* (an observation borrowed from Leibniz) designates the idea of dissolution: *smelen, smoke, smunk.*[34]

— *cl* or *gl,* a "hollow and slurred inflection, labors to paint a sliding descent mechanically," as in *glisser* {to slip}, *couler* {to flow down}, *calare.* "*Clin d'oeil* {wink} is the descent of the eyelid over the eye. *Clignotement* {blinking} is the habit of this movement. *Climax,* in the Greek language, is a ladder permitting gradual ascent or descent."[35]

— *gr,* the "reaction of the throat when roughly touched," paints the effort of climbing up: *gravir* {to climb up}, *grimper* {to clamber up}, *gradus* {Latin, step}.[36]

— finally, *tr,* immobility followed by abrupt movement, is the object or pretext of a wonderful etymological reverie which it would be a great shame not to quote in its entirety. First, de Brosses remarks that this articulation is used to form the number three {*trois*}, Latin *tres,* and all the words that derive from it. Then he adds: "If I were pressed as to why this organic inflection, this typical feature *tr* is appropriate by its nature to become the radical seed of *trois,* I would hazard a guess: *tr* is onomatopoetic, a vocal noise through which the speech organ endeavors to render the image of the movement made in order to insert materially one body between two others, in order to *traverse* both of them and to put a third {*tiers*} between them. In fact, I understand that this articulation *tr,* whose noise so well paints the movement of a forced passage and the arrival of a new body where two others previously were, is found in a large number of words that indicate such a passage and, assuming the prior existence of two objects, designate the addition of a third one: *trans* {Latin, to the other side of},

72

intra {Latin, inside}, *extra* {Latin, outside}, *ultra* {Latin, on the far side of}, *citra* {Latin, on this side of}, *praeter* {Latin, except}, *propter* {Latin, near}, *entrée* {entrance}, *travers* {across}, etc." [37] Clearly, here (alone?) the idea of *thirdness* {*troisième*} in no sense originates from an image of peaceful adjunction, in which the third happens to be added afterward to the first two, but connotes the aggression of a *third party* {*tiers*} that interposes itself violently — as if by breaking and entering — between the first and the second parties, with a *body* that "inserts itself materially between a body and a body," *terzo* being essentially *incommodo:* could anyone dream up a more grim formulation of the Oedipal *trio?* [38]

☞ It is immediately apparent that this chart (exactly like those in the *Cratylus* and in Wallis) is unsystematic and that it does not cover all the French consonants, nor *a fortiori* all the consonantal groups. But the symbolic values of phonemes do not exhaust the mimetic capacity of language. They do not even hold first place in the list of what de Brosses calls the "five orders," or five stages in the constitution of the natural language system, in which an echo, direct or indirect, of Saint Augustine's *On Dialectic* can easily be heard.

The first order, apparently so natural as to preexist conscious mimesis, is that of *interjections,* or cries spontaneously provoked by a strong emotion or an elementary mental state. Pain strikes low cords (*Heu* {ow!}); surprise is expressed by a higher pitch (*Ha*); disgust by the labial articulation (*Pouah* {pooh!}); doubt or disagreement by the nasal (*Hum*), whose negating force has already been recognized. The second order is that of words labeled "necessary," whose form is imposed by the configuration of the vocal organ at a certain stage of its development: thus the child's vocabulary, already referred to, is articulated entirely by vowels(s) and labials: *Maman, Papa, mamelle* {breast}. [39] The third order is that of "almost necessary" words, which are the names of the vocal organs, always drawn from the inflection of the vocal organ itself — or, if you prefer, always made up of consonants articulated on these same organs: *gorge* ({throat} guttural), *dent* ({tooth} dental), *langue* ({tongue} lingual), *bouche* ({mouth} labial) (no need to dwell on the reason for the surreptitious substitution of 'mouth' for 'lip,' for obvious reasons), *mâchoire* ({jaw} mandibular).

The fourth order is that of onomatopoeia properly speaking, or words formed in imitation of the noise produced by the thing they designate. De Brosses does not fail to remind us that, as his etymology shows, onomatopoeia was the supreme act of naming for the Greeks: "This is what the Greeks call purely and simply *onomatopoeia,* that is, *formation of the name;* in recognition of the fact that when they use this emphatic antonomasia, although there may be several other ways of forming names, this one is the true, pristine, and original way." [40] This is because man thereby demonstrates his natural instinct in its pure state, which is to imitate: "It is a quite well-known true fact that man is by his nature inclined to imitation: this can be observed most strikingly in the formation of words. If a name needs to be established for an unknown object and if this object acts on the sense of hearing, which has a direct relationship with the vocal organ, the person neither hesitates, nor thinks it over, nor makes a comparison in order to form the name of this object: he imitates vocally the noise that has struck his ears, and the resulting sound is the name that he bestows on the object." Proof of this instinct is given by children, whose "natural and general tendency" is to name noisy things "by the name of the noise they make," a tendency they lose only as the result of education and adult example, both of which "deprave nature."[41] Paragraph 79 "Examples of words that paint things by the impression they make on the senses," offers a list of twenty-eight nouns (such as *bruit* {noise}, *galop* {gallop}, *tambour* {drum}, *choc* {thump}) and seventeen verbs (such as *siffler* {to hiss}, *tomber* {to fall}, *hurler* {to yell}) which originate from this necessary facture.

But if onomatopoeia is the purest form of verbal mimesis, it is perhaps also the most limited. The voice, as a noise, can directly imitate noises only: "Noise is its proper operation, and, if I may say so, the only color that nature has given it for representing external objects."[42] Now not all external objects are acoustic, and a vast portion of the universe runs the risk of remaining unnamed: for example, that portion which falls exclusively under the visual sense, whose operation is so subtle and quiet that no noise accompanies it. Probably all kinds of movement could be annexed to the acoustic domain, "for there is hardly any movement without some noise": for instance, words that designate the wind, *pneuma* {Greek, air}, *spiritus* {Latin, breeze}, *ventus* {Latin, wind}, etc.; and in this way the visible world is reclaimed, inasmuch as the gaze includes a movement of the eye or eyelid: *nictare* {Latin, to wink}, *clignoter* {to blink}.[43] Yet one must finally tackle the domain of completely silent "objects," which no direct onomatopoeia enables us to imitate. The fifth order of original words enters in here, and defining them obviously puts our author in a predicament: "words sanctioned by nature for the expression of certain modalities of creatures." This order is illustrated by the majority of the symbolic values allocated to the consonants (with the exception of purely onomatopoetic relations such as *s* for hissing). The principle of this allocation is as mysterious to de Brosses as its effect seems obvious to him: experience proves that there are verbal figures "linked to certain modalities of creatures, sometimes without its being possible to sort out clearly the principle of this linkage between things in which no relationship can be seen, such as certain letters and certain figures or modalities of external objects. But even though the cause remains unknown in this case (for it is not always so), the effect is no less strongly felt. Plato recognized this full well, and he remarks on it in the following terms: *quandam nominum proprietatem ex rebus ipsis innatuam esse.*"[44] Whence the interrogative cast given to some of

74

these equivalences: "Why are firmness and fixity most often designated by the character *st*? ... Why are hollowness and excavation designated by the character *sc*?"[45] These questions remain unanswered, or receive only an evasive reply: "Some hidden necessity must have cooperated in the formation of words."

De Brosses seems to have forgotten about his initial principle of articulatory mimesis (the vocal organ taking on, as it were, the form of the object, independently of any phonic utterance) or at least to back down before its concrete and detailed application. He returns to it, but in a vague and tentative fashion, in paragraph 81: "So many examples ... lead us to posit as a principle that certain movements of the vocal organs are appropriate for designating a certain class of things of the same type or same quality," and he plainly hesitates to accept Publius Nigidius's theory on the mimetic articulation of personal pronouns. Nigidius "pushes this system too far, perhaps," he says.[46] And elsewhere, wondering about the "primary origin" of prepositions, he advances with the same reserve an analogous hypothesis on the formation of particles expressing interiority and exteriority: "I will not be saying anything very helpful if I say about the particles *in* and *ex*, which mark the *inside* and the *outside*, the same thing that Nigidius suggests about the pronouns *nos* {Latin, we} and *vos* {Latin, you}: to wit, that the vocal organ moves the sound inward in the first case, and pushes the sound outward in the second."[47] The principle of direct organic mimesis (despite Nigidius) was one of de Brosses's most original contributions to the Cratylist edifice, and also one of the most profitable, since it enabled him to get around the major "theoretical" difficulty (how can things that do not produce sounds be imitated by sounds?). This principle, however, is abandoned on the threshold of its application, apparently for the simple reason that it is inapplicable; once it has been posited in general that the tongue or the throat or the palate must take the form of the "object" to be designated, de Brosses shies away from giving any specific evidence. This retreat is typical of our author, who is that very rare phenomenon since Cratylus (including Cratylus) himself: a Cratylist with common sense — and good breeding.

But de Brosses is also a man of the Enlightenment, who hardly enjoys bowing down before mystery and resigning himself to ignorance. Consequently, we see him elsewhere, as if despairing of his cause, return to purely auditory onomatopoeia as if it were the source and the principle of all (or nearly all) linguistic mimesis: "There is reason to believe that *all* purely organic roots ... from whatever inflection of the vocal instrument they may proceed, *nearly all* come, in their primary origin, solely from an aural onomatopoeia. The spoken word acts directly and naturally upon the ear. Since the first original and radical principles of nouns probably had their source in some initial impression made on the senses by the things named, it is natural for the human voice to have brought back this impression, as far as it was able, to the sense of hearing, in order to copy

75

the object that had to be depicted through a similar noise."[48] Thus, one could, to a certain extent ("as far as it was able"), *bring back* and *reduce* every impression to the sense of hearing. Here a new avenue seems to open up—obvious to us: this is the principle of correspondence, or synaesthesia, between the sensations of different sense organs. This principle will be the great resource of mimologism in the nineteenth and twentieth centuries, and we will see it elaborated in Charles Nodier, with reference to the testimony of the famous blind mathematician Nicholas Saunderson (or, more plausibly, that of another person born blind), who imagined the color red to be analogous to a trumpet sound. For an entire era, this testimony constitutes the point of departure, at least a symbolic one, for a current of thought whose poetic culmination, in Baudelaire and French Symbolism, is too familiar to dwell upon here. Typically, then, de Brosses, for his part, does not refer to it in other than a concessive, almost negative manner, showing no interest in it: "With the exception of bright light, harsh or rough objects, even those from which we turn our sight away through a feeling of aversion, do not cause the eye to shudder—although a person born blind, when asked about his sensations, did once imagine that vivid red resembled a trumpet sound. Objects are painted on the retina almost as imperceptibly as on a mirror. The vocal organ therefore has no basic means of painting visible objects at all, since nature has granted it only the faculty of painting noisemaking objects."[49]

Here we have, then, a door no sooner cracked open than shut again; without seeing it, de Brosses skirts alongside the principle of correspondence, so to speak. The reasons for this missed opportunity—whether refusal or misunderstanding—doubtless belong to the history of ideas, neoclassical sensualism quite naturally being hostile to the idea of synaesthesia.[50] Anyway, the fact is that we owe to this lacuna one of the most remarkable reorientations of Cratylism.

This reorientation, then, which we will follow closely in the very text in which it is implemented, finds its *raison d'être* in an acknowledgment of a deficiency, at the very least an inadequacy, in vocal mimesis. It is as if the impossibility of *explaining* (through correspondences) the functioning of the fifth order (phonic imitation of nonacoustic objects) erases its very existence, despite its being illustrated at length in paragraphs 80 to 84.[51] For de Brosses, exacting mimologist that he is, an inexplicable "appropriateness," a "secret" necessity, are not altogether an appropriateness or a necessity worthy of consideration. Consequently, he does not hesitate here, as we saw previously, to deny the spoken word all mimetic power over noiseless objects. "However," he adds, "objects that are visible [read: and only visible] are countless, the sense of sight being the most wide-ranging of all. They have to be named. How will the voice go about this?"[52]

It is in trying to answer this question that paragraph 91 closes off the field of vocal imitation and opens up that of *derivation,* in which the human system of language will gradually deviate from its mimetic vocation and enter the path of

76

corruption, or arbitrariness. Here in its entirety is the crucial text, boundary and mainspring of the whole inquiry:

As I have said, the voice will do this by comparison, by approximation if possible, while deviating as little as it can from the proper road. A *flower* offers nothing that the voice can represent figuratively {*figurer*}, unless its mobility might represent the stem as it bends with every gust of wind. The voice seizes upon this circumstantial aspect and figuratively represents the object to the ear through the liquid inflection *fl,* which nature has given it for characterizing fluid and mobile things. When the voice names the object *flos* {Latin, flower}, it does execute what lies within its power to perform the best it can. But who does not see how this painting {*peinture*}, which fastens on only a minor, almost foreign circumstantial aspect, is unfaithful and far removed from what is represented by the words *cymbale* {cymbal}, *fracas* {crash}, *gazouillement* {warbling}, *racler* {to scrape}, and so on. Nevertheless, imperfect as it is, we are rarely in the situation where we can make use of this approximation. We must resort to a comparison: calling a flower *immortelle* {everlasting} because of its longlastingness; *balsamine* {impatience} or queen of the heavens (in Phoenician); *oeillet* {carnation}, little eye, because it is round like an eye; *anémone,* or windswept, because it opens up on the side where the wind hits it; *ranunculus* or *grenouillette* {Solomon's seal}, little frog, because it grows in swamplands and its pawlike leaf resembles a frog, and so on. Let us observe a very remarkable thing here. The flower is a being that acts directly on one of our senses, through its sweet-smelling quality. Why, then, has it not taken its name from the direct relation with this sense? Because man sees things from far away and smells them from up close: because he saw before smelling, and because ever in a hurry to name things he sees again, he fastens on the first circumstantial aspect, strong or weak, that catches his attention.

First, let us take up this parting remark, whose function is once more to preclude any recourse to synaesthetic motivation: man, "in a hurry to name," did not have time to find, for the olfactory sweetness of flowers, an equivalent in the sweetness of certain sounds. Therefore, de Brosses will not make what would be the easiest claim: for example, that the words *rose* or *reseda* transpose the essential feature of these objects into the auditory order. The very path of transposition, as we have seen, is condemned. Only two possible ways out remain, then: those de Brosses calls *approximation* and *comparison,* which clearly refer to the tropes classified by rhetoric as metonymy and/or synecdoche, on the one hand (naming the flower by the flexibility of its stem), and metaphor on the other (naming the *oeillet* by its resemblance to the eye {*oeil*}).[53] There is a very appreciable difference in value between these two rhetorical devices, marked from the

77

beginning by the interpolated phrase "by approximation if possible." The figure of approximation is "unfaithful" and "imperfect" in that it merely fastens on a "minor, almost foreign" — in any case, secondary — "circumstantial aspect" of the object it designates: its flexibility, and not its color or its perfume. Still, it does reflect a *circumstantial aspect:* that is to say, a detail actually linked to the existence of the object.[54] Such is not the case with naming by comparison, for there the name is borrowed for the occasion from a completely "foreign" object: the eye {*l'oeil*} resembles the carnation {*l'oeillet*}, but it is in no way a "circumstantial aspect" of the carnation. This is probably an echo of the neoclassical mind's well-known distrust of metaphor, whose mimetic nature de Brosses here goes so far as to ignore, or minimize.[55] The whole virtue of the language system resides in imitation, but for de Brosses, *to make a comparison is not to imitate.*

With naming by metonymy and by metaphor, then, we are already well on the road to derivation, which is the decadence of language. The beginning of paragraph 92 bluntly confirms this: "By this arbitrary and comparative method (that is, metaphor), so common in all kinds of derivation, nature is even more depraved than by the preceding one (metonymy), and the object even more disfigured." We might therefore expect de Brosses to devote the ensuing chapters to the history of this decadence, or else to stop right here, having exhausted the topic of original mimeticism. He does neither one nor the other, and *Formation mécanique des langues* {Mechanical formation of natural languages} takes up barely two-thirds of his first volume. This is because an unexpected and spectacular twist occurs here: just when all avenues seem closed to it, linguistic mimesis is going to make a new departure and embark upon a new career — in fact, the one most consonant with its true nature, which for de Brosses, let us recall, is "to paint" {*peindre*} and "to figure" {*figurer*} objects. When every resource of verbal imitation has been exhausted, the human mind discovers another form of mimesis, of an entirely different kind and with an entirely different potential: writing.

Let us take up paragraph 92 where we left off, in order to appreciate the force of this sudden turnaround, which will put us back on the traces of Wachter's mimography. We have just seen how metonymical derivation and, even more, metaphorical derivation deprave nature and *disfigure* the object named. The text continues as follows: "It was therefore necessary to have recourse to another [method], and man soon found it. Here nature opens up to him a new system of an entirely different type, primitive like the preceding one (for reflection and the act of combining have no share in it), and almost as *necessary,* although to tell the truth, human will does have a slightly greater share in this one than in the other. With his hand and some paint he represented in figures what he could not figure with his voice. He spoke of things visible to the eyes through sight, since he could not speak of them to the ears through sound, as with noisemaking things. Thus nature recovered its due, offering to each sense what it was capable of receiving. Consequently, the primitive writing system was born, in an almost *necessary* manner, from the impossibility of doing otherwise."

The (partial) bankruptcy of vocal mimesis thus has two very different results, which have diametrically opposed values but which de Brosses states in one breath, so to speak: the fall into derivation, which is the progressive abandonment and forgetting of original mimesis; and a recourse to writing, which is the discovery and exploitation of another mode of mimesis. A treatise on the *principles of etymology* cannot fail, no matter what the repugnance felt, to study in detail the phenomenon of derivation, which is the very history of natural language and what will later be called the "life of words"; the bulk of the second volume is devoted to this. The study of the writing system, which in this perspective is a sort of parenthesis, occupies the last two chapters of the first volume. Given that our perspective here is quite different (since the etymologist's work interests us less than his mimological reverie), we will reverse this order and finish with verbal (hence vocal) derivation before returning to scriptural mimesis.

② Under the concept of derivation de Brosses assembles two series of facts, neither of which exactly coincides with what modern linguistics understands by this term: "material" derivation, which is the evolution of the form of words, as in the transition from Latin *fraxinus* to French *frêne* {ash tree}, or from Latin *flagellum* to French *fléau* {whip}; and "ideal" derivation, or derivation "of ideas," which is the evolution of their meaning, the slippage of signification that occurs between the original root and the words that "derive" from it. We will see several examples of this further on.

Material derivation is due to the fragility of vowels and the capacity of similarly articulated consonants for inter-substitution;[56] in other words, it does not compromise the identity of the word, which phonetic analysis reconstitutes without difficulty. Thus, assuming that the Latin word *fort* and the "Teutonic" word *valde* {intensely} have the same origin, the difference between *o* and *a* will be disregarded as insignificant, since all the vowels are really one single vowel, uttered to various degrees of "fullness"; and it will be easy to recognize the articulatory identity of *f* and *v* ("hissing labials"), *r* and *l* ("linguals"), *t* and *d* ("dentals"), the difference between the two words being a general weakening from Latin to the Germanic (from *f* to *v*, from *r* to *l*, from *t* to *d*).[57] Whence the following basic principle: "In etymology, in the comparison of words, no attention should be paid to the vowels, and none to the consonants unless they are produced by different vocal organs. If the variation in the consonant comes only from different inflections of the same organ, one should boldly state that it is … the same letter."[58] Clearly, de Brosses's etymology is still quite close to Gilles Ménage's and in keeping with that tradition, ridiculed by Voltaire, for which "vowels count for nothing and consonants for very little." The comparison between these "physical principles of etymology" and the admirable lesson in methodology given at the same point in time by Turgot in the *Encyclopédie* is rather cruel to our author when judged in terms of lucidity and scientific rigor.[59] But that is not our quarry.

"Derivation of ideas" is more difficult to limit, and as we have seen, de Brosses would sooner exaggerate it in order to "thunder against" it with the vehement indignation of a Cato denouncing the decadence of morals. Derived meanings are tropes, hence "diverted" meanings, that stand opposed to the proper and original meaning as dissonance opposes consonance: "Words taken in their true, physical, proper, and primordial sense can be called *consonances,* and words taken in a diverted, relative, figurative, abstract, moral, and metaphysical sense, *dissonances.*"[60] The musical comparison, as well as the insistent accumulation of epithets, is revealing: the "primordial" meaning is endowed with all the virtues of Nature and the Origin; the derived meaning is loaded down with all the degenerations of a depraved civilization. The first meaning is simple like the triad {*accord parfait*}, or, better, like the unison dear to Rousseau it is consonant with the natural expressive value of the word, with what Mallarmé will call its "radical virtue"; the derived meaning is dissonant, perverts the original *harmony* of the language system, which is an *accord* of sound and sense, and destroys its symbolic unity.

At the end of the sixth chapter, as we saw above, two basic rhetorical devices were assigned to derivation: approximation and comparison, of which the second is the more condemnable. Oddly, chapter 10 ("De la dérivation et de ses effets" {On derivation and its effects}) insists almost exclusively on the first one, which seems to have become the main agent of the drift in the language system.[61] Paragraph 179, headed "Prodigieux effets de la métonymie dans la dérivation" {The extensive effects of metonymy in derivation}, begins as follows: "All these derivations, born from the habit of transferring a word of one signification to another signification bordering on the first through some real or imaginary place, are an end result of metonymy, a very routine figure of speech for man." Regarding the root *dun,* mountain, which he finds in *Lugdunum,* Lyon, a city nonetheless situated on a plain by the water, he reproaches Wachter for not having "sensed the metonymy, the most important trope of diction to notice. It is through its mediation," he adds, "that the radical words, which are small in number even in the richest natural languages, are extended without being multiplied, to the point of designating things whose significations appear to be very far apart,"[62] even opposed: thus Latin *altus,* "which signifies equally a high place and a low place," or French *hôte,* which designates both the stranger welcomed in a city, and the citizen who gives him lodging.[63] In this way we end up uttering unwitting oxymorons like "young senator" (from *senes,* old men), or "footman" ({*écuyer à pied*}, from *equus,* horse, according to de Brosses) — real etymological monsters.[64]

Metonymy also accounts for the variety of words designating the same object, depending on the different "aspects" or circumstances under which we are able to view it. Thus in Latin the priest is called *sacerdos* as he performs sacred offices, *presbyter* for his age, *antistes* because he stands before the altar, *pontifex* for being charged with the maintenance of bridges, *praesul* for dancing before others, and so on.[65] For analogous reasons, in French the same thing is called *région, province, contrée, district, pays, état,* and so forth.[66] Even the original (and organic) roots sometimes seem affected by this metonymic proliferation: thus, a ladder can be represented by the articulation *cl* (Greek, *climax*), which denotes its incline, or by *sc* (Latin, *scala*), which indicates the hollow place where one puts one's foot, or by *gr* (Latin, *gradus*), which expresses the effort of climbing, of *gravir* {struggling up}, of *grimper* {clambering up}. This triple root comes from "different ways of looking at the same object and of grasping it by one or the other of its effects."[67] There is something about this that puts into question the very notion of an original proper meaning, since each one of these three "roots" appears in a metonymy in which a sort of *originary derivation* can be seen at work. But such a criticism could shake the entire edifice, and de Brosses prefers to read a unity of function and "mechanics," or vocal imitation, beneath the obvious diversity of rhetorical device: "There is no difference in the goal being proposed, or in the mechanics used to reach it. The purpose was always to represent the object by a sound comparable, as much as possible, to its effects."

The most typical and most expansively discussed example[68] of this "deviation" of the mind and the "misuse it makes of roots by employing them to express things which they are not at all appropriate for depicting" is the derivation that leads from the root *st,* indicating fixity, to the legal term *stellionat,* designating a fraudulent contract. This started with the application of the root to designate the stars (Latin, *stellae*) with regard to their apparent fixity. Then, because its skin is a mosaic of star-shaped spots, the name for a lizard, *stellio,* was derived from *stella;* next, since another peculiarity of this lizard is its cunning or trickery, *stellionat* was derived from *stellio,* but its meaning no longer has anything in common with the initial idea of fixity: quite to the contrary. Here we see how the mind, led astray by the oblique concatenation of secondary circumstantial aspects, "without losing sight of the radical key, the primordial and characteristic figure that it had grasped, goes merrily along and wanders around from one idea to the other, from one object to the other. . . . In this way, the operation of the mind, perverting the operation of nature which had set aside a certain kind of analogy for depicting fixity, decides to go and use it again in order to depict spottedness and trickery, which the dental articulation *st* just does not figuratively represent to the ear at all."

81

Such are the paths of corruption. When a natural language has reached this point, it has lost its essential virtue, which can only be *truth,* the "fidelity of the relationship between the name and the object it designates." This truth "is no longer found in languages once their nature has been depraved by ideal allusions foreign to it, and once the word derived from its primordial root has been estranged to such an extent that the connectedness which ought to be easily perceptible between them is no longer so." [69]

Ⓑ This lost truth, it should definitely be remembered, is a truth of *painting* {*peinture*}. A natural language no longer holds any truth when it can no longer *paint objects.* And it is at this point that writing intervenes, charged in its own way with *remunerating* the failing in natural languages, as Mallarmé will say. For to write is to paint, according to de Brosses and Plato both, but for completely different reasons based on completely different connotative values: "[The hand] could figuratively represent { *figurer*} objects to the sight by gestures or by tracing their image. This was a new route opened for the transmission of ideas; and nature, recovering its rights without deviating from its method, guided man there as it had done along the preceding path of the voice, in a simple, necessary way imitative of the objects signified." [70]

This mimeticism of the writing system compensates for and neutralizes the infidelity of the spoken word, and in a sense it could be said to encourage this infidelity by rendering it innocuous. With the truth of painting now assured by written language, vocal language can drift as much as it wants to. Henceforth, "the essential lies in the painting and no longer in the name of the object. Thus the imposition of its name can become conventional and much more arbitrary than it had previously been in the purely vocal method of imitative sounds." [71] Mimesis, chased out of the world of sounds where it had been able to lead only a precarious and somewhat uncertain existence, from that moment on takes refuge, or rather is repatriated, in what had always been its true domain: that of "figures presented to the eye."

It stands to reason that in presenting writing (all writing) as a "painting of objects," de Brosses takes as his model not phonetic writing systems, which he labels "verbal," but directly representational systems, which he calls "real" writing. But the existence of an indirect written form, a simple notation (mimetic or not) of the spoken word, obviously does not escape him. There exists not one single writing system but several, with totally different principles, and this plurality requires a typology and, if possible, a genetic hypothesis.

De Brosses's theory here is very close to that proposed by Warburton some thirty years earlier. [72] It is summarized in the following chart, which is both taxonomic and historical, since the six basic types appear in the order of their successive arrival, according to de Brosses.

I. Real writing systems
   A. *Figurative*
      1. Simple painting, or isolated images (Australian drawings)
      2. Continuous painting, writing *in rebus,* representing the things themselves, or written characters in the Mexican style
   B. *Symbolic*
      3. Allegorical symbols, hieroglyphics representing the qualities of things, or written characters in the Egyptian style
      4. Line strokes, representational keys for ideas, or written characters in the Chinese style
II. Verbal writing systems
      5. Line strokes representing syllables, or written characters in the Siamese style: syllabic writing
      6. Separate organic and vocal letters, or written characters in the European style: writing by letters.[73]

"Of these six orders," comments our author, "the first two refer to external objects; two others to internal ideas; the last two to the vocal organs. There exist, therefore, two types of writing based on two absolutely different principles. One is figurative writing {l'écriture figurée} for representing objects, which indicates through the sense of sight what is to be thought and said; this type includes the first four orders mentioned above. The other, to which the last two orders belong, is organic writing representing the articulations of the vocal instrument, which also indicates through the sense of sight what is to be performed and pronounced. One type, by intently setting the sight on objects, stimulates production of their name: the other type goes further, setting the sight on the very name of the object. By this means is effected that admirable juncture of hearing and sight which I have discussed." [74]

We will return to the *admirable juncture* mentioned in this last sentence and the text to which it refers, but from this point on we can observe a completely unexpected valorization of verbal writing, described here as *organic* and credited with a representational efficacy superior to that of real writing. Apparently, this contradicts the principle of graphic mimesis and writing-as-painting {écriture-peinture}. Further on, we will see how this new twist in the tortuous progress of de Brosses's Cratylism is positively justified, but its primary motivation is purely negative: this is the precariousness of the real writing system or, more precisely, its meager mimetic resources. However numerous and sizable visible objects are, they do not exhaust the totality of the representable universe any more than do "noise-making" objects. "Qualities of things," abstract ideas, elude direct graphic representation as much as they do vocal imitation, and we see inevitably reproduced in the writing system the tropological process through which the work of the "derivation of ideas" laid hold of spoken language. The hieroglyphic writing system will therefore use "natural figures" as "symbols and allusions to various things that cannot be painted, through an arbitrary method of approximation and comparison altogether similar to that whose results I have shown in the fabrication of words formed by the vocal organ. ... Being unable to paint *foresight,* one paints an eye, and a bird for *speed.* The road is the same and the graduated process alike in what the hand has done for the sight and in what the voice has done for the hearing. Nature and necessity did first what arbitrariness and convention have continued to do according to the same plan."[75]

Approximation and comparison, metonymies (the eye for foresight) and metaphors (the bird for speed), therefore reopen the path of decadence — arbitrariness and convention — which always stems from the principle of *allegory:* using the sign of one thing to *talk about another.* Once again, the derivation of ideas, an abuse of the signified, entails and feeds material derivation, a usury and degradation of the signifier. Here, phonetic erosion (*fort—vald*) corresponds to the graphic impoverishment of figures, a progressive schematization that leads from the Egyptian hieroglyph to the Chinese ideogram, in which the principle of picture writing peters out through simplification: "When natural figures were once accepted as symbols of other objects, they were called upon to express so many things that it was necessary to shorten, to alter, to deprave their nature and to reduce the figures to simpler line strokes that make them unrecognizable."[76] We have come full circle; the great resource of writing turns out to have been merely a quickly used-up expedient, and the second reign of linguistic mimesis, a brief reprieve. No attempt at a "hieroglyphic" interpretation of the modern alphabet will be found in de Brosses, then, as in Rowland Jones. Here again, the originary "painting" has been effaced.

Within the quite Rousseauistic logic of this thinking, one might expect a condemnation without appeal of the "verbal" writing system as an unfaithful representation of an unfaithful representation, treason to the second degree. As we have already seen, there is none. The alphabet is indeed invented in the wake of this new "depravation" that leads from picturesque writing *in rebus* to the schematic "keys" of Chinese writing, but it apparently inherits none of the defects. Quite to the contrary, it is as if the movement of decadence comes miraculously (and paradoxically) to a halt here. This axiological reversal is very noticeable in the beginning of paragraph 98: "Finally, when it was accepted into common usage that formless lines could signify things, a powerful genius, troubled by the multiplicity of things and line drawings, experimented with the possibility of making some lines signify the syllables of words and the different articulations of the vocal organ, which are limited in number." And it is even more noticeable in the beginning of paragraph 99: "Now, this is the most sublime invention to which the human mind has ever risen, and the most difficult thing it has ever undertaken to accomplish."

84

The surprising thing here is not (need it be said?) the tribute paid to the "sublime invention" of writing by letters, or, rather, the surprise is not this tribute in itself: we know that Saussure himself will describe the Greek alphabet as a "discovery of genius," [77] and its inventors have been hailed as the first masters of phonological analysis. But all this is, if I may say so, Hermogenes' department, and clearly there is nothing over there to arouse Cratylus's enthusiasm. And Rousseau reproaches the alphabet precisely for *analyzing* the spoken word without *painting* it.[78] There is no trace of this criticism in the *Traité;* for de Brosses, the merit of writing by letters is to have succeeded "in reuniting, to the extent possible, in a single art two completely disparate things whose nature seemed to make the juncture impossible; I mean the sense of sight and that of hearing. Or, if it has not reunited them in themselves, it has at least subjected their objects to the same fixed point at the same time, as these two types of objects remain quite separate from each other in the two effects of the art that joins them; for writing and the reading that is its speech are two completely different things, as much as are the two organs that rule with sovereign power over each one of the two: the eye in one, the ear in the other." [79]

This praise will probably be thought to be as sibylline as it is enthusiastic. Perhaps it is simply cautious. Writing by letters can "reunite" hearing and sight, or at least their "objects" (the represented sound and the representational letter), but nothing here—or at any point in the *Traité de la formation mécanique des langues*—indicates the one thing that would satisfy Cratylian desire, which is that writing should constitute a genuine *painting of the spoken word*, a graphic representation resembling some noises of speech or some movements of the vocal organ. Such a mimetic reading of the alphabet—Wachter's—requires a boldness of interpretation totally alien to our author. For him, there is nothing but a de facto linkage between "sight" and "hearing," an obscure linkage whose mimetic character is not confirmed by anything—quite the contrary.

Quite the contrary: for if de Brosses refrains from all criticism—in theory or in particulars—regarding the real alphabet, one chapter that we have left aside until now reveals without any possible ambiguity that he is not personally satisfied. This is his chapter 5, "De l'alphabet organique et universel, composé d'une voyelle et six consonnes" {On the organic and universal alphabet, composed of one vowel and six consonants}. Here the issue is indeed a mimetic alphabet, in which every letter *depicts* {*dépeint*} the movement of the organ it designates. But this alphabet is neither Latin nor Greek nor Phoenician; none of these or any other approaches it. It is wholly factitious, and its inventor, who does not at all claim to substitute it for existing graphic systems, reserves it for the technical and, so to speak, professional use of "etymologists."

In actual fact, de Brosses proposes not one but two "organic alphabets," the first of which alone entirely merits the adjective "mimetic." In this one, the voice (or vowel) is represented by a straight vertical line {see chart, page 86}, marked

La voix, ou les voyelles du nouvel ·
alphabet organique.

Voix pure ou franche.	*Voix allongée.*	*Voix nasale*
⌐ a	⌐ a a	⌐ an
⌐ ai ŋ	⌐ aiai ŋ̃	⌐ ain
⌐ e	⌐ ee	⌐ en
⌐ i	⌐ ii	⌐ in
⌐ o	⌐ oo ω	⌐ on
⌐ ou ȣ	⌐ ouou ȣ̃	⌐ oun
⌐ u	⌐ uu	⌐ un

Voix sourde, et Voix aspirée.

e *muet*	eu		ȣ *Aleph*	h.
			simple	*Aspira-*
			ouverture	*tion pro-*
			de la trombe	*fonde et.*
			vocale.	*gutturale.*

by a horizontal dash placed more or less high up depending on the "length to which the vocal cord or the windpipe is drawn," from *a* (the lowest) to *u* (the highest in pitch). The lengthening of the vowel is marked by a lengthening of the horizontal dash, its nasalization by the presence of a kind of diagonal prong at the upper end of the vertical line.

The consonants {chart, page 87} are represented by a drawing imitating the shape of the articulatory organ (a lip, a throat, a tooth, a palate, a tongue, a nose) and may be assigned a dot whose position indicates the articulatory force (a dot on the right for a soft articulation, on the left for a harsh one, in the center for a "middle" articulation). The consonantal groups combine two, even three drawings: thus, *scl* is figuratively represented by a nose (for the *s*, whose nasality never flags in de Brosses) combined with a throat (for the *c*) and a tongue (for the *l*).

The theoretical value of such an alphabet obviously lies in its iconic character, which the inventor does not fail to point out: "This tablature owes something to the diagrammatic and hieroglyphic writing system, in that I represent

Les six lettres ou consonnes du nouvel alphabet organique.

LEVRE.	GORGE.	DENT.	NEZ
P.	C.	D.	S .
B.	Gh.	Th.	st.
M.	K.Qu.	T.	
F.	cl.	Dgh.	ts .
V.	cr.	Dj.	s cr.
Bz.	Cs.	Dz.	sc.
Bl.	Cz.	Dr.	
Pr.	ct.	Tr .	sp.
Ps.	Gl.	PALAIS.	Spr.
Pt.	Gr.	J.	spl.
Fl.	Cn	Z.	str.
Fr.		ch.	s cl.
Vr.		LANGUE.	sr.
		L.	sm.
		N.	sf.
		R.	sl.
		gN.	s n.
		gL.	

each articulation by an approximate image of the organ that produces it."[80] This alphabet's practical interest, once it has been admitted that it "will never be established in common usage," is to facilitate verification of etymologies by showing the kinship of words through the resemblance of their figures: thus, the "organic" written forms of *peregrin* and *bilgram* {see chart, page 88} are nearly identical — much closer in any case than their traditional written forms.

Unfortunately, this direct representation is bought at the price of an evidently difficult implementation, given the complexity of the figures. Consequently, de Brosses immediately proposes a second "tablature," much less iconic but much simpler, in which "lip" is figuratively represented by a vertical dash, "throat" by a diagonal dash leaning to the left, "tooth" by one slanting up to the right,

"tongue" by a vertical crook, "palate" and "nose" by crooks leaning to the right and to the left {chart, page 89}. Ironic remarks could be made about the way in which he in his turn steps out onto the fatal path of "material derivation," but it must be observed that the practical virtue of his alphabet is not affected, since in this tablature as in the first one, two related words give rise to two analogous drawings. The organic alphabet here loses what C. S. Peirce will call its value as an *image,* but it fully retains its function as a *diagram:* the relation of the figures continues to correspond, homologically, to the relation of the vocables. At the very least, through the kinship that it demonstrates between the different articulations of the same vocal organ, it remains at once more logical and more "talky" {*parlant*} than any real alphabet.

In President de Brosses's approach to language, then, we have, clarified by the bright light of retrospection,[81] a typical illustration of what we have previously seen in Socrates and baptized *secondary mimologism.* Like Socrates (and Cratylus), de Brosses *would prefer* a mimetic language system; like Socrates (and Cratylus), he believes in the mimetic capacities of the phonic (and graphic) elements of the real "natural language"; like Socrates (and unlike Cratylus), he states with regret that this natural language is not always constituted according to its capacities—he even adds that it continuously deviates from them. Thus, in de Brosses, an idealist Cratylism conflicts with a pragmatic Hermogenism. The logical outcome of this contradiction is plainly an attempt to make fact agree with the ideal, or to correct natural language. We have seen that Socrates did not deign to follow this path. As for de Brosses, he goes further, at least on the—for him essential—ground of the writing system, in proposing an "organic" alphabet capable of exploiting the imitative capacities of (vocal) sounds through an appropriate graphic system. As expected, the realistic optimism of the Enlight-

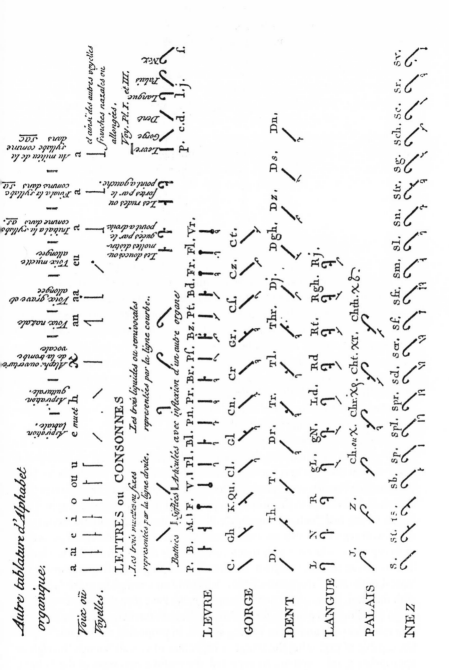

Autre tablature d'Alphabet organique.

Voix ou Voyelles.

a ā i e i o ou u

Aspiration labiale. e muet h
Aspiration gutturale.

ℵ *Aleph ouverture vocale.*
& de la trompe

Voix nasale. an
Voix grave et allongée. aa
Voix muette allongée. eu

a *Tixit à la syllabe conune dans aȝ.*
a *Rivale la syllabe conune dans ȝaȝ.*
a *Au milieu de la syllabe conune dans ȝaȝ.*

Les doux ou molles distin-guées par le poul à droite.
Les rudes ou fortes par le poul à gauche.

Lévre — *P. b. c. d.*
Gorge —
Dent — Langue —
Palais —
Nez — f.

et ainsi des autres voyelles franches nazales ou allongées. Voy. Pl. I. et III.

LETTRES ou CONSONNES

Les trois muettes ou faces representées par la ligne droite.

Les trois liquides ou semivocales representées par la ligne courbe.

Battics J. Sifflés L Articulés avec inflexion d'un autre organe.

P. B. M. ¡ F. V. ¡ Pl. Bl. Pn. Pr. Br. Pf. Bz. Pt. Bd. Fr. Fl. Vr.

LEVRE C. Gh. K. Qu. Cl. Cl Cn. Cr Gr. Cf. Cz. Ct.

GORGE D. Th. T. Dr. Tr. Tl. Thr. Dj. Dgh. Dz. Ds. Dn.

DENT L. N. R. gL. gN. Ld. Rd Rt. Rgh. Rj.

LANGUE J. Z. Ch. ou X. chr. χꝗ. cht. χτ. chth. χ ℰ.

PALAIS S. St. Ts. sb. Sp. spl. spr. sd. scr. sf. sm. sl. sn. Str. sg. sch. Sc. Sr. Sv.

NEZ

enment here leads to an initiative, albeit a limited "symbolic" one. The question posed by the famous linguist Iosif Vissarionovich Dzhugashvili, so relevant to our own discussion, is well known: "Who would benefit if water were not called water any more?" Neither Cratylus nor Hermogenes (nor Socrates) is concerned with such a plan: not Cratylus, because for him all names worthy of that name are perfect imitations; not Hermogenes, because in his opinion a convention is always sufficiently reliable. Both are conservatives, for opposite reasons—and Socrates for a third reason, which is perhaps that all this is not worth an hour of his trouble. The accomplished secondary mimologist, for his part, decides that natural language should be *more mimetic,* and he dreams of *reforming* it. Before Raymond Queneau, de Brosses demonstrates in his own way the paradoxical possibility of a reformist Cratylism: why shouldn't water be written as ~ †?

CHAPTER 7

Generalized Hieroglyphics

⚕ *Origine du langage et de l'écriture* by Antoine Court de Gébelin, published in Paris in 1775, is the third volume of a sort of historico-philological encyclopedia, *Le Monde primitif.*[1] The full title of this third volume is *Le Monde primitif, considéré dans l'histoire naturelle de la parole; ou, Origine du langage et de l'écriture* {The primeval world, examined through the natural history of speech; or, The origin of language and writing}. In the very next year, Gébelin would publish a kind of digest of both this volume and the preceding one (*Grammaire universelle*) under the title *Histoire naturelle de la parole; ou, Précis de l'origine du langage et de la grammaire universelle* {The natural history of speech; or A summary of the origin of language and universal grammar}.[2]

Gébelin's topic is indeed the origin of language and writing, and he addresses it in a much more direct, or central, way than does de Brosses. The first of the volume's five books is actually devoted to the *art of etymology,* but this clearly serves as a mere preamble,[3] and historical etymology here is only a means, a necessary path, for retracing origins, the primeval tongue, the sources of speech. Gébelin, therefore, much less than de Brosses (who saw himself essentially as an etymologist), deals with the disastrous history of *derivation,* or the decadence of the language system. He is spared, or perhaps rather he saves himself from, the negative aspect of the Cratylian approach, and this is a primary difference to keep in mind when comparing the two works.[4]

If, as we have seen, de Brosses is quite often, like Socrates, a disappointed and discontented Cratylist, Gébelin, troubled by nothing, is the very image of the happy mimologist.

⚕ "Our overarching principle, that all is imitation ..."[5] It is not surprising to come across the principle of imitative language again here, based, as in Plato, on the categorical opposition (implicitly excluding any third term) of the *arbitrary* and the *mimetic.* Socrates' dilemma returns here in full force: the language system can only be arbitrary (that is, an effect either of chance or of individual whim) or "necessary" (that is, justified by a direct relation between "name" and "object"). The first hypothesis is untenable on principle; it is a logical and moral monstrosity: "Never were the seeds, the principles, the developments of an art

91

as essential and as wonderful as speech, which could be called *the glory and pre-rogative of the human race,* abandoned to arbitrariness."[6] We are thus left with the second hypothesis: "Never [would men assign a name to an object] without being guided by some relationship between the name chosen and the object to be named." And on its heels comes a specification, imposed with no conceivable way out, that reduces "some relationship" to the single relationship of analogy: "We have said, and it cannot be repeated enough: speech is nothing else but a painting of our ideas, and our ideas, a painting of objects we know; therefore, a *necessary relationship* must exist between words and the ideas they present, as one exists between ideas and their objects. Indeed, *the act of painting cannot possibly be arbitrary; it is always determined by the nature of the object to be painted.* In order to designate an object or an idea, men were thus forced to choose the sound most *analogous* to that object, to that idea."[7] Clearly, the implicit axiom here is, as it were, turned around or turned upside down through a move that initially posits imitation (*painting*) as a factual given, then deduces its necessity as an internal property, hence a logical consequence of mimesis. But imitation itself reverts to a consequence in the last sentence, and this tricky or circular line of argument does not void the postulate it disguises, which is in fact that *there is no necessary relationship but the relationship of imitation.* This postulate can easily be found again a few lines further on in the following supposedly purely descriptive scenario: "Through this analogy between sounds, ideas, and objects, man has always understood ... [that] each word had its *reason,* and this reason was accepted by everyone, because a more picturesque, more expressive, more lucid word could not have been chosen" — put otherwise, a more imitative word. This *forced hand,* which consists of the choice imposed between arbitrary and mimetic, or the absolute assimilation of motivation into imitation, may perhaps be justified (we will return to this). What is surprising in its use by the Cratylian tradition is its ever implicit and virtually surreptitious character; this lies in the continual omission of the following simple and crucial question (for "Cratylus" himself): is it possible, yes or no, to conceive of a "necessary relationship" between signifier and signified which is not an analogical relationship?

ⓔ The mimetic principle is eminently applicable to originary natural language, or the common primeval tongue ("natural languages are merely dialects of one single language"; "the prevailing differences between natural languages do not prevent us from recognizing that they have the same origin": such are the two foremost principles on which the *art of etymology* rests)[8] — but we should add that the mimetic principle irresistibly entails this assumption, since, according to the Saussurean argument taken *a contrario,* a mimetic language system is intuitively presumed to be universal, at least in origin: "Since it is in the nature of things that language is only a painting, and that this painting holds the strongest relationship everywhere, to the extent that the objects to be painted are the same everywhere, the result is that the intuition of a primeval tongue common to all is based on the strongest motives, which can be overruled only by the facts." Now for Gébelin, it happens that the "facts" tend, on the contrary, only to confirm the hypothesis, "since the more carefully one compares the most distant natural languages, the more numerous and astonishing are the relationships one finds between them."[9] The present diversity of languages — reduced to a diversity of *appellations*, and thus to simple synonymy — comes merely from the diversity of the *aspects* of the objects to be named (as for de Brosses): "The different names given to the same object owe their existence merely to the diverse qualities through which each nation views them; in this way, those who called the Supreme Being *Dieu* viewed Him as the source of light and saw in Him a being as pure as light; those who called Him *El* or *Al* intended by this to designate His loftiness; by calling Him *God,* one designated his goodness; by calling Him *Boq,* His powerfulness; by calling Him *Tien,* His superiority and the respect due to Him. But the roots of all these names exist in the primeval tongue, with significations similar to these."[10]

One name, one object: this other postulate of natural language considered as a nomenclature, which already underlies the approach in the *Cratylus* and which we rediscovered in de Brosses, acquires a sort of diachronic inflection with Gébelin. It comprises the idea that all verbs are derivative (from nouns, obviously), that none of them is original, and that therefore the primeval language, at least, was entirely a collection of nouns. "Verbs ... have no place in our investigation into the origin of the language system; since all of them are posterior to the origin of language, since all are borrowed from nouns, and since these are nouns considered from a certain point of view, they cannot be counted among the earliest words. ... All that we are required to do with regard to verbs is to connect them with their true root nouns and to demonstrate that these roots necessarily belong to the primeval language." Let us add that these root nouns are all monosyllabic; this is the third principle of the art of etymology: "The first natural language is composed solely of monosyllables drawn from nature to paint natural or physical objects, and is the source of all words."[11]

Plainly, these root nouns, and thus the natural language they "compose," are reconstituted by comparative etymology, as Indo-European will be later; but the etymological regression is much more ambitious here, for the goal is to return to the universal originary language. This may be ambitious, but it is apparently very easy for Gébelin: "When all the compound words and all the derivative words are removed from natural languages, there remains in each one a very small number of monosyllabic words beyond which we cannot go. This small number of words must be regarded as the elements of natural languages, as the spring from which all other words have been drawn. And since these elements are the same in all natural languages, we cannot help but recognize them as the primeval language, whose existence thus becomes a demonstrated fact, an incontestable principle."[12] Clearly, the primeval language is none other than the sum of elements common to all present-day languages. It is enough to compare the largest possible number of these (this is the fourth principle of the art of etymology)[13] and to apply to them that natural gift, or stroke of genius, which Aristotle calls that which makes us *see resemblances.*

⑨ De Brosses described the speech organ as a wind instrument in which the voice, an unrefined sound, received its form from the different articulations produced by the action of the different organs arranged along the windpipe. In Gébelin, the musical metaphor becomes more defined and systematic. The vocal organ becomes a complete instrument "that combines all the advantages of wind instruments, such as the flute; of stringed instruments, such as the violin; of keyboard instruments, such as the organ, with which it has the closest relationship, and which of all the musical instruments invented by man is the most resonant, the most variegated, and the one most closely approximating the human voice." But as is immediately evident, the parallel with the organ doubles and deflects the comparison, since the organ is itself already a complex instrument, just like the voice: "Like the organ, the vocal instrument has bellows, a soundbox, pipes, keys: the bellows are the chest; the pipes are the throat and nostrils; the mouth is the soundbox, and its inner walls are the keys."[14] Instantly, the role of the vocal cords disappears, and the vocal organ remains—like the organ—essentially a *wind and keyboard* instrument. This reduction is welcome, for it enables Gébelin to hinge the musical comparison directly to the phonic system of natural language: like a wind instrument the vocal organ produces vowels, or *sounds;* like a keyboard instrument it produces consonants, or *intonations.*[15]

This seems to bring us back to de Brosses's opposition between *voice* and *figure,* but the musical analogue here is much more potent than in de Brosses, for it furnishes the phonematic inventory with a principle of systematic organization: the principle of *harmony,* or (according to Gébelin) the natural coordination of sounds into octaves. Quite empirically, de Brosses listed seven vowels and an unspecified number of consonants. The principle of harmony will carve a rigorous order out of this chaos; to begin with, it divides the vocalic continuum just exactly as the tonal system divides the octave into a scale of seven tones: "Since the mouth can be opened to a very great number of degrees, there necessarily exists a very great number of sounds. However, they can be reduced to a small number of basic sounds that together form an octave, drawn from nature, since the vocal instrument is, in relation to the voice itself, a real flute, and since all kinds of harmony are encompassed within the octave. The voice actually differs from song only in its form: it must undergo the same phenomena that song does, then, and a similar tonal series should be found in it. Let us add that since each sound is capable of being divided into an octave, this octave must necessarily contain the other sounds, which therefore reduce to the octave. This would therefore be composed of *seven* main vowels, as the musical octave is composed of seven pitches."[16] De Brosses's vowels were degrees of fullness or intensity; for Gébelin, the mouth's aperture is inversely related to the length of the vocal "canal" or vocal "pipe" and thus, according to the principle of pan-pipes, directly related to the *pitch* of the sound: the most open vowel will also be the highest in pitch, and conversely, the most closed vowel will be the lowest in pitch. Whence the following descending scale that roughly corresponds[17] to de Brosses's scale, but with the criterion of pitch substituted for that of intensity: *a-è-é-i-o-u-ou,* symmetrical to the musical scale *ti-la-sol-fa-mi-re-do.* "One could say that the sound *a* is to the other sounds what *ti,* the highest pitch in music, is to the other tones, whereas *ou* is to the other sounds what *ut {do},* the lowest pitch in music, is to the other tones."[18]

Here, then, we have got hold of seven "sounds," a number which no longer has anything *arbitrary* about it. For their part, the intonations are determined by the keys of the vocal instrument, which are again seven in number: the five recognized by earlier tradition (labial, dental, nasal, lingual, guttural), plus two others that Gébelin not too implausibly adds in order to reach the harmonic number: the sibilant and the "shhh" sound *{la chuintante}.* Each of these keys, depending on whether it is pressed heavily or lightly, produces two intonations, one strong and one weak. From this comes the accompanying chart.[19]

KEYS	STRONG	WEAK
labial	*p*	*b*
dental	*t*	*d*
nasal	*n*	*m*
lingual	*r*	*l*
guttural	*k*	*g*
sibilant	*s*	*z*
fricative	*ch*	*j*

Seven vowels and fourteen consonants — in other words, 3 × 7, or twenty-one phonemes: such is the ideal system, that of the originary natural language. The "harmonic" motivations of this system are rather obvious, and we will return to them in company with the author himself. But first it is worth our while to look quite carefully at the way in which he arrives at this magic number.

For the consonants, the chart retains only what Gébelin calls the "simple intonations," which for him justifies the exclusion of the two palatals *ll* and *ñ* and also of the two labio-dentals *f* and *v,* which bring into play two articulatory organs and are therefore defined also as compound articulations, even though their two components are simultaneous and not successive and though this type of "compounding" is actually found in all consonantal articulations. Thus, Gébelin himself recognizes that his "nasals" *m* and *n* are pronounced "by means of a movement of the lips for the first one, and by a movement of the tongue against the teeth for the second one,"[20] which makes one a labio-nasal and the other, if I am counting correctly, a linguo-dental-nasal, quite as "compound" as *f* or *v*, if not more so. The definition of the "simple" intonations, therefore, is flexible enough to allow fourteen of them to be listed, neither more nor less.

For the vowels, a similar maneuver allows Gébelin to eliminate the nasals by classifying them as mere "modifications" of simple sounds, just as he does the "aspirated vowels," and to neutralize the opposition between long and short vowels. As for the French sound *eu*, since it is pronounced as more or less open or closed — hence sometimes closer to *e* and sometimes closer to *u* — it is ranked along with *oi, ai, au* as a "mixed sound" or diphthong — unlike *ou*, which "admits of no nuances in its pronounciation, being the effect of a fixed open position of the mouth."[21] The same argument surely holds good for *a* and *o*, which admit of a good many "nuances" in the open position, but Gébelin takes care not to apply it to them: he needs seven vowels. Probably for the same reason, he disregards the confusion, frequent in a good many languages, between *é* and *è* (or *i*), and between *u* and *ou* (or *o*). Moreover, this competition of two systems, with seven or five vowels, paradoxically only confirms his harmonic system: just like the number seven, five is founded in nature, on the number of the five senses and the fingers of the hand; what is more, the relation between five and seven itself also refers back to the system of the musical octave, since this, "in which we count seven notes, actually contains only five full tones, and the two others are merely half-tones, which yields twelve half-tones for the entire octave."[22] In other words, the interval that separates *é* from *è* (or from *i*?) and the one that separates *u* from *ou* (or from *o*?) would, like the intervals *mi-fa* and *ti-do* in the major scale of *do*, be half of that separating the others. As is apparent, the analogy is both muddled, since the position of the vocalic half-intervals is uncertain or variable, and lame, since the second interval in any theory is inside the vocalic scale (between the fifth and sixth, or between the sixth and seventh degrees), whereas the interval *ti-do* is outside the scale of seven sounds, being the twelfth half-tone, not of the scale, of course, but, as Gébelin himself says, of "the entire octave." But no more than this is needed in order to liken the spectrum of vowels to the diatonic model and also to dream of a sort of chromatic, or dodecaphonic, phonology that would account for all the nuances of the human vowel system: "We leave it to those more adept than we to investigate whether or not the vocalic octave might be subdivided into twelve sounds as well, and whether or not examples of this might be found in several language systems: whether or not a few of our sounds which are taken for diphthongs, even though

96

they are not so, do not result from the octave's property of dividing itself into twelve. Perhaps a few problems relating to diphthongs could be cleared up in this way, and much more light could be shed on this interesting subject."

Nevertheless, the essential subject for Gébelin definitely remains the "harmonic" distribution of the phonemes into seven sounds and fourteen intonations, which offers the double advantage of corresponding to a "natural" model (the scale, the spectrum) and of introducing into linguistic phoneticism a specific and somewhat symmetrical order, whose very regularity is both a guarantee of truth and, as in Dmitri Mendeleev's chart, a tool of research. But it is probably advisable to let Gébelin speak for himself here:

This division of sounds and intonations into seven might appear too harmonic to be true to those who have not thought about these things or who have not analyzed them so thoroughly. It might be feared, as has already been intimated, that this would tend to revive the superstitious ideas which the Ancients associated with the number seven.

But supposing it were true that the Ancients formed only superstitious and even false views on this subject (which in itself would perhaps be difficult to prove), no objection to a division drawn from Nature, such as the division of sounds into seven and of intonations into seven strong ones and seven weak ones, need follow from that. Moreover, this division is well suited to giving a clear and accurate idea of the entire range of the vocal instrument, since its intonations operate only two by two and always in contrast.

The other divisions in use up to now combine two main defects, which could only confuse those who took them as guides: on the one hand, the number of intonations that went into each class was not well defined, so that one could never be sure if this number was complete; on the other hand, one was compelled to assume that intonations other than the strong and the weak could be found on the same key, which is impossible, and one was compelled to accept middling intonations, an absurd idea which in any case strayed into areas where nothing was well defined any more.[23] Nature does not act in this way; in Nature everything is calculated and combined with the greatest precision.

Let us add that because speech is the effect of a resonant and harmonic instrument, it must of necessity be subject to harmony.

Since the vocal instrument, considered in its sounds, is a wind instrument, it must of necessity produce an octave like any other wind instrument, like a Flute. And since when considered in its intonations it is a keyboard instrument, it is not surprising to observe the impress of the same harmony upon it.

Speech, created for the ear, becomes more pleasant to it through this very fact, since the ear is itself constructed so that it corresponds perfectly to the harmony of the octave and so that everything not in keeping with that harmony hurts it.

Thus all is in concord in Nature, whatever the amazing variety of her works. And without this concord, could these works survive? Could she herself go on? Seeing that she took the proportion of the octave for the harmonic rule of the World in which we live, this harmony had to exist everywhere; and far from being surprised at recognizing it in the vocal instrument, we should be very surprised, on the contrary, if this harmony were not found there, and if this instrument, the model for all others, were created according to proportions that had no relationship to the one we are obliged to follow in any other instrument.

It is this harmony which the Author of Nature has put into the colors and into a large number of other things; in this way, the same harmony animates all of Nature and spreads its wonderful influence everywhere. In this way, the eyes of the Master of the Earth, His mouth, His lips, His ears, the air He breathes, the light that shines on Him, the tones that delight Him, the colors that charm Him, and so forth, all have the same analogy, were all weighed in the same balance, according to the same harmonic proportions, and were all created for His sense organs as well.

This is the harmony which the Egyptians celebrated, which sent Pythagoras into raptures,[24] which Cicero did not disdain to mention, which seems a dream to us only because we have almost lost sight of these relationships, and without which the entire analysis of the vocal instrument and consequently that of natural languages cannot be carried out and will never be anything but what it has been up to the present — a veritable chaos.[25]

As we saw previously, only the primeval language realizes this harmonic system in its purity and its integrity. Everywhere else, the fundamental identity of natural languages is masked by the diversity of what Gébelin discreetly calls the "*modes* of which the vocal instrument is capable,"[26] or the variants of *pronunciation*. This identity is masked but not destroyed: a phoneme does not lose its nature just because it is "pronounced" differently from one natural language to another, and the etymologist need only recognize the general principles of these substitutions in order to rediscover everywhere, beneath its misrepresentations, the unity of the human language system. Here are those principles, reduced to six according to the synthesis given in *Histoire naturelle de la parole*:

1. Vowels tend to become weaker as they descend the steps of the "octave": *a* becomes *e*, *e* becomes *i*, *i* becomes *u*, etc.

2. Metathesis of syllables occurs: *am — ma*.

3. Aspiration disappears or becomes a consonant: *hordeum — orge, huper — super.*

4. A few vowels change into consonants: *u — v, i — j;* as in *Ioupiter — Jupiter.*

5. Intonations of the same key continually substitute for each other: *lusciniola — rossignol, peregrinus — pèlerin.*

6. Intonations of neighboring keys or keys "having some relationship between them" often substitute for each other: *gamba — jambe, caballus — cheval.*[27]

The causes of these variations are themselves diverse, but their common characteristic is that they are, in a way, extra-linguistic: different customs, the influence of fashion, embellishment, individual whim, the "desire to distinguish oneself,"[28] and so on. Apparently, the most powerful cause — also the most "natural" — is climate, and we recognize here one of the most constant themes of eighteenth-century thought (although it goes back to Epicurus). Like the sheep's tongue dear to Montesquieu, the human tongue tightens up and dilates its "fibers" depending on variations in temperature, with very direct effects on speech production. But note that to the purely physical influence of heat and cold, or of topography, is added a sort of analogical determinism of the landscape, which is not accounted for by direct or indirect causation but acts instead through mimetic influence or — probably better put in the words of Jacques-Henri Bernardin de Saint-Pierre — through natural harmony. The speech of the mountain people is precipitate *like* the flow of streams; the man of the valleys produces a quiet murmur, all in "liquid" and "wet" or "palatal" intonations, which matches the sound of the slow and peaceful rivers. The final chapter of Gaston Bachelard's *Water and Dreams,* titled "The Words of the Water," is not far away. Let us listen to Gébelin's charming *speech of the climate {parole du climat}*:

The vocal instrument is composed of fibers which heat relaxes and cold tightens up, in the same way that these elements act upon all other bodies; but the effects for speech when heat and cold relax or tighten up the fibers of the vocal instrument are always very different from one another.

In Lands where the air is burning hot and the blood runs impetuously in the veins, the fibers of the vocal instrument are extremely dilated and as a result have a good deal of play: hence, sounds can be pronounced, and consequently aspirated, very forcefully. Even aspiration can be much stronger because the mouth muscles have more play, opening up more easily and using the innermost area of the mouth more often. Thus the voice ascends the highest octaves more easily, letting aspirations, strong intonations, guttural or extremely open vowels, be heard; it runs through all the nuances of the aspirations in order to vary its continual use of them.

If high Mountains cut across these warm climates, they increase this im-

99

petuosity by interrupting the flow of the blood, thinning it out by jolting it on their rugged and steep roads, and facilitating the play of the lungs by these frequent jolts. There, the language or speech is precipitate like the Torrents that descend from these Mountains, which sweep away every obstacle in their path: there, the vocal instrument resonates on the shortest, most sharply pitched, most sonorous keys.

In Lands where wintry weather has established its sway, where the pace of all that moves is slow, occasionally suspended, because of the extreme cold, where all the fibers are tightened, shortened, deprived of nearly all their play, the vocal instrument opens up with more difficulty. It therefore rises less, it relies less on the inside area and much more on the outer extremity of the mouth: it thus tends to produce labial, dental, and sibilant intonations; the people seem to speak only from the tip of their teeth.

In more fortunate Lands between these extremes, where the air is temperate, where the Rivers run with slow majesty without rushing down the Mountains, and as if they regretted leaving their tranquil home, the springs of the vocal instrument are neither overly dilated by heat nor overly tightened by cold; they are thus in a moderate state of tension that produces gentle, calm, flattering intonations. Since these do not jump to the extremes of the vocal instrument and since their operation extends more or less equally over its entire range and consequently occupies its center, the language abounds in liquids, palatals, linguals, nasals, in pleasant and gentle sounds. It is, so to speak, merely a faint murmur, a sign of the delightful dwelling place inhabited by those who make these pleasant sounds.

It is, above all, the vowels that are climatically influenced because these are capable of longer duration and greater diversity in their range of pitch. Consequently, vowels are fast-moving, lively, and varied in some climates, slow-moving, weak, and monotonous in others; sharp and high-pitched in the former, unrefined and harsh in the latter, and sweetness itself in the middle group.[29]

Like his predecessor de Brosses and like many others after him, Gébelin assigns to vowels a completely minor role in the material composition of words. The sixth principle of his "art of etymology" is extremely stark where vowels are concerned: "Vowels count for nothing in word comparisons"; as we have seen, their pronunciation is "inconstancy itself," and the "Orientals" are truly inspired in taking so little account of them in their writing system. Consonants are subject to variations, too, but most often within the limits of their corresponding articulatory organ. As a result, consonants remain the "essential aspects of words, making up their framework, and without consonants nothing would remain."[30] Here is an appearance, or a reappearance, of that almost inevitable comparison of the word to a body whose flesh is the vowels and whose skeleton is the consonants, a simile that we will see again quite often in other authors. But unlike what happened in de Brosses — and, it must be said, contrary to all logic — this morphological inferiority of the vowel does not entail any semantic inferiority: albeit secondary and "inconstant" in the constitution of the word, the vowel, in Gébelin, remains as important as the consonant in producing the word's meaning. Nothing escapes Cratylian imperialism here: nothing can be insignificant.

Let us begin with the very opposition between "sounds" and "intonations," which is invested with crucial symbolic value. Physically, the main difference between the two classes lies in the contrast between the "liveliness" of the vowels (resonant by definition) and the "quietude" of the consonants (said to be "unvoiced" and silent): "A major difference [between sounds and intonations] can be observed relative to their nature, a difference to which not enough attention has been paid, at least not enough to draw the important consequences that follow from it. Sounds tend to be ringing and loud, to be very lively, very animated, whereas intonations are unvoiced and quiet, as calm as the sounds are impetuous. As a result, these two can paint, each according to its nature, objects endowed with absolutely different qualities: through sounds one can paint noises, movements, collisions, earthquakes, the restlessness of the whole Universe and its parts, whereas through intonations one can convey the fixed and inherent qualities of objects. The latter are more appropriate for designating physical objects, the former for moral and intellectual objects that fall less under the realm of the senses."[31]

The division of labor between vowels and consonants follows from this physical opposition and from the general mimetic principle, restated in the most vigorous way this time: "As the model is, so the copy shall be."[32] The universe of signifieds, "what the spoken word must paint" — namely, "the faculties of our soul, what it feels, what it desires, what it perceives or discovers, the impressions it receives from outside or those it wants others to feel" — can all, it turns out, be reduced to two classes: *sensations* ("impressions we receive from outside and the different states of feeling they produce in our soul") and *ideas* ("the different states of our soul that are the effect of our own faculties"). "The language system, then, is composed of two types of modifications: one to make our sensations known, the other to paint our ideas." That being the case, the mimetic affinity between the two classes of sounds and the two classes of senses thus defined is more than clear, and the correspondences emerge by themselves: "Our impatient readers will have already anticipated this; they will have concluded that sounds or vowels paint sensations, and that intonations or consonants paint ideas." Lively, animated, loud, the sounds wonderfully paint the movement and restlessness of the senses; in contrast, the intonations, unvoiced and quiet, perfectly express the calm and inner silence of reflection.[33]

But this overall division obviously does not exhaust the mimetic capacities of the spoken word; each vowel has to evoke a particular order of sensations, each consonant a particular order of ideas. Here is this division as it is laid out and illustrated in chapters 11 and 12 of book 4.

Vowels

— *a*: as the highest-pitched sound, hence the first one of the descending octave, this is the most immediate cry, hence the "natural sign" of "one's present state," hence the sign of identity and property, possession, and domination. Above all, this is the sound constitutive of the verb *avoir* {to have} ("*il a*" {he has}), and of the "preposition that marks the relationship of possession, of property": "*Cela est à lui*" {That belongs to him}.[34]

— open *è* (apparently always aspirated) is the sign of the sensation of life and everything contributing to it (Latin *vis, vita;* Greek *bia*), particularly Earth.

— closed *é*, "borrowed from respiration, of which it is the sign and name," symbolizes existence and is universally used to form the verb *être* {to be}.

— *i* (usually long, hence *ei*): this is the natural name of the hand, of touching, "and, because of this very fact, of everything related to it, protection and caretaking": Hebrew *id;* French, *aide.*

— *o*, the "cry of admiration, became the name of light, whose sensation is so pleasant," whence *soleil* {sun}, *feu* {fire}, *yeux* {eyes}, *vue* {sight}; thus, Latin *sol, focus, oculus.*

— *u* "paints the action of attracting liquids and odors"; this is the vowel of water (Greek *udor;* Latin *humor;* French *humide;* English *water*) and of perfumes: *odor, humer.*

— *ou* "is the very sound produced on the ears by an ordinary noise, especially by the wind," whence *oreille* {ear}, *le sens de l'ouie* {the sense of hearing}, and everything connected with these; French *oui* {yes}, which properly signifies: "*C'est entendu*" {I heard you; I understand}.

Quite clearly, this list claims to organize the whole of the sensible world and the sensory apparatus in one single gesture: "The sounds express at once the senses, the elements, the sensory organs, impressions, and the kinds of knowledge that result from these." But quite clearly also, it shows the effects of the difficulty Gébelin experienced in distributing the five traditional senses (and the four elements) among the seven vowels: *i* plainly corresponds to the touch, *o* to the sight, *u* to the sense of smell, *ou* to the hearing, but which vowel is related to the taste is uncertain; *a, è* and *é* are too many left over, with values that are sometimes hard to distinguish. As far as the elements are concerned, once *è* is attributed to earth, *o* to fire, *u* to water, and *ou* to air, three unassigned vowels are left over.

As to the consonants, Gébelin seems to have hesitated to divide the world of "ideas" among the fourteen simple intonations. Thus his chart distinguishes only seven "keys," almost without taking account of the opposition between strong and weak intonation.

Consonants

— The *labial* key (*p, b,* to which are linked the labio-nasal *m* and the labio-dental *v*), as requiring the slightest effort, is the natural sign of gentleness. Like de Brosses, whom he quotes liberally here, Gébelin sees this as the supreme example of the childlike articulation: *papa, maman, fanfan, bonbon, bouillie, baiser, poupon, poupée, bobo, bibi, beau, bon, bien, ami, amie, bambin.*

— The *dental* key, in contrast, is the hardest, thus producing the strongest intonations,[35] the loudest possible (*t, d*): "They might be called the consonants par excellence."[36] They are intended for "painting everything that is resonant and noisy, whence come a vast number of the earliest picturesque words. It is with this key that we thunder {*tonner*}, ring out {*retentir*}, astonish {*étonner*}, give the pitch {*donner le ton*}; with this key we designate noisemaking instruments, drums {*tambours*}, timpani {*timbales*}, dulcimers {*tympanons*}, trumpets {*trompettes*}: hence the nouns *tympan* {eardrum}, *tintin* {clinking}, and *tintinnabulum* {tinkling}, the name for clocks in Latin; also, the very nouns *touches* {keys}, *intonation, tact,* and so on. It is with this key that we egg on the dogs at the chase, make our voice ring out from afar, penetrate the density of a forest." Consequently, this key designates quantity, totality, perfection; the friendly form of the second person {*tu*}; the head {*tête*}; and also (*Ta, Atta*), the father "in all nations that do not use the labial for this appellation": the Name-of-the-Father vacillates, then, between strength and tenderness.[37]

— The *nasal* intonation *n,* pronounced by pushing air out through the nostrils, is an "unvoiced and repulsive" consonant, whose function is therefore to paint repulsive objects; no example is given.

— The *lingual* key is generally that of movement, but here the distinction between strong and weak intonation becomes relevant again, as in Leibniz: *r* is produced by a rough scraping; it is the consonant of rough, abrupt, and noisy movements, expressed either by *r* alone or by the groups *fr, tr, cr*; it is also the consonant of rugged, high, steep things. *L,* which is pronounced with "a very gentle and very smooth-flowing explosion" of air, therefore designates "gentle movements with a continuous and peaceful gait," and liquid and smooth-flowing things: *liqueurs, limpidité, lymphe, lait* {milk}, *lac* {lake}; *fluide, fleuve* {river}, and so on.

— The *gutturals* (*k, g*), pronounced from the bottom of the throat "as if from the bottom of a hole," are assigned to "deep" objects which have been "dug out into canals": *col* {neck}, *canal, caverne*.[38]

— The *sibilants* (*s, z*) apparently have a purely onomatopoetic function, form-

103

ing the name of "hissing or whistling noises"; as for the *"shhh"* sounds (*ch, j*), they discouraged our commentator for some reason.[39]

Clearly, the most striking thing about his chart and the pages of examples illustrating it is the completely material aspect of the values assigned to the intonations, whose exclusive relation to the world of "ideas" Gébelin had so strongly asserted. Indeed, we should recognize that nothing here serves to confirm in detail the general division of the phonemes into vowels-sensations and consonants-ideas. Certainly, after having marked out their dividing line so sharply, Gébelin betrays in several awkward statements that he had trouble keeping it watertight. Thus: "Vowels were not so completely limited to sensations and consonants so completely limited to ideas that they never worked together in order to designate either sensations or ideas. This probably happened all the more readily because sensations and ideas are themselves continually merging in their effects on human understanding, so much so that they must have constantly merged with each other in the vocal painting of these effects also."[40]

In the end, then, the division of semantic labor between sounds and intonations is an abortive endeavor, an affirmation of principle that does not succeed in getting back to any linguistic reality and that is inspired solely by the desire to give a meaning to everything. No doubt this desire is hyper-Cratylian, in Gébelin's case, since Socrates attributed no symbolic value to his distinction between vowels, semivowels, and silent vowels and did not even bother to separate them in his list of significations. Further on, we will encounter other manifestations of this extremism, this excessive mimological zeal.[41]

One last remark concerning these phonematic interpretations. As in Plato or de Brosses, the symbolic values of the consonants here are deduced from physical — mainly articulatory — particulars: the gentleness of the labial key, the hardness of the dentals, the roughness of the *r*, and so forth. On the other hand, the interpretation of the vowels seems more gratuitous, or more abstract: *a* expresses identity because it is the "first vowel," and *o* expresses light because it is the cry of admiration; *ou*, the windy noise, is the only vowel with a properly phonic (auditory) value. Here again, nothing indicates a conscious recourse to synaesthetic associations, such as we will commonly find in the twentieth century regarding the semanticism of light in "high-pitched" vowels and of darkness in "low-pitched" vowels. Like that of the majority of his predecessors and contemporaries, Gébelin's symbolism remains tied in theory[42] to the concept of direct mimesis, without either mediation or transposition.

On the other hand, notice the considerable share of the *Origine* given over to lists of confirmatory examples that attempt, with uneven success, to prove that the majority of words in a great number of natural languages (which supposedly

stand for all of them) correspond to the semantic values attributed to the phonemes. Compared with the tact of Plato or de Brosses, this strain is obviously
a feature of primary mimologism: Gébelin not only believes in the mimetic capacities of the phonic elements of the language system but is also convinced of
the good constitution of the lexical material in all known natural languages. In
this he is the direct heir of Cratylus, and perhaps his most faithful disciple.

⑨ Nevertheless, these vocables, "born of the relationship of sounds and intonations with Nature," do not exhaust the bulk of the universal lexicon. "However
numerous these words might be, they were not enough for painting the whole
set of ideas; it thus was necessary to add other sources of words to those we
have just discussed."[43] Chapter 13 of Book 4 is devoted to these other processes.
But we must not mistake the meaning of this addition; it most definitely does
not come from a failure of vocal mimesis, as in de Brosses, or from some linguistic decadence. Simply, the basic lexical material, made up of monosyllables,
is not copious enough to enable everything to be "painted"; a purely quantitative exhaustion of the number of signifying forms therefore makes it necessary,
but also sufficient, to augment or, if you like, to multiply them. These "other
sources," or supplementary processes, are five in number:

1. Onomatopoeia pure and simple. Here Gébelin faithfully follows the exposition in de Brosses's *Traité de la formation mécanique des langues.*
2. The "mixing or combining of intonations": that is to say, recourse to consonantal groups of the type *fr* or *st.* "The basic sounds and intonations were
too small in number not to have been rapidly exhausted; various expedients
were needed to supplement them. One of the first, equally basic and no less picturesque, was the combination of two intonations. In this way, we saw *l* and *r*
joining together with *f* and *t* to form words in *fl, fr, tr* that were as energetic, as
imitative as those in *f* or in *r.*" Clearly, the combination of two consonants does
not release a composite meaning for Gébelin; one of the intonations (sometimes
the first, sometimes the second)[44] loses all its symbolic value here in order to
provide the other with a simple means of combinatory multiplication. There is
nothing comparable to those semantic complexes which produce the group *gl* in
Plato or the group *tr* in de Brosses. At the most, we can observe the role of signal
or call which has devolved upon *s* in the group *st,*[45] or the reinforcing function
granted to the initial consonant in the groups *fr, tr, cr.*[46] The semantic atom is
indeed the word-syllable, whatever the number of its consonants, and Gébelin
makes no attempt, despite his principles, to account for both the idea-consonant
and the vowel-sensation: in point of fact, one or the other dominates absolutely.
3. Complex meaning therefore makes its appearance only with the third process, which is compounding. "Any word of two syllables [or more] is a com-

pound of two other words." But for all that, the mimetic principle is not tra-
duced; a simple painting is merely succeeded by a complex painting: "Complex
words create pictures {tableaux} as precise as simple words; only they are complicated, whereas the pictures created by simple words are not."

4. Simple or complex, all these pictures paint physical objects only; the shift
to intellectual objects demands recourse to *figurative words* {mots figurés}, which
here amount to metaphors of the spiritual taken from the corporeal. But here
again, the change of register does not entail any loss of mimesis. Metaphor for
Gébelin is not what it was for de Brosses: a step on the path of "derivation."
On the contrary, metaphor demonstrates all the more brilliantly the imitative
powers of the human language system, which is capable of painting even invisible things. "In this way, by means of the senses, mankind ascended to the
most invisible objects, and nothing could escape the effects of speech; the spoken word paints even things unseen by us in the most vivid and most energetic
manner, and it makes them known as precisely, as deeply, and as thoroughly as
the very things we see."

5. The last process, which is double besides, replies without any trouble to
that still more formidable question: "How can we paint what does not exist?"
It is this process that presides over the creation of *negative words*. In accordance
with the principle of mimesis, it consists very simply in taking the opposite of
the corresponding positive word, either by a sort of metathesis—"*a* placed at
the end of a noun marked the existence or possession of an object [this apparently refers to the ending of the first declension in Greek or Latin]; *a* placed at
the beginning of the same noun marked the nonexistence, the deprivation of
an object [doubtless the privative *a*, but Gébelin gives no example here]"—or
else by switching from strong intonation, which designates the positive, to the
opposite or weak intonation, which designates the negative. Thus, Latin *gelu*,
French *glace* {ice}, "is merely the weak version of *calor, chaleur* {heat}"; opposite
Greek *hēdonē*, French *plaisir* {pleasure} is Greek *odunē*, French *douleur* {grief or
pain}; opposite Greek *lukē*, French *lumière* {light} is Greek *lugē*, French *obscurité*
{darkness}; opposite Greek *leipo*, French *laisser* {to leave} is Greek *lēbo*, French
prendre {to take}; and so on.

"In these ways arose that incredible mass of words furnished by natural languages, effortlessly, without difficulty, without convention, as man needed them:
the nature of the ideas that he wanted to paint enabled him to find instantly the
most appropriate words, and these words were preserved, transmitted, spread
through colonization, because they were so well adapted to the object they designated that trying to assign it another word was pointless." Such is more or less
the conclusion of this fourth book, devoted to the origin of speech.[47] It evinces
a characteristic euphoria, one that never fails. The idea of linguistic decadence

is as alien to Gébelin as that, mentioned by Socrates, of an initially bad constitution or a birth defect in language. Everything has always been and everything
always is for the best in the best of all possible languages: there is a good deal of
Pangloss in this optimistic polyglot.

The shift from speech to writing, therefore, will not be for Gébelin, as it was
for de Brosses, a palliative or a last hope; there is nothing to be palliated or anything to be rescued. The sole defect of speech, or rather its sole weakness, and
one that in no way challenges its mimetic virtue, is the shortness of its reach
in time and in space: "There is nothing less durable than the spoken word; it
strikes the air and leaves no trace; and if it makes some impression on those
who hear it, this impression is nil for those who are not enclosed within the
tiny circle it travels." A way of *extending* the language system, in distance and
in temporality, had to be found, then, without losing any of its natural evocative power. "This wonderful way of immortalizing one's thoughts and making
them travel over all time and over all space is WRITING {*Écriture*}, that Art which
speaks to the eyes, which paints to the sight what speech paints to the ear; which
is as fixed as spoken language is fleeting, which lives on while those who are its
engineers descended several centuries ago into the night of the tomb; that Art
which perpetuates the Sciences, which facilitates their acquisition, which enables the knowledge of time past to serve in the perfection of the knowledge of
time present, and which will enable all the Sciences together to serve as a foundation for the vast edifice of knowledge to be formed in future time."[48]

A human invention, symbol of all civilization, writing must nonetheless remain, like speech, "drawn from Nature," from which come all its virtues. There
is a small problem here that Gébelin thinks he has solved by linking this invention to the birth of agriculture. Actually, only *agricultural man* "needed a Writing System {*Écriture*} in order to meet all the demands of his station: to keep
a record of his servants, his flocks, his fields, his revenues, his expenses, those
who owe him and those to whom he owes a debt; to teach all his dependents
what they must do themselves in order to fulfill the duties of their own station;
to lay down an order, laws, a cult, ceremonies for everything that makes up
his Empire, whose members increase daily; to preserve his observations on the
stars, on the seasons, on the best methods for turning a profit from his land; to
record his treaties with all his neighbors."[49] Now this farmer, whom we see here
in charge of an entire economic, social, political, and cultural organization, is
paradoxically the only authentic *natural* man for Gébelin. He is the true son of
Nature, for whom "savage man" is merely a bastard or an aborted creature. The
following demonstration of this is not without disturbing implications, since,
in short, the legitimacy of the son is proved by incest: "Savage man is not the
darling child of Nature; she is only a stepmother to him, he is only an aborted
Creature to her. The Child of Nature, her darling Son, he who is the object of

her tenderest care, on whom she smiles, for whom she displays all her riches, all her magnificence, all her charms, is agricultural man: he alone lifts her veil, penetrates her womb {*pénètre dans son sein*}, enjoys her favors." [50]

As we have seen, the spoken word (the sign of air) "strikes the air and leaves no trace"; on the contrary, writing (the sign of earth) is linked—by filiation, perhaps also by resemblance, by some obscure identity—to that supreme trace which is the furrow hollowed out by agricultural man in the "womb" of his mother, Nature.

ⓑ "We will set out from our overarching principle that everything is imitation; we will show how writing is related to this principle and confirms it." [51] Such a passage foreshadows the true color of Gébelin's work. It goes without saying that for him as for de Brosses (or rather, as we will see, much more so), all writing is painting, hence imitation. "Man wanted to paint an idea, but this idea painted an object; he therefore had only to paint that object, only to trace its figure, and the idea was painted: in this way, man wrote by the same means with which he spoke. Writing, like Language, was founded on imitation; Nature footed the bill." [52]

Gébelin's taxonomy of writing systems is more rudimentary than his predecessor's. It includes only three historical categories: the Chinese, the Egyptian, and the "Cadmean" or alphabetic. These boil down to two formal types: ideographic writing, which he calls *hieroglyphic* ("real," in de Brosses), illustrated by both Chinese and Egyptian; and phonetic writing, which he calls *alphabetic* ("verbal," in de Brosses), without taking syllabaries into account. Even then, this formal distinction is only provisional, as we will see.

Gébelin's theory of "hieroglyphic" writing is neither very developed nor very original.[53] Again we find the idea, previously borrowed by de Brosses from Warburton, of the figurativeness {*figurativité*} (in the rhetorical sense) of ideograms, through synecdoche, metonymy, and metaphor,[54] and the idea of the progressive simplification of written characters.[55] Gébelin's great innovation in relation to de Brosses lies in his theory of the alphabet. Moreover, it is typical that book 5 as a whole, which he devotes to the writing system, has for its title *Du langage peint aux yeux, ou de l'écriture, de son origine, et surtout de l'écriture alphabétique"* {On language painted for the eye, or on writing, its origin, and especially on alphabetic writing}; and that its second section ("Origine et nature de l'écriture alphabétique" {The origin and nature of alphabetic writing}) is four times longer than the first section ("De l'écriture en général et des hiéroglyphes en particulier" {On writing in general and on hieroglyphs in particular}).

The basic principle of this theory is simple and its exposition lapidary. The title of chapter 4 is "Toute écriture est hiéroglyphique" {All writing is hieroglyphic}; the title of chapter 5 is "Que l'écriture alphabétique est hiéroglyphique" {That alphabetic writing is hieroglyphic}; the first sentence of this chapter says: "Since all writing is hieroglyphic, it necessarily follows that the alphabetic writing system is, too." It would be impossible to be more categorical.

From the tradition made famous by Rowland Jones, whom he himself mentions,[56] Gébelin picks up the ideographic interpretation of the phonetic writing system. Alphabetic characters are for him true "hieroglyphs": that is, pure picto-ideograms, "each letter being the painting of an object,"[57] with the suggestiveness of the spoken word having a secondary and in a way derivative function. He rebels against the idea that the phonetic writing system "was born out of disgust for the hieroglyphic system, and that among the hieroglyphic characters was arbitrarily chosen the number of written characters sufficient to paint vocal sounds,[58] thereby substituting for the *painting of things* line strokes that would *replace sounds* and would *note* the spoken word simply as one notes music by line strokes that have no relationship to it. But is it true that the spoken word is simply *noted* by alphabetic letters? And was the spoken word not *painted* by this means as much as by hieroglyphs?"[59] But this wording should not lead us to believe that the alphabet for Gébelin is a direct "painting" of the sounds of speech — any more than Egyptian hieroglyphs are. The letter-ideogram paints an object for the eye; the phoneme, which is for him a genuine *ideophone,* paints this same object for the ear — and the resemblance between these two portraits results solely from their equal fidelity to their common model.

℘ Just as there exists an originary shared natural language, clearly there must exist a shared primeval alphabet, from which all the others derive. According to Gébelin, this primeval alphabet comprised sixteen letters, a number that ill matches the harmonic number of twenty-one phonemes. The reason for this clash seems to be that the earliest natural language, still rudimentary, did not distinguish between certain sounds such as *f* and *v, u* and *ou,* and so on.[60] On this point there are considerable ambiguities in the demonstration. Gébelin's plate 6 identifies these sixteen primeval written characters as A-B-C-D-E-F/V-I-K-L-M-N-O-P-R-S-T, but the chart (plates 4 and 5) baptized "Alphabet hiéroglyphique et primitif de seize lettres" {the earliest hieroglyphic alphabet of sixteen letters},[61] which illustrates the ideographic value of these characters (and their kinship in all writing systems), actually contains eighteen,[62] or even twenty through the doubling of the A and the T.

In its first three columns the chart of this alphabet indicates the origin and the signification of written characters plainly enough (if not always convincingly) that no commentary is needed on this topic. On the other hand, it is worthwhile to examine somewhat closely the relation between these ideographic values and the phonic symbolism established in book 4.

In fact, this comparison is made difficult by the several disparities in classifi-

Pl. IV.

Orig. du Langage &c.

ALPHABET HIÉROGLYPHIQUE ET PRIMITIF DE XVI. LETTRES

Lettres	Sens qu'ils Objets les désignent qu'ils peuvent	Caractères au single trait	Caractères CHINOIS Correspondant	Alphabet Espagnol	Hébreu des Médailles	Inscription Phénicienne de Malte	Samaritain	Hébreu carré	Grec ancien	Étrusque	Nombre
A	MAITRE celui qui A		L Lui Homme								I
(seconde)	BOEUF		Boeuf								
H	CHAMP et Source de la Vie		champ								II
E	EXISTENCE VIE		Arbre Vie								
I	MAIN m'Orinal ID l'ii AIDE		Main								III
O	OEIL		œil								IV
OU	OUIE Oreille		Oui Oreille un Clou								V
P	LE PALAIS		Bouche								VI
B	BOUE neuve		Boste ce qui contient								VII
M	ARBRE Ervé productif		Plante la Montagne								VIII

Alphabet Étrusque / Memoir de l'Eccl... du Decript. — Biblie Hébraÿ et Diction... — Alphabet Samarit. — Inscript de Malte Reptégé par Barthélemi — Médaille Hébraÿ par Swiston &c. — Alphabet Espagnol Del Velaxque. — Vieux Chinois de MM. Bayer et Fourmont

ALPHABET HIÉROGLYPHIQUE ET PRIMITIF DE XVI. LETTRES

PLANCHE II.

Lettres	Sens qu'elles expriment	Objet qu'elles peignent	Le même au simple trait	Caractère Chinois correspondant	Alphab. Phénicien d'Hypponne des Médailles de Malte	Inscription Hébraïque Phénicienne	Hébreu Phénicien	Samaritain	Hébreu carré	Grec ancien	Étrusque	
N	Ivre Produit Né Fruit			# Attaché l'un-à-l'autre Nœud &c.								IX
G	Gorge Cou Canal			] Borgne								X
C	Creux de la Main Cave. &c.											XI
Q	Coupe-et Bout ce qui Coupé			P Tout ce qui sert à Couper								XII
S	Scie Dents			~~~ Mortier Mâchoire à broyer à briser								XIII
T	1 er. Toit, Abri			— Toit Couvert							+	XIII
T	2 d. Parfait Grand			+ Perfection Dieu								XIV
D	Entrée Porte			P Porte Maison								XV
R	Nez Pointe			L Angle Aigu								XVI
L	1 re. aile Flanc			] Aile &c.								
	2 d. bras											

| | | | | | | | | | 4000 ans | 4000 ans | 4000 ans | 2400 ans | 3200 ans | 2700 ans | 2800 ans |

111

cation between the two systems. First, all the letters are interpreted individually, whereas the phonemes-consonants were usually mixed up with the intonational keys. Next, the distinction between *è* and *é* seems neutralized here to the advantage of the single grapheme E, barring cases where H corresponds to the sound *hè;* the letter Q is one too many with respect to the chart of intonations; finally, *a* and *t,* single phonemes, double as graphemes.

Allowing for these obstacles and for the obscurities they produce, we ought to give Gébelin credit for having partially succeeded in the difficult tuning of phonic and graphic values (whether this tuning comes from legitimate or improper interpretations is of course another question). Thus the sound *a* and the letter A, image of a man standing up, agree nicely in the idea of human rule over the Earth; the second A, derived from the Semitic *aleph,* associates the field ox with the fruitful labors of "agricultural man." The H, image of a ploughed field, agrees with the sound *hè,* symbolizing life, just as the E, derived from the shape of the human face, agrees with the idea of existence evoked by the sound *é.* The I symbolizes the hand, both sides; the O is the cry of admiration at light, here in the form of the eye. The digraph OU is supposed to represent an ear, like the sound it records, and the exemplary noise of the wind. P and B, letters of the labial key, are inspired by the form of the lips and mouth, whence *boîte* {box}, whence *maison* {house}. M, derived from the outline of a tree and symbol of production, hence of maternity, brings together the main values of the labial intonation (*maman* {mama}, *mamelle* {breast}). G (the camel's neck) and C (the hollow of one's hand) remain faithful to the idea of a cavity suggested by the guttural articulation. The image of the S, fragment of a saw, corresponds to the noise of the sibilant. The T as roof or cross and the D as door (of a tent) go with the idea of stability and closure brought out by the dental intonation. The R, derived from the form of a pointed nose, evokes harshness like the sound *r;* and the L, wing or arm bent "in order to run better," evokes movement, characteristic of the sound *l.* The only letters remaining without a phonic equivalent are N, symbol of fruit, hence of the child, even though the corresponding intonation designated "repulsive objects" (but who knows?); and, of course, Q, missing from the table of phonemes. Derived from the form of the cleaver, Q designates the action of cutting and, more generally, "any dividing up: it is from this last meaning that this letter got the name it bears in French" — a cleft in which the motivational instinct finds its niche.[63]

The motivational instinct will crop up one last time in Gébelin in connection with the order of the letters in the alphabet. This bright idea seems to have to come to him as an afterthought, for it appears only in the *Histoire naturelle* of 1776. We have seen that for de Brosses the arrangement of the alphabet corresponded approximately to the order of acquisition of vocal sounds by the individual and the species. Gébelin's interpretation is more complex and more ambitious in its symbolism. Here is the entire passage:

It only remains for us to point out the reasons that may have determined the assignment of these letters to the order in which they were arranged. A was placed at the head {*tête*} as the highest of the sounds, and as the designation for man, head {*chef*} of everything.[64] T, designating perfection, the end, had to bring up the rear. This final letter, being a strong intonation, easily attracted the other strong intonations to its side: consequently, N, P, Q, R, S, the strong intonations, were placed near the end of the alphabet, while the weak intonations B, C, D, G, etc., are at the head right after A. Let us add that the weak intonations designated large objects: B for building, G or C for camel, D for door of the house, etc., so that they had to be placed together. The strong intonations also had to be placed together because they designated parts of the human body: O for the eye, P for the mouth, R for the nose, S for the teeth, etc. It is not at all surprising, either, that several letters often exchanged their pronunciation and value; that T and Th changed their places; that D and S exchanged their values, as did F and P; that the French X replaced the Greek X, though it is pronounced differently, the Greek letter being an aspirated K, because these letters never differed from each other except in slight nuances of pronunciation. Quite far from being surprised at these slight changes, we should be surprised instead that after so many centuries and so many revolutions the ancient alphabet has altered so little that it lives on among us in only slightly different form. This is because man is imitative, and because he always adheres as closely to his model as he can.[65]

As we have been able to observe on several occasions, Gébelin's work, in which the share of hermeneutic frenzy is quite visible, is characterized by a tight alliance between the most rigidly systematic mind and the most offhand inconsistency. This alliance is sometimes troublesome for the reader but less paradoxical than it appears, since a certain inattention in the application of principles is often necessary in order to safeguard them. The principles displayed in the *Origine* show an ambition rarely attained in the history of the linguistic imagination: not only is a mimologism of writing added to the traditional mimologism of speech, as previously in de Brosses, but it is extended to the very characters of phonetic writing in a heroic attempt to make them agree with each other and, as it were, to make the paths of phonic imitation and graphic imitation coincide. The Cratylian utopia culminates here in what Gébelin, still more intrepid than Rowland Jones, does not hesitate to call a hieroglyphic alphabet. And this alphabet is hieroglyphic not merely as a list of written characters but

113

also already as a collection of phonemes. Not only all writing systems but all linguistic signs are "hieroglyphics." According to Gébelin, the language system is like a generalized ideomimography in which the symbolic relation, transparent and unbroken, circulates constantly between the "thing" perceived, the perceiving organ, the spoken word, and the written word. At the same time, O is—all in one—the sun, light, an eye, a star design, a cry of admiration and of pleasure. This has a gratifying circularity but a dangerous one, too, as Socrates previously warned, since the very distinction between sign and thing tends to disappear— such being the well-known risk of overly perfect imitation—and with this distinction, perhaps, every kind of difference. Innocently, Gébelin caresses a dream, with somewhat incestuous implications (as we have briefly seen) of a return to the womb (maternal, of course) of "earliest" indifferentiation. This totalizing mimologism is in a certain way *just short* of language—or even of birth itself.

CHAPTER 8

Onomatopoetics

⊛ From 1808 (the first edition of *Dictionnaire des onomatopées* {Dictionary of onomatopoetic words}) to 1834 (*Notions élémentaires de linguistique* {Elementary concepts of linguistics}), the philological activities of Charles Nodier span a good fourth of the early nineteenth century.[1] Perhaps we need to go back even a bit further if we allow, as he was later to aver, that the *Dictionnaire* was written five years before its publication.[2] In any case, we have no reason to be suspicious of the description he gives of the background and motivations of his enterprise, on a page from the second edition of 1828: "My initial studies were devoted to the philosophical investigation and analysis of natural languages. Very early on, I had dreamt of plans for perfecting grammar and achieving unity in the language system, from which I quite naturally thought a great amelioration of society would ensue — the eternal peace of Abbot Saint-Pierre and the universal confraternity of peoples. All that was needed to accomplish this childish utopia was an alphabet that I had invented and a language that I was in the process of putting together. I tossed the basic ideas of my method into a published book [the *Dictionnaire*] ... and boldly pursued my ambitious career, for there were no obstacles whatever to the ventures of an eighteen-year-old and no limit at all to his powers."[3]

These few lines situate Nodier's work squarely within the ideological climate of the preceding century, and the *Archéologue* {The archaeologist} of 1810, which is probably very close to his initial intentions, refers to de Brosses and Gébelin, among other precedents, in a tradition transmitted to the author by his teacher David de Saint-Georges. De Brosses and Gébelin are quoted several times in the *Dictionnaire* and in *Notions*,[4] and the obvious continuity is also confirmed by the very Gébelinian subtitle of the latter work: *Histoire abrégée de la parole et de l'écriture* {Short history of speech and of writing}.

Even so, one prime difference shows a crucial change in attitude: whereas in de Brosses, and still more in Gébelin, the mimetic principle of the language system culminated in writing (in theory for the former, in both theory and practice for the latter), in Nodier we are going to see the mimetic principle turn its course back entirely toward speech. That characteristic feature, the word "painting," which continually serves to designate the mimetic relation between words

115

and things, very nearly disappears from the lexicon. Admittedly, the principle of imitation continues to preside over the origin of both oral and written language systems: "The names of things, when spoken, were an imitation of their sounds, and the names of things, when written, were an imitation of their shapes. Onomatopoeia is thus the type of spoken languages, and the hieroglyph is the type of written languages."[5] But unlike his predecessors, Nodier does not think that the "real" (ideographic) writing system holds a large place in history; its theoretical superiority is too quickly undermined by its practical drawbacks, which force it to yield to the writing system based on letters: "The strange multiplicity of its signs, and the arbitrary vagueness of their figurative acceptations, make investigation too time-consuming and difficult for a society that burns with impatience to advance from discovery to discovery and that conquers ideas and new sciences every day."[6] This being the case, the main part of the expositions devoted to the writing system will consist of a *critique* of the alphabet.[7]

Nodier does not in any way pursue the dream of a "hieroglyphic" alphabet in which the letters would directly represent objects at the same time as they transcribe sounds. The phonetic writing system is indeed for him a representation of vocal sound and speaks to thought only "through the intermediary of the ear, by reminding the ear of the spoken word."[8] For him as for de Brosses, a good alphabet would therefore be an "organic" or phonomimetic alphabet, and he is pleased to discover a few traces of it in the Greek writing system, the remains of an anterior, more fortunate state of the syllabic or "radical" writing system, halfway between ideography and phonematic alphabet: "Thus, the *xi* [ξ] of the Greeks has the figure of the saw whose whirring sound it expresses; their *psi* [ψ], which reminds the ear of the arrow's whizzing sound, figuratively represents it accurately to the eyes; and their *theta* [θ], which is the onomatopoeia for a sucking action, represents a breast with its nipple."[9] Even in our Latin alphabet, which has become totally "monogrammatic" (phonematic), a few letters preserve for Nodier the value of a "rational sign" that awakens "the idea of sound through a visual analogy and which might be called its *rebus* and its hieroglyph."[10] In this way, "the serpentine figure of the S and the Z, the T that resembles a hammer, the B that represents the lips in profile and paints the lips forming it, the O that grows round under the pen as the mouth grows round at the moment of its utterance, are very rational signs because they are expressive and picturesque."[11] Others are the Greek φ and the French *f* (lower-case cursive), a "hieroglyph that expresses the snake, which this consonant paints to the eye at the same time as it expresses the snake's breathing {*souffle*} or its hissing {*sifflement*} to the ear."[12] These detours through a "rebus"[13] (the saw, arrow, breast, hammer, serpent) should not lead us to assimilate Nodier's whole interpretation of certain elements of the alphabet to the one proposed by Gébelin: the function of the letter here is not the mimesis of extralinguistic objects but actu-

116

ally that of vocal sound, even though we have to pass through the representation of an object which produces an analogous sound. The letter is an indirect hieroglyph of the sound. This mimesis, phonographic in function, ideographic in method, synthesizes Wachter and Rowland Jones, de Brosses and Gébelin, into an especially clever (but, let us remember, highly limited) form of *visible speech*.

The alphabet, then, is not lacking in mimetic potential, and it would not be impossible to forge an "organic" writing system by borrowing from various existing alphabets their most *eloquent* {*parlants*} characters; we will meet with this hypothesis again further on. But the principal defect of the present-day phonetic writing system lies elsewhere, and it is more radical: "There is no good alphabet; I will go further: ... there is no alphabet. We cannot really give this name to the haphazard mixture of vague, ambiguous, inadequate signs of which all alphabets are composed."[14] This condemnation should not be seen simply as a hyperbolic opinion. The defining principle that it supports is energetically explicated elsewhere: "Ambiguous signs are not legitimately signs." In other words, the sign can be only a one-to-one correspondence, linking without excess or deficiency *one* signifier and *one* signified, and the alphabet would be a genuine system of signs only if each letter corresponded to one single phoneme and vice versa.[15] This is not the case, and in every known natural language the alphabet is not a coherent system but a veritable chaos. "To define orthography as *the art of representing sounds by picturesque signs proper to them* would therefore be an absurdity, for man almost completely forgot his spoken word while composing his alphabet. There is incoherence everywhere and, so to speak, an antipathy between the elements of his language as uttered and the elements of his language as written."[16]

This criticism, which foreshadows the well-known passages in Saussure's *Course in General Linguistics* on the "discord between the written form and sounds," supports its argument with an examination of the French alphabet, taken as an example of the defects of all the others.[17] According to Nodier, the French language has fourteen vowels, yet "we know how to write only five of them, that is, a little over one third." We have a letter for the sound *e* in *patrie* {homeland} but not for the sound *eu* in *heureux* {happy}: "Thus, the insignificant and dubious vowel sound has a letter in the alphabet, and the positive and determinate vowel sound has none." There is no letter either for the sound transcribed by "our so-called diphthong *ou*, a complex sign of a very simple vowel";[18] the same situation pertains to the nasal vowels transcribed as *an, en, on, un*. Conversely, "if, of the fourteen vowels of our alphabet there are nine that have no proper sign, we can flatter ourselves, by way of compensation, that we have several vowels overabounding with artificial signs": thus, the sound *o* "is represented in French in forty-three ways, and I may well have forgotten to count some of them." As for the consonants, C has a double value, guttural or sibilant, the latter competed for by the S, the former by K and Q, with Q receiving yet another value when it combines with a U, "so that this unfortunate sign Q, which recommends itself neither by its name nor by its shape nor by its origin, since it does not even have the distinction of being Greek, fulfills two different functions without a particular aptitude for either one of them, a situation that may indeed be found outside the field of linguistics." The "shhh" sound has CH for its digraph {in French}; the "labio-dental" fricative has PH in competition with F; X is ambiguous, being theoretically the equivalent of *ks,* but *gz* in *exempt, ss* in *Bruxelles* {Brussels}, simple *k* in *excès* {excess}, *s* in {French} *six, z* in *sixain* {sestet}, and nothing at all in *dixme* {a tenth}: "All told, we have found for the sign X, which is not a sign, seven different acceptations, one of which is negative." Again, the ambiguous sign is not a sign, and the system of signs in which certain ones (the majority) are not signs — is not a system of signs. Ergo, the French alphabet does not exist, nor for that matter does any other. Notice that here Nodier is more severe than Saussure, who at least grants the merit of rigorousness to the ancient Greek alphabet, in which "each sound unit is represented by one symbol, and conversely each symbol invariably corresponds to a single sound."[19] In Nodier's injustice we can see the resentment of the disillusioned mimologist, a resentment that is expressed elsewhere through invective: "The letter is the most sublime of inventions; the alphabet is the most stupid of turpitudes."[20]

The perfect or "philosophical" alphabet — one that is both rigorous (one letter per sound) and *rational* (each letter *imitating* a sound, as Wachter claimed) — therefore exists nowhere, but it could and hence it should exist; consequently, it must be invented. Such a plan typically falls within the province of secondary mimologism, and we know that it reiterates de Brosses's proposal (among others) of an organic alphabet. Nodier is aware of this, too, as he mentions de Brosses's proposal in his 1810 Prolegomena to the *Archéologue,* whose very title is borrowed from de Brosses. One might then wonder why he is not content with one or the other of the tablatures of the *Traité de la formation mécanique des langues:* the reason is probably that Nodier, as we have seen, has not given up the hope of drawing an equally useful tablature solely from the resources of various existing alphabets, resources partial and disorganized and everywhere blighted by the incoherence of the alphabetic systems. Whatever the case may be, this plan, announced in 1810 and taken up again in 1824, would never see the light of day, and despite the hint quoted above ("an alphabet I invented"), we cannot be positive that he even fully conceived it. But this alphabet is above all valuable *as a plan,* and it is worth lingering awhile over its successive formulations. Here is the one in the *Archéologue:* "A philosophical alphabet must offer, within the distribution of the signs of which it is composed, a kind of implicit history of the phenomenon of speech; that is to say, its signs must be positioned in accordance with the order of their mechanism and the simplicity of their arti-fice, beginning with the scale of the vocal letters [= vowels], and ending with the consonants that are the most difficult to utter. It must allocate clearly de-fined usages to signs: that is, it must allow neither two acceptations for one sign nor two signs for one acceptation, and it must neither represent a single sound by a compound sign nor a compound sound by a single sign. Finally, as far as possible, it must assemble a number of signs equal to the number of sounds that mankind has agreed to employ in language and that have been part of a stan-dard natural language, either ancient or modern."

Clearly, the point here is a universal phonetic writing system, including all the sounds existing in all natural languages. Clearly, too, the requirement of graphic mimesis is not yet formulated; on the other hand, the philosophical alphabet has to fulfill another criterion, the very one de Brosses found approxi-matively realized in the Latin alphabet: the order of the alphabet must figura-tively represent {figurer} an "implicit history of speech," or reproduce the order of acquisition of phonemes by the individual and by the species. This require-ment crops up again in the 1834 plan of a "grammatory" {grammataire}, put forward along with others in the last chapter of Notions under the characteristic title "Ce qui reste à faire dans les langues" {What remains to be done in natu-ral languages}: "A universal alphabet, a comparative alphabet, a philosophical alphabet of natural languages, in which all the vocalizations and articulations of the speech organ were classified in their natural order and represented by well-characterized, well-analyzed, and properly agreed-upon phonographic signs, would be a magnificient introduction to the study of all natural languages taken separately; and I do not hesitate to say that this alphabet (or, speaking more exactly, this grammatory), uniquely suitable to our European languages, would also be one of the most important monuments of civilization."[21] Of course, the "natural order" is the order of acquisition. Here again, the mimetic principle remains unformulated, or formulated in a timid and ambiguous manner; but already in chapter 8 Nodier had unequivocally expressed his preference in the following terms: "The adaptation of the sign to articulation is a very easy opera-tion, since it is arbitrary, every conventional sign being as good as another for its signification, when it is clearly defined and accepted by unanimous consent. Yet the rational sign is to be preferred and will not cost us more trouble to write out."[22] According to Nodier, then, the philosophical alphabet will imperatively be both historical and systematic, and preferably rational: that is, mimetic.

However, no more than de Brosses does Nodier intend to have this ideal dream of an alphabet adopted as practice in the current writing system. Like de Brosses's tablature, Nodier's would be only a scientific and technical aid: "An alphabet of this sort, whatever the degree of perfection to which it might be brought, would never enter into everyday use, and we would need this alphabet only as an instrument of understanding and a means of communication for natural languages."[23] Even more, far from wishing for a more "phonetic" writing system, Nodier is an intransigent opponent of any reform of French orthography in this direction. The reason for this is simple, and easy to guess besides: our modern spelling system, phonetically inept, is nevertheless excellent evidence for the phonics of the past and hence an excellent etymological index. Now etymology is the key to meaning: "What orthography has to preserve is not a short-lived pronunciation, . . . it is the filiation of the word, without which no word has a fixed signification."[24] Thus, between the two main direct heiresses of Latin, the cultural superiority of French over Italian stems from the fact that French has much better preserved the "aphonic but etymological letters" that in everyone's eyes demonstrate the radical filiation of its words. The conclusion is that "the oldest orthography is the best, which does not prevent it from being faulty."

Mimography in Nodier, then, no longer exists except in the state of erratic traces or aborted plans. The mimetic principle returns to the ground it occupied in Plato, Saint Augustine, or Wallis, that of the sounds of speech; but we will see further on that this does not mean simply a journey backward.

ⓔ Paradoxically enough, for Nodier the idea of an "organic" and natural language system does not entail that of a universal primeval tongue. In the tenth chapter of *Notions,* dreaming of the "pure gold" that the etymologist, who represents the alchemist of language for him, might find at the bottom of his crucible, Nodier takes care to specify: "I am far from believing that this philosopher's stone of etymology would be the primeval tongue. The tongue spoken in the earliest tribe of man expressed such a small number of necessary ideas that if it has remained in its radical form somewhere, it has done so in a very small number of words. Its discovery would be a highly interesting event that would confirm, I have no doubt, my theories on the way in which all natural languages were formed, but this perhaps would not add even ten important ideas to the philosophical history of speech. The family of words that would remain in all natural languages, after this amicable restitution *quarum sunt Caesaris Caesari,* would not be the primeval tongue in absolute terms; it would be the autochthonous language of each country—that is to say, the primeval tongue proper to each."[25] For the notion of a *common primeval tongue* he thus substitutes that of *autochthonous natural languages,* which presupposes an original differentiation, a natural heterogeneity of languages. This upsets (without erasing) two complementary myths: that of the Adamic language and that of the scattering of Babel[26]—which is to say, the myth of an *ulterior* and *unforeseen* differentiation. Languages are at once natural and diverse.

However, this very novel inflection proceeds from a nearly imperceptible displacement in the line of argument, or rather in the mimologist counterargument that we previously encountered in Gébelin. For him, as for de Brosses also, the hypothesis of a common primeval tongue was inevitably linked to the mimetic principle. Simply, the diversity of aspects or "qualities" of each object would open up from the beginning the possibility of several names for the same thing. The relationship of interlinguistic equivalence (translation) between French *Dieu*, Arabic *Allah* and English *God* would refer back to a relation of synonymy (denotative, with connotative nuances) between these same words, or their "roots," in the common primeval tongue in which their coexistence was exactly of the same type as the one de Brosses pointed out, in the Latin language, between *sacerdos, presbyter, antistes, pontifex*, and *praesul*, or, in French, between *région, province, contrée, district, pays, état*, and so on. The plurality of (present-day) natural languages thus issued from the richness of the originary language, and this itself stemmed from the multiplicity of aspects of the extralinguistic referent; in other words, this plurality was purely and simply neutralized, at least at this phase and at this level. It cropped up again further on as the diversity of the *pronunciation* of basically homogeneous lexical material, and it is here that the influence of setting and climate intervened, through a determinism at once causal and analogical. But quite plainly, the difference (of "pronunciation") between, let us say, *Deus* and *Dieu*, which reflects a difference of environment between Latium and the Ile-de-France, has nothing to do with the difference between *Dieu* and *God*, which reflects a difference of aspect between the divinity as light and the (same) divinity as goodness. What is *proper* to each people (its setting) produces only a slight and quite superficial modification ("pronunciation"). As for deep and distinctly *radical* differences, these are already contained in the primeval language, and consequently, they do not affect its unity in any way; one might even be prepared to say that they confirm it.

Diversity in the aspect of the things named, diversity in the situation of the peoples doing the naming: these two motifs are found again almost unaltered in Nodier — but instead of being separated and acting separately and in distinct points of the mechanism of language, they will join and combine their effects, with a resulting radical modification of the system. Here is approximately how this strategy functions in *Notions*. First, in its pure state, the argument of the diversity of aspects is as follows:

It should not be concluded ... that the earliest natural language would have had to become universal, and that all natural languages succeeding it would have had to be identical because they were cast in the same mold and obeyed the same mode of formation. If one were to accept this hypothesis, man's intellectual will would no longer count for anything in the act of naming things, and it would not enter into the designs of the Power who gave him the spoken word as an explicit sign of intelligence. It is only that the simpler the perceptible nature of the creature and the less varied the aspects it offers to the mind, the more noticeable will be the conformity between the radicals that the different natural languages applied to the denomination of the same creature. Animals with only one cry have, so to speak, only one name throughout the world, but these polyglot homonyms are rare, as are their types. On the contrary, it will come as no surprise that the nightingale has received ten names with different roots, since the patient bird lover Bechstein — the German Dupont de Nemours — has taken the trouble to represent up to twenty articulations belonging to it.[27]

Then, ten pages further on, the same argument appears, this time linked to the theme of the natural dispersion of national peoples: "It does not follow from this system that all creatures ought to be designated by universal homonyms, because for this it would be indispensable for each creature to offer in itself only one single character and to be potentially judged by only one single sensation, a ridiculous limitation. Customs, inclinations, habits, susceptibility to impressions: all these are of great consequence in the function of the person doing the naming, as are the perceptible aspects, forms, qualities, behavior in the object named, and as are the place, time, circumstances in which the name emerges." Thus, the multiplicity of aspects of the object "named" translates into a multiplicity of denominations only when it meets and agrees with the multiplicity of attitudes of the "persons doing the naming": that is, different national peoples. Far from containing the whole subsequent lexicon in germ, as Gébelin assumed, the primeval tongue — which is no more than the language spoken "in the earliest tribe of man," as we have seen — was an impoverished language,[28] expressing a "small number of necessary ideas." And in one sense, every "autochthonous" language is impoverished: the richness of the lexicon, corresponding to the variety of aspects of reality on one hand and to the variety of human situations on the other, cannot be found except in the sum total of existing natural languages.

Under the decisive influence of its setting, then, each people works out not only its characteristic "pronunciation" of a universal language, as Gébelin claimed, but in fact its own language, distinct from all the others in what is for Nodier, as for the entire Cratylian tradition, the *heart of natural language:* the lexical material. This is a cardinal difference and one that ought not to be obscured by the evident kinship of tone between the following passage from Nodier and Gébelin's comments on the same subject:

Every people, then, made its language as a single man, in keeping with its organization and the predominant influences of the settlements it lived in. Quite naturally, the outcome of this was that the languages of the Orient and of the South generally would have been limpid, euphonic, and harmonious, as if they had received the impress of the transparency of their sky and had been married through a marvelous concord to the sounds

122

that emanate from the palm trees swayed by the wind, to the trembling of the savannahs that bow down and lift up the forehead of their undulating harvests, to the rustlings, to the hummings, to the whisperings which the growth of a quick, exuberant, and fertile life supports in a countless multitude of invisible creatures under the enameled tapestries of the earth. In its resonant syllables Italian rolls the rippling of its olive trees, the cooing of its doves, and the skipping murmur of its little cascades {*cascatelles*}. In contrast, the languages of the North show the effects of the energy and the austerity of a harsh climate. In their raw and clashing vocabularies they merge with the cry of the cracking fir trees, with the rumbling rush of crumbling rocks, and with the downward crash of the falling cataracts. Consequently, there is no primeval and innate language for the human species at all, but as many innate aptitudes for composing a language, and as many languages that are more or less different from each other, as there are autochthonous societies: that is, societies attached to a particular soil. It is for this reason that the confusion of tongues and the scattering of peoples are presented by the Scriptures as two synoptic events in the magnificent story of Babel, which we might perhaps be allowed to see merely as one of those sublime parables so frequent in sacred writings.[29]

For Nodier as for Gébelin, and even more so, geographic influence considerably outweighs the mechanical action of climate: the transparency of the sky, the murmur or crash of waters, the rustling of plants, the buzzing of insects, and the song of birds merge into a "marvelous concord" and subtly participate in the working out of the autochthonous language. Another chapter of *Notions* will insist more exclusively on the role of the imitation of animal cries: the famous experiment of King Psamtick, according to an already classic observation,[30] would only prove the influence of the bleating of goats on the spontaneous language system of the savage children whom they nourished, and from that point on no more than "a slight effort" is needed "in order to arrive ... at the belief that the imitation of animal noises was the main element in the beginning of natural languages." This experiment therefore strengthens "the universal opinion of lexicologists, who have always related the invention of our first consonant to the *bique* {nanny-goat} or the *brebis* {ewe}." But the *bique* and the *brebis* do not exist everywhere (why Nodier is careful not to name *chèvres* {goats} and *moutons* {sheep} here is clear), and every phonological system thus depends on its own particular *faunologic:* "In American languages there are strident consonants that are plainly formed upon the hissing of certain snakes unknown in our temperate regions, and the clicking of the Hottentots recalls, so well that it is difficult to tell them apart, a kind of cry peculiar to tigers that *ranquent* {make a "rau" noise}, a properly Latin onomatopoeia that I am borrowing from Buffon."[31]

Climate, countryside, surrounding fauna, characteristic temperament: all this makes each language, although or rather because it is natural, a specific, original, irreducible creation—in the full sense of the term, an *idiom*. We are a long way not only from de Brosses's and Gébelin's universal natural language but also from the linguistic Hellenocentrism of the *Cratylus*. Indeed, there are several languages; none is "barbaric," each is autochthonous, and all are natural. Saussure's argument on the plurality of natural languages is refuted in advance, and with this is ruled out Mallarmé's disappointment at the "diversity of idioms on earth" that prevents us from uttering words "in a single stroke, itself materially truth." Natural languages are not "imperfect in that they are several"; they are several, and they are (or at least they were) perfect. And it is probably not forcing Nodier's thought to add: they are perfect because several. For the "truth" is multiple, and it is the "single stroke" that would be a sort of lie here. The truth of the language system, the "appropriateness" of names, does not lie in the univocal nomenclature mythically produced by Adam, assigning every name to every creature in the presence of the Creator; it would instead lie in this "confusion," this plurality of tongues of which Babel, a *felix culpa*, is the misunderstood symbol.

Clearly, this is paradoxical in relation to the entire previous tradition,[32] which so strongly (and so unwisely) connected the naturalness of the language system to its original unity. Nevertheless, this mimologism of Babel, or the mimologism of idioms, corresponds to another deep temptation of Cratylism, which is to naturalize and to *mimeticize* everything, and hence also the present-day diversity of ways of speaking. If language is the mirror of the world, it is equally seductive to make it reflect the variety of settings and the colorful medley of races, and to see in each natural language the faithful image of a people's individuality. Unitarianism and pluralism are the two opposite and complementary postulates of mimologism, and the emphasis shifts from one to the other according to external pressures on its internal equilibrium. Between the strongly pluralist inflection mimologism receives in Nodier and the *nationalist spirit* that permeates the new European movement of Romanticism, the relation is plain enough: the same spirit is at work in Wilhelm von Humboldt's *Sprachphilosophie* at the same moment, and we will see that it is not alien to the very birth of comparative grammar.[33] Each natural language describes a countryside, tells a Story and expresses a *genius*, all specific and linked to one another by a "marvelous concord." Every idiom is the condensation of a folklore.

ⓑ In Nodier, the mimetic theory of speech or of the language system as *onomatopoeia* is not grounded on a phonetic analysis as complete and precise as that in de Brosses and Gébelin. The assimilation of the vocal organ to a musical instrument is repeated in full: the speech organ is a "keyboard, a string and wind instrument [that possesses] ... in its lungs an intelligent and sensitive bellows; in its lips, an outward-curving, mobile, extensible, retractable rim that projects the sound, modifies it, reinforces it, makes it supple, constrains it, veils it, quells it; in its tongue a supple, flexible, sinuous hammer that curls itself up, shortens itself, stretches itself out, that moves around and interposes itself between its valves, depending on whether the voice is to be held back or poured forth, that attacks its keys fiercely or skims over them idly; in its teeth a solid, pointed, strident keyboard {*clavier*}; in its palate, a low-pitched and resonant tympanum."[34] But in Nodier the breakdown of the sounds and the articulations is much more careless and does not aim at a system. The same goes for his dictionary of their symbolic values.

As an individual or a species,[35] man begins with the vowel: "His linguistic expression was at first simply vocal, like that of the animals, which merely happen upon poorly articulated consonants in their bellowing, mooing, bleating, cooing, hissing."[36] This comparison, it will be remembered, had appeared previously in Gébelin; it agrees more or less with the idea that *b* is borrowed from the bleating {*bêlement*} of flocks. The vowel is therefore the language of the nearest thing to animal instinct in man: "the surge of a desire, instinctual appetite, need, terror or anger."[37] It is the vocal substance of the exclamation or the interjection: in short, the cry. But it is nonetheless the vowel that marks "the shift from the state of simple animateness to the state of intelligence. In fact, from that first period, and without any other resource but the vowel or the cry, man rose up, amazingly enough, through the power of thought, to ideas of admiration, veneration, contemplative prescience, spiritualism, worship and religion" — perhaps because the simple cry was enough to express the intensest admiration, which is man's spontaneous feeling in the presence of light, Gébelin claimed, and hence in the presence of the divinity. But the great piece of evidence is that God's name, in the most ancient natural languages, those "of earliest origin," is written entirely in vowels — and if possible, by using all of them: "The sacred word of the Hebrews, which it was forbidden to utter and which was probably quite difficult to pronounce, contained all the vowels of this natural language of ancient days when the vowels were not written out; and I would really like to know with what *Jovis* was made so long afterward, unless it was with *Jehovah!* — because searching for the *Jesus* of Christianity in the *Zeus* of the Greeks, the *Esus* of Gallic fables, and the *Isis* of Egyptian fables is such a common deduction that it does not even need to be mentioned. It is clear from these examples, however, that the consonant was gradually being introduced into the vocable of ancient times which must have bequeathed it to our Orientals and to our Celts; but this was the most vocalized consonant, the sweetest, the most flowing, and consequently the most primitive consonant that could glide between man's lips, like the warbling of birds, like the zephyr that makes the reeds whisper without ruffling them in its graceful flight." The "divine monosyllable," therefore, at least in its earliest forms,[38] is "the most primeval of all names," since it is as yet merely an exclamation: "the first cry to represent thought," "the first exclamation of admiration to be uttered from a man's heart at the sight of nature," "an immense interjection that embraces all feelings, that contains all ideas. ... Yes, God is the first of all the words produced in the progressive series of words, or all grammar is false."

From animal need to an idea that is at once the most primitive and the highest: such is the repertory of "this age of society's childhood which might be called the age of the vowel." Coming next, opening up the era of *articulated* or *consonantal* but apparently equally childlike natural language[39] (as in de Brosses and Gébelin) is the age of the "first consonant," or the *b*, and by extension all the labials. Rather than reel off examples, here Nodier resorts to statements illustrative of imitative harmony: "I propose that we look for our first lessons by the child's cradle as he tries out the first consonant. This will bound forth from his lips at the mother's kisses {*baisers*}. The *bambino*, the babe-in-arms, the brat has discovered the three labials: he broods, he pouts, he mopes; he babbles, blabbers, prattles, blathers, bleats, blabs, bawls, broods, smacks his lips; he grumbles over a bauble, a bagatelle, a piece of rubbish, something stupid, a baby, a bonbon, a booboo, the cup-and-ball game hanging from the display at the *bambelotier* {baby-goods store}.[40] He names his mother and father with affectionate mimologism,[41] and although he has as yet discovered only the simple key of the lips, his soul already moves in the words which he haphazardly mouths. This Cadmus in swaddling clothes has just glimpsed a mystery as great by itself alone as the whole rest of Creation. He is speaking his thought out loud."

Here, in conformity with the rhetorical usage of the period, "mimologism" is nearly synonymous with *onomatopoeia*. But this nuance in meaning forces us to digress slightly. The *Dictionnaire* defines these two terms as follows: "We have said that the majority of the words of primitive man were formed in imitation of the noises that struck his hearing. This is what we call *onomatopoeia*. Taught how to hear and to speak, he figuratively represented his own vocal noises, his cries, his interjections. This is what we call mimologism." This definition occurs in regard to the word *Haha*, a "mimologism of an exclamation of surprise and, by extension, the name of a barrier or ditch {sunk fence} that appears unexpectedly and wrenches this exclamation from the travelers. There is no other word in the language that so well captures what is understood by mimology."[42] Nodier gives another example of mimology two pages further on with *haro* {hue and cry}: "one of those secondary-formation onomatopoeias called *mimologisms* because they were made in imitation of the spoken word itself." Finally, here is a corresponding definition borrowed from the *Examen critique*: "*Mimologism, mimologic*: these two words have been newly but very usefully introduced into the grammar in order to describe the construction of a word formed upon the human cry. *Huée* {boo!}, *brouhaha*, and so on, are mimologisms or mimological substitutes, and as such they differ from onomatopoeias formed on elementary and mechanical noises, such as *fracas* {crash!} and *cliquetis* {clink}." [43]

Strictly speaking, then, an onomatopoeia is a word created through imitation of an external noise (including animal cries), while a mimologism is a word created through imitation of a human cry, or more usually a "vocal noise." "Mama" and "papa" are therefore not onomatopoeias but properly "affectionate mimologisms," formed from the first bilabial blabberings, or the sucking noises at the maternal breast, or kissing noises. Clearly, the opposition between onomatopoeia and mimologism almost exactly reproduces the one between onomatopoeia and interjection, familiar to theoreticians of the origin of language. But what interests Nodier here is not the relation (of cause and effect, and hence of temporal contiguity) that unites the "object" (a barrier, a mother) with the cry or oral noise it arouses ("ha-ha!" "mama!") but the relation (of analogy) that unites this cry or noise with the word created *in imitation of it* (a *haha*, a *mama*). The specificity of mimologism, in its production, is thus not as radical as one might have at first believed; there are questionable cases, like *brouhaha*, that do not properly speaking imitate any cry, and Nodier sometimes uses one of the terms for the other. In his system, then, mimologism can be considered a special case of onomatopoeia, the latter considered an "imitation of natural sounds" in general.[44] His evident interest in the former, however, and his attention to distinguishing it theoretically are not in the least insignificant: in the actual functioning of natural language, imitation by mimologism is much more *important* for him than imitation by onomatopoeia. Words such as *fracas* or *cliquetis* are not vital to common usage, and Nodier would probably put up hardly any resistance to Saussure's objection, which relegates onomatopoeia to a very limited and very marginal sector of natural language.[45] In contrast, *papa, mama,* and other words we are going to run across constitute for Nodier the true heart of natural language; I mean its rock bottom and its central core. Therein lies what he calls "the *organic language,* the one that is structured on its instruments and that applies through a natural process to all language acquisition, to all forms of thought." [46]

The fact that language "is structured on its instruments" signifies, among other things, that there is no rupture between the cry and the word, between the child's prattling and articulated speech, even between the sheer movement of breathing and the greatest "mysteries" of language and thought. This idea is probably what is alluded to in the somewhat obscure statement: "His {the baby's} soul already moves in the words he mouths." Since the soul is at once the simple breath of life and the highest form of the spirit or mind {*esprit*}, the word *âme* {soul} is a perfect example of a highly spiritual word formed on the most basic "organic" gesture, that of breathing. Quoting Gébelin, the *Dictionnaire des onomatopées* opposes the movement of exhalation in the syllable *am* to the movement of inhalation, and hence of taking possession, produced by the syllable *ma*—whence *am* = spirit or mind; *ma* = matter.[47] For its part, *Examen critique* suggests a slightly different opposition, but one with a corresponding effect, between the exhalation {*expiration*} of *âme* {soul} and the inhalation {*inspiration*} of *vie* {life}: "I do not know which etymologist advanced the idea, more ingenious than it is reliable, that there is here something other than a contraction of the Latin *anima*, to wit, a vivid mimology of *expiration*. In the formation of this word, the lips, barely parted to let the breath escape, fall back against one another, closed and passive. In contrast, in the word *vie*, they part gently and seem to inhale {*aspirer*} the air: this is the mimology of breathing {*respiration*}." [48]

As everyone knows, Bachelard—a great admirer of Nodier, whom he does not hesitate to call, precisely at this point, "our wise teacher"—developed and commented upon this double etymology in a long passage of *Air and Dreams* on the "respiratory dialectic of the words *vie* and *âme*." Bachelard faithfully carries on what one hardly dares, in this context, to call Nodier's inspiration: "If we pronounce the word *âme* in its aerial plenitude and with a belief in the imaginary, at just the right moment, when word and breath are one, then we realize that it takes on its exact value only at the end of our breath. In order to express the word *âme* from within the depths of the imagination, our last reserves of air must be expended. It is one of those rare words that ends as our breath ends. A purely aerial imagination would always prefer that this word come at the end of a sentence. In the imaginary life of the breath, our soul is always our *last sigh* {*dernier soupir*}. A little bit of our soul is reunited with a universal soul." [49]

The age of the labial key, then, is not confined to purely material impressions any more than the age of the vowel was: to one belongs the idea of God; to the other belong thoughts of life and death. The preface to the *Dictionnaire* also assigns to the age of the labial those "essentially primary" ideas "typical of children's minds": not only *to drink, to eat, to talk*, and *family* but also *good* and *evil*. *Notions* extends this repertory further, from the "babbling of the child in the cradle" to the "language system of the first society," which "already embraces all the fundamental ideas of civilization.... Consequently, from that time on, an already complete society is in existence, for it has a fortress raised against God, called *Babel*, a capital city called *Biblos*, a king called *Bel* or *Belus*, a false god called *Baal*, and even a mystagogue who makes animals talk and who is called *Balaam*. Given a few more days, if this society is faithful to its early traditions, its first book will be called *Biblion* and its first empire will be *Babylon*." [50] Such is the empire of the labial.

The next stage is that of dental articulation: this is still an organic mimologism, since it comes from the noise of sucking at the breast. "We are taught how to articulate this letter (*t*), in a way, from the first day of life, since sucking at the mother's breast is necessarily done with a slight clicking of the tongue against the teeth, or rather around the place they should occupy, and since this noise can only be represented by a soft or a hard dental letter."[51] Despite this tender origin, the dental letter marks an advance toward solidity and toughness, even the hardness and harshness of the adult age and of civilization at its height: "Mainly proper to sounds that are tenacious, tonic, tumultuous, to keystrokes, to sustained notes, to intonations, to twitterings, to tinklings, to stirring sounds that require a pronunciation that is strong, loud, strident, and firmly stopped; ... the firmest key, and the most solid keyboard of speech, consists of the teeth."[52] Here we recognize the word image *clavier* {keyboard}, which makes the dental the key {*touche*} par excellence, according to a readily suggested analogy, and as if each tooth produced a specific articulation: even Gébelin himself had not dared this much. But let us pursue this interpretation of the third age: "This period is also the one in which the name of God and that of the father, who always follows Him in the chronological order of words in thought, begin to rely on the dental consonant of secondary natural languages. In its turn, this new discovery imposes the memory of its reign and of its conquests on civilization, which does not cease its onward march as long as the alphabet is incomplete; and it is often here that popular traditions halted when they wanted to go back to the natural origins of speech. This period gave us the *Thoth* of the Egyptians, as also the *Theutat* of the Gauls and the *Thevatat* of Siam, a confluence of homonymies that would be unfathomable to philosophy did not these explanations rationalize them. These Titans of speech were regarded as the inventors of the letter among five or six peoples who designated the linguistic faculty by the name *Tad* or *Taod,* and the human race, forgetful of its primeval history, took them to be gods."

The alphabet is not yet complete, but the effort at reconstituting that "implicit history of speech" which is figuratively represented by a well-formed alphabet stops here. The rest of the text is more erratic. Yet let me quote the following illustration of the lingual consonant, the supreme key of language: "This liquid, limpid, fluid and flowing, flexible and flattering articulation had to lend its pliable elocutionary nature to the elucidation of lexicons, to the elegance of locutions, to all select intellections that rely on eloquence; ... as the principal lever of the language system, as that of logic, of dialectic, and of law, the letter *l* has left its name to language itself."[53] Let me also quote the following interpretation of the aspirated letter *h:* "Taking into consideration the way in which it was formed, which has something assiduously eager and impatiently rapacious about it, one would dedicate it to representing ideas that are related to the activity of seizing or of stealing." And here is Nodier's interpretation of the "rolling palatal" *r,* which "painted for the ear the mechanical noise produced by the circular motion of bodies; and since this sound cannot be rendered through the lingual key by a simple and indivisible motion of the tongue, but only by a rapid and repeated brushing against this instrument, the *r* has become the written character of all signs through which the idea of continuity, of repetition, of renewal has been rendered."[54] Finally, let us cite the following rather subtle motivation for the negative value of *n:* "The written character is quite remarkable. This letter, alien to all the others, formed by another means, has a speech organ located outside the entire ensemble of the vocal instrument. It is the only consonantal letter striking the nasal key and capable of being pronounced with the mouth almost closed, because it does not use the mouth for its path of utterance. Last, it is an unmodifiable consonant that can be neither strengthened nor softened. Thus, it is a unique letter, an abstract letter in a way, a *negative* letter [note this term], and suitable for characterizing all ideas of negation and of nothingness."[55]

Nodier's focus in these phonematic interpretations, let us remember, is still just the mimetic *capacities* of speech. The next question, which will mark the dividing line between primary and secondary mimologisms, is whether the actual lexicon of natural language respects these potentials of phonetic symbolism, as Cratylus believed, or not. Nodier's implicit answer, as it can be gleaned from his comments on imitative harmony, is clearly affirmative, and his explicit answer places him unambiguously, in this regard, in the most progressive wing of the Cratylian party. If natural language were perfect — that is, "adequate to translating one's thought," as Mallarmé will put it — then everyone would be a poet: this extreme hypothesis and its extreme consequences are assumed without hesitation by Nodier at the outset. For him, imitative harmony is so "naively" inscribed in natural language that the problem instead would be to avoid it:

Why would natural languages be so naively imitative, then, if not because imitation created them? Not only do I not view the effects of imitative harmony as a great stylistic problem, but I would find it extremely difficult to name perceptible creatures without making them appear to some degree before my mind's eye. The poet should attempt to do just that: he should make the breezes rustle across the heather, the streams murmur as their waters slowly roll along between the flower-covered river banks, the undulating branches sigh as they sway, as they groan, the fresh foliage tremble and shiver, the turtledove coo or the owl hoot from afar; he should make the plaintive winds lament and roar in fury; he should mingle their fearsome clamor with the muffled rumbling of the tempest, with the crash of the torrents dashed from rock to rock, with the tumultuous fall of the cataracts, with the crack of thunderclaps, with the cries of creaking pines. ... he cannot ever escape the necessity of an imitation that arises from the very elements of speech, and the same applies to all the nomenclatures of natural languages whose secret has been unlocked for man. It can hardly be supposed that the poet has contributed much to the terminologies of the arts and trades, for example; nevertheless, it is equally difficult to speak of these without encountering the true name of things: the arrow vibrates, whistles, and flies; the slingshot ruffles the air and makes a rumbling noise; the tympanum rings out; the tocsin chimes and peals; the fire crackles under water that sputters, bubbles over, and boils; the hammer bangs, the felling axe thuds, the saw grates, the blunderbuss explodes, the cannon roars, and the bronze bourdon shakes and booms. All of this is not really a matter of style, for style would be too easy if it amounted to this; quite simply, we have here speech as man found it and as he drew it from Nature.[56]

Imitation, therefore, lies not only in basic sounds but also in words: the passage on imitative harmony that we have just read is not an artificial exercise in alliterations for its author; it is a repertory of onomatopoeias "found in natural language" and put in context. Again, there is a very noticeable displacement of emphasis in the Cratylian project: the focus of attention no longer falls on the sounds and the letters but on the words themselves. Whence the purpose of the *Dictionnaire*, which manifests — for the first time with such intensity, it seems — an attitude we will find again in Claudel or Leiris, for example: that of the "dreamer on words" {*rêveur des mots*} (to use Bachelard's phrase). Yes, Nodier has "often daydreamed between words and things, all for the joy of naming,"[57] and more than a century before Proust's *Noms de pays: Le Nom* or Leiris's *Biffures*, the *Dictionnaire raisonné des onomatopées françaises* presents a collection of word dreams {*rêveries de mots*}. So strong is the convergence of the two lines of thought that we need to borrow from Bachelard again the most accurate description of the activity (for it is an activity, of course, however passive it may claim to be) developed here by Nodier: "But do we know how to welcome into our mother tongue the distant echoes that reverberate in the hollow centers of words? When reading words we see them and no longer hear them. What a revelation the good Nodier's *Dictionnaire des onomatopées* was for me! It taught me how to explore with my ear those syllabic cavities that constitute the sound structure of a word."[58]

This nearly unobtainable book is no longer read, if it was ever read.[59] I therefore have little misgiving in reprinting here, in alphabetical order, a few items from it, chosen entirely according to what delights me personally. Like any exercise in lexical mimologism, the phenomenon called "suggestion through meaning" is too obvious to dwell on here. To this phenomenon is due, moreover, the interest of the verbal game, in which one pretends to seek and to find what was never lost, or how a signification known in advance invests (is invested in) a sequence of sounds by erasing the conflicting semes or by bending a bit to their demands. There is always a little complacency and bad faith in these semantic compromises, as in many others, and therein lies their seduction. We will be careful, then, not to disrupt the game in any blatant way: we will not ask for the mimology *bise* {north wind} and then for its paronym-antonym, *brise* {breeze}; we will not bring up the Latin etymology of *murmure,* which is the rumbling *murmur* of thunder; we will not disrupt the charming vocalic concert of *oiseau* {bird} by some crudely phonetic written form; we will not contrast *catacombe* {catacomb} with the rustic *combe* {coomb, a hollow}, a word revived by Nodier himself;[60] we will not verify, with an intrusive concern for history, whether or not the catacombs actually contained coffins and tombs; we will not inquire whether or not this onomatopoeia could be made more evocative through some ill-sounding metathesis, like the "witty man" who objected to Banville, saying that if *citadelle* {citadel} is a "great big terrible word," then *mortadelle* {mortadella} really ought to be still more terrible.[61] Here, then, "true" or "false,"[62] are a few French onomatopoetic words from Nodier's *Dictionnaire.*

Achoppement {stumbling}: noise of one body striking another.

Agacement {irritation}, *agacer* {to irritate}: sound used to arouse or irritate animals, or else noise produced by an acidic fruit against the teeth, or a fruit that has not reached ripeness and whose effect is to set one's teeth on edge.

Agrafe {hook}, *agrafer* {to grab}: imitation of the noise produced by the ripping apart of the object which the pointed tips of the grappling hook grab hold of.

Asthme {asthma}: noise of breathing abruptly interrupted.

Bedon {potbelly}: onomatopoeia of the noise of a drum.

Biffer {to scratch out}: noise made by a quill pen passed rapidly over the paper.

Bise {north wind}: a dry and cold northeastern wind that sounds like the noise from which this word was formed, when trembling among dry plants, when lightly grazing stained glass windows, or when gliding through cracks in walls.

Bouillir {to boil}, *bouillie* {porridge}, *brouillon* {muddle}: noise made by a liquid heated up to a certain temperature.[63]

Briquet {tinder}: noise of two hard bodies that violently collide with each other, breaking one into pieces.

Brouter {to graze}: noise made by animals in breaking off plants at the root and tearing them up with their teeth.

Broyement {grinding}, *broyer* {to grind}: noise of a slightly resistant substance when broken up between two hard bodies.

Cascade {waterfall}: the first syllable is an artificial sound that causes the second one to ricochet, and this effect vividly represents the redundant noise of the *cascade.*

Catacombe {catacomb}: the union of these two happily married words produces one of the beautiful imitative effects of the {French} language. It is impossible to find a more picturesque sequence of sounds for rendering the ringing of the casket, gradually rolling down on the sharp angles of the stones and suddenly coming to a halt in the middle of the tombs.

Cataracte {cataract}: raging and noisy waterfall that tumbles down and shatters from rock to rock with a great crash.

Clignoter {to blink}: many onomatopoeias were formed, if not on the noise produced by the movement they represent, at least on a noise determined by the one that movement seems likely to produce, considered in analogy with some other movement of the same kind and its usual effects; for example, the action of blinking the eye, about which he [de Brosses] offers these conjectures, produces no actual noise, but actions of the same kind evoke quite well, through the noise accompanying them, the sound that served as the root for this word.[64]

Dégringoler {to tumble}: noise of a body rolling down from a height.

Éclat {fragment}, *éclater* {to explode}: noise of a hard body violently divided into pieces when punctured, split, broken up.

Écraser {to crush}: This word is generated by a sound analogous to the one that produced the word *éclater* but that represents a less simultaneous breaking apart, and for this reason it is lengthened by the rolling consonant {r}. The crack of chalk bursting apart and being pulverized underfoot reproduces this root very distinctly.

Fanfare: The majority of the wind instruments are characterized by the letter F because this consonant, produced by the emission of air pushed out between the teeth, is the expression of breathing or of whistling. Whence *fanfare,* which is the song of the trumpet.

Fifre {fife}: The vowel squeezed in between the two whistling letters gives a very accurate idea of the high-pitched noise of this instrument, and the rolling ending {-re} registers its somewhat raucous outburst.

Fleur {flower}: noise made by the air inhaled by the organ that draws in the flower's perfumes.

Froissement {crumbling}, *froisser* {to crumble}: noise of creasing when a stiff material is pressed somewhat strongly.

Murmure {murmur}, *murmurer* {to murmur}: perfectly paints for the ear the vague and gentle noise of a brook that rolls over the pebbles in little waves, or of foliage swayed by a light wind to which it gives way tremblingly.

Oiseau {bird}: the construction of this word is imitative in the extreme; it is composed of five vowels linked by one softly sibilant letter, and this combination results in a kind of warbling very appropriate for giving us an idea of the birds. (It should be noticed, as a very rare and singular case in our language, that the word *gazouillement* {warbling} is formed, like the word *oiseau,* from the same vocal sounds, linked by the same consonant. It is distinguished only by its intonation, which is drawn from a guttural letter and is consequently very well suited to the idea it expresses.)

Rincer {to rinse}: noise of the fingers against the inside of a glass that one is rinsing.

Ruisseau {brook}: perfectly paints to the mind's eye the little gentle and continuous murmur of running water as it rolls among the pebbles.

Susurration, susurre, susurrement {whispering}, *susurrer* {to whisper}: Here I venture to suggest these three substantives and this verb as probably quite felicitous latinisms for expressing the trembling of the foliage and the murmuring of the reeds stirred by the wind.[65]

Taffetas {taffeta}: drawn from the noise of the material it designates.[66]

Disregarding alphabetical order, I have left aside the entry *roue* {wheel} in order to discuss it last. Actually, unlike all the preceding entries, this one goes beyond the home territory of onomatopoeia or mimology properly speaking: that is, beyond the territory of the vocal imitation of external or internal noises. As we saw above, for Nodier as for his precursors, the *r* sound is naturally linked to the idea of movement through a well-defined articulatory peculiarity (the "rapid and repeated brushing" of the tongue). Here, the notion of "circular movement" — that is, the linkage established between the movement and the circular form — is perhaps a bit less obvious. The privileged site of this linkage is the wheel, and it is in the mimological analysis of this word that we will see the beginnings of the line of thinking through which the constitution of natural language oversteps the circle of pure phonic mimesis. First of all, with evident care for practical illustrations, Nodier states that this word *roue* comes "from the noise of the wheel and generally from the noise of a round body rolling rapidly over a resonating surface." Several derivations borrowed from Gébelin come next (among others, *rouer* {to put on the wheel or rack, to beat or thrash}, *rotule* {kneecap}, *rôder* {to run in}, *rouler* {to roll along}, *roulade* {a roll, trill}, *roulis* {rolling [nautical]}, *rôle, rotonde* {rotunda}, *rond* {round}, *ronde* {circle}, *route*). Then comes a scholium whose opening sentences I will now quote: "To my mind, this root suggests, besides, a thought that lends support to my theory of the extension of natural sounds to the description of soundless beings. As we have seen, two families of words that are quite distinct from each other, one belonging to the idea of movement and the other to the idea of form, are composed of one radical sound which is the sign of movement, and which itself is effected through the rotation of the tongue on the palate. It was not hard to recognize the point of contact of these two families, and I understood that the sign of noises resulting from a circular movement must have become the indicator of round forms in the language system."

134

Let us pause here: in following the course of this symbolic or exemplary wheel, we are precisely at the limit of the capacities of direct imitation. The *r* sound (apical or dorsal) is the effect of a "palatal rotation {*roulement*}," or of a vibration, or of a beating of the tongue on one point or another of the roof of the mouth. Already contained in this very term *roulement* (as, of course, in the familiar phrase "to roll one's *r*'s") is one of those "phonetic metaphors"[67] that include and anticipate a symbolic interpretation, or that even in some obscure way derive from such an interpretation. In the present instance it does not matter: we have encountered motivations of this type before in de Brosses and Gébelin, including exactly this one, which goes back to Plato, and the entire Cratylian tradition will maintain positively that the movement of the tongue while pronouncing the sound *r* is directly analogous to that of a body rolling along on an incline. But here is something that sounds completely different, and more or less new, at the very beginning of the nineteenth century:

But if the relationship of movements and forms at first seems quite a natural explanation for the resemblance of the expressions that characterize them, it is equally true that nature has established striking harmonies between these two sorts of sensations and sensations of colors. Figurative language offers us adequate proof of this. I have mentioned, among other examples, *dark* groans {*sombres gémissements*} and *piercing* gleams of light {*lueurs éclatantes*}. The first of these turns of phrase presents an idea of noise specified by a condition derived from the order of colors, and the second one an idea of color defined by an epithet belonging to the idea of noise. The famous Saunderson, blind from birth, after having tried for a long time to get an accurate feeling for colors, finally compared the color red to the sound of a trumpet; and just a few years ago the interesting deaf-mute Massieu, when asked about his idea of noises, the trumpet's in particular, unhesitatingly compared it to the color red. If there is harmony between these effects, why would they not have been expressed by the same kind of sounds?

In my opinion, therefore, the word *rouge* {red} and its derivatives are onomatopoeias constructed by extension from the radical sound of *roulement* {rotation}. In Old French, *ro* was said instead of *rouge*, and *roe* instead of *roue* {wheel}. All natural languages could provide examples of similar relationships.

Bernardin de Saint-Pierre has recognized the harmony of circular movement, round form, and the color red. He takes pleasure in supporting this ingenious relationship with the most charming observations, too; and if he has paid no attention to proving that the words designating this movement, this form, and this color among the majority of peoples have a common root, it is probably because this kind of demonstration, borrowed from dull grammatical studies, seemed to him too dry for so elegant and so poetic a subject.[68]

As we ultimately discover to our astonishment, the specific purpose of this mimological speculation, then, is the derivation *roue — rouge,* an expression of the "striking harmony" between roundness and the color red. This harmony is so striking, let us point out, that it needs no other argument except Bernardin's authority, and it exempts Nodier from inquiring into the harmonic relations between circular movement and the sound of the trumpet. But what interests us here is the very idea of a harmony between the sensations of different organs, and especially between sounds and colors. The feeling for this genus of "correspondences" is very familiar to us today, if not entirely clear, and the corroborating testimony of the blind man and the deaf-mute should not surprise us, even if it by no means elicits unanimous agreement; its principle (synaesthesia) is obvious. But the same does not apply in Nodier's time, and we must remember that Gébelin, even though he was so keen on harmonies, did not discuss synaesthesias at all; and that de Brosses himself mentioned "Saunderson's" statements only to reject them out of hand; and that the mimetic deficiency of this kind of derivation (by metaphor) was for him the seed of all linguistic decadence. In contrast, for Nodier as for Augustine, nothing could be more legitimate than these extrapolations, which permit the sounds of speech to imitate — indirectly, of course, but faithfully and without any breakdown of mimesis — even objects devoid of any dimension of sound. The preface of the *Dictionnaire* explains this with great clarity:

> The extension of the radical sounds that express a noisemaking object to sensations of another order is not hard to understand. Among man's sensations, only a certain number are proper to the sense of hearing, but since speech is addressed to this sense, and since it is through this sense that the sign of the object that strikes us is transmitted, all expressions would seem to be formed for the hearing. Sounds by themselves cannot express sensations of sight, touch, or smell, but these sensations can be compared to a certain extent with those of hearing and can be conveyed through their assistance. Moreover, these comparisons contain nothing that is not natural and spontaneous. It is to such comparisons that all natural languages owe their figures, and everything points toward the conclusion that the language system of primitive man was highly figurative.
>
> For example, when we say that a color is loud {*éclatante*}, we mean by this not that a color is capable of producing the sensation of a violent noise on the auditory organ, like the noise expressed by the root of the word

éclatant {*éclat:* explosion} but rather that this color produces on the visual organ a sensation as lively and strong as the one to which it is compared.

The impression made on the organ of taste by acrid, bitter, or sour substances is not accompanied by any noise that would reproduce for the ear the root of these descriptive words, but this root recalls for the organ of hearing impressions that have affected it in an analogous fashion. If one were inclined to think that these ideas are exaggerated and that the mind does not easily make comparisons between sensations, it would be enough to glance at primitive poetries, which are full of such comparisons, or to pay a little attention to an intelligent but simple man. The language of children abounds in figures of this kind, and for lack of the proper word they often use the sign of a different sensation to represent their own. Women, who have a more delicate sensibility and who apprehend the subtlest parallels more quickly, also make wide use of figures. Finally, it can be said that it is so necessary for the senses to operate through each other that without such mutual borrowings we could barely and only imperfectly paint the effects proper to them, and that nothing else makes their perception more exact and more penetrating.[69]

For the moment, let us set aside the typical reference to *primitives, children,* and *women,* given as favorite subjects of synaesthetic sensibility. Clearly, the principle of metaphorical expression here enables one — in a quite "natural" way — *to compare* sensations of different orders: that is, to find their *shared feature.* For instance, between a bright color {*couleur vive*} and a loud sound {*son éclatant*}, the shared quality of *intensity* (a "lively and strong sensation") permits one to posit a homology of the following type: *éclatant : son :: rouge : couleur* {loud : sound :: red : color}, and then to pass via a simple permutation of extremes and middles to a second proportion: *éclatant : couleur :: rouge : son,* which permits us to say "a loud color" {*une couleur éclatante*}, or "the red sound of the trumpet" {*le son rouge de la trompette*}. *Notions élémentaires* will return to the linguistic productivity of this "brilliant faculty of comparing sensations and figuratively representing the spoken word"[70] (plainly, Nodier considers these to be one and the same "faculty"), and to the "assistance which the organs lend each other in order to convey sensations without a name": whence metaphors or "allusions" such as a light that *bursts forth* {*éclate*}, colors that *shout aloud* {*crient*}, ideas that *clash* {*se heurtent*}, a memory that *falters* {*bronche*}, a heart that *murmurs* {*murmure*}, stubbornness that *rears its head* {*se cabre*}. "All of these expressions are onomatopoetic" — but *transposed,* just like *pallid* {*pâle*} music, a *faded* {*décolorée*} imagination, *fishy* {*louche*} explanations, *biting* {*âpre*} pain, *bitter* {*âcre*} kisses. Moreover, the relation of analogy need not be objective and scientifically verifiable (those proposed by "Saunderson" and Massieu, quoted again to this effect, are obviously not). It is enough for the metaphor to have, like the Proustian remembrance, a community of *impression:*

The initial operation of thought, when seized by a new perception, is in fact to compare it with previous perceptions that resemble it, if not by their very nature, at least by the way they affected the soul when they were felt for the first time, and it is this comparison that names the new perception. The more delicate the senses serving the individual organization in which this comparison works, the more instantaneous it is, and such instantaneousness in embracing the relationships of things is precisely what we call the mind. Given this, we can easily see why all flattering ideas have been expressed by fluid sounds, all harsh ideas by rough sounds. The man who witnesses a crime or hears a story about it cries out in the same way as he who burns himself with a hot iron or steps on the tail of a poisonous snake; and his spoken word {*verbe*}, in this case as spontaneous as his cry, paints analogous though different sensations through homophonic, or closely connected, articulations. Natural languages could not have originated in any other way.[71]

The principle of analogy by transposition, which founds metaphor, is therefore "the main facilitating element in the creation of natural languages," just as the principle of onomatopoeia is its organic and mechanical element. The virtue of mimesis loses nothing in the exchange—I mean, in the shift from one to the other—which, besides, is noticeable only when analyzed, since the metaphorical "spoken word" {*verbe*} is as spontaneous as the cry. Unlike de Brosses, and like Augustine before, Nodier plainly holds that a comparison is still an imitation. Consequently, Cratylian desire suffers no setback in the statement of this fundamental law, which sums up the entire Cratylian theory of spoken language: *natural languages name through mimology, enrich themselves through comparison; there is no other way; they do not go beyond these bounds.*[72]

But what is a comparison, or a metaphor, if not a figure, and a poetic figure? The initial progress of natural language, which is the passage from a simple material nomenclature to a genuine intellectual activity, is linked to the poetic capacities of the human mind: "The species would never have reached a positive degree of perfection if it had not been born poetic. To compare ideas one with another, to apprehend instantaneously their finest relationships, to represent them through animated and picturesque names whose acceptations multiply according to the different aspects the mind wishes to give them, this indeed is poetry."[73]

The "species" (and, moreover, the individual) is "born poetic"; it did not become so. Quite the contrary: the poetic power—that is, the aptitude for apprehending relationships and arranging them in figures — is linked for Nodier to that childhood of humanity and of nature when every occurrence was an event and every event a miracle, when man, before all logic and science, "was a poet just by being human, because he could not be otherwise." The poetic power is linked equally if not more closely to that childhood of natural language which is the age of "poverty," or the shortage of words. One of Nodier's favorite themes is that poetry is possible only in a natural language that is poor: "there is no poetry at all without linguistic poverty." "To rich languages belong art and taste; to rich languages belong the luxury of erudition and the profuseness of synonymns. To poor languages belong liveliness of expression and picturesque imagery; to poor languages belongs poetry."[74] Conversely, a poor language "can be nothing else" but poetic because it has to compensate for the dearth of words by the richness of their meanings, which, by definition, are all *figurative* meanings (except one). The earliest natural language, "poor in words, was at least rich in fantastic acceptations, like that coin of the cursed wayfarer, which takes on the impress of the reigning king in every country and which always reproduces itself for all usages. ... Poetic expression was to the first men what a fragment of colored glass is in the kaleidoscope. It changed position and effect with all the emotions that stir the language and lent itself with ever new brightness to all the new combinations of thought."[75] This is recognizably the (pre)-Romantic topos already illustrated in various ways by Vico, Hugh Blair, Herder, Rousseau, and so many others, according to which poetry preceded prose, precisely to the extent that passionate and figurative expression is more "natural" to savages, as to women and children, than the exact language of our civilizations, which require "one exclusive sign for each one of the perceptions of the senses and notions of the soul."[76] Such a language (the very one dreamt of by Leibniz) no longer has anything poetic about it; it is an algebra, and "with algebra, one can only make calculations."[77]

The inflection Nodier gives to this topos — at least in 1834 — reveals an extreme pessimism that is essentially literary, I think, and linked to an intense disenchantment with French Romanticism. For him, classicism is dead and Romanticism has failed. The quarrel between them reminds him of "that between thoughtless children who have an argument over the image of the moon reflected in a pail of water, and who refuse to understand that the moon is not there. The classics have forever lost what the Romantics will never find. Poetry in France has died from the sterile opulence of the language, and from several other causes. It has breathed its last gasps over a small number of lyres that have already ceased vibrating. Everything that inspired poetry has vanished with it. The Gods have departed, and the poets have gone away along with the Gods."[78]

To these disillusioned words we might contrast, among others, a note from the 1808 *Dictionnaire*, which conversely exhibits great confidence in the perpetual renewal of expression, if only the worn-out figures knew how to move aside before the new ones or, better, before the return of the proper word and the literal style, which are, during times when rhetoric is exhausted, the great and supreme resource of the poet:

A new figure is full of charm because it gives a new point of view on the idea. A hackneyed figure, having become a commonplace, is no more than the cold equivalent of the proper meaning. We should therefore avoid lavishly producing figures in a worn-out language. They afford no more than an insipid parade of verbal gestures and rhetorical tricks. That being the case, the purely descriptive style would be preferable to the figurative style because the figurative meaning has for some time caused us to forget the proper meaning, and because the proper meaning appears new to us. Without a doubt, dawn with her rosy fingers, opening the gates of morning, her tears rolling down in moist pearls onto all the flowers, offers a felicitous and excellent image; but today a much greater effect will be produced if one paints the rising sun, covering with unsteady reddening light the high mountain peaks, the mists of the plain as they clear away, the contours of the horizon that stand out against the brightening sky, and the flowers that bend down under the weight of the dew.[79]

This passage contains a sort of precocious manifesto of the "new school"[80] — more lucid than many others that would follow — which explains in one decisive stroke the frequently obscured connection of Romanticism and "realism" by unveiling their shared rhetorical source ("terroristic" in this case; it's all the same): the "effect of Romanticism" and the "effect of realism" here both boil down to a reversal of the figural code. But the dominant tendency in Nodier is not toward this active attitude of the writer determined to reorient and to command the course of his writing. Most often, it is indeed natural language itself that *creates* {*fait*} poetry, in all senses. Basically, for Nodier, there are no poets; there are more or less poetic states of a language, and as he says without further refinement, "poetry has become identified with man's language in general."[81] The two features constitutive of all poetry, *harmony* and *figures*, are equally constitutive of natural language. "The first languages were formed of the most essential elements of poetry: in their physical mechanism they were imitative, and this produced harmony; in their application to abstract ideas they were allusive, and this produced figures. Now as a rule, poetry is harmonious and figurative language."[82] We should really take this last sentence literally: poetry is none other than a harmonious and figurative *language* {*langue*}; it is not a collection of *works* {*oeuvres*} but a state of the language system {*langage*}. Whence that major concept of *a natural poetic language* {*langue poétique*}, which provides the title for the fourth chapter of *Notions élémentaires* and which heralds, albeit misleadingly, the "modern" (if one can call it that) concept of *a poetic language system* {*langage poétique*}. I say a misleading herald because, for Nodier, there is not exactly, as there will be for others later, a "language within the language" that is reserved for or, rather, elaborated by poetic expression. Poetry is natural language itself; for him, the true poems are the *words*, and the true "masterpiece" {*chef-d'oeuvre*} is a simple dictionary.

Ⓔ Of all the distinctive characteristics of Nodier's mimologism discussed above — the emphasis placed on speech at the expense of writing and on the individuality of idioms at the expense of the natural unity of the language system; the (re)discovery of the principle of correspondence, which extends and exalts the mimetic virtues of onomatopoeia through a theory of figures; the displacement of the inquiry from the level of constituent sounds to that of constituted vocables — of all these specific features, some of which revive the ancient tradition and some of which inaugurate or herald, not without conflicts and ambiguities, subsequent variants (Romantic, Symbolist, and beyond), it seems to me that this one, which in a sense includes and sums up all of them, is the most significant and the most important. Nobody before Nodier had identified the fate of natural language so totally with that of poetry, and perhaps nobody after him would do so as unequivocally. In Mallarmé or Valéry, the relation will be at once direct and inverse, since the verse line {*le vers*} corrects (or compensates for) the failing of natural languages; for Nodier that would be a senseless proposition. The verse line, for him, is natural language; nothing needs to be corrected. Consequently, he lends a full and absolute value, in its ambiguity, to the following formula out of which we might construct, in a broader and more abstract sense, the watchword of all Cratylism: "*When [the poet and the linguist] do not agree with each other, it is because one of the two has not understood his art and does not know its scope.*"[83]

But which one?

CHAPTER 9

White Bonnet/Bonnet White

In order to explain the nature of articles, one French grammarian uses a simile that he finds both apt and striking: the article, he says, precedes the noun just as the lictor precedes the consul. If this grammarian had known that the article follows the noun in many natural languages, surely he would have said: In that case, it is a page carrying his mistress's train.[1]

⊗ Up to now, we have encountered forms of mimologism involving only the most elementary levels of linguistic integration: that of phonic or graphic "elements" properly speaking, and that of words. But the question of linguistic mimeticism can also arise, of course, on the larger scale of the sentence. Mimesis at the sentence level can be thought of in terms of an overall *image* (in the Peircean sense), as is sometimes the case in expressivist linguistics. Thus, it is said that a short sentence expresses liveliness, a long sentence expresses vastness, and so on. Mimesis can also be thought of in terms of a *diagram,* or a homological relationship between two sets whose elements do not have a one-to-one correspondence but whose internal relations are identical. In this way, in *veni, vidi, vici* the sequence of the verbs imitates that of the actions though each verb does not imitate each action; and in *The president and the minister took part in the meeting,* the sequence of the two nouns in the subjective case imitates the hierarchical relation between the two persons, whom each noun designates in a purely conventional manner.[2] As presented here, mimesis at the sentence level, whether intentional or not, is objectively indisputable, but such utterances are not very frequent, and the typical subject-verb-object proposition presents a trickier problem. In *The cat eats the mouse* or *Alexander conquered Darius,* the

---

The French title of this chapter is "Blanc bonnet versus bonnet blanc." Idiomatically, *bonnet blanc et blanc bonnet* means "six of one and half a dozen of the other." To the grammarians embroiled in the debate of the Ancients versus the Moderns over correct word order (*rectus ordo*) and natural word order (*naturalis ordo*), however, the question of whether the adjective precedes or follows the noun was of the utmost importance; during the Enlightenment, word order was taken to reflect the degree of accuracy with which language represents the world. Genette adumbrates the comical aspect of this debate: after all is said and done, *blanc bonnet versus bonnet blanc* is "six of one and half a dozen of the other."

construction of the sentence—that is, its word order—can be considered mimetic only if one accepts such premises as "the agent is anterior to the act," "the agent is superior to the patient," and so forth.

Even though Plato makes no mention of it, let us agree that this type of motivating interpretation belongs to the field of Cratylism taken in the broadest sense. We are about to discover this form of mimologism—let us call it syntactical mimologism—in a debate that set the partisans of French (word) order against the partisans of Latin order for over a century. This debate, called the quarrel over *inversion,* has already been analyzed in a variety of ways.[3] I need not point out that this phenomenon will be studied here solely from the viewpoint of the mimological imagination.

℗ The specific context of the debate over inversion is the Quarrel between the Ancients and the Moderns, which entailed a comparison of the respective merits or advantages of two natural languages, French and Latin. A quick review of the origins of the issue seems indispensable here. As is well known, in classical Latin, as in other languages that have nominative inflections, word order in the proposition remains unrestricted: theoretically, *Alexander conquered Darius* can be said as *Alexander vicit Darium, Alexander Darium vicit,* and so on, without damaging intelligibility. In fact, at least in prose, Latin usage privileged certain of the six possible constructions, especially those that put the verb at the end, which Quintilian recommends for their effectiveness.[4] The same goes for the positions of the noun and the adjective: *bonus pater* {good father} is preferred to *pater bonus.* These favorite constructions defined a norm of usage often baptized *rectus ordo* (the right or proper order).[5] On the other hand, the term *naturalis ordo* (the natural order) is applied only to nonsyntactical, enumerative sequences (*asundēta*), either in the name of a principle of progression ("theft and sacrilege" instead of "sacrilege and theft"), or by virtue of a chronological or hierarchical order that is self-evident or customary, of the type "birth and death," "day and night," "men and women."[6] Among the classical grammarians and rhetoricians, not the slightest relation between these two ideas seems to have been recognized, and hence not the slightest mimetic motivation of the *rectus ordo.*

At the end of the Classical Age and the beginning of the Middle Ages, however, usage itself was to undergo a modification, linked to the erosion of the morphological system of the Latin language. Admittedly, until the fifteenth century, medieval French literary language attests in its own way to the survival of classical inflections (at least in the rudimentary form of the opposition of subject-object) and to the preservation of a Latin type of construction: *le filz le pere amet* {the son loves the father}. But vulgar Latin appears to move rather early toward a fixed order similar to ours. Alfred Ernout and François Thomas

give as an example the following sentence from *Peregrinatio Aetheriae* (fourth
to fifth century): "Item ostenderunt locum ubi filii Israel habuerunt concupis-
centiam escarum {And so they found a place where the sons of Israel had a
strong desire for food}."[7] As a result, the *rectus ordo* becomes the determining
order of subject-predicate, interpreted as a "logical" or "natural" order, imitative of the sequential order lent to the objects of thought. Aristotelianism intervenes in a timely fashion, providing this construction with a philosophical basis
and guarantee: the noun must precede the adjective because substance precedes
accident (*prius est esse quam sic esse*), and for the same reason the subject must
come before the verb and the verb before the complement: "The right order
(*recta ordinatio*)," says Priscianus, "requires that the pronoun or noun be placed
before the verb ... because the substance or person of the agent or of the patient,
which is designated by the pronoun or noun, must naturally be anterior to the
action, which is an accident of the substance."[8] Consequently, the grammarians
and commentators of this period came to regard the syntactic constructions of
the classical Latin writers, and especially those of the poets, as artificial and deviant in relation to an *ordo rectus* or *ordo naturalis*—henceforth synonymous—
which was simply and plainly called *ordo* {order} and implicitly, even explicitly,
reestablished, preceded by the ritual formula *ordo est* ... {the order is}, whenever one wanted to decipher some utterance whose original construction had
become obscure; the *ordo* is used in this way by Donatus for Terence, and by
Servius, Priscus, and Isidore of Seville for Virgil.[9] Under the later and somewhat
antiphrastic term "construction," this practice persisted in medieval scholastic
education, and even well beyond, as we will see: "to render the construction"
{*faire la construction*} is actually to arrange a Latin sentence into French word
order—or, more generally, into the word order of modern Romance languages.

The naturalness of this word order is essentially understood to lie in its fidelity
to the (temporal) order of ideas as they succeed each other in the thought process. The metaphysical priority of substance over accident or of subject over
action is transposed into a diachronic anteriority (*prius esse*), and by the same
token the structure of the sentence is assimilated into that of narrative {*récit*}.
The "natural" order of the modern sentence is comparable to a simple or natural
narration, which recounts events in their order of occurrence, and the "artificial" order of the classical Latin sentence is comparable to a literary narration
of the epic type, marked by a beginning *in medias res* and by flashbacks.[10]

This coincidence of French construction and "natural" construction—hardly
the result of chance alone—ought to have furnished a nice theme for ethnocentric self-praise, which, as we know, is often linked to Cratylist discourse. This
motif, however, appears to have remained unexploited for centuries, for obvious reasons: the belated awakening of national consciousness, the respect for the
Ancients maintained in medieval culture and consolidated by the Renaissance

and by neoclassicism, the continuing dominance of categories from Latin grammar even in the study of European languages. For example, despite its title, du Bellay's *Defense et illustration de la langue française* is typical in not attempting any glorification of the French language in the name of its mimetic superiority. Similarly, the *Port-Royal Grammar* devotes its chapter "On Syntax, or the Unified Construction of Words" to the problems of agreement and correctness, and not at all to word order: this "general" grammar is still in large measure a Latin grammar.[11]

ⓑ As I have mentioned, the real defense and illustration of the French language appeared in the context of the Quarrel between the Ancients and the Moderns.[12] As stands to reason, it emerged from the party of the Moderns, and straightaway, the supposed superiority of French word order would form one of this party's favorite arguments.

Pierre Le Laboureur's book *Avantages de la langue française sur la langue latine* {Advantages of the French language over the Latin language}, is chronologically the first of these apologies.[13] Its overall positioning typifies the clever strategies of the modern party: Le Laboureur acknowledges the Latin filiation of French and deduces from this an argument in favor of the latter, in the name of progress and the well-known "advantage of those who come last" (Perrault). In practice, the great weakness of Latin is the "confusion" caused by its "transposition of words"; the highest quality of a natural language lies in clarity, to which contribute both the appropriateness {*propriété*}, or univocality, of its terms and their "appropriate arrangement" {*arrangement juste*}, or faithfulness to the order of thought: "If it is true that spoken words ought to represent thoughts, then the construction of spoken words that most imitates the order of thoughts must certainly be the most reasonable, the most natural and consequently the most perfect. ... When we want to say that a man has carried out some action, we start with that man's name; we go on to the verb signifying that action; and we finish with the name of thing in which this same action was terminated. Thus, we say 'The king has captured the *Franche-Comté*,' instead of the Roman version, 'The *Franche* the king *Comté* has captured.' This order, we observe, is true to what the philosophers are explaining about Nature when they say *actiones sunt suppositorum:* this is an axiom on which everybody agrees and one that makes it clear that an action cannot be understood without conceiving of a subject who causes it, whereas one can conceive of a subject without action." The French, therefore, speak "as they think, and the Romans think differently from the way they speak," unless they actually spoke "differently from the way they wrote": "Their linguistic expression was not a true image of their thought; and when the sign is different from what it signifies, that is a sure stamp of its defectiveness" (clearly, this is a Cratylian valorization). From this argument comes the follow-

146

ing celebrated formula, whose immediate success shows that it was not thought to be comical at the time: "You must remain in agreement with me that Cicero and all the Romans thought in French before speaking in Latin." This risky but striking formulation set the tone for more than a century.

As we have seen, one of Le Laboureur's arguments was that a "construction by interposition" entails permanent obscurity in the worst case, and most often at least a temporary obscurity: frustrated, the mind has to wait for the end of the sentence in order to understand what it is about. Linked here, as they will be for a long time, are two motifs that are by rights quite distinct: *clarity,* and the faithful imitation of thought, which Dominique Bouhours would call *naïveté.* The chapter "The French Language" in *Entretiens d'Ariste et d'Eugène* {Conversations of Aristo and Eugenius}, by such a typically "middle-of-the-road" author, already testifies to the constitution of a sort of vulgate favorable to French. Unlike Italian, which "is more concerned with making beautiful paintings than good portraits," heedless as it is of "that imitation in which the perfection of natural languages as well as that of painting consists," French "represents naively what takes place in the mind"; it is the sole language "that really knows how to paint after nature and that expresses things exactly as they are," and this is so because French is "perhaps the only language that accurately follows the natural order and expresses thoughts in the manner in which they arise in the mind." The Greeks and Romans, for example, "reverse the order in which we imagine things; most often, they finish their sentences where reason dictates that we begin. The nominative, which ought to be at the head of the discourse according to the rule of common sense, is almost always found in the middle or at the end.... Only the French language follows nature step by step, so to speak."[14]

The expression *direct construction* appears with François Charpentier as a rather tendentious translation of the classical *rectus ordo* and one that will become, in this form or in its variant *direct order,* the key formula of the modernist grammarians.[15] As Scaglione says, the title of Charpentier's chapter 30 in *De l'excellence de la langue française* {On the excellence of the French language} is highly peremptory: "That direct construction such as the type found in the French language is incomparably more sound than the inverted construction of the Latin language, and that even the Greeks and the Romans thought so." The Greeks' approval is demonstrated by the order of the first sentence in the *Republic,* the Romans' approval by the very term *rectus ordo,* as interpreted above; further on, we will reencounter these misprisions of testimony, which bring Cicero and Quintilian into alignment with Donatus and Priscus. For Charpentier, the two principal merits of direct construction are clarity, "which is the sovereign perfection of discourse," and the transparency of naturalness, which emphasizes the content of the message by avoiding artificial formal devices: "The orator appears to have troubled himself not over words but only over things, and nothing makes him more likely to persuade us than this apparent simplicity which closely imitates Nature and which encourages us to follow his good faith" — a good faith whose guarantee is precisely the naturalness of the discourse. Natural word order, then, confers a rhetorical advantage. As for the uniformity of this construction, it should not be considered an aesthetic defect: "For there is indeed a difference between the beauties of art and the beauties of nature. The former can sometimes produce distaste, the latter never. Therefore, because the direct construction is a natural beauty of the French language, we should not fear that it might become tedious. Thus, we are not bored seeing the same sun and the same stars every day; we are not bored seeing the same green color reborn in the meadows and trees every year, or seeing the same crystal water flow continually from fountains and rivers, and therein does nature surpass art: we always demand variety of art, and in this we are not always sure of getting what we want; we always expect the same beauties from nature, and we do not find them distasteful." Natural word order also confers an aesthetic advantage, and doubtless a bit more than that, in this perpetuity of natural pleasure.

⊛ Up to this point, the glorification of "direct" word order relied solely, in a completely empirical way, on taking stock of its practical advantages, real or imagined. In Jean Frain du Tremblay, this valorization is integrated into a general theory of language for the first time.[16] Traditionalist on the ideologically fundamental question of the origin of natural languages and modernist in its assessment of it, his *Traité des langues* {Treatise on natural languages} would exercise a great influence over the remainder of the debate and, more generally, over the linguistic philosophy of the eighteenth century. From Augustine, Frain borrows a distinction between the spoken word properly defined and the material of natural language: "The articulated sounds that compose languages are not properly speech; they are merely the voice of speech, as Saint Augustine says somewhere, *vox verbi*. True speech is wholly spiritual because it is pure thought." Material signs ("articulated sounds") have no necessary link with their signification; they are wholly *positive* (conventional) and *institutional*. Yet this institution cannot be human in origin, since any convention, in order to become established, already presupposes a previous language system: "Speech is the means through which men agree upon everything; they therefore would not be able to agree upon speech itself without speech. If one cannot make eyeglasses without seeing, neither can one invent language without speaking."

To my knowledge, this is the first instance of an argument which is found again in Rousseau, Beauzée, and Bonald,[17] to mention a few, and which, indirectly and probably unwittingly, makes the Cratylian theory the only alternative to the theory of the divine origin of language — as was apparently already the case in Epicurus. The only possible Hermogenist logothete is God; without His help, men can come to terms with each other (without speaking) only through a natural language system that institutes itself, as it were, by itself.[18] This sophistical argument (by the same means, it could be proved that no one can learn how to swim, and so on) seems to have carried great weight for a hundred years, and it is undoubtedly part of the mimologist commitment of such enlightened minds as that of Charles de Brosses: the choice was between Cratylus and Yahweh (Condillac alone, or nearly alone, rejected this choice).

As for Frain himself, he clearly lines up with the opposite camp, that of theological conventionalism. But this option, let us recall, concerns only the material signs of which natural language is composed. By contrast, speech, in the movement that constitutes it and wrests it from the materiality of natural language, is and ought to be imitative of thought. It is here, then, that Frain is in his way closely akin to both the Cratylian camp and the modernist theory: words are arbitrary, but their "arrangement" can and ought to be mimetic. For this to be so, it is necessary and sufficient for the order of the sentence to correspond faithfully to that of thought: this is where the French sentence succeeds and the Latin sentence fails — or at least the Latin writers' sentence, "for I {Frain} cannot believe that the Romans ordinarily spoke in that manner. Men naturally speak as they think." The *ordo artificialis* of Latin is therefore merely a "work of art," an unfortunate effect of writing, an aberration of style. In general, human speech is an imitation of thought, it cannot be anything else, and no language can absolutely block this necessity. "There is no natural language in which the words cannot be put into an order and made to agree with grammatical regularity, and in which one cannot consequently speak with that precision which is always accompanied by clarity, and that naivete which never fails to please. When a man clearly sees what he wants to say, when thought is well organized, his discourse follows the order of his ideas, and words assume their places naturally. Now clearness of mind and of conception is not a talent peculiar to men of one country or one language; it is common to men of all countries and all languages, and so, as a result, is clarity of style." Frain thus sets forth in his *Traité des langues* what will become the implicit principle of nearly all eighteenth-century speculation on the *ordo*: conventionalism at the level of the linguistic elements (sounds and words), mimeticism at the level of their "arrangement" — that is, at the level of the sentence and discourse. At the end of this chapter we will come back to the very special theoretical status of this version of Cratylism.

In order to lend this principle of syntactic mimeticism its full force, Frain du Tremblay does not hesitate to minimize the difference between French and Latin, even granting the latter a natural capacity for the mimetic *ordo*. The opposite attitude is exemplified by Abbot Gabriel Girard's *Les Vrais Principes de la langue française* {True principles of the French language}[19] — the major work of French linguistic theory in the eighteenth century and the one whose influence on this point was to be decisive. Already present — within a hair's breadth — is the methodological principle that will preside over the practice of comparative grammar half a century later, to wit, that the essential characteristic of a natural language is to be sought not in its lexicon but in its grammar. But according to a definition that already reflects the privileging of a certain model of linguistic functioning, grammar here is understood to mean not merely the grammatical form given to words by inflection, affixes, and everything that will be termed morphology in the time of Friedrich von Schlegel and Franz Bopp, but rather syntax and, even at that, a syntax reduced mainly to the order of words, which Girard calls the "turn of phrase": "The most conspicuous difference in natural languages is the one that first strikes our ears; it comes from the difference of the words; but the most essential difference appears only to our reflection: it arises from the distinct taste that each people has in turns of phrase and in the modifying concept of word usage. … When this distinctive taste is considered in its universality, then it is what linguistics calls *genius,* with whose nature it is important for the grammarian to be thoroughly familiar." [20] Thus, the central notion of the *genius of a natural language* makes its appearance here, defined, let us note (we will return to this point), as a specific arrangement that is purely formal. For Girard and for all eighteenth-century thought, difference in *genius* — that is, fundamental syntactical pattern — commands both the classification and the filiation of languages.

Classification: "Every natural language has [its genius]; nevertheless, they can be reduced to three kinds, and in this way languages are divided into three classes." In fact, these three classes boil down to two ideal types, the third one constituting only a mixed state. *Analogue* languages "ordinarily follow, in their construction, the natural order and the gradation of ideas: the acting subject goes first, the action accompanied by its modifications next, whatever makes up its object and end after that"; these languages are French, Italian, and Spanish. *Transpositive* languages "follow no order other than the light of the imagination, putting now the object, now the action, and now the modification of the circumstance in first place": Latin, "Slavonian," and "Muscovite" behave in this way.[21] The mixed class, which includes Greek, is the one for languages that have both inflection like Latin and the article like French — which tells us nothing about their construction. But Girard clearly does not attach great importance to this type; for him, the main point lies in the opposition between the first two classes, which represents the confrontation of French and Latin, now theorized and, as it were, idealized.

Filiation: Because this opposition is irreducible and immutable, typology determines genealogy here (in contrast to what will happen in the next century). The difference of genius prevents any relationship of filiation between a transpositive and an analogue language. The principle of the pertinence of syntax recurs here, for the kinship of vocabulary between the two languages, as established by etymology, in no way guarantees the kinship of these languages themselves: "Etymology only proves borrowings and not origin.... We should not, therefore, pay too much attention to either borrowings or etymologies when investigating the origin and the kinship of languages; we should concentrate on their genius, following step by step their development and changes. The fortunes of new words and the ease with which the words of one language pass into another, especially when peoples mingle, will always put us off the track on this subject, whereas genius, independent of the speech organs and as a result less susceptible to distortion or change, holds its own amid the inconstancies of words and preserves a language's true pedigree." From this general principle ensues an inevitable consequence, the absence of kinship between French and Latin: "The difference in construction stands in the way of the opinion of those who contend that French, Spanish, and Italian are daughters of Latin.... Observing ... these living languages adorned with articles, which they could not have derived from Latin, in which there never were any, and finding these languages diametrically opposed to the transpositive constructions and to the inflections of ordinary cases found in Latin, one cannot claim, on the basis of a few borrowed words, that these languages are its daughters, unless one wants to give them more than one mother." [22] Hence, there can no longer be any question, as with Le Laboureur, of a linguistic advance by which French would benefit in relation to its imperfect ancestor; all the lines between Latin and French are cut, and since the latter is apparently in need of a "mother," all (other) paths are opened up to speculation, some traces of which we will encounter further on.

This radical separation—whose extravagance we can hardly take credit for recognizing [23]—also commands for Girard what was then deliberately referred to simply as *method*: that is, the method of teaching languages. Here we find one of the early French reactions—if not the first one—like Wallis's, against the tyranny of the Latin model in the teaching of French grammar. Girard actually congratulates himself on the fact that his classification, by loosening

the bonds by which our language is attached to Latin, (might) provide an opportunity to break the chains under which French method now labors— chains so strong that no one has yet undertaken to burst them asunder. Everything published on this subject has been couched solely in a docile tone, submissive to the lessons of the early schools: no one has wanted even to entertain the possibility of proposing a model other than the Latin rudiments of secondary school.... Grammar must form its definitions on the nature of things, draw its precepts from the practice and from the proper genius of the language that it treats, and must especially avoid that common pitfall of adapting for analogue languages what is suitable only for transpositive ones. ... In general, grammar is neither the Latin method nor the French method nor that of any particular natural language; rather, it is the art of treating each language according to its usages and its proper genius. Let us free ourselves, then, from the habit of discussing grammar exclusively after the Latin taste, since other tastes may be applicable to this art; and since each one of them has its suitability depending on the different genius of the languages, these tastes neither can nor should be substituted for one another.

Clearly, this declaration of independence for the "French method" is accompanied by a solemn recognition of the rights of every natural language to its own proper method, and by a warning against any reverse excesses. These cautions were all the more necessary because a backlash had already manifested itself in *Exposition d'une méthode raisonnée pour apprendre la langue latine* {Exposition of a reasoned method for teaching Latin}, the early work of the philosopher-grammarian and future collaborator on the *Encyclopédie*, César Chesneau Du Marsais.[24] The most important feature and innovation of this method is the emphasis placed on what Du Marsais calls "routine," or practical language learning through direct contact with texts, as opposed to "reason," which is the theoretical study of structures and rules. But in the present case such a method runs up against the difficulty of the "inversions" and "ellipses" that crop up throughout genuine Latin texts. One cannot ask young pupils to read these texts in their original order, which is so contrary to the "natural order that French nearly always follows. ... Only at a later age can they survive this trial, and only after, by way of exercise, they form the habit of intuiting Latin word position[25] through its ending alone. It is in order to facilitate early formation of this habit, and in order to make the most of their younger years, a time so favorable to building language skills, that I remove the difficulty entirely by assigning them authors whose works I have organized according to simple construction and without any inversions."[26] Beyond Port-Royal, this is plainly a return to *ordo est* and to scholastic "construction," but taken to the extreme of a substitution pure and simple of the *ordo rectus* for the order of the text. By way of direct contact with Latin texts, the teacher would thus offer beginners sentences by Cicero or verses by Horace arranged in the French syntactical order, once all of the "understood" words had been reestablished.[27] In an appendix, Du Marsais himself presents such a version of *Carmen saeculare;* for the amusement of Latinists, here is an example of the treatment of the first stanza:

Phoebe, sylvarumque potens Diana,
Lucidum caeli decus, o colendi

Semper, et culti, date quae precamur
Tempore sacro

becomes *O Phoebe, atque Diana potens sylvarum, (o vos) decus lucidum caeli, o (vos) colendi semper, et culti semper, date (ea negotia) quae precamur (in hoc) tempore sacro.*[28]

ᔥ "Until now there used to be only one terminology for what is commonly called sentence construction. We thought we were agreed, and in fact we were. In recent days, Abbot Batteux has risen up against universal feeling and has put forward an opinion that is exactly the opposite of the common view."[29] Although partial and summary, Beauzée's retrospective appraisal describes the state of opinion at the beginning of the eighteenth century quite well. The resistance of the party of the Ancients had in fact been weaker and less articulate in the linguistic arena than in that of the works and principles of literary aesthetics. Maybe the partisans of Latin were not outnumbered within the circle of cultivated opinion, but they seemed short of arguments. An initial sign of recovery can be detected in Bernard Lamy's *La Rhétorique; ou, l'Art de parler,* and more precisely between the first three editions (1675–88) and the fourth, which dates from 1701.[30] Until this date, the chapter "On the Order and Arrangement of Words" opened with a very resolute declaration in favor of French word order: "As for the order of words and the rules that must be retained in the arrangement of discourse, the light of natural reason shows so sharply what needs to be done that we cannot ignore what those whose mistress we have made her would have done if they wished to follow her. The meaning of a discourse cannot be understood unless its subject matter is known beforehand. The natural order therefore requires that in all propositions the noun expressing the subject be placed first, and so on." The rest of the chapter restored the equilibrium somewhat by showing that the existence of the case system legitimately exempts Latin from "subjecting itself to the natural order as we do" and the advantages that ensue: an aesthetic advantage, residing in the freedom of construction which "affords {Latin} the means of rendering discourse more flowing and more harmonious"; and an expressive advantage, coming from the fact that thought is not actually as successive as is claimed but is "like an image made of several brush strokes linked together to express it. Thus, it seems felicitous to present this image in its entirety so that one may consider the features all at once linked together as they are, as is the case in Latin, where everything is linked, as things are in the mind ... consequently, Latin expressions are stronger, being more closely interconnected." In 1701, Lamy reinforced the advantage of Latin, first by a much more cautious introduction on the evidence for "direct" word order: "It is not as easy as is believed to tell what the natural order of the parts of speech is, or what the most reasonable arrangement for them might be. Discursive speech is an image of what is present in the mind, which is lively. The mind contemplates several things all at once; it would thus be difficult to determine the position and rank held by each, since the mind embraces them all and sees them all at a single glance." Further reinforcement came from the addition of a new defense of Latin word order, described in its turn as "natural" insofar as it "presents all the parts of a proposition unified with each other as they are in the mind"; and, finally, from a direct and explicit reply to "that person [Le Laboureur] who has written about the advantages of our language" and who "had not made these reflections" when he so inopportunely attempted to ridicule the language of Cicero.

Thus, the Moderns' offensive did not convince Lamy; to the contrary, his counterattack quite clearly outlines in advance what will become the two lines of defense for the partisans of Latin word order: the aesthetic line (a freer construction, hence a more "harmonious" or readily euphonic discourse), and the mimetic one (a more closely bound sentence, hence more faithful to the essence of thought, which is not successiveness but rather unity and simultaneity). The first line of defense does not concern us: this is the one that Abbot Jean Baptiste du Bos adheres to, for example, in his *Réflexions critiques sur la poésie et la peinture* {Critical reflections on poetry and painting}: "The Latin construction makes it possible to reverse the natural order of words and to transpose them until an arrangement is found in which they can be pronounced without difficulty and even produce a pleasant melody."[31] The first line of defense is also taken by E. S. Gamaches in his *Agréments du langage réduits à leurs principes* {The charms of language explained in their principles}, which makes an inventory of cases where, even in French, "inversion" contributes to the clarity and balance of the sentence.[32]

℗ This aesthetic valorization is also present in Condillac.[33] For him, the two leading advantages of Latin inversions are discursive harmony and stylistic vivacity: the distance between words that agree with each other "excite{s} the imagination; and the ideas are dispersed only that the mind, being at the trouble of joining them, should be more sensible of their connection or opposition."[34] But a third advantage lends more importance to mimetic values. Inversions "form a picture: I mean that they unite in a single word the circumstances of an action, in some measure as a painter unites them upon a canvas; if they presented them in succession, it would be only a plain narrative {récit}. This will be better understood by means of an example. *Nymphae flebant Daphnim extinctum funere crudeli.* Here is a simple narrative. I learn that the nymphs wept, that they wept for Daphnis, that Daphnis was dead, etc. Thus the circumstances succeeding each other make but a slight impression on me. Change but the order

of words, and say: *Extinctum nymphae crudeli funere Daphnim / Flebant;* it produces quite a different effect, because having read *extinctum nymphae crudeli
funere,* I am still in the dark; but at *Daphnim* I see the first stroke of the pen-
cil, at *flebant* I see the second, and then the picture is finished. The nymphs in
tears, Daphnis dying, and this death attended with every doleful circumstance,
strike me all at once. Such is the power which transpositions {*inversions*} have
over the imagination." [35] Clearly, the narrative model that implicitly inspired the
partisans of *naturalis ordo* is abandoned here, and even depreciated ("plain"
and "simple" narrative), not, as in Lamy, in the name of the instantaneousness
of thought but in favor of another objective model: that of the picture or painting {*tableau*}. In its rejection of temporal succession, the Virgilian order — or, if
you prefer, disorder — is better than ours at miming the simultaneity of the object or, rather, of the group of objects that continually present themselves to our
perception and solicit our discourse. Notice that this absence of linearity, this
atemporal breakup of the sentence, refutes in advance the central thesis of G. E.
Lessing's *Laocoön,* or at the very least limits its application: it would appear that
certain natural languages are spontaneously narrative, and others naturally destined for description.

Such is the main advantage of what Condillac persistently calls *inversions,* as
do the opponents of Latin. But this concept does not have the same meaning in
his work as it does in the Moderns' doctrine: it stands opposed not to the concept of "natural order" but to that of the *connection of ideas:* inversions "distort"
or "do violence to the connection of ideas." What is this all about, then?

"We flatter ourselves," says Condillac (and this "we" indicates rather nicely
the *dominant* character of the Moderns' theory, even according to their opponents), into believing that the order subject-verb-object is more in keeping with
the succession of ideas in the mind. In fact, it does not work this way at all,
for the "operations of the mind" are either simultaneous (see Lamy), in which
case "there is no order between them," or successive in which case their order
may vary, "because it is every whit as natural that the ideas of *Alexander,* and of
overcoming, should be revived by that of *Darius* as it is that the idea of *Darius*
should be revived by the other two." [36] What counts is not the succession of ideas
but their connection, and even their "greatest connection": the idea of the subject on one hand and that of the object on the other are most closely linked to
the idea of action. Consequently, the most natural constructions — both equally
natural — are *Alexander vicit Darium* or *Darium vicit Alexander.* And even if one
wanted to determine absolutely which one of these is the more natural no longer
according to the connection of ideas, in which they are equally matched, but according to the original order in which they appear in the mind, one would settle
on the second one.

This conclusion takes us back from Condillac's chapter 12, "Of Transpositions," to chapter 9, "Of Words," where he gives his own account of the origins of articulated language and, more precisely, the successive invention of the parts of speech. At first, men discovered the names of tangible objects (*tree, fruit, water, fire,* and so on), doing what was both easiest and most urgent; next came adjectives designating perceptible qualities; then came the verbs, which designate actions. This order of acquisition is quite naturally reproduced in that of the primitive sentence. The savage first designates the object of his thought, which is, generally, the object of his desire: *fruit* is a nominal sentence, in a sense already complete and sufficient. If he wants to be more precise, or more explicit, he will say *fruit to want.* From that point on, in the third stage, "the verb coming after its government, the noun that governed it — that is, the nominative — could not be placed between both; for this would have rendered the relation dubious [here already is the principle of connection]. Neither could it begin the sentence, because its relation to its government would have been less obvious. Its place therefore was after the verb."[37] Thus, *fruit want Peter* {Pierre} (the obligatory name for a man of that era), complement-verb-subject, or in keeping with the terminology of Condillac's time, *régime-verbe-nominatif: Darium vicit Alexander.* Or again, regarding the successive order of noun and adjective: "A person surprised at the tallness of a tree, would say, *tall tree* {*grand arbre*}, even though on other occasions [but are there any others?] he had made use of the words *tree tall* {*arbre grand*}: for the idea which strikes us most is that which we are naturally inclined to pronounce first."[38]

Finally, then, it is really the order of succession, or possibly the order of the nonsuccession, of ideas that for Condillac justifies the order of Latin words (or pseudo-Latin, since the classical *Alexander Darium vicit* is extremely unfaithful to its model). This order is natural because it imitates the simultaneity of the perceptual picture sometimes, and at other times the originary successiveness of thought. Here we again find — but reversed, of course — the mimetic principle of the *ordo naturalis.*

⊕ This same principle presides even more explicitly over Abbot Charles Batteux's demonstration in *Lettres sur la phrase française comparée avec la phrase latine* {Letters on the French sentence as compared with the Latin sentence},[39] a text that was received as the true manifesto of the Latinist party, despite the precedence of Condillac's essay. For Batteux, speech is a "portrait in which our soul sees itself from the outside, completely, such as it is, in all of its positions, in all of its motions." It is a portrait, hence a faithful image, not only of the soul but of the world, and it depends on a chain of resemblances that links ideas to things and expressions to ideas: "Expressions are to thoughts what thoughts are to things: there exists between them a kind of generation that carries resemblance step by step from the originating principle up through the last term."

Now the fidelity of the portrait demands not only a resemblance to every detail of the model but also a diagrammatic correspondence to their overall arrangement: "The perfection of each image lies in its resemblance to that of which it is an image, and this resemblance, when perfect, must present not only things, but the order in which things appear. For example, if my thought represents a man to me, it is not enough for arms, a head, legs to be painted; my thought must also put these members in the place where they belong: that is to say, as they truly are in the man being represented. Otherwise, the image is judged to be false. It is, therefore, on the order and arrangement of things and their parts that the order and arrangement of thoughts depends, and it is on the order and arrangement of thought and its parts that the order and arrangement of expression depends. And this arrangement in thoughts and in expressions, which are images, is natural or unnatural according to whether it is or is not true to things, which are models."

Thus, sentence order is, or rather should be, the image of the order of thoughts and indirectly the image of actual things. But here, through a provisional concession to the Moderns, Batteux distinguishes two orders of construction: the *metaphysical* one, which is none other than the traditional subject-predicate *ordo,* and the *moral* one, "based on the interest of the person who speaks" and embodied in a descending order of importance; the main object must come at the head, "since this one leads all the others." The metaphysical order is suitable for ideal situations, as it were, where the relationship between two objects is considered only "speculatively." In any case involving the interest of the speaker in the broad sense — that is, in fact, almost always — the "moral" order is required. I can state *the sun is round* in a metaphysical context, but if I really am addressing an interlocutor in order to convince him of this roundness, the "subject" of my utterance thereby becomes simply a shared presupposition (we agree on the sun's existence), and it is clearly the predicate that matters and that must come at the head of the sentence: *rotundus est sol.* The moral order, therefore, is at once the most frequent and the most natural one, also in the sense of being the *originary* order, as two examples (after Condillac) should prove: "If I want to make a man other than myself understand that he must flee from or seek some object, I will begin by showing him that object. Next, I will give him to understand what he must do with it. ... It is necessary for me to show him the snake first; next, if needed, I will make the gesture that depicts {*peint*} the action of fleeing. If, at the table, I wanted to ask for some bread by gesturing, when my eyes met those of the person who could give me some, would I begin by pointing to myself first? Would I not point to the bread first and myself afterward? Here, then, is the order that we follow when we are only thinking to ourselves, and the order that we follow when we are speaking to others through gestures alone; this order is prescribed by nature itself. Now whether the signs are gestures or words does not matter: the order and arrangement must always be the same. In this way, Latin, which says *serpentum fuge, panem praebe mihi,* follows the natural order; and French, which says *fuyez le serpent, donnez-moi du pain,* reverses the natural order. This is a type of inversion of which we may not have been aware." Even the narrative principle of the temporal anteriority of the subject cannot motivate the French order: *le père aime le fils* is a hysteron proteron, for "the sight of the object, the son, necessarily exists before the father's love does. We know the old axiom: *ignoti nulla cupido"* {we don't want what we don't know about}. It takes a scholastic to know a scholastic.

The naturalness of the moral order thus establishes the superiority of Latin, which is as a rule confirmed in its most standard constructions. Besides, Latin can bend its constructions as needed to all the variations of the field of interest, reflecting the diversity of situations or of contexts (which amounts to the same thing). Thus, after praising Rome, Cicero naturally goes on to say: *Populus enim romanus sibi Pontum aperuit,* "for it is the Roman people that has opened up the kingdom of Pontus"; if the kingdom of Pontus and not the Roman people had been the main object of the discourse, Cicero would have written: *Pontum sibi populus,* and so on. Obviously, it follows from this double justification that except when pressing reasons of euphony conflict with it, the Latin order is *always* natural and *always* mimetic: "Their language took on all the shapes of their ideas and represented them without any alteration, as in a mirror." For Batteux, then, the commentary of a Latin text essentially consists of a *motivating analysis* of its construction. Thus, for the exordium of *Pro Marcello:* the orator's initial thought necessarily reflected the long silence which he was in the act of breaking, so his first words had to be *Diuturni silentii,* and so on. His second thought: "to seek the reason for this long silence. It could have been fear. But the orator does not want us to think it was, so he rules this idea out: *non timore aliquo.* What was the real reason, then? *Partim dolore, partim verecundia.* A natural order therefore exists for thoughts themselves: an order regulated by a principle that is the same in the person speaking and in the person listening." We will see this identity contested by Diderot, who is, however, far from opposing the principle of expressiveness that founds an entirely new stylistics.

"Reversal" is found not in Latin, then, but actually in French; habit and prejudice alone lead us to take the "established" order of our language for the natural one. Why French betrayed nature in this way remains to be explained. According to Batteux, it cannot be an effect of the "genius" of French, for if it is true that every natural language has its own genius, it must be immediately concluded, or even established first of all, "that there is a general genius, growing out of man's very nature." The diversity of geniuses which, for Batteux as for Frain, results from the diversity of climates cannot effect any change in the natural order, because interest is identical in all cases. The sole possible explanation, therefore, is purely material and somewhat mechanical: it stems from the "particular form and constitution of the sounds that make up what we call a natural language." All such languages have the same goal, "which is to paint with clarity and exactitude," but they do not have the same "colors" {*couleurs*} — that is to say, the same "figurative sounds" {*sons figurés*} — at their disposal. The greater or lesser number of these articulations can cause differences of construction, depending, for example, upon whether or not a language has at its disposal the inflexional elements that lend Latin its perfect suppleness. To paraphrase Lamy's earlier observation, then, French word order is merely a defect made into a virtue.

Such a reversal, if not of values (we will return to this), at least of their systematic functioning and application, necessarily entails practical consequences. The main one for Batteux, who does not concern himself directly with pedagogy, is a precept for translators: always respect the order of the text and imitate it as faithfully as possible in the translation. Of course, this principle conflicts with the then widespread practice of *belles infidèles* translations, but also, indirectly, with Du Marsais's "method" — even though the latter had never proposed to extend his recipe to literary translation. Despite its being indirect, Batteux's opposition is nonetheless flagrant in spirit; he himself would later write: "When the *Lettres sur l'inversion* appeared for the first time, it came back to me that Monsieur Du Marsais was not at all of my opinion. I had anticipated this. What he wrote in his *Méthode* is precisely the opposite of what I had tried to establish in these letters."[40] Batteux's disciples went on to deepen the conflict by attacking Du Marsais's method, if not always by name, at least always in a transparent way. Abbot Noël Antoine Pluche does this in his *Mécanique des langues et l'art de les enseigner* {The mechanics of natural languages and the art of teaching them},[41] especially in a section headed "The order of Latin must not be altered in translation"; the issue is indeed, by now, the pedagogical exercise of translation. Pluche is as attached as Du Marsais to the principle of "routine," but he is anxious to put the beginner into contact with authentic texts, whose mimetic superiority he proves in the style of Batteux. Pierre Chompré does likewise in his *Introduction à la langue latine par la voie de la traduction* {Introduction to the Latin language through translation}[42] and other pamphlets from which it is enough to quote the following vengeful passage: "A Latin sentence by a classical author is a little monument of antiquity. If you decompose this little monument in order to make it understood, instead of constructing it, you are destroying it: thus, what we call construction is really destruction."[43] It is 1757, and as can be plainly seen, the battle — all the rage — rages on.

⊛ Meanwhile, in fact, the philosophes (Diderot, d'Alembert) and their grammarians (Du Marsais, then Beauzée) entered the controversy. Their participation dominates the entire period from 1751 (Diderot's *Lettre sur les sourds et muets*

{Letter on the deaf and mute}) to 1767 (Beauzée's *Grammaire générale* {General grammar}). Powerful though not decisive, it clearly shows where, on this point, the dominant opinion in the French intelligentsia then lay.

The *Letter on the Deaf and Mute*,[44] addressed to Batteux, is really a reply to his *Lettres sur la phrase française*. But, as usual with Diderot, it is impossible to reduce this text to a simple and univocal aim. It is complex, sometimes muddled, nuanced enough for Beauzée to have seen in it the exposition of a "third opinion,"[45] and, of course, digressive (Diderot himself describes it as a "labyrinth") — the most important points perhaps appearing in the digressions.

Somewhat like Batteux himself, Diderot distinguishes in principle between a *natural* order and a *scientific* or *institutionalized* order. As in Condillac, the first one is defined by the initial order of acquisition of the parts of speech, in which perceptible qualities necessarily had to precede abstractions: the adjective must thus come before the noun, as in Latin. According to the scientific order, on the other hand, the substantive, being the philosophical "foundation" of the adjective, must precede it, as in French. Up to this point, then, the scales are balanced. But new tests are about to destroy this balance: to begin with, the investigation of the gestural language of a deaf-mute (hence the title) demonstrates (against Batteux) that the subject must come first: the advantage falls to French. Next, a new analysis of the exordium of *Pro Marcello* proves that Cicero, delivering the initial words in oblique grammatical cases, necessarily had the last ones (which determine these grammatical cases) in mind already: "What made him use the genitive case in *Diuturni silentii,* the ablative in *quo,* the imperfect tense in *eram,* and so on, was the order of ideas pre-existing in his mind which did not coincide with the order of the words—an order he obeyed unconsciously, from a long practice in transposition"—the very definition of inversion.[46] Next, the interest of the speaker is not as sure a guide as Batteux believed: "For example, if I ask you which one of the two ideas contained in the sentence *serpentum fuge* is the main one, *you* will tell me that it is the serpent; but he who fears the serpent less than he fears for my death thinks only of my flight: one takes fright and the other warns me."[47] Nor is the speaker's interest as relevant as Abbot Batteux's purely expressive stylistics would have it; it does not always coincide with the hearer's, whose interest must prevail in good rhetoric. Finally, thought is always simultaneous, for did "our mind not allow of several perceptions at one and the same time, it would be impossible to think and speak; for thought and speech consist in the comparison of two or more ideas."[48] Therefore, no order of succession exists in the mind; consequently, "there is not, and perhaps there cannot be, inversion in the mind"[49]—a lame formulation, for no one has claimed that there was inversion in the mind; rather it was in speech in relation to the order of the mind. This is what Diderot aims to contest now, and his contestation here works to the advantage of French word order. In the final tally, it is undoubtedly

Latin that reverses the natural order. "We express things in French in the order the mind has to consider them, whatever the language. Cicero, if we may say so, followed the French order before obeying the Latin." [50] This is more or less Le Laboureur's formulation. Latin is conceded the advantage of "imagination" and the "passions," but French has that of "common sense": "If truth return to earth, I believe French would be her chosen speech, while Greek, Latin, and other tongues would be the language of fables and falsehoods. French is the language for teaching, enlightening, and convincing; Greek, Latin, Italian, and English for persuading, stirring the passions, and hoodwinking. Speak Greek or Latin to the multitude, but speak French to the philosopher. ... Thus, all things considered, our *pedestrian* language has the advantage of the useful over the pleasant in relation to the others." [51] Let us note in passing the sudden extension of inversion to all natural languages other than French—a generalization that heralds Rivarol's.

As a pamphlet on inversion, the *Letter* ends here—but here it starts moving again in an altogether different and very unexpected direction, although one not unrelated to the topic: that of a theory of poetic language. From the interlinguistic opposition between utility and aesthetic charm, Diderot suddenly slips into the intralinguistic antithesis between prose and poetry. Up to this point we had one clear language (French) and numerous expressive languages (all the others). Now we have every natural language divided into two levels of expression: the level that suffices for "informal conversation" (clarity, purity, precision) and oratorical style (choice of terms, symmetry, and harmony), and the level required by poetry. In this case, "the spirit states and paints objects at the same time; it appeals not only to the understanding but to the soul that it stirs and the imagination that sees and the ear that hears. The poetic lines are not merely a string of energetic words that express the thought both forcefully and nobly but also a many-layered tissue of hieroglyphs that paint thought. In this sense, I would say that all poetry is emblematic." [52] This theory of poetry as a tissue of *emblems* and *hieroglyphs,*[53] or a mimetic language system, is illustrated by several motivating readings that pursue Batteux's but do so on the level of phonic values. For instance, in the following couplet by Voltaire,

> *Et des fleuves français les eaux ensanglantées*
> *Ne portaient que des morts aux mers épouvantées*
> {And the bloodied waters of French rivers
> Bore only the dead to the terror-stricken seas}

Diderot sees in the "first syllable of the word *portaient* ... the waters swollen with corpses and the streams choked, as it were, by this obstacle," and in *épouvantées* the dread of the seas and their vast expanse." [54] Or, in another example, there are the "hieroglyphic beauties" of the death of Euryalus: "the image of gushing blood, *it cruor*" [further on: "*it* is analogous both to the gush of blood and to

161

the small movement of the drops of water on the leaves of a flower"]; "and that image of the drooping head {Diderot: *tête*} of a dying man, *cervix* {neck} *collapsa recumbit;* the sound of a scythe sawing away, *succisus;* the languor of death, *languescit moriens;* the limpness of the poppy stem, *lassove papavera collo;* and the *demisere caput,* with the *gravantur,* complete the picture. *Demisere* is as limp as the stem of a flower; *gravantur* is as heavy as its chalice weighed down with rain; *collapsa* expresses an effort and a fall. The same double hieroglyph is found in *papavera:* the first two syllables show the poppy with head erect, and the last two its drooping."[55]

This is a major detour, whose anticipatory value by far surpasses the limits of its forgotten pretext: not only does Diderot here inaugurate, but more ingeniously, the often naive practices of so-called modern stylistics, for which the supreme beauty of style seems always to lie in doubling signification by imitation,[56] but he also anticipates by more than a century an idea of "poetic language" in which we will find one of the great future refuges of Cratylism. As is apparent, the separation proposed by Frain du Tremblay between a conventional phonics and lexicon, on the one hand, and a mimetic construction, on the other, is entirely overturned by the new division here: in poetry, everything becomes or seems to become a "hieroglyph," including elementary sounds. Poetry transmutes and transfigures language, wresting it completely away from its arbitrary status as social convention, and returning it miraculously to nature.[57]

⑨ Whereas Diderot exceeded the boundaries of the quarrel between the Ancients and the Moderns through his anachronistic genius, Jean Le Rond d'Alembert attempted to rise above it and arbitrate it as a philosopher would, but while eschewing scholastic categories.[58] To begin with, like Lamy, Condillac, and, to an extent, Diderot, d'Alembert accepts the simultaneity of thought at the level of the simple proposition, and hence the impossibility of founding any order on the supposed succession of elementary ideas. Yet the proposition must certainly follow an order, and it is important to determine which is the most natural. Let us take a simple judgment like *God is good:* d'Alembert compares the two ideas of *divinity* and *goodness,* and he takes note of their partial identity. The proposition expressing this partial identity can analytically reflect the operation itself (comparison), and in this case one could say equally well *God good is* or *Good God is* (juxtaposition of two ideas, in any order, then judgment of identity). Or, the proposition can synthetically reflect the result of this operation; in that case it is necessary and sufficient to place the verb in the middle, "as one places between two bodies the bond that serves to form and to indicate their union": either *God is good* or *Good is God.*[59] Thus, the two constructions that place the verb at the beginning are already excluded, for one would be unable to make judgments about what one does not know. But also, every comparison is like a measurement, in which it is more natural to grasp the greater object first and to approach the smaller one afterward, placing "the foot against the height gauge and not the height gauge against the foot."[60] So, *God* being obviously greater than *goodness*, since He is greater than all things (the facility lent by the choice of example is clear), one will naturally place this word at the head of the proposition. Hence only two constructions, both with an initial subject, remain: the analytical *God good is* and the synthetic *God is good.*

This first inquiry considered things in a "metaphysical" way without taking syntactical relationships into account. In a second stage, d'Alembert, in order to integrate these relationships, changes the example and returns to the canonical statement about Alexander and Darius. Here, the verb-object relationships require one order and one only: *régissant-régi* {subject-object, or governing-governed}. "*Alexander vicit Darium* ... alone is true to the natural order because the verb *vicit* presupposes the nominative *Alexander* on which it depends, and because the accusative *Darium* presupposes the verb *vicit* by which it is governed." The syntactical subordination establishes and motivates a hierarchical order of decreasing autonomy that is also a pragmatic order, since at whatever point it is cut, the sentence so constructed "presents, as far as possible, a meaning or at least a complete idea."[61]

As for d'Alembert's third stage of inquiry, once the order subject-verb-complement is motivated in this manner, analogy enters in: "This rule, required for the clarity of the discourse in certain cases, has been extended even to those cases in which the clarity of the discourse does not require such an arrangement" — whence finally: *God is good.* "French grammar of necessity requires that the verb be placed before the object, and by analogy that it be placed before the adjective."[62] Q.E.D.

This contribution, original in its approach but wholly orthodox in its conclusion, was to remain almost without echo.[63] The mainstream of the "metaphysicians'" party is represented and even constituted by the successive interventions of two philosopher-grammarians of the *Encyclopédie*, Du Marsais and then Beauzée. The *Encyclopédie* is more directly engaged here, for several of its articles ("Construction," "Grammaire," "Inversion," "Langue") would take part in the controversy, always on the side of the Moderns.

֍ Du Marsais's demonstration[64] is based on a major distinction between two functions or "objects" of speech or "elocution": one purely intellectual ("to make oneself understood"), and the other aesthetic or affective ("to please or to move": though two different actions, these are apparently inseparable here).

Elocution has three objects. The first, which can be called the essential or principal object, is to excite in the mind of the person who is reading or listening the thought one intends to excite. We speak in order to be understood: this is the primary goal of speech; this is the primary object of every natural language; and each language has established a proper means of attaining this end independently of any other consideration. We often set ourselves one of two other objects in speaking, either to please or to move. These two objects always presuppose the first one as their necessary instrument, one without which the others cannot attain their goal. What can be said of a young person can also be said of speech: if she wants to please, if she wants to move and to excite interest, that person must begin by making herself seen. If you want to please through rhythm, through harmony, through symmetry (that is, through a certain fittingness of syllables), through the connection, sequencing, measure, or proportion of words among one another, so that a cadence pleasant to the ear results, be it in prose or in verse, you must begin by making yourself understood. The most resonant words, the most harmonious arrangement can only please as would a musical instrument; but this is no longer, then, to please through speech, which is exclusively the question here. It is equally impossible to move and to excite interest if one is not understood.[65]

The intellectual function determines one type of construction, called *simple* construction (or *necessary, significant, enunciative, natural, analogous*); obviously, this is the scholastic *rectus ordo*, regulated by the "successive order of relations," with the modified word always preceding the modifier, the sole construction that is natural and "true to the state of things."[66] In fact, this construction is so natural that it commands syntax and the formation of meaning in all languages, since inflection exists in "transpositive" languages merely to aid the mind in reestablishing what Du Marsais calls the *significant order:* "All natural languages agree in that they form meaning only through the link or relation that words have between them in the same proposition. These links are marked by the successive order observed in simple construction. . . . [This order] must be reestablished by the mind, which understands meaning only through this order and through the successive determination of words, especially in natural languages that have cases: the different endings of these cases aid the mind in reestablishing the order when the whole proposition is finished."[67] The order alone produces signification because it alone indicates, or rather constitutes, syntactical relationship. Inflection is not an autonomous grammatical instrument; it is a substitute, an index of the place which the word must occupy and which it ideally does occupy in every natural language. A grammatical case is an ordering number, a corrective expedient, through which a transpositive language unwittingly pays homage to the power of the analogue languages. This conception of syntax, let us note, merely formalizes and theorizes Le Laboureur's old formula: the Romans thought according to the simple construction before speaking according to the *figurative* {*figurée*} construction.

Indeed, this is what Du Marsais baptizes any construction that does not respect the necessary order of simple construction—we will return to this significant baptism. Figurative construction corresponds to the second, aesthetic-affective function of discourse. The shift from one function to another thus coincides with the shift from one discipline to another, from grammar to *rhetoric:* "The work of grammar is a rough diamond polished by rhetoric, which has led one of our most judicious grammarians to say that just where grammar ends, rhetoric begins."[68] Invested with such a wide-ranging mission (everything that, in speech, goes beyond the basic concern for intelligibility), rhetoric is nevertheless defined in the narrowest way, as a repertoire of figures of construction — ellipsis, pleonasm, grammatical syllepsis, hyperbaton or inversion, idiom, attraction[69]—themselves conceived of as so many infractions of, or deviations from, the *ordo rectus:* "First, there is in (all) natural languages an analogue and necessary order through which alone the assembled words produce a meaning. Second, in everyday language we deviate from this order, and there is even some virtue in deviating from it; so these deviations are authorized, provided that when the sentence is finished, the mind can easily relate all the words to the analogue order and supply even those that are not expressed. Third and last, it is chiefly from these deviations that elegance, grace, and vivacity of style result, especially the high style and poetic style."[70]

Yet the status of this deviation must be explained; a detour, as is befitting, will come in handy here. To this point we have considered only two types of constructions; in actual fact, the article in the *Encyclopédie* distinguishes a third type "in which all the words are arranged in keeping with the order neither of simple construction nor of figurative construction. This third kind of arrangement is the one most often used; this is why I call it *ordinary construction.* ... I am calling it ordinary construction because I understand by this the arrangement of words that is commonly used in books, letters, and the conversation of educated people {*honnêtes gens*}. This construction is often neither entirely simple nor entirely figurative."[71] This construction, whose field is coextensive with the whole field of speech and writing, as the adjective "ordinary" shows, is therefore theoretically a *mixed* state but one that leaves to the two other constructions the status of merely ideal types, equally without real practical existence. In point of fact, this equality is illusory, for the only pure type is, of course, simple construction: opposite this stands no "purely figurative" construction, and all partially figurative discourse is quite simply, if I may say so, figurative discourse; between presence and absence there is no middle term. Moreover, the two other articles reject this tripartition; they oppose the simple construction alone to the "ordinary and elegant" construction, the "elegant, everyday, usual, or ordinary" construction, which is always by definition figurative — to a greater or lesser degree, it does not matter — through the very fact of not being "completely simple."[72]

Thus, figurative construction is deviation not in relation to usage, since usage itself is riddled with deviations, but in relation to an ideal norm of simple construction, "the one whose sole aim is to communicate and the one that, although less common, is the unique foundation of the usual construction."[73] It is the norm that underpins usage and not the reverse, then, and this is so not because usage follows the norm but precisely because it deviates from it and because this deviation, which defines usage, is itself defined in relation to the norm. The rhetorical division is not *usage-norm* versus *figure-deviation* but rather *norm* versus *figure-deviation-usage* — as illustrated by the entire Latin language, which is nothing but an immense web of figures.

This theory of construction therefore sheds light, in passing, on an obscure section of the treatise *Tropes* (which predates the article "Inversion" by a quarter of a century). In chapter 1 ("Idée générale des figures" {The general idea of figures}), Du Marsais mentions the opinion, widespread at least since Quintilian, that figures are "ways of speaking removed from ... ordinary ways," in order to reject it immediately in the name of the patently obvious fact (no less widespread) that nothing is more ordinary than the use of figures.[74] Finding himself without a convenient definition of figures, Du Marsais proposes another that is quite empty and fairly tautological, and that, as Pierre Fontanier will not unreasonably surmise, did not completely satisfy its author: "Figures are ways of speaking that are distinguishable from the others through particular modifications, each one of which lends itself to classification into a separate species, and each one of which renders the figures livelier or nobler or more pleasant than ways of speaking that express the same basic thought without any particular modification."[75] Du Marsais is going around in circles: in sum, the figure is distinguished from the nonfigure, which remains undefined as a result of his rejecting the criterion of usage and his being unable to formulate another one. The detour through the *ordo* finally provides us with a specific definition: the figurative construction is indeed a "distant" way of speaking, and we now know what it is distant from: not from usage but from an ideal *simple state*. This criterion need only be extended to the whole field of figures in order to obtain the following definition, which Du Marsais would propose in the article "Figure": "The various deviations made in the primary and, as it were, primitive state of words or sentences, and the various changes introduced in these, are the various figures of words and of thought"[76] — as well as this other definition, which Fontanier wrongly but faithfully attributes to him: "a particular modification through which words or sentences move to a greater or lesser degree away from the *simple, primitive,* and *fundamental* state of language."[77]

Clearly, then, the Moderns' position truly deserves the label of "metaphysical" in the case of Du Marsais: progressively freed from the initial apology for French usage, the *ordo rectus* delineates the mythical "nature" of a language system of pure intelligibility, governed by an ideal grammar that is betrayed continually, and perhaps at its origin, by the rhetoric omnipresent in usage and actual discourse. The philosopher-grammarian has pure speech, but he does not speak.

ⓢ Du Marsais's successor and direct heir went on to systematize this extreme position, which remained oddly empirical and incomplete, by developing all its implications and by integrating it into a monumental *Grammaire générale* {General grammar} and a general theory of language.[78]

For Beauzée the *ordo naturalis*, which he prefers to call the "analytical order" (for reasons to be discussed), is natural in three senses and on three grounds:

Natural because mimetic: It is not directly mimetic of the order of thought, which is simultaneous, hence indivisible and impossible to represent, but mimetic of the order of its analysis as logically carried out. "Speech should paint {*peindre*} thought and be its image: thought, since it is indivisible, cannot by itself be the immediate object of any image because all images presuppose corresponding and proportionate parts. Therefore, only logical analysis of thought can be figuratively represented {*figurée*} by speech. Now it is the nature of any image to represent its original faithfully: thus, the nature of language demands that it paint the objective ideas of thought and their relations exactly. These relations presuppose a succession in their terms; priority properly belongs to one, posteriority is essential to another. This succession of ideas, based on their relations, is then actually the natural object of the image speech must produce; and the analytical order is the true natural order that must serve as the basis for the syntax of all natural languages."[79]

So Beauzée agrees with Batteux here in requiring from speech a complete, detailed, and well-ordered representation of its object: not only must each detail be represented, but it must be in its place. Consequently, Beauzée is not satisfied, as Condillac is, with a simple "connection of ideas"; this connection now must appear in one and only one order: "Since speech must be the image of the analysis of thought, can it be a really perfect image if it confines itself simply to sketching the most general outlines of thought? Your portrait needs to have two eyes, a nose, a mouth, coloring, and so forth. Enter any artist's studio and you will find all of these: is that your portrait? No, because putting together eyes, nose, mouth, and so on is not enough to represent you. All these parts must be like those of the original, proportioned and located as in the original. The same goes for speech: to paint the analysis of thought, it is not enough to make the connection of words perceptible, even if we model speech on the greatest connection, on the most immediate connection of ideas; a particular connection, based on a particular relationship, must be painted. Now this relationship has a

first term, then a second one: if one follows the other directly, the greatest connection may be observed. But even then, if you name the second first and the
first second, you are palpably reversing nature, much like a painter who presents
us with the image of a tree having roots at the top and leaves at the bottom: this
painter would be as faithful to the greatest connection between the parts of the
tree as you would be to that between ideas."[80] There can be no mimesis, then,
without a mimetic order.

Natural because universal: This is the rationalist criterion of universality that,
as Diderot had foreseen, disqualifies the principle of interest so dear to Batteux.
"I would ask if decisions of interest are constant, uniform, and invariable enough
to serve as a basis for a technical framework. ... In fact, there is nothing more
mobile, more irregular, more changeable, more uncertain than interest: what
interested me yesterday no longer interests me today, even if I am not interested
in something diametrically opposite; the interests of individuals are opposed to
one another and to those of society, and those of society can change from one
moment to the next, as do those of each individual. How can one presume to
make so variable a principle the permanent and natural rule of elocution?"[81]
Even Latin inversions are inspired in no way by this supposed principle but really
by a concern for harmony. The only universal and constant principle, therefore,
is the analytical principle, which despite appearances is respected by all natural
languages, including the "transpositive" ones, for in transposition "the analytical order is transgressed but respected as the primitive and natural order." Since
all transgressions confirm the code, inversions "certify the rightfulness of analysis by departing from it."[82] Like Du Marsais, but more insistently, Beauzée treats
inflection as a simple substitute for the analytical order, a palliative that enables
us to recognize and reestablish it underneath the misrepresentations of inversion. In transpositive languages "the movement of the mind is not imitated by
the succession of words" but is "perfectly indicated by the *liveries* they are wearing"; the endings "bear the *imprint*" of the analytical order; they are "the *label*
of the position befitting them in the natural succession."[83] These metaphors
plainly state the secondary and "relative" function of inflection, which assigns
each "transposed" word its place in an order of which it is unaware, as the serial
number does for a lost soldier.[84] The opposition between analogue and transpositive languages, then, is not symmetrical at all: the former *follow* the natural
order; the latter *refer to* it indirectly through their inflections. As second-rate
languages with a derivative status, somewhat parasitical, like so many dialects
or rather like slang,[85] they permanently bear the mark of their fundamental defect, which is the absence of mimesis: whereas the other languages *imitate* the
movement of the mind, these can only *indicate* it. But this difference in no way
calls into question the universality of the analytical principle, for difference is
not diversity but inequality and subordination, recognized and marked, as with

a branding iron, through inflection. The analytical order is definitively "the invariable prototype of two general kinds of natural languages and the unique foundation of their respective communicability," since meaning comes about only through grammatical relationships, and these in fact are identified with the analytical order.[86] Thus, "across these considerable differences in the genius of natural languages, we are sure to recognize the uniform imprint of nature, which is one, simple and immutable."[87]

Finally, *natural because originary:* Here, Beauzée very clearly parts ways with Diderot, who assigned to inversion the period, whether desirable or not, of the earliest "stammerings" of language. "In contrast," objects Beauzée, "I would think that these inversions are the effects of art, an art considerably later than the age of stammering, if men ever were stammerers in the first place." And if the analytical order "presupposes a metaphysics superior to the resources of the earliest men, the only conclusion to be drawn from this is that the earliest men were not its inventors. But the fact that they did not follow this order is an opinion incompatible with accepted ideas on the mechanism of natural languages; everything points toward the conclusion that the analytical is the true order of nature and that it is anterior to all the variations of usage and to the innovations of art."[88]

As we find out here, Nature, which Beauzée sees as presiding over the constitution of the language system, is not and cannot be the same as human nature left to its own resources. The "metaphysics" presupposed by the analytical order of words is superior to Nature's resources and can only be divine. The *ordo naturalis* thus becomes one of the proofs of the divine institution of language — the other one being, paradoxically, the conventionality of its elements. Indeed, in his article "Langue," Beauzée — basing his argument on Rousseau's assertion of aporia in *Discours sur l'inégalité* {Discourse on inequality} — pushes this notion to its implicit conclusion (previously set forth by Frain du Tremblay, as we have seen), stating that an instituted language system presupposes an instituting society, which in its turn presupposes a "means of communication" that can only be this very system. "What follows from this? That if we stubbornly persist in wanting to ground the first natural language and the first society on human abilities, we have to entertain the idea of an eternal world and eternal human generations, and to abandon the idea of a first society and a first natural language properly speaking. ... If mankind had started life without speech, we would never have begun to speak. ... It is therefore God Himself who, not content with giving the first two members of the human race the precious faculty of speech, immediately put that faculty into full use."[89]

Beauzée is betting on both tables, then, invoking both the conventionality of words and the mimeticism of sentences, in order to rehabilitate the orthodox thesis. As a result, not surprisingly, he appoints "the Hebraic language" as the prototype of analogue languages, "the oldest of all those known to us through monuments that have survived to our time and that by this fact seem to remain closest to the primitive tongue," assuming that the Hebraic language is not simply identical to the primitive tongue.[90] This has a foreseeable consequence for the general filiation of natural languages. On one hand, for Beauzée as for Girard, the unbridgeable gap of syntax absolutely excludes a filiation of Latin with French: "We must have recourse to the way in which words are used in order to recognize the identity or difference of the genius of *natural languages* and in order to determine whether or not they have some affinity.... If there is no connection between two languages other than the one arising from the analogy of words, without any resemblance of their genius, they are alien to each other: that is what Spanish, Italian, and French are with regard to Latin."[91] On the other hand, the "modern languages of Europe that have adopted the analytical construction" apparently go back to Celtic, which probably goes back to Hebrew.[92] "Thus we see our modern French language, Spanish, and English linked by Celtic with Hebrew; and this linkage, confirmed by the analogue construction that characterizes all these languages, is in my opinion a much more reliable index of their filiation than all the etymologies imaginable relating them to transpositive languages;"[93] and we see all of these analogue languages taken back step by step to the one taught to the first pair of humans long ago.

But this originary natural language is poles apart from the popular eighteenth-century idea of a "savage" language described as expressive, eloquent, poetic, dominated by the imagination and the passions, full of the naive figures of a spontaneous rhetoric. This idea of natural expressiveness, found in Condillac, in Diderot, in Blair, in Rousseau, in Herder, and previously in Vico, and which Beauzée inevitably encountered in Batteux, is constantly fought and held up to ridicule in his work. Against Du Marsais, Batteux maintained that a construction "contrary to liveliness, to the quickening of the imagination, to eloquence and harmony" was necessarily "contrary to nature."[94] For Beauzée, this conclusion "assumes what is neither acknowledged nor true. The nature of language consists essentially and principally in the manifestation of thoughts through a faithful exposition of the mind's analysis of them.... Elegance and harmony, which have their own natural principles, if you like, are nonetheless purely accidental to the utterance of thoughts and secondary to the nature of language.... Analytical word order can thus be contrary to eloquence without being contrary to the nature of language, for which eloquence is merely an artificial accessory."[95]

Actually, the sole and true end of language is "the clear exposition of thought."[96] Everything that does not belong to this pure intelligibility is already eloquence (Beauzée never discusses poetry) and comes under a totally artificial rhetoric, even more radically separated from grammar than it was in Du Marsais, if that is possible. Taking Batteux severely to task, Beauzée sees the great

WHITE BONNET / BONNET WHITE

mistake of the "mechanists" precisely in their confusion of "passions with truth, rhetoric with grammar, and the accidental portrayal of feelings of the heart with a clear and exact exposition of the mind's intuitive perceptions."[97] For his part, poor Chompré finds himself accused of overstepping his competence: "You are supposed to teach me the Latin language, and instead your mania for preserving harmony and meter retards the progress I might have made. Leave this job to my rhetoric teacher; it is his proper place. Yours is to make as clear as possible the thought that is the object of the Latin sentence, and to lay aside all that might prevent or delay this understanding."[98] The separation between the two domains is therefore absolute, and any crossover is harmful and blameworthy. "Once and for all, what is natural in grammar is accidental or alien to rhetoric; what is natural in rhetoric is accidental or alien to grammar."[99]

For Beauzée as for Du Marsais, this rhetoric consists of an artificial and rule-governed set of "figures," or infractions of a norm that is itself defined not by usage but by Nature: that is, the originary and fundamental state of language. Batteux believed he could define the hyperbaton of the Latin rhetoricians by contrasting it with standard linguistic constructions. His line of reasoning, objects Beauzée, "presupposes a more general principle: that *a figure . . . is a locution removed from the ordinary and common way of speaking in a natural language;* and I acknowledge that this is more or less the notion that all the rhetoricians and grammarians have of it, but it seems rather ill considered to me. . . . A figure is a locution that is removed not from the *ordinary and common* manner but from the *natural* manner of conveying the same ideas in any given idiom."[100] Here is the formulation that Du Marsais was groping for, one that gets at the core of their shared thinking.

Thus, in Beauzée, the Moderns' doctrine culminates in a rigorously intellectualist philosophy of language, which in its natural state is reduced to the "pure exposition of thought," or an algebraic function. The inevitable counterpart of this fanatical intellectualism is an extraordinary inflation of rhetoric, responsible for taking over everything to which grammar turns a deaf ear: that is, all the pragmatic functions (expressive, affective, persuasive, and so on) of speech and the written text. But as we know, this rhetoric, of which so much is asked, is no longer the vast discipline, the science and art of discourse, that the Ancients saw in it; it is no more than a repertoire of figures, tropes, and "turns of phrase" treated as so many artificial, accidental, and accessory ornaments. In this way the "exposition of thought" represses its proper *motive* {*motif*} — that is to say, all the reasons one might have for making one's thought known — behind the ornamental frame of figures.[101] There is a blindness here, a fatal paradox and disequilibrium, to which we shall return after glancing at a few last episodes.

🕮 In 1763 Batteux had indirectly replied to Du Marsais — or rather he had reaffirmed his position against Du Marsais's arguments — in his treatise *De la construction oratoire* {On oratorical construction}, which was a reprise and development of *Lettres sur la phrase française* enriched with a few examples and provided with new terminology. *Moral order* becomes *oratorical construction*, defined more resolutely than ever as "that of the heart and its passions; grammatical or metaphysical word order is that of art and method." It would have been impossible, in advance, to refute Beauzée more effectively. After the publication of Beauzée's "Inversion" and *Grammaire générale*, Batteux engaged in a dispute, directly this time, with the person who really seems to be his perfect opponent: this occurs in *Nouvel Examen du préjugé sur l'inversion, pour servir de réponse à M. Beauzée* {A reexamination of the bias toward inversion, intended as a reply to Beauzée}.[102] A synthesis and testament of the mechanist party position, this reply is framed in both historical and theoretical terms. On the historical level Batteux dismisses the evidence from Latin referred to by Du Marsais and Beauzée: that is, their interpretation of the term *rectus ordo.* He declares that if classical Latin paid no attention to analytical word order, it was not through concern for euphony but in fact because of its own more expressive order; inversely, he declares that if French respects analytical word order, it is not through a love of clarity but for lack of inflections. On the theoretical level, he denounces his opponents' unacknowledged confusion between syntax and construction, "syntactical relationships" and "syntactical order." Batteux reproaches Beauzée for presenting as natural a construction that reflects only the order of analysis of a thought process that he himself declared indivisible: this analysis can therefore be only a "work of art, factitious and artificial." Finally, and above all, Batteux absolutely contests the idea that "the essential and almost unique end" of language is the clear exposition of thought: we never speak simply to express our thought but also "to convey to others' minds our feelings, just as we experience them." Thus, the order of nature is not that of reason alone but also and in the first place "the order of the heart." The opposition between two interpretations of Nature had probably never been so clear-cut.

℗ No reply from Beauzée would appear, and the *Nouvel Examen* seems to close the debate. But its echo, direct or indirect, was to persist for quite some time yet, with nearly everyone wanting at least to lend support to one of the two parties. Thus, Charles de Brosses supports the mechanists[103] and Voltaire the metaphysicians,[104] but there is also Antoine Rivarol, who brings the question back to its point of departure (the praise of "French clarity") — successfully, as is well known: a reward for audacity, since in the *Discours sur l'universalité* {Discourse on universality} he does not hesitate to reserve the privilege of "direct word order" for French alone.[105] These Gallocentric claims provoked the next-to-last Latinist reaction, on the part of Garat, who reverses the argument of clarity in favor of "natural languages with inversion";[106] and the last Latinist reaction, from Urbain Domergue, who takes up the old *serpentum fuge* again in order to ridicule the academicism of the kind of French that was being praised: "Whether I shout in Latin *serpentum fuge* or in French *un serpent, fuyez!* I am being equally faithful to direct word order. And may the cold and absurd language be hanged that in this present danger would have us say: *Monsieur, prenez garde, voilà un serpent qui s'approche* (Sir, look out, there is a serpent drawing near). That language, if it were possibly to exist, would be the most intolerable of languages. Rivarol, though, has a Frenchman speaking this way, in what he calls direct order."[107]

The final word ought to be given to Destutt de Tracy, the last of the philosopher-grammarians and the first of the Ideologues, who, following Diderot's example, negotiates a compromise by granting all the constructions some quality of naturalness. The quality of "sangfroid" belongs to one type of construction, that of passion to another or, rather, to all the others, since if there is only one reason, there are a thousand passions or "ways in which one feels moved and preoccupied"; there is a "direct" construction, then, for moments of sangfroid and a thousand "inverse" constructions for moments of passion, but all are "equally natural, according to the circumstances."[108] De Tracy offers a cautious synthesis that at best locates the point of separation between the doctrines and in so doing pinpoints their shared bias (I will come back to this).

But all wars have their fanatics or crackpots who shoot or fall after the cease-fire; and we are reminded of Napoleon's old-guard soldier who, preserved by his very desiccation, reawakens forty-six years later with the cry "Long live the Emperor!" The Colonel Fougas of the quarrel over inversion reawakens a century later with the cry "Death to Latin!" This exemplary fossil is none other than Jean-Pierre Brisset, whose *Grammaire logique* {Logical grammar} (a typical title) was published in 1883 at the height of historical linguistics, a time when the question of word order has completely left the field and an Indo-European filiation is universally accepted. Like Girard and Beauzée, Brisset refuses to acknowledge the slightest kinship between French and Latin, whose constructions are strictly inverse, and he pushes the devaluation of Latin word order to its ultimate conclusion: for him, Latin is not a natural language but the slang of brigands and, more specifically, a mechanical slang, like *le louchebem* or *le javanais* {pig Latin}, which operates simply by inverting the sentences of native Italian. "Latin is Italian in reverse. ... Latin no more comes from Latium than slang does from Slangia or Double-Dutch from Holland." *Latinus* comes from *latus* (carried) and/or from *latere* (to hide), and it means "hidden transposition" or, if you prefer, *secret inversion*. And "despite the masterpieces of those who have practiced the transposed writing style — Virgil, Cicero, Horace, and so many other great writers — the Latin language has always merely been a language contrary to nature, a slang that like the gang who invented it was civilized, perfected, ennobled, and finally welcomed, studied, and appreciated with an admiration that is all the more natural because the human mind recognizes it as its own work. As for nature, she rejects Latin. She will not adopt anything that is not her child: indifferent, she pursues her straight, simple, and logical path. Whatever does not issue from nature can, of course, through care, have a semblance of life for some time, but it must finally vanish. In all the so-called Latin countries, look for a province, a region, a town, a village, a valley lost in the mountains, a family at least, where Latin is the natural language: you will find none. Latin is what it has always been: an artificial language system, the work of men, a slang."[109] This last episode can be seen as comical: it is the party position of the *ordo rectus* pushed to paranoia.

⑨ We have come to the end of the overly long story of an overly long debate, a literally *interminable* one that is unable to find internal resolution either in mutual agreement or in the victory of one of the two camps—but suddenly evaporates with the collapse of the very ground of debate, the site of agreement and disagreement: the mimetic motivation of word order. The quarrel is false, then, in the double sense that the problem posed is a false problem and that the two parties agree on the essential issue, which is, of course, the very act of posing the problem. Consequently, we see the oppositions gradually diminishing, as, through syntheses, the crux of the question is approached.

At the practical (and, in this instance, aesthetic) level of what might be called the *function of discourse,* there is, as we have seen, an absolute opposition between an *intellectualist* conception—that of Du Marsais and Beauzée, for whom the end of discourse is essentially to "display" thought in the plainest way possible, according to its own proper order or according to the necessary order of its analysis—and a conception that I would like to term *sensitivist,* for which speech serves first and foremost to express sensations (Condillac) or feelings (Batteux), always according to the order of their succession. The first conception of the function of discourse, which is the dominant thesis here, probably best reflects the spirit of the Enlightenment in France, marked by a strong rationalist heritage in which Descartes has not yet completely eclipsed Aristotle. Through ossifying it a bit, this conception extends the aesthetic inspiration of French classicism, which will become that of neoclassicism and Laharpian academicism. Its central motive is the absolute separation between linguistics, with its purely intellectual function, and a rhetoric defined as a codified system of anomalies or exceptions[110] called *figures* and made responsible for taking on all the tasks refused by grammar. This separation is ruinous, and rhetoric, at once restrained in definition and generalized in function, becomes a dangerous supplement: everything that is not the impossible zero degree of style is held to be a figure and is marked and classified as such—whence the familiar proliferation of figures, a tumorous growth that will kill "classicism." (Isn't the "Sir, look out, a serpent is drawing near," at which Domergue scoffed, already too vivid for the grammarian? Could it not be seen as something like a lively and brilliant *apostrophe*? Wouldn't the pure exposition of thought instead be, after the interval necessary for analysis: "This man is probably going to die from a snake bite"? Not at all, for to speak to oneself is a *monologue*.)

The second conception of the function of discourse, held by the minority in France, represents an engaging double anachronism: it is archaic in its attachment to ancient languages and literatures but innovative in its valorization of sensation and affect, and through this it is actually much closer to the (pre-)Romantic movement that dominated the rest of Europe, from Vico to Herder. Here, a conscious and artificial rhetoric is not needed, since the expressive and the poetic are considered to be spontaneous and originary characteristics of the language system. Consequently, in Batteux (and occasionally in Diderot), rhetoric disappears in favor of a simple reading of immediate expressiveness, which prefigures both "modern" stylistics and, more directly, the disappearance of a *technē* now simply become (not to put too fine a point on it) useless and burdensome. On this level, then, no reconciliation is possible; as it turns out, history has settled this unresolved debate to the advantage of the opposition.

At the descriptive (and properly linguistic) level of the *system of natural languages,* the conflict between the partisans of "analogue" and "transpositive" languages seems insurmountable. But in actual fact, the two parties share the criterion of "construction" as the essential feature of a natural language, and they share a generally *creationist* conception of this characteristic, which identifies genealogy and typology and which blocks, for example, any research comparing modern and classical languages — that is to say, of course, any progress toward a scientific linguistics. The fixity in creationism is crystallized in an utterly typical fashion in the key idea of the *genius* of a natural language, which aptly marks the hereditary and immutable aspect of the syntactic schemata or "turns of phrase" proper to an idiom. This aspect is all the more noteworthy because, at that time, the genius of a language was generally not taken as expressing the character of the people who speak it: an expressive function was instead fulfilled by "pronounciation" — that is, the phonological system, determined by climate and environment (see Bouhours, Lamy, Gébelin, and others) — and by the lexicon, whose distribution of words reflects that of the centers of interest.[111] (This is the topos of the thousand synonyms for designating camel, sword, lion, and so forth in Arabic — a hackneyed and ubiquitous topos, at least since Chardin.) In contrast, syntactical genius is almost always a purely formal notion that does not seem to refer to extra-linguistic reality. Condillac alone attributes the antithetical geniuses of analogue and transpositive languages to the "dominant taste" for analysis or for imagination in a given people.[112] On the other hand, Beauzée and

Batteux are agreed on a purely immanent definition, which renders them equally incapable of explaining the existence of the language type whose naturalness they respectively deny. Beauzée goes no further than a concern about harmony, responsible for Latin inversions and, indirectly, for compensatory inflections; Batteux stops at the lack of inflections, which could well account for the regularity of the modern *ordo* but not its direction, which for him goes against nature. In either case, each natural language is consubstantial with its syntactical genius: no mutation can affect it; no influence can modify it, not even the intervention of the community of speakers. The absolute "synchronism" for which Saussure is sometimes reproached is present here: for the mechanists as well as for the metaphysicians, speech has no effect on the fate of a natural language.

On the face of it, early nineteenth-century linguistics sides with the mechanist party by once again espousing this party's valorization of classical languages. Yet the encounter is superficial, for on the one hand the criterion of identification will be no longer syntactical but morphological: Latin, Greek, and above all Sanskrit are no longer languages "with inversion" or with "natural order" but instead languages *with inflections,* and this technical change in criterion entails, or translates, an ideological displacement of the principle of evaluation, as we shall see. And, on the other hand, the typological barrier will no longer impede comparisons and the filiation of one type of natural language with another. Quite to the contrary: in those comparative linguists who are the most attached to typology, such as Schlegel and Schleicher, the shift (the decadence) from the inflectional type to the analytical type becomes the very principle of the general evolution of human languages. On this level, then, despite appearances, Batteux is closer to Beauzée than to Schlegel, from whom the first two are divided by the same historical abyss.

At the theoretical level, let us say, of the *nature of the language system,* the agreement becomes clear, and in our perspective it bears upon the central issue: the mimeticism of sentence construction. For both sides, the order of the sentence imitates the order of thought, and it could be said that the point of divergence, located downstream from this shared proposition, concerns not the nature of the language system any longer, but that of thought itself, viewed by some as a chain of ideas and by others as a succession of affects or sensations. Characteristically, in the two camps the fetishistic respect for the mimetic principle wins over the concern for rhetorical effectiveness. As we have seen, the metaphysicians valorize and advocate a uniform logical order, at the obvious risk of monotony and inexpressiveness; the "conative" function is yielded up, like many others, and in this way it is relegated to a figural supplement. But for their part, the mechanists, motivated by a naively conceived hierarchical bias (the most important word is always at the beginning), do not hesitate to establish an order of decreasing interest that goes against the most obvious requirements of attention — at the risk, this time, of seeing the hearer slip away before a conclusion that is not necessarily devoid of *interest*.

㉚ Syntactical mimeticism, constantly reasserted and reinforced across (and thanks to) a century of debate over a false problem, is a very specific variant of Cratylism: a secondary mimologism. For the purely diagrammatic iconicity of the sentence, superimposed on the arbitrariness of its elements (generally recognized here), is in every case a fact of speech, an individual performance burdened with abolishing or surmounting what Mallarmé would call the "haphazardness {*hasard*} remaining in verbal terms." But the syntactical schemata exploited by this secondary mimologism are also linguistic facts, proper to each idiom or group of idioms and inscribed in the rules of the speaker's grammatical "competence," wherein lies a primary mimologism. The situation is mixed, or ambiguous: in a way, language itself is supposed to correct itself and to "remunerate" its own proper "failing" {*défaut*} without any external intervention other than a utilization consonant with its resources. A "genius" is indeed needed in order to save language, but it is its own genius.

Such a consensus between two camps that appear to be so opposed clearly shows the deep ambivalence of a valorized theme like linguistic mimeticism and its capacity for multiple and even contradictory investments (or motivations): the rationalist motivates and justifies mimology through logic, the sensualist through the flux of emotions, but the theme of mimesis supports and commands these opposite "philosophical" motifs. It is precisely this *common place* — the ground, stakes, and condition of the debate — that will be suddenly engulfed on the threshold of the nineteenth century. As we shall see, in "Romantic" linguistics the theme of mimology almost completely disappears. For instance, Schlegel exalts natural languages with "internal inflections" no longer because they are mimetic but because they are *organic:* this term (as well as *morphology*) still betrays a naturalist valorization, but it is a new type that itself reflects a new conception of naturalness, which resides no longer in imitation, similarity, or "faithful painting" {*peinture fidèle*} but in a language's internal dynamism and capacity for autonomous development. Classical languages are "organic" because the very "root" of their words contains in "embryo" or "germ" a capacity for expressing grammatical relationships, which amounts to a capacity for internal differentiation and for constitution into a paradigmatic system. Grammatical relationships are expressed no longer by a hierarchical ordering of succession but by a specific system of arbitrary and rule-governed differences. The reader will recall that one of the errors for which Batteux rightly reproached his opponents was their confusion of syntactical relations and syntactical order. This criticism is probably the point on which the mechanists come nearest to the comparative grammarians, but it remains purely negative; nowhere did these defenders of

Latin express or probably even experience a genuine *feeling for inflection* as the synoptic and instantaneous expression of grammatical relationships. The closest thing to this would be the exaltation — not in Batteux, but in Condillac and especially Lamy — of the *simultaneous unity* of the Latin sentence, which presents all its parts "united together as they are in the mind," which "sees several objects at a single glance" (Lamy), so that its different objects, producing a "picture" {*tableau*} for us, "strike all at once" (Condillac). But Condillac immediately adds: "Such is the power of *inversion* over the imagination" — the syntactical model remains dominant. From Schlegel through Saussure (and hence beyond), while the syntagmatic imagination gives way to a far-reaching reverie on paradigms, the theme of the valorization of resemblance at the same time necessarily fades away before the theme of difference. Language-as-organism, then language-as-structure, wipes out speech-as-reflection.

Despite all this, it cannot be said that Cratylus has definitively and absolutely lost the game. For if over one century some have agreed to see in the order of discourse a faithful image of (individual) thought as a succession and, through thought, a faithful image of the world as event, others will soon be able to find in the system of natural language the image — more complex, less immediate, but equally *representational* — of this (collective) capacity of thought, which is also a system and a construction and which is about to be called the *spirit* (*Geist*) of a people.

CHAPTER 10

Internal Inflection

⊗ Perhaps no event in the entire history of linguistic thought has had a more decisive influence on the course of the mimological imagination than the "turning point," at the borderline between the eighteenth and nineteenth centuries, created by the "discovery" of Sanskrit and the birth of comparative grammar for Indo-European languages.[1] Max Müller has wisely pointed out the impact of this important discovery upon that era's prevailing ideas about the filiation of natural languages; he recalls the typical refusal—Dugald Stewart's for example—to admit a kinship between the classical languages and the tongue "of the black inhabitants of India." He rightly emphasizes the merit of Friedrich von Schlegel, "the first who dared boldly to face both the facts and the conclusions of Sanskrit scholarship" and whose essay "On the Language and Philosophy of the Indians," published only two years (1808) after the first volume of Johann Adelung's *Mithridates*, "is separated from that work by the same distance which separates the Copernican from the Ptolemaic system. Schlegel was not a great scholar. Many of his statements have proved erroneous; and nothing would be easier than to dissect his essay and hold it up to ridicule. But Schlegel was a man of genius; and when a new science is to be created, the imagination of the poet is wanted, even more than the accuracy of the scholar. It surely required a somewhat poetic vision to embrace with *one* glance the languages of India, Persia, Greece, Italy, and Germany and to rivet them together by the simple name of Indo-Germanic. This was Schlegel's work; and in the history of the intellect it has been truly called 'the discovery of a new world.'"[2]

Of course, the definition of causes and effects is always a risky business, in this domain as in the entire field of the history of ideas. Certain intellectual attitudes that are in the air at the time manage very well without the objective determinations believed indispensable to them: thus, we have come across some inflections of ideas in Charles Nodier which could easily be attributed to Schlegel's or Wilhelm von Humboldt's influence, if the details of his investigation did not tend to invalidate this hypothesis, and we already find some analogues for this in Herder and Daniel Jenisch.[3] And conversely, as everyone knows, a "discovery" can remain a dead letter so long as it has not struck its resonance and therefore found its historical relevance. Between the "new fact" that is the introduction of

Sanskrit at the end of the eighteenth century, and the much more diffuse and elusive circumstance that is the birth of a "new spirit" in linguistics, it is impossible to distinguish which one contributed more to the development of comparative grammar and, directly or indirectly, to this turning point of Cratylism which is now going to occupy our attention.[4] At least we can try to take stock of the influence of certain specific features of the new "science" for its own sake.

The most monumental feature, with the weightiest effect, is obviously the very notion of an *Indo-European family:* that is, the discovery of the historical kinship and ultimately the original identity of those natural languages, "classical" and modern, which in preceding centuries were readily lumped together under the optimistic label of "the greatest number of natural languages." The consequence for the debate over the nature of the sign was to weaken a whole set of arguments based on certain semantic correspondences between these languages. To take the usual example, the (natural) signification of "stop" or "immobility" assigned to the consonantal group *st* had once found ready proof, or confirmation, in the remarkable extension of the phenomenon across so many natural languages, as "diverse" as Greek, Latin, French, Italian, Spanish, German, English — so numerous and so diverse that they could represent the "majority" of human languages for certain thinkers (with the help of a little Eurocentrism and a lot of ignorance). The value *st* = "stop" could then be finally considered, with negligible exceptions, one of the "universals of language" and one index of its mimetic nature. At least this could be done at the level of those hasty inferences that satisfied prescientific speculation, which in the present case identified universality with naturalness, naturalness with necessity, and, more specifically here, necessity with mimeticism. In rigorous theoretical terms, of course, the (supposed) universality of a linguistic fact does not *prove* its naturalness, and conversely, besides, its restriction to a single family of natural languages by no means settles the question of its original motivation: the value *st* = "fixedness" could quite easily both be peculiar to a language and nonetheless have been selected in that language for its mimetic nature — a quality that would have evaded the "namemakers" of all the other languages. But at the level of verisimilitude and common presupposition, these disjunctions have no force. Here was the Cratylian argument, in all its simplicity: "That so many diverse natural languages chose to designate fixedness by words including the group *st* cannot be the result of chance; there is therefore a necessary relation between this sound and this meaning; this relation is, moreover, natural, and so on." It is this line of reasoning that collapses with the constitution of the Indo-European "family": Greek, Latin, French, and the rest, are suddenly restored to unity (of origin), and consequently their correspondence no longer proves anything: *st* = "fixedness" (like so many other connections of meaning) is no more than an "Indo-European root" and therefore ceases to be one of the universals of language; by the same token, its mimetic motivation loses a great deal in the way of probability.

Paradoxically, then, the discovery of the unity of Indo-European, which historically reduces to one single language a fairly large number of the most important and best-known natural languages, ends up weakening the Cratylian idea of the unity of language. This is because in fact the thesis of the original unity of natural languages can be interpreted in two highly different ways — only one of which serves Cratylus's purpose. The first consists in saying that there was at the origin only a single natural language, that of the first human group, a group and language from which arose all groups and all human languages. This hypothesis, which was Herder's, for example, leaves wide open the question of the nature of this original language, which could just as well be conventional as motivated — and of course it deprives of their indexical value for motivation any universal correspondences that might proceed simply from a unity of origin. The second assumes that all men, as scattered as they originally might have been, spontaneously, without realizing it and without having *passed the word around,* invented the same natural language at various points on the globe; here, of course, the thesis of the naturalness of language is considerably reinforced. This second hypothesis, for rather obvious reasons, has never to my knowledge been as clearly formulated; but the Cratylian party's preference for the unitarist thesis, up through the end of the eighteenth century, has always been due, it seems to me, to an implicit confusion and a surreptitious shift from one to the other. By demonstrating the common origin of most European languages, and by letting the imagination glimpse (momentarily) a progressive reduction of all the "families" to a single one, comparative grammar seems to approach the first hypothesis; but in fact it contributes above all to discredit the second one, since it reduces a large number of correspondences to a simple historical filiation. "It is not by any means my intention to dispute," says Schlegel, "the spontaneous origin of language generally, but merely the theory that *all* were originally similar."[5] This is already much, and it inevitably reinforces the conventionalist argument for the diversity of natural languages.

A second feature, with a subtler effect, comes from the very method of comparative grammar and can also be inferred from its name. For centuries, people most often compared natural languages by putting the words side by side, intuitively reckoning that the lexicon is the whole of a language. The only counterview to this attitude was, above all in the eighteenth century, an attempt to define natural languages by their syntactic "genius"; an apparently grammatical consideration, this was itself, in fact, as we have seen, also inspired by the mimetic *parti pris.* Comparative grammar accords a decisive relevance to what began to be called the grammatical *structure* of natural language, which is not identical, as we will see, with the syntagmatic structure of the proposition but presages the Saussurean notion of *system* or of implicit paradigmatic organization. From the first page of his essay, Schlegel, observing that the resemblance between Sanskrit and European languages "is not only found in a large number of common roots but also extends into the internal structure of these languages, and into the grammar," immediately draws the following conclusion: "This conformity is therefore not at all an accidental one, which might be explained by borrowing; it is an essential, fundamental conformity, which reveals a common origin." This principle of the relevance of grammatical structure, still implicit here, would be made explicit six years later and erected into a methodical rule by Rasmus Rask. We will describe it in more detail further on.

Lexical considerations thus pass into the background of linguistic thought: an unfavorable circumstance for Cratylian speculation, which has always been essentially concerned with the relationships between "words" (and more precisely *nouns*) and "things." With comparative grammar, a new reversal of values will operate inside the lexicon itself. "The levers of all words," Jakob Grimm will claim, are not the nouns but the "pronouns and verbs."[6] This is as much as to say "the verb and its satellites," or else "the action and its supports." This turn is clearly decisive for the Cratylian imagination. The reverie on the *appropriateness of nouns* cannot, without deep mutation, become a reverie on the *appropriateness of verbs*. Michel Foucault, quoting this same formula from Grimm, has rightly shown how natural language, henceforth characterized in this way, will speak essentially no longer about objects but about actions, and will from then on be "'rooted' not in the things perceived, but in the active subject."[7] This revolution, itself Copernican also, will have to be taken into account by Cratylus.

But the substitution of the verb for the noun as the fundamental element of the lexicon is nevertheless not the most decisive aspect of the mutation. For this, we will borrow from Oswald Ducrot, who gives the clearest statement: "Linguists hesitated for a long time in deciding which were the words whose resemblance in two different languages proves their kinship, and which words were therefore the least likely to have been borrowed and must be inherited. A doctrine was finally established according to which the key lay in the grammatical signs, endings, affixes, prepositions, shifters, and so on."[8] Here we again encounter the primacy of grammar, but embodied in the lexical material, in *grammatical signs:* connectives, affixes, inflectional elements. It is now time to recall, for confirmation, Rask's precept: "Grammatical correspondence is a much surer indication [than any lexicons] of original kinship or identity, because one natural language that is mixed together with another borrows only rarely, or never borrows, its *morphological* changes or inflections."[9] This is the decisive comment: the grammar in question here, which would hold the foreground of debate for more than half a century, is not that grammar of the sentence which had so intensely occupied the supporters of classical "general grammar," from Port-Royal to Beauzée; it is the grammar present *in the words*, embodied in words or parts of words—that is, *morphology*. Comparative grammar, as everyone knows, was essentially a comparative morphology, and this promotion of the morphological had as its immediate consequence the projection of the grammatical being of natural language—or its relational being and its capacity for abstraction—onto the lexical material. The most striking instance of this is Humboldt's theory of "grammatical forms" (inflections and connectives), which constantly valorizes the grammaticalization of the word as the imprint of the *mind* on language and, conversely, as the (only) way to access the highest forms of abstraction. In the state of what he calls "formalness" (the use of pure morphemes, without concrete signification), the word "has not only a lexicological but also a grammatical individuality; the words charged with the representation of the form no longer have an accessory signification, which clouds the understanding; they have become pure signs of *relationships*."[10] I have underscored the key word here, which recurs again and again, and not only in Humboldt: the relational character of grammatical significations symbolizes and guarantees their high level of abstraction. "Relationships" are not things, and the definition of natural language—and of the lexicon itself—as a "nomenclature" is henceforth finished for good.[11]

Yet there are several degrees to this integration of the grammatical, and the system of values promoted by the first comparatists will have the effect of emphasizing the most integrated forms possible. One of the reasons for the fascination exercised by Sanskrit is this language's capacity for marking grammatical relations by what Schlegel narrowly terms inflection, "or internal variations of the primitive word."[12] This extreme restriction will not be retained by Bopp and his heirs; it is nonetheless revelatory of a desire.[13] The ideal linguistic state would be one in which the entire morphology could be concentrated in the play of vocalic alternations "inside" the radical, excluding any play of affixes. A passage from Schlegel's essay on the Indians makes this *parti pris* wonderfully explicit in a comparison between the morphological devices of ancient Greek and Sanskrit:

In the Greek, the annexed syllables, now blended inseparably with the primitive word, were originally distinct particles and auxiliaries; but this hypothesis cannot be carried out without the assistance of an etymological skill and subtlety which must be unhesitatingly rejected in every scientific investigation or historical contemplation of the origin of language; even then, indeed, the theory could hardly be maintained. Not the slightest appearance of any such amalgamation can be traced in the Indian language; it must be allowed that its structure is highly organized, formed by inflection, or the change and transposition of its primary radical sounds, carried through every ramification of meaning and expression, and not by the merely mechanical process of annexing words or particles to the same lifeless and unproductive root.[14]

We recognize here the organicist metaphor that will burden the theory of the evolution of natural languages for such a long time, but we should be aware of the nature of the linguistic position expressed through this biological image: a "lifeless" root is an *immutable* root—that is, one incapable of internal inflections—which must resort to the play of affixes.[15] A fertile root, in contrast, is a root that contains in itself all the resources necessary for the work of morphology and derivation. It is obviously, therefore, more than a root: it is a "living productive germ," the "living germ essential to a copious development."[16] The valorization is so strong here that the Greek inflections, although actually "organic" (according to Schlegel), find themselves nearly disqualified simply because they are not so in an adequately conspicuous way and because they could, like Caesar's wife, foster suspicion. This valorization of course commands Schlegel's typology of natural languages, which Schleicher will merely refine: there exist natural languages with inflections, in the strong sense, which are the Indo-European languages; and there exist all the others, all those which, to various degrees, separate the radical and the morphological tools.[17] It also commands Schlegel's idea of linguistic evolution, less "pessimistic" because more complex than his successors' (Bopp's in particular): whereas inflected languages degenerate (for example, from Sanskrit to English) by betraying the (supposed) absolute syntheticism of Sanskrit in favor of more and more analytical devices (articles, prepositions, word order, and so on), the other languages on the contrary progress (from Chinese to Arabic) by integrating their originally external morphemes more and more into the radical. The foreseeable result is a stabilization into general mediocrity.

I recall these well-known hypotheses here only for the illustration they provide of the fundamental *parti pris,* that of the "internal inflection." In a very significant manner, this valorization comes to occupy exactly the position of the analytical *ordo naturalis:* "languages of inflection" are nothing other than the philosopher-grammarians' "languages of inversion" but rehabilitated and even praised to the skies for the inspired abstraction of their grammatical method, which no longer owes anything to the vulgar, even puerile, imitation of the relation of ideas by the arrangement of words. What is really overthrown and discredited here through this redistribution of the linguistic palm is therefore the mimeticist *parti pris.*

Moreover, and in a perhaps even more decisive way, the promotion of the inflectional order ends up compromising the privileged object of mimetic reverie: the word. The expression of relations by the order of words presented the following double advantage: not only did it institute an imitative syntax, but it also left every word intact, free from any tie and devoid of all grammatical taint. Say *the king loves the people* or *the people loves the king:* every "whole" word preserves its lexical autonomy and physiognomy, and therefore its eventual mimetic power; say *populus regem amat* or *rex populum amat*, and already you see the declensional inflection encroaching upon the two substantives. Move on to the ideal state of the internal inflection, conjugate the Greek *leipo, elipon, leloipa* or the English *sing, sang, sung*, and you suppress almost the entire demarcation between morphemes and semantemes, and therefore disintegrate the traditional "word" from the inside by stuffing even the very heart of its semantic core with "grammatical" elements. It is true that de Brosses and (to a lesser extent) Gébelin (but not Plato or Wallis or Nodier) safeguarded themselves somewhat against this infringement by abandoning the vowels — the site par excellence of the internal inflection — to accidental historical mutations and by concentrating the essence of the immutable sematic value in the consonantal "scaffolding," whence *peregrinus = bilgram.* But it is one thing to consider the vowels as semantically empty and therefore transparent; it is another thing to recognize them as filled with a decisive grammatical value, which once noticed can no longer be ignored. The mimologist solution would consist, then, in motivating the vocalic alternation itself, by attributing (in Gébelin's style, for example) the mimetic value of the present (*existence*) to the degree *e* of *leipo*, the aorist (zero tense) to the zero degree *elipon*, and the perfect (because of its circular perfection) to the degree *o leloipa;* or (in Wallis's style) by reading in the progressive "darkening" of *sing/sang/sung* the image of the temporal distancing of present/preterite/perfect. But this type of hypothesis hardly seems to have been used, and this relative neglect is no accident: morphological Cratylism is a historical oxymoron or, rather, an anachronism.[18] Thus, the "lifeless and unproductive roots," once reduced to a semantic core, well served the purpose of the mimetic imagination, which found in them pure elements of "meaning" rid of all relational dross and given over to the blissful *tête-à-tête* between "word" and "thing." The "living germs" put an end to this isolation: the word is no longer merely the sign of an object; it is permeated by both more abstract and more subjective notions, caught in a network of relations, modalities, and aspects in which the "activating subject" finds himself inevitably implicated.

Three other considerations, themselves also inspired by the study of Sanskrit and closely linked to one another, complete our mining of the linguistic ground of the mimologist thesis. One of the most widely granted propositions in the neoclassical age, admitted even by the staunchest Hermogenists, was that at least at its origin language must unavoidably have arisen out of natural sounds (cries), onomatopoeia, and/or spontaneous exclamations, even if it then gradually lost the traces of this origin by making an increasingly greater allowance for convention. Another was the necessarily figurative character of the earliest language, whose incapacity for abstraction compelled it to metaphorize the abstract through the concrete, the idea through the sensation, with the "flowery" style of Iroquois or Algonquin harangues generally bearing the brunt of the argument.[19] The third, which almost went without saying in this context, was the absence of grammar in primitive languages. Grammar, linked to the capacity for abstraction, could only be an acquisition (good or bad) of civilized man. "Since every grammar," said Herder, for example, "is only a philosophy of language and a method for its use, it follows that the more primordial a language is, the less grammar must there be in it, and the oldest language is no more than the... dictionary of nature."[20]

These three points are triply refuted by the study of Sanskrit, regarded by Schlegel as the probable ancestor of all the "Indo-Germanic" languages and so as an authentic example of primitive language.[21] On the last point, the striking grammaticality of Sanskrit passes without comment; as for the first two — other natural languages might originate in imitation and figuration, but not "ours."[22] Sanskrit shows neither onomatopoeia nor interjection nor metaphor in its formation; from its first steps, it ascends to the purest abstraction:

The earliest language was not the mere instinctive cry of physical nature, nor was it from an indiscriminate imitation of natural tones, nor from fancy indulging in a sportive experimental combination of sounds that it arose, gradually engrafting on its first rude commencement a more rational expression and reasonable form. The structure of language, on the contrary, is but one proof added in confirmation of so many others, that the primitive condition of mankind was not one of mere animal instinct, which by slow degrees, and with many a weary effort, at length attained some slight glimmering of reason and intelligence; it rather confirms the opposite belief, proving that, if not in every country, at least in that which is now the subject of our investigations, the most profound study and the clearest intelligence were early called into operation; for without much labour and reflection it would have been impossible to frame a language like the Indian, which, even in its simplest form, exemplifies the loftiest ideas of the pure world of thought, and displays the entire ground plan of the consciousness, not in figurative symbols, but in direct and immediate clearness and precision.... This lofty spirituality is at the same time extremely simple, not originally conveyed through the medium of representations of merely sensual expressions, but primarily based upon the peculiar and appropriate signification of the fundamental elements as originally established. The distinct genus of many, which, though quite clear in meaning, yet admits only of a purely metaphysical interpretation, allows us to determine a high antiquity either historically from the employment of the terminology, or etymologically from the compounded words. It is a most unfounded idea that in the earliest epoch of each language a bold and irregular fancy alone predominated; it may have been the case with many, but certainly not in all, nor in the Indian especially, in which a profound philosophical signification and perspicuity of expression are even more striking than poetical inspiration or imagery.[23]

Even if it is in fact reserved for a single family of natural languages (and peoples), this is a reversal of topos quite comparable, in the linguistic domain, to the one Lévi-Strauss will perform one day in the field of social anthropology: to wit, the discovery of a "savage" mind that in its capacity for abstraction rivals the more elaborate forms of the "modern" mind. That this reversal proceeds from a false hypothesis (that of Sanskrit's primitiveness) is perhaps a ruse of reason; that it is, by virtue of another error or of an ethnocentric prejudice, limited to the Indo-European group, with all the ideological (and other) consequences that flow from it in their turn, is perhaps a ruse of madness, which is not lacking either. What matters to us here is once again the effects of these "new facts," true or false (true *and* false), on the Cratylian debate. One obvious consequence: on a limited but (for a thousand reasons) central point of the linguistic atlas, the thesis of originary mimesis is now refuted for the first time by "fact."

ⓑ A setback, then, for the mimologist thesis—at least for those whom the new linguistic doctrine will reach, sooner or later.[24] For Cratylian reverie is by nature a trammeled reverie, constantly relative to the linguistic information of the dreamer and therefore, indirectly, to the state of science in his time as much as to the dynamics of his mimological desire. The observable result is always a specific equilibrium between these diverse forces, which are much more difficult to measure separately. With knowledge supposed to be appreciably similar, Cratylus and Hermogenes, de Brosses and Turgot, Jespersen and Saussure are respectively differentiated by the intensity of contrary *partis pris,* which determine the divergent interpretations of nearly identical information. With a supposedly similar prejudice (all highly cavalier suppositions, to be sure), Gébelin and Mallarmé, for example, are separated by a century (and what a century!) of the history of linguistics, each one being approximately on a par with the knowledge of his time. One could obviously say this about Jean-Pierre Brisset, who was chronologically contemporary with Mallarmé but fossilized by his ignorance (and delirium) into an intellectual lag of several centuries. A defeat, then, of mimologism in general and in its most ambitious guises—but also, and perhaps through an unconscious maneuver to avoid or delay defeat, a transformation or a displacement.

Transformations and displacements. From the nineteenth century onward (and we have seen the broad outline in Nodier), in order to survive, Cratylism will without doubt have to modify itself more profoundly than ever before. Later, we will find other metamorphoses, which will have as their common feature the transference of the mimological dream from the domain of "science" to that of "literature": poetry, fiction, the game recognized and assumed as such or projected into "childhood memories." Let us consider beforehand the most immediate mutation, which not only is provoked, as if mechanically, by the upset of comparatism but directly invests one of its fundamental inspirations in a new form of mimetic reverie. Comparative grammar is not only, or not exactly, a manifestation of conventionalism pure and simple; if it were, it would concern us here in a much less direct manner. It is also or, rather, it performs a subversion, an inversion {*retournement*}, and a diversion {*détournement*} of mimologism. In its course it determines what I would like to call, straining the meaning of this key notion a bit, an *internal inflection* { *flexion interne*}.[25]

We have observed, in all the areas in which its influence is felt, that the comparatist revolution tended to displace the accent of linguistic representation from the object designated toward the activity of the designating subject, from spoken "things" to speaking thought, from the unity of the extralinguistic world to the diversity of natural languages and peoples. This displacement could only have favored and intensified a feature of thought in the epoch from which, once again, it was partly derived; let us call this feature, a bit hastily, Romantic subjectivism.[26] Clearly, it hardly jibes with the traditional forms of the Cratylian imagination, which are entirely oriented toward the "objective" relation that unites word and thing. But if, as we have already observed, Cratylism proceeds from a universal and somewhat protean desire to find a mimetic motivation for every signifying relation, it can attempt as well, when the occasion presents itself and/or when every other path is momentarily blocked, to motivate that other signifying relation which unites the sign to its producer. If we are willing to admit every interpretation of a conventional sign as an image based on resemblance into the notion of mimologism (authentically and legitimately extensible), we perhaps can agree to define and baptize as *subjective mimologism* the attitude that consists of finding in a way of speaking (idiolect, sociolect, idiom) the faithful "expression" of an individual, a group, a nation — or, as formerly and highly imprudently claimed, a "race." Here we reencounter the "genius of natural languages," but this time indissolubly associated, through resemblance (and reciprocal determination), with the *genius of national characters*.

CHAPTER 11

Desert Languages

@ For Ernest Renan as for so many others, the advent of "comparative philology" invalidates beyond return all previous debates on the origin and the
nature of language: "From the day when the science of natural languages became one of the sciences of life, the problem of the origins of language was
transferred to its true ground, the ground of the creative consciousness. Its birth
still remained mysterious, but at least it was clear to which order of facts it had
to be connected and from which sorts of conceptions it was properly deduced."[1]
To begin with, Renan dismisses as equally unsatisfactory both the hypothesis of
a progressive formation of language (Condillac, Herder) and that of a conscious
invention (Plato) or divine revelation (Beauzée, Bonald) of language. Language
could take shape only "at one stroke," from a single *jet,* in the image picked up
again by Friedrich Schlegel: *Hervorbringung im Ganzen.*[2] "The invention of language was the result not of a long process of trial and error but of a primitive
intuition, which revealed to each race the general cut of its discourse and the
great compromise that it had to make once and for all with its thought."[3] But
on the other hand, this "primitive intuition" could not be deliberate: as Turgot
had already understood, "natural languages are not the work of a reason present
to itself."[4] This sudden creation, immediately complete, at least *in posse,* just as
"the bud already contains the entire flower," belongs to a category that for Renan
transcends the opposition between the conscious and the unconscious, and also
between the human and the divine: that of the *spontaneous.* "The spontaneous
is divine and human at the same time. Herein lies the point of reconciliation
for incomplete rather than contradictory opinions, which, according as they are
tied to one aspect of a phenomenon more than to another, possess their share
of truth by turns." The instrument or, rather, the site of this creation is of the
order neither of the senses nor of the reason but of the collective *genius:* "Individuals are not up to it, whatever their genius; as a medium for transmission of
thought, the *scientific language* of Leibniz would probably have been less convenient and more barbaric than Iroquois. The most beautiful and the richest
idioms have come with all their resources out of a silent elaboration that was unaware of itself. In contrast, the languages plied, tormented, fabricated by human
hands bear the mark of this origin in their lack of flexibility, their laborious

189

construction, their want of harmony. Every time the grammarians have tried to reform a natural language from a premeditated plan, they have succeeded only in making it clumsy, expressionless, and often less logical than the humblest patois." Nodier expressed much the same view, but he happened to misunderstand the consequences in proposing at least some reform of writing. Now, the exclusive competence of the collective genius (the people, the race) forbids any kind of secondary mimologism. "The people is the true artisan of natural languages because it best represents the spontaneous energies of humanity."[5]

As is quite clear, this new positioning of the problem is already entirely oriented not toward the object of linguistic communication but toward its subject, creator, and user. The term communication itself is too objective and, as it were, too distant to specify what is at issue. Through language, or rather *in* language, man does not merely communicate; he shapes and elaborates a thought that would otherwise remain unworthy of the name: "To speak is always to transform intuitions into ideas," and to reduce natural language to the role of a simple instrument of transmission is to misunderstand "another no less important function of speech, which is to serve as formula and boundary for thought."[6]

The classical hypothesis of the onomatopoetic origin of language is not exactly rejected ("imitation or onomatopoeia seems to have been the common procedure according to which the first nomenclators formed appellations"). It is, in a quite characteristic fashion, turned back toward the true source of mimetic appellation, which is no longer the nature — superficial or deep — of the object imitated but the soul of the imitator. First — and this has rarely appeared in the Cratylian tradition and here distantly echoes Schlegel — because the mimetic "method" is more or less active, depending on the peoples and therefore depending on the natural languages in question: it is "very perceptible in the Semitic languages and in Hebrew in particular, . . . rarer or more difficult to discern in the Indo-European languages."[7] In short, it would seem that there exist Cratylian peoples and Hermogenist peoples, which reconciles two theses by subsuming them into an equally frustrating one. Second, above all — and this is openly presented as a reply to Plato — because "the appellations do not have their unique cause in the object named (without which they would be the same in all natural languages) but in the object named as seen through the personal proclivities of the naming subject."[8] Hence the emphasis laid on the argument, often used before from Epicurus to Nodier — but becoming here a central element of the system — of the diversity of appellations linked to the diversity of aspects according to the diversity of temperaments: "It is pointless to raise as an objection against this theory [of onomatopoeia] the difference of the articulations through which diverse peoples have expressed an identical physical fact. In effect, the same object presents itself to the senses under a thousand aspects, among which each family of natural languages chooses to its taste that which appears typical. Let us take thunder, for example. However well determined such a phenomenon might be, it strikes man in various ways and can be equally depicted as a muffled noise, as a crackling, as a sudden explosion of light, and so forth. Adelung claims to have collected more than 353, all taken from European languages, and all obviously formed on nature."[9] Moreover, the sensibility of the primitive nomenclators, more delicate than ours, enabled them to discover a thousand "imitative relations which elude us and which struck the first men vividly." Arabic (the observation is proverbial) is supposed to have had 500 words to designate the lion, 1,000 for the sword, 5,744 for the camel. "The faculty of interpretation, which is only an extreme acuity in grasping relationships, was more developed in them than in us; they saw a thousand things at once. No longer needing to create language, we have in a way unlearned the art of giving names to things; but primitive men possessed this art, which the child and the common man apply with such boldness and felicity. Nature speaks to them more than to us, or rather they find in themselves a secret echo that responds to all the voices of the outside and returns them as articulated sounds, as words."[10] Let us note this characteristically regretful tone: *or rather* — it is no longer nature that speaks; it is the interior echo that responds in words to the speechless voices of the outside; and this "secret" echo is clearly more and better than an imitation.

This subjectivist reversal of the Cratylian theme is concentrated and symbolized in what might, in another context, seem to be a terminological subtlety. Juxtaposing the onomaturgic activity of the first men, who were guided by analogies imperceptible to us, with the comparable activity of children and common people, Renan concludes his chapter 6 with a strange formula: "The connection of meaning and word is never *necessary,* never *arbitrary;* it is always *motivated.*"[11] Here Cratylus and Hermogenes are both dismissed, because both are victims of the *same* illusion, the one affirming ("necessary"), the other denying ("arbitrary") an objective, universal, and permanent connection between meaning and word, whereas this connection can only be subjective: *motivated, but from the inside.*

@ Such a philosophy of language obviously leaves no room for the hypothesis of an originary common natural language: "To suppose that there was at the origin of humanity a single primitive tongue, from which all the others derive by direct descent, is to impose a hypothesis, and the least probable hypothesis, onto the facts."[12] This refusal springs a priori from the premises that we have just seen, but it is corroborated by the discoveries of modern "philology" besides:

At first glance, the science of natural languages appears to bring a decisive weight into the balance. If the outcome is indeed incontestable, it is because the network of natural languages which have been or are still spoken on the surface of the globe is divided into families absolutely irreducible to each other. Even supposing that the Semitic family and the Indo-European family could one day be merged one with the other (a supposition that I do not grant, and which good philology is closer and closer to rejecting), and supposing (which I also do not grant) that the two African families, one represented by Coptic, the other by Berber or better by Tuareg, could one day be reunited to the above-mentioned languages, one can at least argue that it will absolutely never be possible to classify in the same group Chinese and the languages of east Asia. . . . There is here an abyss that no scientific effort is able to bridge. Whatever might be the future hypotheses of science on questions of origin, one can lay down the following proposition as an axiom henceforth established: language does not have a unique origin; it was produced concurrently at several points. These points could have been very near in space; their appearances could have been almost simultaneous; but certainly they were distinct, and the principle of the old school — *all natural languages are the dialects of one single natural language* — must be forever abandoned.[13]

If one wanted to envisage a unity of human language, it would have to be situated not at the beginning of evolution but at its endpoint, after a long labor of winnowing and thinning out, just as Greece in the long run established its *koine,* or Italy adopted the *lingua toscana.*[14] Even so, under the circumstances it was a matter of unifying several dialects (through fusion or exclusion). But a true natural language cannot lend itself to such an assimilation, because a natural language is a system, or rather an autonomous and irreducible organism, which evolves solely by developing the virtualities contained in its original "seed," which "unfolds itself through its innermost force and through the urgent bidding of its parts." "A seed is put into place, keeping hidden *in posse* all that the creature will one day be; the seed unfolds itself, the shapes constitute themselves in their orderly proportions, what was potential becomes actual; but nothing is built up, nothing is added: such is the general law of creatures subject to the conditions of life. Such was also the law of language."[15] The image of the seed, which Schlegel applied to every "fecund root," is now extended to the entire idiom and dominates Renan's whole idea of linguistic evolution, viewed not as a history but as a simple passage from potentiality to action: a natural language can become only what it has always been.[16]

This crucial seed, this indestructible genetic patrimony, cannot be the lexicon; it is the "rational form without which words would not have been a *natural language:* in other words, grammar. . . . The error of the eighteenth century was to take too little account of grammar in its analyses of discourse. Sounds do not form a natural language, any more than sensations make a man. What makes language, just as it makes thought, is the logical link that the mind establishes between things." This is a highly unjust appraisal of the century of Harris and Beauzée, but we have already seen all that separated the grammar of the philosopher-grammarians from that of the comparative philologists. For Renan, eighteenth-century linguistics remains essentially that of de Brosses and Gébelin, and he does not hesitate to attribute entirely to the new school the great methodological principle, previously that of Abbot Girard, according to which "in the task of classifying natural languages, grammatical conditions are much more important than lexicological considerations."[17] As a result of this, the new notion of grammatical structure receives in him the same absolutist interpretation that Girard or Beauzée gave to that of syntactic "genius." There is nothing here of the pessimism of a Schlegel or a Bopp, nothing either of the future optimism of a Jespersen: nothing budges. Chinese, born "without grammar," remains forever without grammar. The Semitic languages, deprived at the origin of a "satisfactory system of tenses and of modes," will remain forever thus deprived. "Each natural language is imprisoned once and for all in its grammar; it can acquire, through the passage of time, more grace, elegance, and smoothness; but its distinctive qualities, its vital principle, its soul, if I dare say so, appear completely fixed right away."[18] A natural language cannot, any more than a creature, change its *soul*.

℗ The specific point of application for these principles was to be Semitic languages. Professor of Hebrew at the Collège de France from 1862,[19] Renan had given himself as early as 1847 a task and a model for the first outline of *Histoire générale et système comparé des langues sémitiques* {General history and comparative method of the Semitic languages}: "I set out to produce, to the best of my ability, *for the Semitic languages what Mr. Bopp did for the Indo-European languages:* that is to say, a chart of the grammatical system which would show in what way the Semites succeeded in giving complete expression to thought through speech."[20] He explains in his preface {to the *Histoire*} of 1855 how the systematic aim found itself gradually supplanted by a historical purpose — a provisional supplantation in principle but one that remained definitive, since the "theoretical" volume that ought to have followed never saw light. In fact, we have already been able to observe that theory is anything but absent from this first part (which largely repeats the material of *De l'origine du langage* {On the origin of language}) and to recognize the limits (theoretical, precisely) of his historical point of view. Perhaps the difference from Bopp (or Schlegel) does not lie exactly where Renan sees it, and perhaps it comes precisely from an excessive fidelity to his model. This will be clarified, I hope, in the upcoming pages. For the moment, let us remark only that Mr. Schlegel or Mr. Bopp, for their parts, never gave themselves models — and for a reason — in their work on the Indo-European languages: their contribution could only have been self-contained. Renan's is not and, in short, could not have been. To do for the Semitic languages what others had done for the Indo-European languages (that is, to produce a comparative grammar) almost inevitably meant attempting to apply to this new "family" the methods tested on the other, thus to set out on its discovery with the character-istic features of the other constantly in mind, and finally to be able to describe the former only in opposition and in contrast to the latter. So we will find not a "chart" of the Semitic languages in Renan, as we found a chart of the Indo-European languages in the Germans, but a sort of *inverse* of the latter, based on a perpetual comparison in which the Aryanocentric valorizations already per-ceptible in Schlegel will be developed in a somewhat unfortunate manner.

It should be pointed out right away that although Renan constantly uses the terms "Semitic race" and "Aryan race," the difference, for him, is not of an anthropological order: "The division of the Semites and the Indo-Europeans has been created by philology and not by physiology. Although the Jews and the Arabs have a highly pronounced type, which prevents confusing them with the Europeans, never would scholars who envisaged man from the viewpoint of natural history have dreamed of seeing in this type a mark of race, had not the study of natural languages, confirmed by that of literatures and religions, made recognizable here a distinction that the study of the body did not reveal." Even more clearly: "The individuality of the Semitic race having been revealed to us only through the analysis of language, an analysis singularly confirmed, it is true, by the study of customs, literatures, and religions, this race being, in a way, created by philology, there is really only one criterion for recognizing the Semites: language." [21] Aryans and Semites constitute for him (over against "Mongols" and "Negroes") a unique race ("white" or "Caucasian") native to the region of Imwas, which apparently split into two groups before the creation of language. The linguistic difference would then reflect a nonoriginary opposition without biological basis, and therefore, despite some equivocal statements, an opposition of a historical, geographical, and cultural order. [22]

The many facets of this obsessive comparison can be reorganized under three principle headings. First is the opposition between Indo-European diversity and Semitic unity. The Aryan mind is pluralistic, polytheistic, and naturally tolerant. The Semitic mind is (therefore) essentially unitarian and intolerant: "Mono-theism sums up and explains all its characteristics." [23] From this comes the con-trast between the plurality of the Indo-European languages, stretched out in an "immense string from Ireland to the islands of Malaysia" and infinitely divided into branches, subgroups, and dialects, and the unity of the Semitic languages, "confined in a corner of Asia" and differing no more among themselves than the varieties of any one European group, the Germanic for example. The Semitic civilization is uniform from Hejaz to Andalusia: "In everything, the very simplicity of the Semitic race makes it seem incomplete to us. It is, if I dare say so, to the Indo-European family what *grisaille* {gray monochrome} is to painting, what plainsong is to modern music; it lacks that variety, that breadth, that superabundance of life which is the condition of perfectibility."[24]

Indeed, to this unity in space corresponds a unity in time, which is the immutability or sterility of the Semitic mind, opposed to the capacity for evolution and fertility of the Indo-European mind. Aryan Asia and Europe are lands of history, of mutations, and of progress. The Orient is said to be immutable only because we generally attribute to it "what belongs only to the Semitic peoples; ... the nomadic peoples are distinguished by their essentially conservative spirit." With their delicate vowel system constantly being eroded, the Indo-European languages crumbled away little by little and were periodically reconstituted on new foundations, thus passing (one recognizes Schlegel's evolutionary schema here) from an original synthetic state to the modern analytic state. The "Semitic speech organ" itself, which pays little attention to vowels, "never eased off from its twenty-two fundamental articulations. ... the three fundamental articulations of each root remained like a sort of bony scaffolding that preserved them from any softening. The Semitic system of writing, for its part, contributed quite a bit to this phenomenon of persistence. It cannot be said that the Semites write in as perfect a manner as the Indo-Europeans: they represent merely the skeleton of the words; they render the idea instead of the sound." The Semitic languages have therefore not budged for centuries. "They have not grown, they have not lived; they have endured. Arabic today conjugates the verb in exactly the same way as Hebrew did in the most ancient times; the essential roots have not changed by one single letter up to our day, and one can maintain that in matters of primary importance an Israelite of the time of Samuel and a Bedouin of the nineteenth century would be able to understand each other." The Semitic languages are thus as incapable of "differing from themselves in their successive eras" as of "differing among themselves."[25]

The connection between these two contrasts is obvious, and moreover explicit. The third appears more independent at first: it is the opposition between the Indo-European spirit of abstraction and "idealism" (again a theme of Schlegel's) and the Semitic incapacity for abstraction. Aryan civilization is essentially turned toward science and philosophy. Semitic civilization shuns these: its preferred domain is poetry, prophetic discourse, religion. At the linguistic level, the same distribution pertains: to the completely "metaphysical" abstraction of Indo-European roots is opposed—in the Koran as in the Bible—the perpetual metaphor of the spiritual through the physical. "If only the Semitic languages were considered, one might suppose that sensation alone presided over the first acts of human thought and that language was at first merely a sort of reflection of the external world.[26] In looking over the series of Semitic roots, one hardly runs across a single one that does not bear a primary material meaning that is applied, through more or less immediate transitions, to intellectual things. In order to express a feeling of the soul, one has recourse to the organic movement which is usually its sign." Anger is rapid breathing, heat, fracas; desire is thirst or pallor; to forgive is to cover up or wipe away, and so on. "I am not unaware that analogous facts are observable in all natural languages and that the Aryan idioms would furnish nearly as many examples in which one could likewise see pure thought engaged in a concrete and perceptible form [Renan here parts company with Schlegel]. But what distinguishes the Semitic family is that the primitive union of sensation and idea is always preserved in it, that one of the two terms has not eclipsed the other, as has happened in the Aryan tongues; in sum, that an idealization was never fully carried out, so that in every word one feels one can still hear the echo of the primitive sensations that determined the choice of the first nomenclators." With their supple and complex syntax, their inflections, their particles, their inversions, their immense and yet solidly constructed periods, "the Aryan tongues transport us straightaway to the height of idealism, and would make us envisage the creation of speech as an essentially transcendental act." By contrast, the Semites do not have, so to speak, any syntax. "To join words into a proposition is their utmost exertion; they do not dream of subjecting propositions themselves to the same operation." They do not know how to subordinate; they juxtapose, they go as far as coordinating, and the copula *and* "is the secret of their period and takes the place of almost all the other conjunctions for them." Their eloquence is "merely a lively succession of urgent turns of speech and bold images; in rhetoric as in architecture, the arabesque is their favorite stylistic device." [27] Their only period is the verset, itself merely the arbitrary division made by a breathless prophet: "The author pauses not out of any feeling for a natural period of discourse but out of the simple need to take a pause." Such a language, so materialistic in its lexicon and so minimally relational in its grammar, obviously does not lend itself to any intellectual speculation. "To imagine an Aristotle or a Kant with such an instrument is hardly more possible than to conceive of a poem like that of Job written in our metaphysical and reflective languages." [28]

Such, reduced to its essential motifs, is this trying parallel. As the last example shows, the determination of a natural language by the national genius is not without its reciprocity. Subjective mimologism always oscillates between two poles: that of the *Volksgeist* stamped into the idiom, and (as earlier in Humboldt, more recently in Sapir and Benjamin Whorf) that of the natural language imposing its categories on the mind of the speakers. This is a "dialectical" relation if ever there was one, and Renan himself puts it most incisively: "The mind of each people and its language are in the closest of relationships: the mind creates language, and language in its turn serves as the formula and boundary of the mind."[29] The first determination, nevertheless, belongs to the mind: the action of language is an action *in return,* through which the *Volksgeist* is confirmed and locked away in its work.

Yet, as usual, these theoretical formulas do not restore very faithfully the true progression of the linguistic imagination, which they rationalize after the fact. In this case, the true point of departure seems to me to be a sort of global, and *physical,* intuition of the Semitic being, in both its natural language and in what cannot here be called its culture, so manifestly dominant is nature's share (geographical, climatic, physiological). This is a tangible theme, that of the mineral and the osseous: dryness, hardness, aridity; sterile monotony of stone and of sand. Its most revealing formulation is this bit of pure Michelet: "The desert is monotheistic."[30] Linguistically, the following key formula is no doubt the underlying cliché: "consonantal *skeleton.*" Neither flesh nor fluid: no vowels (written and fixed), a tongue all of consonants for a people all bone and sinew (the archetypal Semite is always the Bedouin), nourished on wild honey and locusts.[31] Instead of Schlegel's "fecund seed," every Semitic root (and, at the level of discourse, every biblical or Koranic verset) presents a sort of hard and dry *kernel,* immutable, incapable of relationship and of development. This dryness is not that of abstraction (which, on the contrary, Renan valorizes under the unctuous kinds of *idealization*); it is the "tangible" in its most concentrated, burning, and, as it were, parched form. The physical impression (thinness) and its linguistic projection (gutturalness, dominance of consonantism, parataxis) are indissociable here: they create one and the same image.

But this image, it must be said, however immediate and spontaneous it may be, is anything but innocent. A cultural complex is conspicuously present here, one that fully deserves to be labeled ideological, in a sense other than that of Destutt de Tracy, and in which we again find the consequences, difficult to avoid, of the initial plan "to do for the Semitic languages what Bopp had done for the Indo-European languages." Renan's Semitic is Semitic *viewed from here,* bearing all the weight of an inevitably crushing comparison, since the very terms, descriptive categories, and implicit valorizations are borrowed from one of the systems being compared. Renan was not, and could not be, the Bopp of Semitic languages, quite simply because unlike his model he analyzed these languages within the terms elaborated for (and by) another analysis.[32] The ideal linguistic type remains the Indo-European, and it is by this, and according to its norms, that another system is going to be measured. It follows that any difference will be a *lacuna* and a deficiency, and the picture can no longer be anything but negative. This is expressed with a truly caricatural clarity by one sentence from the *Histoire:* "The Semitic race is recognized almost exclusively in its negative characteristics: it has neither mythology, nor epic, nor science, nor philosophy, nor fiction, nor plastic arts, nor civic life."[33]

There is here a (pairing) structure in the strongest sense: that is to say, one capable of transfer or of translation and paradoxically (if we consider the intensity of the invested images), independent of its contents. The evidence for this is that the pair is quite ready to neutralize its opposition, no matter how violent it appears, in order to constitute in its turn one of the terms of a new oppositional pair. It suffices to compare both of these two branches of the "white race" or "civilized family,"[34] which are after all twins, to another such group that is further removed: the Chinese, for example (or the Egyptians). Immediately, the enormous contrasts that separated Aryans and Semites vanish, and a "great and profound analogy" emerges: "the existence of a *grammar*. In contrast, the Chinese have only one thing in common with the other languages of Europe and of Asia: the goal to be attained. Chinese attains this goal, which is the expression of thought, just as well as the grammatical languages but by completely different means.... If the planets whose physical nature seems analogous to that of the earth are peopled with beings organized like us, one can argue that the history and the natural languages of these planets do not differ more from ours than Chinese history and language do. China thus appears to us as a second humanity that developed almost without the knowledge of the first one."[35] But this new dichotomy can itself be eclipsed in favor of a vaster one, which would oppose Aryans, Semites, and Chinese as a group to the "inferior races of Africa, Oceania, the New World": as for the latter, which apparently remain at the threshold of humanity and of articulated language, "an abyss separates them from the great families which we have just discussed." We watch the mechanism of contrastive valorization being put back into gear: now Chinese, that language "without grammar," becomes rehabilitated in the face of ways of speaking still more deprived — just as Semitic, a language without syntax, was rehabilitated in the face of the poverty of Chinese. And so on without end, I suppose, and just as well in the other direction, as illustrated by the following passage, verging on the fantastic, in which, to the "absolute" idea that certain philosophers such as Hegel have conceived of the development of humankind, Renan opposes an essentially related idea that might appear to be a belated realization of the illusions of ethnocentrism, did it not confine the diversity of cultures to the irrepressibly axiological perspective of a sort of gigantic distribution of prizes:

If the Indo-European race had not appeared in the world, it is clear that the highest degree of human development would have been somewhat analogous to Arab or Jewish society: philosophy, great art, high thought, political life would have barely been represented. If, besides the Indo-European race, the Semitic race had not appeared, Egypt and China would have remained at the top of humanity: moral feeling, refined religious ideas, poetry, the instinct for the infinite would have been almost entirely lacking. If, besides the Indo-European and Semitic races, the Hamitic and Chinese races had not appeared, humanity would not have existed in the truly sacred sense of this word, since it would have been reduced to the inferior races, nearly devoid of the transcendent faculties that make up the nobility of man. Now for what reason was there not formed a race as superior to the Indo-European race as the latter is superior to the Semites and to the Chinese? It seems impossible to say. Such a race would judge our civilization to be as incomplete and as defective as we find the Chinese civilization incomplete and defective.³⁶

Renan had criticized this sort of prejudice beforehand, but he attributed it, through a detour typical of ethnocentrism, solely to primitive peoples: "We find that in the most ancient natural languages the words serving to designate foreign peoples are drawn from two sources: either from verbs that signify *to stammer* or *to stutter,* or from words that signify *mute.* The people is always led to see only an inarticulate jargon in tongues that it does not understand; likewise, for primitive man, the characteristic sign of the stranger was speech in an unintelligible tongue, one that resembled formless stammering."³⁷ The stammerer or the mute is always the *Other,* the interchangeable barbarian always shut outside {*forclos*} the egocentric circle, and this idea also, of course, is already present in the monolingualism of the *Cratylus.* When it is applied to a foreign tongue (which was not really the case for the founders of "Indo-Germanic" grammar), subjective Cratylism — in a manner no doubt particularly marked here, but always marked to some degree — bears the weight of what Jean Paulhan would call "the illusion of the explorers," which is one of the traps of exoticism: a fascination with the Other and an incapacity to *understand* (in all senses) the Other otherwise than by forcing alterity into a contrast that suddenly permits one to *reduce* it.³⁸ Solipsism, or barbarism.

CHAPTER 12

Failing Natural Languages

The true writer is a man who does not *find* his words.[1]

 If an autobiographical letter to Paul Verlaine is to be credited, Stéphane Mallarmé did not attach great value to his *Mots anglais:* "a neatly done piece of work and that's all, about which it is unbecoming for me to speak."[2] But should we believe him? For Paul Valéry, quite on the contrary, this book "may well be the most revealing document we possess concerning his secret research."[3] Others have found in it "the source of all his poetry,"[4] and this hypothesis has inspired more than one commentary. Perhaps the *Petite Philologie* of 1877 merits neither such disdain nor such honor. It is a telling document, to be sure, and not only for the Mallarméan theory of language but more generally for the Cratylian imagination at a turning point in its history. But this document, far from being

---

In the French title of this chapter, "Au défaut des langues," the word *défaut* is rich in connotations relevant to Genette's argument. First, it can denote the "flaw" or "imperfection" in a mineral or precious metal. Applied to languages, this meaning is central to secondary Cratylism, or the attempt to motivate language in relation to things no longer through the hypothesis of a divine or natural origin but "artificially" through belated human intervention. In this sense, the "flaw" in languages is a *felix culpa,* since it legitimates the philosopher's and the poet's (re)invention of a more mimetically exact or correct (*juste*) verbal system.

Second, the *défaut* in languages is a "default" or "lack" in mimetic exactitude or correctness (*la justesse*), which threatens the assumption that language can be used as an instrument of truth either in philosophy or in poetry. This idea entails a network of economic metaphors: the "default" in verbal mimesis must be "compensated for" and also "remunerated" by the invention of a better (more strictly motivated and less arbitrary) sign system. Words are tokens ("coins") of meaning that have been exchanged or circulated so long without careful attention to exact correspondence between sign and referent that language has become misleading and/or arbitrary in relation to the objects it is supposed to designate.

Third, *défaut* in the sense of a "flaw" or "failing" in languages carries metaphysical undertones that implicitly return us to the Socratic question of the original error of the divine name-maker and law-giver. For Christian thinkers, too, this "failing" in languages became implicated in the notion of original sin—the falling away of humanity from God and of human language(s) from Nature (unity); see Genette's discussion of the myth of Babel in chapters 4, 6, and 8. Here, I have most often translated the key word *défaut* by the more general term "failing" so as to evoke all the foregoing connotations.

self-sufficient, lends itself to interpretation only in light of its context—certain other pages by Mallarmé—and its situation: the very special relation of a poet to an idiom that is neither his mother tongue nor his natural language for writing (even if, in this case, he knows it well enough to teach and to translate it). As much and more than the article on Wagner, this book could be subtitled *Rêverie d'un poète français* {Reverie of a French poet}.[5] English as dreamed of, in short, or—to paraphrase yet another Mallarméan title—*English as seen from here*.

Now then, the complete title is *Petite Philologie à l'usage des classes et du monde: Les Mots anglais* {Short Book of philology for classroom and general use: English words}.[6] The publisher announced a second volume under preparation, devoted to the *Étude des règles* {study of Rules}, or to grammar, and several other allusions in the text confirm this promise—which would never be kept.[7] The baptism of the whole enterprise as philological[8] and its immediate restriction to the lexicon alone indicate clearly enough the ambiguity of the work, which extends and deflects the Cratylian tradition at the height of historical linguistics. Typical of the nineteenth century is the awareness of the plurality of natural languages and, at least for the Indo-European family, their complex network of kinships and differences. "What is English?"[9] The inquiry will focus not, as in the past, upon language *in general* {le *langage*} but on *one* natural language {une *langue*}, situated in its place in the general historical chart[10] and defined more by its filiation than by its structure. On the final page Mallarmé belatedly tries for a typological characterization in the manner of Schleicher, but he does so with a purely rhetorical, or ludic, air: English will be simultaneously "monosyllabic" (isolating) like Chinese, "and even interjectional, one and the same Word often serving as both verb and noun"; agglutinative in its compound words; and inflected in a few vestigial case endings and verb conjugations. Elsewhere, and with a cooler eye, Mallarmé sees it as above all monosyllabic and "radical": "Whoever wants to speak wisely can say only one thing about English, which is that this idiom, thanks to its monosyllabism and to the neutrality of certain forms capable of marking several grammatical functions simultaneously, presents its Radicals almost in their naked state."[11] But this is not the essential point, and as characteristic as it may be, this structural feature is merely an effect that refers back to its historical cause: "a result mainly achieved in the shift from Anglo-Saxon to English."[12] This shift, a crucial moment in a diachrony that goes back to the primitive Indo-Europeans of the Oxus Valley, itself results from a historical event: Hastings,[13] the conquest of England by William's Normans, the encounter and the progressive fusion of the two tongues.

Therein lies the key, and the true answer to the initial question, "What is English?" It is a mixture of Anglo-Saxon and French-Norman. We will return to this, but it should be noted immediately that such an answer, despite its obvious historicism, is conceivable only in the eyes of a linguistics still caught in the categories and the implicit valorizations of an older attitude, for which the essence of a natural language resides in its lexicon. In order to clarify things in this respect, it suffices to point out that J.-P. Thommerel, in his *Recherches sur la fusion du franco-normand et de l'anglo-saxon*,[14] after having counted only 13,330 Germanic words against 29,854 Roman words, nevertheless endorsed Abel-François Villemain's opinion: "The English language is still today a wholly Teutonic tongue," for the German words constitute "the essential, indispensable part of the language system; without them there would be, as it were, no more than an undigested list of nouns, adjectives and verbs, without number, or tense, or modes, or persons."[15] This grammatical awareness of natural language, which gives the premier role to the construction of sentences and to relational words, is obviously absent from *Les Mots anglais:* "It is best to pass over the Grammar in order to think only about the Lexicon."[16] Albeit methodical and theoretically provisional, this neglect is no less typical. It comes in fact less often from a deliberate decision than from an unnoticed slippage. Here, Mallarmé asks himself "what is Language?" and answers "the life of words"; elsewhere, he switches from one category to the other in the same sentence, clearly identifying natural language with the lexicon.[17] This valorization of the word (but not of the *noun* here, since, as we have seen, the distinction, for Mallarmé, is not always pertinent in English)[18] is a characteristic feature of mimologism, and therein lies the other face of *Les Mots anglais.* The question "What is English?" thus definitively boils down to another question: What is the English lexicon?

So defined, the English idiom offers the inquiring poet-linguist a rather rare and, as we shall see, obscurely emblematic spectacle: that of a *double* language, in which the respective heritages of Northern Old French {*langue d'oil*} and Anglo-Saxon are mingled and compounded without ever fusing, according to secret laws. This "Anglo-French dualism"[19] is at first translated by the well-known division that reserves Norman, tongue of the conquerors, for the political and seignorial vocabulary, and conquered Anglo-Saxon for the "humble and private" realities. Thence come those "parallel" vocables that designate in both languages the living animals of peasant reality (*ox, calf, sheep, swine*), and the meat offered "on the lord's table" (beef {*boeuf*}, veal {*veau*}, mutton {*mouton*}, pork {*porc*}): a classic example of sociolinguistic cleavage or social resistance to the fusion of languages.[20] But what interests Mallarmé above all is the aesthetic aspect of the phenomenon, the picturesque juxtaposition of the idioms, the immediate expressiveness of their division[21] — and even more, its strange poetical investments: those bilingual doublets, "unique modes of rhetoric" characteristic of the language of Chaucer, which originate in an obvious need for direct translation (*act* and *deed* {*acte*}, *head* and *chief* {*chef*}, *mirth* and *jollity* {*joliment*}), and those adjectival framings (*the woful day fatal*), from which derives "one of the most exquisite forms of style in modern English poetry."[22]

But this segregative and redundant dualism is joined by another, with subtler although entirely spontaneous effects: that resulting from the inevitable absorption of one natural language by another, from the forced anglicization of the French words adopted since the eleventh century, "our words hindered by the strange obligation of speaking a tongue other than their own." Mallarmé devotes an entire chapter (book 2, chapter 1) to these adulterations of form and to the "laws of permutation" that regulate them.[23] Here, a natural language is seen not next to its rival but behind it, by virtue of etymological transparency: *napperon* under *apron, chirurgien* under *surgeon, asphodile* under *daffodil*, and so on. These are adulterations of forms but also of meanings, whence those misleading vocables, the famous *faux amis* {false cognates; literally, "false friends"} where the resemblance of the signifiers dissimulates the conflict of the signifieds: "library," which is and is not *librairie* {bookstore}, being, without being, *bibliothèque* {library}; "prejudice," not *préjudice* {harm} but *préjugé;* "scandal," not *scandale* {outrage} but *calomnie* {slander}. Such words institute an odd to-and-fro movement of identities and differences from one language to another. "Most often extension or restriction are what can happen, as well as the passage from a proper acceptation to an almost rhetorical figure" (that is, metonymy); this spontaneous tropology is constantly at work in all natural languages, but here it plays above their borderline. Finally, there are double adulterations, "truly bizzare cases in which signification and orthography are merged in order to form new products"; this is the well-known mechanism of popular or "folk" etymology, where an opaque term—in the present case, opaque because foreign— finds itself reinterpreted, hence remotivated, by means of a paronymic collision. The collision may be partial, as when *femelle* becomes "female" (versus "male"); *lanterne*, "lanthorn" (from "horn," *la corne*, used as glass); or *écrevisse*, "{shell} fish"—if you like, "crayfish". Or it may be complete, as in *asparagus*, "sparrow grass"; *buffetier*, "beef-eater"; *Bellerophon*, "Billy Ruffian"; and that masterpiece of phonic transposition, the famous signboard *Chat Fidèle* {The Faithful Cat}, which has become "The Cat and the Fiddle." These "felicitous wordplays" are genuine plays on languages, an ironic, pre-Joycean subversion of the very concept of translation and of the signifying relationship.[24]

Such is English, a completely original formation, "neither artificial nor absolutely natural," the "graft" of a "virtually finished" language on a "nearly finished" language,[25] a language with a double base and a false bottom, perhaps with two usages, one of which would be pure play—pure poetry.

⑤ But of these two basic stocks, one is clearly privileged—not, as we have seen, insomuch as it commands the joining of words and the construction of sentences but insomuch as it is the original, the earliest treasury of "words of the soil." It is the "Gothic or Anglo-Saxon" element to which Mallarmé devotes his

Book 1 {of *Les Mots anglais*}, and the whole of the mimological inquiry is the subject of the first chapter. In itself, this *parti pris* is by no means peculiar to Mallarmé, since we have already observed it at work in John Wallis.[26] But we shall see further on that in passing from the earlier author to the later one, this restriction, already contrary to Cratylian universalism, takes on a still greater and more paradoxical significance.

Once the field has been thus narrowed down, the mimetic principle, the *correctness of words* {*la justesse des mots*}, is rediscovered at work. It comes up with regard to onomatopoeia, whose state of "inferiority" in present-day natural language Mallarmé (like de Brosses) clearly detects, but which he sees as "perpetuating in our idioms a process of creation that was perhaps the first one of all"[27] — words so pristine that they escape all history (all filiation) and appear to have been "born yesterday. Your origins? one asks them; and they merely display their correctness" (this is the gist of Socratic eponymy). How can one talk about their origin, since these "right words {*mots justes*}, issuing fully formed from the instinct of the very people who speak the language," are simply the origin itself of everything *that speaks*? Mallarmé hardly specifies the nature and the workings of this mimetic correctness, unless it is by a highly discreet, almost dubious, recourse to the principle of organic vocal imitation dear to his predecessors in the past century, alluding to the "relations between overall signification and the letter — which, if they exist, do so only by virtue of the special use, in a word, of one or the other of the speech organs."[28] He is still more reserved when he describes the link "between the spectacles of the world and the spoken word charged with expressing them" as "one of the sacred or perilous mysteries of Language, and one that it will be advisable to analyze only on the day when Science, mastering the vast repertory of all idioms ever spoken on earth, writes the history of the letters of the alphabet across the ages and approximately what their absolute signification was, sometimes divined, sometimes misunderstood by men, the creators of the words."[29]

Sometimes misunderstood: this is the very hypothesis of the law-giver's error, invoked by Socrates against Cratylus, and the foundation of what we have agreed to call secondary mimologism: namely, that the elements of language have an "absolute signification" — in other words, a natural one — but that the words of the actual lexicon can betray it. This includes the English language, itself not always above reproach: "Yes, *sneer* is a nasty smile and *snake* a perverse animal, the serpent, *sn* therefore[30] impressing a reader of English as a sinister digraph except, however, in *snow,* etc. *Fly? to flow?* but what is less soaring and fluid than the word *flat?*" In any case, the expressive "link" between word and spoken word, alluded to just now, was not given in natural language but "established by the imagination" thanks to the "magisterial effort" of alliteration: that is to say, a factitious imitative harmony, even if its process is said to be "inherent in the northern genius." Here Mallarmé's secondary Cratylism appears already nearly fully fledged: the poet (or the "erudite prose writer") is to be entrusted with compensating for the mimetic inadequacy of natural language. But this is to anticipate.

Limited, then, to an idiom within an idiom, and not without possibly premonitory precautions, the mimetic principle will undergo anew a series of reductions that will restrict, but probably also concentrate, its effect. First, there is a crucial separation of the phonemes into vowels and consonants according to a very widespread metaphorical equivalence that sees "something like flesh" in the vowels and the diphthongs, and "something like a skeletal frame that is difficult to dissect" in the consonants.[31] Here we rediscover the "consonantal skeleton" of Semitic vocables and Indo-European "roots," in which is centered the power of signification. "What is a root? An assemblage of letters, often consonants, displaying several words of a natural language as if dissected, reduced to their bones and their tendons, removed from their ordinary life, so that a secret kinship between them may be recognized."[32] *Bones* and *tendons,* framework and musculature: the site of all power lies there. The vowels, of "middling importance" at least in the "northern languages,"[33] retain only a purely grammatical function, as variations on and derivations from the semantic *theme* furnished by the consonants alone: "On the inside, vowels or diphthongs; there is nothing simpler than these, with their relative insignificance, which receive the effort of the voice straining to differentiate the grammatical value of the word."[34] Clearly, "grammatical value" is closely linked to insignificance, which amounts to the presupposition of a radical antinomy between grammar and signification. Thus, as in de Brosses, the vowels, pure morphemes, are henceforth out of semantic play.

But a new distinction will now subdivide the consonants themselves, not according to their mode of articulation but according to the position they occupy in the word. The final consonants "appear as good as suffixes that are not always discernible,"; "these end consonants coming to add something like a secondary sense to the notion expressed by those at the beginning. What? not yet Affixes: no, but indeed very ancient endings, rough and abolished." They are thus confined, in their turn, within a grammatical function as simple agents of inflection. There remains, then, the initial consonant, the last refuge of semanticity: "It is there, *in the attack,* that signification truly resides"; "the initial consonant remains immutable, for in it lies the radical power, something like the fundamental meaning of the word."[35] The consonant and not, as in Wallis, the consonantal group: there is here an extreme reduction, therefore, that leaves to the consonants of the second and third rank merely a subordinate semantic value, nuance, or modulation. Jean-Pierre Richard quite rightly compares this decisive valorization of the initial position to another, parallel or homothetic, valorization: that of the initial position in the verse line, itself also baptized as the *letter of attack.*[36] "I despise you," writes Mallarmé to F. Champsaur, "solely because of the capital letter removed from the verse line; the letter of attack there holds, in my view, the same importance as the rhyme." Elsewhere, he calls it the "alliterative key,"[37] and the inferential role of this musical metaphor is quite plain. The first letter of the word, as of the verse line, is indeed "the key that harmonizes it" (Richard), the key signature at the head of the score that gives the pitch, that regulates and dominates the semantic alliteration. It is this "dominant Consonant" through which he will attempt "to explain the Signification of more than one vocable"[38] — thus does Mallarmé himself define his purpose. As for words with an initial vowel, necessarily doomed to contingency and arbitrariness, they will have the merit of discretion: "Everyone will notice how few words having a vowel for the initial letter belong to the original English — that is, to the Anglo-Saxon base; it is mainly a consonant that performs the attack in the vocabularies of the North."[39] Let us leave it at that, then.

The system of semantic values attributed to the consonants in initial position is presented, as everyone knows, in a list (called a *table*) of vocables grouped by families[40] (plus, each time, an accessory list of "isolated" words that defy this grouping) according to their consonant of attack, the latter being themselves arranged no longer in alphabetical order but according to a phonetic classification: labial, guttural, sibilant, dental, aspirated, liquid, and nasal. Here we need to recall the features of these values.[41]

— *b* signifies heaviness or roundness: "meanings, diverse and yet all secretly linked, of production or childbirth, fecundity, amplitude, puffiness and curviness, boastfulness; next, of bulk or ebullience and occasionally of benevolence and blessing ... significations more or less implied by the basic labial."

— *w* indicates oscillation, perhaps on account of the "vaguely double nature of the letter," whence wateriness, fainting, and whimsy; whence weakness, charm, imagination. But Mallarmé seems more sensitive to the "diversity" of this family than to its unity. The group *wr* is assigned, as in Wallis, but equivocally, to the sense of torsion.

— *p*: piling up, stagnation, sometimes a clear-cut act. The groupings with *l* and *r* do not seem to produce any specific meaning.[42]

— *f*: strong and fixed grip; *fl*: flight, whence through "rhetorical transposition" light, flowing; *fr*: strife or estrangement, and various other things.

— *g*: desire; *gl*: satisfied desire, whence joy, light, gliding, enhancement; *gr*: seizing of the desired object, crushing (cf. Wallis).

— *j*: very rare in first position, "placed nowhere but before a vowel or a diphthong, it thus shows a tendency to express some lively, direct action rather than possessing in itself alone one of these meanings" — which is to say, no doubt, that its position always *directly* before the vowel is what gives it this value.

— *c:* "swift and decisive attack," spirited acts; *cl:* to clasp, cleave, clamber up; *cr:* crash, cracking (cf. Wallis); *ch:* violent effort.

— *k,* before *n:* knottiness, knuckles; "moreover, notice the group *kin, kind, king,* whence springs a notion of familial benevolence."

— *q,* before *u:* quick and violent movement.

— *s:* to place or, on the contrary, to look for. Here again we find the well-known principle, previously encountered in de Brosses, of the equivalence of "opposite meanings." Mallarmé had announced this beforehand: "The tacking back and forth in the signification can become absolute to the point of matching an authentic analogy in interest; it is thus that 'heavy' seems suddenly to rid itself of the sense of *weightiness* which it marks, in order to supply *heaven,* the sky, high and subtle, considered as spiritual abode"; to separate is to equalize.[43] But the important aspect of the significations comes from their diverse groupings — *sw:* swiftness, swelling up, absorption; *sc:* scission, gash, scraping, shock; *sh:* shooting forth; shadow, shelter, and, "contradictorily," the action of showing; *st:* stability, as "in many natural languages" (cf. Wallis), instigation, "perhaps the principle meaning of the letter *s*";[44] *str:* strength, yearning (cf. Wallis); *sl, sn:* slackness, slipperiness, sneakiness; *sm:* honesty, smiles; *sr:* very delicate work; *spr:* springing out (cf. Wallis);[45] *spl:* split.

— *d:* steady action without showiness, dullness, obscurity; *dr:* an effort that drags on.

— *t:* stop, stasis, a fundamental signification "admirably expressed by the combination *st.*" Admirably, but in flagrant infraction of the general principle of the predominance of the initial position. Whence *th:* objectivity (in demonstrative and second person pronouns, and the definite article); and *tr:* moral trustiness, whence truth.

— *h:* direct and simple movement; hand, heart, head; power, domination.

— *l:* longing without result, slowness, lengthiness, dullness; but also to leap, listen, love.

— *r,* "articulation par excellence": raising, removal, richness, rending, radicalness.

— *m:* "power to make, therefore virile and maternal joy"; measure, duty, number, meeting, mingling, mediator; by "transfer," inferiority, mildness, mad.

— *n:* neat and incisive character; nearness.

One cannot help being struck by the heterogeneity of these items, an aspect that Mallarmé takes a perverse delight in emphasizing:[46] only *b, w, g, c, d,* and *t* seem provided with a stable and coherent signification. This diversity in interpretation should be compared with two other characteristic features, equally deviant with respect to the Cratylian tradition. First, there is the extreme restraint concerning physical motivations. The only one that is clearly indicated remains doubtful: this is the "double nature" — graphic, in the present case — of *w*, which would determine its value of oscillation. The link between the bilabial articulation of *b* and its value of puffiness is suggested in a highly uncertain way, and that between the "swift and decisive" nature of the attack *c* and its signification of spiritedness is hardly drawn more clearly. Even values as univocal as those of *g*, *d*, or *t* are given without any attempt at explanation; they are *a fortiori* the most heterogeneous. There is nothing that recalls the traditional motivations, from Plato to Nodier, of the values attributed to *r*, *t*, *l*, and the groups *gl* and *st*. The significations are simply noted and recorded, just as the (rudimentary) statistics of the word lists suggest, and not without some confusion. Indeed, it is typical for the semantic interpretations to come after the catalogues of vocables,[47] which therefore function not simply as illustrative examples (chosen as such) but as the real material for observation.[48] The approach of this chapter is properly inductive, whence its often uncertain and almost hesitant character. Here, the signification of the letters is offered no longer as *absolute* but indeed as relative to the (often capricious) givens of an existing corpus. The connection between this multiple signification and the physicality of the signifiers is not intended to be properly mimetic, or even otherwise necessary: things just are that way in English, and nothing more. And when by exception Mallarmé observes a more widespread value, such as *st* = stop, he carefully refrains from declaring it to be universal; it is merely attributed to "many natural languages," and the "kinship of these idioms" is directly inferred from that. This is a typical illustration of the trammels imposed on the Cratylian imagination by historical linguistics. The relation *st* = stop is no longer a fact of nature, extensive with all of human language; it is more modestly, and definitively, an Indo-European root.

Thus, Mallarmé tacitly renounces, simultaneously, the two key principles of Cratylism — universality and mimeticism — without, for all that, renouncing its overall trend or, above all, its deep desire. On the one hand, he poses the "correctness of words" (in the English language); on the other hand, he assigns to every English consonant one or several meanings whose correctness almost nothing confirms and still less guarantees and which could ultimately be based on pure convention. So we have — once again contrary to Socrates' hypothesis, and apparently against all logic — "right" (necessary) words composed of arbitrary elements.

In this paradoxical form of mimologism are combined (at least), on the one hand, the *feeling for onomatopoeia*, or mimetic correctness, with respect to a large number of English words,[49] and, on the other hand, the impossibility of *explaining* (and therefore grounding) this correctness at the level of the linguistic elements. This is quite close to the situation foreseen and criticized by Socrates, predicting the discomfiture of anyone who claims to explain the derivative forms (by the simple ones) without being able to explain the simple ones (by the most basic ones), and who ends up talking only "nonsense." In fact, for Socrates, these elements of language will become the only solid ground for mimetic motivation, a ground too often abandoned by the name-maker. For Mallarmé — not, to be sure, in practice but in theory — the problem here is that the necessary foundation slips away, as if the English lexicon had in part been for the foreign observer the site of an illusion or, more precisely, of a mirage.

Finally, then, we must (re)turn to that peculiar feature of *Les Mots anglais*, perhaps the most peculiar and probably the most important — in any case, the most paradoxical: that it is (partly) a mimological reverie *applied to a foreign {étrangère} language* (and, what is more, to the "strangest" {*plus étranger*} stuff in this language). To assign, implicitly or explicitly, a special — nay, even exceptional — mimetic virtue to a natural language is not, once again, a new thing, since this was Wallis's main intention regarding English. And, after all, national prejudice readily inspired several inflections of this type in Gébelin and Nodier (of whom the latter experienced the feeling for onomatopoeia with respect to the French dictionary), and in another area (that of syntax) in the classical supporters of the order of French words — not to mention the spontaneous Hellenism of the *Cratylus*. But just so, in all these cases and in many others, the valorization always focuses on the "mother" tongue — let us say, perhaps more exactly, one's *own proper* tongue {*la langue propre*} — as an image, faithful to a more or less exceptional degree, but always an image, of *the one* natural language {*la langue en soi*}, therefore always privileged as the quintessential language, whose high degree of mimeticism in a way represents the fundamental mimeticism of all language.[50] If need be, many degrees and many fluctuations in the excellence of language in general could be admitted, but to exclude oneself by excluding one's own idiom or by assigning it an inferior rank in this scale of values is quite obviously an act contrary to mimological desire. Cratylus said, in essence, "Natural language is right," meaning by this his own language, modestly considered to be the only one. Most of his heirs said, "Natural languages are right and are, besides, basically identical; (so) look at mine." Wallis explicitly said: "My language is the only right one, the others are an odious hodgepodge," a chauvinism born no longer, as among the Greeks, from the conqueror's disdain but from resentment vanquished. In all these cases, the identification of the linguistic principle with the mimetic principle remains intact (I do not say complete) through the quite natural intervention of one's own language. Clearly, such is no longer the case when the mimetic value finds itself, albeit implicitly, reserved for a foreign idiom, projecting *a contrario* onto other languages and especially onto one's own the shadow of the reverse failing.

Ⓥ For the moment, such an interpretation might seem very extreme; in a sense it is, and we need to correct it immediately, or at the very least qualify it, before (re)producing the texts, other than *Les Mots anglais*, that argue for it.

First, let us remark that the chart of the originary lexicon includes no trace of subjective mimologism, unless the very aptitude for mimeticism should be considered as a feature (the only one) of Anglo-Saxon *Volksgeist.* The sole hint in this direction is fugitive and a bit oblique; it is the description, previously mentioned, of alliteration (and hence of imitative harmony) as a process "inherent in the northern genius." As for labeling onomatopoeia the "very soul of English," it goes without saying that this formula applies to the idiom without necessarily implicating its speakers.

This description of the English language calls into question the nature (the "soul") of this language and the (linguistic) point of view that inspires such a judgment. A first question, then, would be whether or not the English language is especially mimetic. We do not pretend to answer this question here, or even to decide if it really has meaning. Let us merely note the agreement between a native speaker[51] and an outside observer, and the widespread impression of an especially high number of onomatopoetic terms and words whose structure resembles that of onomatopoeia, or expressive exclamations, in this language. The very marked monosyllabism is evidently a familiar part of this impression, and Mallarmé, like Wallis, refers to it constantly.

Another question, which must first be posed in the most general way, is whether the impression of mimeticism, true or false, is stronger in regard to one's own language or a foreign language. Here again, the answer is not obvious, and opinions seem divided. It is conceivable that the very opacity and the greater intensity (phonic or graphic) of a foreign word might lead, through an effect of exoticism, to an overvaluation of its expressive value. This would be a special case of the "explorers' illusion," and such a meaning could be wrung from Mallarmé's statement: "A word is never seen so steadily as from the outside, where we are; that is to say, from abroad, the foreign side {de l'étranger}."[52] But conversely, the familiarity of one's own proper language, the transparency of its vocables, the almost innate, sometimes exclusive, obviousness of their signification can promote belief in their naturalness, and it is quite plainly this tendency that is expressed in classical Cratylism. Mallarmé mentions this fact in regard to his "fellow poets" and appraises it in the following rather ambiguous terms: "It is a fact that those reclusive in their meaning or faithful to the sonorities of the language whose instinct they glorify have a secret distaste for, as it were, admitting any other; from this angle and more than anyone else, they remain patriots. A necessary infirmity that perhaps reinforces, in them, the illusion that an object uttered in the only way that to their knowledge it can be named, springs forth itself, ingenerate; but, what a strange thing, is it not?[53] The object springing forth ingenerate at the mere utterance of the vocable believed to be uniquely capable of designating it: this is indeed mimologism of one's own language — but treated here as an illusion and an infirmity, an illusion but one necessary to the poet. In short, it is the idea, common in our day, that the poet, at least, needs to believe or to make others believe in a motivation for language — for his own language. We will encounter this again in a moment, in a text just slightly more recent, but so subtilized that it will be nearly reversed. It is not yet time to follow that text's beckoning in this other direction; let us note here that such a critique of Cratylian "patriotism" confirms the presence (conscious or not) of an opposite attitude in Mallarmé, which inclines him instead to emphasize the mimetic features of a foreign language. For him, therefore, the "foreign" point of view really seems the most favorable to the Cratylian illusion.

But this conclusion must still be dialecticized. We have already come across that preliminary text in which Mallarmé envisages a possible "misunderstanding" of elementary significations by words — even English ones: *sn*, the sinister digraph, is thoroughly out of place in *snow*, as is the soaring *fl* in *flat*. These criticisms, which herald others, confirm that no natural language is without its failings and that "correctness" is not a matter of the idiom. Conversely, one finds here and there a few Cratylian reveries on French or Frenchified proper nouns (note this restriction): *Voltaire*, the "arrow's departure and bowstring's vibration," an ideal eponym for that "archer consumed by the joy and anger of the brilliant dart he looses"; *Théodore de Banville*, "a predestined name, as harmonious as a poem and as charming as a stage set"; *Hérodiade*, "that gloomy word, red like an open pomegranate," to which Mallarmé claimed to owe all the inspiration for his poem of that name.[54] These are applications to his own language of that "worship of the vocable" or "infatuation with the power of words" which until now we have seen invested solely in English as he dreamed it.

© But the chief text, in which Mallarmé's most profound — and also most paradoxical — linguistic thought is expressed with all its force, is obviously the famous passage from "Crisis in Poetry" {"Crise de vers"}, which really must be quoted one more time, after so many others.

> Languages are imperfect because multiple, the supreme one is missing: to think is to write without accessories, without even whispering, but since the immortal word remains tacit, the diversity of idioms on earth prevents anyone from uttering words which, otherwise, were they to appear in a single flash, would be truth itself incarnate. This express prohibition holds sway over nature (one stumbles on it with a smile), to the effect that we have no grounds for equating ourselves with God; but, then, from the aesthetic perspective, I regret to see how discourse fails to express objects by means of keys that would correspond to them in coloring or in aspect — keys that do exist in the instrument of the voice, among languages and sometimes in one language. When compared to the opacity of the word *ombre* {shadow}, the word *ténèbres* {gloom} does not seem very dark; how disappointing is the perversity that contradictorily assigns dark tones to *jour* {day}, bright

212

tones to *nuit* {night}. We long for words of brilliant splendor in sound and sense or, conversely, for words whose light has died in sound and sense; for a luminous succession of elements—*Only* let us remember that were it so, *verse would not exist:* philosophically speaking, verse remunerates the failing of natural languages, being their superior complement.[55]

Faced with this inexhaustible text, we will point out first its unambiguous formulation of the Hermogenist argument—the very one that Saussure will take up later[56]—for the plurality of natural languages, "imperfect since there are several," the imperfection or "flaw" here clearly being the absence of *correctness* ("truth"): that is, of mimetic necessity. The diversity of the idioms "prevents {anyone} from uttering the words which otherwise (if there were only one natural language on earth) might take the form of one single stroke, itself materially truth": that is to say, the very image of the thing. Here again, note that linguistic unity and motivation are linked to the point of identification in a line of thinking more plausible than it is rigorous. The plurality of natural languages does not absolutely preclude the mimetic hypothesis (and we know how often the Cratylian tradition has refuted this argument). Conversely, the unity of human language does not necessarily entail its correctness; perhaps it only gives the illusion of correctness. Whatever the case may be, the strong hypothesis of mimologism is very explicitly repudiated here: not being "unique," language cannot be "perfect."

The reversal, however, does not go as far as absolute conventionalism, since Mallarmé still maintains the mimetic *capacity* of the phonic elements of language, "touchkeys corresponding (to objects) in coloring or in rhythm, which exist in the instrument of the voice." If natural languages are not accurate, they could be so at least partially, on the condition that those touchkeys, the vowels and the consonants, be correctly used.[57] Unfortunately, save for erratic exceptions "among the languages," and maybe more numerous "within one of them" (symbolically, in this case, English), "discourse"—that is, real natural language —"fails to express objects" in this manner. A double illustration of this failure, significantly borrowed from his own native language, is the "perversity" of the pairings *jour/nuit* {day/night} and *ombre/ténèbres* {shadow/darkness}, where the "darkest" timbres are assigned to the brightest objects and vice versa. This linguistic misdeal gives rise to disappointment and regret. We find here again, therefore, the position previously indicated at the beginning of *Les Mots anglais:* the mimetic capacity of the phonemes, too often "unrecognized" by the lexicon. This position, let us recall, is exactly that of Socrates in the second part of the *Cratylus,* who without hesitation assigns a value of hardness to the sound *r,* then criticizes the word *sklērotēs* {hardness}, which should have been something like *skrērotēs.*

However, three features distinguish Mallarmé's attitude from that of Socrates. The first, which we have already pointed out in *Les Mots anglais,* is a greater hesitation in the assignment of basic symbolic values and a very great reserve as to their physical motivation. One day, says Mallarmé, maybe all of this will become an object of scientific inquiry,[58] but for the moment conjectures are uncertain and inadequate; thus, the values of light at play in *jour/nuit, ombre/ténèbres* are easily guessed at but not specified. The second distinguishing feature is obviously the exception — highly discreet here, but which we saw illustrated in *Les Mots anglais* — made for *one* natural language, one that is not our own. No such exception is found in Plato — quite the contrary. Let us remark, however, that English tends to play in the Mallarméan system the role held in the *Cratylus* [59] by the "language of the gods," borrowed from Homer: the role of a nostalgic or consolatory myth into which are projected from afar all the virtues in which one's own language is lacking as a *real* natural language — the one that I write in and speak in. A linguistic paradise lost or, if you prefer, a *linguistic utopia* almost recognized and accepted as such. For Mallarmé, therefore, English (as he dreams of it) is the site and the object not of true *jouissance,* but of regret: the specular image of a lack. And all things considered, as certain reservations allowed us to foresee, all of this — I mean the whole game — has little to do with real English as it exists and is spoken. And all other natural languages, or rather any *other* language, would have done just as well — that is, served the office of "supreme" language: the very one that is "lacking," and whose lack and (in the strong sense) *failing {défaut}* are embodied, if I may say so, in real language. Moreover, the English-French relation could ultimately be reversed, the supreme language always being, for every natural language, the one facing or opposite it.

By thus situating English in Mallarmé's linguistic reverie, perhaps we avoid a rather strong temptation, which is, by exploiting the dates, to reduce its different aspects to kinds of diachronic stages.[60] First of all, there would be Mallarmé the naive mimologist in *Les Mots anglais,* converted a few years later to a more realistic attitude. We have already seen that nothing of the sort occurred, and that the author of *Les Mots anglais* was no more naive (nor more fanciful) than the one of "Crise de vers," and that he merely pretended he was, while taking care to drop a few contradictory clues here and there — which have not always been picked up. At the risk of going too far in the other direction, then, let us say this: *Les Mots anglais* is a fable or symbol, *a contrario,* of the universal *failing in natural languages.*

A universal but not incurable failing or, more precisely, one not impossible to compensate for. Here the third difference between Socrates and Mallarmé's secondary mimologism becomes manifest, a difference which, moreover, further justifies this term. Once the failing of the language system (the error of the law-giver) is established, Socrates more or less contents himself with warning Cratylus, and everyone else, against an instrument as misleading and definitively discredited as this one. On the same bases and according to the same values, however, a reform of the language system could be undertaken or advocated, or at the least dreamed about, which would give or return to it all the rightness of which it is presumed capable. Here we have secondary Cratylism in the full and also the obvious sense, in the wish to (re)establish artificially a nonexistent or vanished ideal state. A few traces or outlines of this are found in such authors as de Brosses and Nodier: for them, it is strictly a question of correcting the language system. Mallarmé's attitude is comparable but more subtle and oriented in an entirely different direction: "verse" is charged, "philosophically," with "remunerating" the default of natural languages: that is to say, not with correcting it—poetry does not alter the language; it does not decide to call *nuit* {night} *jour* {day} and vice versa—but with *compensating for* it through some use of an order and a level ("superior complement") other than that of natural language, which for Mallarmé is always that of words. To compensate for, but also to recompense, since the failing of natural languages is the *raison d'être* of "verse," which exists only for—and *from*—this compensatory function. If natural language were "perfect," "verse" would have no reason for being; or, if you prefer, language itself would be a poem: poetry would be everywhere and consequently nowhere. More specifically, a spontaneous poetry—a naturally mimetic language system—would render useless the poet's art, which is the creation of an artificially motivated (artificially natural, all in all) language system: "verse." This is confirmed still more clearly by the following rejoinder in the "spoken sketch" by Francis Viélé-Griffin, a report (we hope) of a real conversation, in which Mallarmé ascribes to his interlocutor a thought that is his own: "If I understand you, you rest the poet's creative privilege on the imperfection of the instrument on which he must play; a natural language hypothetically inadequate to translate his thought would do away with the literary writer, who, for that reason, would be named Mister Everyman?"[61]

The secondary mimologism that Mallarmé illustrates here, then, is no longer a Cratylism of natural language but a Cratylism of "verse" that surmounts a Hermogenism of natural language and more precisely of words, which itself surmounts a (semi-)Cratylism of elementary sounds. In this integrative structure each level is opposed in value to the one it integrates; the accompanying diagram schematizes things in a necessarily approximative way.

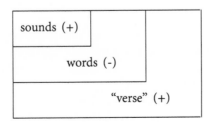

"Verse," therefore, is charged with reestablishing, at a level justly described as "superior," the accuracy of which phonemes are capable and which words have betrayed. Unable to "correct" natural language by altering the words, one arranges them into more comprehensive units that will form something like synthetic vocables, collectively right and necessary, "the verse being nothing but a perfect, comprehensive, ingenerate word."[62] *Comprehensive* because composed of several words from natural language; *perfect* and *ingenerate* — two adjectives we have met previously — because approximating the originary or the mythical correctness of the language system. Or to turn to the most famous formulation: "Verse that out of several vocables reforges a total word, new, alien to natural language and as if incantatory ... denying, with a sovereign gesture, the element of chance left to the terms despite the artifice of their retempering, alternating in the sound and the sense."[63] The *element of chance {hasard}* in these terms, which the sovereign gesture of the "verse" denies (without annulling it, since it *remains* there), is what we call the "arbitrariness" of the sign, the nonnecessary character of the connection between *sound* and *sense*. What a note of 1869 says about the "Word" *{Verbe}* might, then, be applied to "verse": "a principle that develops itself through the negation of all principle, chance."[64] "Chance," also states a letter to François Coppée, "does not enter any line of verse."[65] Failing to abolish chance, which, besides, it perhaps disdains, "verse" surmounts it by integrating it, in the manner of Hegel, like a throw of the dice in which every face may remain indeterminate but the total is ineluctable.

This overly facile metaphor will not excuse us from looking a little more closely at what, for Mallarmé, this "sovereign" synthesis consists of, which the word "verse" has so far designated in a somewhat sibylline manner (hence our awkward quotation marks). That the issue here is not merely regular verse in the narrow and traditional sense ("official" verse, Mallarmé says) is explicitly confirmed by the following reply to Jules Huret: "Verse exists everywhere in language where there is rhythm, everywhere — except in advertising posters and the back page of the newspaper. In the genre we call prose, there are verses, sometimes admirable ones, in all sorts of rhythms. But, really, there is no such thing as prose: there is the alphabet and then there are verses, more or less closely knit, more or less diffuse. Every time there is an effort at style, there is versification."[66] Mallarmé, then, defines as "verse" a *poetic language*[67] that extends very widely beyond official poetry. But neither should this term be stretched into an overly wide sense, extending to any syntagm or any sentence. The following statement by Jean-Pierre Richard might lead to such an interpretation: "The pessimism of the word in Mallarmé is ... succeeded by a{n} ... optimism of the verse *and of the sentence.*"[68] Or else the parallel with Abelard suggested by Édouard Gaède: "a nominalist with respect to words and a realist with respect to sentences."[69] The idea that each sentence adjusts at its level the failure of correctness in the words it integrates would be perfectly conceivable (there was something of this in the diagrammatic mimologism of the *ordo naturalis*); but such is not Mallarmé's way of thinking. For him, not every sentence is verse (otherwise, the poet would find himself "Everyman" again); at the very least, as we have just seen, an "effort at style" and rhythm is necessary. An effort: verse is *worked.*

The definition of this work, theoretically and practically, belongs no longer to Mallarmé's poetics of language but to his poetics simply and plainly—his poetics of verse and of the poem, albeit in prose; rather fortunately for us, then, it is out of our field of inquiry. As a matter of fact, it remains largely unformulated by Mallarmé himself and is thus almost entirely in his practice. For attempts at more precise articulation of the principle of "remuneration" with regard to *jour* and *nuit,* I refer the reader to Roman Jakobson and a few others—all this being, as was realized a bit late, already in Albert Thibaudet. Unfortunately, the examples, here and there, are taken not from Mallarmé but from Jean Racine or Victor Hugo. To tell the truth, they illustrate a somewhat superficial idea of "remuneration," consisting of what Jakobson calls a "phonological palliative" for the discord between sound and sense. Thus, says Thibaudet, "the dark timbre of *jour* will be brightened up in a verse of monosyllables with the interstices bathed in light: '*Le jour n'est pas plus pur...*'"[70] Of course. These corrective harmonies have a nice effect, but it is a little difficult to reduce Mallarmé's poetics to that. His poetics is of another order, and maybe indefinable; Valéry will say this later on (as we shall see). Without slipping (too quickly) from one to the other, it is advisable to ponder this cautionary note: the necessity of Mallarméan verse is different from the verbal mimeticism (quite crude, when all is said and done) whose failing it remunerates: perhaps, all in all—*felix culpa*—a welcome failing. Language, even poetic language—especially poetic language—has better things to do than to imitate the world. To paraphrase Proust, mimological reverie lies on the threshold of the poetic life: it can usher us in; it does not constitute it.

ⓟ Finally, then, Mallarmé's position is the exact opposite of the Romantic concept of spontaneous creation, illustrated for example by Nodier's *Dictionnaire des onomatopoées françaises,* and no doubt nothing is more contrary to his "artless" poetics than the very widespread temptation to apply the symbolic values of *Les Mots anglais* to his poems.[71] This is so not only because of the unwarranted passage from one natural language to another, and the excessive generalization of values detected solely *in the initial position,* but also, and more radically, because Mallarmé's poetic work is itself situated, as deliberately and firmly as possible, at the level of the verse line and not of words. The very notion of the "Mallarméan word" seems regrettable to me. Probably, there are, in Mallarmé as in all writers—moreover, this is widely known[72]—words privileged by frequency and/or structure; but in his poems, there is no Cratylian game at the level of the words, since he recognized the impossibility, and maybe the futility, of that too. It would therefore be a strange diminishment of his poetics to reduce it, following the unsophisticated taste of the day, to effects of alliteration, imitative harmonies, homophonies, and other anagrams. As he reminded Degas, it is indeed "with words" that he wrote his poems, and by letting them take "the initiative."[73] But an initiative is not a decision, and the poem does not equal the sum of its words. Likewise, one can observe that the "spatial" poetics of *Un Coup de dés* does not rely on any graphic mimologism.[74] Here, poetic creation absolutely transcends the linguistic given, bestowing—in a familiar phrase—a *purer* meaning on the words of the tribe.

So, Mallarmé's linguistic speculation ends up in a veritable scission of language into what he calls the "double condition of the spoken word, unrefined or immediate here (in everyday language), essentialized there"[75]—in poetic language. The first state of language, serving only to "narrate, teach, even describe" —in short, for "universal reporting"—merely fills the "function of an easy and representative currency." The arbitrariness of the sign is no drawback, since this completely fiduciary function wears out in a circulation similar to that of a "coin," which one constantly exchanges without ever trying to *convert* it: therein lies the Hermogenist's necessary sacrifice. The second condition, which Mallarmé still calls the Enunciation {*le Dire*}, or the Word {*le Verbe*},[76] does not put up with any such "element of chance" (that of linguistic convention) and seeks to (re)constitute, at a "higher" level and in a "higher" form, the irrefrangible necessity of a perfect, "supreme," and, if you like, divine language.[77] Hence the emblematic value of the linguistic "dualism" manifested by English, as we have seen. A little (very little) like the Anglo-Saxon base in modern English, poetry is a language within a language, being its purest form and the one most faithful to the original truths. The idea of a double language is not, as a matter of fact, completely new (nothing ever is in this story, where History merely shifts the emphases around); we found a few premonitions of it previously in Diderot and others. It will not remain without its echoes, either; let us listen to some of them resonate.

℗ As is well known, Paul Valéry's poetic thinking took shape from the first as an extension of Mallarmé's, as a reflection on the *example* offered by the man who had been his master teacher and in whom he admired above all else what he called "the identification of 'poetic' meditation with the mastery of language, and the minute study in himself of their reciprocal relations." In a revealing statement further on, Valéry remarks: "Mallarmé understood language as if he had invented it."[78] So one can say that his own poetics of language is articulated as a reprise and a new elaboration of Mallarmé's idea of *double language*.[79]

In particular, everything goes along as if the experiment of *Les Mots anglais*,

218

whose importance to Valéry we have seen, had spared him from any of the temptations of primary Cratylism. It would be hard to find a trace of it in him, even in those reveries on words in which he every so often indulges like everybody else. Here are two instances, *a contrario* as it were, both in regard to foreign words. The first one concerns the Scandinavian word for "thank you," *tak,* "which makes the noise of a watchcase when snapped shut." The second one, more developed, evokes the port of Anvers, from which André Gide was writing letters to Valéry: "ANTWERP! a Baudelaire, all wild and black lies in that word. A word full of spices and pearls unloaded, under a rainy sky, by a drunken sailor, in the doorway of a tavern. ... The rose-colored lantern attracts the Negroes to the sad streets where the woman in underclothes tramples through the mud. And the prolonged echo of songs in a distant language, aboard boats enshrouded in silence. As you can see, I am letting these foreign words carry me off to you." [80]

Upon closer inspection, it is easy to see that neither of these two reveries follows the paths of the mimological imagination. The first one does compare the sound of a word to a noise, but this noise has no relationship with its signification: *tak* is therefore not (heard or understood as) an instance of onomatopoeia — or if it is, this onomatopoeia has adopted the wrong object and is already an illustration of the failing of natural languages. Conversely, the second one turns away entirely from the resonances of the vocable in order to evoke images of the city that it designates, without claiming to find a necessary relationship between them. A phonic description on one hand, a semantic description on the other, and no possible interaction. "There is no relationship between the sound and the sense of a word. The same thing is called HORSE in English, HIPPOS in Greek, EQUUS in Latin, and CHEVAL in French; but no manipulation of any of these terms will give me an idea of the animal in question; no manipulation of the idea will yield me any of these words — otherwise, we should easily know all languages, beginning with our own." [81]

Again, we recognize the Saussurean argument of the plurality of natural languages, in the service of the thesis known as the arbitrariness of the sign. The term itself appears elsewhere, redoubled by its Mallarméan equivalent: "We realize that there is hardly an instance in which the connection between our ideas and the groups of sounds that suggest them each in turn is anything more than arbitrary or purely chance." Also: "Each word is an instantaneous coupling of a *sound* and a *sense* that have no connection with each other." [82] Valéry's Hermogenism is apparently seamless. For him, any natural language reduces to a system of conventions: "The French language is a system of conventions among the French people. The English language ... among the English people." [83] This line of thought about natural language, as is known, had been corroborated very early on by his reading of Michel Bréal's *Sémantique,* published in 1897, which was reviewed by Valéry for the *Mercure de France* of January 1898. In this article we find one of the earliest formulations of his linguistic conventionalism ("the signs of language are absolutely distinct from their meaning; no rational or empirical pathway can lead from the sign to its meaning"), and the sketch of a general theory for "all symbolic systems taken together. Algebra, written music, certain types of ornamentation, cryptography, etc. can be subjected to semantic analysis." [84] This is more or less Saussure's program for a general semiology, including his distinction between "signs that are entirely natural (mime, for example)" and "systems based upon the arbitrary nature of the sign." [85] "Considered from the viewpoint of the significations, all these systems and language must lead, in my opinion, to a major distinction among the modes that are matched up with mental states. Let us designate by a and b two of these matched states, such that if a is given, b is given. In certain cases it will occur that a relation other than that of sequencing between a and b can be found. In these cases b can be construed with the help of a, and reciprocally, a with b. It will follow, in general, that any variation in one of the terms will determine a variation in the other. But in other cases, it will occur that the two terms proposed will have between them only a pure sequential relation. One can then say that this association is symbolic or conventional. Language is formed out of this second kind of relation." [86]

A letter from Valéry to Gustave Fourment, just a little later, develops and illustrates this opposition, whose terms are now labeled, as was previously the case in Nodier, as *rational* (for motivated signs) and *irrational* (for arbitrary signs). An example of the first kind is "all metaphors. I touch the warm stove; *afterward* I think of a woman's ass. The shared term is the warmth, the smoothness of the enamel, etc. Conversely, I might pass from the abovementioned backside to the pleasant warmth of a stove. ... The verbal metaphor would be this one: *vol* {flight} is like *val* {vale}; *sol* {soil} is like *cil* {cilium}. But the ideas corresponding to these words do not go along with the slight variation in their sound; they differ *subsequently* much more. I will give you a rather curious example. Draw a small house: this is the hieroglyphic system. Well! you can pass directly from this object to a real house; make it larger and color it in, and it's finished. Write the word *maison* {house}, and you can tinker with it as much as you like, but if I do not know the *signification* of this picture riddle or sound riddle, I will never be able to read it. The drawing, inasmuch as it represents the objects, is not irrational. Language is." [87]

Irrational signs are baptized here, in accordance with scientific usage (and contrary to the literary connotations of the term), as *symbols:* "Languages in general are all symbols." One can infer from this that the plan of studying "symbolic systems" in general, mentioned above, anticipated Saussure's highly controversial restriction of semiological analysis solely to "arbitrary" signs, deemed able to realize better than the others "the ideal semiological process": in other words, the a priori identification of the semiotic with arbitrariness, in which an anti-Cratylian valorization of the conventional can be seen. This is, let us recall, the furthest point that Hermogenism can reach: not only to "state the fact" of the conventionality of the sign, more or less resignedly, but to attribute to it a sort of fundamental superiority over any other mode of representation. In Valéry, the Hermogenist *parti pris* is clearly linked to a very explicit epistemological conventionalism, evidently inspired by Raymond Poincaré, and to a no less flaunted aesthetic conventionalism. The sciences are indeed "useful conventions" for Valéry, and we know how the major failing of history or of philosophy lies in not recognizing their own conventions at all. In literature, formal rules please him because they are arbitrary ("Rhyme has the great advantage of infuriating simpleminded people who naively believe there is something more important under the sun than a convention"), and classicism appeals to him because it "is recognized by the existence, the clarity, the imperative character of {its} conventions." [88] His preference for the established nature {*thesei*} of language is clearly expressed in the *Cahiers:* "The greatest progress was made the day conventional signs appeared. ... The immense improvement lay in the conventionality." [89] This is the exact opposite of the decadence of language according to de Brosses: true language begins with arbitrary signs; all that precedes is prehistoric and shows us nothing about its essence. Moreover, in any field, "the origin is an illusion." [90]

The same rigor is found again in other aspects of the discussion: there is, for example, no trace of that valorization of the word, of that overestimation of the lexicon in the functioning of natural language, which is still so evident in Mallarmé. The mistrustful declarations regarding such terms as *Temps* {Time}, *Vie* {Life}, "and all the others," which are useful only in proportion to the "swiftness of our passage," like "those light planks that are thrown across a ditch, or across a mountain crevice," are familiar, and it would be foolish to dwell on them. It is no more necessary to dwell on the words "on pain of seeing the most lucid discourse decompose itself into enigmas and more or less learned illusions." [91] Isolated words (and "likewise, a great number of word combinations") are fiduciary, incontrovertible, and "insolvent" values.[92] This critique does not arise only from a sort of fundamental "skepticism" with regard to language; more precisely, it takes aim at the traditional linguistic attitude that reduces natural language to a collection of vocables. If a word that is "clear when one uses it is obscure when pondered," this is not exactly because its use is based on an imposture but because the "weighing" of meaning in dictionaries refers to a fictive state of the word furnished by the set of its definitions and by its virtual uses. It is the actual — that is, contextual — use that removes the word's "enigmas" and determines its meaning each time: "Once words are isolated, we look at them — we seek to substitute for them the indeterminate set of their relations — whereas this set is determined in the act of composition."[93] Therefore, it is not the word that makes meaning but the sentence (and so forth).

This leads to the following conclusion, as un-Cratylian as it can be: "*There is no such thing as an isolable word.*"[94] Within the lexicon, Valéry makes the same break with the classical valorization of the noun. Preference goes to verbs ("The majority of verbs express *true* things, while substantives are ... a paradise of hollow formations") and to grammatical connectives: "What characterizes the language system are not the substantives, the adjectives, etc., but the words of relation, the *if* {*si*}, *that* {*que*}, *now* {*or*}, and *therefore* {*donc*}."[95] This is obviously the lesson of comparativism. The ideal linguistic system would ultimately be a language without words, made entirely of combinations of minimal elements as abstract as possible, the farthest away from the singularity of the proper name or the noun, that Cratylian object par excellence. Here is a picture of the deterioration of language: "It becomes less articulated. The sentence gives way to the word—and the word becomes a proper name. And here is a picture of its progress: "Language as combinations was able to develop only when it became constituted into short and simple elements. If it contains words with very complex signification—like those words of primitive peoples that are translated by three sentences in a modern language—its combinatory is impracticable. It gradually changed in such a way as to render its words more and more combinable. As a result, the possible became firmly established, being nothing but the combinatory capacity of a system."[96] In Valéry's "perfect language," which is obviously a "philosophical" language in the style of Leibniz, there is no longer any room for resemblance.

🕭 You are probably wondering what such a resolute rebel is doing in Cratylian country. It happens that we have so far considered only one facet of his doctrine, that part which holds good exclusively for what he calls "*ordinary,*" or "common," or "*demotic*" language or simply "prose," and which, at its ideal limit, would be the most functional and the most transparent of the instruments of thought, even substituting itself for that thought and taking away its entire *raison d'être:* "If the language system were perfect, man would cease to think. Algebra does away with arithmetic reasoning."[97] We are therefore at the extreme opposite of Mallarméan "perfection," the lack of which is resolved in the poem. Valéry's system is more complex (in this respect), for he entertains two antithetical perfections, both apparently meriting the term "absolute language" or "pure language."[98] Over against algebra there is what Valéry, suddenly renewing ties with the Homeric-Platonic tradition, does not hesitate to call the "language of the gods": "The poet is a peculiar type of translator, who translates ordinary speech, modified by emotion, into 'language of the gods.'"[99]

As in any system with a polar axiology, the main thing is first not to confuse the two poles in the name of their equal value but rather to acknowledge that the two perfections are antithetical, incompatible, and exclusive: to distinguish between them at any cost and by almost any means whatsoever. Sometimes this distinction is really so stark, and so little substantiated, that Valéry seems to intend to set aside a different language for each one of these states. Thus, he attributes to Mallarmé the intention "*of keeping the language of poetry always firmly, and almost absolutely, distinct from the language of prose,*" and he declares in his own name: "For me, since the language of the gods should be as distinct as possible from the language of men, all means of differentiating it should be retained so long as they also conduce to harmony." [100] In fact, poetry does not aim to be another natural language but, in a well-known formula, "a language within language": that is, a different use of the same natural language. More subtly, what poetry implies is "a decision to change the function of language." [101] Of what, then, does this *poetic function* of language (as Jakobson will later say) consist?

A first answer, a purely functional one in fact, consists in saying that the aim of the poem is to create in the reader a certain state, baptized the *poetic state:* "A poem is ... a sort of machine for producing the poetic state of mind by means of words." [102] Of course, such a definition cannot escape tautology unless the poetic state is in its turn defined and described otherwise than as the effect produced by the poem; therefore, it must also be possible for this state to be produced by something other than the poem — even if its specificity must suffer. This is just the case in Valéry, who describes it on at least two separate occasions [103] as an "emotion" capable of transfixing any spectacle or moment of existence whatsoever, by "musicalizing" it: that is to say, by making its elements "resonate through each other" and correspond with each other "harmonically." Thus is born a *"feeling of the universe,"* a perception of a *"world,"* in the strong sense, or a "complete system of relationships, in which creatures, things, events, and acts, although they may resemble, *each to each,* those which fill and form the tangible world — the immediate world from which they are borrowed — stand, however, in an indefinable but wonderfully exact relation to the modes and laws of our general sensibility. At that point, the value of these familiar objects and creatures is in some way altered. They respond to each other, they combine with each other quite otherwise than in ordinary conditions. They become ... *musicalized,* somehow commensurable, resonating through each other." [104] These privileged perceptions, then, are dominated by the feeling of relation and harmonic unity, and this feeling is clearly euphoric in itself. Its relation to the poetic message remains to be defined.

A first definition, of a Proustian type, is present in Valéry: like the ecstasy of reminiscence, the euphoria of the poetic state is essentially fortuitous and ephemeral; one can neither provoke it nor prolong it at will. The poetic state, like the dream (to which it is also akin in other features), is "wholly *irregular, in-*

constant, involuntary, fragile, and we lose it, as we acquire it, *by accident.* There are times in our life when this emotion and these highly precious formations do not manifest themselves. We do not even think them possible. Chance bestows them on us, chance takes them away."[105] We therefore need to find a way to "restore the poetic emotion at will, outside the natural conditions where it is produced spontaneously, by means of the artifices of language." This means is the poem. "All the arts have been created in order to perpetuate and change, each according to its nature, an ephemeral moment of delight into the certitude of an infinity of delightful moments. *A work of art is no more than the instrument of this potential multiplication or regeneration.*"[106]

The analogy with Proust's approach is quite striking, but it should not disguise an important difference. In Proust, the literary work can perpetuate the ecstasy of memory because it constrains itself in principle to transmit it by describing it and by giving a strict equivalent for it in the form of metaphor. On this point, Valéry's position is much more hesitant. All the texts just cited seem to imply such a transmission, and so the necessity for the poet himself first to feel the poetic emotion that he claims to communicate. Doesn't he justify the very term *poetic states* by the fact that "few among them are finally fulfilled in poems"? (On the other hand, it is true that nothing proves that these poems had any relation of content with the emotion that "fulfilled" itself in them and that produces an analogous state in their readers.) But here is a more ambiguous remark: when Valéry talks about the ways of "producing *or* reproducing a poetic world," he implies at the very least that one could produce it without reproducing it. And above all — corroborated as we know by a hundred other anti-Romantic professions of faith on this subject — he says: "A poet's function ... is not to experience the poetic state: that is a private affair. His function is to create it in others."[107] If, then, it happens that he creates it without having experienced it, this could still mean one of two things: either his poem is a sort of feigned transmission, a fictive description of the poetic state; or the poem in itself constitutes a (verbal) object capable of eliciting a poetic state in its reader, as independently from its subject matter as from the circumstances of its composition. This last interpretation seems the most consistent with the overall context. Naturally, it entails a direct application to the poem of the properties just now attributed to the poetic state, or more precisely to its cause: musicalization, the harmonic resonance of the elements, capable of engendering a "feeling of the universe": that is to say, a lively consciousness of relations. Used in this way, the recourse to the poetic state appears no longer as a tracing back to the cause but instead as a metaphorical description: a preliminary sketch for a description of the poetic message.

The *poetic state*, therefore, is also a state of language: there is a poetic state of language that differs from the "normal" state of everyday language. A new detour, a new comparison, will enable us to pin down the nature of this difference and thus of the specific operation that produces the poetic message. This time, the comparison is borrowed directly from the musical domain, to which the terms "musicalization" and "harmony" previously referred. Its clearest formulation is found in one of the texts on Mallarmé: "Just as the world of pure sounds, so easily recognized by our hearing, was selected from the world of noises to stand in opposition to it and constitute the perfect system of Music, so the poetic mind would like to do with language."[108] We meet with it again, considerably developed, in Valéry's two lectures on poetry, where the notion of the *musical universe* enters to throw a sidelight on that of the poetic state or universe. The world of *sounds* stands in opposition to that of *noises,* in which we ordinarily live, through a contrast between "the pure and the impure, order and disorder." But the "purity" of the sounds (which stands in opposition to the forever mixed-up and confused character of natural noises) is only a means in the service of "order": that is to say, the constitution of a regulated network of relations. The sounds are defined as "elements that have relations between them which are as palpable to us as these elements themselves. The interval between two of these privileged noises is as clear to us as each one of them."[109] Whence their capacity for reciprocal and generalized evocation (*"a sound evokes, of itself, the whole musical universe"*); whence the feeling of the *universe*—that is, a coherent system—which they infallibly elicit.[110]

The poetic state will then be to the ordinary state of language what the world of sounds is to that of noises: a state in which the internal relations will be as regular and as perceptible as those of music. An ideal illustration is furnished by Mallarmé's poems: "These marvelously polished little compositions imposed themselves as types of perfection, so sure was the movement from word to word, verse to verse, from rhythm to rhythm, and so strong was the sense that each poem gave of being an absolute object, as it were, produced by an equilibrium of intrinsic forces, shielded by a prodigious number of reciprocal forces from those vague impulses to alter and improve which the mind in the act of reading unconsciously devises when faced with the majority of texts."[111]

But in performing this transposition from the musical to the poetic, we have overlooked a considerable obstacle, which Valéry by no means overlooks and which we could already glimpse in that qualifying phrase quoted earlier: "so the poetic mind *would like* to do." This obstacle lies in the fact that the separation between noise and sound—the physical, technical separation that the musician finds already in place when he starts his work—has no equivalent in the domain of language: "The poet is deprived of the immense advantages possessed by the musician. He does not have before him, at the ready for the service of beauty, a set of resources made expressly for his art. He must borrow *language*—the public voice, that collection of traditional and irrational terms and rules, oddly created and transformed, oddly codified, and very diversely understood and pronounced. Here, there is no physicist who has determined the relationships among these elements; there are no tonometers, no metronomes, no inventors of scales and theoreticians of harmony. On the contrary, there are the phonetic and semantic fluctuations of vocabulary. Nothing pure; but a mixture of totally incoherent auditory and psychic sensations."[112] So, the musical metaphor has the function not only of describing the poetic state of language but also, and rather, that of illustrating *a contrario* the poet's difficulties: "Nothing gives a better idea of the difficulty of his task than a comparison of his initial givens with what the musician has at his disposal. ... Far different, infinitely less favorable is the poet's endowment."[113] Or, to approach it from another angle, this comparison has the effect not of throwing light on the difference between poetry and prose (according to the implicit formula *poetry : prose = sound : noise*) but rather of obscuring and taking the edge off it by insisting on the unity of the linguistic material common to the two types of discourse. In fact, therefore, *poetry : prose ≠ sound : noise* — because in a certain fashion and on a certain plane, *poetry = prose*, whereas *sound ≠ noise*.

This difference between poetry and music or, if one prefers, this identity (of means) between poetry and prose will be illustrated in its turn by a new comparison: the well-known parallel between poetry and dance, borrowed from François de Malherbe. It, too, is presented as a relation of four terms: *poetry : prose = dancing : walking*. Or, more precisely, just as dance utilizes for other ends "the same organs, the same bones, the same muscles" as walking, but "differently coordinated and differently motivated," so poetry utilizes for other ends (and with other coordinations and motivations) the same linguistic material as prose.[114]

Apparently, then, this new detour has no other function than to illustrate the (partial) inadequacy of the first one, and to substitute an exact comparison for a lame one. In fact, the comparison of poetry and dance is going to supply us, as an unexpected bonus, with a new piece of information regarding the essence of the poetic message: the difference in function between walking and dancing is that the latter "goes nowhere"; it is "a system of acts ... whose end is in themselves"; it aims not at a goal to be attained, an object to be taken possession of, but a state to be produced, a euphoria to which it does not *lead* but which coincides with it, consists of it, and dies away with it in such a way that one can only prolong or renew the one by prolonging and indefinitely repeating the other. In contrast, "when the man who is walking has reached his goal ... when he has reached the place, the book, the fruit, the object of his desire, the desire for which has drawn him out of his state of repose, at once this possession definitively cancels his entire act; the effect swallows up the cause, the end has absorbed the means; and whatever the act was, only the result remains."[115]

Now the same happens with language: in its ordinary use (prose), it is also merely a means that is absorbed into and canceled by its end. Its only goal is to be *comprehended:* that is, "completely replaced by its *meaning.*" "I ask you for a light. You give me a light: you have understood me."[116] In other words, your "comprehension" of my sentence *consists of* something completely different from it: an act of yours that removes from it all reason for lasting and for reproducing, and so abolishes it. "And here is the counterproof for this proposition: the person who has not understood *repeats* the words, or *has them repeated* to him." Or again, I could have pronounced my sentence in a certain way that is itself perceptible and noticeable, "with a certain tone, and in a certain timbre of voice—with a certain inflection and a certain languor or briskness." In that case, even if you have understood it, the sentence survives its own comprehension, returns in you, causes itself to be reiterated, "can yet go on living, though with an altogether different life. It has acquired a value; and it has acquired this *at the expense of its finite signification.* It has created the need to be heard and understood again. ... Here, we are on the very threshold of the poetic state."[117] Such, in effect, is the mark of the poetic message: it refuses to cancel itself out in its signification. "The poem ... does not die for having lived: it is expressly designed to be reborn from its ashes and to become indefinitely what it has just been. Poetry can be recognized by this property: it tends to get itself reproduced in its own form; it stimulates us to reconstitute it identically."[118]

Herein is posed, therefore, the great difference—the only crucial one—between the message of prose and the poetic message: the first is abolished in its function, the second survives itself and reproduces itself perpetually *in its form:* "If I may be permitted a word drawn from industrial technology, I should say that poetic form is automatically salvaged."[119] This cardinal thesis has an obvious consequence, or rather another possible and equivalent formulation: prose discourse is essentially translatable, and poetic discourse essentially untranslatable.[120]

All of this is well known and has declined long since into doctrine. On the face of it, this theme of the indestructibility (I choose this somewhat awkward term for its neutrality) of the poetic text is simple and unambiguous—whence perhaps its success. In fact, we are going to see it specified in Valéry—and perhaps in others—into two quite divergent and finally almost contradictory variants.

The first is that of the "intransitivity" or, if one prefers, the *autonomy* of the poetic form in relation to its signification. We have previously encountered this in passing, when it was a question of the value taken on by a sentence "at the expense of its finite signification"; the need for repetition is in inverse proportion to comprehension, and the most solid instance of this is that "the person who has not understood repeats, or has the words repeated to him." Ultimately, then, the obscurity or the total insignificance of a message could be a sufficient condition for its poetic value: "It should not be forgotten that for centuries poetic form was used for the purpose of spell-casting. Those who took part in these strange operations must have believed in the power of the spoken word {*parole*}, and far more in the efficacy of its sound than in its signification. Magical formulas are often meaningless, but their power was not thought to depend on their intellectual content. Now let us listen to verses like these: '*Mère des souvenirs, maîtresse des maîtresses* {Mother of memories, mistress of mistresses} ...'; or '*Sois sage, ô ma douleur, et tiens-toi plus tranquille* {Be wise, o my grief, and keep yourself more calm} ... '. These words work on us (at least on some of us) without telling us anything much. They tell us, perhaps, that they have nothing to tell us." [121]

This autonomy of form is itself articulated in two ways. One way (as we have just seen) is through the *secondary* and nonpertinent character of signification in poetry. The "quasi-creative, fiction-making" role of poetic language "is evidenced most clearly by the fragility or arbitrariness of the *subject*"; "first and foremost was not meaning, but the existence of the verse": this is the well known apologue of Mallarmé explaining to Degas that poetry is made "not ... with ideas, but with *words*." [122] Sometimes the autonomy of form is articulated through its multiple character, through the *polysemy* of the poetic message — a theme that has itself also, since then, turned into a cliché. "*There is no true meaning to a text*": Valéry applied this to "*Le Cimetière marin*" in regard to Gustave Cohen's commentary, and it essentially holds good for the poetic text. [123] We come back to it again when Valéry responds to the new commentary by Alain on *Charmes*: "My verses have the meaning attributed to them. The one I give them suits me alone and does not contradict anyone else. It is an error contrary to the nature of poetry, and one that might even be fatal to it, to claim that for each poem there is a corresponding true meaning, unique and conformable to, or identical with, some thought of the author's. ... Whereas solely the content is exigible from prose, here it is solely the form that commands and survives." [124] Recalling the statements on the essential translatability of the prose text, we see a perfectly symmetrical opposition taking shape between the polysemy of the poem and the polymorphousness of prose. The peculiar property of prose is always to tolerate *several forms for one meaning;* that of the poem, in contrast, is always to propose *several meanings under one single form.*

Poetic "meaning" is therefore either multiple, or of secondary importance, or else ultimately absent. In all these cases, the form remains autonomous and stands on its own; it cannot be linked to such an evanescent function. Up to this point, therefore, Valéry's theory of poetic language is as un-Cratylian as his theory of "ordinary" language. But here is an unexpected reversal that is going

228

to lead us back to Cratylism, or nearly: it is the second variant indicated for the central theme — that of the indestructibility of the poetic message.

⑨ In actual fact, the reversal arises from an almost imperceptible slippage, which can be reconstructed roughly as follows: since the poetic form is not, like the other one, sacrificed to its meaning, it is not *subordinated* to it; it enjoys an (at least) equal importance. This equal importance is illustrated by a new comparison: the image of the pendulum. We have seen that, once "comprehended,"[125] the poetic text requires resumption in its form: in the poetic experience, the mind thus goes from form to meaning, then returns from meaning to form (or "sound"), and so forth, like a pendulum. "Between Voice and Thought, between Thought and Voice, between Presence and Absence, oscillates the poetic pendulum. It follows from this analysis that the value of a poem resides in the indissolubility of sound and sense."[126] The slippage indicated has therefore led us from autonomy to equality, from equality to equilibrium, from equilibrium to perpetual oscillation, and from oscillation to inseparability, or indissolubility. At the start the poetic form was independent of its content; at the end it is substantially joined to it. The distance covered disguises the volte-face, but the volte-face is there. Departing from an ultraformalist poetics, we find ourselves back in a (quasi-)Cratylian poetics: that is, in the definition of poetic language as *motivated* language.

For it goes without saying that the *indissolubility of sound and sense* is the motivation of the sign. This is confirmed, should it need to be, by the way in which this text leads into an argument already familiar to us. Let us go over this development: "The result of this analysis is to show that the value of a poem resides in the indissolubility of sound and sense. Now this is a condition that seems to demand the impossible. There is no relation between the sound and the meaning of a word. The same thing is called HORSE in English ... (etc.)." This is indeed the opposition of poetic mimologism to the ordinary conventionality of natural language, and suddenly here we are (again) in familiar territory. That this return is not merely a chance mishap, a metaphorical concatenation, or a simple slip of the pen is indicated by many analogous and, furthermore, well-known statements such as Roman Jakobson's use of the following formula from Valéry: "The poem — that prolonged hesitation [still the oscillation of the pendulum] between the sound and the sense."[127] To tell the truth, other statements are more forceful. Thus, regarding the lines from Baudelaire cited above, Valéry again shifts from the "equal importance" of sound and sense to their "indivisibility" and the "possibility of their innermost and indissoluble combination." Elsewhere: "The sound and the sense, no longer separable, correspond to each other inexhaustibly within our memory."[128] Elsewhere still: "The art {of poetry} implies and demands an equivalence, a perpetually exercised exchange between form and content, between sound and sense, between act and matter." [129] The equivocation in this position is as if concentrated here in the ambiguous term *equivalence*, which, strictly speaking, designates the equality of value and importance, apart from any resemblance, but which in fact almost inevitably gives us to understand: similitude. We will find a parallel equivocation in Jakobson.

Here we are, then, on the threshold of a neo-Cratylian poetics that would, as in Mallarmé, charge poetic language with correcting the conventionality of natural language. But we will not remain on this threshold, for Valéry's position here is even more guarded than that of his master teacher.

A first reservation: the arbitrariness of the sign is now (recognized to be) so strong that it apparently stands in the way of any kind of correction. Contrary to Lessing's wishes, the poet cannot really *transform* his conventional signs into motivated signs: "This ... seems to demand the impossible"; "That is to ask for a miracle." Apparently, all he can do is to give his reader the illusion of motivation: "It is the poet's business to give us the *feeling* of an intimate union between the spoken word and the mind," "to produce a powerful *impression*, sustained for a fixed period of time [in short, momentary], that there is I know not what harmony between the perceptible form of a discourse and its *exchange value in terms of ideas,* that the two are conjoined in I know not what mystical union"; "A poem ... should create the *illusion* of an indissoluble compound of *sound* and *sense.*" [130]

Next, a second reservation: even by way of an illusion, Valéry shrinks visibly from the idea of a poetic form that would be the *image* of the meaning. We should recall here that at least in principle, a motivated sign is not necessarily a sign by resemblance. Cratylian speculation, of course, has never known how to draw this distinction very well and, to tell the truth, has most often misunderstood it; but for a long time tropology has dealt with figures of speech motivated by other types of relations (contiguity, inclusion, contrariety, and so on). We have seen that Valéry readily evokes an (illusion of) motivation for the poetic form, rendered "inseparable" or "indissoluble" from its content, but we have not yet run across any statement that clearly specifies this motivation in terms of mimesis. The furthest step in this direction consists of using the words *harmonie* {harmony} or *accord* {concord}, which evidently connote in standard usage a sort of partial resemblance. But they are modalized each time by a very characteristic style of hedging: "*I know not what* harmony," "a *certain* indefinable concord." [131] These clauses (and especially the second) are not simply careful wordings, as a major text from *Tel Quel* confirms: "The power of verse lines stems from the *indefinable* harmony between what they *say* and what they *are.* 'Indefinable' is basic to the definition. This harmony should not be definable. When it is, it is *imitative* harmony—and that will not do at all. The impossibility

230

of defining this relation, combined with the impossibility of denying it, constitutes the essence of the verse line." [132]

Imitative harmony—which Valéry scorns, not without practicing it himself on occasion [133]—is obviously the poetic form of vulgar mimologism. But just what would a *nonimitative harmony* be? It could easily be defined, by arguing from the musical origin of the term (as with *concord*), as a relation not of resemblance but of regulated difference, one capable of engendering an aesthetic pleasure. But to define it in this way (or in any other way) is already, let us note, to contravene Valéry's formula, which posits, in the manner of an ancient paradox, that any definable harmony, even if nonimitative, is by definition imitative. What must be looked for instead, therefore, is what a *nondefinable* harmony consists of. But the futility of such a question is glaringly obvious. Valéry's poetics ends, deliberately, in an aporia. Perhaps the moment has come to recall this cruel remark: "Most people have such a vague idea of poetry that the very vagueness of their idea is, for them, its definition." [134] At the least, applying this criticism to its author, one might say that in Valéry the vagueness "enters [consciously, which makes it worth something] into the definition."

But on the whole, it is a question not of vagueness but rather of a sort of irreducible core of contradiction: the very one, of course, already noticed, between a "formalist" poetics that decrees the autonomy of the poetic form, and a neo-Cratylian poetics that advocates the indissolubility of sound and sense. Up to this point, these two divergent aesthetics had remained separate in their formulations, scattered in that "chaos of bright ideas" which the Valéryan text is also, and perhaps more than any other. When they inadvertently coincide, their synthesis can only be a paradox.

ⓟ Perhaps there may be another way to resolve this contradiction, but nothing indicates that this solution was in Valéry's mind at any time, and I advance it with all proper disclaimers. Let us recall the properties of the poetic state that enabled the comparison with the musical universe to be brought out—and that were afterward abandoned along the way: structural unity, relations between the elements as perceptible as the elements themselves. These features obviously apply to the poetic text. Such tightly woven relations "of word to word, verse to verse ... rhythm to rhythm" necessarily inspire in the reader the impression of "an absolute object, as it were, produced by an equilibrium of intrinsic forces, shielded by a prodigious number of reciprocal forces from those vague impulses to alter and improve" (I am continuing my consideration of the text on Mallarmé, cited above, in a new light). Such is the *necessity* of the poetic text, clearly a "purely formal" necessity—that is, "intrinsic" to the form. But the temptation seems to be strong to interpret a necessary and thus motivated form *in this sense* (through the mere "equilibrium of intrinsic forces") as necessary and motivated *in another sense:* to wit, as the expression of a certain content. From the internal (musical) necessity of a form, one would then switch, surreptitiously, to the necessity of its signifying function,[135] and therein would lie the key to the "illusion" of mimeticism in poetry—and, incidentally, the key to Valéry's poetics.

Yet it should be remembered that for Valéry this internal immutability of the poetic message is itself illusory: it is an impression of the reader who, unaware of the series of tentative efforts and substitutions from which the work of art arises, does not imagine it (might be) different, and believes it "completed." But in reality, "a poem is never finished—it is always ended by accident," and "*a finished sonnet*" simply signifies "*abandoned sonnet*."[136] No text is therefore unmodifiable, and the internal necessity of its form is always imperfect. The illusion of mimeticism would arise, then, from an illusion of completion. A double misapprehension—a doubly "graceful attribute with which the reader endows his poet: the reader sees in us the transcendent merits of virtues and graces that develop in him."[137] The true Cratylian magicmaker, the truly "inspired one," is not the poet but the reader.

Once again, a like (re)solution is nowhere made explicit as such in Valéry. The contradiction remains unresolved between a very sharp formalist and conventionalist *parti pris* and a sort of hereditary reflex for valorizing mimesis. Today, this contradiction is still at the heart of all "modern" poetics, and we will discover it again. Maybe we should be satisfied, then, to have caught in Valéry a glimpse of what a Hermogenist poetics might be—a poetics *without illusion.*

⑨ Jean-Paul Sartre's theory of poetic language appears in the first chapter of *What Is Literature?* in the context of the famous theme of the writer's "commitment" {*engagement*} and the need to explain why such commitment does not concern, "or, at least, not in the same way," painting, sculpture, music, and even poetry.[138] For poetry is "on the side of painting, sculpture, music" in a division that opposes all these arts as a group to Literature alone, which is obviously reduced to "prose."[139] The principle behind this division is not aesthetic, in the full sense (a difference between the "materials"—acoustic, plastic, verbal, and so on), but properly semiotic. The arts utilize, or rather handle and arrange, *things* that "exist in themselves" and "do not refer to anything outside themselves." In contrast, literature (excluding poetry) deals only with *significations,* and it alone holds this position: literature is "the empire of signs."[140]

These signs, which are plainly linguistic, will once more be reduced here to their single lexical dimension: prose is an activity that utilizes *words* as signs. As the opposite, poetry will therefore be defined as an activity—or rather as an *attitude*—"that looks upon words as *things* and not as *signs*. For the ambiguity of the sign implies that one may traverse it at will like a pane of glass and pursue the thing signified across it, or turn one's gaze toward its *reality* and look upon it as an object."[141] Clearly, Sartre here (for the most part) takes the term "sign" in the current sense (one object representing another), which is approximately the one that Saussure attaches to the term "signifier." To be more precise: I specify *here,* because other uses (as in "the empire of signs, or prose") refer more to the Saussurean sense of the sign: that is, to "the totality formed by the signifier and the signified." I also say *for the most part,* because as we will very soon discover, and perhaps have already discovered, the problem is no longer the ambiguity of the sign but that of the word *sign*—unless these are one and the same thing.

To consider the word as an object would then be (provisionally) to set aside its signification and to treat it as a pure phonic and/or graphic "reality," analogous (or at least parallel) to those acoustic or plastic realities handled by music or painting. Such graphic/phonic aggregates would be for the poet what sounds are for the musician and colors for the painter. Therein lies "formalist" poetics in its crudest—and, as everyone knows, its most untenable—version. Sartre is perfectly well aware of this, too, and immediately justifies his theory by saying that "signification alone ... can give words their verbal unity; without it, they are scattered into sounds or into strokes of the pen."[142] It would be pointless to raise the counterexample of concrete poetry, the ever open possibility of an activity that would effectively utilize the phonic and/or graphic material of natural language for artistic ends. The implicit reply is that this material would then no longer consist of "words," or at least that these words would no longer exist as such. Signification is essential to the definition of the word; it is therefore by definition impossible to treat or consider it as a *pure object,* as a pure thing.

At this point, it becomes clear that the initial opposition between *thing* and *sign,* understood as a rigorous alternative between two exclusive terms, leads to an aporia. Either one has to give up the fight prematurely, or one has to backtrack and make the dilemma somewhat more tractable. First, let us observe that the opposition was asymmetrical, or lame, in any case, since "signs" can only be a certain species of "things": those that do not exist (solely) "in themselves," or rather *for* themselves, but (also) refer to something else outside themselves. A piece of blank paper is a "thing"; a bank note is both a thing (a printed piece of paper) and a monetary sign. Therefore, the opposition *thing* versus *sign* actually opposes things that are nothing else but that (pure things) to those that are also signs: the sign-things. But asymmetry does not prevent the opposition from being exclusive, if one posits that a word must necessarily be considered either as pure thing or as sign-thing. As we have seen, the first hypothesis was excluded by definition, but it is also clear that the second one, in an apparently intolerable cancellation of all opposition between prose and poetry, throws us back entirely upon "prose." Sartre has to invent a third hypothesis, then, which is as follows: "If the poet comes to a halt before words, as the painter does be-

233

fore colors and the musician before sounds, this does not mean that they have lost all signification in his eyes. ... It is only that {signification} becomes natural, too. It is no longer the goal always out of reach and always aimed at by human transcendence; it is a property of each term, analogous to the expression of a face, to the slightly sad or gay meaning of sounds and colors."[143] In this signification "become natural," it is not hard to recognize the Cratylian *physei*, which (re)appears at the appointed time to offer a third path between the insignificance of "things" and the significance — implicitly defined as artificial and conventional — of "signs." The opposition between these two types of significance will be thematized and provided with a terminology later on in a text to which we will have occasion to return.[144] This is the distinction between *signification* (conventional) and *meaning* (natural): "Things do not signify anything. However, each one of them has a meaning. By *signification* should be understood a certain conventional relation that makes a present object into the substitute for an absent object; by *meaning*, I denote the participation of a present reality, within its being, in the being of other realities, whether present or absent, visible or invisible, and by degrees in the universe. Signification is conferred upon the object from outside by a signifying intention; meaning is a natural quality of things: the first is a transcendent relationship between one object and another, the second a transcendence fallen into immanence."[145]

So there we have the symbolist theory of poetic language felicitously reformulated: the words of prose have a signification; those of the poem, like things, like sounds and colors, have a meaning. One notices immediately that the insignificance of things is posited only provisionally, inasmuch as it opposes the significance of signs. As a matter of fact, the third term has been substituted for the first, and there are finally no more than two terms, which are the two significances: that of instituted signs, or signification, which makes up (among others) the "empire" of prose; and that of things, or meaning, which is, or can be, the material of art and of poetry.[146]

About this poetic significance, we know only that it is *natural*, a natural "property" or "quality" of things. It should be carefully distinguished from those marginal semiotic uses that can be made of certain objects upon which one "confers the value of signs by convention," as in the "language of flowers." The signification of "faithfulness" attributed to white roses has nothing to do with their "frothy profusion" or their "stagnant sweet perfume"; it does not belong to them but is "transcendent," "conferred from the outside," as it might have been conferred upon any other species of flowers: such is the arbitrariness of the sign. On the contrary, the naturalness of meaning is the immanent relation between a thing and the significance with which it is "impregnated." For example, the yellow rift in the sky above Tintoretto's Golgotha does not *signify* the agony of Christ but *is* both yellow sky and agony. For another example: "Picasso's attenuated harlequins, ambiguous and eternal, haunted by an indecipherable meaning, inseparable from their lean stooped-over forms and the faded-out diamond shapes on their tights, are an emotion that has made itself flesh and which the flesh has absorbed like a blotter drinking up ink."[147] Likewise: "The signification of a melody—if one can still speak of signification[148]—does not exist outside the melody itself, unlike ideas, which can be adequately rendered in several ways" (one recognizes here an echo of Valéry's definition of prose).

These illustrations, borrowed from art, may still seem quite vague; in fact, they merely express a confused, almost ineffable, intuition of what a signification "fallen into immanence" might be, once it has been "made into a thing," like the agony of Christ "which has turned into the yellow rift in the sky and which, as a result, is submerged in, coated over by the particular properties of things, by their impermeability, their extension, their blind permanence, their externality, and that infinity of relations which they maintain with other things."[149] In this typically "Sartrean" discourse, the semiotician on duty might have a little difficulty recognizing his tools, but he has to go through all this before arriving at formulations that are clearer, probably too clear. Here is a parallel instance taken again from *Saint Genet:* "[Signification] can prepare for an intuition, can orient it, but it seems unable to furnish the intuition itself, since the signified object is, theoretically, external to the sign; [meaning] is by nature intuitive; it is the odor that impregnates a handkerchief, the perfume that vanishes out of an empty, musty bottle. The abbreviation '17th' *signifies* a certain century, but this entire period, in museums, is suspended like a piece of gauze, or a spider's web, from the curls of a wig, or escapes in whiffs from a sedan chair."[150] The examples of Louis XIV's wig or of a sedan chair, with their "immanent," inherent, or at the least *adherent* meaning, aptly illustrate what a "natural" significance might be. Better still, they throw light on the definition mentioned above—one that requires a little further attention: "*participation* of a present reality ... in the being of other realities, present or absent." Between the sedan chair and the meaning "17th century" there exists a necessary relation of "participation," since the chair actually belongs to the century from which it comes. This is a relation of part to whole (synecdoche), or equally well one of effect to cause (metonymy): the object in the style of Louis XIV is basically an *index,* in C. S. Peirce's sense, of the Great Century—a *vestige.*

Something in this choice of examples slightly (temporarily) disturbs our Cratylian habits. For once, the necessary semantic relationship is one not of resemblance but of contiguity or, as Beauzée said, of "coexistence." For once, the model for the natural sign is the index and not the "icon," still in the Peircean sense of an image or reflection. What is more, this specific choice was implicit not only in the examples but already within the very definition. For the moment, then, it is as if for Sartre natural significances boil down to signs motivated by contiguity, to the exclusion of all other types of motivation. This seems to raise the question of a completely new version of Cratylism.[151]

But a considerable obstacle presents itself here. The notion of a sign by contiguity, or participation, is perfectly clear outside the linguistic sphere, but what becomes of it when one wants to transpose it — as one really must in the case of poetry — into the functioning of language? Take the poetic utterance that Sartre has just explained by introducing his distinction between meaning and signification: "In producing his first poem as an object" [above, he said "like a thing"], reasons Sartre, "Genet transforms the *signification* of the words into *meaning*."[152] Let's take a look at this. That first "poem" is the syntagm *moissonneur des souffles coupés* {reaper of gasping breaths}. To answer our question, Sartre's analysis ought to show how these three or four words, which begin as conventional signs in natural language, become, or here at least give the illusion of becoming, indexical signs or natural metonymies linked by "participation" to the things they designate. In fact, there is nothing of the kind in these six otherwise dazzling pages, which turn entirely upon an altogether different idea: that of "the syncretic interpenetration of meanings" in the poetic word and the poetic syntagm.[153] Thus, the poetic mode of meaning, which is one of "indeterminacy," "indistinctness," and "syncretic unity," forbids us to choose between *couper les souffles* {literally, "to cut breaths"; idiomatically, "to cause one to gasp"}, used in this verse, and *couper les tiges* {"to cut the stems of flowers"}, inferred from *moissonneur* {reaper}: "Right out of the blue the two meanings spread through each other and coexist, neither fusing together nor contradicting each other."[154] Breaths are at the same time flower stems: wind, plant, respiration, all at once "in a sort of tourniquet" — until the final operation that will *execute* the signification beyond this syncretic unity, disclosing that a gasping breath is nothing, that a reaper of nothing is no one, and that in this way, with all content canceled out, Genet's verse simply meant: *nothing*. But this double demonstration concerns the nature of the relationships between signifieds (*moissonneur de tiges — moissonneur de souffles*) in the poem, not that of the relationships of signification between signifiers and signifieds (*moissonneur —* "one who reaps"). The interpenetration of meanings has been substituted for the participation of meaning (for meaning as participation), but this substitution is neither legitimate nor efficacious. For all that, the critic can yet rightly argue — in a last echo of the theme —that "*moissonneur* is still completely impregnated with the smell of ripened wheat"; evidently Sartre cannot demonstrate this argument — and apparently he is no longer worried about it, as if he had changed his mind along the way. And maybe it would be very difficult for him simply to make what he means explicit.

Indeed, if the mimetic relation between word and thing is subject to debate, at least it is clearly definable: one can grant or deny that *moissonneur* resembles a reaper; what is at issue is more or less clear. But how can a relationship of "impregnation" or "participation" be granted or denied here? What are we to *understand* by these terms? The only conceivable relation of this type would be the onomatopoetic one that apparently unites the word that imitates the noise with the object that produces this noise. Thus, one could say—very hastily— that the noise-word *cascade* (according to Nodier) participates in the (noisy) object, "cascade." But one immediately sees that the relationship of participation in fact unites the two "objects," the cascade and its noise; and that the linguistic relation lies elsewhere—between the noise and the word; and that it is not participatory but (if one wishes) imitative. Here *cascade* would designate the noise of the cascade through onomatopoeia and the cascade itself through metonymy—that is, through a relationship of participation *between the signifieds.* But between signifier and signified the only possible motivated relation remains the mimetic one. Let us return to our (word) *moissonneur.* It resembles (or doesn't) a reaper: this is a direct imitation. Or else it resembles (or doesn't) a noise produced by the reaper, or by his scythe, or by whatever one wishes: this is an indirect imitation. But the reaper does not produce the word *moissonneur.* One can say, therefore, and even reiterate, that the word *moissonneur* is impregnated with the smell of ripened wheat, or any other odor, but this would-be metonymy will remain what it is: a metaphor. Words have no odor.

The variant sketched out in *Saint Genet* thus turns out to be illusory; it is necessary to return to "classical" poetic Cratylism, to poetic language defined as mimesis. Besides, the text from *What Is Literature?*, as if it had foreseen the uselessness of the detour, passed directly from the general notion of "natural signification" to the particular one of the mimetic relation. First, the poet is "outside language": he maintains a "silent contact" with things; then he turns toward "that other species of things which words are for him" in order to discover their "particular affinities with earth, sky and water and all created things. Short of knowing how to use it as a *sign* of an aspect of the world, he sees in the word the *image* of one of these aspects." *Affinity* remained ambiguous: is it resemblance or "participation"? But the telltale word is obviously *image,* whose italics formally oppose it to *sign* and which sanctions the return to a pure mimetic relation, as the following statement does again, a bit further on: "language is for [the poet] the Mirror of the world." Image, reflection: this is indeed mimesis, a "magical resemblance," but artificially (re)created in the poetic message, beyond the failing of natural languages: "The verbal image that he chooses for its resemblance to the willow or the ash tree is not necessarily the word which we use to designate these objects."[155] It can be the reverse—"willow" for ash, "ash" for willow—as if Mallarmé had dared (or deigned) to call night "day," and vice versa; it can be anything else: the poetic image recreates language.

Thus endowed with a mimetic function, the poetic word begins, for Sartre, to exist "by itself" in a tangible and, as Valéry said, "physical" manner: "Its

237

sonority, its length, its masculine or feminine endings, its visual aspect compose for him a fleshly face that *represents* signification rather than expressing it."[156] In this way, paradoxically (we encountered this paradox earlier in Valéry, but in a less ingenuous form, and will meet it again in Jakobson), far from increasing the transparency of the vocable, its very mimetic virtue seems to be the necessary and sufficient condition for its aesthetic autonomy and opacity. The more "semblant" the poetic word is, the more *perceptible* it becomes. I say *Florence,* "and the strange object that thus appears possesses the liquidity of *fleuve* (river), the soft fulvous fire of *or* (gold), and, for the finishing touch, abandons itself with *décence* (decency), and, through the sustained diminution of the silent *e,* indefinitely prolongs its very reserved opening out."[157] Indeed, the "poetic" word is a strange object, whose whole tangible existence is as if insufflated by the (partial) objects of its signification. The "poetic" word releases a typical series of lexical associations — Socratic etymology or Leirisian gloss[158] — in which the mimetic illusion, without power over the whole noun or name, decides to divide and conquer in order to rule, syllable by syllable, fragment by fragment, over a shattered vocable. The "poetic" word is a mirror — a broken one.

⑨ At the outset, the Russian Formalists have a completely clear, if not entirely specific, idea of what they call "poetic language" (*poeticheskij jazyk*). In opposition to everyday language, the language of pure communication in which phonic, morphological, and other forms have no autonomy, the function of communication in the poetic mode of language recedes into the background and {the} "language resources acquire an autonomous value."[159] This autonomy of the poetic word in relation to its function is manifested by a greater *perceptibility:* "Poetic language is distinguished from prosaic language by the palpableness of its construction."[160] The perceptibility of the form became, as we know, one of the major themes of Formalist theory in all domains. This includes the domain of "literary evolution," whose driving force was taken to be the erosion of old forms as they become habitual, hence transparent, and the need to substitute for them new, hence perceptible, ones: "The new form does not appear in order to express a new content, but in order to replace an old form that has already lost its aesthetic character"[161] — and this also occurs, for example, at the level of dramatic constructions or narrative devices. As I have said, this generalization diminishes the specificity of poetic language but gives it in return, as in Valéry, an exemplary value: poetry is literature par excellence, art par excellence, defined by its deliberate rupture with any "practical" function.

Roman Jakobson's early analyses do not stand out at all in this context, unless it is for their sometimes greater Formalist intransigence. Thus, in "La Nouvelle Poésie russe," he says that in poetry "the communicative function, proper to both daily language and emotional language, is reduced . . . to a minimum.

Poetry is indifferent in respect to the object of the utterance, just as practical, or more accurately objective ... prose is indifferent, but in the opposite direction, in respect to, let us say, rhythm." [162] Poetic devices such as neologism or phonic repetition apparently have no *raison d'être* other than promoting or emphasizing this "opacity" of the verbal forms in the poem. [163] The neologism "produces a dazzling euphonic splash, whereas the old words age phonetically, too, being worn out by frequent usage, especially because their phonic constitution is only partially perceived. One easily loses awareness of the form of words in daily language, which dies, becomes petrified, whereas one is compelled to perceive the form of the poetic neologism." Similarly: "We do not perceive the form of a word unless it is repeated within the linguistic system. The isolated form dies; likewise, the combination of the sounds within a poem: ... we see it only through the repetition." [164] This position is confirmed a few years later and is, above all, justified within a typically conventionalist axiology:

> But how does poeticity manifest itself? Poeticity is present when the word is felt as a word and not as a mere representation of the object being named or as an outburst of emotion, when words and their composition, their meaning, their external and internal form, acquire a weight and value of their own instead of referring indifferently to reality.
>
> Why is all this necessary? Why is it necessary to make a special point of the fact that sign does not merge with object? Because, besides the direct awareness of the identity between sign and object (A is A_1), there is a necessity for the direct awareness of the inadequacy of that identity (A is not A_1). The reason this antinomy is essential is that without contradiction there is no mobility of concepts, no mobility of signs, and the relationship between concept and sign becomes automatized. Activity comes to a halt, and the awareness of reality dies out. [165]

This text is thoroughly exceptional in the history of poetic theory. Not only is the poetic sign presented here as essentially "different" from its object, but this difference is also deemed superior to that of daily language, in which the erosion of habit automatizes, and thereby naturalizes, the semantic relation. Above all, this differentiation is exalted as an instrument for awakening the consciousness of reality. A Hermogenism of fact but also of value is asserted, therefore, whose liberating virtue could not inconceivably be compared to certain Brechtian formulas on this subject. In any case, it is clear that the *perceptibility* of the poetic word is in no way linked here to just any mimetic function — quite to the contrary. Later on, in "Linguistics and Poetics," the poetic function is still defined, among the six functions of language, by "the set ... toward the message as such, focus on the message for its own sake," and not for the sake of its relation, of whatever order this might be, with its object. On the contrary, Jakobson

239

immediately specifies that this function, "by promoting the palpable aspect of signs, deepens the fundamental dichotomy of signs and objects" — a dichotomy that leaves the message completely free to organize itself "for its own sake" and according to preferences totally independent of its signification, as the following example well illustrates: "'Why do you always say "Joan and Margery," yet never "Margery and Joan"? Do you prefer Joan to her twin sister?' — 'Not at all, it just sounds smoother.' In a sequence of two coordinate names, and as far as no problems of rank interfere, the precedence of the shorter name suits the speaker, unaccountably for him, as a well-ordered shape of the message."[166]

Let us work on this example and its commentary a little more. The "well-ordered shape of the message" here is really a question of pure internal arrangement, of rhythm and euphony, without any possible "interference" from the respective positions of "rank" between the two persons meant by the two proper names, twin sisters who are equally liked: clearly, the situation was carefully calculated. The question, therefore, is really one of *formal* affinity. In order to appreciate this fully, another example of "well-ordered shape" has to be adduced, borrowed from another, nearly contemporary essay: "Such a sequence as 'The President and the Secretary of State attended the meeting' is far more usual than the reverse, because the initial position in the clause *reflects* the priority in official standing."[167] And Jakobson goes on to talk about a "correspondence of order between signifier and signified." So there we have, in opposition to the purely formal order of "Joan and Margery," an order that imitates the hierarchy of contents and that belongs to the class of iconic signs that Peirce has baptized "diagrams," or "icons of relation," in opposition to "images," or simple icons. This example belongs to a series of illustrations of the mimetic capacities of common language at the syntactic (as in this case), morphological, and phonic levels. "The President and the Secretary of State" is an utterance of "ordinary," "daily," "prosaic" language, dominated as such by the function called "referential," focused on the "context" or object of discourse. Its evidently mimetic arrangement is in no way a poetic fact; on the contrary, its expressiveness fosters its referential function, and the question here is no longer the euphonic principle of the "precedence of the shorter name," to which this utterance is completely indifferent — just as the poetic utterance (the one illustrating the poetic function) "Joan and Margery" was indifferent to mimetic appropriateness, even at the risk of a serious misunderstanding ("Do you prefer Joan?"). In short, between a prosaic utterance and a poetic utterance, it is the former that aims, as far as possible, at mimetic expressiveness, and the latter that shies away from this. The prosaic utterance "reflects" or traces its object; it puts its diagrammatic transparency at the service of the "cognitive" function. The poetic utterance is more autonomous, less tied down to its content, therefore less transparent and more perceptible as an object; therein lies its function. So goes, once again (one last time), Formalist poetics, or the poetics of Hermogenes.[168]

But this distinction represents merely one facet of Jakobson's theory. In order to see (gradually) the obverse side, we need only return to and continue the reading of "Linguistics and Poetics," moving on to the second, then to the third example of the poetic message.[169] The second example is "Horrible Harry." Why "horrible" instead of "terrible," "frightful," and so on? Because, as Jakobson directly remarks, "horrible" and "Harry" are in a relationship of paronomasia: we are still, then, at the purely formal level. If the person were called, say, "Ingrid," the appropriate expression of disgust would obviously be "Ignoble Ingrid," and so forth. The agreement exists between the two verbal units, and nothing else. However, here is the justification that Jakobson attributes to his speaker: "Horrible fits him better"; "him" obviously represents the person, not the pronoun. The alliteration is therefore felt (by whom?) as an *imitative* harmony. Now for the third example: "I like Ike." Jakobson gives this a phonic analysis at first, then he adds: "The first of the two [vocalically] alliterative words is included in the second ... a paronomastic image of the loving subject [I] enveloped by the beloved object [Ike]." Once more, but this time explicitly by the analyst, paronomasia is described as producing an "image": the relation between the two verbal units reflects the relation between the two individuals.

Here we are (again) in familiar territory: poetic language no longer deviates from the expressive potentials of natural language; it respects and exploits them. One step further, and it will be said, as so often previously, that it develops them, or at least that it shows them off more. This step is taken a little further on: "Poetry is not the only area where sound symbolism makes itself felt, but it is a province where the internal nexus between sound and meaning changes from latent to patent and manifests itself most palpably and intensely."[170] Or else: "The autonomous iconic value of phonemic oppositions is damped down in purely cognitive messages but becomes particularly apparent in poetic language."[171] One final step, and the situation just described (referential mimetic language versus autonomous poetic language) reverses itself totally: mimetic poetic language versus conventional prose. The reference to Mallarmé is thus pivotal, and as a matter of fact it appears in both texts,[172] followed by the well-known remarks on the way in which French poetry can "get around the difficulty" of the pair *jour/nuit* {day/night} by glossing over the "defect" {*défaut*} through an appropriate phonic context or, conversely, by adapting the signifieds to the resonant color of the signifiers: "chaleur lourde du jour, fraîcheur aérienne de la nuit" {heavy heat of the day, airy freshness of the night}. The poetic relevance of these comments, mentioned here for their Cratylian tenor, will not be reexamined. If we add to these the quotations from Pope ("The sound must seem an echo of the sense") and from Valéry ("The poem [is] a prolonged hesitation between sound and sense"), Jakobson's conversion to poetic mimologism will clearly appear — with the slight difference that the role granted to the mimetic capacities of natural language is probably much greater here than in Mallarmé, and certainly much greater than in Valéry: "Sound symbolism is an undeniably objective relation founded on a phenomenal connection between different sensory modes, in particular between visual and auditory experience."[173]

I have used the term "conversion" in order to emphasize the divergence between the two theses, but this term should not be taken too hastily in a uniformly diachronic sense. Tempting as it is to think so, it would be hard to establish that Jakobson's position on this point changed between 1920 and 1960, and that a more personal interpretation of the poetic phenomenon gradually emerged from attitudes shared by the Formalist group. In actual fact, the connection between perceptibility and mimeticism is already suggested in the 1935 lecture "The Dominant," which attempts to define the hierarchy of the different linguistic functions within the poetic work: "In the referential function, the sign has a minimal internal connection with the designated object, and therefore the sign in itself carries only a minimal importance; on the other hand, the expressive function demands *a more direct, intimate relationship between the sign and the object,* and therefore a greater attention to the internal structure of the sign. In comparison with referential language, emotive language, which primarily fulfills an expressive function, is as a rule closer to poetic language (which is directed precisely toward the sign as such)."[174] Clearly, the position here is qualified through the interposition of "expressive" language between the referential and the poetic, with an increasing importance of the signifier each time. Referential discourse dissociates itself from the signifier; the expressive function makes it more prominent through the expressive link itself; the poetic is deliberately "oriented" toward it. But the connection is even closer, as early as 1919, in "La Nouvelle Poésie russe": "In emotional and poetic languages, the verbal (phonetic and semantic) representations attract more attention to themselves, *the link between the acoustic aspect and the signification* becomes closer."[175] Therefore, it can be said that these two themes coexist in Jakobson's discourse from the beginning.

Maybe this coexistence is less paradoxical than it seems at first glance, at least in theory. Indeed, on one hand the "arbitrary" signifier is perceptible because it is arbitrary and therefore made prominent by its very lack of motivation, its mimetic inadequation, ultimately its incongruity, which is a form of defamiliarization (*ostranenie*). Previously, Lessing had said that the conventional sign provokes "an awareness of the sign that is stronger than that of the thing designated."[176] And didn't Mallarmé, in a highly critical way, see vocables like *jour* and *nuit* as "perverse" in themselves?[177] But, on the other hand, the mimetic sign (or the sign considered as mimetic), theoretically "transparent" through its mimeticism, is in fact unusual and therefore perceptible for this very reason, especially if it produces a contrast and an exception within the context and/or within the system: this is another *ostranenie*, the opposite of the preceding one and perhaps equally effective.[178] As always, then, these theoretical rationalizations are perfectly reversible, and the positions actually determine each other and must be evaluated on an altogether different level, that of biases and deep valorizations. It is at this level (unarticulated, and often unthought) that the Formalist attitude enters into conflict with Cratylian desire—to the great advantage, here, of the latter.

Moreover, in Jakobson, the positive investments of these two factors are not at all comparable: in a way, the "Formalist" position is a *point of honor*, a position of principle, whose practical (technical) application remains weak. In contrast, the mimetic valorization penetrates all the elements of Jakobson's poetics, and especially the most important (by far): the principle of recurrence. As we have seen, this appears already in 1919, as one means among others for underscoring the idea of form, under the category of phonic repetition. The 1966 essay "Grammatical Parallelism and Its Russian Facet" considerably extends its modalities (phonic, grammatical, and of course metrical) and its field of action across Hebrew, Chinese, Ural-Altaic, and Russian folk poetries, with the invocation of those "great advocates of parallelism," Herder and Hopkins.[179] Quite beyond any simple phonic and grammatical recurrences, the issue here is a "generalized parallelism," according to Gerard Manley Hopkins's thesis that the whole art of poetry "boils down to the principle of parallelism"—confirmed by the very etymology of the word *versus* (return): "We must consistently draw all inferences from the obvious fact that on every level of language the essence of poetic artifice consists in the recurrent returns."[180]

This principle of generalized recurrence, obviously inspired by a specific consideration of the most traditional forms (folkloric or not) of poetic creation—whose application to some works of another order might have disconcerted the specialists—is again encountered at the center of "Linguistics and Poetics," where, as we will see, it does a bit more than compete with the "set toward the message" as a distinctive feature of the poetic function: "What is the empirical linguistic criterion of the poetic function?" Expanded and reformulated in terms of structural linguistics, poetic parallelism here becomes the well-known projection of "*the principle of equivalence from the* [paradigmatic] *axis of selection onto the* [syntagmatic] *axis of combination.* Equivalence is promoted to the constitutive device of the sequence."[181]

There is a substitution, indeed even a supplantation, here that perhaps has not been noticed as much as it deserves to be. If we ask ourselves what Jakobson's definition of the poetic function is, two answers come to mind equally: the *autotelism of the message* and the *projection of equivalence*. The first is properly theoretical, springing from the general scheme of the six linguistic functions; the second is presented as a simple "empirical criterion," a sort of rule of thumb, a handy means of "recognizing" a text with the poetic function. But this division neither sufficiently nor satisfactorily defines the relationship between the two criteria. Apparently, repetition is only a technical *means* for producing the autonomy of the form (according to the observation suggested back in 1919); but then we may wonder how it happens that the instrument here is more conspicuous, easier to "recognize" than the result aimed at—at the least, it is an index of low efficiency when the effort eclipses the effect. We can wonder, too— as we did above regarding the nature of the semantic relationship—whether the means designated is to such a degree the only conceivable one that its presence might become *the* decisive empirical criterion. What about the other poetic *devices* formerly pointed out by Jakobson himself (like neologism in Velimir Khlebnikov)? Moreover, what about the opposite device, or the systematic absence of repetition? The (greater) perceptibility of recurrent features, like that of mimetic ones, is an easily reversible principle. We know very well that the complete opposite has been maintained with as much probability: to wit, that difference alone is perceptible and that monotony engenders anesthesia. Once more, then, a spontaneous preference covers itself up (poorly) with a retroactive rationalization but gives itself away in the rush of reaction, since hardly is the theoretical criterion posited when it is definitively wiped out in the face of the empirical criterion which is supposed to embody or illustrate it and which it in fact serves to introduce.[182] Moreover, we are really dealing with the same valorization—in the present case, here (repetition) and there (mimeticism), a valorization of *sameness*.

Indeed, the crucial term *equivalence* is remarkably ambiguous, in French as in English, something we previously appreciated in Valéry. In structural terms it designates here, very broadly, the relation maintained by all the terms capable of occupying the same slot in the chain. In this sense, a defective utterance such as "The child —— in its cradle" can be completed by a thousand "equivalent" verbs, among which are "goes to sleep" or "wakes up": "The selection is produced on the basis of equivalence, similarity and *dissimilarity,* synonymity and *antonymity.*"[183] But for ordinary consciousness, equivalence equals similarity, and in fact, when he needs an example to illustrate the notion of selection, Jakobson spontaneously resorts to "semantically cognate verbs—sleeps, dozes, nods, naps," the selection being exercised from that point on only among stylistic variants of the same term. This shift from paradigmatic equivalence to semantic equivalence is clearly already at work in the 1956 essay "Two Aspects of Language and Two Types of Aphasic Disturbance," where the function of selection is interpreted in terms of similarity and related to the "metaphoric pole" of language, with metaphor established as the cardinal figure of poetic diction. "Generalized parallelism," therefore, becomes generalized equivalence (in the strong sense), on all planes and in all dimensions: "the principle of *similarity* underlies poetry," apparently without brooking any opposition.[184] Formal recurrences, described in principle as semantically neutral or, rather, ambivalent ("the metrical parallelism of the verse lines or the phonic equivalence of rhyming words prompts the question of semantic similarity *and contrast*"; "in poetry, any conspicuous similarity in sound is evaluated with respect to similarity *and/or dissimilarity* in sense"),[185] are eventually interpreted in the sense of a reciprocal and generalized symbolization: "The projection of the *equational principle* onto the sequence has a much deeper and wider significance. Valéry's view of poetry as a [prolonged] hesitation between the sound and the sense ... is much more realistic and scientific than any bias of phonetic isolationism. ... *Similarity* superimposed on contiguity imparts to poetry its thoroughgoing symbolic ... nature. ... Anything sequent is a simile. In poetry, where similarity is superinduced upon contiguity, any metonymy is slightly metaphorical and any metaphor has a metonymical tint."[186]

This offers an altogether remarkable condensation of Jakobson's poetics: textual recurrence (formal similarities spread out over the space of the text) induces a sort of parallel recurrence at the level of the signified, which is metonymized metaphor, or similarities of meaning spread out over the space of the content. Ultimately, therefore, a veritable symbolical volume with three dimensions is established within the poem. In actual fact, it constitutes the poem as a horizontal network of signifying equivalences (phonic, metrical, grammatical, intonational, prosodic) that refers to another horizontal network of equivalences signified by means of a series of (vertical) semantic equivalences between each form and each meaning (images), and between each group of forms and each group of meanings (diagrams) — a hyperbolic and flawless state of the Baudelairean "forest of symbols." At this point, the punctilious distinctions of the old rhetoric lose their relevance: the figural link (metaphorico-metonymical) plays vertically as well as horizontally among signifieds, among signifiers, between signifieds and signifiers. Thus, it can be concluded that "the relevance of the sound-meaning nexus is a simple corollary of the superposition of similarity upon contiguity"[187] — and perhaps vice versa: the principle of repetition becomes in its turn a corollary of the mimetic principle, and the poem becomes an infinite play of mirrors.

⊘ "Well now," said Maurice Barrès, "scratch the ironist and you find the elegist."[188] Perhaps modern poetic theory might be quite aptly depicted by risking the following parody: *scratch the Formalist and you find the Symbolist* (that is to say, the Realist), and, pushing it a little further, *scratch Hermogenes and you* (re)discover *Cratylus*. There is even something of this in Saussure: scratch the author of the *Course in General Linguistics* and you find the dreamer of anagrams; and what nicer application of the "principle of equivalence" could there be than the paragrammatic dissemination of the theme word within the poetic message? We know how Jakobson, among others, welcomed these hypotheses, and how he applied them to the last "Spleen" and to "The Abyss" by Baudelaire.[189] Modern poetic consciousness is very largely "governed" by the principles of equivalence and motivation, and the majority of today's theoreticians and critics could be cited in this respect, without excepting, here and there, the humble author of this book. Beyond all the episodic antagonisms and across many displacements of emphasis and balance, we encounter, all over the place, the following triple valorization of the analogical relation: between signifiers (homophonies, paronomasias, and so on), between signifieds (metaphors), between signifier and signified (mimetic motivation). To a great extent such a convergence is probably an index of "truth," but it is also, and maybe above all, a sign of the times and a period theme. It is inevitably accompanied by a choice, conscious or not, within the poetic corpus, which a statistical study of the quotations and the objects of analysis would eloquently demonstrate. Our "poetic language" is the language *of a certain poetry,*[190] and—to keep to just one counterexample—it is easy to imagine what Malherbe, so hostile to all "repetition," so bent upon opening up to the utmost the sonorous and rhythmical range of the verse line and the stanza, would have thought of our generalized similarity. Aside from a few contrastive and coded effects of alliteration and imitative harmony, French poetry of the neoclassical age was governed instead by a principle of dissimilation, or maximal differentiation.[191] A poetics founded through and through on the "demon of analogy" is a typically Romantic and Symbolist idea. It is modern *in this sense,* which is to say that it is neither eternal (and universally valid) nor *very modern,* and maybe it already betrays a certain backwardness (ever the bird of Minerva) in relation to poetic practice—but that's another story. As aesthetic resurgence and last (?) refuge of mimologism, this idea of poetic language as compensation for and challenge to the arbitrariness of the sign has become one of the fundamental articles of faith in our literary "theory." In fact, the *very idea of poetic language* (in general and whatever the specifics) is dominated by this metaphor gone astray which always arises from the dichotomy between poetry and "ordinary language," and which mythically transposes to the linguistic plane (the relation between signifier and signified) characteristics of discursive organization which in fact belong to an entirely different level: figural, stylistic, prosodic, and so on. Surreptitiously, the phenomenon of discourse thus becomes a phenomenon of natural language, and the "art of language" a "language within language."[192] Today, this idea has become so familiar to us, so natural, so transparent, that we have some difficulty imagining that it is one theory among others, that it did not always exist, that it will not exist forever. This doctrine does not go without saying, however, for it is clearly a phenomenon of history; it already belongs to History or, when all is said and done, to the past. The very act of beginning to perceive it and making it (in its turn) into an object of discourse is perhaps the sign of this, if it be true that "the mere perceptibility of the present is already the future."[193]

CHAPTER 13

The Age of Names

℘ In *Remembrance of Things Past* as in the *Cratylus*, the preferred object of mimologically motivated reverie is what Marcel Proust calls the Name {*le Nom*}: that is, the proper noun {*le nom propre*}.[1] The difference between the Name and the Word {*le Mot*} or common noun is established in a famous passage from the third part of *Swann's Way*, in which Proust describes his hero's reveries on the names of several countries where he hopes to spend the upcoming Easter vacation:

> Words present to us little pictures of things, lucid and normal, like the pictures that are hung on the walls of schoolrooms to give children an illustration of what is meant by a carpenter's bench, a bird, an anthill; things chosen as typical of everything else of the same sort. But names— of persons and of towns which they accustom us to regard as individual, as unique, like persons—present to us a confused picture, which draws from the names, from the brightness or darkness of their sound, the color in which it is uniformly painted.[2]

Evidently, the traditional (and questionable) opposition between the individuality of the proper noun and the generality of the common noun is here accompanied by another difference, an apparently secondary one that actually sums up Proust's entire semantic theory of the name: the "image" of the thing presented by the common noun is "clear and ordinary," and being neutral, transparent, inactive, it has no effect whatsoever on the mental representation, the concept of bird, carpenter's bench, or anthill. In contrast, the image presented by the proper noun is *confused* because it borrows its unique color from the substantial reality (the "sound") of this name; the image is confused, therefore, in the sense of being *indistinct* in its unity, or rather its uniqueness, of tone; but the image is also *confused* in the sense of being *complex* as an amalgam of elements coming from the signifier and those coming from the signified. In point of fact, the extralinguistic representation of a person or a town, as we shall see, always coexists with suggestions emanating from its name, and often exists prior to them.

Let us keep in mind, then, that Proust reserves for proper nouns that active relationship between signifier and signified which other authors apply to common nouns as well.[3] Such a restriction might appear surprising on the part of a writer so obviously familiar with metaphorical relationships. The reason for this restriction lies in the highly marked predominance of a spatial or, even better, geographical sensibility in his work, for the proper nouns around which the Narrator's reverie crystallizes are in fact almost always (and not only in the chapter so entitled) names of places—or names of noble families that derive their essential imaginative value from the fact that they are "always place names."[4] The uniqueness, the individuality of places is an article of faith with the young Marcel, as it is with the narrator of *Jean Santeuil*, and despite the eventual counterevidence of experience, he holds on to at least a trace of this faith in his dreams, since he is still able to write with regard to the landscape of Guermantes: "Sometimes, at night, in my dreams, [its] individuality binds me with a power that is almost fantastic."[5] The supposed singularity of the proper noun corresponds to the mythical singularity of the place, reinforcing it: "[Names] magnified the idea that I formed of certain points on the earth's surface, making them more special, and in consequence more real.... How much more individual still was the character that they assumed from being designated by names, names that were only for themselves, proper names such as people have."[6] However, one should not allow oneself to succumb to this linguistic laziness, which seems here to make "person" into the very model of individuality ("towns ... as individual, as unique, as people"): the individuality of places, albeit a mythical one, is actually much more marked in Proust than that of living creatures.[7] From their first appearances on the scene, Saint-Loup, Charlus, Odette, Albertine manifest an elusive multiplicity and the network of confused kinships and resemblances tying them to many other people who are no closer to being "unique" than they are themselves. Moreover, as will emerge further on, their names are not really fixed and do not belong to them in a properly substantial way: Odette changes hers several times; Saint-Loup and Charlus have more than one; even the first names of Albertine and Gilberte are set up so as to become confused some day, and so on. In appearance at least, places exist much more as "persons"[8] than people themselves do; moreover, they *hold on* to their names much better.

We should now specify the nature of that "active relationship" between the name and the thing in which lies the essence of Proust's nominal imagination. If we were to refer to the theoretical statement quoted above, we would be inclined to see a unilateral relation in which the "image" of the place drew its entire content from the "sound" of the name. As a matter of fact, the relation, as it can be inferred from the several examples that appear in *Remembrance*, is more complicated and more dialectical. But first we need to introduce a distinction between the names Proust invents for fictional places, such as *Balbec*, and (real) names for real places, such as *Florence* or *Quimperlé*—with the understanding that this distinction is relevant solely to the author's (real) work and not to the fictitious reveries of his hero, for whom Florence and Balbec are situated on the same plane of "reality."[9] According to a comment made by Roland Barthes, the role of the "narrator" (let us say, for the sake of clarity, the hero) is that of decoding here, while that of the novelist is one of encoding: "The narrator and the novelist cover the same trajectory in contrary directions: the narrator believes he can decipher, in the names given to him, a kind of natural affinity between signifier and signified, between the vocalic color of *Parme* {Parma} and the mauve sweetness of its content; the novelist, having to invent a site at once Norman, Gothic, and windy, must search the general tablature for phonemes, a few sounds tuned to the combination of these signifieds."[10] But it is somewhat misrepresenting the situation to align the hero with a real name (*Parme*) and the author with a fictional name (*Balbec*). Actually, the encoding, on Proust's part, occurs exclusively for coined names: that is, for a very small proportion of the place names (in the passage under discussion, Balbec is the only one). As for real names, the positions of hero and novelist are no longer symmetrically inverse but parallel, with Proust attributing to Marcel a decoding or a motivating interpretation of the nominal form that he himself, of course, has "invented" and, therefore (the two activities being equivalent in this case), carried out. Their positions may be parallel but they are not identical, for on at least one point the hero's experience does not coincide with the writer's: when he thinks of Venice or of Benodet, the young Marcel has not yet even been to either of these places, but when he writes this passage, Proust, in contrast, is already familiar with them; and we will see that he does not completely disregard his own memories—of his real experience—when he ascribes to his hero reveries that purport to be fed by two sources alone: the names of these places and a few bits of knowledge taken from books or acquired by hearsay.

Indeed, a fairly close reading shows that none of these images is determined by the form of the noun alone, that on the contrary each of them results from an interaction between this form and some idea, whether true or false, which is in any case independent of the name and comes from somewhere else. When Marcel says that the name of *Parme* seems "compact and glossy, mauve, soft" to him, it is quite obvious that at least the detail of the color has more to do with the violets in the town than with the sound of its name, and this conspicuous link is confirmed a few lines later: "I could imagine it [the house in Parma where he dreams of staying for a few days] only by the aid of that heavy syllable of the name of Parma, in which no breath of air stirred, and of all that I had made it *absorb* of Stendhalian sweetness and the reflected hue of violets."[11] The semantic analysis here is furnished by Proust himself, who evidently assigns the qualities of compactness and also of glossiness to the proper noun's influence, the color mauve to hearsay knowledge about the violets, and the sweetness to his memory of Stendhal's *Chartreuse de Parme*. The signifier definitely acts upon the signified, causing Marcel to imagine a town where everything is glossy and compact, but the signified acts equally forcefully upon the signifier, causing him to perceive the "name" of this town as mauve and sweet.[12] Likewise, *Florence* owes its image, "miraculously embalmed, and flowerlike," as much to the red lily in its emblem and to its cathedral, *Sainte-Marie-des-Fleurs,* as to the floral allusion in its first syllable, with content and expression here being in a relation no longer of complementarity and exchange but of redundancy, since the name turns out to be positively (although indirectly, through its formation) motivated in this case.[13] Balbec derives its archaic image ("old piece of Norman pottery," "long abolished custom," "feudal right," "former condition of some place," "obsolete way of pronouncing the language") from the "incongruous syllables" of its name, but it is clear that the fundamental theme of "waves surging round a church built in the Persian manner" contaminates, without any reference to the name, two descriptions offered by Swann and by Legrandin.[14] Here, the verbal suggestion and the extralinguistic notion have not completely succeeded in merging, for if the Norman essence of the countryside and even the pseudo-Persian style of its church are both "reflected" in the sonorities of *Balbec,*[15] it is more difficult to find in this name an echo of the storms forecast by Legrandin.[16]

Subsequent references realize more effectively, as in the case of *Parme,* the mutual contagion of the name by the idea and the idea by the name: thus, the highest point of the cathedral of *Bayeux,* "so lofty in its noble coronet of rusty lace," catches the light with "the old gold of its last syllable"; the old-fashioned windows {*vitrage*} of the houses in Vitré justify ("etymologically") the name, whose acute accent, in turn, suggests through its diagonal movement— "a lozenge of dark wood"—the old-fashioned facades (note the operation of the name's graphic form rather than its sound here); the nearly uniform whiteness of *doux Lamballe* {gentle Lamballe} yields nuances moving from the "eggshell yellow" of its first syllable to the "pearly gray" of its second one; the same "diphthong" *an* that appears "fatty and yellowish" in *Coutances* softens the "tower of butter" of its Norman cathedral.[17] But *Tour de beurre* is, in fact, as everyone knows (and for reasons having to do with neither its shape nor its color), the name of the right-hand tower of Rouen; and the mineral rigidity of *Coutances* ill fits this description, which would seem wholly inspired by the sound of the name (with the possible addition of a homophony between *Coutances* and *rance* {rancid}). We will run across this reduplicative association of *an = jaune* {yellow} again; let us observe for the moment that it has a rival in the "old gold" of *yeu* in *Bayeux.* The little picture *Lannion,* which surely lays no claim to the specificity of Tréguier, misappropriates the fable of the coach and the fly as an illustration of the essence of provinciality and rusticity: the "noise of the coach (*Lan-*) followed by the fly (*-nion*)."[18] *Questambert* and *Pontorson* are no doubt connected, as Jean-Pierre Richard remarks,[19] through the identity of their "prosodic mould" but also through the analogy of their consonantal structure, in which the "funny" contortion of *rs* echoes that of *st* (which inevitably suggests another shared patron: *Marcelproust*). The "white feathers and yellow-spotted beaks" probably resonate both with this oral dance and (as in *Lamballe* and *Coutances*) with hearing the nasal consonants as colors — whence that sketch of the duck pond confirmed by the "fluviality" of *Pontorson,* with which the earthling *Questambert* is willy-nilly associated. In *Benodet,* the phonic lightness — or lability — attributed to the name, which is "scarcely moored and which the river seems to be striving to draw down into the tangle of its seaweeds," owes more to geographical fact, as does *Pont-Aven,* "the snowy, rosy flight of the wing of a lightly poised coif, tremulously reflected in the greenish waters of a canal." [20] Finally, the limpid streams that previously spellbound the Flaubert of *Par les champs et par les grèves* correspond to the transparent pearlescence {*perlé*} that ends the name *Quimperlé* in an etymological fantasy.

The same interaction animates other reveries about names scattered throughout the early volumes of *Remembrance,* such as the one sustained by that especially magical name *Guermantes,* evocative of "a dungeon keep without mass, no more indeed than a band of orange light." [21] The dungeon obviously belongs to the fortified castle that is supposedly the cradle of this feudal family, and the orange light "emanates" from the last syllable of the name.[22] This emanation, moreover, is less direct than it would appear at first sight, for the same name of Guermantes elsewhere [23] takes on an amaranthine color hardly compatible with orange, whose resonance derives from the golden blond hair of the Guermantes family. Contradictory from the perspective of "hearing in color," these two descriptions come, therefore, not only from the spontaneous synaesthesia [24] equating *an* and yellow, as in *Coutances* and *Lamballe* above, but also from a *lexical association:* that is, from the shared presence of the sound *an* in the name *Guermantes* and in the names for the colors *orange* and *amarante* {amaranthine} — just as the acidity of the name *Gilberte,* "pungent and cool as the drops which fell from the green watering-pipe," [25] probably derives less from the direct action of its sounds than from the assonance *Gilberte-verte* {-green}. The paths of motivation are often more devious than expected, and we have had occasion to see how often a clandestine (pseudo)etymology acts to supplement the weak link of phonic expressiveness.[26]

One last example: if the name *Faffenheim* conjures up, through its straightforward attack and "the stammering repetition" that punctuates the first two syllables, "the impulse, the mannered simplicity, the heady delicacies of the Teutonic race," and through the "dark blue enamel" of the last syllable, "the mystic light of a Rhenish window behind the pale and finely wrought gildings of the German eighteenth century," it is not only because of its sounds but also because *Faffenheim* was the name of a Prince Elector.[27] Frankness and repetition are clearly inscribed in *Faffen,* but their specifically Germanic nuance comes from the signified and, even more particularly, from the memory, called up by the first version of the same passage in *By Way of Sainte-Beuve,* of the "colored sweets eaten in a small grocery shop on the old German square."²⁸ Hearing the sounds of the final *-heim* in color may evoke the transparency of a dark blue stained-glass church window, but the Rhenishness of this window and the rococo gilding that frames it do not spring full-fledged from what the earlier version called the "variegated sound of the last syllable." Such anticipated and authorially controlled interpretations are organized like program music or like those "expressive" leitmotifs about which Proust remarks that they "paint in splendid colors the glow of fire, the rush of water, the peace of fields and woods, to audiences who, having first let their eyes run over the program, have their imagination trained in the right direction."²⁹ Should this connivance of the signified be found wanting, then the vocable no longer "expresses" anything, or else expresses something entirely different. On the little train that takes him from Balbec-en-Terre to Balbec-Plage, Marcel discovers a strangeness in the names of towns such as Incarville, Arcouville, Arambouville, Maineville, "dreary names, made up of sand, of space too airy and empty and of salt, out of which the termination *ville* always escaped, as the *vole* seems to fly out from the end of the word *Pigeon-vole*"—in short, names whose connotations seem typically marine, without his realizing their resemblance to other names, however familiar, such as Roussainville or Martinville, whose "somber charm" derives on the contrary from the taste of preserves or from the smell of fire associated with the childhood world at Combray.³⁰ The forms are quite similar, but the unbridgeable gap between the contents invested in them prevents him from even noticing their analogy: thus, "to the trained ear two musical airs, each consisting of so many notes, several of which are common to them both, will present no similarity whatever if they differ in the color of their harmony and orchestration."³¹

Marcel's poetic reveries display, therefore, that same tendency to motivate language that also inspires the solecisms of Françoise or of the elevator boy at Balbec; but instead of acting on the material of an unfamiliar word in order to reduce it to a form that is "familiar and meaningful," and thereby justified, this motivation operates, more subtly, both on the form of that word (the way its "substance," phonic or otherwise, is perceived, concretized, and interpreted) and on the form of its meaning (the "image" of the place) in order to make them compatible, harmonious, mutually suggestive. The illusory nature of this agreement between "sound" and "sense" has been discussed above, and we will see further on how the awareness and critique of this illusion is expressed in *Remembrance.* But there is another mirage, involving the meaning itself: Roland Barthes rightly emphasizes the imaginary character of semic complexes suggested by a reverie on names and how erroneous it would be, here as elsewhere, to confuse the signified with the *referent:* that is to say, the actual object.[32] Yet this error is exactly the one Marcel makes, and its correction is one of the central aspects of the painful learning experience that constitutes the plot of the novel. A reverie about names, says Proust, results in making the image of these places more beautiful "but also more different from anything that the towns of Normandy or Tuscany could in reality be, and, by increasing the arbitrary delights of my imagination, this aggravated the disenchantment that was in store for me when I set out upon my travels."[33] The reader will recall, for example, what bitter disillusion Marcel feels upon discovering that the composite image of Balbec that he has made for himself (the Persian-style church beaten by the waves) bears only a distant resemblance to the real Balbec, whose church and beach are miles and miles away from each other.[34] Marcel feels the same disappointment a little later, upon seeing the Duke and Duchess of Guermantes "withdrawn from that name Guermantes in which long ago I had imagined them leading an unimaginable life"; or in the presence of the Princess of Parma, a small, dark (not mauve) woman who is more concerned about pious deeds than Stendhalian sweetness; or in the presence of the Prince of Agrigente, whose name seems "a transparent sheet of colored glass through which I beheld, struck, on the shore of the violet sea, by the slanting rays of a golden sun, the rosy marble cubes of an ancient city," and who himself seems "as independent of his name as of any work of art that he might have owned without bearing upon his person any trace of its beauty, without, perhaps, ever having stopped to examine it"; and even in the presence of the Prince of Faffenheim-Munsterburg-Weinigen, Rheingraf and Elector Palatine, who uses the revenues and sullies the reputation of his Wagnerian fief in order to maintain "five Charron motorcars, a house in Paris and one in London, a box on Mondays at the *Opéra* and another for the 'Tuesdays' at the *Français,*" and whose pathetic ambition is to be elected a Corresponding Member of the Academy of Moral and Political Sciences.[35]

Thus, when Proust states that names, "whimsical draughtsmen,"[36] are responsible for the illusion that encircles his hero, we should not take "name" {*nom*} to mean the vocable alone but rather the sign in its totality, the unity constituted, according to Louis Hjelmslev's definition, by the relation of *interdependence* posited between the form of the content and the form of expression.[37] In *Parme,* it is not the sequence of sounds or of letters that creates the poetic myth of a compact, mauve, and sweet town; it is the "solidarity" gradually established between a compact signifier and a mauve, sweet signified. The "name," therefore, is not the cause of the illusion but more precisely the *locus:* it is in the name that the illusion becomes concentrated and crystallized. The apparent indissolubility of sound and sense, the motivation of the sign, encourages the childish belief in the unity and the individuality of the imaginary place designated. As we have seen, Marcel's arrival in Balbec dispels the first belief. There are two Balbecs;

the car rides with Albertine, in *Cities of the Plain,* will dispense with the second one. In fact, unlike the voyage by train — during which essences are materialized by each station's "signboard" bearing the individual and distinct name of a new place and which entails in Proust an abrupt change (an abruptness brought on by the traveler's having slept between the two stations) from one essential state to another[38] — the voyage by car is an uninterrupted progression that reveals the continuity of the countryside, the interconnectedness of places, and this discovery annihilates the myth of their separation and of their respective singularities,[39] just as Gilberte, at the beginning of *Time Regained,* will abolish the crucial opposition between the "two ways" simply by saying to Marcel: "If you like, we might go out one afternoon and then we can go to Guermantes, taking the road by Méséglise, it is the nicest walk."[40]

Once shattered by contact with geographical reality, the prestige of names undergoes another attack when the narrator, listening to the Duc de Guermantes's self-satisfied genealogical explanations, discovers the seamless network of alliances and inheritances that link so many noble names — place names — which, until then, he had thought to be quite completely irreconcilable, as radically dissociated by "one of those distances in the mind that not only distance, but separate and locate on another plane" as those of Guermantes and Méséglise, Balbec, and Combray. The reader will remember Marcel's surprise, despite Saint-Loup's earlier explanations, upon learning at Madame de Villeparisis's house that Monsieur de Charlus was the brother of the Duc de Guermantes. When the duke reveals to Marcel, for example, that a Norpois married a Mortemart under Louis XIV, that "Monsieur de Bréauté's mother had been a Choiseul and his grandmother a Lucinge," and that "Monsieur d'Ornessan's great-grandmother had been the sister of Marie de Castille Montjeu, the wife of Timoleon de Castille, and consequently Oriane's aunt" — all these names "springing to take their places by the side of others from which I should have supposed them to be remote ... each name displaced by the attraction of another, with which I had never suspected it of having any affinity"[41] — distances are canceled out and barriers broken down; essences thought of as incompatible merge into one another and in so doing vanish. The life of names is revealed to be a series of transmissions and usurpations that removes any remaining basis from onomastic reverie. The name of Guermantes will eventually fall into the possession of the utterly common *Patronne,* formerly Verdurin (via Duras); Odette is successively Crécy, Swann, Forcheville; Gilberte is Swann, Forcheville, and Saint-Loup; the death of a relative makes the Prince de Laumes a Duc de Guermantes, and the Baron de Charlus is "also Duc de Brabant, Damoiseau de Montargis, Prince d'Oléron, de Carency, de Viareggio, and de Dunes";[42] in a more roundabout but no less significant manner, Legrandin will become the Count of Méséglise. A name is really a paltry thing.

Yet Marcel was still able to feel a sort of poetic vertigo when witnessing the onomastic ballet of *The Guermantes Way*.[43] The same cannot be said for one final experience, a purely linguistic one this time, which reveals to him, with no aesthetic compensation, the emptiness of his reveries on place names: this involves the etymologies of Brichot in the last part of *Cities of the Plain*.[44] Critics have often speculated on the function of these etymologies in the novel, and Jean Vendryès, who sees in these tirades a satire on the pedantry of the Sorbonne, adds that they also evince a sort of fascination. There is no doubt about this ambivalence, but the "etymological passion" probably does not have the sense Vendryès gives it when he asserts that "Proust believed in etymology as a rational means of penetrating the hidden meaning of names and consequently of acquiring knowledge about the essence of things. This notion," he continues, "goes back to Plato, but no scholar would defend it today."[45] Vendryès does not hesitate to connect the etymologies of Brichot to those of Socrates and to put them at the service of the "Cratylian consciousness,"[46] for which in fact, as we have seen, the *essence of things* lies in the *hidden meaning* of their names. Now if these etymologies are considered a bit more closely, along with their effect on the hero's mind, it is easy to see that they have exactly the opposite function. Whatever their actual scientific value, it is obvious that they are proffered and understood as so many corrections of errors of common sense (or of the amateur linguist embodied in the priest of Combray), of "popular" or naive etymologies, of spontaneous interpretations of the imaginary.

Against all this, and therefore against the instinctive Cratylism of the young hero, who is convinced that an immediate relationship exists between the *present* form of the name and the timeless essence of the thing, Brichot, symbol of the new linguistics, reinstates the deceptive truth of historical filiation, phonetic erosion — in short, the diachronic dimension of language. Not every etymology is necessarily inspired by *realism:* those of Socrates are because they aim at establishing through arbitrary analyses an appropriateness of sound and sense that is not sufficiently obvious from the total form of the name or noun. By contrast, Brichot's are almost systematically antirealist. If, as an exception, *Chantepie* is really the forest where the *pie* {magpie} sings {*chante*}, the queen {*reine*} who sings at *Chantereine* is a vulgar frog ({Latin} *rana*), with all due respect to Monsieur de Cambremer; Loctudy is not the "barbarous name" that the priest of Combray sees in it but the properly Latin name *Locus Tudeni; Fervaches,* whatever the Princess Sherbatoff believes, is Warm-water ({Latin} *fervidae aquae;* {French *Eaux-chaudes*}); *Pont-à-Couleuvre* shelters no grass snake {*couleuvre*} but really means Tollbridge (*Pont à qui l'ouvre*); Charlus may have his oak tree {*chêne*} at *Saint-Martin du Chêne,* but no yews {*ifs*} at *Saint-Pierre-des-Ifs* (from {Latin} *aqua*); in *Torpehomme, homme* {man} "does not in the least mean what you are naturally led to suppose, Baron," but is *holm,* which means a "small island." Finally, *Balbec* itself has nothing Gothic or stormy or above all Persian about it: this name is a corruption of Dalbec, from *dal*, "valley" and *bec*, "stream"; and even *Balbec-en-Terre* does not signify "Balbec-on-Land," through an allusion to a few leagues that separate it from the coast and its storms, but "Balbec-of-the-Continent," in opposition to the barony of Dover of which it was once a dependency: *Balbec d'outre-Manche*.[47] "Anyhow, when you go back to Balbec, you will know what Balbec means," Monsieur Verdurin says ironically; but his irony does not reach its direct target alone (the pedant Brichot), for it is quite true that Marcel, too, has long believed that he knows what Balbec "signifies," and if Brichot's revelations captivate him, it is because they finally destroy his old beliefs and introduce him to the salubrious disenchantment of the truth.[48] In this way, he will come to see the charm vanish from the *fleur* {flower} that he must no longer seek in *Honfleur* (which instead comes from *fiord*, "port"), and the humor from the *boeuf* {cattle} that he must no longer seek in *Bricqueboeuf* (instead from *budh*, "hut"). Thus, he will come to discover that names are no more individual than the places they designate, and that just as the latter display a continuity (or contiguity) on the "ground," so the former exhibit a kinship through their paradigmatic organization in the system of natural language:

> What had appeared to me a particular instance became general, Bricqueboeuf took its place by the side of Elbeuf, and indeed in a name that was at first sight as individual as the place itself, like the name Pennedepie, in which the obscurities most impossible for the mind to elucidate seemed to me to have been amalgamated from time immemorial in a word as coarse, savory and hard as a certain Norman cheese, I was disappointed to find the Gallic *pen* which means mountain and is as recognizable in Pennemarck as in the Appennines.[49]

Like experience of the "visible world," linguistic apprenticeship depoeticizes and demystifies: the names of countries are "half-stripped of mystery which etymology [replaces] with reasoning."[50] As a matter of fact, after this lesson, nominal reveries disappear for good from the text of *Remembrance*: Brichot has made them literally *impossible*. His etymologies, therefore, do have an "emblematic function," as Barthes says, but not one pointing to the "Cratylian character of the name"; quite to the contrary, Brichot's etymologies constitute a refutation of this nature through the "specifications of linguistic science."[51]

So we should not, without reservation, attribute to Proust himself the *optimism of the signifier*[52] evinced by his youthful hero; belief in the truth of names is for him an ambiguous privilege of childhood, one of those "illusions to be destroyed" which the hero must shed one after another in order to attain the state of absolute disenchantment that precedes and prepares for the final revelation.

We know from a letter to Louis Robert that Proust once thought of calling the three parts of the *Remembrance*, as planned in 1913, *L'Age des noms, L'Age des mots, L'Age des choses* {The age of names, The age of words, The age of things}.[53] Whatever interpretation is given to the last two, the first formula unequivocally designates the fetishism of names as a transitory stage, or rather as a point of departure.[54] The age of names is what *Swann's Way* more cruelly dubs "the age in which one believes that one creates a thing by giving it a name."[55] This remark occurs in the context of Bloch's request that Marcel call him *cher maître* {dear master}, and "to create" should be taken here in its most naively realist sense: the illusion of realism is believing that what one names exists *exactly as one names it.*

A sort of anticipatory mockery of this deceitful "magic" of proper names might be found in *Swann in Love*, in the somewhat tasteless jokes exchanged between Charles and Oriane at the Sainte-Euverte party with regard to the name *Cambremer*, puns {*calembours*} and parodies of Socratic etymology about which one might wish to consult the illustrious Brichot:

> "These Cambremers have rather a startling name. It ends just in time, but it ends badly!" she said with a laugh.
> "It begins no better." Swann took the point.
> "Yes; that double abbreviation!"
> "Someone very angry and very proper who didn't dare to finish the first word."
> "But since he could stop himself beginning the second, he'd have done better to have finished the first and be done with it."[56]

Such are the unseemly consequences of carelessly opening (or breaking) what *By Way of Sainte-Beuve* calls the "urn of the unthought."[57]

🖐 The *Remembrance*, therefore, offers simultaneously a very faithful account of mimological reverie and a critique — sometimes explicit, sometimes implicit, but always severe — of this form of imagination. It is doubly exposed as a realist illusion: first, as the belief in an identity between the signified (the "image") and the referent (the place), or the *referential illusion*, according to current terminology; and second, as the belief in a natural relation between the signified and the signifier, or what could properly be termed the *semantic illusion*. This critique, although it happens to mesh with or to anticipate certain themes of linguistic thought, is nonetheless closely linked in Proust to the development and to the perspective of a personal experience, which is the hero-narrator's apprenticeship to (Proust's version of) truth. As a realization that involves, among other things, the value and the function of the language system, this critical lesson clearly rejoins that of the *Cratylus:* to wit, we should begin not with names, in order to know things, but with the things themselves.[58] Proust's journey faithfully repeats that of Socrates, from the initial mimologism to its final repudiation. And like Socrates, Marcel plays both roles successively.[59] The Cratylist hero becomes (and this becoming is one of the lessons of this novel of apprenticeship) the Hermogenist narrator, who necessarily has the last word, since he "holds the pen." From the critique of language emerges the triumph of Writing {*Écriture*}.

CHAPTER 14

The Stakes of Writing

⟨᱿⟩ Like so many other writers since Mallarmé, Paul Claudel is perfectly aware of the contradiction that brings mimological desire into conflict with the actual functioning of language. The most confident, or the most naive, expression of mimological desire in Claudel is found in a note to his *Poetic Art* which dates from 1904 and revives the classical tradition from the *Cratylus* to *Les Mots anglais*: "Every word is the expression of a psychological state, caused by attention to an external object. It is a gesture that can be separated into its component elements or letters. The letter or, more precisely, the *consonant* is an acoustic attitude sparked off by the generative idea it mimics, the emotion, the word. As S, for instance, indicates the idea of scission, so N, produced by the occlusion of the voice, with the tip of the tongue rising to the palate, suggests the idea of an inner level reached, a willful deafness, a refusal in virtual plenitude. *In, non, hominem, nomen, numen, omnis, nemo, semen, unus, numerus, nos* {Latin}, *nous* {Greek}, and the immense group *noscere, nasci*, about which I spoke above; the form of present participles.... 'Cratylus is right to claim that there exist natural names for things,'" and so on.[1] At the other end of Claudel's career, a passage from 1952 contrasts this spontaneous certainty with the denial of "science," itself immediately rejected by inmost belief: "All language is fiction. Between any object, fact, feeling, or action and its spoken or written representation, there appear to be no relationships (although personally, with Plato, I am convinced of the contrary)."[2] This line of thinking, which without discussion juxtaposes knowledge and belief, is typical, and we will encounter it again.

In his lecture "L'Harmonie imitative" {Imitative harmony}, Claudel faces head on what he calls "one of the fundamental problems of poetry and of language, on which every literary craftsman has been drawn to meditate; I mean the relationships of sound and sense, the letter and the spirit, the idea and its spoken and written representation such as it is delineated by our speech apparatus or by a conventional word which I trace out on paper."[3] In this connection, he mentions (as we already know) the "formidable dossier," begun by Plato and continuing through the Arab mystics, the Jaffir alphabet, the Cabala and Hindu esoterism, and the *Jardin des racines grecques* {The garden of Greek roots} to end in Mallarmé's *Les Mots anglais*—a tradition within which circulates, under

261

various inflections, the magical faith "that one summons a thing by naming it." Here again (or already), the linguist's negative opinion enters in to combat the poet's "fantasy": "I can guess at, understand, and, to a certain extent, approve of all the protests that a principle of this kind, thus brazenly declared and applied, would provoke in the ranks of all rigorously scientific students of language and of the objective laws under which they have tried to arrange, as they would say, its morphology [a typical reference to comparative grammar]. We must recognize that in the proposals occasionally hazarded by someone like Mallarmé, they see only fantasy and arbitrariness. For them, words are the result of a long, careful working-out to which chance, convenience, certain inflections, certain vocal habits, certain attitudes of the race, and, above all, certain historical developments have contributed, so that this old suit has only a wholly conventional relationship to the feelings of the newcomer who is obliged to put it on." But once more, the refutation that he can in principle "understand and, to a certain extent, approve" remains ineffectual before the practical needs of the poet and the language user: "The poet, the artist of words, or quite simply the popular customer of this vast store of terms, which have come from all corners of the world and from the history that is our French language, refrains from replying at all to these solid arguments, to the objurgations of grammarians and philologists — and for good reason. But he behaves exactly as if the opposite principle, that is to say, the adaptation of sound to sense, were an absolute and indisputable truth, because without this it would be impossible to speak, just as it would be impossible to walk without some belief in the truth of space."[4]

Two solutions to this contradiction present themselves at the same time. The first, which is already familiar to us, is poetic language as secondary mimologism, an artificial and/or illusory compensation for the arbitrariness of the sign. According to a metaphor already found in Mallarmé and Valéry, the semantic scheme of "ordinary" language is defined in terms of a fiduciary relation with a purely instrumental function: "In daily life we employ words not strictly as they *signify* objects, but as they *designate* them and, pragmatically, as they enable us to lay hold of objets and make use of them. Words afford us a kind of portable and approximative simplification, a well-worn commonplace value, like money." While Sartre opposes poetic *meaning* to prosaic *signification,* Claudel contrasts this functional *designation* with the poetic order of language which is that of genuine *signification:* "The poet does not avail himself of words in the same way. He uses them not for the sake of utility, but in order to form, out of all those acoustic phantoms which the word puts at his disposal, a picture at once intelligible and delectable."[5] The union of the intelligible and the delectable is the agreement, and, if possible, the melding of sound and sense.

As for Valéry or Jakobson, so for Claudel this agreement presupposes a sort of reactivation of the signifier, in which activity lies the essence of the work of poetry: "Not only in order to express his thought, but in order to lend it the tension, the projective and penetrative force that he wants, an artist discovers ever new and unexpected resources in language. Under his pen everything takes on an emphasis, a relief, and a stylistic turn. If the word called up by the meaning does not have the color and the piquancy that the ear and the imagination require, he heightens it by sharpening its lateral values or through a livelier syntactical turn. If the substantive is faded, the ray of light that illuminates an unexpected adjective next to it prevents the reader from noticing this. Sometimes it is the meaning, the interest in the idea, that carries the visitor on and leads him to glide unawares along a succession of dead and dull vocables; sometimes it is the joyously awakened internal orchestra that invites and beckons him on from room to room and from floor to floor."[6] I have presented this resurrection of language (which brings to mind the verbal hallucinations of Baudelaire's "Poème du haschich") as a condition for poetic Cratylism, in Jakobson's style, and that is certainly the way it operates implicitly in Claudel's text, where it hinges directly upon the poet's faith in the "adaptation of sound to sense." But one need only detach this endeavor from its context in order to see it as a labor with no other end than the aesthetic, as a simple "accentuation of the message" for the pure pleasure of physical delight.[7] As in Valéry and Jakobson, we find again here the ambiguity of "poetic language" so defined, always in an unstable equilibrium between formalist autotelism and mimetic transparency.

But the homage thereby given to the Mallarméan (or pseudo-Mallarméan) tradition remains without any other theoretical investment, and a few significant nuances, or dissonances, can even be detected in Claudel. In the passage quoted earlier, the reader may have noticed the parallel, unexpected in the present context, between the "artist of words" and the simple "popular customer" — not of the poem but of natural language. The distinction between the active mode of language (poetry) and its passive or amorphous mode (prose) is no longer identified, as in the dialogue between Mallarmé and Viélé-Griffin, with the separation between the poet and "Mister Everyman" — and still less with that between the writer and the simple speaker. For Claudel, there is more poetry in the popular manner of speaking than in the majority of written texts: "This labor of accommodation and selection, in which our need for expression works on the ready-made material put at our disposal, is not reserved for the professional. The most cursory glance will reveal the fact that in the working-out of the words that constitute our modern languages, in the storehouse to which we go today to find our means of communication, it is not the pure idea, the intellectual concept, the realized image that has played the main role; it is expressive and phonetic convenience. We want a mouthful, as it were, of words, of expressions. We want to press them under our tongue, between our teeth, and sometimes, if I may say so, to breathe them in deeply like a well-worn tool that becomes one with the worker's hand. Thence come those word games that so often disconcert the scholarly etymologist; and thence comes that dazzling wealth of common and trashed words, like the word *tête*, for example. Thence comes the divorce between written and spoken language, in which the latter, I do not hesitate to say, is almost always right." [8]

Everyone knows in what contempt Claudel held "grammar" as the guardian of "correction" and the castrator of all linguistic invention by the writer, and by the popular speaker as well. [9] In the style of Pascal, he therefore substitutes for the simple opposition between poetry and ordinary language a "gradation" of three terms that reverses pro into con: the people, who follow linguistic instinct, are for this very reason within the realm of poetic truth; the demi-clever ones, who have lost this instinct and follow Léopold Auguste's injunctions, are in error; the poet, in a wise ignorance that knows itself, rejects false, sterilizing corrections and rediscovers the popular instinct for language. The two "extremes" meet in the truth, leaving those "in the middle" to act like know-it-alls and miss the mark. Identified in this way with the "instinctive movement of language," [10] poetry is then no longer a matter for specialists, and one might even hesitate to define it as an *art* in the strict sense (*technē*), since it exists everywhere in the natural state, everywhere that the natural movement of language lives on: "Poetry no more than inspiration is a phenomenon reserved for a small number of privileged persons. ... Wherever language exists, wherever words exist, there lies poetry in the latent state. This is not saying enough, and I would add: wherever silence exists (a certain silence), wherever attention exists (a certain attention), and, above all, wherever a *relationship* exists (that secret relationship, alien to logic and incredibly fertile, between things, persons, and ideas, which is called *analogy* and out of which rhetoric has created metaphor), there poetry is. The very texture of language, and consequently of thought, is made of metaphors. ... Poetry is everywhere. It is everywhere except in bad poets." [11]

Such an attitude does not in itself possess great originality, to say the least: we have here Romantic topos that has been encountered in Nodier, for example, and that ties Claudel to a pre-Mallarméan tradition, like so many other features of the pseudopopulist anti-intellectualism that he shares as well with a large number of contemporaries of all persuasions. But this tradition has some influence on the specific orientation of his Cratylism — and in a direction already rather clearly indicated by the reference to Nodier: to deny or to play down the technical and artifical nature of poetic language is in the same stroke to turn one's back on the solution afforded by *secondary* (poetic) mimologism, since this by definition consists of an artifice, a working-over of natural language that modifies and corrects it, even if the aim be to restore it to its originary virtues. As we have seen, Claudel himself takes natural language as it is (has become), and he wants to return it or rather to leave it to its poetic function in this state. From this comes that foreseeable volte-face which is a return to the only Cratylism compatible with such premises: *primary* mimologism, applied not to "verse" but to natural language itself. But since, for its part, the scientific refutation that has already been acknowledged makes it impossible to entertain such a position "seriously," only one path remains open any longer—the one foreshadowed by this characteristic proposal, mentioned above: the poet or the popular customer of language refrains from challenging the Hermogenist thesis; he just "behaves exactly as if" this thesis had no effect on him; he *pretends* to be unaware of it and thus practices a mimologism that can be described as *fictitious*. Fictitious, not *factitious:* the secondary mimologism of the Symbolist theoreticians is fac-titious in the sense that it acts or claims to act on natural language in order to lend it a mimetic virtue it does not possess or, at the very least (Valéry), in order to give the illusion of such mimetic virtue to the reader. Its specific mode is therefore on the order of *acting in such a way that* {*faire en sorte que*}. Accord-ing to Claudel, the mode of fictitious mimologism consists of *acting as if* {*faire comme si*}, all the while knowing perfectly well, or almost, that nothing of the kind is true. This is no longer work; it is *play* {*jeu*}, a "little game {*jeu*} in which you might indulge this summer in the country, when the rain forbids taking a walk. After all, it is as good as puzzles or crosswords"; it is an "amusement for a rainy day," an "amusement that I would have been glad to share with you," and so on.[12] Of course, the role of play was already evident in *Les Mots anglais,* in *Dictionnaire des onomatopées,* and even in the *Cratylus,* where the ironic ref-erence to inspiration from Eutyphron can be seen as a half-confession, and the ludic component can be regarded as a constant of the Cratylian tradition. But this component has never yet been so clearly displayed, even if this display is mixed, as it must be, with the claim to a "grain of truth."[13] Does not this grain, in its turn, enter into every definition of play {*jeu*}?

ⓢ Now we come to a second typical feature that directly introduces us to the nuts and bolts of Claudel's Cratylism: we will not find in him any sort of mimetic "fantasy" inspired by the phonic reality of language.[14] The Claudelian game {*jeu*} focuses mainly on *writing* {*écriture*}. The lecture on de Piis, even though nec-essarily devoted to "imitative harmony" as its immediate topic requires and its title announces, makes a very revealing displacement in its opening pages. After having explained the general theory with which we are familiar, Claudel acknowledges that it has carried him a bit far from his subject and directly in-vites his audience to consider some "new twists": he quotes Rimbaud's sonnet "Voyelles" (Vowels)[15] and then proposes to extend this "visual interpretation" of the vowels to the consonants. "Naturally," he adds, "one cannot attribute color to a consonant. But isn't it obvious that each one of them, every letter in gen-eral, has a different dynamism, and that each one *works* differently."[16] In the next four pages mimetic interpretations of letters and written words crop up again. Through a paradoxical line of thinking, although it is one seen before in de Brosses and Gébelin and one to which we will return shortly, the valorization of the consonant (a purely phonic notion in theory) is inevitably tied to a valorization of the "letter in general," or to the graphic aspect of the language system.

Here again, of course, and even more so, Claudel in his own way takes the linguistic objection into account. In his own way—that is to say, he points it out, quietly pays his respects to it, and moves on: "I know only too well the objections that the philologists will probably raise. Their arguments against the symbolic value of the written sign will probably be even more overwhelming than those against that of the phonetic sign. And yet no demonstration will convince a poet that no relationship exists between the sound and the sense of a word, or else he might as well renounce his profession.[17] And likewise, is it so absurd to believe that the alphabet is the abbreviated form and the vestige of all the acts, all the gestures, all the attitudes, and consequently all the feelings of humanity in the bosom of the creation that surrounds it?"[18] Once, Claudel even goes so far as to suggest that graphic mimesis is more substantial than the other kind because it escapes (and indirectly replies to) "the philologists' major objection to the analogy, admitted by all poets, between the sound and sense of words—or, homonyms. There is no relationship, for example, between *eau* {water} and *haut* {high}, between *être* {being} and *hêtre* {beech tree}, between *mon* {my} and *mont* {mountain}, and yet the sound of these words is absolutely identical. Now the orthographic anatomy of these vocables, letter for letter, enables us to understand their constitution in a much more discriminating way than does their simple breaking on the ear." Actually, the philologists' "major objection" (in practice) is instead synonymy, and especially interlinguistic synonymy (*cheval/horse*), against which the written form of language offers no counterreply. But within its limits, Claudel's line of argument is still relevant: there are no, or almost no, graphic homonyms, and the written form of language effectively makes it possible to individualize everything that the phonic form of language tends to mix together. Moreover, this recourse is completely spontaneous, for "the perception of a word that we pronounce and hear is not simply a phenomenon involving the ear and the mouth for a civilized person. Always intermingled with it is a certain graphic representation, which prevents us from confusing words with similar sounds but different meanings."[19]

Thus, after an eclipse of more than a century,[20] we have returned (but within a ludic framework) to a Cratylism of the writing system, to mimographic reverie. Here as elsewhere, a choice immediately opens up between phonomimographism (in Wachter's style) and ideomimographism (in Rowland Jones's style). The very title of Claudel's main contribution to the Cratylian corpus, "Idéogrammes occidentaux" {Occidental ideograms}, is enough to indicate the direction of his chosen *parti pris*, but the temptation of "visible speech" is not entirely unknown to him: "Are we to believe that between the phonic act and the written sign, between the expression and the thing expressed, across the entire linguistic genealogy, the relationship is purely formal and arbitrary? — or on the contrary, that all words are made up of an unconscious collaboration of eye and voice with the object, which the hand delineates at the same time as the inner mouth is evoking it? For example, is not each vowel the portrait of the mouth pronouncing it? This obviously holds for the o, and also for the u, which is simply two lips pushed forward. Is not the same true for the {French} a, which is simply a broadened, enlarged o, emphasized by the sideways dash as if by a pointing finger [of course, we must think of a handwritten a here]; for the {French} e, which is a half-closed aperture; and finally for the {French} i, which is the picture of the open slit of a mouth and of the dot placed between the teeth by the tip of the tongue?" [21] Once again, we recognize the age-old theme, down to specific examples made fun of by Molière in *The Bourgeois Gentleman*, but in Claudel it is even more vigorous and more general because it has been extended to the consonants: "It is highly likely ... that letters were originally a kind of schematic drawing of our speech apparatus in the process of pronouncing each one of them. The same reason that led the speaker to use this or that sound to express this or that idea recurs in the graphic representation of the oral act: I mean the letter." [22] But already evident in this last sentence is something that might have been divined earlier in the hypothesis of an "unconscious collaboration of eye and voice with the object," something that unconsciously as well as vaguely goes beyond pure imitation of the sound by the letter, as illustrated by the preceding examples. In fact, the issue here is a joint imitation of the object by the sound and the letter; we are no longer with Wachter but with Gébelin, in the realm of "collaboration" — and *indirect* resemblance — between the ideophone and the ideogram, which henceforth will absolutely dominate Claudelian Cratylism.

Clearly, the model, or at least the origin, for this is the Chinese writing system, such as Claudel had the opportunity to discover and become familiar with (if not actually to use) during his stay in China (1895–1909), and later in Japan (1922–27) — and such as reading Leon Wieger and B. Tchang Tcheng-ming [23] encouraged him to interpret wishfully: that is, as a mimetic ideography without a trace of phoneticism. Typically, in the twentieth century, the Chinese logogram has played the role of confirmatory myth and exotic guarantee that the Egyptian "hieroglyph" played before Jean-François Champollion, both relying on the same mirage. [24] Moreover, Claudel is quite ready to affect a certain detachment with regard to these intermediaries: Wieger's "delightful" book on the transition "from the image to the sign" is "an inexhaustible source of interest and amusement" for him, with its "entertaining" mimetic interpretation; in Tchang Tcheng-ming he finds "little drawings that are infinitely lively and amusing."

But the degree of validity of these conjectures is basically unimportant, for they are always merely the point of departure for another game, a still more risky but much more amusing one: the application of the mimographic hypothesis to the "Occidental" writing system itself, in this case the Latin alphabet — or more precisely, as we will see, to words that are written in the Latin alphabet: "I was led to wonder if in our Occidental writing system as well there were any means of recovering a certain representation of the objects signified"; "Suddenly I was struck by an idea. Yes, we too have ideograms, and our natural languages are just as suitable as Chinese for producing a graphic representation of objects"; "All of this is just a very summary account of a rich and fascinating subject, intended only to preface a sort of discovery — well founded or not — that I, as an inveterate old writer by profession, have made about our Occidental writing system — that it too has ideograms!"[25]

Thus is born the ludic hypothesis of the Occidental ideogram. But if we want to understand quite specifically how it works, we must first take into account everything that differentiates the two writing systems as compared by Claudel. This comparison begins in the wonderful "Religion du signe" {Religion of the sign},[26] which contrasts the "Roman letter," as essentially vertical, with the Chinese written character, as essentially horizontal — features later confirmed by the countervailing arrangement of the Latin writing system into horizontals and the Chinese into vertical columns.[27] The horizontal symbolizes the permanence of "each thing that finds a sufficient *raison d'être* solely in being parallel to its principle." The vertical "indicates action and sets forth an affirmation"; it is discrete, instantaneous. The Chinese written character indicates "a schematic being, a scripted person," and is immobile and synthetic; in contrast, the letter "is by nature analytic, every word that it constitutes being a successive enunciation of affirmations that are spelled out by eye and voice." Taking up this text again in his 1925 lecture "Philosophie du livre" {Philosophy of the book}, Claudel emphasizes the contrast between the "fixity" of the Chinese word — an "abstract image of the thing," with its "stable, radiating signification" — and the mobility of the Occidental word, a "restless portion of the sentence, a section of the pathway toward meaning, a vestige of the transient idea" that "asks us not to come to a standstill ourselves but to continue on up to its furthest reach the movement of our eyes and of our thought."[28]

Stated in this way, the theme of immutable Orient versus dynamic Occident is extremely trite, but we are interested in its implications for writing here. These are confirmed and clarified in 1926 in the conclusion of "Idéogrammes occidentaux," which can be boiled down to the following three basic oppositions: analytic versus synthetic; action, movement versus an immobile state of being;[29] vertical versus horizontal. In 1938 Claudel again discusses "the intrinsic immobility" of Chinese writing, which seems "entirely different from that continuous

furrowing of our personality in the process of explicating itself which is left behind by the metallic tip between our fingers. When I write: 'It is three o'clock,'
by the time my pen gets to the end of the sentence it is no longer three o'clock.
But three strokes of the Chinese brush suffice to inscribe this fleeting moment
on the substance of eternity. Not only is it three o'clock, but every time a human
eye settles on this intellectual drawing, it will always be three o'clock." [30] To this
characteristic Claudel attributes the "sort of fascination" that this sort of writing exercises over him. But as we shall see, fascination is not always the sign of
genuine adhesion.

These various contrastive features can be reduced quite well to a single one,
which opposes the supposedly indivisible *unity* of the Chinese written character to the *divisibility* of its Occidental equivalent. Despite the parallel suggested
once or twice between the written character and the *letter,* it can be easily inferred that this equivalent is not the letter but the *word.* This apparent truism
(since everyone knows that Chinese characters notate words) is not negligible,
for it strongly distinguishes Claudel's attitude from that of Jones or Gébelin, for
example, who inquired first and foremost into the signification of letters, even if
this meant looking for secondary confirmations in vocables considered as additions and combinations of letter values. In contrast, Claudel's graphic mimologism is essentially lexical,[31] like Nodier's phonic mimologism. For Claudel, the
Occidental homologues of Chinese written characters are indeed words, treated
as so many mimographies and, if I may say so, instances of scripted onomatopoeia. Moreover, one can see in his lists of ideograms [32] the graphic counterpart
of Nodier's *Dictionnaire,* except for one slight difference to be discussed in a
moment.

This specific attitude, which, to my knowledge, has no precedent in the Cratylian tradition but does have roots in the communal linguistic imagination,
is aptly described by Charles Bally: "As we know, written words, especially in
natural languages with a whimsical and arbitrary orthography, like English and
French, appear to the eye in the form of total images, of *monograms;* but this
visual image can furthermore be associated either closely or loosely with its
signification, so that the monogram becomes an *ideogram;* these parallels are
most often childish, but the phenomenon is not in itself insignificant. Some
people claim that *lys* {lily} is more beautiful than *lis* {lily} because the *y* figuratively represents the flower stem, which blossoms out into the consonants. Other
people will say that there is a vague resemblance between the eye and the French
word designating it {*oeil*}. For Mr. Paul Claudel ..." [33] We are going to cover
these examples ourselves, but first we should survey the boundary separating
Claudel's ideogram from Nodier's mimology (and the Chinese written character as viewed by Claudel, as above): the distance between them stems from the
analytic, or rather analyzable, nature of the written word. An onomatopoeia is

most frequently understood to be a globally mimetic word, not one whose every phonic element separately imitates a semic element of the object. For example, *ruisseau* is said to murmur like a brook, but a given phoneme is not, at least spontaneously, assigned to a given drop of water or a given pebble. For Claudel, however, the Latin ideogram is a complex symbol whose every letter, theoretically, represents an element of meaning.[34] To read the ideogram is essentially to analyze it,[35] and Claudel's ideograms can be distinguished and classified according to the type of analysis to which they lend themselves.

The first type of ideogram corresponds to the weakest degree of relation established between the graphic figure and the signified: here it is a question of a simple semic analysis in which each letter represents a property or an aspect of the object, but without an apposite correspondence between the spatial organization of either one. This goes without saying for "abstract" words whose signified has no spatiality, such as these.

être {being}: "t is everything that stands up in height and width; e is that which communicates with itself, taking root in its own heart. R is that which turns back on itself, looking at itself. And the second e is existence while the first e is essence; it wears a crown! a triangular aspiration toward God."

âme {soul}: "a[36] is both opening up and desire, the reunion of man and woman, that which exhales and inhales breath; m is a person between walls; e is being."

vie {life}: "v is the meeting of two electrodes, i the spark that jumps out; e is that which draws being from within."

toi {you}: "the t's vertical is the supreme representation of the object that arrests our gaze, of unity, someone toward whom we have turned; the bar of the t indicates direction, interpellation; the union of the o and i is the paradigm of all human diphthongs; the dot on the i is that eye of the other which we catch with our own gaze."

tu {you}: "the same thing, with the two lips reaching out."[37]

Clearly, redundancy plays a considerable part here: the significations of letters are distinct but convergent; a nearly identical signification is imitated differently by each letter.

There is a little more semantic diversification in the treatment of vocables with a more concrete signified, but still without spatial divisions.

vol {flight}: "v is the two wings of the bird, o the circle it describes, and l the bird as it comes and goes."

maison {house}: "m gives us the walls, roofs and partitions; a, the center, is the interior circulation; i is the fire, o the window, s the hallways and stairs, n the door, and the dot [over the i] is the inhabitant who looks in wonder at this magnificent building!"

corps {body}: "c is the mouth breathing in and swallowing, o all the round organs, r the rising and falling liquids, p the body properly speaking with head (or arms), s the piping system or breathing."

pied {foot}: "two footprints, one of which emphasizes the toes, the other the heel; i is the direction, e is the balancing motion on the joints, the heel."

faux {scythe}: "f is the shaft and handle of the scythe; a is the area that has just been mowed with the blade seen moving away; x is everything about the process of cutting, the blade, eager to chop, with its jaw gaping on all sides."[38]

Helter-skelter, the word here offers us a series of descriptive elements whose position is neutral and indeterminate: *vol* would read just as well, and identically, if written *lov, vlo,* or whatever.[39]

The second type of ideogram introduces spatial layout, with the vocable being read as a complex drawing of a complex object, each letter representing, insofar as possible, a part of that object in the corresponding position. This is extremely obvious for OMO, "two eyes underneath superciliary arcades"; and *eye*, "which adds the nose."[40] In *toit* {roof}, "do we not have here a complete representation of a house, not even missing the two chimneys? O is the wife and I is the husband, characterized by their basic differences: care and force; the dot of the i is the smoke of the hearth or, if you prefer, the spirit shut away behind doors and the private life of the home."[41] And *monument* is "a veritable edifice from the time of Louis XIV with its two symmetrical wings and its central loggia completely framed by columns,"[42] in which the graphic symmetry corresponds, more or less exactly, to the spatial symmetry of the object. In *arbre* {tree}, the b "stands up straight in the middle of the typographic island like a cypress tree"; and in *tree*, "t is the big tree in the foreground, and r is the brook at its feet, the double e representing its graceful twists and turns."[43] Finally, locomotive is "a drawing made to order for children. First, in its length, the word is an image of the animal. L is the smoke, o the wheels and the boiler, m the pistons, and t the marker of its speed — as in *auto* — in the manner of a telegraph post, or else a connecting rod; v is the control gear, i the whistle, e the coupling device; and the underlining is the rail!"[44]

The third type of ideogram — the only one that does full justice to the temporal successiveness of the Occidental writing system (according to Claudel) — is scantily represented. This is the highest level of integration and hence the most difficult to concretize, since it takes into account not only spatial relationships but also the diachronic dimension of the object, represented by the irreversible succession of letters running from left to right, whereas words of the second type of ideogram (even <u>locomotive</u>) can be read just as well in reverse, and those of the first can be broken down into any (dis)order. Here, the vocable is no longer a simple collection of descriptive features or even a simple picture; it becomes a faithful imitation of a series of events; it becomes a story {*récit*}. Thus, *quilles* {skittles} contains this story: "The hand holding the bowling ball, five skittles of unequal size, the ball rolling (the dot of the i) and the final ricochet (e)."[45] Or, at a very different level of investment, in *soi* {oneself}, "the S represents a winding staircase like the one seen in that painting called *The Philosopher* by Rembrandt at the Louvre, by which one descends into the conscience. And what will you find there, I ask you? An O and an I, or a flaming torch and a mirror."[46] Or the story in *rêve* {dream}: "Rêve is a complete painting. The circumflex is a butterfly. A hunter armed with a net extends his leg in pursuit of this elusive sliver of a creature. With a ladder, which is the E, he attempts to entrap it. He reaches his arms out toward it, in the reverse of an impalpable sign, and that is the V. In vain, for only the ladder remains."[47]

As these few examples suggest, such analyses impose a more or less constant determination of elementary values at the level of the letter, or even at the level of still more basic graphic features. Some of these values have been brought out by Claudel himself in side remarks or in the conclusion of his lexical interpretations. For example, the letter M, which serves as the thematic index and unifying thread for the article "Les Mots ont une âme" {Words have a soul}, is interpreted as follows: "a wonderful and memorable letter that stands up straight in the middle of our alphabet like an arch of triumph resting on its triple jamb, assuming that the typography does not make it into a spiritual canker on the horizon. The M in *Monde* {World} is an example, and why not the M in *Mort* {Death}?"[48] An unusual fate is allotted to the X in a text dedicated to the École Polytechnique: "X is first a crossroads, the intersection of four directions. I compare it to an aspiring mood that pushes a balanced symmetry of possible outcomes to their extremes. The four angles determined by its two arms constitute the principle of all plane geometry, whereas when they become wings by rotating, they produce a sphere. The X is at the center of all measure and all creation. It is the Tree, it is the Giant with his legs spread apart who holds up the sky. It is the multiplication sign. And it is the sign of the cross used as a signature by illiterates [and so on]."[49] The T "suggests at once the idea of a cross, a lever, a scale, an intersection," and the O "evokes at the same time a wheel, the horizon, the aperture of a vase or a mouth, a pulley, an automobile steering wheel, and so on."[50] Last and above all, the conclusion of "Idéogrammes occidentaux" singles out a posteriori several typical constants: "Some of the letters I have tried to explain are veritable mechanical gadgets. The e is a balance, the u is a piston or a pipe, the L is a lever, the T is a stay, the o is a wheel and a pulley, the r is a siphon or sometimes (r) a hook, the s is a spring or spiral, the f is a blade or—

as a capital (F) — a key, the vowels topped by their accents are regular little explosives: the alphabet puts at your disposal all sorts of ropes and ties, shafts and rods, a complete tool kit."[51]

That last text is very characteristic of Claudel's style of interpretation: the letters, graphic elements, clearly represent basic values, elements of meaning; analysis progresses symmetrically on the two planes of what Hjelmslev (an obligatory reference) would call content and expression. But the elements of meaning here do not consist, as in the Leibnizian type of semantic analysis, of pure abstractions and general categories; they are technological elements, as it were, simple tools and machines (typically, Claudel's term is *engin* {machine}), interchangeable but specialized spare parts of that "huge tool shop," ever at our disposal, that for Claudel is Creation. We will encounter this trait again.

Other basic significations remain scattered about, and their synthesis is left to the reader. To begin with, this task comes up against a certain number of polyvalences, some of which Claudel presents within one and the same article. We have already run across these proposals made at will, such as the dot on the i in *toit*, which is smoke or spirit; or the t in <u>locomotive</u>, which is a post or a connecting rod; or the s in *corps*, which is breathing or piping. Most of these emerge from two or more glosses, and even if we overlook certain ad hoc interpretations that are directly inspired by the verbal context — such as the a in *pain* {bread}, which is a round loaf or "the circular gesture of the baker's boy as he kneads"; the A in *Âne* {donkey}, whose bar could be "the tail the animal holds out straight to help him bray,[52] if we are to believe the Countess de Ségur; or the E that is the ladder in *RÊVE*[53] — we must reckon with a few others that are more constant. Thus, C is sometimes read as concave (= "cavity"), sometimes as convex (= everything that makes itself round "in anticipation of a caress"); V stands for two electrodes, two spread wings, two raised arms, all probably reducible to a dialectic of unity and duality ("unity in the process of dividing itself in two like pine needles"),[54] whose identity or inverse can be found in Y, "the pair of eyes deeply rooted in our unity."[55] The most typical and most significant pattern is that of the couple O-I (almost always grouped into a "diphthong"). Starting from an obvious geometrical value (circle versus vertical line), Claudel obtains relations such as table/light (or fire, the constant being the verticality of the flame); mirror/light; mouth/breath; cropped/raised area; and of course, above all, man/woman, the supreme couple that makes OI "the type of all human diphthongs."[56] The sexual motifs and motives of this interpretation are clear, and Claudel himself draws attention to O as the "female principle" and I as the "phallus,"[57] elsewhere metaphorized or metonymized, as we have seen, as receptivity/desire or care/force.

Once these various polysemies have been reduced, a few relatively constant values can be singled out: c = convexity/concavity; e and j = involution, reflection; i = verticality, unity; l = going to and fro; m = horizon or partitioning off (the latter value being shared with n); o = roundness; r (handwritten) = rise and fall; t = verticality + horizontality; u = cavity open near the top; s = vertical curve, descending spiral; v, y = dual unity; x = intersection; z (seen as a reclining s, in receding perspective) = horizontal curve, meander. The most notably absent items[58] can be analyzed into more basic elements, such as a into o + i or c + i; or b, d, p, and q into o (or c) + a vertical indicator that is more contextual than i, since it is pointed sometimes up, sometimes down. Plainly, then, for Claudel the letter is not quite a graphic atom. It can sometimes be reduced to another simpler letter, sometimes to an infrascriptural but still meaningful grapheme: a curve, a vertical or horizontal or oblique line, a loop, a bar, a jamb — the smallest one (the dot over the i, "the spirit shut away behind doors and the private life of the home") not being the least important.[59]

Ⓢ As has doubtless been noticed, Claudel draws no line here between vowels and consonants, which are consistently treated according to identical symbolic schemata. Of course, this assimilation is legitimate, since the issue is a purely phonic distinction, not translated by anything on the level of writing.[60] This assimilation is nonetheless revealing, for among his predecessors, such as Wachter, Jones, and Gébelin, the influence of phoneticism entails at the very least a bunching together of vowel letters and of consonant letters. But in Claudel, the valorization of articulation — always linked to that of writing, for understandable reasons, as we have remarked[61] — probably goes further than it ever went in the previous tradition, with considerable consequences for the interpretation of the symbolism of writing.

This valorization is already very noticeable on the phonic level. We have observed that Claudel, quoting Rimbaud, slides over from the *color* of vowels to the *dynamism* of consonants; this division is fundamental and has been valorized before. Moreover, he opposes "the timbre that the vowel imprints on the word," and "the form, virtue, impulse, energy, the distinctive action that the consonant confers"; the consonants "are the impulsive, propellent, dynamic ones."[62] He acknowledges having systematically selected from de Piis's alphabetic repertory the illustrations of consonants, "although the vowels play a no less picturesque role there. The reason for this is that, for me, the consonant is the essential element in speech production. It is the consonant that lends the word its energy, its contours, its action, with the vowel representing its exclusively musical element."[63] This chosen *parti pris,* adopted with its characteristic motivations, should be connected to Claudel's own poetics, which — as expressed in "Réflexions et propositions sur le vers français" {Reflections and suggestions on French verse}, for example — is actually more dynamic than musical, essentially rhythmic and articulatory, and founded on what he calls the *motif,* "that sort of dynamic *pattern* or *central power source* that imposes its form and its impulse on the entire poem."[64] The parallel between *form* and *impulse,* which approaches an identification, is typical, just as is the formula *dynamic pattern,* which is almost a paradox elsewhere: for Claudel, form is always dynamized as figure and motional capacity.

As a result, in Claudel the neutralization of the difference between vowels and consonants in the writing system looks distinctly like an assimilation (in the strong sense) of the former into the latter—a highly marked and very significant appropriation. There is no mention here of the luminous and chromatic values traditionally attributed to the vowels;[65] everything stands for form and movement, and the sole generic mention of the vowels, topped by their accents (always?), makes them into so many little explosive charges—yet again a promise of movement.

Now we understand the emblematic value of the seme-machine. The wheel, the lever, the pulley are precisely motor powers that have been materialized, generative or transformative forms of motion: *articulations.* In the workshop of *homo faber,* there is room only for consonants.

⟲ This interpretation of the writing system, and through it that of the language system, extends the traditional theme of the valorization of the *masculine consonant* versus the *feminine vowel* but intensifies it according to the particular givens of an essentially dynamic genius, a genius for action and enterprise whose most symbolic figure is the hero of *The Satin Slipper*—he who cannot go wrong because, like Columbus, he "takes the sun as his guide." The implicit oxymoron of an *Occidental* ideogram acquires its full meaning and its full value here: the Chinese written character, static and seemingly passive, is a writing system that is always already written, *scriptura scripta,* offered up for contemplation and fascination; the Occidental letter, dynamic and active, is a writing system in the process of writing, *scriptura scribens,* symbol of restless energy. To me, it appears highly significant that Claudel treats somewhat ironically the age-old topos according to which "Creation is a written book."[66] The book motif is readily devalorized in Claudel through the apathetic metaphors of "collection," "empty vessel," "jar," "herbarium."[67] Here, as elsewhere, there is a very lively opposition between the Book as a totality that is completed and, as it were, dead or at the very least dormant, and writing as gesture, action, violence.[68] For Claudel, God *has* not written, He is *in the act* of writing, "in the act of creating before us like a painter on a canvas,"[69] and we recall the epigraph of *The Satin Slipper: "Deus escreve direito por linhas tortas."*

Thus, mimologist speculation, habitually tied to what Bachelard has called a *reverie of repose* {*rêverie du repos*}, since it is a reverie on resemblance and hence on the security of the Same, becomes in Claudel the occasion for a dynamic reverie, a *reverie of the will* {*rêverie de la volonté*}, based on motion and energy. Or rather, to use a category common to Claudel and to Bachelard (among others), Cratylus here shifts from the *anima* to the *animus,* from the principle of reverie to the principle of action: he no longer dreams on writing; he *brings it into play* {*met en jeu*}, in the strong sense — that is, he both sets it in motion and puts it into question. In short, he *awakens* {*réveille*} it-and, in a last digression, one is tempted in turn to play on this word, whose Cratylian etymology is a profound paradox, by refiguring it as *rêveille:* for is it not true, sometimes, that *a dream is a waking and a vigilance* {*le rêve veille*}?[70]

CHAPTER 15

Signe: Singe

 Symbolically, in the autobiography of Michel Leiris the beginning is an ending. This symbolism is hardly paradoxical, since a point of *departure* is necessarily a place one is leaving, an epoch drawing to a close in order that another
may be inaugurated. This double term, this both final and initial event, is here,
as elsewhere, a fall; or rather, it comprises, in fact, two falls, the first of which,
an entirely physical one, provokes but also figuratively represents the second,
entirely spiritual one. A child's toy, a fragile soldier made of lead or cardboard,
falls to the floor. The child picks it up, determines that it is not broken, and "expresses" his joy by crying out: *"Reusement!"* {Tunately!}. An adult or a "better
informed" older boy corrects him: we do not say *reusement,* but *heureusement*
{fortunately}. And instantly the child's joy gives way to a strange malaise:

> This word, which I had until that moment used as a pure interjection, with-
> out any consciousness of its real meaning, became tied to *heureux* and,
> through the magical power of a similar parallel, it was suddenly inserted
> into a whole sequence of precise significations. Apprehending all at once,
> in its entirety, this word which I had before always truncated, felt like a dis-
> covery, like the abrupt rending of a veil or the explosion of some truth. This
> vague vocable—which up to this moment had remained mine alone and
> as if sequestered—was now being promoted, by pure chance, to the role
> of link in an entire semantic cycle. It was no longer something belonging
> to me: it participated in that reality which was the language system of my
> brothers and my sister, and that of my parents. No longer something pos-
> sessed by and proper {*propre*} to me, it became common and open. There
> it was, in a flash, having become something shared or—if you like—*social-
> ized.* No longer a confused exclamation that escaped from my lips—still so

---

Genette's chapter title "Signe: Singe" alludes to the wordplays characteristic of the work of Michel
Leiris, especially his *Biffures* and *Glossaire,* which are the focus of discussion here. Since Aristotle,
the sign (*signe*) has been linked to the human instinct for imitation, which we seem to share
with certain apes: hence, *singe* (monkey). Man is a kind of signifying monkey: *signe-singe.* For
a famous intertext behind Leiris's wordplay, see Mallarmé's sonnet "Le vierge, le vivace et le bel
aujourd'hui . . .": *cygne-signe,* "swan-sign" (Genette discusses Mallarmé in chapter 12).

close to my vital organs, like a laugh or a cry—it was, among thousands of others, one of the elements constituting the language system, that vast instrument for communication. ... This ill-pronounced word, which I had just discovered was not in reality what I had believed it was until then, put me in a position to sense dimly—thanks to the kind of deviation, the kind of gap that this event impressed on my mind—the extent to which articulated language, an arachnean tissue of my relations with others, exceeded my grasp, with its mysterious antennae pushing out from all sides.[1]

In order to begin (to end), in our turn, we must consider rather closely this initiatory passage, the last one of the first chapter in *La Règle du jeu* {The rule of the game}. Let us point out right away in what sense this point of departure is (only) symbolic: the rupture in question, which is not otherwise given a date, is in reality one among others, which it represents by synecdoche and delegation. What is ending at this moment has probably already ended several times, and will end several times more, even indefinitely. But, with Leiris, we are going to pretend that this fall is really an isolated, aoristic one and that it divides Before and After at one stroke. A toy has been broken in a fall—hence, joy ceases—and this toy is not, as had been believed, the lead soldier but a "word," and through it a whole language system, or at least a state of language, and more precisely a state of relationship to language, symbolized by that autonomous and (partly) idiolectal vocable: *reusement*. This state, which we will call without ado childhood language, was perfectly unconscious; it reveals itself upon its disappearance—as does paradise when it is lost—and is defined through the negation of what succeeds it: that is to say, of course, adult linguistic consciousness. The two main features of this consciousness are "insertion" and "participation"—in other words features of connection: that of each vocable to "an entire semantic cycle" and, beyond, to an entire natural language that is suddenly perceived, in its immanence, as a coherent system but also, in its transcendence, as a "vast instrument for communication"; and hence, through natural language, to a whole family group and, step by step, to all of society.

As "something common and open," an "arachnean tissue of my relationships with others," adult language reveals at once its internal and external connection, its systematic structure and its social function. In contrast, therefore, childhood language manifests retrospectively its essential characteristic, which was *autonomy:* that of the speaker with regard to others, because he spoke for himself, without addressing anyone; and that of each verbal element with regard to a linguistic system as yet unknown. In point of fact, it is obvious that the former autonomy was illusory, and we will very soon see that the latter is completely relative, and more precisely how childhood consciousness frequently substitutes for the actual connections of the linguistic system other, imaginary

ones. But the fact that they are made up, or conjectured, relieves them completely of the weight of convention and hence of social constraint, lending them
a kind of psychological freedom. The child is master of a language that he believes to be "something possessed by and proper to him," and something that
depends on his decisions alone. We are not yet within the domain of mimologism, but we are already in the Cratylian situation of the sovereign nomenclator,
where social bonds count for nothing, and where everything transpires among
"words," "things," and him who decides on their relation.[2]

Such is the lost linguistic paradise, and it is hardly an exaggeration to see in
the work of Leiris — or at least in the part of his work that interests us here-an
attempt to find it again, or to reconstitute it. He himself has, on several occasions, established an extremely close connection between his literary vocation
and "the supreme importance" he has always attached to "matters pertaining
to language."[3] Here, what might seem like an utter platitude takes on a more
exact and more original meaning indeed: for Leiris, the "world of words" is not
merely — and, above all, not *in the first instance* — the instrument of literary activity. Rather, the "world of words" is the very object of this activity: "One must
appeal to this obscure attraction to language *as such,* I think, to find the earliest
sign of my slowly emerging contact with things literary." Hence, logically, the
belated nature of this vocation: "If you feel yourself drawn toward reading and
writing, you will readily recognize your vocation as a writer; but if you have
language before you, in its sudden immense nudity, chances are good that you
will not recognize any vocation at all."[4] Leiris finds language *before him,* not as
a means but as an end. The literary work is for him a *quest for language,* and this
paradoxical situation clearly cannot be understood unless the language-object
of the quest is in some way hidden, or lost. Whence that other revived cliché of
a "second childhood (rediscovered) under the aegis of poetry recognized and
practiced as such,"[5] a cliché that escapes banality only if the childhood to be
rediscovered is that childhood of language provisionally emblematized by the
inaugural *reusement:* "Misunderstandings, errors as to the very texture or as to
the meaning of a vocable, phonic analogies,... the evocative potential of certain elements of vocabulary, the charm attached to names of characters,... the
double figure of words whose signification for us does not necessarily match
the common definition given them by the dictionary, diverse types of linguistic
'accidents':... such is the set of fragile but intensely felt realities (in childhood
especially, the time of our greatest capacity for being filled with wonder) that
made up the object of my collection and constituted — without my at first having
to leave this verbal domain which had never ceased to be a privileged one for
me — the originary core around which, progressively, the remainder solidified."[6]

This "remainder" {*reste*} is explicitly identified here as the text of *Biffures* and,
more specifically, its first five chapters ("... Reusement!", "Chansons," "Habille-

en-cour," "Alphabet," "Perséphone"), which are mainly presented, in Proustian style, as an essay on the recollection of childhood language. But this recollection, like so many others, is impossible on the part of the adult writer[7] — for whom, as Leiris acknowledges, the "precious Cabala" of childhood having long since lost its luster, "letters and words have become, or virtually, *dead letters*" — unless a degree of artificial reconstitution ("retrospective reconstruction") and perhaps of simulation is added.[8] Unlike the Proustian narrator, who implicitly lays claim to a perfect authenticity, Leiris is the first one to emphasize the factitious aspects of his project, speaking here of "cheating that consists in lending to language, after the fact, a glamour which, ever since I learned how to read, to write, to employ these auditory or visual signs for specific ends (whether utilitarian or not), language has nearly lost for me, now that it has been reduced to the purely human function of an instrument," and speaking elsewhere of "rather idle entertainment" very far removed from the "profound age-old game {*jeu*} whose elements of seriousness and of iron-hard inventiveness I now have great difficulty measuring exactly."[9] As in Claudel, the terms *jeu* and *amusement* recur quite often for describing this retrospective activity. But perhaps the superficial entertainment of the adult remains somehow faithful to the "profound game" of childhood; at least this is what the author of *Biffures,* when all is said and done, wants to believe, "as if I were unable to resign myself to the fact that my game was only a game and as if I could fully enjoy it only by ascribing an almost religious importance to it," taking pleasure in viewing this game-playing as a habit "formed early in childhood." Thus, the artificial entertainment may unconsciously revive lost beliefs, "bring memories alive again — infusing them with new blood, so to speak, or practicing on them something like that artificial respiration by means of which one tries to bring the drowned back to life."[10]

These are contradictory statements, in which a necessarily problematic authenticity takes the typically Leirisian form of scruples and of self-discontent. We will not, therefore, attempt the impossible and perhaps futile distinction {*départ*} between memory and its pastiche,[11] and we will assume straightaway that, regarding the verbal "materials" they share, the young hero and the adult narrator are separated only by the degree of their belief. Nonetheless, the adult's ambiguous playfulness is much less distanced from the child's credulity than is the expressly critical attitude of the Proustian narrator. Proust unequivocally, albeit somewhat indulgently, repudiated the Cratylism of young Marcel. Leiris, as disillusioned as he is, seems rather to regret the loss of his "illusions" — thereby showing that he has not completely lost them, as is moreover confirmed by the following passage, which, with an ambiguity worthy of Claudel, even suggests the search for a sort of scientific guarantee: "I am only amusing myself here, and out of all these correspondences there are few that I take seriously, by which I mean few that impress me as self-evident. But it seems to me nonetheless that, in this direction, something remains to be discovered.... Likewise, it is on the basis of objective data that we have succeeded in specifying the relationships among sounds and colors, providing a rational foundation for a large portion of those correspondences which, for centuries, had no justification save in the realm of mysticism or of poetics." [12]

ⓟ In childhood, linguistic reverie focuses at once on the elements of natural language and on the vocables constituted from them, and it may even begin working on the latter, before any analytical ability. We are going to violate the order of the text a bit, and probably that of lived experience, so as to begin with the *elementary* speculations to which Leiris devotes, almost exclusively, the first fifteen pages of the chapter titled, precisely, "Alphabet."

Precisely, *alphabet*. It goes without saying that for the child, properly phonic analysis remains inaccessible and without doubt inconceivable for a long time. On the other hand, graphic analysis is given, so to speak, in shapes at once simple and seductive, in various presentations (images, blocks, the "sculpted letters of shop signs," and so on) that fall into this category. But a ready-made analysis is no longer (or not yet) a genuine analysis: here, straightforwardly, each letter appears as an autonomous and picturesque shape, even as a concrete object, prior to any consciousness of its possible utilization in a greater linguistic whole, whether syllable, word, or sentence. At the outset {*départ*}, the only perceptible whole is, naturally, the alphabet itself. Letters are therefore concrete objects that belong to a concrete unity that is "the alphabet-object," a thing with "shape and weight," "opaqueness and consistency." [13] This mode of existence directs the child's attention spontaneously to the materiality of the elements of (what is not yet) writing {*écriture*}.

Such materiality is, of course, graphic, plastic (a "lightweight scaffolding of letters", an "impalpable framework of girders," the "book's thickened space"), chromatic (a "yellowish alphabet"), and above all, in the present case, gustatory and, as it were, alimentary. [14] This description may seem absolutely idiosyncratic, and it probably is, given its circumstantial causes: *alphabet* happens to rhyme with *Olibet*, a trademark of sweet biscuits and butter cookies, which transmits its yellowish color (corroborated by the "yellow cover" of the primer of ABCs) and its consistency of "fine and dense crumbs" to "alphabet." Another of its material manifestations also happens to be "pasta for alphabet soup," [15] whence that almost daily experience of "eating an A, a B, a C, a D" and thus "tasting the fruit of the tree of knowledge," from which issues yet another experience, apparently unique but crucial: "One evening, when I was under the weather and had gulped down a little too much soup too fast, I suddenly emitted, greatly to the detriment of the tablecloth and the large, deep breadbasket next to me, an enormous series of letters which I had not digested and which remained as legible as the fat letters that compose, if not the headlines, at least the subtitles of a major daily newspaper."[16]

Baudelaire compared Hugo to the prophet Ezekiel, whom God one day ordered to eat a book. "I do not know," he continued, "in what prior world Victor Hugo swallowed the dictionary of the language which he was called upon to speak, but I do see that the French lexicon, upon leaving his mouth, became a world, a colorful, melodious, and mobile universe."[17] Clearly, in the process, the book (the text, actual discourse) has become a dictionary (the potential repertory of a natural language). At the expense of a further slippage from the dictionary to the alphabet — that is, from the lexicon to its phono-graphic elements — the young Leiris realizes in his own way Baudelaire's metaphor, a profound metaphor according to which to speak would be to regurgitate a previously ingested linguistic treasury that is stored somewhere behind the Homeric gateway of the teeth. "If I believe that I am a language eater {mangeur de langage} when I say alphabet, this illusion is mediated through the book";[18] through a striking detour, which appears to be merely accidental, it is writing that reveals and manifests the profound and irreducible orality of the voice and of articulated language. "In short, alphabet is something that we hold in our mouth when pronouncing it aloud or silently; it is what we call a concrete word that fills up the cavity bounded by the throat, tongue, teeth, and palate with tangible contents."[19] "Ne pas mâcher ses mots {not to mince one's words}, être mal embouchée {to be foul-mouthed}, avoir un ton amer, aigre, sucré, mielleux {to speak in a bitter, sour, sugared, honeyed tone}: these many expressions show, each in its own way, how in everyone's mind the spoken word {la parole} remains attached to its place of origin, the oral cavity."[20] We will hear more about this gustatory and alimentary dimension.

With their material existence confirmed and intensified in this way, the elements of language quite naturally take on an evocative value of their own, a direct and autonomous signification: "Letters do not remain dead letters {lettres mortes} but are shot through with the life force of a precious Cabala." As in Hugo or Claudel, we find here a repertory of formal equivalences between letters and objects: A is a stepladder; I, a soldier or a column; O, the "original spheroid of the world"; S, a winding path or snake; Z, lightning; X, the cross; Y, the fork in a tree or the fragment of a portico. D is a fat stomach; E, a tenon; F, a corbel; J, a fishhook or an inverted crook; L, a chair without legs; N, a zigzag; T, a pillar supporting an architrave; U, the longitudinal section of a vase. "G is a great Florentine lord in a doublet with puffed sleeves, posing with his hand on his hip, very close to the heavy curved guard of his sword or dagger hilt; K, in which a sort of wedge has been driven, or which has been ravaged by a pick that gouged the whole middle of its face, ruined like the face of Carabosse, a {wicked hunchbacked} fairy with her deeply creased mouth and her curled-back nostrils set between a monstrously prominent forehead and chin; Q has the round and jovial face of someone who loves bad puns, with a double chin supported by the little knot of a necktie." [21] Among the secondary graphemes, the cedilla {,} evokes a "small pig tail" and, in a more specific memory, a "crank like the one used by the owner of the bazaar at the corner of Michelangelo and Auteuil Streets, for operating the awning that protected his shop stall." [22] As the reader has noticed, every letter is interpreted solely according to its shape as a printed capital, reconfirming the dominance of the alphabet. In drawing up this list, I have somewhat rearranged Leiris's order and classification, and above all I have reduced each interpretation to a one-to-one match between letter and object by editing out along the way some details or explanatory digressions, to which we will return further on.

As is evident, these letter values are of a purely formal (visual) order: each letter is taken as a simplified drawing of the object it evokes. From the phonic perspective, the relation is more diversified: "If, from the purely logical point of view, the alphabet comes under the visual domain, then vowels and consonants, which are noises that reach the ear after they leave the mouth, come under the auditory domain, of course, but to a certain extent they also belong to the sense of taste because like a stalagmite the tongue alternately rises and falls in the antrum of the throat and under the vault of the palate, giving rise to the aerial movements that constitute the flesh of vowels and consonants, which are like divinities stirred up in this grotto and gently simmering there as if inside the walls of an alchemical vessel. Nothing prevents us from adding an auditory kaleidoscope and even a gustatory kaleidoscope to the visual kaleidoscope of written characters — if that amuses us; only touch and smell would be needed in order to make our pleasure complete." [23] Thus does Leiris set forth his repertory of phonic symbolism, but this declaration is not entirely respected: the "auditory kaleidoscope" is absent from the list, in which no phoneme seems endowed with a direct onomatopoetic value. Taking to an extreme the course of action initiated by Nodier, Leiris proposes only synaesthetic values. Even so, we should note the striking absence of visual values, as if the "kaleidoscope of written characters" had exhausted that resource, or the desire for it; as we saw earlier, Leiris does indeed mention the "correspondence" par excellence, that of the "relationships between sounds and colors," but he does not make any use of it here. [24]

In point of fact, then, the phonic repertory boils down to three types of values: gustatory, olfactory, and tactile. *Gustatory* — on a scale from low to high, the vowels evoke substances varying in weight and solidity: *a,* puree of peas; *o,* mashed potatoes; *e, é, è,* vowels that are "neutral" or "for accompaniment," bread; *i* and *u,* "more acidic and lighter," lemon, green vegetables. All together and without further specifications, the consonants, which are less substantial but more muscular, signify: meat. *Olfactory* — the nasal vowels evoke "organic perfumes" and strong smells (cheese, game), whereas the light vowels *i* and *u* evoke flowers; *t* and *v*, alcoholic or fermented drinks (we will see why). Let us note in passing that except for flowers, the olfactory is in fact bound up with the gustatory. *Tactile* — with vowels excluded because they are "amorphous" (as in de Brosses and Gébelin, the only form here comes from articulation), Leiris distinguishes "frothy" (dull-edged) consonants, which are all continuants (*j* {ʒ}, *l, m, n*), and "pointy" consonants: the velar occlusives *g* and *k* are felt as sharp-edged; the labials and dentals *b, d, p, t* as "cutting and thrusting"; *r* as gnawing (ever the *litera canina*); the labio-dental aspirates *f* and *v* as "having the sharpness of a razor ... and the ambiguous softness of velour"; the sibilants *s, x, z* as "uncoiling springs." Finally, the two semivowels *w* and *y* share the value of lubrication, with *w* being fat and "unctuous" (honey, butter), and *y* being moist ("it is not by accident that the term *mouillure* is used to refer to the palatization of any consonant following a light *y*").[25]

For the moment, as the reader may have noticed, the foregoing are just some "evocative potentials" of the graphic and phonic elements of language, without any mimetic relation between these two systems of expression, and without any application of these potentials to the formation of the actual lexicon. As Leiris himself says regarding one series of letter values: "Here, only shape or form is in play; sight alone is affected; the written character does not benefit from any thieving committed upon complicit words, nor does it merge with the sound that it is the job of the written character to notate."[26] Now the mimetic function of the language system cannot be founded on the potentiality of its elements alone, as we know from the *Cratylus* and as Leiris knows quite well, too. He says as much in regard to the writing system, which cannot be motivated solely by the shape evoked by each letter. This shape must actually serve as well either to refer to the sound it transcribes (phonomimesis) or to imitate the object it helps to designate (ideomimesis): "In the alphabet ... a meeting of elements from various sources occurs: as a writing system, the alphabet is in the first place a catalogue of visual signs addressed to the eye, offering it a stock of images; but as a transcription of the language system, the alphabet also corresponds to acoustic components and, from this fact, acquires a value for the ear, each of its constituent written characters becoming the formal equivalent of a real or hypothetical sound instead of remaining a mere figure, the prey of sight alone; finally, since the alphabet is the means by which we write words, the acoustic signs of things or ideas, it also must receive, from its immemorial commerce with these things and ideas, a little something that overwhelms the intellect by creating the illusion that a certain providential act, which intervened in the development of spoken language to make it an adequate expression of the true nature of things, also played a role in the constitution of written language, making letters — which are ultimately merely arbitrarily chosen marks — the garment, or even the very body, of these words which themselves retain the closest possible relationship to the heart of things (and this, for all eternity)." [27]

As in Claudel, the phonomimetic relation is very skimpily illustrated here: at the very most, we can find a triple similarity between sound and shape for S, "whose hissing resonance agrees with its serpentine shape"; for R, "which makes us hear a hoarse and grating rumble while it stands upright like a rocky escarpment" (notice the agreement with Nodier on S and on the use of illustrative alliterations).[28] As far as Q is concerned, the motivation is more complex, since it uses the double relay of the name of the letter, which is lexicalization in its rough state, and the name of a familiar part of the body, which is a homophone {*le cul*}.[29] This "facile" and inevitable play on words, already encountered in Gébelin and Nodier, authorizes the following gloss: "Q, also a letter that, when spelled out, has a cutting edge to it, like the blow of the axe {*la hache*} that made the deep furrow in the primordial globe, now divided into two buttocks." [30] In other words, the shape of this letter indirectly evokes the sound of its own name through the metonymical relay of a kind of "furrow" that is pronounced in the same way as it is—a situation reminiscent of Nodier's "rebuses" but still more indirect, even if one ignores the inconvenient presence of the name of another letter, which we will see again shortly.[31]

Ideography (or ideophony) is further developed, at least as an apposite—and, in fact, artificially induced—harmony between the value of certain letters (or phonemes) and the signification of the *words* they serve to form. In exactly this way, H combines the shape of the guillotine with a name that is a homophone of the name for another sharp-edged instrument {*la hache*}.[32] W, a mechanical part, appears in "tramway" or "wagon"; *a* and *o* appear in *pois cassé* {split pea} and *pomme de terre* {potato}, *y* in *yeux* {eyes}, *f* and *v* in *ferment* and *vin* {wine}.[33] Here, Leiris himself points out the (circular) course of illusory motivation, implying that the two basic values can be inferred from the meaning of two words.

The same probably goes for other values, not yet mentioned, where the letters "to some extent embody the content of certain words in which they hold the initial position: V is hollowed out like a wing in motion because of the word *vautour* {vulture}, like a stomach sunken by hunger because of the word *vorace* {voracious}, like a crater if one thinks of *Vésuve* {Vesuvius} or simply of *volcan* {volcano}; R assumes the rugged profile of *rocher* {rock}; B takes on the pot-bellied shape of *Bibendum* {the Michelin tire logo}, the blubbering lips of *bébé* {baby}, or the flabby effect of *bémol* {a flat note}; P acquires the loftiness of *potence* {gallows} or *prince;* M, the majesty of *mort* {death} or *mère* {mother}; C, the concavity of *cavernes* {caverns}, *conques* {conches}, or *coquilles* {shells}, like eggs ready to be broken." [34] The digraphs Œ and Æ share in evoking classical Antiquity: *æ* stands for latinity, "with its alternating tintinnabulations of bronze (*a*) and of crystal (*e*)"; *œ* is "more visceral, because of the circularity of the *o* and its thicker sonority, in closer relationship with the stomach and the heavy parts of the body," but also because *œ* is found in *œuf* {egg}, *œil* {eye}, *bœuf* {beef}, *œsophage* {esophagus} (in which one can hear *les ophages,* like *les intestins* {intestines} and *les entrailles* {entrails}) — and because *œ,* "with its convolutions, its two letters imprisoning each other, inextricably tied and tangled up together," evokes "the ever mysterious image of the labyrinth, of original chaos and of life hidden away in the darkest recesses of the organic deep": the ancient Greece of *Œdipus,* of course, whose traces survive in *Philopoemen.*[35] Finally, one last series owes its success to the felicitous convergence of phonic and graphic mimeticisms: *ravin* {ravine}, whose *v* "explains its essence" (the idea of a fissure or cleft) both through its sharp sound and through its acute angle; *mort* {death}, whose only vowel *o* represents the entrance to a tunnel or an underworld (Hades, of course) that reverberates with the echo of a tolling bell; *gouffre* {chasm}, which begins with a "stifled cry" of "frightened surprise" and ends in the noise of a fall and a *"fortissimo* of terror" (*ff*). Last and at last, *calme* {quietude} is a landscape that might have escaped from Claudel's "Idéogrammes occidentaux": "Perfectly calm, with the texture of a placid lake ... the medial L in this word is a solitary tree growing between the undulation of M and the syllable *ca,* the safely nestled cube of a little cabin."[36]

⊚ Gradually, the lexical investment of the values of linguistic elements has led us to a mimetic interpretation of whole *vocables,* read as so many mimological and/or mimographic pictures, in the style of Nodier or of Claudel. Out of the hundred or so reveries on nouns scattered throughout *Biffures,* we might try drawing up a new version of Nodier's *Dictionnaire des onomatopées,* one last juicy example of lexical Cratylism. As a matter of fact, this attempt would come to an abrupt halt, for a reason that, as we shall see, touches upon the essential characteristic of Leiris's linguistic imagination. Here are a few Leirisian mimologies, then: *Noël,* whose dieresis "hardens the second vowel like a frost and shoots its bright double point toward the stable"; *Balthazar,* its "triple *a* set ringing like a gong or a knell by the sturdy frame of consonants"; *bristol* {smooth cardboard}, which imitates the noise of a card bent "first one way, then the other"; *métal,* "jointed by three consonants resting on two very pure vowels and stripped of all traces of gangue"; *bronze,* the "humming of bells"; *airain* {brass}, the "noise of helmets and weapons clanging together"; *chemise* {shirt}, the "slight rustling of my father's starched shirt cuffs when he buttoned them over his wrists or removed them."[37] And that is about all.

Why? Because the vast majority of the lexical glosses recorded in *Biffures* contain something other than a simple imitation of the signified by the phonic or graphic signifier. Let us test out, for instance, *Pâques* {Easter}, a "name crackling like sugar, with an aptly circumflexed *a* that mouths the round shape of a decorated egg." Clearly, the direct and quite effective evocation of the Easter egg by the shape of *a* is, as it were, redoubled and overdetermined by the resemblance between *Pâques* and some other words. These, moreover, are present in the gloss (*craquetant* {crackling} and *sucre* {sugar}), and guarantee its gustatory and tactile value by an entirely different means: that of lexical association or *indirect motivation,* which is quite familiar to us from the "etymologies" in the *Cratylus* and whose main function, as we know, is to palliate or rather to disguise {*sōma-sēma*} the gap in mimesis. *Pâques* does not "crackle," or does not do so enough, but it does rhyme with *craque,* which lends it some of its mimetic value.

Now, let us examine *Caïn* {Cain}: its hiatus "grates aggressively — the scraping of a spiked, spiny mass against another spiked, spiny mass — " a direct mimesis of wickedness. But here is the rest of the gloss: "The dieresis marking the *i* corresponds to a sort of grimace, with fleshy jaws curled up to bare two pointy canines protruding out over the other teeth." In this case, we realize that the mimetic harshness of the hiatus and the dieresis is at the very least confirmed by another harshness — the one induced by the parallel *Caïn-canine,* which has been carefully anticipated by *babines* {fleshy jaws}, without any mimesis other than the resemblance between the two vocables. In a parallel way the antithetical gentleness {*douceur*} of *caillou* {pebble} owes much to its relation with *doux* {gentle} and *mouillé* {wet}.[38] *Nabuchodonosor* {Nebuchadnezzar} grants the Assyrian despot his disproportionately long reign," but the *or* {gold} of his robe belongs to the rhyme.[39] And if *Lannion* "sounds really rustic" and evokes "peasants going to market with their basket handles over their arms," the homophony *Lannion-campagne-panier* {Lannion-countryside-basket} doubtless has some part in it.[40]

In all these cases, lexical association plays a minor role, so to speak, at once masked by an interpretation purporting to be purely mimetic and exposed by the presence — which can hardly be unwitting — of one or more vocables that become associated in the very text of the interpretation, as if the author wanted to set a trap for us and to give us the key for it at the same time. In point of fact, the main purpose of Leirisian reverie is not mimetic interpretation but rather indirect motivation, the play between words {*le jeu entre les mots*}. This emerges quite clearly in the following childhood version of folk etymology, a risky interpretation of "distorted words suggesting riddles." These would be a bunch of words or syntagms, unknown to or misapprehended by the child, usually proper names, which are always more opaque, as we know, or the words of songs or soliloquies, all the more confusing because they are often heard on the old family phonograph. These words are distorted, then, and reinterpreted according to an analysis or an affinity judged to be more true to life than the enigmatic vocable itself: *à Billancourt* becomes *habille-en-cour; Salpêtrière* {the Salpêtrière cemetery} becomes *salle Pétrière* {the Pétrière room}; *en guerre s'en allait* turns into *en berçant la laisse;* Hugo's *étranges syllabes* {strange syllables} becomes *tranche-*

syllabes {syllable-slices}, a perfect emblem of eponymic analysis.[41] Manon's *petite table* {little table} gives birth to a *petit totable,* and immediately the motivating reverie begins searching for homophonies that can make sense of this accidental neologism: *table,* of course, *étable* {stable}, *retable, potable* {water}, whence *lavabo* {washbasin}. On top of all this, the pressure of context (Des Grieux at the seminary)[42] directs the search for the likely object toward church or sacristry furniture, somewhere between a *prie-dieu* and a *guéridon* {pedestal table}. Very tellingly, the latter is rejected despite its mimetic adequacy, "even though the stumbling quality of its first syllable very precisely mimics the noise of the pedestal table's legs — their bumping or scratching sound — when someone pulls it over the floor in order to put it somewhere else." *Totable* (or *tetable*) is thus left half-defined, drawing all its magic from the fact that it "designates nothing while seeming to signify something, and remains the label of pure nothingness or of a forever incomprehensible object."

"It is likely," adds Leiris, "that a little something always clings to the skirts of these words that sound as if they correspond to a particular reality but are actually devoid of any kind of meaning. Herein lies their *revelatory* charm, since they are by definition formulas for what is the most impossible to formulate, the names of incredible beings that seem to fill a world beyond our laws." The *paroles oiseuses* {idle words} of Polin's soliloquy, which become *paranroizeuses,* are initially oriented by their context toward trooper folklore, and to the parade ground of the Boulevard Suchet, an orientation confirmed by rustic phonics ("a hick name, water-wallowing {*pateaugeant*}, rainy, ... a condensation of plain fatigues, hobnailed boots, the wet noise of footsteps, clumsy oafs doing army exercises"). Further support for *paranroizeuses* is sought in *palissade* {palisade}, *barricade, balayeuse* {street sweeper}, *demoiselle* {young lady}, and *arroseuse* {water sprinkler} for an instrumental allusion to men at work on the street; in *octroi* {city toll}, *roi* {king}, *pavois* {bulwark}, and *tournoi* {tournament} for more historical prestige; in *zouave, patois* {dialect}, *ouailles* {flock}, *paroisse* {parish}, and *Fouillis-les-oies* {Hicktown}, only to slide back into provincial or outlying muck. These are various attempts (and errors) made in order to get the floating signified to agree with the homophonic possibilities of the signifier, as if one were to look up the definition of a word in a dictionary of rhymes. In a last example, the signified — or rather the designated person, since we are dealing with a proper name — is already known, and the child assigns him a more nearly correct name by mistake, a *felix culpa:* this is *Dictolétien* for *Dioclétien* {Diocletian}. The epenthetic *ct* fashions a name "of stronger stuff, with a more angular and sharper outline."[43] So much for direct motivation; the rest will proceed by lexical associations: *dictateur* {dictator}, *licteur* {lictor}, *pactole* {pay dirt}, *pectoraux* {pectorals} — connotations derived from physical strength, military imperium, and profitable conquests.

Thus, the majority of the reveries on names and nouns in *Biffures* designate their mediators or motivational triggers, with an accommodating attitude that leaves no doubt as to the nature of the method used or, rather, the *rule of the game {la règle du jeu}*. *Blaise* is as pale as a *falaise* {cliff} — here, exceptionally, the other mediator, *blême* {pallid}, is passed over in silence and perhaps unnoticed; *Abel* is *bel* {handsome} and good; *Moïse* {Moses} drifts on the *Oise* River in a cradle made of *osier* {willow}; *Bethléem* {Bethlehem} "contains the good warmth of the powerful *haleine* {breath} from the *bête* {beast} in the stable"; *Épiphanie* {Epiphany} is adorned with a grace as *fanée* {faded} as "Fanny"; the *Philistins* {Philistines} are "greenish *intestins* {intestines} tangled up in a ball of *fil* {string}, rumbling with *instincts indistincts* {vague urges}"; *Jésus-Christ* evokes *crypte* {crypt} and *cris* {cries} shouted out from the *croix* {cross}; *Éléazar* slips under the belly of an *éléphant* as huge as the Saint-*Lazare* railway station; *Perséphone* combines *perce-oreille* {earwig} and *gramo-phone*, whose *diaphragme* {diaphragm} is linked to *fragment*, an *anfractuosité* {crevice} open to *fracas* {noise}; *laiton* {brass}, the exemplary alloy, evokes the smelting of metals through the *liquidité* {liquid sound} of *lait* {milk}; an *expérience* {experiment} is *patiente* {laborious} and *sérieuse* {serious}, halfway between *espérance* {hope} and *expédient* {expediency}; *éclair* {lightning} is antithetically yoked to *éclipse*; *verglas* {black ice} starts with *verre* {glass} and ends with *glas* {knell}; *Waterloo* rains down bilingually, one drop for Wellington, one drop for Napoleon, and so on.[44] One hesitates to reduce to their lexical analysis in this way such ever so carefully knotted and intertwined patterns, whose subtle convolutions and complicated ramifications sometimes envelop an entire chapter, as in the case of *Perséphone*.

By way of compensation for many other possible examples, let us linger for a while over Leiris's commentary on *Saül*. Omission of the dieresis orients the word toward *roi-saule* {willow-king}, somewhere between King *Candaule* and *roi des Aulnes* but not unrelated to King *Lear* "(or perhaps *roi-lyre* {lyre-king}), mad old monarch who wanders around in the wind that transforms his beard of *saule pleureur* {weeping willow} into an Aeolian harp."[45] Madness brings Saul and Lear together, but the name Lear, which in French is phonetically irregular, is magically recaptured in *lyre* through association with the harp of David, an association motivated in its turn by the analogy between David facing Saul's demons and Orpheus facing the beasts. Now to reconstruct the net spun out of *saule* {willow}: Shakespeare leads us to the *Romance* {love song} of Desdemona, another incantation fated to calm other royal fits of rage; superimposed on this network of literary allusions is a second lexical pattern — a more soothing one (*pendule, scrupule, calcul* {pendulum, scruple, calculation}) — for this noun, "bedecked as if with two silver droplets falling, at *crépuscule* {twilight}, from the small bell on a *mule*"). This association is soothing but "fallacious,"

289

since it assigns gentleness and moderation to an immoderate character, "irascible and cruel"; the gloss must be interpreted, therefore, in an opposite sense, as a mask and a denial. Yet this description does not take into account the pattern of patterns, which is the link that their shared dieresis establishes between the various biblical names — the Hebraic *Caïn, Moïse, Ésaü, Saül,* and *Noël:* the "duality of the dieresis" is "the badge of its ambiguous power," the point of departure for "some of the strangest itineraries I had occasion to travel, in my childhood, through that world of will-o'-the-wisps and fantasies that emanates from the *frondrières* of language." [46]

These interlexical relations, "phonic analogies that establish term by term a network of strange relationships," justify the choice of the "double figure" [47] of the title — *bifurs/biffures* — designating exactly that type of "linguistic accident" which is at once a switching-over, a branching-off of thought riding on the rails of formal analogy, and a straying both of the tongue that "forks" and corrects itself and of the pen that wanders in all directions before crossing out its wrong mark {*trace*}: half-deliberate punning, in which the perpetuation of paternal mannerisms and familial refrains is perhaps more potent than Leiris would like;[48] a half-slip of the tongue or pen ("no sooner unleashed than erased"); the stuff of revelation in the service of an autobiography that is also, in a subtler and deeper way than *Manhood,* a self-analysis.

In formal terms, each one of these *biffures* functions like a partial (dreamed-of) etymology: *laiton* uses *lait* to motivate its essential character as an alloyed metal, writing off the prosaic and vaguely depreciatory pseudoinflection {*-on*}; *Dictolétien* is *dictatorial* only by virtue of its first syllable, and so on. But clearly, in a good many instances, the same vocable benefits from two or three associations that end up concealing it in its totality. We might amuse ourselves, then, by arranging side by side, as in a dictionary of etymologies rather than of onomatopoetic expressions, the word-object and the inferential nodes of its motivation. A series like this,[49] for example, might result:

BLAISE	*blême falaise*
BETHLÉEM	*haleine de bêtes*
ÉCLAIR	*éclipse claire*
EXPÉRIENCE	*expédient d'espérance*
PERSÉPHONE	*perce aphone*
PHILISTIN	*fil d'intestins aux instincts indistincts*
VERGLAS	*verre, glas*
WATERLOO	water, *l'eau*

In these reduced versions of a few *biffures,* readers familiar with Leiris will easily identify the dominant technique of his *Glossaire* {Glossary}, which can be described as a sort of half-humorous, half-poetic formalization of speculations on names and nouns,[50] analogous to those retrieved or reconstructed in the text of *Biffures*. Of course, such a description does not claim to establish an actual filiation between the two works, whose diachronic relationship is, moreover, inverse, since *Glossaire* is quite a bit earlier than *Biffures*.[51] But this description does do justice, as well it should, to the autobiographical character of the latter work: that is, to its status as a *document* (albeit a partly factitious one) on childhood thoughts, which invites us to see these thoughts as the ground, if not the very stuff, of later elaborations, including those in *Glossaire*. Whereas *Biffures* recounts or imitates an *experiment,* with all its trial and error, its multiple enticements, its blind gropings, its revisions, its advances, its impasses, its errancies, its blank desertions, its ambiguous and uncertain results, *Glossaire* offers a series of finished and peremptory verbal objects, stamped with that (illusory) seal of finality which is the mark of the "poetic." Nevertheless, the important point here is not what distinguishes the two works, but rather, as we shall see, what they have in common.

ⓓ From the viewpoint of the formal relationship between the gloss and the word entry, the items in *Glossaire* can be divided into four types.[52] I will arrange these in order of increasing complexity, which coincides with the order of increasing frequency anyway.[53]

The first type operates in the way that the elements of a rebus or a crossword puzzle do, where one letter or a group of letters "phonetically" represents the word to be reconstructed by spelling them out: thus, GN yields *géhene* {Gehenna} and ABC yields *abaisser* {to lower}. For want of a better term, let us baptize this procedure *lexicalized spelling.* Obviously, the distinctive characteristic of the *Glossaire* here lies in the fact that the activity of spelling is practiced on a group of letters that already compose a word; therefore, it consists in spelling out the letters of a word in order to extract from it a group of words, or even a phrase, that will form its gloss. In this way, CHAÎNE {chain} can be read as *c'est hache haïe et noeud;* CHEVAL {horse}, *c'est achevé à ailes* (Pegasus); HOMME {man}, *à chaud, aime et meut;* MER, *émeut aires;* WALHALLA, *double, vais à ailes, hache à ailes est là!* And, in a bit more approximative fashion: OPIUM, *au pays eu, aime et hume;* COEUR, *c'est haut! sa cohue erre.* And still further removed (a metagloss is definitely needed): MÈRE, *et Meuh! exsangue rave, et Reuh! (C'est une vache).*[54]

The second type is that of the *alē theia* in the *Cratylus* — analysis: CONTRADICTION — *contrat d'Ixion;* LIQUEUR — *liecoeur;* MORPHINE — *mort fine;* TRANSCENDANCE — *transes sans danse;* and, slightly disguised, DIEU (*dit oeufs*) — *il dit; ses paroles sont des oeufs.*[55]

The third type is distortion by a metaplasm either of the consonant (RIVIÈRE — *civière;* SOURCE — *course*) or of the vowel (ANTHROPOLOGIE — *en tripes au logis;* JÉSU-CHRIST — *gésier creux*), or by metathesis, which may be graphic (AVE-NIR — *navire;* BAISER — *braise;* SIGNE — *il singe:* this one is truly a mimetic sign) or phonic and generally a bit more approximative: BOURREAU — *beau rouge;* PATRIE — *tripaille.* The very title of Leiris's book belongs in this category: GLOS-SAIRE — *j'y serre mes gloses.* Some of these metaplasms clarify and motivate the reversal as expressive of an inversion of meaning: CLERGÉ — *"j'éclaire" à l'envers;* JARDIN — *retourné, il donne un nid de rage* (nidraj).[56]

The fourth and last type, which is by far the most frequent, uses the resources of the two preceding types in order to build upon the entry word, or the *theme word,* a more developed syntagm that serves as its phonic expansion or paraphrase. Again, one can quite easily recognize the analytical technique, exploited more freely in glosses like the following ones, in which I have offset the epenthetic elements in brackets: PARI — *Pa[scal] rit;* CRATÈRE — *[il] cra[che la] terre;* ÉGLISE — *[des] aigles [s'y en]lisent;* CADENCE — *quad[rature du sil]ence;* or the technique of metathesis in SPERME — *terme du spasme.* The various distributions and substitutions mingle and are redoubled in more complex glosses such as PRINTEMPS — *l'empreinte de Pan;* AQUARIUM — *square humide des requiems;* ARMÉE — *merde amère;* FENÊTRE — *fait nôtre un air neuf.* The redoubling is particularly noticeable in PSYCHANALYSE — *lapsus canalisés au moyen d'un canapé-lit;* then everything is scrambled into multiple anamorphoses in VER-BIAGE — *herbage des mots sans vie;* ALGÈBRE — *abrégé agile des givres cérébraux;* ANTIQUITÉ — *temps inquietant quitté, que hantaient les Titans;* ICARE — *le hic qui le contrecarra, c'est carence de la cire;* OEDIPE — *yeux perdus pour ce peu: le meurtre d'un père hideux, le déduit d'une mère adipeuse;* JUDITH — *Juive judicieuse: tire la tige justicière du gîte putassier de ses jupes;* and, for a finale, the longest one, ACROBATE — *embarqué de bas en haut, de haut en bas, il bat du corps et baratte l'air sans accrocs.*[57]

These paraphrases recall, of course, the most elaborate Socratic "etymologies," such as SÉLÈNE (*sélas aei néon te kaì hénon*); Saussure's paragrams (SCIPIO — *Taurasia cisauna Samnio cepit*); and also — but with the full effect of dissemination reserved for the signifier — those *gloses,* as they are called, or medieval *farcitures* that Paul Zumthor describes as follows: "Discourse is conceived of as implied in a single word ... whose amplification constitutes discourse itself, a word that discourse both deploys and is engendered by."[58] But these distant authorities were probably not on Leiris's mind. *Glossaire* is dedicated to Robert Desnos and bears a direct family resemblance to various plays on language by the Surrealists, especially the poems of Rrose Sélavy, which link the two sides of a spoonerism into one proposition (*Rrose Sélavy se demande si les* Fleurs du mal *ont modifié les moeurs du phalle; Aragon recueille in extremis l'âme d'Aramis sur un lit d'estragon*).[59] To a certain extent, Leiris simply reduces the proposition to its original metathesis by proposing statements of this type: FLEURS DU

MAL: *moeurs du phalle,* or ARAGON: *âme d'Aramis sur un lit d'estragon.*[60] But this formal modification entails a striking functional change, which may probably be deduced from the Socratic precedent alluded to above: the arrangement of wordplay into dictionary item, with the entry word followed by its gloss, inevitably confers on that syntagm an apparently *explicative* function, either in regard to the signifier (etymology) or in regard to the signified (definition). This is exactly how Leiris, in the 1925 preface, describes the operation of ordinary dictionaries, "in which words are catalogued and given a well-defined meaning ... based on usage and etymology," given their "everyday meaning" and their "etymological meaning."[61] Formally, Leiris's glosses look like etymologies, in the sense that they are related to the signifier of the entry word through phonic and/or graphic analogy—as in the various examples just discussed; at the same time, they inevitably have a *definitional* function: that is to say, they are tantamount to an explanation of the entry word's signified.

Following Philippe Lejeune,[62] let us compare a Leirisian gloss to an entry in an actual dictionary for the word *cratère* {crater}. The dictionary gives us, on the one hand, an etymology (Latin, *crater*), a simple (more or less literal) phonic analogue, and, on the other hand, a definition ("mouth of a volcano"), a semantic equivalence without formal analogy. This division makes for a striking demonstration of the conventionality of the signifying relation: the dictionary is essentially (and necessarily) Hermogenist. As for *Glossaire,* it offers us the phonic analogue and the semantic equivalent in one single statement (*il crache la terre* {it spits out earth}: *crache/terre = cratère*}. In other words, *Glossaire* proposes (or imposes) the *coincidence of phonic analogy and semantic equivalence* and hence, implicitly, a reciprocal suitability, the adequation of phonic and semantic levels—in short, the motivation (indirect, in the present case) of the sign. *Glossaire* is a Cratylist dictionary. Accordingly, *cratère,* like a Socratic eponym, is a correct word {*un mot juste*} because it says *exactly* { *justement*} what it wants to say (let us keep in mind, too, this adverb's temporal sense: "coincidentally"), or if you prefer, because it (almost) merges with its own definition, since its signifier (the entry word) is analogous to its signified (the gloss): *estin hoion logos to onoma.*[63]

An objection could be raised here, on apparently good grounds, that this example is too well chosen and that other glosses do not work so readily in this way, because the semantic adequation of the phonic paraphrase is not as strong or as obvious. As a matter of fact, it happens that the pressure of meaning (the horror of a semantic void, a natural frame of mind) on the one hand, and the infinite availability (or plasticity) of associations on the other, allow—as a reading of *Glossaire* indirectly proves—no phonic paraphrase to escape the *effect of motivation.* (This effect of motivation shows up in other Surrealist language games such as *cadavre exquis* {exquisite corpse}: the most haphazard combination of words always makes sense.)[64] Philippe Lejeune deliberately invents a gloss that is as arbitrary as possible: CRATÈRE — *crabe de l'éther;* he is immediately forced to recognize that "even *crabe de l'éther* is not entirely innocent of Cratylism."[65] Here, *éther* {ether} suffices to evoke a volcanic projection into the upper atmosphere, in which *crabe* {crab} survives the best it can. Perhaps *crabe délétère* {noxious crab} would offer more resistance, and so on, but the fact remains that the mind can always establish a meaningful relation between the theme word and its gloss, albeit an incongruous one. Whatever the kind of gloss, *Glossaire* inevitably compels us to enter the Cratylian game, where even a refusal to play already (or still) harbors a degree of acquiescence (we have certainly seen this in Plato's *sklērotēs* and in Mallarmé's *jour/nuit*).

Moreover, Leiris's intention is obviously never to seek out the greatest obstacles to this game; among countless possible paraphrases he most often chooses not the most unimaginatively motivated one, of course, but at least the one that will best combine a certain touch of surprise with a certain degree of perceptible appropriateness. Besides, he has explicitly and repeatedly pointed out the semantic function of his glosses. Thus, in *Manhood,* he describes himself as "decomposing the words of the vocabulary and reconstructing them into poetic puns which seemed to me to *explain their deepest meanings*"; and in a bibliographical note to *Brisées,* he recalls "the distant period at which I hoped that a certain way of pulverizing words would allow me to grasp *the last word in all things.*"[66] Naturally, the exact nuance implied each time by these restrictive superlatives — "the deepest," "the ultimate" — remains to be determined. I will come back to this presently.

The *Glossaire* is to indirect motivation, therefore, what the *Dictionnaire des onomatopées françaises* was to direct motivation, and it resoundingly confirms the predominance of indirect motivation in Leiris's Cratylism, whose overall tendency is to effect a remarkable return to the Socratic position. On the one hand (in "Alphabet"), there is the immediate expressiveness of phonic and graphic elements. On the other hand (in *Glossaire* and most of the lexical motivations in *Biffures*), there is a marked expansion of "etymological" motivation. Between the two there remains a weak link, which is, of course, the central one for a pure mimologism: the lexical investment of the values of linguistic elements, which we have seen disappearing almost entirely in favor of puns and various homophonies.

🖗 We seem, then, to have come full circle, our voyage through Cratylusland having returned to its point of departure. But between the aim of Socratic eponymies and that of the etymologies in *Glossaire,* there exists a crucial distinction whose direction is quite clearly indicated by another Leirisian text: "To designate an object by an expression that corresponds to it not figuratively but literally, one would need to know the very essence of that object, which is impossible, since we can know only phenomena, not things in themselves."[67] Here, we find ourselves at the opposite pole of Socrates' requirement that the name or noun should function only to designate (and, according to the Cratylian hypothesis, to imitate) the *essence* of a thing. We have observed the abandonment of this essentialist requirement, or claim, by the mimologists of the neoclassical period, who, forced to choose between essence and mimeticism, preferred to sacrifice the former to the latter, so that the "right" word {*le mot "juste"*} became for them the imitation of one simple "aspect" among others — or, to speak in the Kantian vocabulary of Leiris, the imitation of a simple "phenomenon." But Leiris not only confirms this abandonment; he emphasizes, motivates, and valorizes it, and therein lies the central justification of his enterprise — in *Biffures* as in *Glossaire* — as it is set forth in the preface of *Glossaire*, which should now be quoted in its entirety:

A monstrous aberration causes people to believe that language came into being to facilitate their relations with one another. It is with this end in mind, of usefulness, that they make dictionaries in which words are catalogued and given a well defined meaning (they believe), based on usage and etymology. Now, etymology is a perfectly ineffectual science that is not at all informative about the *true* meaning of a word, that is, the particular, personal signification that each individual ought to assign to it, as his mind pleases. As for usage, it is superfluous to say that it is the lowest criterion to which one could refer.

The everyday meaning and the etymological meaning of a word can teach us nothing about ourselves, since they represent the collective part of language, which was made for all people and not for each of us individually.

By dissecting the words we like, without bothering about conforming either to their etymologies or to their accepted significations, we discover their most hidden qualities and the secret ramifications that are propagated through the whole language, channeled by associations of sounds, forms, and ideas. Then language changes into an oracle, and there we have a thread (however slender it may be) to guide us through the Babel of our minds.[68]

Clearly, for Leiris, the search for a motivated signification is also, and above all, a rejection of "everyday" and "accepted" signification, a rejection of the "collective part of language." The "*true* meaning of a word," known to neither usage nor etymology, is a meaning "*for each of us individually*," a "particular, personal signification that each individual ought to assign to it, as his mind pleases." This formulation inevitably brings to mind another: "Then if a man speaks as *he fancies* he ought to speak, will he speak correctly? ... Well then, suppose *I* give a name to something or other, designating, for instance, that which we now call 'man' as 'horse' and that which we now call 'horse' as 'man,'" and so on.[69] This utterly individualistic attitude, as the reader may recall, is the position of Hermogenes as caricatured by Socrates the better to reject it; the arbitrariness of the sign as individual "fancy" and whim stands opposed to the universality of the natural sign, itself imitative of essence. Leiris totally (and in a sense, legitimately) reverses this opposition: for him, the conventional sign is "collective," and the motivated sign is "arbitrary" because it comes—in principle[70]—from a wholly personal motivation. By definition, convention is contractual and social; mimetic motivation is "hidden," "secret," and refuses collective constraint. Ludic in the most aggressive sense, it represents caprice and revolt.

Hermogenes is a city fellow: that is to say, a man of consensus. His adversary, having become a "poet"—but has he not been one from the beginning?—removes himself from this city, willingly or not (with a little push from Socrates, as we have seen). He goes into exile and retreats into what he decides is the truth—"his" truth—of language and of the world. Henceforth a stranger to all common *communication,* he devotes himself to exploring his interior universe and his interior vocabulary (these are one and the same), out of which he brings to light strange verbal objects bearing his mark and leaving no room for debate—take it or leave it: *Cratyle, il crache son style* {Ever a Cratylus, he spits out his own style}.[71]

CHAPTER 16

Taking Sides with Words

Ⓢ The theoretical formula for Francis Ponge's mimologism[1] fits into one simple and well-known equation: "*PARTI PRIS DES CHOSES* égale *COMPTE TENU DES MOTS*" {taking sides with things equals taking account of words}.[2] Actually, this equivalence is immediately complicated, even disproved, by the addition of some unequal, if not inversely variable, fractions: "Certain texts will have more PPC in their alloy, others more CTM.... No matter. In all cases some of one *and* some of the other must be present. Otherwise, nothing comes out."[3] Quite clearly, the issue here is the writer's task and not the untouched state of natural language—and it even happens (once) that, like Mallarmé, Ponge seems to make its "failing" {*défaut*} a condition of language's proper use. Thus, he bemoans the perfection of *mimosa*, which leaves him with little to do: "Perhaps what makes my job so difficult is the fact that the name of mimosa is already perfect. Since I know both the bush and the name of mimosa, it becomes hard to find a way to define the thing that is better than this name itself."[4] But this situation remains exceptional, just as the complaint itself remains purely rhetorical and propitiatory: the proof is in the poem. The supposed adequation between the "density of things" and the "semantic density of words"[5] is not really an obstacle to Ponge's writing; it is one of its resources, and often its aim.

Words in themselves constitute "a concrete world, as dense, as real as the external world."[6] Like any object, the word has its density and its three dimensions, not in space but, more subtly, one "for the eye," one "for the ear, and possibly the third one is something like their signification."[7] Further on, Ponge says: "Maybe the word is an object with three dimensions, hence an object in the true sense. But the third dimension lies in this signification."[8]

The first two dimensions display no ambiguity, even though (as we will see)

Throughout *Mimologics*, Genette has used the phrase *parti pris* (deliberate decision, bias) to describe the position of the most devoted mimologists who believe that words are, or should be made to be, phonic and/or graphic equivalents for the things to which they refer. Besides having this theoretical context the French title of chapter 16, "Le Parti pris des mots", alludes to the ambiguous title of one of Francis Ponge's best-known works: Le Parti pris des choses (1942). Has Ponge invested his poetics in things (*choses*) over words (*mots*), or in words over things, or in both at the same time?

the acoustic aspect is barely present in Ponge's work. The third dimension demands a bit more attention. As a matter of fact, it consists of that diachronic density revealed for every vocable by each item in Émile Littré—Ponge's preferred tool, as everyone knows.[9] This historical dimension is deposited and as if crystallized into a proliferating polysemy: "All the words of all natural languages—and especially of languages that have a literature, such as German or French, and that also have (how can I put it?) come from other languages which have already had monuments, such as Latin—these words, each word is a column of the dictionary, each word is a thing with extension, even in space, in the dictionary, but each word is also a thing that has a history, that has changed meaning, that has one, two, three, four, five, six significations."[10] Inversely corresponding to this semantic multiplicity, which tears the vocable apart into disparate *senses,* is the proliferation of homophonic parallels, which provides the basis for the game {*jeu*} of indirect motivations. Thus, etymology, whether fanciful or not, becomes "the poet's most necessary science."[11]

Here, as in Plato, etymology can be approached through the eponymy of proper names. *Claudel* is a cross between *clame* {proclaims} and *claudique* {limps}, while *Braque* combines *Bach* and *Baroque,* but also, through an anagram of one of his favorite subjects, *barque renversée* {an overturned boat}.[12] *Malherbe* is "something male (*mâle*) ... something free (*mauvaise herbe* {weed})"; and AS-SYRIE {Assyria} is "a cosmetic encrustation {*encrassement cosmétique*} [a certain style of trimming one's beard] in Syria."[13] Next, Ponge extends the procedure to the names of things: "There is something to see {*voir*} in *voyage*"; "as there is *tamis* {a sieve} in *tamaris* {tamarisk}, so there is *mima* in *mimosa*"; *olive* is close to *ovale* {oval}; *escargot* {snail} starts as *escarbille* {a bit of grit} and ends up where {the English} 'go on' starts; and, as we know, *cageot* {crate} is in all senses "halfway between *cage* and *cachot* {dungeon}."[14] *Ustensile* {implement} takes after both *utile* {useful} (also, *outil* {tool}) in its frequentative form, and *ostensible* {conspicuous}: it is an instrument we use often and hang up on the kitchen wall. *Ustensile* also has some kinship with *combustion* and, when hanging from its nail on the wall, has some inflectional homophony with *oscille* {oscillates}.[15] As in Varro, *pré* {meadow} is at the same time *paré* {bedecked}, *préparé* {prepared}, "Near {*Près*} rock and brook, / Ready {*Prêt*} to be mown or grazed"; taken alone, *pré* is the "past participle par excellence" and the "prefix {*préfixe*} of prefixes."[16] But suffixes also play their part, for it is no accident that *lézard* {lizard} shares its ending with *flemmard* {idler}, and so on; nor that *gymnaste* {gymnast} shares its ending with *dévaste* {devastates}, *chaste,* and BASTE! {so what!}; nor indeed that *huître* {oyster} has the same ending as *opiniâtre* {stubborn}, *blanchâtre* {whitish} and a few other words.[17] As for *hirondelle* {swallow}, it is analyzed, in Socrates' manner, into *horizondelle* or *ahurie-donzelle,* an analysis that immediately suggests a rewording into some Leirisian gloss, as always: *hirondelle — horizon d'ailes.*[18] Finally, here as elsewhere, ludic etymology leads rather quickly to coinages made out of portmanteau words: *pâtheux,* which conjoins *pâte* {paste} and *pathos;* the damp *amphibiguïté* of autumn; or the *tonitruismes parfumés* {fragrant thundering truisms} of a horse.[19]

We began with the third "dimension" of the word-object, the third route to its "adequation." The second one — phonic motivation — is missing, so to speak. In Ponge, as in Claudel, verbal mimesis in its entirety seems to have taken refuge in the graphic aspect of words: a displacement that comes as no surprise in a writer who is typically "visual" and whose aesthetic is highly pictorial. Ponge "proclaimed" his chosen *parti pris* starting in 1937 and justified it by invoking an evolution of literature itself, from the oral to the written: "There is no doubt that literature *enters us* less and less through the ear, and *leaves us* less and less through the mouth.... There is no doubt that it passes (enters and leaves us) more and more *through the eye.*" What is more, literature has evolved from the written to the printed: "But neither is there any doubt, it seems to me, that literature passes before our eyes less and less in a handwritten form. In practice, the concepts of literature and of typography are at present coterminous.... We are working from this given, much more than we are aware."[20]

Even so, there is nothing systematic in Ponge's mimo(typo)graphy, where all is fortuitous and always unscrupulously ad hoc. Examples include the tortuous Z of *lézard* {lizard}; the vertical I of *pin* {pine}; the B of Braque in the shape of a guitar; the M of *Ministre* {Minister}, with coat and tails and a "procession of official signatures"; the triple s of *Assyriens* {Assyrians}, "like a comb passing with difficulty through a curly fleece of hair"; the "o split into œ" in *œillet* {carnation}, like the bud that splits open and bursts into languets; the *gymnaste* {gymnast} of the Belle Époque, with his G delineating goatee, moustache, and lovelock, and his Y, the leotard with two creases at his groin, hitched up to the left; the medial hollow U of *cruche* {jug,}, rimmed by "fragile, rough and easily crackable clay."[21] The V and U that begin and end *verre d'eau* {waterglass} make it "adequate to the object it designates," as though its A (or {small-case} *a?*) "represents the eye which the presence of the water lends to the glass it fills." In this unusual instance, the same *verre d'eau* offers two phonic motivations: the silent, "gray" *e* matching the neutral taste of water, I assume, and the double rolling of the *rr,* "for it seems that simply pronouncing the word VERRE very forcefully or very intensely in the presence of the object it designates would be enough to shatter the object itself, shaken by the vibrations of the voice pronouncing its name. (This would account for one of the main properties of glass: its fragility.)"[22] In another example, the S of *oiseau* {bird} "looks like a resting bird in profile," while the two groups of vowels flanking it are "the two plump fillets of meat surrounding the breastbone" — and for once the reformatory demon of secondary mimologism shows itself: "*The word* OISEAU: *it contains all the vowels. Very well, I approve.*

But, instead of the S as its only consonant, I would have preferred the L of *aile* {wing}: *OILEAU,* or the V of the breastbone, the V of outspread wings, the V of *avis* {Lat., bird}: *OIVEAU.*"[23] Appearances notwithstanding, this has nothing in common with Nodier's mimology, with its "five vowels linked together by one softly sibilant letter." The vowels are there only for the sake of the fleshy mass of the digraph *oi* and the trigraph *eau,* and the consonant, whether found or dreamed up, is only a drawing, despite the additional pun on *aile;* nothing warbles here, and Ponge's bird is, like those of Braque, a songless bird.

Etymology and mimography dominates, and these two features meet again in the exemplary text called "14 JUILLET," which is none other than a reading and justification of its own title. This time, the whole text needs to be quoted:

That day, an entire people rushed up to write on the album of history, on the sky of Paris.

At first, a pike appears, then a flag stiffened by the rush of the onslaught (some see in it a bayonet), then — along with the other pikes, two flails, and a rake {*râteau*} — against the vertical stripes of the trousers of the *sans-culottes,* a bonnet tossed into the air as a sign of joy.

An entire people in the morning with the sun at their backs. And something hangs in the air, something new, a little vain, candid: it is the smell of the white wood of the Faubourg Saint-Antoine — and the J has the shape of a planing tool as well.

The whole word leans forward when written in an English hand, but when pronounced, it starts out as Justice and ends up just as it should be {*Justice, ça y est!*}, and not even the scowling heads of Launay and Flesselles on their pikes can take away the joyous {*joyeux*} aspect of this forest of tall letters, this trembling poplar wood {*peupliers*} which forever replaces in men's memory the massive prison towers.[24]

The double eponymic reading of {14} JUILLET is an indirect motivation: *joyeux* through paronymy; *justice ça y est* through analytic gloss. The mimography includes the pike of *1:* the stiffened flag or bayonet of *4;* the various pikes or vertical stripes of JUILLET, where the two L's are specified as flails, the T as a rake, the dot on the I {*i*} as a bonnet joyously tossed, and finally, J as a planing tool. No use is found for U and E, just as, no doubt, many aspects of the event have not found their ideograms. As usual, the mimological commentary is a set of compromises that accommodate what they can and ignore the rest. Let us not forget the clever first paragraph which, by literalizing and hence remotivating the cliché *inscrire une date* {to write a date into history}, loops the loop and joins the signifying with the signified face of language in a Möbius strip. Yes, this indeed is what we call a *page d'histoire* {a page from history}.

CHAPTER 17

The Genre and
Gender of Reverie

Marriage is *un mystère,* and what mystery? The emblem of the union
of Jesus Christ with his church. And what would have happened to this
mystery if the word *l'Église* had happened to be masculine in Latin?
Stendhal, *On Love*[1]

⑨ Like Nodier or Leiris, whom he cites and discusses several times,[2] Gaston
Bachelard is what he himself calls a "word dreamer" {*rêveur de mots*}, and we
have already seen the terms in which he acknowledges his special debt to the
Dictionnaire des onomatopées. Today, Bachelard is often reproached for his indifference to poetic craft and to the total structure of those works in which he
seems to look only for a sort of fragmentary pretext for reverie — a line here,
an "image" there, without much attention to their context and even less to their
compositional function. This relative indifference could of course be of the same
nature, and stem from the same motives, as that indifference we were able to detect in Nodier himself, through an anticipatory opposition between his linguistic quietism and his Mallarméan will to "compensate for the failing in natural
languages" by the perfection of poetry. When a language is (envisioned as
{*rêvée*}) flawless, poetically satisfying in itself, the task of the poet is virtually reduced to the function of illuminator or foil of language and educator of our linguistic sensibility. In its more indirect way, but just as much as the mimological
gloss, the "poetic image," through an unprecedented but silently expected parallel, also has the role of "causing to resonate in the hollow of words" a "distant
echo" that it has not invented but merely discovered, as if by chance, through
marrying two words that had never met before (*bûcher de sèves* {a sapling pyre};
feu humide {wet fire}) and revealing their profound resonance: "*Bûcher de sèves*
— words never before spoken, the sacred seed of a new language that must think
the world through poetry"; "An image-thought-phrase like Joubert's ('the flame
is a wet fire' {*la flamme est un feu humide*}) is a linguistic feat. In it speech sur-

passes thought." This is because "we are not able to meditate within a prelin-guistic zone"; "language is always a little ahead of our thought and a little more impetuous than love," always "at the command post of the imagination."[3]

Thus, the poetic event, always instantaneous and free of structural relations, because it is always closer to the single vocable, can be for Bachelard, in Roland Barthes's phrase, an object of reading, of pleasure, of happy reverie, without first having been an object of writing in the strong sense: that is, of craft.[4] The read-ing of poetry can even be reduced entirely to word reveries {rêveries de mots} — in an obviously double sense: first, there are words that dream; we have only to listen to these words dreaming in order to dream them in turn, "just as the child listens to the sea in a seashell." And despite certain protests against the "unfair advantage of sounds," the natural inclination of this reverie really lies, as with Nodier, in mimophonic interpretation.[5] For the person who knows how to "explore by ear those syllabic cavities that constitute the sound-structure of a word," clignoter {to flicker} is "an onomatopoeia for the flame of a candle," in which the "uneasiness of the flame" condenses into clashing and trembling syllables; piauler {to pule} is another, "in the minor mode, with tearful eyes"; vaste {vast} is the "power of the spoken word," a "respiratory vocable," which teaches us to "breathe with the air resting on the horizon," by virtue of that a which is "the vowel of boundlessness." In contrast, miasme {miasma} is "a sort of silent onomatopoeia of disgust." Rivière {river}, grenouille {frog}, gar-gouille {gargoyle}, glaïeul {gladiolus} are "water words," the "waggish" speech of liquid consonants: rivière "never stops flowing"; grenouille, "phonetically — in the true phonetics of the imagination — is already a water animal"; gargouille "was a sound before becoming an image, or at least it was a sound that suddenly found its image in stone," fashioned, like itself, to "spew the guttural insults of water"; and the poets are right — experience notwithstanding — to make glaïeul an aquatic flower, for "where song is concerned, realism is always wrong.... the gladiolus, then, is a special sigh of the river, ... the melancholy water in half-mourning... a soft sob forgotten." It is easy to discern in this last gloss the unacknowledged role of indirect motivation (mourning, sob), but Bachelard's commentary puts it down to "liquid speech": to a, "the vowel of the water"; to "the liquid consonants" (r, l, gr, gl); to the "correspondence between word and reality"; and to the semantic expansiveness of onomatopoeia, which, accord-ing to Nodier's precept, is capable of transposing and "delegating" all sensible qualities into verbal sonorities. Because "the ear is much more receptive than we suppose, it quite readily accepts a certain degree of transposition in imita-tion, and before long it imitates the first imitation. With his joy of hearing man combines the joy of active speaking, the joy of his whole physiognomy which expresses a talent for imitation. Sound is only one part of mimologism."[6]

As we can see, Bachelard merely follows and illustrates one of the familiar paths of Cratylian reverie here. His specific contribution—and also, it seems, the most deeply motivated one—involves a less traditional aspect of linguistic functioning, which is the gender of words: his is a motivating, and therefore sexualizing, interpretation of a phenomenon that two clever grammarians (one a psychiatrist) earlier termed, appropriately, the *sexusemblance* {*sexuisemblance*} of substantives.[7]

Everyone knows that the distinction of grammatical gender is neither universal nor identical in all the natural languages that employ it: some have a system with two levels, or with three terms, in which the neuter (inanimate) intervenes, in principle reserving the masculine/feminine opposition for animate and sexed beings. In the latter case, the phenomenon of sexusemblance cannot occur, since no inanimate signified is marked by a pseudosexual index: this is what happens in English, at least when no expressive or poetic intention occasions recourse to personification, a figure of speech that immediately imposes a choice of sex. (This essentially poetic figure also has a familiar, even popular usage: *car* and *ship*, for example, are often feminized in idiomatic usage.) On the other hand, the effect of sexusemblance can appear once the use of the neuter is no longer rigorously systematic, and once certain inanimate things can be masculine or feminine: this is the most frequent case, for example, in Greek, in Latin, or in German; it happens *a fortiori* in modern Romance languages that do not have the neuter.[8] The distribution of inanimate things into masculine and feminine is thus highly capricious, resulting from purely mechanical reasons, a rather striking illustration of the "arbitrariness" of the sign. That, at any rate, is the common view of linguists,[9] a view of which Bachelard is clearly aware but one that hardly suits his purposes: "I would certainly have benefited from a close study of the grammarians. I cannot conceal my astonishment, however, at seeing so many linguists dispose of the problem by saying that the masculine or feminine of nouns comes about haphazardly. Obviously, no reason at all can be found for this if only logical reasons are sought. Perhaps an oneiric study ought to be undertaken."[10] The implicit hypothesis of this project of study, or *genosanalysis*,[11] seems to be that the distribution of genders originally corresponds to a more or less conscious ("oneiric") motivation on the part of the creators of language. Bachelard recounts the delightful conjecture of Bernardin de Saint-Pierre, according to whom women created masculine words to designate objects endowed "with strength and power," and conversely, men created feminine words for objects endowed "with grace and charm." Less imaginative, and usually very little inclined to speculation on motivation, James Harris himself ventured: "In some words these distinctions seem owing to nothing else than to the mere casual structure of the word itself: it is of such a gender, from having such a termination; or from belonging perhaps to such a declension. In others we may imagine a more subtle kind of reasoning, a reasoning which discerns even in things without a sex a distant analogy to that great natural distinction, which (according to Milton) animates the world." [12]

It is clear how sexualizing reverie gets bound up with the theme of mimology: it consists in *justifying* the gender of a noun through a relation of conformity between that gender and the sexual identity metaphorically given to the object named. This motivation is a partial one, since it bears upon only one aspect and not the entirety of the vocable: with Bachelard, it could be said that the feminine gender of the French word *eau* {water} is well suited to the "femininity" of the aquatic element, but this does not imply that the sound, for example, or the graphism of this word has anything feminine about it. Present also is a purely and, as it were, abstractly grammatical motivation that concerns the gender itself and not its material morphological mark. This kind of motivation, therefore, should not be confused with that variety of classical mimologism which consists in motivating and justifying a morpheme of gender by a phonic characteristic claimed to be "adequate" to its function: just so, Bachelard speaks of the "softness" {*douceur*} or the "unhurriedness" {*lenteur*} of feminine endings. [13] Likewise, Proudhon observed that "in all natural languages the feminine ending [originally, according to him, a mark of the diminutive] was softer, more delicate, one might say, than the masculine: Hebrew, Greek, Latin, etc., use the *a*, French the silent *e*, and it is generally agreed that these two endings give a style of lightness and grace." For Grimm, "the masculine gender was the one that received the strongest and most perfect impress; the feminine gender took on a less sharply defined and more ponderous form; in the masculine gender the consonants and short vowels dominate, in contrast to the long vowels in the feminine gender." And according to Renan, "if *a* and *i* are characteristically feminine vowels in all natural languages, it is probably because these vowels are better suited to the female organ than the virile sounds *o* and *ou*." [14] In principle, this morphophonic motivation applies to properly feminine (animate) nouns such as *lupa* versus *lupus* and *louve* versus *loup*. [15] It may also coincide (as we often see in Bachelard) with the sexualizing motivation of genders for inanimate things, thereby reinforcing their effect, as in, say, *rivière* {fem.: river} versus *ruisseau* {masc.: stream}, or *cuillère* {fem.: spoon} versus *couteau* {masc.: knife}; but the first does not merge with the second. The same psychological projections are invested in both but through completely distinct linguistic processes. Properly speaking, sexusemblance is independent of motivation by the morphemes of gender; it focuses on the notion of gender itself, without involving its morphemes— which are most often, at least in French, external to the word anyway: *eau* {water} is feminine only through its determining marks on other words (its article, its adjective) which "agree" with it; *rivière* {tributary river} is morphologically not more feminine than *fleuve* {main river}, nor *femme* {woman} than *homme* {man}, and *soeur* {sister} is rather less so than *frère* {brother}, just as *fagus* {beech-tree} was less so than *poeta* {poet}.[16]

What we have here, then, is a relatively abstract psycholinguistic phenomenon in which the signifier is not necessarily a phonic or graphemic reality but a grammatical category, whatever its mark or absence of a mark. As for the signified, it is obviously metaphorical, and the role of the imagination lies essentially in the construction of this metaphor.[17] The justificatory motivation will therefore consist of interpreting the object's character, or at least one or the other of its characteristics, in terms of femininity or masculinity. This interpretation itself presupposes an analogical extension of the definition of the sexes, and of course this extension, which is anything but objective, proceeds in its turn from several typically ideological investments that under other circumstances would have attracted the critical notice of Bachelard as an epistemologist. Thus, as Harris writes, "we may conceive such substantives to have been considered as masculine which were 'conspicuous for the attributes of imparting or communicating; or which were by nature active, strong, and efficacious, and that indiscriminately whether to good or to bad; or which had claim to eminence, either laudable or otherwise. The feminine on the contrary were such as were conspicuous for the attributes either of receiving, of containing, or of producing and bringing forth; or which had more of the passive in their nature than of the active; or which were peculiarly beautiful and amiable; or which had respect to such excesses as were rather feminine than masculine.'"[18] Thus, the sun is generally masculine because it gives light, heat, and fecundating energy; the moon is feminine because its reflected beams are more subdued.[19] The sky is masculine as the source of fertilizing rains, the earth feminine as the mother of all living creatures; the ocean could have been feminine as the receptacle of all waters, but its terrible power tipped the scale in favor of the masculine. For the same reason, time, God, sleep, and death are most often masculine; virtue is feminine because of its charm and its beauty; vice, masculine for its ugliness; Fortune, feminine because of its caprices, and so on.[20]

Clearly, the central ground of metaphorical extension is quite simple here, being directly borrowed from the characteristics of (the masculine idea of) the sexual relation: the male is active, powerful, and plain; the female is passive, fertile, and pretty. We have encountered this oppositional theme in Bernardin and Proudhon, and, inevitably, it is again found in Bachelard, except for a few nuances: the feminine value of fertility disappears almost entirely, and when he comes across it in Proudhon, Bachelard rejects it as a superficial rationalization; also, he reproaches Proudhon for leaving the motif of inferior size unresolved, but he hardly deals with it himself. For Bachelard, the real theme of the feminine is revealed by the two characteristics attributed to "feminine sonorities,"

305

which are *softness* {*douceur*} (or sensibility {*tendresse*}), and *unhurriedness* {*lenteur*}. What valorizes femininity is its fundamental character of depth {*profondeur*} and intimacy {*intimité*}. The masculine is the gender of external action and exploitation: "To love things according to their use belongs to the masculine. They are the counters for our actions, for our energetic actions." The feminine is the gender of contemplation and intimate communion with a natural profundity: "But to love things intimately, for themselves, in the unhurried ways of the feminine, is to enter into the labyrinth of the secret nature of things." This fundamental opposition inspires several of the couples [21] that Bachelard so enjoys pairing: *l'angle/la courbe* {angle/curve},[22] *le courage/la passion, le jour/la nuit* {day/night}, *le sommeil/la mort* {sleep/death}, *le berceau/la berce* {cradle/crib} ("in which one knows true rest, since one sleeps in the feminine" — a telling formula), "the faithful wristwatch and the exact stopwatch," "the friendly lamp and the stupid lampstand," "the forbidding gateway and the welcoming door," the "staight and vigorous" fir tree and the palm tree (feminine in the poem by Heinrich Heine), with "all its fronds open, attentive to every breeze." Here, the passage from one language to another permits a "conquest of the feminine" and hence — a typical inference — an "enrichment of the entire poem," fortuitously turning the tables on "the extraordinary inversion" (in German) that makes the sun feminine and the moon masculine, a linguistic scandal, an exceptional failing in a natural language, which gives the (French) dreamer "the impression that his reverie is being perverted."[23] Other scandals include the masculinity of *fleuve* {major river}, of *Rhin* and *Rhône*, "linguistic monsters" that betray the "femininity of true water," which is illustrated in contrast by the names of those true *rivières* {tributary rivers} such as the *Aube*, the *Moselle*, and the *Seine* and the *Loire* (so much for geographical terminology); or further, the masculinity of *Brunnen* {brook}, which contrasts with the correct femininity of *fontaine* {fountain}. Yet, to some extent, Bachelard ends up legitimizing (remotivating) this reverse reverie: "The same water does not flow from *fontaine* as from *Brunnen*," since the latter "makes a deeper noise" and "courses less smoothly"; it hints at what might be the paradoxical truth of water in the masculine, "but it is undoubtedly a temptation of the devil to try dreaming in a language which is not the mother tongue. I must be faithful to my *fontaine* as my source."

Indeed, the theme of femininity presides over all aquatic reverie and suggests a sexualizing reduction of the famous quadripartition of the four elements: water is essentially feminine and thereby opposes fire, which is essentially masculine.[24] Still, in a moment of extreme indulgence and conciliation, Bachelard discovers or welcomes the femininity of *la flamme*, the flame of *la chandelle* {candle}, tardy and silent. For its part, the earth is feminine and at least once is opposed to the sky and thus implicitly to the masculine air: so the earth inspires a (double) *rêverie* {fem.}, whereas the air presides over *fancies* {*songes*, masc.}.

306

Of course, we have to cheat a little here, for feminine water commands masculine *dreams* {*rêves*, masc.}, and earthly reveries come partly from the *will* {*la
volonté*}, a feminine word for a virile reality, and partly from *repose* {*le repos*},
a masculine word for the most feminine of states.[25] (It is true that femininity
is above all the *site* for a repose that is implicitly the man's.) But the essential
bipartition remains clear: air and fire divide the masculine realm above, while
earth and water share the feminine empire below.[26]

Such a division might inspire a unilateral valorization of masculinity as the
force of highmindedness and hence as a sign of superiority, "well founded or
otherwise," as Harris said. As we have seen, however, this is not Bachelard's
way, or more precisely, his emphasis lies almost entirely on the compensatory
countervalorization that exalts the feminine as *profundity* {*profondeur*}: that is,
as inferiority maintained but valorized as such.[27] The empire of the feminine
represents a profundity that is receptive, calming, and conciliatory — that of the
refuge: the maternal "breast," of course; the return to the security and embrace
of the womb. Thus, *The Poetics of Reverie* is not only a sexualizing reverie but
also a *feminizing* reverie, a quest for the femininity of language, in which each
"conquest" is a victory and a gain, a promise of happiness.

It might be tempting to relate this attitude to the usual psychological (or
psychoanalytical) complex, and such an interpretation would not be entirely
groundless. But it should not misrepresent or obliterate in its wake a more topi-
cal peculiarity: the fact that Bachelard's pages on femininity are also and first
of all a chapter on reverie, and that reverie itself is for him an essentially feminine activity (which is not to say a woman's activity). The dominant pair here
is *rêverie* versus *rêve* {imagining versus dreaming} — "in sum, the dream is masculine, the reverie is feminine" — which derives directly from the fundamental
opposition, borrowed from Carl Jung, between *anima* and *animus.* Always feminine, reverie is so because it can invest only a feminine object, and in order to
"invest the core of feminine reverie" the analyst (genosanalyst) in his turn must
"entrust himself to the femininity of words." Only feminine words "are reverie
words, for they belong to the language of the *anima.*" Reverie in the feminine
is thus ultimately a circular, self-contemplative reverie; as aptly suggested in
Bachelard's title, it is a *reverie upon reverie.* We ought, therefore, to interrogate
Bachelard's valorization of the feminine only through this other (and same) valorization which is that of reverie, whose feminization, among other things, is
so strongly opposed to Freud's "daydream" {*rêve diurne*}, itself masculine twice
over, both in gender {*le rêve*} and genre {*le jour*}. Such is not our purpose. On
the other hand, if the "femininity" of reverie is due to the investment of an
"Oedipal" desire for a return to originary intimacy — that is, to the security of
sameness, indifferentiation, identity — then mimological reverie is, as we have repeatedly observed, reverie par excellence, since it is a refusal of and flight from

difference, a desire or nostalgia—projected onto verbal reality—for the reassuring and blissful, even passive, identity between word and thing, language and world. In this sense, mimologism is not just one among many linguistic reveries; it is the reverie of language itself—here again in a double sense, as if language itself, forgetting the "lack" {*défaut*} that constitutes its being, dreams its own (and illusory) intimacy, its proper (and impossible) self-identity, its own proper (and fatal) repose.[28]

CHAPTER 18

Mimophony Restricted

One of the most frequent and most productive among the themes of interpretation and valorization dear to mimological reverie—as we have noted on several occasions—is the opposition between vowels and consonants. Without propounding the phonetic data in detail, let us state immediately that this opposition has more imaginary resonance than objective reality. "In practice," says one linguist, "the boundary is not always clear."[1] But for the naive linguistic consciousness, the antithesis is obvious, and its dominant motif is naturally, as we see clearly in de Brosses, or Nodier, or Claudel, the contrast between a mere vocal emission and an articulatory effort or action—hence a whole network of metaphors that render this contrast as an opposition between content and form, substance and movement, color and line, flesh and bone. To the texts already discussed, I now add a few instances collected somewhat at random during a directed reading. *Form* versus *content:* "I told myself that there are *vowel-words* and *consonant-words*. The first provide the material for expressions and the others, the shape {*figure*}."[2] *Form* versus *color, framework* versus *texture:* "From a general point of view, if we compare poetry to architecture, we could say that the consonants represent the scaffolding of the edifice and the ribs that connect all its parts, whereas the vowels seem to be the splendid metopes on the frieze. If we look for terms of comparison in painting, the consonants will be the forms that cooperate in the same action, from the same or different perspectives, whereas the vowels will be the colors harmonizing with each other to produce a powerful effect of unity and variety." "It is the consonants . . . that constitute

---

The French title of this chapter, "Mimophonie restreinte," has several important senses that cannot be encompassed by any one English word. In the technical sense, it means "restricted mimophony," or the tendency among modern linguists to restrict the hypothesis of sound symbolism to a few specialized areas of natural language, such as onomatopoeia. In the figurative sense, *mimophonie restreinte* suggests the disciplinary restraint of modern linguists such as Otto Jespersen and Ferdinand de Saussure, who feel constrained by new scientific principles to deny or at least downplay the mimetically motivated relation between word and thing, signifier and signified. Finally, the title resonates with one of Genette's previous essays, "La Rhétorique restreinte" (see "Rhetoric Restrained," in *Figures of Literary Discourse,* trans. Alan Sheridan [Oxford: Basil Blackwell, 1982], pp. 103–26).

the framework or armature of words, and this framework calls up operative drives, prompts actions."[3] Thus, *movement* versus *body:* "We know that linguistic creation, of which poetic invention constitutes merely a more perfect state, proceeds by self-driven patterns, and that verbal roots are, in Indo-European languages and even more in Semitic languages, assemblages of consonants, or verbal movements, and not sounds, or verbal bodies. Every root, every verbal movement, can resolve itself as needed into fixed words, into precise vocalizations, can come to a halt by solidifying around vowels; *spirit, inspiration, to respire* represent local and precise realizations in which it does not seem to us that the elementary consonantal root exhausts all the verbal possibilities with which it is alive and pregnant: the hundreds of current Indo-European words that it has as it were deposited along the way are few beside those it could have deposited there. And yet this infinitely fertile reality of the consonantal root is a simple fact. For us it represents the type of the self-driven pattern, the elementary model of all linguistic life."[4]

This apparent relation between the dynamism of articulatory movement and the amorphous stasis of vocalic emission most often ends up erasing from interpretive practice a phonetic feature that nevertheless constitutes the opposition and is the very origin of the word *consonant:* to wit, that the consonants cannot in principle be pronounced alone and cannot form a syllable without using the support of a vocalic sound, which gives vowels the advantage of phonic autonomy. Better still, this dependency is nearly always felt as a feature of superiority, spontaneously translated into terms of *activity* versus *passivity:* the consonant is presumed to lay ("to impress," de Brosses said) its articulatory form on the vocalic material that supports it; in a way, the consonant *articulates the vowel.* Whence the following insistent metaphor, which we find for example in Grimm: "Obviously a feminine base must be ascribed to the vowels all together; to the consonants, a masculine one";[5] or in Gabriel Bounoure, quoted approvingly by Bachelard: "To the consonants that outline the masculine structure of the word are married the changeable nuances, the delicate and finely shaded colorations of the feminine vowels."[6] Here we find once again (despite the identical gender of the terms {*la voyelle, la consonne*}) "distribution by sexusemblance" and the sexist reverie. Such an equivalence, of course, can only consolidate the opposition through overdetermination. It commands a network of symbolic attributions, a few of whose elements we have previously encountered and whose constancy itself is also quite remarkable: thus, as feminine-affective, the vowels express sensations, whereas the consonants, masculine-intellectual, express ideas (Gébelin); as feminine-introverted, the vowels express internal feelings, whereas the consonants, masculine-extroverted, are images or representations of the external world (Swedenborg, A. W. Schlegel).[7]

In the mode of subjective mimology, the evolutionary schema encountered

in de Brosses and in Nodier makes the vowel the most primitive phonic element — that is, at once the most fundamental and the most inchoate: the "age of
the vowel" is the infancy of language. For Rousseau, the "first language" is characterized by "few articulations; a few interspersed consonants would eliminate
the hiatus between vowels, and so suffice to make them smooth and easy to pronounce. On the other hand, its sounds would be extremely varied, and variety
of accent would make the same utterings {voix} greater in number: quantity and
rhythm would make possible still further combinations; so that, since utterings,
sounds, accents, and number, which are by nature, would leave little to be done
by articulations, which are by convention, men would sing rather than speak."[8]
According to Bernardin de Saint-Pierre, the proportion of vowels and consonants indicates quite accurately indeed the age of a natural language: "Vowels
abound in the tongues of emerging peoples: they are often doubled, and consonants are rare and few in number: one can observe this in the vocabulary of the
peoples of the South Seas. In this respect, their language still resembles that of
our children. When languages began to take on a personality and, as it were, to
shape words by articulating them, then the consonants grew in numbers; this is
perceptible in our European languages, which are only the dialects of the earliest
languages. We can observe this above all in the Russian language, derived from
Greek, which has forty-six letters in its alphabet, of which several are merely
our same consonants differently pronounced. The difference between the earliest languages and the dialects, which are only their derivatives, is therefore that
the words of primitive languages abound in vowels, and those of dialects in consonants; that the former are as it were sung, being composed solely of sounds,
and the latter are spoken, being articulated by consonants."[9] More specifically,
for Chateaubriand, the vowel *a* ("first vowel") is the index par excellence of a
purely pastoral and idyllic primitive state:

> We can observe that the first vowel of the alphabet is found in almost
> all the words that paint scenes of the countryside, as in *charme* {charm},
> *vache* {cow}, *cheval* {horse}, *labourage* {plowing}, *vallée* {valley}, *montagne*
> {mountain}, *arbre* {tree}, *pâturage* {pasture}, *laitage* {dairy products}, and
> so on, and in the epithets that usually accompany these nouns, such as
> *pesante* {heavy}, *champêtre* {rustic}, *grasse* {fattened}, *agreste* {countrified},
> *frais* {fresh}, *délectable* {delectable}, and so on. This observation is equally
> applicable to all the familiar idioms. Having discovered the letter A first,
> as being the first natural emission of the voice, men, at that time shep-
> herds, employed it in the words that composed the simple dictionary of
> their life. The regularity of their customs, and the limited variety in their
> ideas, colored by images of the fields, must also have called forth the recur-
> rence of the same sounds in the language. The sound A suits the calm of a

rustic heart and the peace of rural scenes. The tone of an impassioned soul is high-pitched, sibilant, headlong; the A is too long for such a soul; it requires a pastoral mouth, one that can take the time to pronounce it slowly. But nevertheless the A still enters quite a lot into complaints, lovers' tears, and the unsophisticated *hélas* {alas!} of a goatherd. Lastly, nature makes this rural letter heard in its noises, and an attentive ear can recognize it variously accented in the murmurs of certain shady places, like that of the trembling aspen or the ivy, in the first or the last voice of the bleating herds, and, at night, in the barking of the rustic dog.[10]

This evolutionist doctrine is akin to another, more geographically inspired, also illustrated by Rousseau, according to which the vowel dominates in the "tongues of the south" and the consonant in the "tongues of the north," such as Polish, "the coldest of all languages."[11] Likewise, for Hugo,

the sun produces vowels just as it produces flowers; the North bristles with consonants just as it does with ice and crags. The balance of consonants and vowels is established in the intermediary languages, which are born from temperate climates. Here is one of the causes for the domination of the French idiom. An idiom of the North — for example, German — could never become the universal tongue: it contains too many consonants for the relaxed mouths of the South to chew. Italian, a southern idiom, could not, I imagine, adapt itself to all nations either; its countless vowels, barely contained in the words, would disappear in the coarse pronunciations of the North. French, on the contrary, built upon consonants yet not bristling with them, softened by the vowels without becoming insipid, is so constituted that all human tongues can tolerate it.... Examining natural language from the musical viewpoint, and reflecting on the mysterious reasons for the things contained in the etymologies of words, one concludes that each word, taken in itself, is like a small orchestra in which the vowel is the voice, *vox,* and the consonant the instrument, the accompaniment, *sonat cum.* A striking detail, which shows in what lively fashion the discovery of one truth makes all the others emerge from the shadow, is that instrumental music belongs to the countries of consonants, or the North, and vocal music to the countries of vowels, or the South. Germany, land of harmony, has composers; Italy, land of melody, has singers. Thus, the North, the consonant, the instrument, harmony: four facts that engender each other logically and necessarily, and to which correspond four other parallel facts: the South, the vowel, the song, melody.[12]

Primitive and/or meridional man (the two characteristics naturally merge if one assumes, as often happens, that humankind was born in the South) is clearly conceived here, according to the ontogenetic model, as a creature in its childhood, too weak, too indolent, perhaps too contented to make the effort to articulate. By contrast, another image of primitive and savage nature (a blind brute force), in Hugo's work again, dictates the idea of a barbarous and confused first tongue, with interminable words chock-full of consonants: "The more ignorant man is, the more he is charmed by obscurity; the more barbarous man is, the more complexity pleases him. Nothing is less simple than a savage. The idioms of the Hurons, the Botocudos, and the Chesapeakes are forests of consonants across which, half engulfed in the basin of crudely cast ideas, huge and hideous words drag themselves along like antediluvian monsters crawling beneath the tangled vegetation of the primitive world. The Algonquins translate that perfectly short, perfectly simple, and perfectly pleasant word *France*, as *Mittigouchiouekendalakiank*."[13] There are, therefore, two possible primitives: the good savage of the South Seas, who sings softly in the sunshine, and the cruel, savage, or rather, in this context, *barbarous* Indian of the North, who brandishes his consonants like so many arrows and war hatchets. But the phonetic intuition remains the same: it is verticality (bristling, forest, harmony), or the rough virility of the consonantal articulation, opposed to the slack softness of the vowel sound. Rousseau and Hugo do not have the same idea of the savage, but they certainly have the same idea of the vowel/consonant opposition, and this is what produces the system.

This fundamental symbolics naturally entails some contradictory valorizations, or rather it determines an unstable and ever reversible equilibrium of valorization and countervalorization. The male privilege of the consonant is evident in de Brosses, in Mallarmé, in Claudel. We find it again in Clemens Brentano, who jokingly recommended to Bettina a linguistic hierarchy in the Hindu style, "in which the consonants are aristocrats who do not permit the bourgeois vowels to penetrate their caste," and then took pains to write an entire sentence omitting the vowels.[14] But the system is much more balanced in Gébelin and Nodier, who grant vowels a rich expressive value; and it reverses itself completely in Rousseau, for whom, very logically, the primitiveness of the vowel — singing, inarticulate, refractory to writing — is marked as a positive sign — including in politics, since democracy presupposes a language in which an orator can easily make himself understood by the people assembled outdoors, therefore a "sonorous, rhythmic, harmonious" language like ancient Greek; on the contrary, "imagine someone delivering a formal speech in French to the people of Paris in the Place de Vendôme. If he shouts at the top of his voice, people will hear that he is shouting, but they will not make out a single word.... Now, I maintain that any language in which it is not possible to make oneself understood by the people assembled is a servile language; it is impossible for a people to remain free and speak that language."[15]

We have already seen such a reversal of values in Hugo, who casts the consonant back into a barbarous and dysphoric primitive state. We even find at least once, in Herder, an apology for the vowel that is motivated by its phonic anatomy, and a critique of Semitic writing, guilty, as we know, of recording only consonants: "What explains this peculiarity of Hebrew, that its letters are all consonants, and that those elements on which the entire language depends, to wit, the vowels with their autonomous sound, were not written out at all at its origin? This manner of writing down the accessory and omitting the essential is contrary to the course of reason. ... For us, the vowels are the primordial thing, the most vital, the pivot of the language system, so to speak."[16] Here Herder was, in anticipation, diametrically opposed to Brentano.

🖉 It would be unwise indeed to claim that these fluctuations of the axiological equilibrium are related to a simple and univocal historical movement. Nevertheless, it seems that we could, very rapidly, relate the valorization of the consonant to a diathesis of the classical and modern type, in which a formal and dynamic sensibility dominates (de Brosses, Mallarmé, Claudel), and the valorization of the vowel to a Romantic type (in the Baudelairean sense), in which tangible and chromatic values dominate. And we might find it significant that Hugo, whom we have just seen denigrating the consonants so vehemently, would have been one of the first to treat the topos, so hackneyed since, of the "color of the vowels," which in the twentieth century becomes the dominant motif of the linguistic imagination.[17] Look at the accompanying text and chart, recently unearthed.[18]

Could one not [a missing verb] that the vowels exist for the eye as much as for the ear and that they paint some colors? One sees them. A and i are white {blanches} and radiant {brillantes} vowels. O is a red {rouge} vowel. E and eu are blue {bleues} vowels. U is the black {noire} vowel.

It is remarkable that almost all the words that express the idea of light {lumière} contain the a or the i and sometimes both letters.
Thus:

2	1	3
lumière	astre	rayon
briller	ardre	rayonner
scintiller	ange	éclair
étinceler	éclat	éclairer
étincelle	éclater	diamant
pierreries	aube	braise
étoile	aurore	fournaise
Sirius	flamme	constellation
soleil	flambeau	arc-en-ciel
ciel	enflammer	

2	1	3
resplendir	*allumer*	
oeil	*auréole*	
luire	*chandelle*	
	candélabre	
	lampe	
	lampion	
Dieu	*charbon*	
	escarboucle	
	regard	
	lanterne	
	matin	
	planète	
	Aldebaran	

light	heavenly body	ray
shine	burn ardently	radiate
scintillate	angel	flash
sparkle	burst of light	flash out
spark	burst with light	diamond
jewels	daybreak	ember
star	dawn	furnace
Sirius	flame	constellation
sun	torch	rainbow
sky	enflame	
be resplendent	light up	
eye	aureole	
gleam	candle	
	candelabra	
	lamp	
	Venetian lamp	
God	coal	
	carbuncle	
	gaze	
	lantern	
	morning	
	planet	
	Aldebaran	

Fire { *feu*} does not necessarily express the idea of bursting out until it is lit. After that it becomes *flAme* { *flAmme*}.

Neither of these two vowels is found in *moon* {*lune*} which shines only in the darkness. *Cloud* {*nuage*} is white, *thunderhead* {*nuée*} is leaden. One sees the sun through *mist* {*brouillArd*}; one does not see it through *fog* {*brume*}. Words in which the ideas of darkness and the idea of light are mingled generally contain the *u* and the *i*. Thus, *Sirius, nuage, nuit* {night}. Night has stars {*étoiles*}.

It would not be impossible for these two letters, through that mysterious force bestowed upon signs, to play a part in the luminous effect produced by certain words which, however, do not belong to the physical order. Thus:

âme	*esprit*	*royauté*
amour	*intelligence*	*pairie*
	génie	*puissance*
	gloire	*gaîté*
César	*victoire*	*saillie*
sénat	*pouvoir*	*enthousiasme*
	empire	
	joie	

soul	mind	royalty
love	intelligence	peerage
	genius	authority
	glory	gaiety
Caesar	victory	jauntiness
Senate	power	enthusiasm
	empire	
	joy	

This text occasions several remarks, the most obvious of which is that the chart is complete neither for the list of vowels nor for that of colors. Missing among the vowels, for example, are the sound *ou* and the nasal vowels; it is not really clear what the letter E is intended to mark. The usual confusion of the phonic and the graphic is in play here as elsewhere: the sound *i* is totally absent from *étoile* {star}, *gloire* {glory}, *joie* {joy}, which, on the other hand, contain an *a* that Hugo does not detect. Among the colors, *o* = red and *e/eu* = blue draw no example, save perhaps the very names of these two colors {*rouge, bleu*}, which could well be the real triggers of the association; nothing is given for the five other shades of the spectrum. The main point, therefore, rests on two "colors" that are not colors: black and white. The association *u*-black is illustrated by *lune* (if one is willing to transfer onto the heavenly body of night the shadows surrounding it),[19] *nuée, brume*. There is nothing truly black in these, just as the lists responsible for corroborating the values a-white and i-white do not contain a single truly white object: among them we even find *charbon* {coal}, which is the antithesis of white. This is because, in fact, Hugo has passed without say-ing it (without seeing it) from properly chromatic values to luminous values, as announced by "white and *radiant* vowels," then "idea of *light*," and further on, "idea of *darkness*": cloud, fog are not black but dark; stars, dawn, embers are not white but luminous. This slippage, as we will see, is altogether significant.

Besides, we know that Hugo's chart is merely one among many instances. Be-fore him, at least one of the same type is found in A. W. Schlegel and one in Jakob Grimm. After him, Georg Brandes, Arthur Rimbaud, René Gil, Vladimir Nabokov, Matyla Ghyka have proposed some others, to which can be added some individual or collective contributions gathered by various psychologists and linguists. In his chapter "Sonnet des voyelles" {Sonnet of the vowels},[20] René Étiemble compares a few of these charts in a strictly critical spirit, emphasizing their undeniable contradictions and confusions. I will recapitulate the overall thrust of this evidence in the next chart, retaining for each "vowel" the indi-vidual responses and significant dominant features of the statistical responses, without dwelling overmuch on uncertainties brought about by the spelling or the passage from one language to another — confusions between front [a] and back [ɑ] (noted as A); between closed [o] and open [ɔ]; between open [ɛ], closed [e], open [œ] and closed [ø] (E, sometimes EU); between [y] and [u] (U and OU); in English between [i] and [ai] (I); the absence of the French nasal vowels, victims of their digraphy, as are [u] and [ø] — or on the strange bias of the "method" that almost always consists (except once, in Chastaing) of looking for the "color of the vowels" and almost never the vowel of the colors. In such an uncertain subject, the concern for rigor (fortunately?) loses all relevance.[21]

Considering the complete results of several surveys, Étiemble not unreason-ably concludes that "*all* the colors are attributed to *each* of the vowels." The same does not quite go for our chart, because it retains only the majority re-sponses from the collective surveys. On these terms, we find here neither *a* nor *o* for green, nor *e* for red or black, nor *u* for blue, nor *ou* for white, nor *eu* for red, green, or yellow. Inversely, we observe several rather marked dominances, such as *a* for red (12 out of 29), *e* for yellow and white (10 + 6 out of 22), *i* for white and yellow (8 + 7 out of 23), *o* for red (11 out of 25), *u* for green (7 out of 16), *ou* for brown, dark blue, and black (3 + 2 + 2 out of 8), *eu* for blue (4 out of 6; the hypothesis of a lexical influence from the word *bleu* is very tempting here, but we must then note the contradictory absence of *ou* for *rouge*). If these domi-nances are accepted as indicative proof of the strongest inclinations of "hearing in color," one finds that no clear relation is established between the range of the vocalic sounds and that of the colors of the spectrum — at the most there is a privileged association between *a* (and *o*) and red, which Jakobson describes as a "propensity to connect the most chromatic vowels to the purest colors."[22] The qualifier "chromatic" here produces a circular metaphor: it could perhaps more

317

	A	E	I	O	U	OU	EU
SCHLEGEL	red		sky blue	purple	violet	dark blue	
GRIMM	white	yellow	red	blue		black	
HUGO	white	blue	white	red	black		blue
BRANDES	red	white	yellow			dark blue	
RIMBAUD	black	white	red	blue	green		
GHIL	black	white	blue	red	yellow		
FECHNER	white	yellow		red			
NABOKOV	brown	yellow	yellow	ivory	greenish yellow		
GHYKA	black	yellow	white	red	green		
FLETCHER	light/ dark	green	blue	red	purple/ yellow		
LEGRAND	red	white	yellow	black	green		
X	red	white	black	yellow	brown	faded gold	off- white
WERTH	brown	yellow	white	dark blue			purple
LANGENBECK	red	yellow	white	blue	gray	brown	sky blue
S. P.	red	bright green	yellow	blue/ red			dark blue
DEICHMANN	red	yellow	white	red/ brown		brown	
BOAS	red	yellow	white				
ARGELANDER	red white dark	yellow	white	brown		black	
GRÜBER	black blue white	white	yellow red	brown red	black		
COURS	red	gray	yellow	orangey	green		
FLOURNOY	white red black	yellow blue	red white	yellow red	green	brown	
CHASTAING	red	orange	yellow	violet red	green		blue

objectively be said that these vowels are physiologically the most median and the most open, and acoustically the most compact.[23] "*U* and *i*," Jakobson continues, "are, on the contrary, linked to the less chromatic colors, and even to the series white-black." Unlike *a*, *i* is certainly the most closed vowel (minimal amplitude of the buccal resonator) and the most diffuse, but it would be difficult to say the same about *ou;* the relation between vocalic resonance and chromatism therefore remains hard to define. On the other hand, as Jakobson correctly indicates here, the relation between these same resonances and the range of luminosity is very evident: the vowels most frequently associated with "bright" colors (including white) are the vowels with front articulation and (hence) with high frequency, *i, é, è, ü;* the vowel considered dark in the greatest number of cases is the back vowel with low frequency, *ou*.[24]

The shift from the chromatic to the luminous, which we observed previously in Hugo, is again manifest in the conclusions of the survey conducted with the readers of *Vie et Langage* by Maxime Chastaing.[25] The question asked was "Here are six colors: red, orange, yellow, green, blue, violet. Which vowel seems to you to fit each color?" In other words, the chromatic order of the spectrum was followed. The results, on the other hand, place the colors according to an approximate range of decreasing luminosity (yellow-green-orange-blue-red-violet), and demonstrate the following law: "the higher the intonation, the more luminous the color to which it is matched"—or, in articulatory terms, "the bright colors correspond more to the front vowels, and the dark colors to the back vowels." The most distinctive interest of this survey obviously lies in this implicit slippage (one that the investigator does not question at any time) from one range to another, in which we clearly see an excessively bold hypothesis retreating to more cautious and more solid arguments. But in itself—that is to say, without movement in the direction of chromatism—the relation between height (or front position) and brightness had already been noted frequently since the beginning of this century. Thus, Jespersen saw a "natural association between high tones (sounds with very rapid vibrations) and light, and inversely between low tones and darkness, as is seen in the frequent use of adjectives like 'light' and 'dark' in speaking of notes."[26] As is known, Maurice Grammont called back vowels "dark" and front vowels "bright."[27] Benjamin Whorf qualified them as "dark" and "radiant."[28] Several surveys in experimental psychology have shown the constancy of this association, in particular the one whose results Chastaing gave in 1962: thus, thirty students in upper primary school grades assigned on an average the following coefficients of luminosity: *i:* 2.5; *e:* 1.4; *a:* 0.3; *o:* −0.6; *ou:* −1.5.[29] The made-up words *kig, kag, koug* were interpreted as "bright," "neutral," "dark"; *peb, pib, pob, poub* were translated into "dawn," "daytime," "twilight," "darkness"; *i* = "daytime," *ou* = "nighttime"; *limière* would be more appropriate for "light" than the actual French *lumière*, and so on. From all the evidence, there is here a very widespread synaesthetic value, one that owes little to individual whim.

Still more plainly, this value is not the only one, nor perhaps the one most universally recognized; that mark of distinction belongs without doubt to the relation between the range of frequencies and the category of size, to which Jespersen in 1922 devoted a study that can be considered the archetype of the genre[30] and from which I will quote only, for the moment, this amusing observation: "One summer when a serious drought was raging in Fredriksstad (Norway), the following notice was posted in a restroom: 'Do not flush for *bimmelim*, but only for *boummeloum*' — and everyone understood immediately."[31] In 1929, Edward Sapir presented a series of experiments based on neologisms made up "in such a way as to avoid all association with the meaningful words" of the real lexicon: thus, the pair *mil/mal* was interpreted as "small"/"large" by about 80 percent of the subjects.[32] Chastaing tried this again more recently with the same success: *kigen* and *kougon* were divided into "small" and "large" by nearly 100 percent.[33] Around 75 percent of the young children similarly distributed the couples *ibi/aba, pim/poum, kina/kouna,* and the range *pim/pam/poum.* "The children," observes the author, "correlate ... an acoustic order with a semantic order: the clearer the timbre of a vowel, the more it seems to them to fit the expression of smallness; the less clear it is, the less it seems to them to fit." The explanation here seems obvious and is ascribable less to synaesthesia than to direct analogy: high-pitched sounds are produced by a small buccal resonator, low-pitched sounds by a wider one. Sapir had already remarked on this, and Chastaing does not fail to do so either, but the opinion of a linguist as orthodox as André Martinet will perhaps appear more significant:

The existence of a universal symbolism in the case of certain sounds of language, ... which has been merely a very plausible hypothesis for a long time, appears to be well established today. Individuals can be more or less sensitive to it, but their reactions are not found to be contradictory when observation is made with all the requisite guarantees: the timbre of [i], for example, goes together with the concept of smallness {*petitesse*}, which is not invalidated by either *big* or *small* in English; the timbre of [u] (French *ou*) naturally evokes thickness and heaviness. These are only the most striking features of this symbolism, but they suffice for our purposes. One need not be a great scholar of articulatory phonetics to understand the reason for such identifications: [i{ee}] is the vowel for which the speech organs strive to realize the smallest possible resonating cavity toward the front of the mouth by pushing the bulk of the tongue toward the inside portion of the palate and by drawing in the lips to the maximum against the gums; for [u], in contrast, the bulk of the tongue is drawn backward and the lips are pushed forward in such a way that the resonating cavity is as wide as possible. The symbolic equations [i] = thinness {*petitesse*} and [u] = thickness {*grosseur*} have an obvious physiological foundation, and it is this foundation that permits us to assume that they are the reality for all mankind, although the observations on which they are based did not involve the whole of humanity—far from it.[34]

To this scale of sizes, we can no doubt link up a few other symbolic values from the range of vowel frequencies, more or less directly derived from or connected to them: sharp/blunt, whence hard/soft (Whorf); high/low, whence light/heavy,[35] whence perhaps fast/slow; near/far, of which Jespersen found a significant application in systems of deictics such as *ci/ça* or *this/that*. The light symbolism itself is perhaps derived from these spatial values, since the "dark" vowels come from the "bottom" of the phonatory apparatus, its obscure depths, whereas the "bright" vowels come from high in the oral cavity's front regions, those most open to the light—unless the relation between the relative frequencies of acoustic and luminous vibrations is directly established.

And now for the consonants, which, let us recall, are essentially composed of *noises* with nonperiodic vibrations, accompanied or not (voiced or resonant/unvoiced or silent) by *pitches* {*tons*} produced by vibrations of the pharynx, as for the vowels. It seems that, contrary to the a priori speculations of classical mimologism (de Brosses, Nodier, for example), modern investigations accord less symbolic relevance to the consonants' more or less frontal *position* of articulation (bilabial, apico-dental, palatal, and so on) than to their *mode* of articulation: occlusive/continuous, voiced/unvoiced, lateral/vibrating, and the like. Thus, in Köhler's famous experiment[36] where the two neologisms *takete* and *maluma* are compared with two figures, one angular, the other rounded, the group of occlusives quite naturally symbolizes hardness, hence angularity, and the group of continuous consonants symbolizes softness and smoothness, hence rotundity; this association was confirmed by Chastaing's series of experiments on some consonantal variations in onomatopoeias.[37] A homothetic distinction, subject to an analogous interpretation, is that between silent (unvoiced) and resonant (voiced) occlusives and fricatives, which above all contrasts two degrees of effort, hence of articulatory difficulty: "Which is the more delicate? *sata* or *zata*? *Zata* receives 10 out of 10 votes."[38] But the presence/absence of voicing seems to add here a symbolic category previously encountered in the opposition between front and back vowels, that of size, and hence of weight: *ava* is felt as larger than *afa*, *slid* as heavier than *slit*, *mib* as slower than *mip*. Lastly, in the antithesis r/l (vibrating/lateral), we rediscover the Cratylian pair par excellence, the classic opposition between roughness and smoothness.[39] For the Hungarian children questioned by Ivan Fonagy, r is a man and l is a woman: "The r," comments the author, "appears masculine on account of the greater muscular effort that it requires for production." For Chastaing's students, *r* evokes solid, hard, acrid, bitter, rugged, strong, violent, heavy, near; *l*, delicate, sleek, weak, easygoing, light, distant, bright.[40]

Ⓢ As has often been observed,[41] almost all of these investigations are aimed not at bilateral relationships, in which a single sound releases one symbolic value, but at noticeably more complex relations, most often between pairs with a four-term ratio (*i*:*u* :: bright:dark, *r*:*l* :: male:female), sometimes between series with several terms each (*i*:*a*:*u* :: bright:blazing:dark). From this obligatory observation, a negative, or restrictive, conclusion is sometimes drawn (implicitly by Delbouille, explicitly by Todorov) as to the existence of the symbolic relation. The necessity for this sort of *menage à quatre*, or of several couples, is said to reveal the weakness, even the illusory character of the symbolic marriage: "*a* is not big in itself, but when compared to *i*," states Todorov, a qualification plainly connoting a failing, that relative greatness is less great than absolute greatness. "It is therefore not a sound that resembles a form (how could it?), but a relation of sounds that resembles a relation of forms; this refers us back to another type of symbolism, arising no longer from semantic theories but from diagrammatism." But can any symbolism — and semanticism — exist outside of "diagrammatism": that is, the relational and the relative? Greatness "in itself" is obviously only a phantom, and so are brightness, sharpness of pitch, femininity in itself — and on the side of phonic features, front-back placement, occlusiveness, voicing, and so on, are not absolute values either. There exist only relative qualities, and all symbolism aside, the humblest perception presupposes, as is widely recognized, a categorial axis and hence a diagram: if a subject is presented with a round green figure and asked what its main characteristic is, he will legitimately hesitate between roundness and greenness; if it is paired with another figure, green and square, or round and red, he will no longer hesitate. Diagrammatism does not, therefore, eliminate semanticism; it situates it on the plane of categorial relativity which is that of all perception and all description. This is probably what Jakobson meant to emphasize in a well-known passage from *Essais de linguistique générale* that implicitly makes diagrammatism a legitimate, and by no means disqualifying, condition for phonic symbolism:

> Sound symbolism is undeniably an objective relation, based on a phenomenal connection between different sensory modes, in particular between visual and auditory sensations. If the results of research done in this field have sometimes been vague and debatable, that is due to the inadequate care exercised in the methods of psychological and/or linguistic investigation. From a linguistic point of view in particular, the facts have often

been distorted for lack of sufficient attention to the phonological aspect of the sounds of language, or because someone has persisted in working with complex phonematic units instead of placing himself at the level of the basic components. But if, in conducting a test, for example on the phonematic opposition high/low, one asks which of two terms, /i/ or /u/, is the darker, some subjects could rightly answer that this question has no meaning for them, but it will be hard to find a single one to assert that /i/ is the darker of the two terms.[42]

It seems to me, then, that the issue is not to decide whether or not the investigations by Jespersen and his successors succeeded in establishing the existence of a "sound symbolism." The symbolic capacity of the sounds of the language system is a matter of fact, or more precisely an a priori certainty. Like any kind of physical event, the sounds of language have perceptible characteristics; they are more or less high or low, rough or gentle, slight or bold, and so on, and these characteristics are inevitably in a direct analogical relation with those of other sounds and noises of the world, and in an indirect or oblique (synaesthetic) analogical relation with those of other physical events. This relation may be partly stable and universal, partly unstable and subjective, but its objective core is today well established and, moreover, as we have seen, rather trivial. The real issue, as we have known since the second part of the *Cratylus,* is to decide (forever *sklērotēs* — and *kinēsis*) whether or not natural language respects and invests these imitative capacities in its functioning. The investigations mentioned so far do not tackle this point, always being concerned with isolated phonemes or with experimental "neologisms," foreign to natural language and destined to remain so; or more truthfully, up to now we have wanted to bear in mind only this extra- (or *pre-*)linguistic aspect, as the least subject to controversy. It remains for us to consider these investigations in their next application, which bears upon the properly linguistic investment of phonic expressiveness.

The most favorable ground, by which I mean the easiest of access, is obviously that of onomatopoeia in the strict sense: that is to say, words manifestly created "by phonetic imitation of the thing named" (*Petit Robert*). This is almost an overly favorable ground, since the "phonetic imitation" at work in creations such as *bêê* {baa} or *coucou* {cuckoo} do not yet depend on symbolism understood as oblique expressiveness: there is no synaesthesia in these vocables. At the most, as Maurice Grammont rightly shows in a chapter that remains the best discussion of the question, there is a sort of phonematic *interpretation* of sounds or groups of sounds alien to our articulatory system: in short, an interpretation rather like the approximations we spontaneously give in to, alas, when first learning foreign languages.[43] "When we render an external sound by an onomatopoeia, we translate it into our language system. ... Why do we interpret as *coucou* what in reality

323

is *ou-ou?* Because we are hardly accustomed to pronouncing the same vowel twice in a row without a consonant; because at a certain distance we confuse the occlusives or are not even aware of them at all; out of this comes our habit of restoring them to the words we recognize and assuming them in the others. ... The only occlusives that we assume before a vowel are those that have the same point of articulation as it does. The normal introducers of the velar vowel *ou* are the velar occlusives *q* and *g;* but the *g* carries a resonance and a softness that are not suitable if the attack of the vowel is sudden. Only the *q* (*c*) fulfills all the requisite conditions, and *coucou* is an irreproachable translation, but a translation nevertheless." Of course, the same can be said for *bêê* {baa}, *miaou* {meow}, *hi-han* {hee-haw}, *cocorico* {cock-a-doodle-doo} ... and everyone knows that these phonological approximations vary from one natural language to another.

The issue here is not exactly a sensory transposition, but a simple adaptation from one sound system to another. The exploitation of oblique symbolism begins with those expressive apophonies that use reduplicative onomatopoeias such as *tic-tac* {tick-tock} or *pif-paf-pouf* {bing-bang-boom}. Grammont observes, as have many others no doubt, that these "special" apophonies, independent of the system of vocalic alternations invested in the morphology, obey a simple and strict law, which (at least in modern European languages) requires that "their accentuated vowels be in general *i, a, ou,* going from the brightest to the darkest, without that order being capable of inversion." [44] He suggests no factual explanation, but a related remark puts us on the track: "Each one of the syllables in *pif-paf-pouf* also constitutes a monosyllabic onomatopoeia serving to designate a single noise; but they are not employed indifferently for just any noise. Thus, *pif* can designate the one made by a gun hammer hitting the percussion cap, *paf* that of a gunshot, *pouf* that of a man falling and landing on his behind. If we were told that a sack of flour made a *pif* when falling to the ground, we would immediately ask just how it could have produced such an unexpected noise. The quarrymen of Fontainebleau have three onomatopoeias to designate the various qualities of sandstone: they call the very resistant one *pif*, the stone of good quality *paf*, and the one that is reduced to dust under the slightest impact *pouf*." The "irreversible" order of *pif-paf* or *tic-tac* is perhaps not always based on the difference in size, weight, distance, brightness, and so on, that the opposition *i/a* appears to symbolize, but there is in the difference of phonic height at least the indication of an obligatory path *high-low*, which is that of an opening followed by a resolution of the type *question-response* or *dominant-tonic*. For a rather unclear reason, but one that is evidently due to their expressive capacity, the high vowels systematically have the value of protasis and the low ones that of apodosis. *Patati-patata* {blah-blah-blah} is the (euphonic) order of discourse.

With the expressive function of sounds in onomatopoeia being certain and universally acknowledged, the issue of mimology apparently comes down once more to deciding what role onomatopoeia plays in the system of natural language. We rediscover this problematic — classic from Saint Augustine through Nodier — nearly intact in Saussure, who, in a well-known and highly controversial passage, has linked the fate of the "principle" of the arbitrariness of the sign to an attempt at a systematic reduction of onomatopoeia. Here we need to refer to this distinctive text:

> *Onomatopoetic* words might be held to show that a choice of signal is not always arbitrary. But such words are never organic elements of a linguistic system. Moreover, they are far fewer than is generally believed. French words like *fouet* {whip} or *glas* {knell} may strike the ear as having a certain suggestive sonority. But to see that this is in no way intrinsic to the words themselves, it suffices to look at their Latin origins. *Fouet* comes from Latin *fagus* {beech-tree} and *glas* from Latin *classicum* {trumpet call}. The suggestive quality of the modern pronunciation of these words is a fortuitous result of phonetic evolution.
>
> As for authentic onomatopoeia (e.g., French *glou-glou* {gurgle}, *tic-tac* {ticking} of a clock), not only is it rare but its use is already to a certain extent arbitrary. For onomatopoeia is only the approximate imitation, already conventionalized, of certain sounds. This is evident if we compare a French dog's *ouaoua* and a German dog's *wauwau*. In any case, once introduced into the language, onomatopoetic words are subjected to the same phonetic and morphological evolution as other words. The French *pigeon* {pigeon} comes from Vulgar Latin *pipio*, itself of onomatopoetic origin, which clearly proves that onomatopoetic words themselves may lose their original character and take on that of the linguistic sign in general, which is unmotivated.[45]

In an unexpected manner that we will discuss more fully in a moment, Saussure here makes intention the criterion for expressiveness, and diachrony the test for expressive intention — while taking care to make this work to the detriment of motivation every time. When phonetic evolution destroys an "authentic onomatopoeia" (*pipio — pigeon*), this proves that linguistic consciousness is not rooted in expressiveness enough to fight against the erosion of the expressive signifier. When an onomatopoeia is created (*classicum — glas*), this can only be a "fortuitous result," and so, in the absence of intention, it cannot be an "authentic onomatopoeia." Diachrony can therefore only ceaselessly destroy the onomatopoetic stock without ever being able to build it up again.

This enlistment of diachrony in the service of the arbitrariness of the sign constitutes the polar opposite, or rather the axiological negative, of two mimological theses at once — one very old, the other very recent and even subsequent to the publication of the *Course in General Linguistics,* and both resting on the same facts. The traditional thesis, which we have encountered throughout our exploration, except in the *Cratylus*, is the idea of an originary expressivity—onomatopoeia as the source of natural languages—that would be progressively erased under the impact of an irresistible phonetic and/or semantic evolution, and also because of a gradual weakening of the mimetic instinct and sensibility. But instead of emphasizing and implicitly valorizing this infidelity, as does Saussure, this thesis insists upon the origin of language as a revelation from Nature. *Pipio—pigeon* functions here as the universal formula for human language, where forgetting the origin in no way undermines the original essence, and where betrayal itself is nevertheless an acknowledgment: at the source of every "arbitrary" word there could be, and therefore is, an expressive word. Arbitrariness is a supervention; it is a fact of history and not of nature. There was no originary convention, therefore no convention at all, for a series of accidents is not a convention. One can then correctly claim that natural languages are (have become) arbitrary, but not that they are (essentially) conventional. We have seen how the birth of comparative grammar disqualified this classical thesis by showing that a language assumed to be near its origin, like Sanskrit, was not in the least more mimetic than its distant descendants of the present day. The study of the languages of the so-called savage peoples of America or Africa would contribute a parallel "refutation" somewhat later on. Whence, perhaps, the belated appearance of an inverse thesis that aims at exploiting the work of diachrony in the opposite direction, interpreted not as destructive but on the contrary as creative of mimology, and whose emblematic formula could this time be *classicum—glas*. Such is the evolutionist thesis (precisely in the Darwinian sense, as we shall see) of Otto Jespersen.

For *classicum—glas* (or any other filiation of the same type) to have a mimological value, it is obviously necessary to reject the Saussurean criterion of the pertinence of the intention revealed by the origin; in other words, it is necessary (at the least) that the supervening expressiveness not be disqualified by the fortuitous nature of its (involuntary) production. Consequently, we see Jespersen infallibly attacking the weak point in Saussure's line of argument: "Here we see," he writes, "one of the characteristics of modern linguistic science: it is so preoccupied with etymology, with the origin of words, that it pays much more attention to what words have come from than to what they have come to be. If a word has not always been phonetically expressive, then its actual suggestiveness is left out of account and may even be declared to be merely fanciful. I hope that this chapter contains throughout what is psychologically a more true and linguistically a more fruitful view." [46] It would be difficult to come up with a more (perhaps unwittingly) humorous exposure of the clear contradiction between the diachronic argument used by Saussure and his principle of synchronic autonomy. And for good measure, Jespersen permits himself the further luxury of rejecting the two examples proposed by Saussure: "I must confess that I find nothing symbolical in *glas* and very little in *fouet*. ... On the whole, much of what people 'hear' in a word appears to me fanciful and apt to discredit reasonable attempts at gaining an insight into the essence of sound symbolism."[47] Here, then, Saussure is both a pathetic Cratylist in his choice of "expressive words," and a clumsy Hermogenist through his excessive neogrammarian historicism.[48]

And there we have a (re)reversal of de facto onomatopoetic creations of the type *classicum — glas*, to the mimological credit of diachrony, even if Saussure's ear is bad here — or too good. But, *a fortiori*, the intentional creations, if there are any, must be counted among these: that is, of course, the "authentic onomato-poeias" of recent formation, whose existence Saussure implicitly — and impru-dently — denies, such as, let us say (to remain within the *Belle Époque*), *teuf-teuf* {puff-puff} or *vroum-vroum* {vroom-vroom}. But additionally, and much more troubling for the Saussurean thesis, the facts of evolution that seem to trans-gress the laws of historical phonetics in order to produce expressiveness must be counted. This transgression can be purely negative: this is what happens when, contrary to *pipio*, an old onomatopoeia resists phonetic erosion: for example, *coucou*. It would be positive if certain words had not always been but instead were to become expressive by evolving in opposition to the phonetic laws, but there is, apparently, no such instance.

One last possibility remains, therefore, that plays no longer upon the signi-fier but upon the signified: a word gradually adapting its meaning to its form. Jespersen was particularly attached to this phenomenon, which he baptizes, in a phrase recalling our *secondary mimeticism*, "*secondary echoism* or *secondary symbolism*." For example, the English *patter* (Latin *pater*), which in the begin-ning meant "to say one's paternosters," came, under the influence of its hom-onym *patter* ("to tap") and other expressive words like *chatter* or *jabber*, to sig-nify "to speak rapidly and glibly"; or the French *miniature*, originally an "image painted with minium," whose present meaning came about "on account of its *i* sound," the symbol for smallness, as we have seen.[49] Clearly, in both cases, and particularly in the French example (regarding which he does not even mention the evident influence of the *minus* family), Jespersen attributes to phonic sym-bolism what actually, or principally, comes from lexical contagion and from pseudo-etymological reconstruction: a typical confusion, as we know, but one that singularly weakens the hypothesis of *secondary symbolism* here, by depriv-ing it of serious proof. But who is talking about proof? It is a matter of a general theory, entirely speculative and visibly inspired by Darwinian evolutionism, ac-cording to which the most expressive words *must* survive better than the others, on account of a natural selection of the fittest (in this case, the most "appropri-ate" words) which does not necessarily depend on the speakers' knowledge:

But if the sound of a word ... was, or came to be, in some way suggestive of its signification — say, if a word containing the vowel [i] in a prominent place meant "small" or something small—then the sound exerted a strong influence in gaining popular favour to the word; it was an inducement to people to choose and to prefer that particular word and to cease to use words for the same notion that were not thus favoured.[50] Sound symbolism, we may say, makes some words more fit to survive and gives them considerable help in their struggle for existence. ...

In all languages the creation and the use of echoic and symbolic words seems to have been on the increase in historical times. If to this we add the selective process through which words which have only adequate expressions, or less adequate forms of the same words, and subsequently give rise to a host of derivatives, then we may say that languages in course of time grow richer and richer in symbolic words. So far from believing in a golden primitive age, in which everything in language was expressive and immediately intelligible on account of the significative value of each group of sounds, we arrive rather, here as in other domains, at the conception of a slow progressive development towards a greater number of easy and adequate expressions—expressions in which sound and sense are united in a marriage-union closer than was ever known to our remote ancestors.[51]

This inverted myth does not lack for panache in its anticonformism, but like the other one it remains without a real grasp of linguistic reality. Jespersen like de Brosses—Saussure like de Brosses and Jespersen—tries hard to make History speak; but as often happens, between one side of the question and the other, Dame History neither confirms nor denies. The outright truth may be endorsed by the wise Maurice Grammont: "From the viewpoint of onomatopoeia, what phonetic evolution causes a natural language to lose on one hand, it gives back on the other. The losses and gains nearly balance each other out."[52] Now the investigation is thrown back into synchrony.

Here, as opposed to Socratic aversions, it is a question of counting up the voices, as at the Ecclesia, in order to see if the expressive words carry the day, in a statistically "significant" way, in the actual lexicon. Regarding the i, Jespersen continues to use lists of favorable examples without relative measurement, and so without demonstrative value. The attempt at statistics is made above all by Maxime Chastaing, who devoted himself to this question with an optimism tempered by an increasing concern for rigor; I will give only an impression of the overall curve. In 1962, a list of terms indicating light and darkness, taken by Benac from the French *Dictionnaire des synonymes,* yields 36 front to 21 back vowels for the vocabulary of light, and 13 front to 19 back vowels for darkness, disproportions conforming to the recognized symbolic values. An analogous sampling in English yields 41 front, 18 middle, and 5 back vowels for light; 31 front, 11 middle, and 25 back for darkness—a less decisive score, since the front vowels dominate both sides. In 1965 the same dictionary this time yields 61 percent front against 25 percent back (and 14 percent "middle") vowels for the vocabulary of smallness; and for that of largeness, a confirmation through reversal, 33 percent front against 53 percent back vowels. (Here again, English disappoints with 65–35 and 52–48, while Spanish confirms with 56–44 and 46–54.) But Chastaing is wise to the unrepresentative character of such a corpus, in which words with very varied frequencies of usage coexist, so he makes appeal to the actual lexical storehouse of a group of French students. With all the vowels here being distributed into front (*i, ü, é, è,* open and closed *œ, un, in*) and back (open and closed *a* and *o, ou, an, on*), one obtains almost 71 to 29 for smallness, 47 to 53 for largeness. But here, a new qualm arises: "a lexicon [even a living one] is not a natural language," and Chastaing believes he can overcome this difficulty through recourse to tables of frequencies. West's table on the 2,000 most often used English words yields 77 front against 23 back vowels for brightness, but again 53 against 47 for darkness. For French, Dottrens-Massarenti's table yields 48 against 52 for brightness, 25 against 75 for darkness, the latter making up for the former. An average of samplings, this time from the vocabulary for sizes, will yield the overwhelming scores of 90 to 10 for smallness, 20 to 80 for largeness; of 63 to 37 for proximity, lightness, rapidity, height, and 27.5 to 72.5 for the opposite qualities. A comparable mix in English will yield 71.5 to 28.5 and 50 to 50, with English once again belying its reputation, on this ground, as the champion of expressiveness.[53]

This series of investigations, which I have here alluded to in a very summary fashion but not, I hope, too unfaithfully, may not escape certain methodological criticisms. The material for the experiments (the lists of words) is not made known, and the fundamental categories are, here and there, rather fuzzily defined: what exactly is the vocabulary of brightness, smallness, and so on? Where exactly is the boundary between front and back vowels? Why is there sometimes an intermediary class, and sometimes not, and so on? Applied to such vague and fluctuating data, the concern for numerical rigor seems only mimimally pertinent, and so only minimally effective: as Bachelard has rightly shown, it is always easier to refine calculations than to define their basis and to know exactly what is being counted up.[54] Finally, even if the defects or the uncertainties of the method are ignored in order to consider its results, one hesitates at the least to endorse the enthusiastic conclusion that Chastaing draws: "It is therefore no longer merely a truth of the laboratory [as in the experiments on neologisms], no longer merely a stylistic truth [as in the poets' exercises in imitative harmony] or lexical truth [as in the dictionaries of synonyms]: it [the symbolism of sounds] is a truth of the language that we speak."[55] Perhaps it is not enough to integrate indices of frequency in order to make a "lexical truth" into a "truth of natural language"; moreover, one cannot overlook the fact that up to this point this possible "lexical truth" itself boils down to a very scanty part of the lexicon of a very small number of natural languages, whose potential for generalization remains problematic.[56] If, therefore, ignoring all the obstacles, we admit the existence of a seat (or a pocket) of mimology here, we must immediately add that it is at best a situation of *restricted* mimology.

But the very term "mimology" is probably too ambitious here. *Mimophony* would be more apt—but on condition that we recognize that finally neither mimophony nor mimography (nor their sum total), once established, would be sufficient to constitute a true mimology. Let us do a crude parody of the Pascalian dialectic: from all the phonics and graphics taken together, not one single fact about natural language can be extracted; that is impossible, and of another order.

ⓢ Indeed, while Jespersen and his heirs were working hard to establish the objective existence of a phonic symbolism on the basis of experiments, an event took place in the field of linguistic science that could be considered, from the viewpoint we are taking here, as the most important since the birth of comparative grammar, one that can be described as a *rupture between the phonic* (or also the graphic, or any other material support of the functioning language system) *and the linguistic.* This rupture is already virtually present in the Saussurean theory of the purely *formal* and *differential* character of the signifier. If we are not "dealing with a substance when we deal with linguistic phenomenona" but only with "conventional values" that are "distinct from the tangible element which serves as their vehicle" without being able to "determine" them any more than metal or paper does the value of money; if the linguistic signifier is "not physical in any way" but "constituted solely by differences which distinguish one... sound pattern from another," it necessarily follows that this signifier, in its "essence," does not belong to the phonic order any more than to other material orders. Therefore, it is "impossible that sound, as a material element, should in itself be part of the language. Sound is merely something ancillary, a material that language uses." Or again, in other terms, "the essence of language... has nothing to do with the phonic nature of the linguistic sign."[57] These bold but purely theoretical position statements were to find their empirical application and verification a few years later in phonology, which is based entirely on the rigorous distinction between the *sounds of language* (whose study is left to phonetics) and the *phonemes* properly speaking, defined, after some fluctuations, in terms of a pure linguistic function.[58] The autonomy of the phoneme in relation to the sound manifests itself from then on through the specificity of the phonematic choice performed by each idiom on the nearly infinite storehouse of phonetic possibilities, and through the freedom of relations between the two "orders." In French, two sounds as different as the apical *r* and the velar *r* make

up only one phoneme because their physical difference never serves to distinguish two words, but two sounds as close as the apical *r* and *l* make up two
distinct phonemes; open and closed *a* are two phonemes in French but one in
English, and so on. The phoneme is not the sound, and language is constituted
not by sounds but by phonemes. Here then, we see not only, as at the beginning
of the nineteenth century, the crumbling of arguments for mimologism based
on fact but the giving way of its theoretical foundation: linguistics slips away
from phonetics, as it does from any material determination, and the symbolic
capacities of *mimēma phōnē* lose all pertinence for the functioning of the linguistic system. Once again, we find Socrates' final position, but transformed and
in a way radicalized. No longer "Natural language has from its origin betrayed
the expressive capacities of its phonic elements," but instead, "The elements of
natural language as such are not phonic; therefore, phonic expressiveness, if it
exists, cannot penetrate language; or rather, it can penetrate, and even inhabit,
language, but it does not belong to language, and therefore it could never constitute language."

The boldest application of these principles to the Cratylian debate is without doubt to be found in the article that Karl Bühler contributed in 1933 to the
famous special issue of the *Journal de Psychologie*.[59] The great psycholinguist
there fully recognizes the existence of a "tendency to *paint* with the aid of the
sounds of language," present "not only among the poets, but in language in
general," a tendency that expresses a "thirst for concrete reality" and a "desire
to recover contact with tangible reality," and that aims to exploit to this end the
incontestable "*pictorial* potential of the human voice," thanks to its "surprising
richness in timbre." But this tendency cannot actually install itself in the functioning of natural language, which is based on an indirect and conventional system of "representation" (*Darstellung*), and which bars the desire for vocal imitation through three successive "locks": on the *syntactical* level (the fixed order
of words in every natural language), the *lexical* level (the impossibility of individually coining expressive words), and the *phonological* level, which we have
just discussed. Like Socrates, humankind would have liked, and would still like,
to provide itself with a true instrument for vocal imitation, and without doubt
it could have done so; but for a reason that Bühler does not explain, at a certain
stage in its development, "like Hercules at the crossroads of vice and virtue,"
humankind had to settle on the opposite choice. After having probably hesitated for some time at the crossroads where the left-hand signpost read "archaic
logic and onomatopoetic representation of things" and the right-hand signpost
read "symbolic language" (in the scientific sense of the term: that is, nonana-
logical), human language as we know it chose the right path, as did Hercules
once upon a time. Ever since this "original decision," the history of humanity's
belated efforts to return to the left path has been only a "list of lost opportu-

nities": the "pictorial desire" no longer found satisfaction except in the "joints" and the "margins" of the linguistic system, "small, scattered, and sporadic surfaces where some freedom subsists" but which can never and could never ever form a "coherent representational field." These joints and margins (whether "authentic" onomatopoeias or not) are like a bone to gnaw on which the system tosses to mimetic desire.

Despite the kind of legitimacy *within its own sphere* that he is willing to concede to this desire, Bühler, exactly like Saussure, clearly valorizes the somewhat mythical "original decision" in favor of convention, which is really the "right" road, or the one of *virtue*. The Hermogenist valorization of the conventional already encountered in Leibniz is once more recognizable here. If we wished to characterize this position again according to its answers to the three key questions of the debate, the answer would obviously be negative to questions A (should natural language be mimetic?) and C (is natural language mimetic?).[60] But question B now receives an ambiguous or, rather, a complex answer: natural language *could have* been mimetic, but it decided not to be, because one day it realized that it should not be and irreversibly decided not to be; it might still be at the phonic level which is not proper to it, but not at the phonological level which is so. This position, then, can be approximately represented by the accompanying chart:

A	B	C
–	+/–	–

The sole merit of this lopsided formula, perhaps, is to show how modern linguistics, after twenty-five centuries of "hopeless debate," succeeded in displacing this debate or, if one prefers, in displacing its terms. Even Saussure, who readily expresses himself in classically conventional terms in the tradition of Locke or Whitney, does not notice this. But an unspoken discomfort resurfaces in Saussure under other guises: for example, his inability to compose, in 1894, a review of Whitney's work, his contradictory drafts, and this characteristically ambiguous formula: "As soon as discussion concerns only the universal things that can be said about the language system, I do not find myself in agreement with any school in general, no more with the reasonable doctrine of Whitney than with the unreasonable theories that he victoriously fought against."[61] This might be paraphrased by saying that modern linguistics, while in a certain way granting the first a victory over the second, adheres neither to the (reasonable) doctrine of Hermogenes nor to the (unreasonable) theory of Cratylus because *the very ground or, if one prefers, the object of the debate* — the phonic or graphic substance, and so on — *has become extrinsic to it.* There is here a true (for once) "epistemological rupture," which is the abandonment of a realist and substantialist attitude (in Bachelard's sense) in favor of a more abstract model, and a new consciousness of what will be called, in Edmund Husserl's terms, the *ideality* of the linguistic signifier. I specify the signifier, for in a certain way the ideality, or at least the (obvious) abstraction of the signified, was already one of the themes — and one of the arguments — of classical Hermogenism: for instance, James Harris's masterly chapter 3, section 3 in *Hermes.* What comes to light with the Saussurean theory of linguistic *identity* (the exclamation "Sirs!" being identical to itself throughout an infinite diversity of actual occurrences, like "the Paris-Geneva express" through all the modifications of its material elements), and what is illustrated by the phonological method, is precisely the transcendence of the signifier (vocable, morpheme, phoneme, or grapheme) in relation to all its concrete realizations, and therefore in relation to any kind of substance.[62] This is certainly an epistemological decision, a model, like that of the atom in another field, constructed the better to subject the linguistic object to scientific procedures, and in this regard the conventionality of language is really itself a scientific convention: "It is probably because it is arbitrary, and because one can define the condition upon which it attains its power of signification, that language can become the object of science"[63] — and if by chance it were found not to be so, one could count on linguistics to "make believe."

The arbitrariness of the sign is the founding move and *parti pris* of linguistics, and thus inevitably something like the *professional ideology* of the linguist. But it perhaps should be added — and here the facile comparison with the atomic model loses all validity — that the same bias is equally founding for language itself. Once again, the term *parti pris* is given the double meaning suggested by the two different turns of phrase: to make *one's own* choice {*prendre* son *parti*} and to choose *sides with* something {*prendre* le *parti de quelque chose*}. Irrespective of the "original decision" imagined by Bühler, one must conceive of humanity as awakening to the practical *impossibility* of a mimetic language — ultimately, as cumbersome as Balnibarbi's language of objects,[64] and as "laughable" as the double universe conjured up by Socrates, where each word would be the exact replica of a thing, "without our being able to distinguish which is the object itself and which is the name" — and forever doomed to that "betrayal" of the real which founds every natural language and initiates all science.

If one accepts this story, or at any rate the truth that it expresses, it is immediately apparent that this (double) decision exacts a very heavy price, which is the renunciation — in this domain — of all the seductions of the analogical relation.[65] The desire repressed here therefore seeks to satisfy itself, or at least to manifest itself, elsewhere, and its return takes two parallel roads. The first is a practical one, which we have seen described by Bühler as the pressure of the "pictorial" desire, through the phonic substance, on the "joints" and the "margins" of the linguistic system; Jespersen, Chastaing, and others thrive on measuring the effects of this pressure. The other road is "theoretical": it is a phantasmic description of natural language as being *essentially* that analogue of the real which it can never be except in an accessory and marginal way, and this is of course Cratylism itself.

By describing the mimologist theory as "phantasmic," I do not mean to point to its completely relative "falsehood," which is not at all our subject, but simply to suggest the essential role in mimological thought (a typical example of wishful thinking) played by a complex and more or less conscious system of desires or, let us say, of predilections to be satisfied: substantialism (refusal of abstraction); the attachment—often noted here—to the most "concrete" elements of language, sounds and vocables, semantemes rather than morphemes, nouns rather than verbs, proper names rather than common nouns; the need for valorization (refusal of neutrality), which makes one constantly choose sides, *preferring* this or that, one natural language over another, vowels over consonants, consonants over vowels, the *ordo rectus* over the *rectus ordo*, the masculine over the feminine, at the risk of endlessly balancing the first valorization with a compensatory countervalorization, privileging what is discredited; the instinct for motivation (refusal of gratuitousness, horror of the semantic void), which can accept only "necessary" significance, justified and exculpated, as it were, by some *natural* relation between its terms; finally, the dominant taste for analogy (refusal of difference), which irresistibly, and quite obviously, orients this search for "appropriateness" toward that very special variety which is justification by resemblance. At the same time, we have recognized the real difficulty in conceiving of another mode of motivation;[66] but the spontaneous and characteristic movement of Cratylian desire is not even to make the attempt, and to go straight for its object. Another continual slippage (we have found it, for example, in Proust, Leiris, and just now in Jespersen)—parallel or, rather, convergent— quite spontaneously attributes to mimologism what comes from indirect motivation: fanciful etymology, lexical association. This bias toward resemblance is properly the core of Cratylian thought, in which it might not be too risky to hear a few well-known psychoanalytical resonances: the "Oedipal" theme of uterine indifferentiation; the "narcissistic" theme of the mirror relation—which makes mimologism a *speculation* in the double sense of the word; and, in Lacanian terms, the flight from the symbolic and refuge in the imaginary.[67]

Whatever details may have escaped this critic's analytical competence, it is largely on this weight of imaginary investments that the aesthetic savor or, as was recently said, the *literariness* of mimological discourse depends. In twenty centuries of "reasonable theorizing," Hermogenes has produced nothing truly seductive; and his corpus, from Democritus to Saussure, practically boils down to a few laconic negations. In contrast, Cratylus leaves us with a series of picturesque, amusing, sometimes troubling works, some of which we have savored along the way. Here, Nodier's principle of unity — "When the poet and the linguist disagree, it is because one of the two has not understood his art and does not know its scope" — proves inspired by a slightly hasty and finally reductive monism. Rule for rule, I prefer to contrast his with this rather more "dialectical" one from Bachelard's *Psychoanalysis of Fire:* "The axes of poetry and science are opposed to one another from the outset. All that philosophy can hope to accomplish is to make poetry and science complementary, to unite them as two well-defined opposites."[68] As an illustration of this principle, perhaps, I would observe that the explicit or implicit axiology of Cratylism accounts very poorly for the charm peculiar to the Cratylian text, to mimologism as poetic production. Indeed, this charm comes not from the mimetic proof at all — with its inevitable platitude and pointless redundancy — but in each instance, on the contrary, from the surprise at the bringing together of a form and a sense that were previously separated: the ruralness of the *a,* the canineness of the *r,* the femininity of the vowel, the fluvial quality of "Moses" {*Moïse*}, the fatal fall of "catacomb." We feel a fleeting surprise, generally followed or accompanied by a sort of acquiescence, or semi-acquiescence, or marginal protest, which signals just as surely the entry into the game and the effective operation of the trap; failing this variable assent of the reader, mimological discourse sometimes seems to take refuge in a purposeless autistic raving. An unexpected but happy marriage, every successful mimologism is an authentic creation, or both an invention and a discovery: an active disavowal and an immanent refutation of the insipid — and impotent — aesthetic of resemblance.[69]

℘ Despite constant and multiple appeal to so many implicated disciplines (history of ideas, history of linguistics, philosophy of language, epistemology, and others), the nerve of this study, then, turns out to be, instead, the aesthetic seduction of mimologism considered as one of the fine arts — let us say (reiterate), as a literary genre. "The peculiarity of the truly general is its fertility": the fertility peculiar to generality, or Cratylian genericity, is perhaps its providing a context (an intertext) and thus a signification, a relevance, an existence, for texts otherwise and, if I may say so, until now neglected if not unknown — isolated, unsituated, undescribed, without transcendence and hence without function, unworkable and hence imperceptible.

This research certainly does not and could not claim to be exhaustive: for a single tradition, practically a single language, with at least one enormous period of silence (the Middle Ages),[70] even the term *lacunae* would be too flattering here. As announced from the beginning, our enterprise was instead a voyage of exploration and recognizance, useful perchance for preparing other explorers — for others. As such, however, it seems to me that this sampling has permitted us to survey, or nearly so, the typology of the genre and to sketch out the main lines of its history. On the whole it is a very simple history, and consonant with many others. From Plato to Nodier there are twenty-two centuries of immobility—which means, as we have seen, not uniformity but the almost timeless and ever reversible deployment of diverse possible variants—all virtually contained in that *Iliad* of the genre which is the founding text, whose inexhaustible (retrospective) *prescience* has continually astonished us. Then, under the crucial, and nearly disintegrative, shock of the birth of linguistics at the end of the eighteenth century—an event in the strongest sense, a rupture and point of no return—the genre, momentarily threatened with death, bursts forth in a shower of substitutive formations: the "subjective" Cratylism of the romantic *Volksgeist*, the secondary mimologism in the theory of "poetic language," a retreat to the restrained mimophony of sound symbolism, and the fictive mimology of ludic Cratylism, assumed as such or projected onto the handy alibi of the childlike consciousness.[71] With this last avatar, the genre in a way acquiesces to its deep essence by abandoning (almost) all scientific pretension and by moving from an implicit literariness to a conscious and organized literariness. Progress or decadence? Under this guise, anyway, mimology clearly, and legitimately, eludes all "refutation" and accedes to invulnerability, even immortality, if only it can avoid one last peril—the most serious—which would be its suffocation by repetitive proliferation. This, at least, is the reprieve that the belated critic wishes it, wishes us, in the expectation—who knows?—of new and unforeseeable metamorphoses.

Notes

INTRODUCTORY REMARKS

1. Luis Borges, *Other Inquisitions, 1937–1952*, trans. Ruth L. C. Simms (Austin: University of Texas Press, 1964), pp. 101–2.

2. Maurice Grammont, *Le Vers français* (Paris: Delagrave), p. 3.

3. Roman Jakobson, *Problèmes du langage* (Paris: Gallimard, 1966), p. 26.

4. Paul Claudel. "L'Harmonie imitative," in *Oeuvres en prose*, ed. Jacques Petit and Charles Galperine (Paris: Gallimard, 1965), p. 96.

CHAPTER 1

1. *Trans. Note:* Note that Genette has chosen the dative forms of both *thesis* and *physis* in the opening sentence. I have drawn upon two main sources in translating the quotations from Plato in this chapter: Louis Méridier's French translation, *Cratyle* (vol. 5 in Plato, *Oeuvres complètes* [Paris: Les Belles Lettres, 1961]), which Genette used to formulate his arguments; and H. N. Fowler's English translation in the Loeb Classical Library edition (Cambridge, Mass.: Harvard University Press, 1953). In most cases, Genette provides in parentheses the Greek equivalents for key terms; where he does not, I supply the Greek in braces. Where Genette's argument depends on the phrasing in Méridier's French translation, I give both the Greek *and* the French in braces. Finally, throughout the book, I provide in braces the French for the pivotal terms in Genette's theory.

2. See esp. the introduction to Méridier's edition. The main argument of this thesis is the obviously ironic way in which Socrates invokes the inspiration of the charlatan soothsayer Euthyphro.

3. Let us recall that the subtitle is *On the correctness of names* (*peri onomatōn orthotētos*).

4. According to Méridier, Plato wrote the *Cratylus* between the *Euthydemus* (c. 386) and the *Symposium* (c. 385).

5. This is what Victor Goldschmidt calls the "entreptic refutation" (*Essai sur le Cratyle: Contribution à l'histoire de la pensée de Platon* [Paris: Champion, 1940], p. 45).

6. Plato *Cratylus* 384d. *Trans. Note:* All quotations from Plato's *Cratylus* are from the Fowler translation unless otherwise noted.

7. {Ibid., modified.} *Trans. Note:* Although Fowler renders the Greek *orthotēs* some-

times as "correct" and sometimes as "right," I have preferred the former for the sake of consistency. The English translation of the subsequent quotation from Plato's 384d in this paragraph follows Méridier's reading rather than Fowler's.

8. {Plato *Cratylus* 385a, modified.}

9. {Ibid., 385a-b.}

10. Ibid., 387b-d. *Trans. Note:* Méridier and Fowler differ here: the question seems to be whether Plato is saying that things can name themselves as well as be named (Méridier), or only the latter (Fowler).

11. Plato *Cratylus* 390a, {modified}. *Trans. Note:* Fowler renders the Greek *tithenai* (imposes) as "embodies," while Méridier (hence, Genette) has *imprimer* (to imprint).

12. Plato *Cratylus* 388e-389a.

13. Ibid., 390d-e.

14. Let us note in passing the ambiguity of this verb, which applies equally, in French {*nommer*} as in Greek (*onomazein*), to the creation of the name and to its subsequent use.

15. Plato *Cratylus* 387c.

16. Of course, there is something naive about treating Hermogenes and Cratylus as real interlocutors of Socrates, in whom we can recognize this or that dialectial strength, when in fact Plato manipulates them at will as Socrates' foils. All remarks of this kind should therefore be taken simply as figures of speech, through which the reader pretends to accept the game of the Platonic dialogue as dramatic fiction.

17. See Méridier, *Cratyle*, p.55 n.1.

18. Ferdinand de Saussure, *Course in General Linguistics*, trans. Roy Harris (London: Gerald Duckworth, 1983), p.65. *Trans. Note:* All notes citing Saussure refer to Harris's English text, which also provides pagination for the original 1916 edition of the *Cours de linguistique générale* (Paris: Payot).

19. The Greek lexical field here is a bit more muddled than the French. There is no general term corresponding to the French *mot* {word}, the position of which is indiscriminately filled by *onoma* {name, word} and *rhēma* {saying, phrase}. But when they are placed in opposition to each other, as Plato does right here (425a), *onoma* stands for "noun" and *rhēma* for "verb." *Trans. Note:* The French word *nom* covers two different meanings in English: "name" (as in "proper name") and "noun" (as in "substantive"). Depending on the context, therefore, I have rendered *nom* as "name" (one sense of the Greek *onoma*), as "noun" (another sense of *onoma*), or as both together. Thus, the French title of chapter 1, "L'Éponymie du nom," may mean "eponymy of the name" in regard to determining correctness of names (is "Hermogenes" a suitable name or not?) and also "eponymy of the noun" in regard to the larger debate on language (do words refer to things, or are words merely arbitrary conventions?).

20. Plato *Cratylus* 391d.

21. *Trans. Note:* Genette is punning on the subtitle of the *Cratylus* — *peri onomatōn orthotētos* — in several senses here, each of which points to a main line of his argument

in this chapter. Given Méridier's translation of *orthotētos* as *justesse* (accuracy, appropriateness), *propriété* refers to the correctness of word choice, or the right assignment of names to things, which is the issue at the heart of the debate in the *Cratylus*. In the ordinary sense, however, *propriété* means the legal ownership or possession of a thing, hence a piece of property. The "proper name," which, as Genette observes, best satisfies the Cratylian theory of exact correspondence between signifier and signified, entails a notion of language as proprietary power. (See Hermogenes' example in 384d: masters always correctly name their slaves.) *Propriété* also means something that "belongs to" someone, suggesting in turn the Proustian idea of the *nom* (proper name) as the key to the individual and unique identity of a thing or a person. Finally, *propriété* recalls Greek *ousia*, the "essence," "substance," or "Being" (in Plato) of a thing. And *ousia* can also mean someone's wealth or "substance" — which brings us back to the French *propriété*. In this way, Genette's playful subtitle *de la propriété des noms* is multiply overdetermined and infinitely interpretable — just the kind of eponymous pun that Plato enjoys in the *Cratylus*.

22. For his purposes, Tzvetan Todorov distinguishes between "etymologies by filiation" (this being the current sense), of the type *cheval-caballus* {horse}, and "etymologies by affinity," of the type *sōma-sēma* {body-sign} (*"Introduction à la symbolique,"* *Poétique* 11 [1972]: 288). The line of reasoning put forward in order to include these kinds of connections in the notion of etymology is that "as much as kinship, etymology was preoccupied, in the past anyway, with relationships by affinity," and that in the nineteenth century these were designated as "popular etymologies." This argument seems rather sophistical to me: by this explanation, the philosopher's stone could be taken for a legitimate object of modern chemistry. Above all, this is to forget that for the "etymologists" of yesterday, relationships "by affinity" were actually taken for filiations. Likewise, "popular etymology" is really most often a naive filiation.

23. According to Bailly, it will appear only in Dionysius of Halicarnassus.

24. *Psychē* (soul) is explained successively by *anapsychon* (refreshing) and by *echei physin* (holding nature) (*Cratylus* 399d-400b). *Apollōn* is explained by *apolouōn* (purifying), *haploun* (simple), *aei ballōn* (ever-darting), and *homopolōn* (accompanying) (405c-406a).

25. Or rather in the sense of the historical etymology of the nineteenth and early twentieth centuries: thus, says Max Müller, "each word can have only one etymology, just as each living creature can have only one mother" (*New Lessons on Language*, vol. 2 [1863]). Today, Pierre Guiraud and Paul Zumthor think somewhat differently about this and give more consideration to phenomena of collusion — which in any case remain accidental, having nothing in common with the methodical overdetermination of the *Cratylus*.

26. Saussure, *Course*, p. 137.

27. Plato *Cratylus* 421b.

28. Ibid., 414b-c. *Trans. Note:* Where Fowler gives the Greek name for a letter, I have

used the letter itself—as does Genette. The individual examples from the *Cratylus*, in order of appearance in Genette's text here, are 421b, 406c, 395c-d, 395a-b, 411d, 414b-c. References for further individual examples are given below.

29. Plato *Cratylus* 411e-412a, 399c, 416b, 409b {modified}.

30. Ibid., 410c.

31. Ibid., 414a, 420c, 418c-d, 400b.

32. Ibid., 400b. Cf. Plato *Gorgias* 493a.

33. In the present context, this explanation is "overdetermined" in the strict sense, since the *same* "etymology" is explained in two ways at once, whereas the parallel *sōma-sōma* suggests another determination. This fine point might be illustrated by the following schema:

On the other hand, the schema for *Apollōn* would be, without a double linkage:

34. *Trans. Note:* Apparently, *sōzēma* is a coinage, fabricated from *sozein* (to preserve, safeguard)—but by which name-maker?

35. {Plato *Cratylus* 383b.}

36. {Ibid., 384c.}

37. Ibid., 395b. For other instances of the word, see Plato *Parmenides* 130e; *Sophist* 225d; *Phaedrus* 238a. *Trans. Note:* According to Fowler, *hé tou onomatos epōnymia* means "the form of the name." For Genette's argument, the most important meanings of *eponymia* include "derived" or "significant name"; "nickname"; "title" (e.g., of a god).

38. Jean Bollack, "*L'En-deça infini: L'Aporie du* Cratyle," *Poétique* 11 (1972): 310.

39. *Atechnōs gar estin hoion logos to tou Dios onoma:* "For the name *Zeus* is just like a definition" (*Cratylus* 396a {modified}).

40. *Trans. Note:* Genette is referring to Martin Heidegger's etymology.

41. Plato *Cratylus* 421c.

42. {Ibid., 421d-422c.}

43. Ibid., 426a-b, modified. *Trans. Note:* Fowler's variable translation of three main terms here has been made consistent: *onomata* are "names", *rhēmata* are "words," *logoi* are "sentences."

44. *Theos* {god} (a "component" of *alētheia*) is related to *thein* (to run) in 397d. This,

although said in passing, would give *alētheia* a tautological value: "running wandering." Why not?

45. Plato *Cratylus* 425d.

46. Ibid., 422d {modified}.

47. Ibid., 422e, 423a-b.

48. {Ibid., 423c.}

49. *Trans. Note:* Literally, *onomatopoeia* means "name-making." Genette seems to be punning: in fact, Socrates denies that onomatopoeia is the making of an *onoma*.

50. But only in its way, as we will see later on. In the meantime, the use of the term *phoneme* must not be understood in a rigorously phonological sense — that is, as a pure abstraction — but more roughly as a phonic element of natural language. Likewise, *grapheme*, like *letter*, designates an element of writing.

51. In fact, to *one* natural language — but considered here, in typical Greek fashion, to be the only one worthy of that name. Aristotle proposes the same criterion in another form in his definition of the phonic element (*stoicheion*): "An element {letter} is an indivisible sound, not every such sound but one of which an intelligible [composite] sound can be formed. Animals utter indivisible sounds but none that I should call an element {letter}" (*Poetics* 1456b, trans. W. Hamilton Fyfe, Loeb Classical Library [Cambridge, Mass.: Harvard University Press, 1932], p. 75). *Trans. Note: Stoicheion* can mean both "element" and "letter." The sense of the French rendition of this passage from Aristotle, from which Genette is arguing, is given in braces.

52. Plato *Cratylus* 423e.

53. According to Goldschmidt, this chart "is certainly not Plato's invention. The names of Democritus or Hippias, both of whom had studied individual letters, might be put forth" (*Essai*, p. 151). But according to Proclus, Democritus is elsewhere considered a supporter of the conventionalist thesis.

54. Plato *Cratylus* 424-427.

55. {Ibid., 424c-d, modified.} *Trans. Note:* This difficult passage has been retranslated (by Rachel Rue) in order to capture the sense of Méridier's (hence, Genette's) reading of it. Since the famous chart of letter values follows directly, I have retained Fowler's rendition of *stoicheia* as "letters" rather than Méridier's "elements."

56. In the *Cratylus* itself, I mean. We will find in Court de Gébelin an attempt to assign a generic signification to vowels (sensations) and to consonants (ideas).

57. Plato *Cratylus* 437d.

58. Goldschmidt, *Essai*, p. 168.

59. Plato *Cratylus* 432c-d. Cf. 434a: "Cratylus: 'Representing by likeness ... is absolutely and entirely superior to representation by chance signs.' — Socrates: 'You are right.'" And, in *Theaetetus* (206d), the following very Cratylian definition of *explication* {*logos*} is given: "to express one's thought in verbs {*rhēmata*} and nouns {*onomata*, names} by means of speech, forming an image of one's belief, in this oral emission, as if in a mirror or a pond" (trans. Robin A. H. Waterford [Suffolk: Penguin Books, 1987]) {modified}.

60. Saussure, *Course*, p. 68.

61. Plato *Cratylus* 432b–c.

62. On the other hand, through its very rigor, the Socratic definition will be more vulnerable than others to the conventionalist argument of the plurality of natural languages (*hippos/equus/cheval* ...), which the sensualistic mimologists of the neoclassical period will reject by appealing to the variety of aspects in the objects named, and thus by reducing the plurality of languages to a simple parasynonymy. This is impossible when one identifies, as Socrates does, the signified with a necessarily unique *essence*.

63. Plato *Cratylus* 434d. Obviously, an analogous critique would hold good for (against) the absence of *r* in *kinēsis*.

64. Ibid., 437a, 437b–c.

65. Ibid., 436c–d (emphasis added). *Trans. Note:* Genette emphasizes all the words having to do with the temporal sequence of the name-maker's error(s) in Méridier's translation of this passage from Plato: *au début, suite, point de départ, première*.

66. *Trans. Note:* Genette is punning here. The French text reads "pour un oui ou pour un ... nom." The idiom *pour un oui ou pour un non* means "at the drop of a hat" or "for a mere trifle." But the negative *non* (no) sounds the same as *nom*, "name" or "noun." Genette is inviting his readers to play the game of sound symbolism, or mimologism.

67. Plato *Cratylus* 429b.

68. Ibid., 439b.

69. "Every natural language being imperfect," Voltaire will say in a perhaps analogous reaction, "it does not follow that one ought to change it" ("Langues" [Natural languages] in *Mélanges*).

CHAPTER 2

1. On the Stoics' hermeneutic etymologies, esp. concerning names of the gods, see Jean Pepin, *"L'Allégorisme stoïcien"* in *Mythe et Allégorie: Les Origines grecques et les contestations judaeo-chrétiennes* (Paris: Aubier, 1958), pp. 125–31.

2. Let us recall that if Democritus was taken for one of the supporters of the conventionalist thesis, by contrast Epicurus, in his "Letter to Herodotus," and Lucretius, in Book 5 of *De rerum natura*, defend the naturalist thesis.

3. See Paul Zumthor, "Étymologies," in *Langue, Text, Énigme* (Paris: Seuil, 1975), pp. 144–58. Indeed, etymological speculation seems to have been the most active part of the Cratylian heritage throughout the Middle Ages.

4. Dionysius of Halicarnassus, *Peri sunthēseōs onomatōn* (late first century B.C.), p. 14.

5. Jean Collart, *Varron, grammarien latin* (Paris: Les Belles Lettres, 1954), p. 285. All the examples quoted here from Varro are taken from this work.

6. Aulus Gellius *Noctes Atticae* 10.4.

7. Ibid., 10.5 and 13.10. Aulus Gellius compares this last etymology to the one proposed by the jurisconsult Marcus Antistius Labeo: *soror* comes from *seorsum* (outside), because a sister is not destined to live within the family into which she is born.

8. Lucius Aelius Stilo Praeconinus, in *Grammaticae Romanae Fragmenta* ed. Gino Funaioli (Stuttgart: B. G. Teubner, 1969), 1 (sec.76): 59–76. Cf. Quintilian *Institutiones oratoriae* 1.6.33–34. *Trans. Note:* See the bilingual edition, *The Institutio Oratoria of Quintilian*, trans. H. E. Butler (Cambridge, Mass.: Harvard University Press, 1976–80), p.127.

9. Saint Augustine (Aurelius Augustinus), *Opera omnia*, in *Patrologia Latina cursus completus*, ed. J.-P. Migne (Paris: Montrouge, 1841), 1 (App.): 1411–13. Obviously, the point here is not to settle the question of this contested attribution (although it is less and less so); nor that of the relationship between the linguistic theory in this chapter and the whole of Augustinian semiotic, itself generally of a more conventionalist turn; nor, finally, the question of the degree of the author's fidelity to the Stoic doctrines which he claims to report, and on which he is today our sole source of information, along with a sentence — a corroborating one, moreover — from Origen: "According to the Stoics, primitive sounds, from which come the deduced names and the elements of etymology, imitate things" (Origenes Adamantius, *Contra celsum* 1.18). This text is taken here as a raw and, as it were, absolute document — neither more nor less so than the *Cratylus* itself. *Trans. Note:* All quotations from *On Dialectic* are taken from the bilingual Latin/English edition by Jan Pinbord, trans. B. Darrell Jackson (Dordrecht: Reidel, 1975); chap.6 appears on pp.90–99.

10. {Augustine, *On Dialectic*, p.93.}

11. "Breviter tamen hunc locum notatum esse de {notatum, hoc est de} origine verborum, volo paulisper accipias, ne ullam partem suscepti operis praetermisisse videamur. Stoici autumant..." {"Nevertheless I do wish for you to consider for a little while this topic which we have indicated briefly, namely, the origin of words, so that we might not seem to neglect any part of the work we have begun. The Stoics...think..." (ibid., pp.92–93)}.

12. {Ibid., p.95.}

13. {Ibid.}

14. {Ibid.}

15. {"From this point they believed that the license for naming had proceeded to the similarity of things themselves to each other" (ibid. pp.94–95).}

16. {Ibid., pp.95, 97.}

17. The example is not very accurately analyzed: in fact, the derivation moves by metonymy from *piscis* "fish" to *piscina* "fishpond," then by metaphor to *piscin[a]e* "swimming-baths" (or maybe by ascending synecdoche from *piscina* "fishpond" to *piscina* "pool in general").

18. The text adds a final example of *vicinitas* {neighborhood}, from whole to part, which is not very clear: *capillus* (hair), *quasi capitis pilus* (hair of the head) {Augustine, *On Dialectic*, pp.96–97). In this form it is merely a contracted compound word; there would not really be any derivation unless *capillus* were derived from *caput*, without the intervention of *pilus* — which, besides, is the true etymology.

19. One notices here, as in Aristotle, the assimilation of the relation of inclusion to the relation of proximity, which prefigures the modern annexation of synecdoche to

metonymy. On the other hand, and even though the exposition on "contrariety" occurs parenthetically in the study of *vicinitas,* the derivation through antiphrasis preserves its complete autonomy.

20. {Augustine, *On Dialectic,* p. 97.} "Quorum {origo, de qua} ratio non reddi possit, aut non est, ut ego arbitror, aut latet, ut Stoici contendunt" (ibid., p. 96). "Motivation" might seem an anachronistic and tendentious translation, but the *aut non est* precludes a more liberal interpretation such as "cause" or "origin." Augustine cannot mean that certain words have no origin; that would be an absurdity. The only plausible interpretation is, therefore, that their origin is not *motivated:* that is to say, it is purely conventional. *Trans. Note:* Bearing in mind Genette's translation of the word *origo* as "motivation," one can appreciate the Latin phrase that he has chosen for the title of chapter 2 of *Mimologics.* Besides echoing — if not parodying — the title of chapter 6 in Augustine's chapter title, "De origine verbi", the phrase *de ratione verborum* underscores Genette's central argument concerning mimologism here: "On the Reason for Words" or "On the Motivation of Words."

21. An essential conclusion, for in fact the chapter continues and ends with a last illustration, a bit muddled, of the impossibility of tracing back beyond phonic expressivity. This time, the point of departure is more elementary: it is the "thick and powerful" sound of the labio-velar *v,* whence *vis* (violence), *vincula* (chains), *vimen* (withe), *vitis* (vine, because of the tendrils), *vietum* (an old man bent over with age {withered}), *via* (a winding or well-beaten road). If an inverse procedure is adopted, one can backtrack, for example, from *vietum* to *vitis,* from *vitis* to *vincire,* from *vincire* to *vis,* and from *vis* to that *ultima ratio* which is "the congruence between the... powerful sonority of this word and the thing it signifies, beyond which there is nothing more to explain" (ibid., p. 99). It is clear that the return route no longer even goes as far back as the phonic element *v* and stops with the onomatopoetic word *vis.* The endpoint of the analysis would therefore really be phonic expressiveness at the *lexical* level, which would mark a conscious refusal to follow Socrates onto the ground of elementary sounds; but the contradiction between this stopping point and the interpretation attached to the *v* remains open, and with it the ambiguity of the text.

22. Aristotle *Peri mnemes* 451b.

23. We have detected another weak link, between *prōta* and *hustata,* which is due to the fact that etymological motivation does not always proceed by analysis but sometimes becomes locked in an apparently indefinite play of lexical associations (*sōma-sēma*) and therefore incapable of leading back to the primary elements. This weak link remains unacknowledged, but perhaps an unspoken awareness of it partly determines its final abandonment.

24. For there will be adversaries, of course, after as before *On Dialectic* — and the *Cratylus.* The special attention granted to the Cratylian tradition here should not make us forget that it was always contested, and was besides almost always a minority position in the opinion of scholars: the names of Aristotle, Boethius, Saint Thomas Aquinas, Roger Bacon, John Locke, A.-R.-J. Turgot — well-known and influential supporters

of the conventionalist thesis—suffice to illustrate this fact, even before the birth of scientific linguistics.

CHAPTER 3

1. John Wallis, *Grammatica linguae anglicanae* (Oxford, 1653), 3d ed. (Hamburg, 1672), pp. 148–64. Wallis (1616–1703), a mathematician, logician, theologian, and grammarian (considered by Nicolas Beauzée to be one of the founders of general grammar), is one of the great phoneticians of the neoclassical period. His mimologisms are cited by Bernard Lamy and Hugh Blair. *Trans. Note:* The most recent English edition of Wallis is *Grammar of the English Language*, trans. J. A. Kemp (London: Longman, 1972), but it omits chapters 14 and 15. Therefore, since Genette's examples come from chapter 14, "On Etymology," I have translated them from his French.

2. The Latin verb, as neutral as the noun *index*, is *innuere*, here and throughout the text.

3. I am giving the essentials from the list of examples for this first group, in order to give an idea of the sequence of derivations; the other lists will be much more selective.

4. *Canina litera* comes from Persius, *Satires* 1.109; it is the sound of a dog growling. "When dogs challenge each other, before biting one another, by putting on a menacing look and drawing back their teeth, they seem to pronounce the *r*, for which reason the poet Persius, the most elegant among the satiric and caustic writers, called it *litera canina*, the canine letter, the one pronounced by dogs, when he said in his first satire: '*Sonat hic de nare canina litera*,' that is to say, 'the canine letter reverberates from one side of the nose in this place.' When a man is angry, or jibing, or becoming incensed, we say that he is irritated by some annoyance, or exasperated. And this is so because he cannot say a nice word but only harsh, injurious ones, full of strident letters, which are the letters *rr* repeated and harshly pronounced" (Geoffroy Tory, *Champ fleury; ou, l'Art et science de la proportion des lettres* [1529], ed. Gustave Cohen ([Paris: Charles Bosse, 1931]), bk. 3 (n.p.).

5. Not counting analyses of the type *grind = grate + wind*, or *greedy = gripe + needy*, which call to mind the "portmanteau words" of Lewis Carroll or James Joyce, but in reverse. From *fuming* and *furious*, Carroll creates *frumious*. If there is mimologism in this neologism, it is clearly *secondary*, since it modifies (adds to) the natural language. As for Wallis, he applies a fanciful analysis to an existing word (even though the process incontestably exists within the English language), and long before *brunch* or *stagflation*: cf. Otto Jespersen, "Blendings," in *Language: Its Nature, Development, and Origin* [London: Allen & Unwin, 1922], chap. 16, sec. 6). Thus Wallis in fact falls within the tradition of Socratic "etymology" and within the system of primary mimologism.

6. A few do appear, as if by accident, in the examples of final consonants. One could also question the group *wr*, which phonetically reduces to one single consonant; but conversely, of course, an initial consonant like that in *jump* is a group [dž] hidden by the written form.

7. Let us recall that already for Socrates, *i* stands for lightness and thinness.

8. The same articulatory feature and the same semantic value are assigned to *r* here, but without any lexical confirmation.

9. On English monosyllabism, cf. Otto Jespersen, "Monosyllabism in English," *Linguistica: Selected Papers in English, French, and German* (Copenhagen: Levin & Munksgaard, 1933), pp. 384–408.

10. Only ultimately, because Wallis, acknowledging that some Romance words could have slipped into his lists, immediately adds that "the English, just as they themselves form their words with sounds of this type, eagerly seize those which they find already formed in that way." As we have seen, he also has occasion to propose {Latin} etymologies such as *crepo, curvo, crux* (and also a few Greek ones).

CHAPTER 4

1. Let us recall that Locke's *Essay concerning Human Understanding* appears in 1690. Leibniz immediately undertakes a critical reading of it; this undertaking is revived in 1700 by Coste's French translation. Locke, {as if} in a hurry to evade the dialogue with "the gentlemen in Germany," dies in 1704 when the main portion of the critique, a sustained commentary in the form of a pseudodialogue, is already written. But *New Essays* will finally appear only in 1765, half a century after the death of Leibniz himself. *Trans. Note:* The standard English version of Leibniz's *New Essays on Human Understanding*, trans. and ed. Peter Remnant and Jonathan Bennett (Cambridge: Cambridge University Press, 1981), has been used for citations throughout this chapter; bk. 3, chap. 2, sec. 1 begins on page 273. For Locke's essay, see John Locke, *An Essay concerning Human Understanding*, ed. Peter H. Nidditch (Oxford: Clarendon Press, 1975).

2. {Locke, *Essay*, p. 405.}

3. A remark made by Hans Aarsleff in "Leibniz on Locke on Language," *American Philological Quarterly* 1 (1964): 165–88; rpt. in Aarsleff, *From Locke to Saussure: Essays on the Study of Language and Intellectual History* (Minneapolis: University of Minnesota Press, 1982), pp. 42–83.

4. The Latin text was published by Louis Couturat, ed., *Opuscules et fragments inédits de Leibniz* (Paris: Presses Universitaires de France, 1903; rpt., Hildesheim: Georg Olms, 1961), pp. 151–52.

5. See Leibniz, *New Essays*, p. 278: "Perhaps there are some artificial languages which are wholly chosen and completely arbitrary, as that of China is believed to have been, or like those of George Dalgarno and the late Bishop Wilkins of Chester." And *Brevis designatio* {see note 6}, p. 187: "I except [from motivation] the artificial languages, like that of Wilkins, Bishop of Chester, who was a person of intelligence and knowledge without peer." See George Dalgarno, *Ars signorum, vulgo character universalis et lingua philosophica* (London: Hayes, 1661); John Wilkins, *An Essay towards a Real Character and a Philosophical Language, with an Alphabetical Dictionary* (London, 1668).

6. Leibniz, *New Essays*, pp. 274, 278; *Brevis designatio meditationum de originibus*

346

gentium, ductis potissimum ex indicio linguarum, published in 1710 in *Miscellanea Bero-linensia ad Incrementum Scientiarum,* vol.1; rpt. in *Opera omnia,* ed. Louis Dutens (Geneva: 1768), 4, pt.2: 186-87.

7. Leibniz, *New Essays,* p.274. The mathematician and orientalist Jacques Golius (1596-1667) taught at Leyden and colloborated in Martini's *Atlas sinicus* (noted in Jacques Brunschwig, ed., *Nouveaux Essais* [Paris: Garnier-Flammarion, 1966]).

8. *Trans. Note:* Genette does not identify his Baron de Montesquieu source.

9. See Madeleine V. David, *Le Débat sur les écritures et l'hiéroglyphe aux XVIIe et XVIIIe siècles et l'application de la notion de déchiffrement aux écritures mortes* (Paris: SEVPEN {Service d'Édition et de Vente des Publications de l'Éducation Nationale}, 1965), pp.79-80.

10. Letter to P. Bouvet, quoted in David, *Débat,* p.65.

11. The *New Essays* makes room here for an exception almost symmetrical to that of Chinese: slang (*Rothwelsch, lingua zerga, narquois*) and composite languages like the Mediterranean *lingua franca.* For Leibniz, these are artificial but nonetheless (partially) motivated languages, but this is because they were forged out of natural languages, through deformation ("either by replacing the accepted significations of the words with metaphorical ones or by compounding or deriving new words according to their fancy") or through blending ("either by the haphazard mingling of neighboring languages or, more often, by taking one language as a base and—through neglecting or changing its rules and even by grafting new words onto it—mangling and garbling and mixing and corrupting it"). These languages are therefore entirely naturally "a mixture of chosen features and natural and chance features of the languages upon which they are built" (*New Essays,* pp.279, 278).

12. In *New Essays, ex instituto* is given in parentheses as a gloss on the adjective "arbitrary."

13. Leibniz, *Brevis designatio,* p.187: "Talis etiam fuerit, si quam mortales docuit Deus."

14. Ibid.: "At in linguis paulatim natis orta sunt vocabula per occasiones ex analogia vocis cum affectu, qui rei sensum comitabatur: nec aliter Adamum nomina imposuisse crediderim."

15. See Leibniz, *New Essays,* p.281. On the theory of natural language in Jacob Böhme, see the article by Wolfgang Kayser, "*Böhmes Natursprachenlehre und ihre Grundlagen,*" *Euphorion* 31 (1930): 531-62; trans. as "La doctrine du langage naturel chez Jacob Boehme et ses sources," *Poétique* 11 (1972): 337-66.

16. Leibniz, *Brevis designatio,* p.187: "Neque vero ex instituto profectae, et quasi lege conditae sunt linguae, sed naturali quodam impetu natae hominum, sonos ad affectus motusque animi attemperantium. Artificiales linguas excipio."

17. {Leibniz, *New Essays,* p.283.} *Trans. Note:* Leibniz's French reads: "comme disant par exemple mon lévélend pèle."

18. Let us recall that Leibniz accepts the paleo-comparatist theory called the "Scythian hypothesis"—maintained in the sixteenth century by Goropius Becanus and

NOTES TO PAGES 48-50

taken up again at the end of the eighteenth century by Andreas Jäger—on the original unity of the greater part of natural languages and European peoples, descendants of the Scythians who came from the shores of the Black Sea. See George J. Metcalf, "The Indo-European Hypothesis in the Sixteenth and Seventeenth Centuries," in Dell H. Hymes, ed., *Studies in the History of Linguistics: Traditions and Paradigms* (Bloomington: Indiana University Press, 1974), pp. 233-57. On the body of Leibniz's ideas in historical linguistics, and their "sources," see Sigrid von der Schulenburg, *Leibniz als Sprachforscher* (Frankfort, 1973).

19. Leibniz, *Brevis designatio,* p. 187: "Tales detegunt sese primae origines vocabulorum, quoties penetrari potest ad radicem τῆς ὀνοματοποιίας."

20. {Leibniz, *New Essays,* p. 283 (emphasis added).}

21. {Leibniz, *Brevis designatio,* p. 187 (emphasis added).}

22. "Optimism of the signifier" (*optimisme du signifiant*) is how Jean-Pierre Richard describes René Chateaubriand's mimologism (*Paysage de Chateaubriand* [Paris: Seuil, 1967], p. 162).

23. See Louis Couturat, *La Logique de Leibniz d'après des documents inédits* (Paris: Germer Baillière, 1901); and Couturat and Leopold Léau, *Histoire de la langue universelle* (Paris: Hachette, 1903).

24. But also natural, since it is just simply, in Rowland Jones, a matter of English erected into a universal natural language.

25. David, *Débat,* p. 63 {original emphasis}.

26. A position apparently much closer but more complicated (or more confused) is that of Marin Mersenne in his treatise *Harmonie universelle* (Paris: Sebastien Cramoisy, 1636-37). Like Socrates and Leibniz, Mersenne assigns an expressive value to the sounds of natural language ("*a* and *o* are appropriate for signifying what is large and fullbodied, ... *e* signifies sharp and subtle things, ... *i* very thin and very small things, ... *o* serves to express the grand passions ... and to represent round things, ... *u* signifies dark and hidden things." Among the consonants, *f* can represent wind and fire; *l,* laziness; *r,* roughness; *m,* magnificence; *n,* dimness). But contrary to Leibniz, he does not believe that these capacities manifest themselves in the development of natural languages; his illustrations are composed not of simple vocables, but—we will encounter this cleavage again—of complex imitative harmonies borrowed from Virgil: that is, from poetic art. And finding that no affection of the senses inspires in us "vocables that would signify naturally, of which one could compose a natural language," he comes to conclude: "I do not think that there is any natural language" (bk. 2, pp. 75-77). There is no mimetic natural language, despite the mimetic capacities of the sounds: so far we are within pure Socratic orthodoxy. But here is the Hermogenist reversal: "If one were able to invent a language whose diction (vocables) had a natural signification, so that all men understood the thought of others solely from the pronunciation without having learned the signification, as they understand that a person is happy when he laughs and sad when he cries, this language would be the best of all possible languages. ... But since the sound of spoken words does not have a relationship with natural, moral, and

supernatural things, such that their pronunciation alone could make us comprehend their nature or their properties, because the sounds and the motions are not tokens attached to the things they represent until men agree together and impose on them whatever signification they want ... we need to see if men's artfulness and intelligence can invent the best of all possible languages. That can happen only if one first assumes that the best language is the one that explains intellectual notions most succinctly and clearly" (p. 65; cf. p. 12). The "best language possible" is therefore not mimetic language — which is impossible; it is simply the most succinct and clear language, and as we know, Mersenne finally locates this ideal of economy and effectiveness — and much earlier than Dalgarno and Wilkins — in an artificial algebraic language based on the analysis of concepts and a combinatory of conventional signs. He would, then, represent quite well the rather twisted trajectory from secondary Cratylism to secondary Hermogenism: that of a Socrates converted *in extremis* to "philosophical" language.

CHAPTER 5

1. This is the "visible speech" of the Bell Company researchers; see Ralph K. Potter, George A. Kopp, and Harriet C. Green, *Visible Speech* (New York: Van Nostrand, 1947).

2. Articulatory phonomimesis is used by artificial alphabets as well: this is the "visible speech" of Melville Bell (not to be confused with the above), recast by the phonetician Henry Sweet under the name of an "organic" system; see Sweet, *A Primer of Phonetics* (Oxford: Clarendon Press, 1906).

3. Geoffroy Tory, *Champ fleury; ou, l'Art et science de la proportion des lettres* (1529; Paris: Charles Bosse, 1931), bk. 3, n.p.; Julius Caesar Scaliger, *De causis linguae latinae* (1559; Heidelberg: Petrum Santandreanum, 1580), bk. 1, p. 39.

4. This lesson is known to have been inspired by Geraud de Cordemoy's *Discours physique de la parole* (1668), but the mimetic interpretation is not in Cordemoy.

5. R. P. Bernard Lamy, *La Rhétorique; ou, L'Art de parler* (Paris: Pralard, 1675), bk. 3, chap. 2, p. 161. *Trans. Note:* Since Genette quotes sometimes from the first edition of Lamy's *Rhétorique* (1675) and sometimes from the fourth (1699; Brighton: Sussex Reprints, 1969), all translations throughout are mine for the sake of consistency.

6. To be read as a block capital; the variants in script, even mechanical script, are so important that it is sometimes necessary to specify these details.

7. The text from Galeotus comes from the chapter "De literis" in *De homine* (Taurini: Joannem Angelum & Bernardinum de Sylva, 1517).

8. Franciscus Mercurius Van Helmont, *Alphabeti vere naturalis hebraici brevissima delineatio* (Sulzbaci: Typis Abraham Lichtenthaleri, 1657).

9. Johann Georg Wachter, *Naturae et scripturae concordia* (Leipzig, 1752). Wachter, a German philologist and archaeologist, lived from 1673 to 1757. His major work is *Glossarum germanicum*, published in 1736-37.

10. Paul Claudel, "The Religion of Letters," in *The East I Know*, trans. Teresa Frances and William Rose Benet (New Haven: Yale University Press, 1941), p. 65.

11. Rowland Jones was an English philologist (1722–74). The texts discussed here are *The Origin of Language and Nations* (1764; Menston, England: Scolar Press, 1972); *Hieroglyfics* (1768; Menston: Scolar Press, 1972); *The Circles of Gomer* (1771; Menston: Scolar Press, 1970); *The Io-Triads* (London, 1773). *Trans. Note:* The full title of Jones's last work reads: *The Io-Triads; or, the tenth muse, wherein the Origin, Nature, and Connection of the sacred Symbols, Sounds, Words, Ideas and Things, are discovered and investigated, according to the Platonic numbers. AND The Principles of all Human Knowledge, as well as the First Language, are retrieved in the English.* For the descriptive subtitle of *The Circles of Gomer,* see note 13, below.

12. Samuel Bochart, a major supporter of the Hebraicist thesis, wrote *Hierozoicon* (1663). For his part, Jones rejects the derivation of Celtic from Hebrew. Substituting one ancestor for another, he happens to propose the Phrygian language, following the hypothesis attributed to Psammetichos (Psamtik) by Herodotus.

13. Jones, "Preface," *Origin,* pp. 18–19, 1; *Hieroglyfics,* p. 5. The *Io-Triads* reiterates this superiority of English and carries on a controversy with Court de Gébelin over the comparative merits of French (p. 47). Of course, here again we encounter the national *parti pris* already present in John Wallis, but reoriented by a jealous protectionism toward a kind of imperialism, which is clearly marked, too, by the subtitle of *The Circles of Gomer: An Essay towards an Investigation and Introduction of English as an Universal Language,* and the presence of an appendix titled: "An Universal English Grammar."

14. Let us recall that in the neoclassical period, and up to Jean-François Champollion, the Egyptian writing system is thought to be purely ideographical and without a trace of phoneticism; for that time, the "hieroglyph" is the very type of the mimetic sign. We will come across this motif again, which survives all the way up through Charles Baudelaire. Cf. Liselotte Dieckmann, *Hieroglyphics: The History of a Literary Symbol* (St. Louis, Mo.: Washington University Press, 1970).

15. Jones, *Hieroglyfics,* p. 12. In *The Io-Triads,* Jones, after Leibniz, defends the principle of the mimetic origin of language against the attacks of his illustrious compatriot "Mr. Locke, who, after furnishing the human soul with many new faculties, in order to be consistent in his new system of metaphysics, has ventured to define language to be nothing more than a set of words, which any people have arbitrarily agreed upon to record and communicate their thoughts to each other, without any natural connection betwixt sounds and ideas or things" ("Preface," pp. 4–5; the phrasing from Locke's *Essay concerning Human Understanding,* bk. 2, chap. 2, is recognizable). Thus, against Locke, Jones maintains regarding the natural signification of the word *life* that "it now appears to be a matter of fact, that words and ideas have a natural connection with each other and the word *life,* in particular, as a compound of *l-if,* signifying the flowing or springing up of parts or things" (p. 5). The Cratylian debate coincides with the philosophical and religious debate here quite consistently, with Locke's conventionalism being directly (and very inaccurately) related to his alleged impiety: "lacking a correct notion of the divine origin of speech."

16. Unless otherwise indicated, the following examples are from Jones, *Origin. Trans.*

Note: Genette's examples are located in the section "Of Letters and Characters," pp. 2–8.

17. Jones, *Origin,* p. 2; *Hieroglyfics,* p. 15.

18. "It is also remarkable, that man of all animals in the expression of joy and admiration makes use of the o, which signifies eternity; but other animals seem to sound the letter a, signifying the earth; man also is upright, with his countenance towards heaven; but beasts look downwards upon the earth, as if their utmost joy and pleasure are centered there" (*Origin,* "Preface," p. 17). We will reencounter this telluric interpretation of the A in René Chateaubriand.

19. The letter F is treated merely as an "auxiliary" to M; not being Celtic letters, K, Q, V, X, and Z receive no commentary. As for S and, more vaguely, R, these are simple "letters of sound": that is, apparently purely phonetic signs. But S offers an interesting case of indirect phonomimesis: drawn in the form of waves, it notates a sound that itself imitates their whistling or hissing noise. So, phonic mimesis and graphic mimesis rejoin here through the object imitated, which is both visible and audible. We will find such obviously forced convergences again elsewhere.

20. Jones, *Io-Triads,* p. 44.

21. The *Origin* actually presents two series of particles — vowel + consonant, then consonant + vowel — which doubles the signifying capacity, for the reversal modifies or particularizes the semantic synthesis. Thus, *ac* signifies an "earthly action"; *ca,* more precisely, the action of surrounding or enclosing the earth (pp. 8, 10).

22. Jones, *Hieroglyfics,* pp. 24–25.

23. Another attempt at ideographical interpretation of the alphabet, apparently inspired by Jones's, is found in *An Essay towards an Investigation of the Origin and Elements of Language and Letters,* by L. D. Nelme, published in 1772 (rprt., Menston: Scolar Press, 1972). For Nelme, the two basic graphemes are, once more, the vertical feature, whence the letter l, symbol of height and extension in general, and the circle, whence the letter O, symbol of the horizon and all boundaries, starting with that of the Garden of Eden. Then O + l yields Saxon *Ol,* "whole" (unlike Jones, Nelme derives English not from Celtic but from Anglo-Saxon; Jones refutes this heresy in *The Io-Triads*).

CHAPTER 6

1. Charles de Brosses, *Traité de la formation mécanique des langues,* 2 vols. (Paris: Saillant, Vincent & Desaint, 1765; rev. ed., 1800). Jean Roudaut has reproduced a few pages from the book in his valuable *Poètes et grammairiens au XVIIIe siècle* (Paris: Gallimard, 1971). The short book by Hippolyte Sautebin, *Un linguiste français du XVIIIe siècle: Le Président de Brosses* (Berne: St. Aempfli, 1899; Geneva: Slatkine Reprints, 1971), is merely a basic summary.

2. De Brosses, *Traité,* 1:30–31. *Trans. Note:* All quotations from de Brosses's *Traité* are translated from the 1800 revised edition. Since Genette has not modernized the punctuation, I have followed suit in preserving de Brosses's style of neoclassical periods and much of his idiosyncratic punctuation.

3. Ibid., 1:255.

4. Ibid., 2:368. This very widespread valorization of the noun as the most "concrete" vocable probably originates in a spontaneous intuition, as witnessed by the child's imagination: "There are some words that I see," says a little girl of five years old. "I can really see 'window,' for example, but there are other words that I don't see. I don't see 'I love you'" (reported by Brice Parain in *Recherches sur la nature et les fonctions du langage* [Paris: Gallimard, 1942], p.52).

5. De Brosses, *Traité*, 1: chap.16.

6. De Brosses's position on the then highly controversial issue of the mother tongue is very cautious, but it is marked by at least one quite decided rejection of the traditional Hebraicist thesis (of Guichard, Bochart, Thomassin, etc.): "There is no evidence in favor of Hebrew or of any other language as being the original language" (*Traité*, 1:209). The Hebraicist thesis was still upheld in 1764 by Nicolas Sylvestre Bergier (*Les Éléments primitifs des langues, découverts par la comparaison des racines de l'hébreu avec celles du grec, du latin, et du français* [Paris: Brocas & Humblot, 1764]) and was not ruled out by Nicolas Beauzée in the article "Langue" {Natural language} in the *Encyclopédie* (1765). De Brosses's position is also marked by a clear preference for Greek, regarded as the language closest to the "system of nature, which is none other than this penchant she has given to man for combining the form of a vocal inflection with the form of a physical object in order to assimilate one to the other: a system whose development is the topic of the Treatise that I am writing" (1:84-85) — in other words, the most mimetic natural language in the world. This gives a certain accent to the topos, inherited from a tradition going back to Estienne, of the "correspondence" of Greek and French (1:69).

7. De Brosses, *Traité*, 1: chap.14; cf.1:19: "Everything depends essentially on two material principles; the imitation of objects by the voice, and the movement proper to each vocal organ in keeping with its structure."

8. *Trans. Note:* Much of de Brosses's theory and Genette's analysis of it depend upon the semantic field shared by two cognate verbs: *peindre* (to paint) and *dépeindre* (to depict). The verb *peindre* and the noun *peinture* (painting), which appears in the French title to Genette's chapter 6 ("Peinture et dérivation"), cover the English notions of "paint" and "portray," "painting" and "portrait," respectively. The verb *dépeindre* means "paint" in the sense of "depict" or "describe."

9. De Brosses, *Traité*, 1:12.

10. Ibid., 1:9-10.

11. Ibid., 1:111-12.

12. Ibid., 1:109.

13. *Trans. Note:* The several concepts designated by the word *figure* are crucial here. As Genette points out, for de Brosses the first sense of *figure* is visual "shape" or "form," specifically the form of the written letter as it represents or "figures" the consonants, which in turn "figure" or represent the vowels, which are the originary basis of language as speech. However, *figure* also means "figure of speech" or "rhetorical figure." The slippage between *figure* as perceptible, hence natural, form and *figure* as rhetorical

device, hence unnatural "deviation," is an important aspect of de Brosses's contribution to the Cratylian tradition. There are also important resonances between the noun *figure* and the verb *figurer*. Since the first sense in English of *figurer* is simply the general verb "to represent" I have most often translated it as "to represent figuratively" in order to bring out the important connection between rhetoric and representation in de Brosses's *Traité* and in Genette's analysis. Sometimes, where this connection is pointedly thematized, I have translated *figurer* as "to figure."

14. De Brosses, *Traité*, 2:37-38.

15. "The sound with its figure" (ibid., 2:45) stands for the vowel with its consonant; BA is a "full voice figuratively represented by the lip"; CA is a "full voice figuratively represented by the throat" (2:511-14). *Trans. Note:* The previously quoted sentence to which Genette refers is at 1:112.

16. Ibid., 1:114.

17. Ibid., 2:48. As is well known, the connection between the consonant and writing is already present in Jean-Jacques Rousseau, *Essay on the Origin of Languages*, trans. Victor Gourevitch (New York: Harper & Row, 1986), pp. 249-54. Cf. Jacques Derrida, *Of Grammatology*, trans. Gayatri C. Spivak (Baltimore: Johns Hopkins University Press, 1976), pt. 2, chap. 3.

18. De Brosses, *Traité*, 2:423.

19. Ibid., 2:44, 49.

20. Ibid., 2:46-148; cf. p. 231.

21. Ibid., 1:233, 243. In contrast, La Hontan asserts that in four days he was unable to get a Huron to articulate a labial; it is true that the subject was not a child. Previously, Paul Lejeune, in his *Relation de 1634* (ed. Guy Laflèche [Montreal: Presses de l'Université de Montréal, 1973], p. 111), had marveled at a similar infirmity, "for this letter seems almost natural, so great is its use." Max Müller will extend the observation to the Mohicans (*New Lessons on Language*, 1:46). Those Indians sure were ornery.

22. De Brosses, *Traité*, 1:123.

23. Ibid., 1:262-63.

24. Ibid., 1:263.

25. Ibid., 1:265-66. Notice here the double agreement with Plato and Leibniz (movement) and with Persius, Martianus Capella, Wallis, and so on (roughness). In his exactly contemporaneous *Encyclopédie* article "Langue," Beauzée adds this note to the chorus: "We can very probably attribute the fact that the Chinese make no use of the rough articulation *r* to the lethargic character, already well known, of this people."

26. De Brosses, *Traité*, 1:267. "Nasal letter," *s*; "labial letter," *b* or *f*.

27. Ibid., 1:158-59.

28. Ibid., 1:267-69.

29. Ibid., 1:261; cf. 2:367. Cf. Wallis.

30. Ibid., 1:261-62.

31. Ibid., 1:263-64; cf. 2:367-68, 378.

32. Ibid., 1:265.

33. Ibid., 1:266.

34. Ibid., 1:267.

35. Ibid., 2:383-84.

36. Ibid., 2:385.

37. Ibid., 2:131-32. Cf. Varro.

38. We can append to this list a certain number of original mimetic "roots" including a vowel (always *a*): *ac,* which designates things sharpened to a point and things that forge ahead, whence Latin *ago; tac,* "onomatopoeia imitative of the noise made by striking the tip of one's finger on something," whence Latin *tago, tango,* and Greek *thigo;* and the following pretty derivation, itself "œdipal" too: "The labial root *am* is the indispensable word by which the child names his mother or his nurse; for it is this syllable alone that nature allows him yet to pronounce. [The canonical form, as for de Brosses himself, is obviously *ma,* but we will see directly the reason for this metathesis.] It was used to express the feeling of tenderness for a beloved object, thereupon producing the verb *amo*" (ibid., 2:367-68). A. R. J. Turgot says more cautiously: "It would not be unlikely were the Latin word *amare* to derive its origin from this" ("Étymologie," in *Oeuvres de Turgot et documents le concernant, avec biographie et notes,* ed. Gustave Schelle [Paris: F. Alcan, 1913-23], 1:498).

39. Paragraph 73, "On the words *Papa* and *Mama,*" and paragraph 76, "In all centuries, and all countries the *lip*-letter is used or in its absence the *tooth*-letter or both together to express the child's first words *Papa* and *Mama*" (this is the title).

40. De Brosses, *Traité,* 1:252.

41. Ibid., 1:253.

42. Ibid., 1:258.

43. Ibid., 1:259.

44. Ibid., 1:260-61.

45. Ibid., 1:261.

46. Ibid., 1:270-71.

47. Ibid., 2:406. Cf. *Cratylus* on *n.*

48. Ibid., 1:257-58 (emphasis added). Another symptom of this predicament is the following change of heart, or ruefulness, regarding the fifth order: "The fifth order, which is a hidden consequence of the preceding one, and better known by its numerous effects than by its cause, is born from the fact that the mechanical structure of certain vocal organs naturally suits them for naming certain classes of things of the same genus; the inflection proper to each organ is indicated by nature as the characteristic of that class: this basically results from the fact that things ... have some quality or some motion similar to the one proper to the organ" (1:285-86). Clearly, de Brosses maintains at once that the fifth order is a consequence (but a "hidden" one) of the fourth order or of onomatopoeia, that its cause is not fully known, and that "basically" this cause is not of the auditory order but stems from a direct analogy between organ and object. De Brosses is going around in circles, and quite obviously he cannot make up

his mind to choose between "onomatopoeia of the ear" and organic mimesis, neither of which in fact satisfies him.

49. Ibid., 1:290–91.

50. Locke had previously shown the same disdain for the reaction of the man born blind, which he compared (in *An Essay concerning Human Understanding*, bk.3, chap.4) to knowing the taste of pineapple through hearsay. (But in 1690, Saunderson was only eight years old, so he could hardly have been the subject; the testimony is anonymous in de Brosses also, and the identification inserted by Nodier is therefore suspect: between Locke and Diderot, many blind persons were made to talk — or to keep quiet.)

On the lukewarm reception given to P. Castel's "ocular harpsichord," see Roudaut, *Poètes et grammariens*, pp.21–29; and Rousseau, *Essay*, chap.16, "False Analogy between Colors and Sounds." Denis Diderot, who belongs more among the partisans of synaesthesia, cites the testimony of Mélanie de Salignac, who "distinguished between *dark* voices and *fair* voices" (appendix to *The Letter on the Blind*, in *Diderot's Early Philosophical Works*, ed. and trans. Margaret Jourdain [Chicago: Open Court, 1916], p.146, and *Éléments de physiologie*, in *Oeuvres complètes de Diderot*, ed. Assézat-Tourneux [Paris: Garnier, 1875], 9:335). Regarding metaphors such as "sharp" taste or "vivid" light Turgot writes: "There is a certain analogy between our different senses, an analogy whose particulars are little known and that in order to be known would require discriminating observations and a rather subtle analysis of the operations of the mind which it greatly influences and which it often directs without our being aware, either because this analogy is founded on the very nature of our soul or only on the connection which we put between certain ideas and certain sensations due to our habit of experiencing them at the same time; or because it is the same in all mankind; or because it differs depending on time, place, and mind. It is always certain that we feel some affinity between very different sensations, between sensations and ideas" (*Les Autres Réflexions sur les langues*, in *Oeuvres*, 1:354).

In the field of theories on the origin of language, the principle of correspondence appears in very general terms in Johann Gottfried Herder (*On the Origin of Language* [1770], trans. Alexander Gode [New York: Frederick Ungar, 1967]); and in more detail, in Abbot Copineau, *Essai synthétique sur l'origine et la formation des langues* (Paris: Rualt, 1774), pp.34–35: "Whatever the organ affected, [sensations] always act through some disturbance, some vibrations in the nerves, comparable to those which sounds, by reason of their different nature, produce on the ear. Thus, although these sensations are not at all perceptible to the hearing, they may be expressed by sounds that work nearly the same effect on the ear as they work on their own proper respective organs. Consequently, the impression of the *color red*, which is vivid, lively, harsh to the sight, can be very aptly rendered by sounds where *r*, which makes an analogous impression on the hearing, is used. A gentle and weak light can also, for the same reason, be very aptly rendered by sounds or words containing *l*, and so on." But Copineau, though he heralds Nodier here, is not a mimologist. Very close to Condillac, he assumes four stages: language that is *mimed* {*mimique*} (gestures), *emotional* {*pathétique*} (interjections), *imitative* {*imitatif*} (onomatopoetic), *analogical* {*analogique*} (by correspondences). But the final, properly linguistic stage is that of *conventional* {*conventionnel*} language, and Copineau explicitly criticizes de Brosses for making the whole lexicon derive from the resource of imitation (p. 50).

51. See Roudaut, *Poètes et grammairiens*, pp. 276-81. To tell the truth, the original natural language includes yet a sixth order, that of prosodic *accents*, which for their part, unlike the spoken word that "paints objects," express "the manner in which the speaker is affected by objects, or the manner in which he wants them to affect others" (de Brosses, *Traité*, 1:278). But de Brosses himself proposes to consider this order as an "appendix to the first one" (that of interjections).

52. De Brosses, *Traité*, 1:291.

53. Notice that in *flos* or *fleur*, the articulation *fl* is directly mimetic in de Brosses's system, standing for the flexibility of the flower stem, but there is nothing mimetic in *oeil* (Paul Claudel will dispute this). Likewise, *anémone*, given as a comparison or simile, is in fact a metonymy.

54. In the *Cratylus*, Socrates already condemns the idea of naming through mimesis based on appearance; it is the *essence* of the object that the name must imitate (422b–423e). But unlike Plato, de Brosses keeps mimesis at the perceptual level.

55. De Brosses does so while knowing full well that "any metaphors and any oratorical figures, in which ... the terms with a meaning diverted from the proper sense of the root come from some feature of the imagination, which always has resemblance at its foundation" (*Traité*, 1:288): this was the implicit argument of Augustine's *On Dialectic*, but here it is stripped of its effect.

56. Bergier makes the same remark in *Éléments primitifs*, p. 31.

57. De Brosses, *Traité*, 2:322-23.

58. Ibid., 2:158-59.

59. Moreover, the historical relation between the two texts is significant: a manuscript of the future *Traité* was sent to Turgot for the article "Étymologie"; Turgot thought it better suited to an article on "Onomatopoeia" and he himself decided to write the text we know (though too little, to tell the truth) today. Since he had been very incorrectly accused of plagiarism, de Brosses was anxious to exculpate himself, lucidly adding: "We differ essentially on the basic issue" (see Turgot, *Oeuvres*, 1:516–17). Clearly, the basic issue is the debate over the nature of the sign. Let us recall that Turgot's article opens with one of the most resolute conventionalist proclamations in the entire history of the debate: "Words do not have a necessary relationship to what they express at all."

60. De Brosses, *Traité*, 1:28.

61. The role of comparison here seems confined to the transposition from the physical to moral: thus, from *mihr* (sun) to *admire*, originally "to look at the sun"; from *templum* (sky) to *contemplate;* from *sidera* (stars) to *consider;* from *moun* (moon) to

monere {to warn}, *admonition* (ibid., 2:241). "This application of a method, already very imperfect, to entities whose comparison was still further removed made it still more defective" (1:239).

62. Ibid., 2:119.

63. Ibid., 2:112–15. The same idea appears in Bergier, *Éléments primitifs*, pp. 23–27. Everyone knows about the subsequent fortunes of speculation on "opposite meanings," in Abel and then in Freud, and Émile Benveniste's clarification in *Problems in General Linguistics*, trans. Mary Elizabeth Meek, Miami Linguistics Series 8 (Coral Gables, Fla.: University of Miami Press, 1971), pp. 68–72. De Brosses anticipates this rather well by remarking that "contrariety establishes between [contrary things] a sort of relation," which is surely the semantic category inside of which the opposition is articulated: this is the case for *verticality*, to which *altus* refers, apart from any distinction between high and low. "Let us see how men could have fallen into expressing diametrically op-posed ideas by the same term *Alt*. They wanted to render the first idea that an object was quite out of reach along a perpendicular line; and after having used this word for things quite out of reach above, they also used it for things out of reach below, only stopping at the generalization of this idea, an abstraction made out of the contrariety found relative to the contrary positions of the object."

64. Ibid., 2:106, 110.

65. Ibid., 2:59–60.

66. Ibid., 2:56.

67. Ibid., 2:395. This theme of a mimesis diversified according to the variety of as-pects and ways of perceiving — an inconceivable theme, let us recall, for Platonic essen-tialism — is one of the naturalist replies to the conventionalist argument of the diversity of natural languages at least since Epicurus (*Letter to Herodotus*) and Lucretius (*De re-rum natura* 5.1056ff.). Previously, Bernard Lamy illustrated it in the following terms: "It is up to us to compare things as we wish, which causes that great difference between natural languages that have the same origin. . . . French, Spanish, Portuguese come from Latin, but the Spanish, seeing that windows are the passageway for wind, call them *ven-tana*, from *ventus*. The Portuguese, having regarded windows as little doors, call them *janella*, from *janua*. In the past our windows were divided into four sections by stone crosses, for which reason they were called *croisées*, from *crux*. The Romans thought that the function of windows is to receive light; the word *fenestra* comes from the Greek *phainein*, signifying 'to shine.' In this fashion different ways of seeing things lead to their being given different names" (*La Rhétorique; ou L'Art de parler* [Paris; Pralard, 1675], bk. 1, chap. 5, p. 19). And Giambattista Vico: "As the peoples have certainly by di-versity of climates acquired different natures, from which have sprung as many different customs, so from their different natures and customs as many different languages have arisen. For by virtue of the aforesaid diversity of their natures they have regarded the same utilities or necessities of human life from different points of view, and there have thus arisen so many national customs, for the most part differing from one another and at times contrary to one another; so and not otherwise there have arisen as many

different languages as there are nations" (*The New Science* [1725], 3d ed. [1744], rev. and trans. (abr.) Thomas G. Bergin and Max H. Fisch [Ithaca, N.Y.: Cornell University Press, 1968], p.105). We will come across this theme again, with equally diverse inflections, in Court de Gébelin, Charles Nodier, and Ernest Renan.

68. It takes up the entirety of paragraph 230: de Brosses, *Traité*, 2:333-38.

69. Ibid., 2:54-55.

70. And vice versa: "The Australians of Magellan, a people of the most brutish nature, who can be regarded as being on the threshold of human knowledge, had represented the ship of an English captain on the heather in figures of red clay. Now, I call that true writing. Any painting deserves this name. Any activity carried out in order to excite ideas through the sight is a genuine form of writing; and it is not a metaphor to say that in this sense the world is a great living book opened up under all our eyes" (ibid., 1:304).

71. Ibid., 1:301. Observe that de Brosses places writing both as anterior to speech, which becomes more arbitrary after writing (and thanks to it), and as posterior to speech, since the method of vocal imitation presided "before this" over the imposition of names. Such a double relation is not in the least contradictory here, since it clearly involves three stages: (1) that of a purely vocal language system, whose mimetic resources are very quickly exhausted; (2) the invention of a "new way," which is that of writing-painting, supremely mimetic; (3) the vocal language system after the in(ter)vention of writing, from then on given over to deviation without harm. But certain expressions are more difficult to reduce to this evolutionary scheme. Thus: "The picture {*figure*} of the object presented to the eyes in order to give rise to the idea, it seems to me, must have come from the imposition of the name given to this same object in order to fix or to awaken the idea each time this word was uttered" (1:301). And furthermore: "The convention of applying names to objects, of signifying them by words that do not paint them, necessarily presupposes some anterior familiarity with these same objects reached through one of the senses; otherwise, the word is merely a vague noise, completely devoid of relation, without which its effect is nonexistent. Therefore, mankind began by representing to the sight in crude figures {*figurer*} some portrait {*portrait*} of the object" (1:302). The theme of writing anterior to (or at the very least independent from and contemporaneous with) speech is not new in the eighteenth century. Thus, Vico said: "The difficulty as to the manner of origin was created by the scholars themselves, all of whom regarded the origin of letters as a separate question from that of the origin of languages, whereas the two were by nature conjoined" (*New Science*, p.97). Or Rousseau: "The art of writing does not in any way depend on that of speaking. It depends on needs of a different nature, which develop sooner or later depending on circumstances that are altogether independent of how long a people has been in existence" (*Essay*, p.251). De Brosses's theme of writing-painting clearly admits of the same hypothesis.

72. Their relation is hard to describe. De Brosses claims (*Traité*, 1:295) to have written his chapter 7 before having read Warburton's *Essay on Hieroglyphics* (translated into

French in 1744), but he admits having added to this chapter "a few observations that had escaped me and which I draw from the English author and his commentator." The relative proportions of confluence and of borrowing are therefore indistinguishable.

73. This chart, as it appears here, is not found in the *Traité*. I am synthesizing several classifications scattered throughout chapter 7, from hierarchical levels that are different but undeniably compatible despite terminological uncertainties. The list of the six orders takes up paragraph 101 and dominates all following paragraphs until the end of the chapter. The opposition *real/verbal* appears on 1:346, but elsewhere it is blurred, particularly by two symmetrical synecdoches. One is the use of *symbolic* to designate the whole set of real writing systems, including the "figurative"; the other is the use of *literal* for all verbal writing systems, including the syllabic, whence the general title of chapter 7, "De l'écriture symbolique et littérale" {On literal and symbolic writing}. The reasons for these terminological extensions are themselves symmetrical, too: symbolic writing is the most widespread of the real writing systems; literal writing is the most widespread of the verbal ones. "Moreover, I do not end with treating syllabic writing and literal writing separately. Both of them are organic, and to tell the truth there is hardly any difference between them. My observations on one apply to the other almost equally well" (1:435–36).

74. Ibid., 1:311–12. "Figurative" {*figurée*} here designates all real writing systems.

75. Ibid., 1:305–6.

76. Ibid., 1:307.

77. Saussure, *Cours de linguistique generale* (Paris: Payot, 1916), p.64. *Trans. Note:* The translation from Saussure's "C'est une découverte de génie" is my own. Cf. *Course in General Linguistics*, trans. Roy Harris (London: Gerald Duckworth, 1983), p.40. My more literal rendering captures an important mimological theme: the "genius" of the first name-giver (divine or human).

78. Rousseau, *Essay*, p.253. *Trans. Note:* What Rousseau says here is "Writing ... substitutes precision for expressiveness. One conveys one's sentiments in speaking, and one's ideas in writing."

79. De Brosses, *Traité*, 1:309.

80. Ibid., 1:181.

81. Clearly, it is a question of a logical and not a real outcome, since the project of an organic alphabet was presented already in chap.5.

CHAPTER 7

1. The set appeared from 1773 to 1784. The topics of the other volumes are allegory, universal grammar, the history of the calendar; the etymology of French, Latin, Greek; heraldry, coins, games, and miscellanea. Although famous in his time, Gébelin remains marginal and unclassifiable in relation to the intellectual mainstream of the eighteenth century. Baldensperger ("Court de Gébelin et l'importance de son *Monde primitif*," in

Mélanges Huguet [Paris: Boivin, 1940]) situated him rather aptly between Vico, whose influence is patently obvious, and Romantic "ideorealism."

2. Antoine Court de Gébelin, *Histoire naturelle de la parole; ou, Grammaire universelle à l'usage des jeunes gens* (Paris, 1776 [published by the author]); revised in 1816 with rather critical notes and preface by Count Lanjuinais, and plates corrected by Remusat (Paris: Plancher). The main argument of the present study has to do with the 1775 volume of *Le Monde Primitif, analysé et comparé avec le monde moderne, considéré dans l'histoire naturelle de la parole; ou, Origine du langage et de l'écriture* (Paris [published by the author]); all references are to this work {cited as *Origine*} unless otherwise indicated. Jean Roudaut has given long excerpts from its book 5 (*De l'écriture*) in his *Poètes et grammairiens au XVIIIe siècle: Anthologie* (Paris: Gallimard, 1971), pp. 288-310. *Trans. Note:* Genette modernizes Gébelin's spelling and punctuation; I have followed suit.

3. Book 1 occupies 64 of 510 pages. The titles of the other books are 2. *De l'origine du langage* {On the origin of language}; 3. *Des divers modes dont est susceptible l'instrument vocal* {On the various modes of which the vocal instrument is capable}; 4. *Développements du langage, source des mots, base du dictionnaire primitif* {Word expansions, source of words, basis of the primeval dictionary}; 5. *Du langage peint aux yeux, ou de l'écriture* {On language painted for the eye, or on writing}.

4. Plainly, Gébelin has read Charles de Brosses, and if he does not exactly call himself his disciple, he does not fail to pay tribute to de Brosses several times, or rather to grant him the prerogative in their "similarity of viewpoints"; see pp. 335-51. But we will observe a few nearly explicit disagreements, too.

5. Gébelin, *Origine*, p. 376.

6. Ibid., p. 275. The humanist phrasing (emphasized by the author himself) ought not to conceal the fact that for Gébelin (a Genevan Calvinist, but one who would join the Free Masons in 1776), speech is a gift from God: this is the argument of bk. 2, chap. 2.

7. Ibid., p. 275 (emphasis added).

8. Ibid., pp. 38, 40.

9. Ibid., p. 363.

10. Ibid., p. 362; cf. Louis de Bonald, *Recherches philosophiques sur les premiers objets des connaissances morales,* in *Oeuvres de Monsieur de Bonald,* vol. 8 (Paris: A. Le Clerc, 1818), bk. 1, p. 176: "If there are, in the same natural language, several terms to express the same object, and terms that are not properly synonymous with each other, why would not several languages have different words to signify the same thing, too?" *Trans. Note:* As so often in mimologism, Gébelin's argument here depends on a play on language. For instance, the French name for God reflects an important "aspect" of the Creation, or light: French *Dieu/lumière,* Latin *dies* (day). It is doubly related to the venerable classical language of Latin not only through "light" (*Dieu-dies*) but also through "divinity" itself: French *Dieu,* Latin *deus* (god). And so on, at each mimologist's own pleasure.

11. Gébelin, *Origine,* pp. 361-62. These two ideas (a primeval tongue made up of monosyllables, and the appearance of verbs) are already present in Giambattista Vico,

The New Science (1725), 3d ed. (1744), rev. and trans. (abr.) Thomas G. Bergin and Max H. Fisch [Ithaca, N.Y.: Cornell University Press, 1968]), pp. 107, 109–10). The second, very widespread, is found in, among others, Étienne Bonnot de Condillac, *An Essay on the Origin of Human Knowledge* (1746), trans. Thomas Nugent (1756; rpt. Gainesville, Fla.: Scholars' Facsimiles & Reprints, 1971), pt. 2, sec. 1, pp. 182, 241; and in Abbot Nicolas Sylvestre Bergier, *Les Éléments primitifs des langues, découverts par la comparaison des racines de l'hébreu avec celles de grec, du latin, et du français* (Paris: Brocas & Humblot, 1764; rpt. Paris, 1850), bk. 1, p. 1. In this particular instance, Johann Gottfried Herder (*On the Origin of Language* [1770], trans. Alexander Gode [New York: Frederick Ungar, 1967]) formally took exception to mainstream opinion: first, man observed that the lamb "bleats" (*bêle*), then he called it by a noun formed on this imitative verb — "the bleater" (*le bêleur*). But Herder did add a remark that maintains the valorization of the noun: to wit, that the anteriority of the verb is for him evidence of the human origin of the language system; God, on the contrary, in all His perfection, would have started with the nouns.

12. Gébelin, *Origine,* p. 42.

13. Ibid., p. 44. In fact, the linguistic knowledge flaunted by Gébelin seems to be very wide ranging for his time — if not very reliable. His examples cover almost all the European natural languages, plus Hebrew and Chinese.

14. Ibid., p. 74. Of course, the comparison of the vocal instrument to the organ is not new; along with the comparison of consonantal articulation to the "keys" of a flute, it is found in, e.g., Bernard Lamy, *La Rhétorique; ou, L'Art de parler* (Paris: Pralard, 1675), bk. 3, chap. 1.

15. Gébelin, *Origine,* p. 122. As a rule, Gébelin reserves the terms *vowels* and *consonants* for graphemes (p. 111). As for phonemes, he had at first considered baptizing them *sounds* (vowels) and *tones* (consonants). His earliest readers' confusion over these made him give up this symmetry (p. 122). Finally, his terminology returns to Nicolas Beauzée's in the *Encyclopédie* article "Grammaire" {Grammar}, which subdivides the *elements* (of speech) into *sounds* and *articulations,* and the *letters* (of writing) into *vowels* and *consonants,* even while recognizing that current usage is likely to confuse these terms. Today, of course, the latter division is no longer pertinent except on the phonic level.

16. Gébelin, *Origine,* pp. 111–12.

17. Except for the inversion of position between *u* and *ou.*

18. Gébelin, *Origine,* pp. 112–13.

19. Ibid., p. 123. *Trans. Note:* In order to preserve its strong onomatopoetic aspect, the French term for "(palato-)alveolar fricative," *la chuintante,* has been rendered colloquially as "the shhh sound." In the chart of the consonants, the English-speaking reader should remember that Gébelin is working with the sound system of French. Thus, for example, among the fricatives, the French *ch* is pronounced like the English *sh* or [s], while the French *j* is not the English *j* (soft *g*) but rather [ʒ]. In the later discussion of vowels, French *i* is pronounced much like English *ee.*

20. Gébelin, *Origine,* p. 140.

21. Ibid., pp. 118, 125.

22. Ibid., p. 327.

23. This criticism, made in a typically "binarist" spirit, is clearly addressed to de Brosses, who distinguished strong, middling, and weak articulations.

24. The quite Pythagorean inspiration of this entire passage is perhaps to be connected with the author's Masonic sympathies.

25. Gébelin, *Origine*, pp. 126-28. The following paragraph introduces a new numerical hypothesis which again reinforces the principle of harmony: "A new relationship between these different harmonies might be found as well, in that the sounds can be reduced to three main ones, the guttural *a*, the dental *e* and *i*, and the labial *o* and *u*, as Amman understood very well, following the method of the Arabs who reduced their vowel points to these three. In this way, the tones of music are reducible to the third, and the seven primary colors are also reducible to three, with which all the other colors are produced." From seven to three, the mysticism of numbers still prevails.

26. Ibid., p. 142.

27. Gébelin, *Histoire naturelle*, rev. ed. (1816), pp. 94-96. For details, see *Origine*, pp. 152-260.

28. Gébelin, *Origine*, pp. 143-47.

29. Ibid., pp. 144-45. This geomimology, which we will find again in Nodier, is plainly a constant theme of the linguistic imagination. I found a recent manifestation of it in the work of Pierre Viansson-Ponté, who declares that the Auvergne dialect is "a way of speaking as rocky as the nearby volcanic slopes." R. Lafont, specialist in the *langue d'oc*, replies: "I leave you to your linguistic geology, with the suggestion that Flemish is flat like Flanders and Eskimo is crystalline like an iceberg" (*Le Monde*, 16 and 30 March, 1973). Edward Sapir, rising up against these supposed climactic influences, dutifully noted the Eskimos' "agreeable phonetic system," very ill suited to their harsh living conditions (quoted in Otto Jespersen, *Language: Its Nature, Development, and Origin* [London: Allen & Unwin, 1922], chap. 14, sec. 2, p. 256).

30. Quite clearly, Gébelin is analyzing all consonants — including *sifflantes* {sibilants} and *chuintantes* {"shhh" sounds} — as occlusives: "Being merely the effect of pressure or of instantaneous movement, intonations last only a moment. The noise cannot be prolonged at will, but only reiterated" (*Origine*, p. 124).

31. Gébelin, *Origine*, pp. 124-25.

32. Ibid., p. 283.

33. Ibid., pp. 283-86. *Histoire naturelle* provides a valuable confirmation here: animals, who have sensations only, utter only vowels (p. 103). So much for the bleating lamb and the *litera canina* {canine letter}. In his *Cahier des langues*, Louis Claude de Saint-Martin will take exactly the opposite view of this division: for him, vowels express ideas, and consonants express sensations (*Les Cahiers de La Tour St. Jacques* 7 [1961]: 186).

34. This last sentence is in Gébelin's *Dictionnaire étymologique de la langue française* (vol. 5 of *Monde primitif*), p. 2.

35. Clearly, the nature of the key matters much more here than the degree of articulation: the "weak" dental *d* is assumed to be stronger than the "strong" labial *p*. In point of fact, for Gébelin, every dental is strong and every labial is weak.

36. Let us note in passing that this value contradicts the general characteristic of consonants, which was, as we have seen, to be "silent and quiet."

37. *Trans. Note:* Genette is referring here to Jacques Lacan's psychoanalytic theory. *Le nom du Père,* the "Name-of-the-Father," plays a central role not only in the Oedipus complex of the young man, according to Lacan, but also later in the symbolic structures of authority (the Law, the Word) and masculinity (the Name-of-the-Father, legitimacy) which the adult internalizes as a member of Western society and culture. For further discussion of the Name-of-the-Father and its place within the "symbolic order," see Jacques Lacan, *Speech and Language in Psychoanalysis* trans. and ed. Anthony Wilden, (Baltimore: Johns Hopkins University Press, 1968), esp. pp. 270–73, 293–98.

38. Cf. de Brosses.

39. Of course, like de Brosses, Gébelin also brings up the imitative character of the names given to the speech organs themselves: *bouche, dent, gorge,* and so on (*Origine,* p. 349).

40. Gébelin, *Origine,* p. 329. Cf. p. 287: "In this way, so thorough a commutation occurs from sensations to ideas and from ideas to sensations that a good deal of shrewdness and attention is needed to disentangle these different faculties, to recognize the properties that characterize them in order to distinguish the influences of each one. But it cannot be concluded from this that these faculties do not differ from one another at all, and that the language of one is the language of the other; this hasty conclusion would muddle everything and lead us away from the truth forever."

41. Let us recall that de Brosses, for his part, rejects any semanticism of vowels, just as he denies them any phonetic identity. Stéphane Mallarmé, in *Mots anglais* {see chapter 12} will further restrict "radical virtue," reserving it for initial consonants. Gaston Bachelard, however, will hazard the following unequal division: "The voices of earth are consonants. Vowels belong to the other elements" (*La Terre et les rêveries du repos* [Paris: José Corti, 1948], p. 197).

42. In theory only, for it is plain that here, as elsewhere in de Brosses, semantic values are not always as direct as claimed; this is so for the translation of the articulatory "softness" (*douceur*) of the labial into a gustatory sweetness (*bonbon*) or an affective tenderness (*maman*). In actual fact, a certain amount of metaphoric "derivation" (among other figures) enters in almost from the first lexical investment, but it is not recognized and still less theorized.

43. Gébelin, *Origine,* p. 350.

44. The wording is not the clearest; apparently, *fl* equals *f* here, *tr* equals *r, fr* is ambiguous. In the other examples cited, the amalgam works to the advantage of the second consonant; thus, *bl, cl, gl, br, cr, gr* "participate equally in the values proper to these lingual intonations," *l* and *r* (ibid., p. 353).

45. "This word (*st*) designates the property of being fixed, stopped, remaining in

place: it is the movement or cry of those who want someone to stop, to stay still; why is this so, if not because in pronouncing *s* one produces a sort of hissing or whistling sound {*sifflement*} which excites the attention of the person up ahead, and because the intonation *t*, coming afterward, is harsh, abrupt, short, and fixed and naturally indicates the fixed position that one wants this person to adopt" (ibid., p.353).

46. Ibid., p.343.

47. Ibid., pp.360–61.

48. Ibid., pp.374–75.

49. Ibid., p.407; the same line of argument appears on p.378. According to Lanjuinais, "the show of limiting the use of this art to agricultural peoples … is an exaggeration that comes from the author's strong attachment to systems, to the language of the economists": that is, the physiocrats (Gébelin, *Histoire naturelle*, p.114n).

50. Gébelin, *Origine*, p.378.

51. Ibid., p.376.

52. Ibid., p.379.

53. Ibid., pp.381–91.

54. Ibid., p.382.

55. Ibid., p.386.

56. Gébelin mentions Rowland Jones in chap.2 of *Origine*, along with Nelme, but also with Wachter and Van Helmont, who "sought to demonstrate that each alphabetic letter was merely the painting of the shape the tongue adopted in order to pronounce that letter." The apparent confusion of these two types (ideographic and phonographic) can be explained by the fact, pointed out above, that as writing and speech in his system are both mimetic, they are in an indirect mimetic relation with each other.

57. Ibid., p.402.

58. Of course, the ideographic interpretation of the alphabet, defended by Gébelin, must not be confused with the much more modest hypothesis (one adopted by modern grammatologists, moreover), that all or part of the alphabetic characters derive *in their form* from certain ideograms. On this, de Brosses says: "If attention is paid to the figure of the Samaritan *aleph*, some crude image of an ox head with its two horns can be found in it. One sees here a trace of the shift from hieroglyphs to our present letters" (*Traité de la formation mécanique des langues*, 2 vols. [Paris: Saillant, Vincent & Desaint, 1765; rev. ed., 1800], 1:450). For Gébelin, the *aleph* preserves not only the form but also the signification "ox head."

59. Gébelin, *Origine*, pp.401–2 (emphasis added). Clearly, Gébelin here ignores the partially diagrammatic nature of classical musical notation.

60. Ibid., p.416.

61. This is confirmed in Gébelin, *Histoire naturelle*, where the letters are arranged in a logical order: vowels, then consonants grouped by keys — labial, nasal, guttural, sibilant, dental, lingual.

62. The chart adds three (H, Q, and OU) and omits one (K).

63. Gébelin, *Origine*, p.411. We will encounter this inevitable play on words again in

Charles Nodier and in Michel Leiris. *Trans. Note:* The letter Q invites both phonetic and visual mimology in the French language. One of several possibilities would be to associate *cul* (ass) and *queue* (1. tail of an animal, tail end of an object; 2. line of people; 3. French slang for penis). Genette himself makes a joke here: the sexual instinct and the mimological instinct ("the instinct of motivation") alike find a "niche" in the letter Q and in the *cul.*

64. *Trans. Note:* There is another pun here, this time based on synonymy between the French words *tête* {head} and *chef* {chief}. A.-J. Greimas uses *tête* as an example of a simple word with a complex lexical field (*Structural Semantics*, trans. D. McDowell et al. [Lincoln: University of Nebraska Press, 1983], pp. 47–55). The *effets du sens* (meaning effects) of *tête* change contextually, and one of its metonymic uses is precisely as a synonym for *chef* or "head" as in "leader," "boss." *Chef* itself is the Old French term for the body part, head; hence, the *chef* (chief) of a tribe and the *chef* in a kitchen. Perhaps not even modern structural semantics is entirely free of mimologism.

65. Gébelin, *Histoire naturelle*, pp. 145–47.

CHAPTER 8

1. Charles Nodier's corpus mainly includes:

— *Dictionnaire raisonnée des onomatopées françaises,* published in 1808 (Paris: Demonville); the second edition, "revised, corrected, and considerably enlarged," in 1828 (Paris: Delangle), mainly consists of additional entries, but the general preface remains nearly unchanged.
— *Notions élémentaires de linguistique* (Paris: Renduel, 1834), vol. 12 in the so-called *Oeuvres complètes.* This volume gathers together a series of columns that appeared in *Le Temps* from September 1833 to July 1834 (Geneva: Slatkine Reprints, 1968).
— the prospectus titled *Archeólogue,* or *Système universel et raisonné des langues: Prolégomènes,* dating from 1 February 1810 (printed without a date by Didier).
— a few entries from *Examen critique des dictionnaires de la langue française* (Paris: Delangle, 1828).

2. To be exact, Nodier says: "The *Dictionnaire des onomatopées,* written when I was eighteen years old, published when I was twenty-three" (preface to *Examen critique,* p. 5). But in 1808, Nodier was in fact twenty-eight years old. Given his habit of underestimating his age, we should probably translate this twenty-three into twenty-eight, and eighteen into twenty-three: the *Dictionnaire* would then have been written around 1803. But in a note in the second edition (p. 147), Nodier points out that his theories on style "were new in 1805." And again, the *Prolégomènes* of 1810 talks about the "very premature publication" he gave his *Dictionnaire;* this expression ill applies to a piece of work that had spent five years in a drawer. This chronological labyrinth is indeed typical of this precursor — so neglected today — of Lewis Carroll and Jorge Luis Borges.

3. Nodier, Preface, *Examen critique,* pp. 5–6.

4. And the description of the vocal organ as a complete musical instrument, according to Gébelin, is conjured up in "La Fée aux Miettes" (in *Contes de Nodier*, ed. Pierre-Georges Castex [Paris: Garnier, 1961], pp. 321–22).

5. Nodier, *Dictionnaire* (1828), p. 11. All references to the *Dictionnaire* cite this second edition. *Trans. Note:* The most recent reprint of Nodier's *Dictionnaire raisonné des ono-matopées françoises* [*sic*] of 1828 is edited, with introductory essay, by Henri Meschonnic (Mauvezin: Trans-Europ-Repress, 1984); the pagination given for Genette's quotations corresponds to Meschonnic's edition.

6. Nodier, *Notions*, pp. 90–91.

7. Ibid., chaps. 6–9.

8. Ibid., p. 91.

9. Ibid., p. 93. This last notation, which seems novel, had already appeared in the 1808 *Dictionnaire*, and a note of 1828 strongly confirms it, extending it to "the majority of the ancient alphabets of the Orient" (p. 261).

10. Nodier, *Notions*, p. 140. "Rational" obviously signifies *motivated* here.

11. The motivation of O deliberately agrees with the remarks of the philosophy teacher in Molière's play *The Bourgeois Gentleman*, which Nodier quotes besides (ibid., pp. 23, 25): "Here we are quite close, you will think, to that philosopher teacher called Monsieur Jourdain who proves through sound arguments that one pouts {*fait la moue*} when one says a U. I would not disagree, but it is not really my fault." *Trans. Note:* Here is the relevant section of dialogue from Molière, *The Bourgeois Gentleman*, trans. Albert Bumel, in *The Actor's Molière* (New York: Applause Theatre, 1987), 2:60:

Philosophy Teacher: The vocal sound U is formed by almost closing the teeth and protruding the lips: U.

Monsieur Jourdain: U, U. By God, it's true. U.

Philosophy Teacher: You push your lips forward as if you were sulking. That's why, when you want to yell at someone, you simply say, "O, U."

12. Nodier, *Notions*, p. 126.

13. The term is obviously not used here in its strict sense.

14. Nodier, *Notions*, p. 126.

15. Ibid., p. 155. The *General and Rational Grammar of Port Royal* (1660; Eng. trans. 1753 [Menston: Scolar Press, 1968]), in pt. 1, chap. 5 ("Of Letters Considered as Characters"), previously posited this condition as necessary "in order to give {written characters} their utmost degree of perfection" (p. 14).

16. Nodier, *Notions*, p. 154.

17. For details, see ibid., pp. 109–33.

18. In connection with this topic, Nodier criticizes the improper use of *diphthong*, which he proposed to replace by *digraph* (*Examen critique*, p. 144).

19. Ferdinand de Saussure, *Course in General Linguistics*, trans. Roy Harris (London: Gerald Duckworth, 1983), p. 40.

20. Nodier, *Notions*, p. 116.

21. Ibid., p.296 (emphasis added).

22. Ibid., pp.139-40 (emphasis added).

23. Ibid., p.297.

24. Ibid., pp.167-68.

25. Ibid., pp.191-92.

26. Babel as the symbol of the dispersion of peoples and the confusion of tongues is not absent in Nodier — quite to the contrary — and we are going to encounter this symbolism soon. It is the *ulteriority* of Babel that disappears: that is to say, the hypothesis of prior Adamic unity. But the theological implications of this disappearance are apparently too grave for Nodier as a Christian; consequently, he tries to accommodate the theme of the original dispersion (what else is *autochthony?*) and the references to Genesis and to Adam's invention of names.

27. Nodier, *Notions*, pp.39-40.

28. Further on, we will see what the importance of poor natural languages is for Nodier.

29. Nodier, *Notions*, pp.51-53. The seeds of this development are to be found in the preface to the *Dictionnaire*, pp.12-13.

30. We find this observation, for example, in Claude Fauchet: "What would he [Psamtik] have replied to some scoffer who maintained that it was the voice of the goats, the nurses of these children?" (*Recueil de l'origine de la langue et poésie française* [1581], p.4). Or again in Bernard Lamy: "This king reasoned incorrectly, for it is probable that these children, never having heard any voice other than the cry of the goats that suckled them, imitated that cry, which this Phrygian word resembles merely by chance" (*La Rhétorique; ou L'Art de parler* [Paris: Pralard, 1675], 1:13). The same interpretation recurs in Nicolas Beauzée's article "Langue" and again in Count Volney's *Discours sur l'étude philosophiques des langues* (1819). Let us recall that according to Herodotus, the story concerns children raised alone in the desert, at the pharaoh's command, whose first word was supposedly the Phrygian *bekos*, "bread": this instance was put forward as proof of the primitiveness of that language.

31. Nodier, *Notions*, pp.78-79. Cf. Jacques-Henri Bernardin de Saint-Pierre, *Harmonies de la nature* (1815), 3:232-33: "Men at first imitated the cries of the animals and the songs of the birds proper to their climate. The language of the Hottentots clicks like ostriches; that of the Patagonians has the sounds of the sea breaking against the coastline; and one can still find traces of this process in the languages of various civilized peoples of Europe: the language of the English whistles like the cries of the marine birds of their island, that of the Dutch is full of breck-keeks and croaks like the cries of their marsh frogs." The role of the imitation of animal cries in the genesis of the human language system is itself also a very old idea that goes back at least to Lucretius, and it is found again in Lord Monboddo (*The Origin and Progress of Language* [Edinburgh: J. Balfour, 1774-1809], pt.1, bk.3, p.6).

32. Let us recall that for Socrates, however, the plurality of "etymologies" for every name does not invalidate its appropriateness. Apollo is properly at once *apoulōn*, *haploun*, *aei ballōn*, and *homopolōn*, and this multiplicity of possible analyses does in-

deed designate a multiplicity of aspects and of functions, as between *sacerdos, praesbyter,* and so on, but this multiplicity is nonetheless gathered into the apparent unity of a name — as if this single natural language (Greek), secretly containing several languages, were therefore perfect — precisely in being multiple.

33. Apparently, Nodier does not know Humboldt's work at all (in 1834, Nodier's linguistic baggage is still typically eighteenth-century), but he shares at least certain motives with Humboldt.

34. Nodier, *Notions,* pp.12–13.

35. "Society proceeded ... like the infant in his cradle, who is its natural type" (ibid., p.15).

36. Ibid., pp.13–14. Here "vocal" signifies *vocalic.* The vowel is always the voice in its pure state, no more differentiated here than in de Brosses, although Nodier approvingly quotes the famous passage from Chateaubriand's *Genius of Christianity* on the vowel *a,* to which we will return later on.

37. It is, says the *Dictionnaire* (p.17), the language of the elementary passions: desire, hatred, fear, pleasure.

38. Later, it will come to rely on consonants but always those that are "earliest formed" (labials and dentals), and almost always keeping to monosyllables.

39. Nodier, *Dictionnaire,* p.17.

40. Nodier, *Notions,* pp.24–25. *Trans. Note:* For Cratylists who will treasure it and for Hermogenists who will smile at it, here is Nodier's original masterpiece in the labial key of *b:* "Je vous propose de venir chercher nos premiers enseignements près du berceau de l'enfant qui essaye la première consonne. Elle va bondir de sa bouche aux baisers d'une mère. Le bambin, le poupon, le marmot a trouvé les trois labiales; il bée, il baye, il balbutie, il bégaye, il babille, il blatère, il bêle, il bavarde, il braille, il boude, il bouque, il bougonne sur une babiole, sur une bagatelle, sur une billevesée, sur une bêtise, sur un bébé, sur un bonbon, sur un bobo, sur le bilboquet pendu à l'étalage du bimbelotier."

41. "*Papa:* this word and many others belong to the series of the first articulations of childhood. Initially, they are merely a vague, uncertain, purposeless utterance, which we gradually learn to make into the expression of an idea, itself at first quite vague and ill defined. Children utter *papa* and *mama* for a long time before linking the idea of these articulations to that of two specific persons, and it is not until quite long afterward that they begin to realize their parents' relationship to them in a passably clear way. ... And since what is true for one idea is necessarily so for all the others, it is self-evident that human intelligence always works from the word to the idea and not from the idea to the word" (*Examen critique,* pp.297–98).

42. Nodier, *Dictionnaire,* p.169. This suspect etymology is accepted by Littré and Darmesteter as well; I find nothing in the *Französisches Etymologisches Worterbuch* (Basel: Zbinden Druck). Alexandre Dumas (*Ange Pitou* {1853}, p.6) proposes the following variant: the bourgeois of Villers-Cotterets take as the goal of their daily stroll "a wide ditch separating the park from the forest, located a quarter of a league from

the town and called, probably because of the exclamation that the sight of it drew from asthmatic chests gratified to have traveled such a long way without becoming too winded, the Haha!"

43. Nodier, *Examen critique*, p. 264.

44. "Natural languages name through mimology... there is no other way.... Man created his speech through imitation: his first language is onomatopoeia, or natural noises" (*Notions*, pp. 39–40). Clearly, it is in this broad sense that we should understand the title of the *Dictionnaire*.

45. Saussure, *Course*, p. 69. Let us recall that de Brosses and Gébelin themselves gave onomatopoeia only a limited place in their systems.

46. Nodier, *Notions*, pp. 29–30 (emphasis added).

47. Nodier, *Dictionnaire*, pp. 45–46.

48. Nodier, *Examen critique*, pp. 33–34. *Trans. Note:* The etymological punning involved in Nodier's plays on the monosyllables *am* (as in *âme* [soul, spirit]) and *ma* (as in *matière* [matter]) is quite complex and can be traced back not only to the Latin *anima* (the vital principle or soul, spirit) but also to the Latin roots for *expiration* (= *âme*) and *inspiration* (= *vie*), where *spirare* means to breathe or draw breath, *inspirare* means to breathe life or soul into or to inspire, and *expirare* means to breathe out, exhale, or to "give up the ghost" (soul) or die.

49. Gaston Bachelard, *Air and Dreams: An Essay on the Imagination of Movement*, trans. Edith R. Farrell and C. Frederick Farrell (Dallas, Tex.: Dallas Institute of Humanities and Culture, 1988), p. 240 {modified}.

50. {Nodier, *Notions*, pp. 25–26.}

51. Nodier, *Dictionnaire*, pp. 21–22.

52. Nodier, *Notions*, p. 27.

53. Ibid., p. 29.

54. Nodier, *Dictionnaire*, p. 23.

55. Ibid., s.v. *nez* {nose}, p. 200 (emphasis added).

56. Nodier, *Notions*, pp. 36–38.

57. Gaston Bachelard, *The Poetics of Reverie*, trans. Daniel Russell (New York: Orion Press, 1969), p. 31.

58. Gaston Bachelard, *The Flame of a Candle*, trans. Joni Caldwell (Dallas, Tex.: Dallas Institute of Humanities and Culture, 1988), p. 28 {modified}.

59. *Trans. Note:* It was not until after the 1976 publication of Genette's *Mimologiques* that Nodier's 1828 *Dictionnaire* was newly edited by Henri Meschonnic (see also note 5, above).

60. Nodier, *Contes*, p. 547.

61. Auguste Dorchain, *L'Art des vers*, rev. ed. (Paris: Garnier, 1933), p. 290. *Trans. Note:* The pun on *mortadelle*, a kind of sausage, depends on the French word for death, *la mort*, which is indeed "more terrifying" than *la citadelle* (the citadel).

62. Quite plainly, the distinction between "true" and "false" is not relevant here: the

present-day feeling for onomatopoeia is independent of the "real" etymology, whether the latter is known or not. We will come across this issue again further on, in connection with Saussure's remarks concerning the origin of *fouet* {whip} and *glas* {knell}.

63. *Trans. Note:* Genette has modernized the spelling that appears in the Nodier text of 1828 (see the Meschonnic edition) and has modified two of the entry word(s): in Nodier, *bouillir* is followed by *bouillonnement, bouillonner* (bubbling, to bubble), whereas in Genette the entry reads *Bouillir, bouillie, brouillon.* Further on, Nodier uses the plural *catacombes* where Genette has inserted the singular.

64. Again, see Gaston Bachelard, *Water and Dreams: An Essay on the Imagination of Matter,* trans. Edith R. Farrell (Dallas, Tex.: Dallas Institute of Humanities and Culture, 1983), pp.189-90 {modified}. *Trans. Note:* Genette is here quoting Bachelard, who in turn is quoting from Nodier's *Dictionnaire,* p.90.

65. Perhaps Chateaubriand remembered this suggestion in the famous *Journal de Carlsbad à Paris:* "It is only the susurration of the reeds."

66. *Trans. Note:* Following are the page numbers (Meschonnic edition) for the foregoing words from Nodier's *Dictionnaire: Achoppement,* p.36; *Agacement,* p.37; *Agrafe,* p.38; *Asthme,* p.48; *Bedon,* p.54; *Biffer,* p.59; *Bise,* pp.59-60; *Bouillir,* p.64; *Briquet,* p.69; *Brouter,* pp.70-71; *Broyement,* p.72; *Cascade,* pp.80-81; *Catacombe(s),* p.81; *Cataracte,* p.81; *Clignoter,* pp.90-91; *Dégringoler,* p.118; *Éclat,* p.118; *Écraser,* p.121; *Fanfare,* p.125; *Fifre,* pp.126-27; *Fleur,* p.129; *Froissement,* pp.138-39; *Murmure,* p.196; *Oiseau,* p.205; *Rincer,* p.223; *Ruisseau,* p.234; *Susurration,* p.251; *Taffetas,* pp.255-56. The entry for *Roue* is cited in the next paragraph from pp.225-26, 229-30.

67. Ivan Fonagy, *Die Metaphern in der Phonetik: Ein Beitrag zur Entwicklungsgeschichte des wissenschaftlichen Denkens* (The Hague: Mouton, 1963).

68. Nodier, *Dictionnaire,* pp.230-31. This is an allusion to the tenth study in *Études de la nature* (Paris: Didet, 1784-88), in which Bernardin de Saint-Pierre compares the "five primary colors" (white, yellow, *red,* blue, black), the "five basic forms" (line, triangle, *circle,* ellipse, parabola), and the "five main movements" (rotational, "perpendicular," *circular,* horizontal, static), the middle term of each series being the most perfect and the most euphoric.

69. {Nodier, *Dictionnaire,* pp.13-15.}

70. Nodier, *Notions,* p.57.

71. Ibid., pp.47-48.

72. Ibid., p.39.

73. Ibid., p.58.

74. Ibid., pp.66, 251.

75. {Ibid., pp.64-66.}

76. Or more correctly, a topos reactivated and reinterpreted at that time, since it goes back to Strabo and Plutarch (at least). On the movement (and its limits), see M. H. Abrams, *The Mirror and the Lamp* (Oxford: Oxford University Press, 1953), chap.4, sec.3, "Primitive Language and Primitive Poetry."

77. Nodier, *Notions,* pp.58-59. Clearly, Nodier disapproves of this univocity in natu-

ral language which, on the contrary, he regretted not finding in the alphabet; this is because he sought in the writing system a genuine system of signs (of speech), as transparent as possible. Natural language, on the other hand, interests or captivates him in proportion to its poetic ambiguity. The opposite extreme of algebra is *slang*, an essentially figurative language: "There is a hundred times more wit in slang itself than in algebra, which is the masterpiece of artificial languages, and slang owes this advantage to its property of figuratively representing expression and imaging the language. With algebra, one can only make calculations; with slang, however ignoble its origins, a people and a society could be remade." Another opposition of parallel value is set up between pedantic scientific nomenclatures and popular appellations: the best model "is the the nomenclature of astronomy, the *Milky Way* {*chemin de lait*}, the *chariot*, the *dragon*, the *shepherd's star* {*étoile du berger*}. Thus, it was shepherds who created this nomenclature" (p. 209).

78. Ibid., pp. 72-73.

79. Nodier, *Dictionnaire* {1828}, pp. 146-47.

80. In 1828, Nodier adds this characteristic note: "Permit me to point out here that these theories, which have become rather commonplace, were new in 1805, and that they could be expressed without fear of getting bogged down in hackneyed ideas" (ibid., p. 147). In twenty years, rejuvenation itself had grown old.

81. Nodier, *Notions*, p. 60.

82. Ibid., pp. 61-62.

83. Ibid., p. 51. In conclusion, let me draw attention to the amusing "Lettre sur les origines de l'alphabet," addressed by Nodier to his friend Jacques-Nicolas Vallot on January 27, 1808, and published by Marius Dargaud in *Cahiers du Sud* 304 (1950): 379-81. This is a short parody of several commonplaces of the period (from Vico to Nodier himself) on the subject of a language exclamatory in origin and a succession of "hieroglyphic," syllabic, alphabetic writing systems-all on the occasion of oysters, of which his correspondent had promised him a few dozen, perhaps in exchange for this humorous piece. Nodier says, among other things, that "the earliest name of the oyster {*huître*} was probably the exclamation, the cry of pleasure aroused by the oyster's sweet taste," and not, as one could have sworn, a *live mimology* of the act of gulping it down.

CHAPTER 9

1. Pierre Joseph Proudhon, "Essai de grammaire générale" (1837), appendix to Abbot Nicolas Sylvestre Bergier, *Les Éléments primitifs des langues découverts par la comparaison des racines de l'hébreu avec celles du grec, du latin, et du français* (Paris: Brocas & Humblot, 1764; rept., Paris, 1850), p. 272. *Trans. Note:* For the publishing history of this rare work by Proudhon, see his *Oeuvres complètes*, ed. Theodore Ruyssen (Geneva: Slatkine, 1982), 14: 79-81.

2. These examples are proposed by Roman Jakobson in "Quest for the Essence of Language," in *Selected Writings of Roman Jakobson* (The Hague: Mouton), 2: 350.

3. The best guide here is "Direct Order and Inversion" {in chap. 4} in Aldo Scaglione, *The Classical Theory of Composition from Its Origins to the Present: A Historical Survey,* University of North Carolina Studies in Comparative Literature, 53 (Chapel Hill: University of North Carolina Press, 1972), pp. 222-82. For a philosophical explanation, see Ulrich Ricken, "Rationalismus und Sensualismus in der Diskussion über die Wortstellung," in *Literaturgeschichte als geschichtlicher,* ed. Werner Bahner (Berlin: Rutten & Loening, 1961); and from the strictly grammatical viewpoint, see Jean-Claude Chevalier, *Histoire de la syntaxe: Naissance de la notion de complément dans la grammaire française* (Geneva: Droz, 1968).

4. Quintilian *Institutionis oratoriae* 9.4 (*De compositione*): "Verbo sensum cludere multo, si compositio patiatur, optimum est: in verbis enim sermonis vis est" {If the demands of artistic structure permit, it is far best to end the sentence with a verb: for it is in the verbs that the real strength of language resides}. *Trans. Note:* See the bilingual edition by H. E. Butler, *The "Institutio oratoria" of Quintilian* (Cambridge, Mass.: Harvard University Press, 1976-80), pp. 520-21. Page numbers hereafter refer to this edition.

5. Ibid. Bornecque translates *rectus ordo* here as the "normal order of words" {*ordre des mots normal*}.

6. Ibid., pp. 518-19. The priority of the principle of progression over the chronological principle is clearly marked a few lines below: "Nec non et illud nimiae superstitionis, uti quaeque sint tempore, ea facere etiam ordine priora; non quin frequenter sit hoc melius, sed quia interim plus valent nate gesta ideoque levioribus superponenda sunt" {Another piece of extravagant pedantry is to insist that the first place should always be occupied by what is first in order of time; such an order is no doubt often the best, but merely because previous events are often the most important and should consequently be placed before matters of trivial import}, (pp. 518-519, 521).

7. Alfred Ernout and François Thomas, *Syntaxe latine* (Paris: Klincksieck, 1964), p. 9.

8. Quoted in Scaglione, *Classical Theory,* pp. 82-83. These philosophical justifications were advanced previously in the classical period by the Greek grammarians, who were perhaps more directly under the influence of the Peripatetics, but who were also thereby more in keeping with Greek sentence construction, nearer to ours than to Latin. Demetrius of Phalerum deems it true to the *natural order* (*physike taxis*) to begin the sentence with the subject and proposes as an example the following sentence from Thucydides (*History of the Peloponnesian War* 1.24), whose word order is almost exactly like that of French: "Epidamos esti polis en dexia eispleonti eis ton Ionion kolpon" (an example that was often invoked by the defenders of the French word order, up through Rivarol). And Dionysus of Halicarnassus writes: "The noun indicates the essence (*ousia*), the verb the accident (*sumbēbēkos*); it is therefore natural for substance to precede accident"; see Scaglione, *Classical Theory,* p. 78. *Trans. Note:* The quotation from Thucydides appears in Scaglione, *Classical Theory,* p. 277 n. 149. See the bilingual edition of *Thucydides* by Charles Foster Smith (Cambridge, Mass.: Harvard University Press, 1962), p. 43.

9. Servius quotes the *Aeneid* 2.347 ("Juvenes, fortissima frustra / Pectora, si vobis au-

dendi extrema cupido, / Certa sequi ...), and adds: "Ordo talis est: juvenes, fortissima pectora," and so forth. Isidore of Seville intensifies the commentary: "Confusa sunt verba; ordo talis est ..." and resumes Servius's "construction." Priscianus, commenting on the opening line of the *Aeneid,* "Arma virumque cano" {Of arms and a man I sing} restores the text to "Cano virum" {I sing of a man}. All these examples are cited by Nicolas Beauzée, *Grammaire générale, ou exposition raisonnée des éléments nécessaires du langage, pour servir de fondement à l'étude de toutes les langues* (Paris, 1767; rpt. Stuttgart: Friederich Frommann Verlag, 1974), 2:475-78.

10. "Naturalis hic est ordo, quando nominativus precedit et verbum cum suis determinationibus et attinentibus subsequitur. Et iste ordo rem, prout gesta est, ordine recto, plano modo declarat et exponit. Artificialis ordo est ... qui rem gestam vel ut gestam a medio incipit narrare, et postea res narratas de principio ducit ad finem. Et hoc ordine Virgilius utitur in Eneide" (Konrad von Mure, quoted in Scaglione, *Classical Theory,* p.114). The slippage from syntactical structure to narrative structure here is quite spectacular.

11. The paragraph on the "figures of construction" associates hyperbaton with figures such as ellipsis or pleonasm, which do not affect word order, and syllepsis (*turba ruunt*), which is typically a figure of grammatical agreement.

12. It also emerges in the context of a closely related debate on the appropriate language for composing inscriptions of public monuments.

13. Pierre Le Laboureur, *Avantages de la langue française sur la langue latine* (Paris, 1667), esp. the second essay, pp.112-72.

14. Dominique Bouhours, *Entretiens d'Ariste et d'Eugène* (Paris: S. Mabre-Cramoisy, 1671), {pp.59, 60-61, 68, 69}.

15. François Charpentier, *De l'excellence de la langue française* (Paris: Bilaine, 1683).

16. This integration is clearly shown by Jean Frain du Tremblay's title: *Traité des langues; ou L'On donne des principes et des règles pour juger du mérite et de l'excellence de chaque langue, et en particulier de la langue française* (Paris: J.-B. Delespine, 1703).

17. Jean-Jacques Rousseau, *Second Discourse* {*Discourse on Equality*} (1755); Nicolas Beauzée, "Langue" ("Natural Language") in *Encyclopédie; ou, Dictionnaire raisonné des sciences des arts et des métiers* (1756); Vicomte de Bonald, *Recherches philosophiques sur les premiers objets des connaissances morales,* in *Oeuvres de M. de Bonald* (Paris: A. Le Clerc, 1818), 8: chap. 2, "De l'origine du langage." Beauzée's and Bonald's obvious, and acknowledged, "source" is Rousseau. The same applies to the Marquis de Saint-Martin, *De l'esprit des choses; ou, Coup d'oeil philosophique sur la nature des natures et sur l'objet de leur existence* (Paris: Laran, 1797), 2:217. Fabre d'Olivet sums it up as follows: "If man's language system is a convention, how was this convention established without language?" (introductory essay to *La Langue hébraïque restituée* [Paris; 1815-16], sec.1). Less expected, and probably preceding Rousseau's *Second Discourse,* here again is A.-R.-J. Turgot, who is, however, a conventionalist, as we know, in the article "Étymologie": "Are we not seeking the origin of natural languages in an arbitrary convention that would, moreover, presuppose some previously established signs, for how

can this convention be produced without speech?" (*Autres réflexions sur les langues* [c.1751] in *Oeuvres de Turgot et documents le concernant, avec biographie et notes,* ed. Gustave Schelle [Paris: F. Alcan, 1913–23], p.351). This false evidence is the very type of an ageless, authorless commonplace; more noteworthy is the belief, at the turn of the century that Rousseau had to be given all the credit for this idea.

18. Of course, the dilemma of divine institution versus human motivation was already present in Leibniz, but not in the context of the same argument of the necessity of a language system prior to any convention; instead, the implicit reason was the necessarily "philosophical" character (for Leibniz) of a conventional language.

19. Abbot Gabriel Girard, *Les Vrais Principes de la langue française; ou, La Parole réduite en méthode conformément aux lois de l'usage* (Paris, 1747; rpt., Geneva: Droz, 1982), esp. pp.21–40.

20. {Ibid., pp.21–23.}

21. {Ibid., pp.22–24.}

22. {Ibid., pp.27–30.}

23. In the seventeenth century and at the beginning of the eighteenth (see Le Laboureur; or Bernard Lamy, *La Rhétorique; ou, L'Art de parler* [Paris: Pralard, 1675], 1: chap.13), the Latin filiation was really not in doubt. The criterion of the *ordo* entails a certain regression of genealogical "knowledge" {*savoir*}.

24. César Chesneau Du Marsais, *Exposition d'une méthode raisonnée pour apprendre la langue latine* (Paris: E. Ganeau, 1722), rpt. *Oeuvres* (Paris: Pougin, 1797), 1:1–41.

25. This position, of course, is the one that the word would occupy in a French-style construction and is, consequently, the function it indicates. As we shall better see further on, for Du Marsais, "position" and function are one and the same thing.

26. {Du Marsais, *Exposition,* p.9.}

27. Here are some examples of ellipsis according to Du Marsais: *maneo (in urbe) Lutetiae* or *(sub) imperante Augusto.*

28. Du Marsais, *Exposition,* Appendix, pp.46–47.

29. Beauzée, *Grammaire générale,* 2:464.

30. The 1699 "fourth edition {of Lamy's *Rhétorique*}, revised and enlarged by one third" (Amsterdam: Paul Marret; Brighton: Sussex Reprints, 1969), is in fact identical to the preceding ones, at least in the chapter cited here. The genuine revised and enlarged fourth edition is that of 1701 (Paris: Delaulne).

31. Jean Baptiste du Bos, *Réflexions critiques sur la poésie et la peinture* (Paris: J. Mariette, 1719), p.310.

32. P. Etienne Simone de Gamaches, *Agréments du langage réduits à leurs principes* (Paris: G. Cavelier, 1718).

33. Étienne Bonnot de Condillac, "Of Transpositions," pt.2, sec.1, chap.12 in *An Essay on the Origin of Human Knowledge, Being a Supplement to Mr. Locke's Essay on the Human Understanding* (1746), trans. Thomas Nugent (1756; rpt., Gainesville, Fla.: Scholar's Facsimiles & Reprints, 1971), pp.264–72. *Trans. Note:* Although the spelling in Nugent's translation has been modernized, the expressive punctuation has not. Nugent renders the French *inversion* as "transposition."

34. {Ibid., pp. 268–69.}

35. {Ibid., pp. 269–70.}

36. {Ibid., pp. 264–66.}

37. {Ibid., chap. 9, "Of Words," pp. 240–41.}

38. {Ibid., p. 245.}

39. Abbot Charles Batteux's *Lettres sur la phrase française comparée avec la phrase latine* was published in 1748 as an appendix (139 pp.) to the second volume of his *Cours de belles-lettres; ou, Principes de la littérature*, 2d ed. (Paris: Desaint & Saillant, 1753). A Hellenist, a Latinist, and a translator of Aristotle, Dionysus of Halicarnassus, and Horace, Charles Batteux, through his *Beaux Arts réduits à un même principe* (Paris: Durand, 1746), also represents one of the main transition points between classical and Romantic aesthetics (and poetics).

40. Charles Batteux, *De la construction oratoire* (Paris: Desaint & Saillant, 1763), chap. 3.

41. Noel Antoine Pluche, *Mécanique des langues et l'art de les enseigner* (Paris: Estienne & Fils, 1751). The title *Mécanique des langues* gave a group name to the partisans of Latin: they were called the "mechanists"; their opponents were called the "metaphysicians" because of the metaphysical order they defended. I will employ these convenient labels as needed.

42. Pierre Chompré, *Introduction à la langue latine par la voie de la traduction* (Paris: Guérin et Delatour, 1751).

43. Pierre Chompré, *Moyens sûrs d'apprendre facilement les langues et principalement la latine* (Paris: Guérin et Delatour, 1757), p. 44.

44. Denis Diderot, *Lettre sur les sourds et muets à l'usage de ceux qui entendent et qui parlent* (published anonymously in 1751), in *Diderot's Early Philosophical Works*, ed. and trans. Margaret Jourdain (Chicago: Open Court, 1916), pp. 158–225. *Trans. Note:* Unless otherwise indicated, subsequent quotations are from the Jourdain text. For a more recent but abridged translation, see *Letter on the Deaf and Dumb for the Use of Those Who Hear and Speak* in *Diderot's Selected Writings*, ed. Lester G. Crocker, trans. Derek Coltman (New York: Macmillan, 1966), pp. 31–39.

45. Beauzée, *Grammaire générale*, p. 465. Diderot's capacity for contradictory statements can be illustrated by juxtaposing the following two excerpts from his article, "Encyclopédie": "the double convention that attached ideas to the voice and the voice to written characters," and "the idea is to the sign as the object is to the mirror that repeats it." These statements are contradictory for us, of course; I assume that for him, conventionality and mimeticism in no way exclude each other, which enables him to don the hats of Cratylus and Hermogenes alternately.

46. {Diderot, *Letter*, p. 180.}

47. *Trans. Note:* Since the Jourdain version (ibid., p. 181) omits part of this colorful and amusing passage, the translation here is mine.

48. {Ibid., p. 188.}

49. {Ibid., p. 189.}

50. {Ibid., p. 190.}

51. {Ibid., pp.191, 217 (modified).} *Trans. Note:* Since the word Genette emphasizes, *pedestrian,* does not appear in the Jourdain version of the last sentence quoted here, the translation is mine.

52. {Ibid., pp.194-95 (modified).}

53. "Fleeting emblems," "accidental hieroglyph," and so on. In keeping with a popular idea at that time, the hieroglyph for Diderot is the type of the mimetic sign; *emblem* evidently carries the same sense. *Accidental* is more complicated: it mixes the everyday acceptation (an accidental hieroglyph is a word that apparently owes its mimetic character to chance) and the philosophical sense (a hieroglyph paints an accident: that is, a perceptible quality of the object it designates), and also the grammatical sense later explained by Du Marsais in the article "Accident" in the *Encyclopédie:* any nonessential property of a word is accidental, such as its acceptation (literal or figurative), its type (primitive or derivative), its form (simple or compound), its pronunciation.

54. {Diderot, *Letter,* p.195.}

55. Virgil, *Aeneid* 9.433-37; {Diderot, *Letter,* p.198 (modified)}.

56. See Paul Delbouille, *Poésie et sonorité: La Critique contemporaine devant le pouvoir suggestif des sons* (Paris: Les Belles Lettres, 1961), pt. 2: "Quand la critique s'égare" — a collection of foolish quotations that has been quite surpassed by the "aberrations" of the last fifteen years. Let us recall that ten years after Diderot's *Letter,* Rousseau found in "The Fox and the Crow" a "splendid line whose very sound suggests a picture: I see the big ugly gaping beak, I hear the cheese crashing through the branches" (*Émile,* trans. Barbara Foxley [London: Dent, 1972], bk. 2, p.79) {modified}. *Trans. Note:* The mimologically rich line from La Fontaine's fable is "Il ouvre un large bec, laisse tomber sa proie."

57. Indeed, before Diderot, several outlines of a similar conception can be found in du Bos or Harris (see Tzvetan Todorov, "Ésthetique et sémiotique au XVIIIe siècle," *Critique* 29.308 [1973]: 26-39), in Lamy, even in Gabriel Du Bois-Hus: "When highly active geniuses speak or write, their language and discourse seem to have taken on the colors they depict; their words look red and incarnadine when they speak of carnations and roses, yellow when they sketch their worries, white when they describe lilies or swans, green when they depict hedgerows, forests, and plains for us" (*Le Jour des jours* [1641], quoted in Jean Rousset, *L'Intérieur et l'extérieur: Essais sur la poésie et sur le théâtre au XVIIe siècle* [Paris: Librairie José Corti, 1968], p.113). This conception can be found especially in Lessing, for whom poetry "must necessarily seek to raise its arbitrary signs to natural ones" (letter to Nicolai, 26 May 1769). But in an unexpected deviation Lessing reserves this privilege for the genre of drama alone, where the words uttered by the actors perfectly "imitate" — for good reason — the words exchanged by the characters. Of all the precursors of Symbolist poetic mimologism, Diderot remains the most striking.

58. Jean Le Rond d'Alembert, "Éclaircissements sur l'inversion, et à cette occasion sur ce qu'on appelle le génie des langues," chap. 10 in *Essai sur les éléments de philosophie; ou, Sur les principes des connaissances humaines* (Paris, 1759; rpt. Paris: Fayard, 1986), pp.295-314.

59. {Ibid., pp. 298, 305.}

60. {Ibid., p. 300.}

61. {Ibid., pp. 303-4.}

62. {Ibid., pp. 305-6.}

63. Unless we count the chapter "Inversion" in Abbot Copineau's *Essai synthétique sur l'origine et la formation des langues* (Paris: Rualt, 1774), which devotes a faithful and approbatory summary to it.

64. See Du Marsais's article "Construction," in the *Encyclopédie*, vol. 4 (1754), reprinted in *Oeuvres*, 5:1-96; "Principes de grammaire; ou, Fragments sur les causes de la parole" {cited as *Fragments*}, published posthumously in *Logique et principes de grammaire* (Paris: Librairies Associées, 1769); and the piece "Inversion" (also published posthumously in *Logique et principes*), probably the draft of an article for the *Encyclopédie* and used as such to a large extent by Beauzée after Du Marsais's death in 1756. These three texts support one another and ought to be studied together. I am leaving aside the purely pedagogical aspect of his works, in which Du Marsais defends his method against the criticisms of Pluche and Chompré, and his recourse to the testimony of "old Latin grammarians" who, he says, defended the "natural order" at the time when Latin "was still a living language," and did so independently of any influence of a modern language. As was previously the case in Charpentier, this is a debatable assimilation of the classical *rectus ordo* to the scholiasts' *naturalis ordo*. For a general critique, see Gunvor Sahlin, *César Chesneau Du Marsais et son rôle dans l'évolution de la grammaire générale* (Paris: Presses Universitaires de France, 1928), chap. 3, "La construction."

65. Du Marsais, "Inversion," pp. 196-97. Notice the very obvious play on the ambiguity of the verb *entendre* {to hear, to understand}.

66. Du Marsais, "Construction," pp. 7, 3.

67. A very sharp distinction between syntax and construction is posited from the beginning of the article: "*Accepi litteras tuas, tuas accepi litteras, litteras accepi tuas:* there are three constructions here, since there are three different word arrangements; however, there is only a single syntax, for in each of these constructions the same signs of relationships exist between the words" {ibid., p. 2}. But as a matter of fact this distinction is forgotten, and from the next page on, Du Marsais speaks of syntactical relationships as "*successive* relationships that obtain between words," thereby folding all syntax back into "construction" and assuring the universal hegemony of the *ordo* {p. 3}.

68. Du Marsais, "Inversion," p. 206; the wise grammarian is Father Buffier.

69. Du Marsais, "Construction," pp. 19ff.

70. Du Marsais, "Inversion," p. 204.

71. Ibid., pp. 4, 36.

72. Ibid., p. 204; Du Marsais, *Fragments*, pp. 78, 83.

73. Du Marsais, *Fragments*, p. 84.

74. {César Chesneau Du Marsais, *Des tropes: ou, Des différents sens dans lesquels on peut prendre un même mot dans une même langue*, in *Oeuvres* (Paris: Pougin, 1797), 3:15.}

75. Ibid., p. 23.

76. Du Marsais, "Figure," in *Oeuvres*, 5:262. In this way, Du Marsais supplements Scaliger's definition ("A figure is nothing but a special arrangement of one or several words"), which is more or less the one he was content to use in *Tropes*.

77. Pierre Fontanier, *Commentaire raisonné sur les "Tropes" de Du Marsais*, p.3. Fontanier claims to have found this definition in the *Encyclopédie méthodique, ou par ordre de matières; Par une société de gens de lettres, de savants et d'artistes; Precédée d'un vocabulaire universel* (Paris: Chez Panckoucke, 1782-1832). I do not find it there, and at any rate the additions to the *Encyclopédie méthodique* as far as rhetoric is concerned are Beauzée's.

78. Nicolas Beauzée (1717-89) was a professor of grammar at the École Royale Militaire; his articles for the *Encyclopédie* were written in collaboration with Douchet, and each author's contribution is difficult to pin down exactly. The corpus discussed here includes the article "Grammaire" (1757) and the article "Langue" (1765), both quoted from the new edition provided by Sylvain Auroux (*L'Encyclopédie "grammaire" et "langue" au XVIIIe siècle* [Paris: Mame, 1973]); the article "Inversion" (1765), which takes up in part the project left behind by Du Marsais; and *Grammaire générale* (Paris, 1767; rpt., Stuttgart: Friederich Frommann Verlag, 1974), vol.2, bk.3, chap.9, "De l'ordre de la phrase" (pp.464-566). This is the only grammar from the entire age of neoclassicism that has an explicitly *Cartesian* aim: "With regard to general grammar, I have followed the method of investigation proposed by Descartes for all philosophical matters" (Preface, p. xxvii). Beauzée is the perfect embodiment of the "philosopher-grammarian," but his philosophy is closer to classical rationalism than to Enlightenment sensualism.

79. Beauzée, *Grammaire générale*, 2:471-72.

80. Ibid., pp.535-36.

81. Ibid., pp.496, 501.

82. Ibid., pp.538, 539.

83. Ibid., pp.470, 474, 515 (emphasis added).

84. "Words cannot abandon the posts assigned to them (by the natural construction) without putting on the uniform of inflections that plainly summon them back to it" (ibid., p.502).

85. Beauzée, of course, does not use this notion, but we will run across it again in one of his distant heirs.

86. Beauzée, "Langue," p.140.

87. Beauzée, *Grammaire générale*, p.471.

88. Ibid., pp.509-11. This repudiation did not escape the notice of Diderot, who immediately replied in a review in *Correspondance Littéraire*, November 1767. After highly praising the book, he added: "There is not one word of truth in the chapter on inversions, in which the author claims that French syntax lines words up in the order that is the most natural and the most consonant with the birth and succession of ideas" (*Oeuvres complètes de Diderot* [Paris: Club Français du Livre, 1970], 7:432).

89. Beauzée, "Langue," pp.110, 114.

90. Ibid., pp.140-41.

91. {Ibid., pp.160, 161 (original emphasis).}

92. This linguistic myth, in which the "Hebraicist" and the "Celtist" theses are conjoined, goes back at least to the seventeenth century. Beauzée here cites more recent authorities: Jean-Baptiste Bullet, *Mémoires sur la langue celtique* (1754-60) and Charles de Grandval, *Discours historique sur l'origine de la langue française* (1757).

93. Beauzée, "Langue," pp.141-42.

94. {Beauzée, *Grammaire générale*, pp.529-30.}

95. Beauzée, *Grammaire générale*, pp.529-30.

96. This wording reappears on several occasions; Beauzée systematically avoids the term "expression," which is probably too affective for him.

97. {Beauzée, *Grammaire générale*, p.526.}

98. {Ibid., p.517.}

99. {Ibid., p.531.}

100. {Ibid., pp.545-46 (original emphasis).}

101. "Whether it is true *or not* that we always speak out of some interest, it is a *prior and still more certain* truth that we speak in order to make our thoughts known" (ibid., p.532). The repression of motives is typical.

102. Charles Batteux, *Nouvel Examen du préjugé sur l'inversion, pour servir de réponse à M. Beauzée* (Paris, 1767), 78 pages.

103. Charles de Brosses, *Traité de la formation mécanique des langues et des principes physiques de l'étymologie* (Paris: Saillant, Vincent & Desaint, 1765; rev. ed., 1800), chap. 22.

104. François-Marie Arouet de Voltaire, "Langues" (1771), in *Questions sur l'Encyclopédie*, vol.5 (Geneva, 1777). This is above all a critique of the *Traité de la formation mécanique* and part of the long quarrel with de Brosses.

105. Antoine Rivarol, *De l'universalité de la langue française* (Paris: Bailly & Destenne, 1784), par.64-72.

106. "The direct word order, it is said, greatly favors clarity. It would be truer to say that clarity is more necessary to the direct order. In natural languages enslaved by this order, there often is only one single construction for expressing oneself completely clearly. ... In natural languages with inversion ... there are twenty ways of constructing the same sentence. ... Therefore, languages with inversion favor clarity, since they have so many ways of being clear" (M. Garat, "De l'Universalité de la langue française," *Mercure de France*, 6 August 1785, pp.10-34).

107. Urbain Domergue, introduction (the only part published) to *Grammaire générale analytique* (Paris: C. Houel, 1799), p.73.

108. Destutt de Tracy, *Éléments d'idéologie*, pt.2, *Grammaire* (Paris, 1803; rpt. Paris: Vrin, 1970), pp.158-60.

109. Jean-Pierre Brisset, *La Grammaire logique, résolvant toutes les difficultés et faisant connaître par l'analyse de la parole la formation des langues et celle du genre humain* (Angers: Lachèse et Dolbeau, 1883; rpt. Paris: Tchou, 1970), sec.97, pp.87-90. Brisset is not completely unaware of the linguistics of his century, since he mentions at least

the existence of Sanskrit (which is also labeled an artificial language), but the linguistic baggage of this autodidact is typically eighteenth-century. Besides, he quotes Du Marsais. His quarrel with Latin, halfway between Beauzée and Obélix ("They are mad, those Latins!"), may have some personal motives: "Latin has never been more in demand than today. An official diploma certifying you in Latin is worth more than half a lifetime passed in doing military service, more than the blood spilled on the fields of battle, and more than the education, whatever kind it be, acquired while defending one's own person amidst the difficulties of life" {p.89}. Plainly, there is a theme of administrative persecution here. Brisset suffered a final snub, itself also highly symbolic: *Grammaire logique*, put up for a prize at the Academy (a *salle aux prix* or a *saloperie?* {a "room of prizes" or "trash?"}), was rejected by Ernest Renan (see Michel Foucault's preface, p. xviii). Brisset is a true victim of the new linguistics.

110. Or *special* cases, as we say of certain courts: "Allow me to compare simple construction to common law and figurative construction to preferential law" (Du Marsais, "Construction," p.18).

111. "Accordingly as the peoples pay more attention to things, their verbal terms possess more distinct ideas and increase in number" (Lamy, *Rhétorique*, 1: chap.5).

112. Condillac, *Essay*, pt.2, sec.1, chap.15, "Of the Character of Languages" (pp.283-300).

CHAPTER 10

1. The decisive date is of course that of Sir William Jones's address to the Asiatic Society of Bengal, 1786. But it must be remembered that Sanskrit was not then altogether unknown in Europe and that the hypothesis of Indo-European unity, for its part, had been maintained since the sixteenth century: this was Goropius Becanus's so-called "Scythic" hypothesis, which we reencountered in Leibniz. Jones's outstanding contribution lay in connecting the two lines of thought.

2. Max Müller, "The Classificatory Stage in the Science of Language," lecture 4 in *Lectures on the Science of Language* (1861; London: Longman, 1862), pp.164-65 {original emphasis}.

3. Johann Gottfried Herder, *Essay on the Origin of Language* (1770), in *On the Origin of Language*, trans. Alexander Gode (New York: Frederick Ungar, 1967); Daniel Jenisch, *Philosophischekritische vergleichung und wurdigung von vierzehn altern und neuern sprachen Europens* (Berlin: F. Maurer, 1796).

4. Let us recall that Rasmus Rask, early in his career, practiced comparatism without knowing Sanskrit, but not without projecting onto Old Icelandic the same enthusiasm that Shlegel or Bopp did onto Sanskrit—and with the same theme of the perfection of the inflectional system. In a mind reputed to be matter-of-fact and rigorous, this fervor for the language of "our ancestors" definitely has a certain accent of Romanticism.

5. Friedrich von Schlegel, "On the Language and Philosophy of the Indians," in *The*

Aesthetic and Miscellaneous Works of Friederick von Schlegel, trans. E. J. Millington (London: Henry G. Bohn, 1849), p.455.

6. Jakob Grimm, *On the Origin of Language* (1851), trans. Raymond A. Wiley (Leiden: E. J. Brill, 1984), p.17. On the history of this reversal of values at the end of the eighteenth century in Monboddo, Hermsterhuis, and Herder, see Edward Stankiewicz, "The Dithyramb to the Verb in Eighteenth- and Nineteenth-Century Linguistics," in Dell H. Hymes, ed., *Studies in the History of Linguistics: Traditions and Paradigms* (Bloomington: Indiana University Press, 1974), pp.157-90. We have already noted Herder's ambiguous position; more clearly, Copineau already sees "the most important part of discourse" in the verb (*Essai synthétique sur l'origine et la formation des langues* [Paris: Ruault, 1774], p.54).

7. Michel Foucault, *The Order of Things: An Archeology of the Human Sciences* (New York: Random House, 1970), pp.287-91. *Trans. Note:* The quotation here is from p.290. On the motif of the "correctness" (*justesse*) of words, and of nouns in particular, for referring to things, see Genette's chapter 1, "Eponymy of the Name."

8. Oswald Ducrot, *Qu'est-ce que le structuralisme?* vol.1, *Le Structuralisme en linguistique* (Paris: Seuil, 1968), p.30.

9. Rasmus Rask, quoted in Georges Mounin, *Histoire de la linguistique des origines au XXe siècle* (Paris: Presses Universitaires de France, 1967), p.165 (emphasis added).

10. Wilhelm von Humboldt, *De l'origine des formes grammaticales,* trans. Alfred Tonnelle (1823; Paris: Ducros, 1969), p.46.

11. As previously cited, Saussure used the word "nomenclature," whose (re)appearance here is not entirely anachronistic. Already in the implicit linguistic theory of the first comparatists we find more than a little Saussureanism or, if one prefers, structuralism, which will be lost later on, through the historicist "atomism" of the neogrammarians at the end of the century. Saussure, who is not for nothing the author of *Mémoire sur le systeme primitif des voyelles dans les langues indo-européenes* (1879; rept., Hildesheim: G. Olms, 1968), will rediscover this inspiration and take it further; but we must not underrate all that his idea of natural languages as a differential system owes to comparatist practice.

12. Schlegel, "Indians," p.447.

13. Humboldt's position is more complicated. He readily defines inflection in a manner rather close to Schlegel's, ideally, as "modification of words," "adjunction and insertion of elements devoid of signification, changes of vowels and consonants" (*De l'origine,* pp.23, 29). But he does not think that this "authentic inflection" was ever originary in a natural language: it always derives from an agglutination, from an "adjunction of significant syllables" (pp.31-32); and consequently the division into natural languages with (internal) inflections and with agglutinations does not seem to him "defensible from any point of view" (p.35). Cf. Oswald Ducrot, "Humboldt et l'arbitraire linguistique," *Cahiers Internationaux de Symbolisme* 26 (1974): 15-26.

14. Schlegel, "Indians," p.445.

15. See Judith E. Schlanger, *Les Métaphores de l'organisme* (Paris: Vrin, 1971), pp. 126ff.

16. Schlegel, "Indians," p. 449. The *parti pris* is energetically denied elsewhere — "It must not, however, be supposed that I desire to exalt one chief branch of language exclusively, to the neglect or disparagement of the other" (p. 451) — only to be immediately confirmed: "It must undoubtedly be admitted, after adequate investigation and comparison, that languages in which the grammar is one of inflection are usually preferable, as evincing higher art in their construction" (p. 451). In short, the superiority of natural languages with inflections is not "absolute," because no superiority, by definition, can be so; it is just overwhelming.

17. Let us recall that for Schlegel the class of "noble" natural languages, that is, those with internal inflections, is closed to the Semitic languages, Arabic being merely the most evolved of the languages with affixes. As for Humboldt, he will place the Semitic languages "alongside" Sanskrit; but it is to Greek that he accords the "highest point of perfection in its structure" (*De l'origine*, p. 57). And Ernest Renan, quoting Humboldt, judges that the Semitic languages typically have their inflections "inside the words," expressing "the gist of the idea through the consonants and accessory modifications through the vowels" (*Histoire générale et système comparé des langues sémitiques* (1855) in *Oeuvres complètes*, vol. 8, ed. Henriette Psichari [Paris: Calmann-Levy, 1958], p. 545).

18. Anachronistic in the sense that, roughly speaking, interest in morphology is born just when (classical) Cratylism is dying. But in duly scrutinizing the fringe period, one can find several traces of this hybrid. Thus, in de Brosses, there are the following reflections on adjectival degrees: "When they want to mark the superlative degree of something, all nations use the natural and common method of redoubling their effort in pronunciation, and of adding more to the composition of the noun. To this end, the Americans repeat the simple word twice in succession. The Greeks and Latins extend the word by ending it with a highly stressed motion of the mouth, but with the same purpose of expressing the superlative degree mechanically, the Greeks depict it by *tatos*, the Latins by *errimus* or *issimus*. All of them achieve the same thing, but through various means of the same type" (*Traité de la formation mécanique des langues* [Paris: Saillant, Vincent & Desaint, 1765; rev. ed., 1800], 1:47). But this is a mimeticism of a rather diagrammatic type, which we will encounter again in Roman Jakobson discussing the same subject (*high-higher-highest, altus-altior-altissimus*): "Morphology abounds in examples of substitutive signs that present an equivalent relation between their signifiers and signifieds" (*Problèmes du langage* [Paris: Gallimard, 1966], p. 30). More classically Cratylian, because the morphological motivation this time applies the hypothesis of phonic symbolism only to the affixes (as in my imaginary examples in Gébelin's or Wallis's style), is the interpretation of case endings which Humboldt attributes to Bopp himself: "In the third person pronoun, the light *s*-sound is obviously accorded symbolically to the living, and the dull *m* to the genderless neuter; and the same alternation of letters in the endings now distinguishes the subject considered as agent, the nominative, from the accusative, the object of agency" (Wilhelm von Humboldt, *On Language: The Diversity of Human Language-Structure and Its Influence on*

the Mental Development of Mankind, trans. Peter Heath [Cambridge: Cambridge University Press, 1988], p.106). I cannot locate such a statement, evidently contrary to all the methodological principles of comparatism, in Bopp; if a natural (and therefore universal) symbolism can inspire the selection of morphological elements, their value as indices of filiation disappears by the same token. This sort of inconsistency is certainly not unprecedented (and we will run across one or two instances in Grimm), but the typical attitude of the comparatists is rather to refuse any interrogation of the object of the Cratylian debate, which is pushed outside the field of linguistic pertinence: "One point I shall leave untouched, the secret of the roots, or the foundation of the nomenclature of the primary ideas. I shall not investigate, for example, why the root *i* signifies 'go' and not 'stand'; why the combination of sounds *stha* or *sta* signifies 'stand' and not 'go'" (Franz Bopp, *A Comparative Grammar of the Sanskrit, Zend, Greek, Latin, Lithuanian, Gothic, German, and Slavonic Languages,* trans. Edward B. Eastwick, 3d ed. [London: Williams & Norgate, 1862], 1:v). *Trans. Note:* Humboldt's *Diversity of Human Language-Structure* is the general introduction to a three-volume work, *On the Kawi Language on the Island of Java,* and was published separately in 1836.

19. See, e.g., Hugh Blair, *Lectures on Rhetoric and Belles-Lettres* (London: W. Strahan & T. Cadell, 1783), 1:114. *Trans. Note:* Genette is paraphrasing Blair, who says: "The Iroquois and Illinois carry on their treaties and public transactions with bolder metaphors, and greater pomp of style, than we use in our poetical productions."

20. {Herder, *Origin,* p.159.}

21. Tentatively on p.454 (Schlegel, "Indians") but categorically on p.429: "It is further proved by comparison that the Indian is the most ancient, and the source ... whence others of later origin are derived."

22. "In many languages, indeed, instead of that highly organized and artistic construction which is produced by significant syllables and prolific roots, we discover merely varied imitations, and almost sportive combinations of sound—the cry, as it were, of instinctive feeling and impulse, to which the exclamatory, the interjectional, and distinctive terminations and additions in time became annexed, and invested by constant use with a certain conventional and arbitrary signification" (Schlegel, "Indians," p.456). This is the classical thesis (Condillac, Copineau, etc.) but—a crucial distinction—deprived of its universality and confined to a few inferior idioms.

23. Schlegel, "Indians," pp.454 and 457 {modified}.

24. Particularly well known is the time lag in France, during the whole first half of the century, in a domain that was to remain a Germanic specialty for a long time.

25. *Trans. Note:* Genette's concluding argument here involves several senses of the key phrase *flexion interne,* which is the title of this chapter. First, it refers to the central "discovery" of nineteenth-century comparative grammar that the origin of languages might be traced through structural changes in words—the "internal inflections" of roots. Second, *flexion interne* alludes to Genette's own methodology throughout *Mimologics,* which he makes explicit in this chapter. In the continuous series of "transformations and displacements" that constitutes the history of Cratylism, comparative

grammar provides an exemplary case of a *flexion interne,* an "internal twist" that is simultaneously "subversion," "inversion," and "diversion."

26. Naturally, the presence of Schlegel, Humboldt, or Grimm leads one to exaggerate slightly here the relevance of the notion of Romanticism. In fact, as we will see further on, Jakob Grimm and especially A. W. Schlegel at times lean toward a more classical mimologism. Humboldt makes an allowance for "symbolic" motivation (*st* = solidity, *l* = liquidity, *n* = "cut and dried division," *w* = fluctuation), in which "a *feeling* of conceptual unity has actually passed over into the sound," and in which "the influence of this inner feeling of unity still remains the primitive one" (*On Language,* pp.104, 115; original emphasis). And, on the other hand, one finds from Novalis's pen this quite Hermogenist warning: "On the exchange made between the symbol and the symbolized (on their identification), on the faith in the veracity, in the full totality of representation (and the relation of the original and the image, of appearance and substance), on the consequences drawn from external resemblances for the unison and the correspondence commonly rediscovered within: in short, on confusions between object and subject are based all the superstitions, the false beliefs, and the errors of every era in every people and for every individual" (*Fragment* 6.555, in *Oeuvres complètes* [Paris: Gallimard, 1975], 2:343).

CHAPTER 11

1. Ernest Renan, *De l'origine du langage* (1848), p.47 in *Oeuvres complètes,* vol.8, ed. Henriette Psichari (Paris: Calmann-Levy, 1958), which also includes *Histoire générale et système comparé des langues sémitiques* (1855). These two texts, which frequently overlap, constitute the essential part of Renan's linguistic work. The *Origine* occupies pp. 11-123; the *Histoire,* pp.129-589.

2. This is the extension to natural language itself of the famous formula that Duclos reserved for writing: "born all at once, like the light" (chap.5, *Remarques sur la grammaire générale* [1754], in *Oeuvres complètes de Duclos,* ed. M. Auger [Paris: Janet et Cotelle, 1820-21; Geneva: Slatkine Reprints, 1968], 8:38). *Trans. Note:* Genette is referring to Schlegel's description of the origin of language in Lecture 3 of *Philosophy of Language:* "It came forth ... at once and in its totality [*hervorbringen im Ganzen*] out of the full inner and living consciousness of man" (trans. Rev. A. J. W. Morrison [London: Henry G. Bohn, 1847]), p.402.

3. Renan, *Origine,* pp.16, 53, 18.

4. Quoted in Renan, *Origine,* p.49. This sentence is found in A. R. J. Turgot, "Remarques critiques sur les réflexions philosophiques de M. de Maupertuis" (1750), in *Varia linguistica,* ed. Ducros (1970), p.50.

5. Renan, *Origine,* pp.17, 50-51. We are a long way from Plato's professional onomaturge. But after all, had he not, from the end of the dialogue, revealed his fallibility?

6. Ibid., pp.24-34.

7. Ibid., p.71; cf. p.74: "Almost exclusively dominant among the hypersensitive races as among the Semites, it appears much less in the Indo-European tongues."

8. Ibid., p.76.

9. Ibid., p.71.

10. Ibid., pp.72-74.

11. Ibid., p.76.

12. Ibid., p.162.

13. Ibid., pp.101-2 (this is taken up again in *Histoire*, p.537).

14. Renan, *Histoire*, pp.228-29.

15. Renan, *Origine*, p.54; and *Histoire*, pp.560-61.

16. Remember, this conception in no way prevents the use of the word *history* (even in the title), nor the declared conviction that "the true theory of natural languages is in one sense merely their history" (Renan, *Histoire*, p.134).

17. Ibid., p.548.

18. Ibid., p.559.

19. This appointment was immediately suspended, then reinstated in 1870.

20. Renan, *Histoire*, p.134 (emphasis added).

21. Renan, *Origine*, p.102; and *Histoire*, p.180.

22. If one wants to appreciate by contrast the subtlety of Renan's determinism, here is an example of a genuinely racist theory of language: "By *race*, I mean a primitive variety of the human species. By *natural language*, I mean the primordial syllabic organism in which each race spontaneously embodied the products of its particular intellectual organization. Thus, each language is merely a natural complement of the human organization anatomically, physiologically, and psychologically specialized in each race. The different characteristics of the productive cause (any given cerebro-mental organization) find themselves necessarily reflected in the effects produced. To put into its natural language what was in its head, and in the manner in which that head felt and understood, therein lies the common, first, spontaneous, and inevitable achievement of each race. Whence, for example, some corollaries such as these: The Chinese race is to the Chinese language as the Indo-European race is the Indo-European language. To each race, its language; and to each language, its race" (Honoré Joseph Chavée, *Les Langues et les races* [Paris: Chamerot, 1862], p.7).

23. Renan, *Histoire*, p.146.

24. Ibid., pp.155-56. It is necessary, however, to contrast these declarations with a passage in which, carried away by another topos (that of the influence of the climate), Renan insists to the contrary on the diversity of the three great Semitic languages: "Whereas the tongues of the South abound in varied forms, in sonorous vowels, in full and harmonious sounds, those of the North, comparatively poorer and looking only for the necessary, are burdened with consonants and with harsh articulations. One is surprised by the difference which a few degrees of latitude produce in this regard. For example, the three main Semitic idioms, Aramaic, Hebrew, and Arabic, although dis-

tributed over a considerable area, are in an exact relationship, in richness and beauty, to the climatic situation of the peoples who have spoken them. Aramaic, in use in the North, is hard, poor, without harmony, heavy in its constructions, without aptitude for poetry. In contrast, Arabic, situated at the other extreme, is distinguished by an admirable richness. No natural language possesses as many synonyms for certain classes of ideas, none presents as complicated a grammatical system; so that one would be sometimes tempted to see overabundance in the almost indefinite expanse of its dictionary and in the labyrinth of its grammatical forms. Finally, Hebrew, situated between these two extremes, maintains the middle ground between their opposed qualities as well. It has what is necessary but nothing superfluous; it is harmonious and easy, but without attaining the marvelous flexibility of Arabic. Its vowels are arranged harmonically and moderate one another in order to avoid overly harsh articulations, whereas Aramaic, searching for monosyllabic forms, does nothing to avoid the collisions of consonants, and in Arabic, on the contrary, the words seem, literally, to float in a river of vowels, which bubbles over them from all sides, follows them, precedes them, unites them, without suffering any of those clashing sounds that other languages, even the most harmonious, tolerate" (*Origine*, pp. 95-96; repeated in *Histoire*, pp. 572-73). We will have to come back to this curious versatility of the topos, which reverses itself in displacing itself or, rather, in changing levels: here, Aramaic is to Semitic in general what Semitic is to Indo-European; and Arabic, opposed to Aramaic, suddenly has nothing Semitic about it any more.

25. Renan, *Histoire*, pp. 527-30. But here is the inverse theme (Schlegel's again): "Contrary to the Indo-European languages, the Semitic languages have enriched and perfected themselves through aging. For them the synthesis does not lie at the origin, and it is only with time and through long efforts that they have succeeded in giving a complete expression to the logical operations of thought" (p. 522).

26. We can see how precisely Renan applies to the Semitic languages alone the very idea that the "old school" had formed of the origins of all language. Classical mimologism is not refuted; it is simply relegated—but for him, of course, this relegation is equivalent to a refutation.

27. *Trans. Note:* The French word *tour*, which Renan uses here to describe the "lively succession of urgent turns of speech" (*une vive succession de tours pressants*) that characterizes Semitic languages, carries the full weight and ambiguity of his latent racism. *Tour* means not only a "turn" or "twist" of thought that produces a rhetorical figure, but also a "trick," as in *un sale tour*, ("a dirty trick")—evoking the stereotype of the "sneaky" or "dirty" Jew or Arab. These negative connotations are carried over into Renan's next sentence: "the arabesque is their favorite stylistic device" (*l'arabesque est leur procédé favori*). *Procédé* is any rhetorical device and, as the history of rhetoric since Plato shows, "device" implies a tricky or deceptive use of language—another *sale tour*.

28. Renan, *Origine*, pp. 96-98; and *Histoire*, pp. 157-62. The last sentence here is from the *Origine*. The *Histoire* offers an interesting variant: "To imagine an Aristotle or a Kant with such an instrument is as impossible as to conceive of an *Iliad* or a poem like

that of Job ..." (p.157). Placing Homer on the same side as Job here upsets the antithesis a bit, unless one classifies the Homeric "dialect" among the Semitic tongues. Regarding the metaphysical incompetence of the Semites, let us recall that in 1852 Renan wrote a doctoral thesis on Averroës. But for him Arabic philosophy is not a creation of the Semitic mind, since it derives entirely from Aristotle.

29. Renan, *Origine*, p.96.

30. Renan, *Histoire*, p.147.

31. This traditional information on John the Baptist is mentioned in Renan's *Life of Jesus* (1863; New York: Modern Library, 1955), chap.6. For Renan, John the Baptist is the incarnation of the Semitic spirit in its purity, the heir of the "Bedouin patriarch preparing the faith of the world." We know the role played in *The Life of Jesus* by the geo-ethnographical opposition ("Every nation called to high destinies ought to be a little world in itself, including opposite poles") between arid Judea, the Semitic country par excellence, and blooming Galilee, whose "less sharply monotheistic" spirit is the natural source of Christianity (p.113). The attempt to pull Christianity away from its Semitic origins is evident. On the other hand, Islam will be "a sort of resurrection of Judaism in its most Semitic form" (p.218); the antithesis Semite/Aryan is thereby perpetuated in an opposition between an essentially Semitic Islam and an Aryanized Christianity. *Trans. Note:* There is a geomimological wordplay involved in the contrast between *la sèche Judée,* the "dry" and "barren" land of Judea with its "humorless" people, and *la riante Galilée* — the "smiling" land of Galilee with its "laughing" waters and the fertility that these suggest. Such chiasmus typifies the genre of mimology, or reverie on words, with its slippage back and forth between geographical fact and motivated fiction.

32. This danger had been pointed out before by Humboldt: "Since, to study an unknown natural language, one usually situates oneself from the viewpoint of another known natural language, whether the maternal tongue or Latin, one tends to look for the ways in which the grammatical relations of the latter are expressed by the former; then one applies to the inflections or to the combinations of words of the foreign language the very name of the grammatical form which, in the language already known, or according to the general laws of language, serves to express the same relationship. Now it happens very often that these forms do not exist in any way in the new natural language but are replaced there by some others or are expressed by some circumlocutions. To avoid this error, one must study each natural language separately, in its own distinctive character, and, through an exact analysis of all its parts, attempt to recognize what special form it possesses, according to its constitution, in order to represent each grammatical relationship" (*De l'origine des formes grammaticales, et de leur influence sur le développement des idées,* trans. Alfred Tonnelle [Paris: A. Franck, 1859], p.19). But here Humboldt merely applied to the study of "unknown" natural languages the principle of respect for the "distinctive genius," formulated by Girard against the imperialism of Latin. A principle, to be sure, that is easier to set forth than to apply.

33. Renan, *Histoire*, p.155.

34. Ibid., p.577.

35. Ibid., p.580.

36. Ibid., p.588.

37. Renan, *Origine*, p.90.

38. *Trans. Note:* Jean Paulhan is the author of *Causes célèbres* (1950) and other works, an Orientalist, linguist, writer, and eventual member of the Académie Française (1963).

CHAPTER 12

1. Paul Valéry, *Cahiers*, ed. Judith Robinson (Paris: Gallimard, 1974), 2:487 (emphasis added).

2. Stéphane Mallarmé, letter to Paul Verlaine (November 16, 1885), facsimile, also known as *Autobiographie* (Paris: Albert Messein, 1924).

3. Paul Valéry, "A Kind of Preface" in *Leonardo, Poe, Mallarmé*, trans. Malcolm Cowley and James R. Lawler, in *The Collected Works of Paul Valéry*, vol.8, ed. Jackson Mathews, Bollingen Series 45 (Princeton: Princeton University Press, 1972), p.306.

4. Maurice Monda and François Montel, *Bibliographie des poètes maudits*, vol.1, *Stephane Mallarmé* (Paris: Giraud-Badin, 1927), p.23.

5. *Trans. Note:* Genette is referring to Mallarmé's essay on Richard Wagner, "Rêverie d'un poète français" (1885).

6. Stéphane Mallarmé, *Petite Philologie à l'usage des classes et du monde: Les Mots anglais* (Paris: Truchy-Leroy, 1877; reprinted in *Oeuvres complètes*, ed. Henri Mondor and G. Jean-Aubry [Paris: Gallimard, 1945]), pp.885–1053. *Trans. Note:* All citations from *Les Mots anglais* refer to the Gallimard edition; I have replaced many of Genette's group page references with separate notes. Further, when Genette cites Mallarmé's other works, I have supplied the titles; these references also cite the Gallimard edition.

7. Mallarmé, *Mots anglais*, pp. 889, 903, 911, 926, 953. The manuscript of *Thèmes anglais* (pp. 1055–1156) in *Oeuvres complètes*) probably has some relation to this plan, but it was intended for inclusion in another framework (*Cours complet d'anglais*); and it is much more a phraseology than a grammar, being a collection of "proverbs and typical locutions" translated into French and meant to be rendered idiomatically. *Trans. Note:* The subtitle of Mallarmé's *Étude des règles* is *Une Mythologie nouvelle, d'après l'anglais* (A new mythology, in the manner of the English language).

8. This is the French term used at the time to designate comparative and historical grammar. Renan speaks of "comparative philology."

9. Mallarmé, *Mots anglais*, p.889.

10. Ibid., p.1050.

11. {Ibid., p.963.}

12. Ibid., p.962.

13. Antedated by twenty-four years [to 1042]: see Mallarmé, *Mots anglais*, p.911.

14. J.-P. Thommerel, *Recherches sur la fusion du franco-normand et de l'anglo-saxon* (Paris, 1841), pp.115, 104.

15. Abel-François Villemain, *Cours de littérature française* (Bruxelles: Société Belge de Librairie, 1830).

16. Mallarmé, *Mots anglais,* p. 911. *Trans. Note:* Mallarmé's capitalization has been restored throughout.

17. Ibid., pp. 901, 903.

18. Another formulation appears in Mallarmé, *Mots anglais:* "Many words, reduced to their simplest expression, are Nouns and Verbs at the same time" (962).

19. Mallarmé, *Mots anglais,* p. 913.

20. {Ibid., p. 911.}

21. This distribution is both a historical phenomenon—an originary trace—and a phenomenon of diagrammatical mimesis at the general structural level of the lexicon, which is divided up *like* society.

22. Mallarmé, *Mots anglais,* p. 913.

23. *Trans. Note:* Genette draws all examples in this paragraph from Mallarmé, *Mots anglais,* pp. 979-97 (bk. 2, chap. 1).

24. Mallarmé here adds a comment of a different nature, which manifests without acknowledgment the direct influence of Max Müller's theses on the linguistic origin of "modern myths": "This is Mythology, as much as Philology: for it is through an analogous process that, over the course of the centuries, the Legends accumulated and were propagated everywhere" (*Mots anglais,* p. 997). *Les Dieux antiques* of the 1880s was clearly inspired by Max Müller also, indirectly (through Cox's original text) and directly (one sentence is obviously borrowed from *New Lessons on Language* of 1863), but always without acknowledgment. (See Pierre Renauld, "Mallarmé et le mythe," *Revue de l'Histoire Littéraire de la France* 1 [1973]: 48-68). The Oxford professor is therefore one of the hidden sources of Mallarmé as linguist and mythographer, and—for him as for many others in this period—the agent of transmission for German comparative grammar.

25. Mallarmé, *Mots anglais,* p. 915.

26. At present there is no basis for saying whether or not Mallarmé had even indirect knowledge of Wallis. Paul-Gabriel Laserstein ("Stéphane Mallarmé professeur d'anglais," *Les Langues Modernes,* January–February 1947) believes he has discovered some borrowings from Hugh Blair, which in fact would refer to Wallis, but it could be a simple matter of confluences, as we shall see.

27. Mallarmé, *Mots anglais,* p. 920.

28. Ibid., p. 923. As often, the use of the word *letter* (for *sound*) disguises an essentially phonic (articulatory) conception of linguistic mimesis.

29. Ibid., p. 921.

30. Ibid. This "therefore" aptly marks the inductive character of these phonematic interpretations (we will return to this), imposed by the real lexicon.

31. Ibid., p. 901.

32. Ibid., p. 962.

33. Ibid., p. 926.

34. Ibid., p. 965.

35. Ibid., pp. 926, 965. *Trans. Note:* Genette is quoting alternately from these two in the foregoing sentences.

36. Jean-Pierre Richard, *L'Univers imaginaire de Mallarmé* (Paris: Seuil, 1962), p. 576.

37. Mallarmé, *La Musique et les lettres*, p. 654.

38. {Mallarmé, *Mots anglais*, p. 921.}

39. Ibid., p. 923.

40. Let us note in passing that this grouping permits, as in Wallis, the association of indirect motivation by etymology with direct motivation by phonic symbolism, thus reconciling the two lines of inquiry in the *Cratylus*, but by an inverse process: starting from the root word, one follows the derivation (quite far along) as de Brosses does, without finding any deplorable deterioration in it. Here are two or three picturesque examples: *to break — brook* "of a thousand bends," *to brake* a car, "to break in horses," *bread* "which one breaks"; *to pick,* to sew up, to gather — *pocket; to feed — father* "or foster-father"; *to grow — grass, green,* "when the leaves grow out"; *shell — skull; short — shirt.*

41. *Trans. Note:* The page references for consonants in Mallarmé's chart of semantic values are as follows: *b,* pp. 926–29; *w,* pp. 929–32; *p,* pp. 932–34; *f,* pp. 934–36; *g,* pp. 936–38; *j,* pp. 938–39; *c,* pp. 939–41; *k,* pp. 941–42; *q,* p. 942; *s,* pp. 942–49.

42. Mallarmé adds the following phonetically odd remark, perhaps stemming from some faulty transcription, that "among the dentals, one would only rarely recognize (in *p*) the counterpart of the labial *b*" {*Mots anglais*, p. 933}.

43. Ibid., p. 919.

44. The discrepancy between this "main" meaning and that indicated at the beginning of the entry is noticeable. See this other definition, again divergent, in a note of 1895: "*s* ... is the analytical letter; [it is] supremely dissolvent and disseminating" ("Notes," p. 855).

45. Clearly, the points of agreement with Wallis (*wr, gr, cr, st, str, spr*) turn on a few consonants, strongly marked but reducible to etymology.

46. But, on the other hand, this heterogeneity is necessarily underplayed by the foregoing summary's simplification.

47. More precisely, the semantic interpretations come after each list of families and before that of isolated words.

48. Let us not forget that the work's official function is to be a sort of English vocabulary *raisonné,* in which etymology and motivation play a mnemotechnical role.

49. Indeed, it is in reference to onomatopoeia, it seems, that Mallarmé writes, "It is a question of the very soul of the English language" (*Mots anglais*, p. 920).

50. *Trans. Note:* The opposition in French between *propre* and *étranger* is important here. Mallarmé's mimology is peculiar in choosing *une langue étrangère* (a foreign, strange, or other language) instead of privileging, as Plato, Wallis, and others do, *la langue propre* (one's own, proper, natal language). Note that *langue* means not only "language" but "tongue" (both literally and figuratively, as in *la langue maternelle,* "mother tongue"). At the same time, Genette is punning intertextually on *propre,* which appears in the idiom *le mot propre* ("the right or proper word", synonymous with *le mot juste* — a key to Mallarmé's poetics) and which also recalls the ludic subtitle given to Plato's *Cratylus* in chapter 1: *peri onomatōn orthotētos* (on the correctness of names) =

de la propriété des noms (on the propriety, ownership, or properness of names).

51. Wallis, of course, and Rowland Jones, but also George Campbell, who judged the English language the most capable, and the French language the least capable, of imitation (*Philosophy of Rhetoric* [London: W. Strahan and T. Cadell, 1776], bk. 3, chap. 1, sec. 3); and Lord Monboddo, who rejects the idea of a mimetic origin of language in general but notes the peculiar frequency of these kinds of words in English, "such as crack, snap, crash, murmur, gurgle, and the like" (*Of The Origin and Progress of Language* [Edinburgh: J. Balfour, 1774–1809], pt. 1, bk. 3, chap. 5); and Leonard Bloomfield himself in *Language* (New York: Henry Holt, 1933), pp. 227–30. Otto Jespersen (*Language: Its Nature, Development, and Origin* [London: Allen & Unwin, 1922], chap. 20), a Danish student of English, would instead be comparable to Mallarmé as a foreign observer, but his theory of "sound symbolism" goes beyond the scope of the English language.

52. Mallarmé, *Mots anglais*, p. 975. A more specific form of the question would be whether or not something in one and/or the other of the two languages can render English especially mimetic for a *French* ear.

53. Mallarmé, "*Tennyson vu d'ici,*" p. 528.

54. Mallarmé, "Sur Voltaire," p. 872; "Symphonie littéraire," p. 265; *Correspondances,* ed. Henri Mondor and Jean-Pierre Richard (Paris: Gallimard, 1959), p. 154. On the key name Hérodiade, see the suggestive comparisons made by Robert Greer Cohn, *L'Oeuvre de Mallarmé: Un Coup de dés* (Paris: Librairie Les Lettres, 1951), p. 278; and by Richard, *Univers,* pp. 120, 144. *Trans. Note:* See Cohn's earlier publication of this study in English: *Mallarmé's "Un Coup de dés": An exegesis,* a Yale French Studies Publication (New York: AMS Press, 1949).

55. Mallarmé, "Crise de vers," pp. 363–64. This passage dates from 1895. *Trans. Note:* The translation of this famous passage, and of other quotations from the same essay, is my own. For the full text in English, see "Crisis in Poetry" in Bradford Cook, *Stéphane Mallarmé: Selected Prose Poems, Essays, and Letters* (Baltimore: Johns Hopkins University Press, 1956), pp. 34–43. From this point onward, Genette encloses the word *vers* in quotation marks to indicate its special place in Mallarmé's poetics. *Vers* (sing.) refers to one line of verse, while *vers* (plur.) may mean versification or poetry in general. Like Plato's word-maker, Mallarmé's poet is a skilled artist (*technikōn*).

56. Ferdinand de Saussure, *Course in General Linguistics,* trans. Roy Harris (London: Gerald Duckworth, 1983), pp. 67–68.

57. The absolute privilege of the consonant is not in play here.

58. Yet Mallarmé adds here that "there will no longer be, in that era, either Science to sum this up, or anyone to tell about it" (*Mots anglais,* p. 921).

59. Plato *Cratylus* 391d.

60. These stages are occasionally presented as Hegelian "moments": see Édouard Gaède, "Le Problème du langage chez Mallarmé," *Revue d'Histoire Littéraire de la France* 1 (1968): 45–65.

61. Francis Viélé-Griffin, "*Stéphane Mallarmé: Dialogue,*" *Mercure de France,* November 15, 1924, pp. 30–31. Griffin's reply: "Yes, I make the accidents of linguistics the sole

excuse and the condition for our efforts; in the imaginary projection, if you will be good enough to allow me this hypothesis, with each person employing what the poet calls his 'finds,' the latter gets lost in the crowd." Mallarmé: "What's the problem?" In other words, if *the poet did not exist*, one would still be able—after all—to console oneself with the perfection of language, which in turn would remunerate the *default of verse*.

62. Mallarmé, "Villiers de L'Isle-Adam, II," p.492.

63. Mallarmé, "Variations sur un sujet," p.368.

64. Mallarmé, "Notes," p.854. *Trans. Note:* Within Mallarmé's poetics, both main senses of the term *le Verbe* are in play: "the Verb" (as a part of speech), and "the Word" (as divine Speech). Regarding the latter, see chapter 1, where Genette discusses Plato's theory of the origin of names (*onomata*), verbs (*rhēmata*), and speech (*logoi*) in the *Cratylus*.

65. {Letter to François Coppée, December 5, 1866, in *Selected Letters of Stéphane Mallarmé*, ed. and trans. Rosemary Lloyd (Chicago: University of Chicago Press, 1988), p.69 (modified).}

66. Mallarmé, "L'Evolution de la littérature," *Écho de Paris* (1891); rpt., *Oeuvres complètes*, p.867.

67. This phrasing appears in "Notes" (1869), p.853.

68. Richard, *Univers*, p.544 (emphasis added).

69. Gaède, "Problème du language," p.61. The relationship between mimologism and realism, conventionalism and nominalism, is clearly another matter and of another import...

70. Albert Thibaudet, *La Poésie de Stéphane Mallarmé* (Paris: Gallimard, 1926), pp. 230-32.

71. Despite some rhetorical precautions (p.98), the archetype for this is obviously Cohn's chapter "Le mot mallarméen: La Signification des lettres," in *L'Oeuvre de Mallarmé*, pp.89-116. This attempt has been previously criticized by Richard, *Univers*, pp. 576-77.

72. See Pierre Guiraud, *Index du vocabulaire du symbolisme*, vol.3, *Index des mots des poésies de Stéphane Mallarmé* (Paris: Librairie C. Klincksieck, 1953).

73. Mallarmé, "Crise de vers," p.366. *Trans. Note:* Mallarmé's key word *l'initiative* appears in the following statement: "A pure work implies the locutionary disappearance of the poet, who yields the initiative to words."

74. *Trans. Note:* Genette is referring to the experimental long poem *Un Coup de dés n'abolira jamais le hasard*, pp.455-77.

75. Mallarmé, "Crise de vers," p.368.

76. "Never confuse Language {*le Langage*} with the Word {*le Verbe*}" (Mallarmé, "Notes," p.858).

77. Let us recall, nevertheless, that the hypothesis of a divine creation of natural language (one of the themes of the Cratylian tradition) is explicitly rejected in *Les Mots anglais*, p.921: "men, the creators of words."

78. Paul Valéry, "I Would Sometimes Say to Stéphane Mallarmé..." in *Leonardo*,

Poe, Mallarmé, pp. 287, 290. *Trans. Note:* Throughout this section Genette quotes freely from many separate titles by Valéry, most of which are available in *The Collected Works* (the standard Bollingen translation, 15 vols., by diverse hands), henceforth *Works;* I have added specific titles and page numbers. Translations from Valéry's *Cahiers*, however, are mine.

79. *Trans. Note:* Genette's description of Valéry's poetics as a "reprise" of Mallarmé's is a significant choice of words. As repetition, renewal, or return, *"reprise"* suggests Valéry's great debt to Mallarmé (direct influence). At the same time, however, *"reprise"* carries a negative sense of mending or repairing, as if the "failing" in natural languages had been repeated in the predecessor and so required correcting by the new poet. Like another "round" (*reprise*) in boxing, or like the "reentry" (*reprise*) of an instrument or the "repetition" of a motif in an orchestral score, Valéry's *reprise* of Mallarmé's ideas on language (and some of his analogies) is both harmonious and agonistic.

80. Valéry to André Gide, July 1891, in *Self-Portraits: The Gide/Valéry Letters, 1890–1942*, ed. Robert Mallet, trans. June Guicharnaud (Chicago: University of Chicago Press, 1966), p. 78 {modified}.

81. Valéry, "Poetry and Abstract Thought," in *Works*, vol. 7, *The Art of Poetry*, trans. Denise Folliot (Princeton: Princeton University Press, 1958), p. 74 {modified}.

82. {Valéry, "I Would Sometimes Say," p. 277 (modified); "Abstract Thought," p. 68.}

83. Valéry, *Cahiers*, 1:425.

84. {Valéry, "Michel Bréal, *La Sémantique*," *Mercure de France* (January 1898): 254–60; rpt. in *Oeuvres*, ed. Jean Hytier (Paris: Gallimard, 1960), 1:1448–54.}

85. Saussure, *Course*, p. 68; cf. pp. 15–20.

86. Valéry, "Bréal," p. 1453.

87. Valéry to Gustave Fourment (January 4, 1898), in *Oeuvres*, 2:1463–64. *Trans. Note:* Valéry's use of italics has been restored throughout.

88. Valéry, *Odds and Ends* in *Works*, vol. 14, *Analects*, trans. Stuart Gilbert (Princeton: Princeton University Press, 1970), p. 102 {modified}; "The Place of Baudelaire," in *Works*, 8:201. Cf. *Cahiers*, 2:1089. *Trans. Note:* Valéry's collection titled *Tel Quel* includes several subdivisions which have been rearranged in *Works*, vol. 14.

89. Valéry, *Cahiers*, 1:418, 457. There is a conspicuous discrepancy on p. 429: "Language has the following flaws: (1) it is conventional — (2) being so insidiously, clandestinely — hiding the conventions in its first infancy"; but the brunt of the criticism obviously falls on the second feature. It is known that in any subject matter Valéry detests hidden conventions, not as conventions but for being hidden. *Trans. Note:* Genette's remark on Valéry's preference for *l'être **thesei** du langage* underscores the latter's conventionalist position. See chapter 1 on Plato.

90. Valéry, "Bréal," p. 1450.

91. Valéry, "Abstract Thought," pp. 55–56 {modified}.

92. {Valéry, *Cahiers*, 1:475.}

93. Ibid., 1:386.

94. Ibid., 1:454.

95. {Ibid., pp. 455, 397.}

96. Ibid., p. 397.

97. Valéry, "Variations on the 'Eclogues,'" in *Works*, 7:300; *Cahiers*, 1:426-28. Here, *prose*, it should be emphasized, designates not literary prose (whose special status Valéry quite overlooks) but everyday language. It is, moreover, precisely this inattention to the art of prose that permits the convenient antithesis *prose/poetry*, and the very notion of poetic language.

98. Valéry, *Cahiers*, 1:426.

99. Valéry, "Variations," p. 301.

100. Valéry, "Stéphane Mallarmé," in *Works*, 8:260 {modified}; "Variations," p. 306.

101. Valéry, "Baudelaire," p. 209, and "Abstract Thought," p. 64 {modified}; "Remarks on Poetry," in *Works*, 7:208. *Trans. Note:* For Valéry's key statement, "*un langage dans le langage*," Cowley and Lawler have "a language within the language," while Folliot (in *The Art of Poetry*) renders it as "a language within a language."

102. Valéry, "Abstract Thought," p. 79. Cf. p. 60; and "Remarks," p. 197.

103. These are two versions of the same lecture—"Abstract Thought" (1939), pp. 52-81, and "Remarks" (1927), pp. 196-215—that contain the essential points of Valéry's poetic theory. Many of the following citations are taken from this double text. *Trans. Note:* Both versions can be found in *Works*, vol. 7, as cited above. Because Genette frequently quotes passages that are identical or nearly identical in both, however, the reader is advised to consult the French originals.

104. {Valéry, "Abstract Thought," p. 59; and "Remarks," p. 198 (modified).}

105. {Valéry, "Remarks," p. 199 (modified).}

106. {Ibid., p. 199 (modified).}

107. {Valéry, "Abstract Thought," p. 60.}

108. Valéry, "I Would Sometimes Say," p. 277 {modified}.

109. Valéry, "Abstract Thought," p. 66 {modified}.

110. {Ibid., p. 67 (modified).}

111. Valéry, "Letter about Mallarmé," in *Works*, 8:247 {modified}.

112. {Valéry, "Abstract Thought," pp. 67-68 (modified).}

113. {Ibid., pp. 201, 204 (modified).}

114. {Ibid., p. 71 (modified).}

115. {Ibid., pp. 71-72 (modified).}

116. {Ibid., pp. 72, 64.}

117. {Ibid., pp. 64-65 (modified).}

118. {Ibid., p. 72 (modified).}

119. Valéry, "Remarks," p. 209; cf. "I Would Sometimes Say," pp. 280-81, 289-90; "Variations," p. 301; *Cahiers*, 2:548. And: "A beautiful line of verse repeats itself all by itself and remains as if mingled with its meaning, halfway preferable to it—its ceaseless origin" (*Cahiers*, 2:1086).

120. Valéry, "Problems of Poetry," in *Works*, 7:87; *Odds and Ends*, pp. 19, 106; "Variations," pp. 298-99; *Rhumbs*, in *Works*, 7:213.

121. {Valéry, "Abstract Thought," pp. 74-75 (modified), quoting Baudelaire.

122. Valéry, *Odds and Ends,* p. 97 {modified}; "Mallarmé," p. 667; and "Abstract Thought," p. 63 {modified}.

123. {Valéry, "Concerning *Le Cimetière marin,*" in *Works,* 7:152.}

124. Valéry, "Commentaries on *Charmes,*" in *Works,* 7:155–56, 157–58 {modified}.

125. Valéry forgets here, intentionally or not, that there could be nothing to comprehend—a possibility that no longer has a place at this point in the demonstration.

126. {Valéry, "Abstract Thought," pp. 73–74 (modified).}

127. *Trans. Note:* Genette mentions the importance of Valéry's formula for Jakobson's theory of poetry again later in this chapter. The passage in question occurs in "Closing Statement: Linguistics and Poetics," in *Style in Language,* ed. Thomas A. Sebeok (Cambridge, Mass.: MIT Press, 1960), p. 367: "Valéry's view of poetry as 'hesitation between the sound and the sense' ... is much more realistic and scientific than any bias of phonetic isolationism."

128. {Valéry, "Baudelaire," p. 209 (modified).}

129. Valéry, "I Would Sometimes Say," p. 291 {modified}.

130. Valéry, "Abstract Thought," p. 74; "I Would Sometimes Say," p. 277; "Variations," p. 299 {modified}. *Trans. Note:* Genette alternates quotations from the first two texts, then adds the last one from the third. All italics are Valéry's except Genette's emphasis on the word "illusion."

131. Valéry, "I Would Sometimes Say," p. 277; "A Kind of Preface," in *Works,* 8:304 {modified}.

132. Valéry, *Rhumbs,* p. 211 {modified}.

133. An inevitable example: *L'insecte net gratte la sécheresse.*

134. Valéry, *Odds and Ends,* p. 96 {modified}.

135. A fragment from *Cahiers* (2: 1117) regarding the poetic state conjures up a "necessity both formal and significant, whence its both *necessary* and *improbable* character—the connection of *form* and *content* is the result."

136. Valéry, *Odds and Ends,* p. 104; "Remarks," p. 212.

137. Valéry, "Abstract Thought," p. 60.

138. Jean-Paul Sartre, *What Is Literature?* (1947), trans. Bernard Frechtman (New York: Philosophical Library, 1949), p. 7. *Trans. Note:* chapter 1 of *What Is Literature?,* to which Genette refers throughout his discussion of Sartre, appears on pp. 7–19. Quotations from this English edition have been slightly modified.

139. {Ibid., p. 11.}

140. {Ibid., pp. 8, 11.}

141. {Ibid., pp. 12–13.} *Trans. Note:* The first two emphases are Genette's; the third is Sartre's.

142. {Ibid., p. 13.}

143. Ibid., p. 13.

144. Jean-Paul Sartre, *Saint Genet: Actor and Martyr* (1952), trans. Bernard Frechtman (New York: Pantheon, 1963), p. 283. This entire section ("Language," pp. 276–310) in the chapter titled "Cain" is a sort of illustration of or live experiment on Sartre's theory of poetic language. A "delinquent" child, exiled from the communal utilitarian

language, finds himself successively condemned to silence ("a convict does not speak"; however, if he does speak, words — "prison," for example — do not have the same meaning for him as they have for Society); to lying (thus to a paradoxical language of noncommunication); to slang (a parasitic language, out of line, typically figurative and therein already "poetic"); to a homosexual subversion of slang (see the bilingual pun on "making pages" {*On fait les pages*}); and finally to a poetic play on certain "prestigious words" or "word-poems" ("turnabout" {*virevolte*}), in which "a secret affinity of language with the hidden aspects of things" is revealed.

145. {Sartre, *Genet*, p.304.}

146. I am diverting the term *signifiance* in order to include the concepts of *sens* {meaning} and *signification*.

147. {Sartre, *Literature*, pp.8, 11.}

148. {Ibid., p.10.} Remember that Sartre does not yet have at his disposal here (in 1947) the term *sens* {meaning}.

149. {Sartre, *Literature*, p.9.}

150. {Sartre, *Genet*, p.304.}

151. For example, we have seen how Socrates opened up this perspective without really entering into it, and how Gébelin closed it off by reducing the genus to the species, all motivation to imitation — which is, consciously or not, the habitual and probably natural movement of the Cratylian imagination.

152. {Sartre, *Genet*, p.304.}

153. {Ibid., p.308.} *Trans. Note:* The "six dazzling pages" are pp.304-10 in *Saint Genet*.

154. {Ibid., p.305.}

155. {Sartre, *Literature*, pp.13-14.}

156. {Ibid., p.14.} In order to translate the same nuance, perhaps others might write that he *expresses* more than he *represents*. For opposing mimetic to conventional signification, the lexicon has a perpetual revolving door of denominations that in its own somewhat ironic way illustrates the arbitrariness of the sign: *meaning* versus *signification, to represent* versus *to express, to express* versus *to represent, symbol* versus *sign* (Hegel, Saussure), *icon* versus *symbol* (Peirce), *to signify* versus *to designate* (Claudel), and so on.

157. {Sartre, *Literature*, p.15.}

158. According to Sartre's own description, "a *poetic definition* of certain words, that is, one that may be in itself a synthesis of reciprocal implications between the sonorous body and the verbal soul" (ibid., p.16).

159. Leo Jakubinsky (1916), quoted in Boris M. Eikhenbaum, "The Theory of the Formal Method," in *Readings in Russian Poetics: Formalist and Structuralist Views*, ed. and trans. Ladislav Matejka and Krystyna Pomorska (Ann Arbor: Michigan Slavic Contributions, 1978), p.9.

160. Victor Shklovsky (1919), quoted Eikhenbaum in ibid., p.9.

161. Shklovsky, quoted in ibid., p.17.

162. Roman Jakobson, "Fragments de 'La Nouvelle Poésie russe,' [1919], esquisse

première: *Velimir Khlebnikov,*" trans. from the Russian in *Questions de poétique* (Paris: Seuil, 1973), p. 14.

163. Osip Brik, in an essay of 1917, explicitly refused to interpret the phonic repetitions, which he was content to list and classify.

164. Jakobson, "La Nouvelle Poésie," pp. 20, 21.

165. Roman Jakobson "What Is Poetry?" (1934), trans. from the Czech in *Language in Literature,* ed. Krystyna Pomorska and Stephen Rudy (Cambridge, Mass.: Harvard University Press, 1987), p. 378 {modified}.

166. Roman Jakobson, "Linguistics and Poetics" (1960), in Sebeok, *Style in Language,* pp. 356–57 {modified}. For Jakobson, the poetic function extends widely beyond the official poetic corpus.

167. Roman Jakobson, "Quest for the Essence of Language," in *Selected Writings of Roman Jakobson* (The Hague: Mouton), 2:350 (emphasis added).

168. In a manner of speaking, of course, but Hermogenes has ever broad shoulders.

169. *Trans. Note:* The second and third examples are both in Jakobson, "Linguistics," p. 357.

170. Jakobson, "Linguistics," p. 373.

171. Jakobson, "Quest," p. 356.

172. Jakobson, "Linguistics," p. 373; "Quest," p. 356.

173. Jakobson, "Linguistics," p. 372.

174. Jakobson, "The Dominant," in Matejka and Pomorska, *Russian Poetics,* p. 84 (emphasis added).

175. Jakobson, "La Nouvelle Poésie," p. 14 (emphasis added).

176. Gotthold Ephraim Lessing, *Laocoön: An Essay on the Limits of Painting and Poetry,* trans. Edward Allen McCormick (Indianapolis: Bobbs-Merrill, 1962), p. 75.

177. This fact alone, let us say, somewhat upsets the reassuring and ill-considered topos (Grammont, Dorchain, Bally, Nyrop, Whorf, Delbouille, Mounin) according to which the discord between sound and sense is never perceived; and it is difficult to understand how Jakobson ("Linguistics," p. 373) can so serenely compare two opinions as contradictory as Mallarmé's and Whorf's.

178. A piece of evidence among many in this context, but a particularly explicit one, is the following: "The motivated sign may never be able to claim the transparency of the unmotivated sign (Ullmann, *Semantics,* pp. 80–115), of the pure sign that is born from the sacrifice of a substance consuming itself in order to transform itself into reference" (Ivan Fonagy, "Motivation et remotivation," *Poétique* 11 [1972]: 414). *Trans. Note:* Fonagy is referring to Stephen Ullmann, *Semantics: An Introduction to the Science of Meaning* (Oxford: Oxford University Press, 1962).

179. Jakobson, "Grammatical Parallelism and Its Russian Aspect," in *Selected Writings,* 3:128.

180. Ibid., pp. 129, 98; cf. Jakobson, "Poetry of Grammar and Grammar of Poetry," in *Verbal Art, Verbal Sign, Verbal Time,* ed. Krystyna Pomorska and Stephen Rudy (Minneapolis: University of Minnesota Press, 1985), p. 39.

181. Jakobson, "Linguistics," p.358 {original emphasis}.

182. Ibid., pp.358-59.

183. Ibid., p.358 (emphasis added).

184. Roman Jakobson, "Two Aspects of Language and Two Types of Aphasic Distur-bances," in Jakobson and Morris Halle, *Fundamentals of Language* (The Hague: Mouton, 1956), p.81 (emphasis added).

185. Ibid., pp.81-82; "Linguistics," p.372 (emphasis added). Cf. "Linguistics," pp. 367-68, concerning the semantic value of rhymes.

186. Jakobson, "Linguistics," pp.367, 370 (emphases added). Note the shift from *equivalence* (but the English term here is already *equational principle*) to *similarity.*

187. Ibid., p.372.

188. Maurice Barrès, *Sous l'oeil des Barbares* (Paris: Plon, 1921), p.192.

189. Jakobson, "La Première Lettre de Ferdinand de Saussure à Antoine Meillet sur les anagrammes," in *Selected Writings*, 2:190; and Jakobson, "Une microscopie du dernier 'Spleen' dans *Les Fleurs du mal*," in *Questions*, pp.434-35. *Trans. Note:* Baudelaire's poems, "Spleen" (IV) and "Le Gouffre" (The abyss), can be found in the bilingual edition *The Flowers of Evil: A Selection,* trans. Marthiel and Jackson Mathews (New York: New Directions, 1955), pp.62-65, 146-49.

190. A good example is the privilege Jean Cohen explicitly grants to "modern," which actually means symbolist, poetry (*Structure du langage poétique* [Paris: Flammarion, 1966]). Another example is Julia Kristeva's situating of the "revolution in poetic language" in the nineteenth century.

191. Here is a rather random example from Bernard Lamy: "Among the flaws in the arrangement of words is included similitude: that is, an excessively frequent repetition of the same letter, the same ending, the same sound, and the same cadence. Variety gives pleasure; the best things become boring when they are excessively commonplace. ... It is not caprice alone that makes variety necessary: nature loves change, and the reason for this is as follows. A sound wearies the parts of the organ of hearing that it strikes for too long a time; this is why variety is necessary in all actions, because the labor is divided up, each part of an organ is less fatigued by it" (*La Rhétorique; ou, L'Art de parler* [Paris: Pralard, 1675], bk.3, chap.8, p.184, and chap.9, pp.190-91.

192. The two statements, not at all equivalent, are from Valéry.

193. Boris Pasternak, quoted in Roman Jakobson, "Marginal Notes on the Prose of the Poet Pasternak" (1935), trans. from the German in *Language in Literature*, p.317.

CHAPTER 13

1. This chapter includes, with several additions, pages 232-48 of *Figures II* (Paris: Seuil, 1969). If any excuses be needed for this somewhat irregular practice, here are two: the first is self-evident; the second is that sometimes one has to repeat oneself in order to be understood. *Trans. Note:* Those pages in *Figures II* belong to the essay "Proust et le langage indirect," translated by Alan Sheridan as "Proust and Indirect Language" in

Figures of Literary Discourse (Oxford: Basil Blackwell, 1982), pp. 229-95. Since Genette recast his analysis of Proust's Cratylism for *Mimologiques,* however, I have translated the text anew, keeping the Sheridan version in mind throughout.

2. Marcel Proust, *À la Recherche du Temps Perdu* (Paris: Gallimard, 1955-56), trans. as *Remembrance of Things Past* by C. K. Scott-Moncrieff (vols. 1-6) and Andreas Mayor (vol. 7) (New York: Random House, 1970), 1:296. *Trans. Note:* The syntax of the 1970 Moncrieff-Mayor translation (the edition cited here) has been slightly modified in a few instances and the spelling Americanized.

3. To the best of my knowledge, Proust's only remark concerning the form of a common noun (which is anything but common!) has to do with *mousme* {Japanese girl}: "When you hear this word, you get a toothache, as if you had put a large piece of ice into your mouth" (*Remembrance,* 3:257). But this is plainly a description of mere physical sensation, and not the beginnings of semantic motivation.

4. Marcel Proust, *Contre Sainte-Beuve* (Paris: Gallimard, 1954), p. 274. See the passage in *Cities of the Plain* where Marcel receives an invitation to a funeral which has been signed by a host of names of the Norman nobility ending in -*ville,* -*court,* and -*tot:* "Garbed in the roof tiles of their castle or in the roughcast of their parish church, their nodding heads barely reaching above the vault of the nave or banqueting hall, and then only to cap themselves with the Norman lantern or the dovecote of the pepperpot turret, they gave the impression of having sounded the rallying call to all the charming villages straggling or scattered over a radius of fifty leagues" (*Remembrance* 4:135).

5. Marcel Proust, *Jean Santeuil* (Paris: Gallimard, 1971), p. 570; *Remembrance,* 1:142. *Trans. Note:* On the available English translation of *Jean Santeuil,* see Sheridan, p. 288 n. 34, in Genette, "Proust and Indirect Language."

6. Proust, *Remembrance,* 1:296.

7. {Ibid.}

8. Proust, *Santeuil,* pp. 534-35.

9. An intermediate case is that of names borrowed from reality and assigned to a fictional place, such as *Guermantes:* here, the novelist exercises his freedom not through the combination of phonemes but through the overall choice of an aptly suited vocable.

10. Roland Barthes, "Proust and Names," in *New Critical Essays,* trans. Richard Howard (New York: Hill & Wang, 1980), p. 62.

11. Emphasis added. This word, which quite plainly shows the effect of the signified on the signifier, already possesses the same value at the beginning of this passage: "If their names thus permanently absorbed the image that I had formed of these towns it was only by transforming that image, by subordinating its reappearance in me to their own special laws" (*Remembrance,* 1:296). The reciprocity is very noticeable here. *Trans. Note:* As Genette points out in chapter 18, one of the main sites of mimological reverie is the equivalence between vowel sounds and the color spectrum. In this spirit, I have rendered *mauve* as such in English, whereas Scott-Moncrieff translates it "violet-colored." In the long quotation from Proust above, I follow Sheridan's translation: see "Proust and Indirect Language," p. 288 n. 39.

NOTES TO PAGES 252-54

12. Proust, *Remembrance*, 1:296. Note also: "Its compact and almost cloying name" (3:307). This is an extreme case of "sense suggestion," in which the mimetic relation is asserted through the most minimal attempt at justification: "*Fontainebleau*, a name sweet and golden as a cluster of grapes raised to the sky!" (Proust, *Santeuil*, p. 570). Or again: "*Versailles* (in the autumn), a grand name, rusty and mellow" (Proust, *Plaisirs et les jours.*) *Trans. Note:* The relatively weak mimetic motivations here seem to be a semantic one — *Fontaine* (fountain) + *bleau* (read: *bleu*, blue) — and a pseudophonetic or orthological one: *Versa-illes/rou-ille* (rust).

13. {Proust, *Remembrance*, 1:297.}

14. {Ibid.}

15. The Norman essence comes through an analogy with Balbec, Caudebec, etc. The Persian style of the name (*Remembrance*, 2:172: "The name — almost Persian in style — of Balbec") probably derives from its homophony with names such as Usbeck in Montaigne's *Lettres persanes* {*Persian Letters*}, not to mention the Lebanese Baalbek. These lexical associations are again classifiable under indirect motivation.

16. Unless, as Barthes suggests ("Proust and Names," p. 63), we pass through the "conceptual relay ... of the word *rugueux* (rugose)," which would enable him to evoke "a complex of high-crested waves, steep cliffs and bristling architecture."

17. {Proust, *Remembrance*, 1:297.}

18. {Ibid.}

19. Jean-Pierre Richard, *Proust et le monde sensible* (Paris: Seuil, 1974), p. 90 n. 3.

20. {Proust, *Remembrance*, 1:297 (modified).}

21. Proust says "a yellowing tower" in *Remembrance*, 3:6, and a "golden name" in *Sainte-Beuve*, p. 273.

22. Proust, *Remembrance*, 1:132: "the orange light which glowed from the resounding syllable -*antes*."

23. Proust, *Remembrance*, 3:149: "That amaranthine color of the closing syllable of her name."

24. As does, it would seem, the association *i* = purple, instanced at least twice (Proust, *Remembrance*, 1:32, and *Sainte-Beuve*, p. 168), noted in Barthes, "Proust and Names."

25. Proust, *Remembrance*, 1:109.

26. On other aspects of the Guermantes network, see Claudine Quémar's invaluable note in *Cahiers Marcel Proust* 7:254.

27. Proust, *Remembrance*, 3:183. See Jean Pommier, *La Mystique de Marcel Proust* (Paris: Droz, 1939), p. 50.

28. The fact that in this case, curiously enough, the name has been analyzed without being cited might lead one to think (though it is hardly likely) that it was invented afterward (Proust, *Sainte-Beuve*, p. 277).

29. Proust, *Remembrance*, 2:291.

30. {Ibid., 2:174.}

31. Ibid.

32. {Barthes, "Proust and Names," pp.60-64.}

33. Proust, *Remembrance,* 1:296 {modified}.

34. Ibid., 2:172.

35. Ibid., 3:374, 311, 184.

36. Ibid., 2:90.

37. Louis Hjelmslev, *Prolegomena to a Theory of Language,* trans. F. J. Whitfield, 2d rev. ed. (Madison: University of Wisconsin Press, 1961), p.60.

38. Proust, *Remembrance,* 2:161.

39. Ibid., 4:363.

40. Ibid., 6:193.

41. Ibid., 3:387.

42. Ibid., 4:243. At Balbec, Saint-Loup had already warned Marcel about this instability: "In that family they change their names as you'd change your shirt" (2:243).

43. "The name Guermantes itself received from all the beautiful names — extinct, and so all the more glowingly rekindled — with which I learned only now that it was connected, a new sense and purpose, purely poetical" (ibid., 3:387).

44. The functional relation between these etymologies and Basin's genealogies is clearly pointed out by Proust: noblemen are "etymologists of the language not of words but of names" (*Remembrance,* 3:380); but Brichot, too, confines himself to the etymology of names (of places). We should remember that his etymologies can be found scattered throughout *Remembrance,* 5:205-41. Before this, the priest of Combray offered a few etymologies (1:79-81), but these were still lacking in critical value; besides, Brichot often refutes them. In regard to the linkage between genealogies and etymologies, one might note Marcel's somewhat hybrid "revelation" when he learns that the name Surgis-le-Duc derives not from a ducal filiation but from a misalliance with a rich manufacturer called Leduc (4:78).

45. Jean Vendryès, "Proust et les noms propres," in *Mélanges Huguet* (Paris: Boivin, 1940), p.126.

46. Barthes, "Proust and Names," p.68.

47. {Proust, *Remembrance,* 4:206, 209, 229, 231, 236-37, 239, 355.}

48. {Ibid., 4:248.}

49. {Ibid., pp.354-55.}

50. Ibid., 4:355.

51. Barthes, "Proust and Names," pp.67-68.

52. Jean-Pierre Richard, *Paysage de Chateaubriand* (Paris: Seuil, 1967), p.162.

53. André Maurois, *À la recherche de Marcel Proust, avec de nombreux inédits* (Paris: Hachette, 1947), p.270.

54. Moreover, traces of a parallel course can be seen in the outlines for *Contre Sainte-Beuve* collected in chap.14 ("Names of People") of the Fallois edition and in the final version of *Remembrance.* In the former, the onomastic refutation does not yet exercise its power of disillusionment: the name of a given Norman family "is actually Provençal. That does not prevent its evoking Normandy for me"; and the "inevitable disappoint-

ment of our encounter with things whose names we know" ought not to destroy, or even depreciate, the "imaginative charm" of nominal reverie. Perhaps Cratylian optimism died out only late in Proust, as did other kinds.

55. Proust, *Remembrance*, 1:69.

56. Ibid., 1:262.

57. Proust, *Sainte-Beuve*, p. 278.

58. For all that, this final critical attitude does not invalidate all research on Proust's onomastics, especially as it applies to places or to fictional beings. Whether borrowed (like *Guermantes*) or coined (like *Verdurin*), the names in Proust are indeed chosen according to an expressive structure, precisely the one that arises from secondary Cratylism. Yet we need to recognize and take into account this secondariness, and hence the critique it presupposes and entails: to coin or to borrow (that is, to displace) "appropriate" names is to correct, and therefore to admit the "defect" {*défaut*} of, most real names. We should not confuse Proust's work (of factitious motivation) with Marcel's "illusions" about natural motivation, which is, in a sense, the exact opposite.

59. Whence, perhaps, the double misreading, the persistent double myth, of Plato's and Proust's Cratylism.

CHAPTER 14

1. Paul Claudel, *Poetic Art* (1907), trans. Renée Spodheim (1948; rpt. Port Washington, N.Y.: Kennikat Press, 1969), p. 111 n. 1 {modified}.

2. Paul Claudel, "La Poésie est un art" (1952), in *Oeuvres en prose*, ed. Jacques Petit and Charles Galperine (Paris: Gallimard, 1965), pp. 51–52.

3. Paul Claudel, "L'Harmonie imitative" (1933), in *Oeuvres en prose*, pp. 95–110 {quotations, p. 96}. This is a florilegium from de Piis's poem "L'Harmonie imitative de la langue française" (1785–88), a web of expressive alliterations.

4. {Claudel, "Harmonie," pp. 97–98.}

5. Paul Claudel, "Lettre à l'abbé Bremond sur l'inspiration poétique," in *Oeuvres en prose*, pp. 47, 48.

6. Claudel, "Harmonie," pp. 98–99.

7. This aspect, among others, becomes clear in Claudel's "Réflexions et propositions sur le vers français," in *Positions et propositions*: "Written speech {*la parole écrite*} is used for two purposes: we wish to produce in the reader's mind either a state of knowledge or a state of joy.... In the first case we have prose; in the second we have poetry" (in *Oeuvres en prose*, p. 4).

8. {Claudel, "Harmonie," p. 99.}

9. See Claudel, "Réflexions," p. 41; *Oeuvres complètes*, vol. 18, *Accompagnements, discours et remerciements* (Paris: Gallimard: 1961), p. 355; and, of course, *The Satin Slipper* {1928–29} Third Day, sc. 2.

10. Claudel, "Réflexions," p. 41.

11. Claudel, "Poésie," pp. 54–55. The paradox lies in this text's title: *La Poésie est un art*.

12. Claudel, "Harmonie," p.102; "Idéogrammes occidentaux," p.90; and {fragment in} *Oeuvres complètes,* 18:457.

13. "Idéogrammes," p.457.

14. This is so with the exception of the note to *Poetic Art,* cited above {see note 1}.

15. *Trans. Note:* The sonnet "Voyelles," by the Symbolist poet Arthur Rimbaud, is one of the major documents in the history of mimology. Since Genette refers to it again in chapter 18, I provide an English version here (trans. Wallace Fowlie, in *Rimbaud: Complete Works, Selected Letters* [Chicago: University of Chicago Press, 1966], pp.120-21):

A black, E white, I red, U green, O blue: vowels,
One day I will tell your latent birth:
A, black hairy corset of shining flies
Which buzz around cruel stench,

Gulfs of darkness; E, whiteness of vapors and tents,
Lances of proud glaciers, white kings, quivering of flowers;
I, purples, spit blood, laughter of beautiful lips
In anger or penitent drunkenness;

U, cycles, divine vibrations of green seas,
Peace of pastures scattered with animals, peace of the wrinkles
Which alchemy prints on heavy studious brows;

O, supreme Clarion full of strange stridor,
Silences crossed by worlds and angels:
— O, the Omega, violet beam from His Eyes!

16. {Claudel, "Harmonie," pp.99-100.}

17. Notice the disagreement here with Mallarmé, who, in contrast, made the failing {*défaut*} of natural languages the *raison d'être* of poetry.

18. {Claudel, "Idéogrammes," p.90.}

19. Claudel, {fragment in} *Oeuvres complètes,* 18:457.

20. Among others, Hugo did indeed try his hand at a "hieroglyphic" reading of the alphabet, but one that did not claim to invest the "signification" of letters (a simple — and obvious — figurative virtuality) even in the case of the constitution of written words. Nevertheless, I quote the following text (*Voyage de Genève à Aix* [September 24, 1839], in Victor Hugo, *Oeuvres complètes,* ed. Jean Massin [Paris: Le Club Français du Livre, 1968], 6:715-16) which is unintentionally echoed here and there in Claudel, in Leiris, and in Ponge:

Have you noticed how the Y is a picturesque letter with innumerable significations?

The tree is a Y; the branching of two roads is a Y; the confluence of two rivers is a Y; a donkey's or ox's head is a Y; a glass on its base is a Y; a lily on its stem is a Y; a supplicant raising his arms to the sky is a Y.

Moreover, this observation can be extended to all the constituent elements of the human writing system. Everything in demotic language has been poured into it by hieratic language. The hieroglyph is the necessary root of the written character. All letters were at first signs, and all signs were initially images. Human society, the world, all of mankind exists within the alphabet. Freemasonry, astronomy, philosophy, all the sciences take it as their imperceptible but real point of departure; and this is as it should be. The alphabet is a fountainhead. A is a roof, a gable with its crosspiece, the arch {*arche*}, *arx;* or it is the *accolade* of two friends who kiss each other on the cheek and shake each other's hand. D is the back {*dos*}; B is D on D, a back on a back, the hump {*bosse*}; C is a crescent {*croissant*}, the moon; E is a solid foundation, the right foot, a console and sternpost {*étrave*}, the whole of basement architecture within one single letter; F is the gallows, a pitchfork {*fourche*}, Furca; G is a horn; H is the façade of a building with its two towers; I is a war machine throwing a projectile; J is the plowshare and the cornucopia; K is the angle of reflection equal to the angle of incidence, one of the keys of geometry; L is the leg and foot; M is a mountain {*montagne*}, or a camp with paired tents; N is a closed door with its diagonal bar; O is the sun {*soleil*}; P is a porter {*portefaix*}, standing with his burden on his back; Q is a rump with a tail {*queue*}; R is rest {*repos*}, the porter leaning on his staff; S is a *serpent;* T is a hammer; U is an urn {*urne*}; V is a *vase* (which is why we confuse them so often); I have already said what Y is; X is crossed swords, a fight — who will be the victor? we do not know; so, the hermetics took X for the sign of fate, the algebraists took it for the sign of the unknown; Z is a flash of lightning, it is God.

Thus, first there is man's house and his architecture, then man's body, both its structure and its deformities; next, justice, music, the church; war, harvest, geometry; mountains; the nomadic life, the enclosed life; astronomy; work and rest; the horse and the serpent; the hammer and the urn, which can be inverted and joined to make the bell; trees, rivers, pathways; finally, fate and God: there you have what the alphabet contains.

For some of those mysterious constructors of languages who built the foundations of human memory, and whom human memory forgets, it could be that the A, E, F, H, I, K, L, M, N, T, V, Y, X, and Z were none other than the various ribs of the framework of a temple.

21. Claudel, "Idéogrammes," pp. 90–91.

22. Claudel, {fragment in} *Oeuvres complètes,* 18:457.

23. Leon Wieger, *Chinese Characters; Their Origin, Etymology, History, Classification, and Signification: A Thorough Study from Chinese Documents* (1923), trans. L. Davrout, rev. 2d ed. (New York: Paragon Book Reprint, 1965); B. Tchang Tcheng-ming, *L'Écriture chinoise et le geste humain: Essai sur la formation de l'écriture chinoise* (Paris: P. Geuthner, 1937).

24. Also well known is the use made by Ezra Pound and a few others of Ernest Fenollosa's shaky theories and the persistent recourse (passim) to Chinese logography as the model of a writing system independent of speech, even of natural language.

25. Claudel, "Idéogrammes," pp. 81-82; "Harmonie," p. 101; "La Figure, le mouvement et le geste dans l'écriture en Chine et en Occident," in *Oeuvres complètes*, 18:455.

26. Paul Claudel, "Religion du signe" (1896), in *Connaissance de l'Est* (Paris: Mercure de France, 1945), pp. 61-66. *Trans. Note:* This text was published in English as "The Religion of Letters," in Claudel, *The East I Know*, trans. Teresa Frances and William Rose Benet (New Haven: Yale University Press, 1914), pp. 42-46.

27. Claudel, "Idéogrammes," p. 89.

28. Paul Claudel, "La Philosophie du livre," in *Positions et propositions*, pp. 68-81 {quotation, p. 72}.

29. Claudel, "Idéogrammes," pp. 89-90. Here Claudel neutralizes an opposition between vertical = action, and diagonal = motion, set forth in 1896. The Occidental writing system may be either straight or "tilted."

30. Claudel, "Figure," p. 454.

31. But Claudel's graphic mimologism is not exclusively lexical, as we shall see.

32. Claudel's lists include some sixty items, of a few lines each, in "Idéogrammes" (1926), pp. 82-89; about fifty more cursory items in "Les Mots ont une âme" (1946); in *Oeuvres en prose*, pp. 92-95; a dozen or so in "Harmonie" (1933), pp. 97-103; around twenty in *Oeuvres complètes*, vol. 18; then a few scattered here and there in *Conversations* and the *Journal*—altogether, eliminating the repeats from the total (but certain variants deserve attention), well over 120 glosses. See Jean-Claude Coquet, "La Lettre et les idéogrammes occidentaux," *Poétique* 11 (1972): 395-404; rpt. in *Sémiotique littéraire: Contribution à l'analyse sémantique du discours* (Tours: Mame, 1973), pp. 131-45.

33. Charles Bally, *Linguistique générale et linguistique française*, 4th ed. (Berne: Francke, 1965), p. 133. Notice that Bally, like Claudel, clearly gives *ideogram* the strong sense of *mimetic ideogram:* this slippage reveals a spontaneous and more or less universal interpretation, whereas both in theory and in practice, the ideogram or logogram can perfectly well be purely conventional, or motivated nonmimetically.

34. As in all graphic mimologism, this symbolism presupposes a general or specific definition of the type of graphic form: handwritten or typed, in capital or lower-case letters, and so on; little formal relationship exists between r and R, or between g and G. As we shall see, Claudel's practice varies but is usually explicit.

35. The only (partial) exceptions to this rule of "letter-for-letter orthographic anatomy" are *locomotive*, whose overall length imitates that of the thing (but an analysis follows); *pain* {bread}, whose "four letters form one single syllable like the dough" (but the idea of the syllable is purely phonic, and an analysis precedes); and, if you like, *mouvement* {movement}, because its elements seem undifferentiated and equivalent, so that this word evokes "either a line of the little legs of marching foot soldiers, or the row of pistons [*sic*] that appear before our eyes when we raise the hood of our car" ("Idéogrammes," p. 83; "Harmonie," p. 103).

36. This letter must again be read as a handwritten α, which breaks down into *o + i*, as we will see.

37. {Claudel, "*Idéogrammes*," pp. 85, 82.} *Trans. Note: Tu* is the nominative case of "you" (singular form) in French, while *toi* may be emphatic or dative. Both designate

a relationship of familiarity, if not intimacy, between addresser and addressee; more formal usage employs *vous*.

38. {Ibid., pp. 86, 84, 83, 85.}

39. Claudel maintains (ibid., p. 89) that "in French the main symbolic representation is usually in the middle of the word, around which the rest is symmetrically organized. For example, the b in *arbre* {tree}, the o in *noir* {black}, and so forth." But this principle is hardly applied beyond these examples. "In each word, it is convenient," he goes on to say, "to draw a distinction between the essential sign and what I will call the connective tissue of the body and the clothes, for instance, endings that are a sort of all-purpose machine without specific character." As a matter of fact, in the majority of the glosses, all the elements function, for better or worse, including the most *omnibus* inflections, like the *-ir* in *courir* {to run}. The ideogram does not distinguish the root from the inflection.

40. Claudel, "Harmonie," p. 101.

41. {Ibid.} Claudel's handwritten manuscript emphasized this mimetic value by means of a more evocative graphic form: tôît {roof}. This demonstrates a secondary mimologism no longer produced by an artificial alphabet, as with de Brosses, but by an ad hoc deformation of the existing writing system, the graphic equivalent of phonic intensifications such as *immmense* or *pitit pitit* {teeny tiny}. This technique occurs frequently in paraliterary forms (advertising, comic strips, graffiti), especially in the United States: examples are LOOK and NIXON. The status of a deformation such as Flaubert's *hénaurme* {for *énorme*, enormous} is more subtle, for here the graphic metaplasm, which does not necessarily correspond to a phonic metaplasm, alters not the form of the letters but only their use. As for Apollinaire's calligrams, they play, properly speaking, not on the written form but solely on the spatial arrangement of the word or sentence. All these effects would probably be worth a more rigorous and more systematic analysis.

42. Claudel, "Mots," p. 95.

43. {Claudel, "Idéogrammes," p. 84.}

44. {Ibid., p. 83.}

45. {Ibid., p. 82.}

46. Claudel, "Harmonie," pp. 1419-20 n. 13. Cf., among others, ibid., p. 88; "Figure," p. 456; and the commentary on Rembrandt's painting in "Seigneur, apprenez-nous à prier" and in "Introduction à la peinture hollandaise" (in *L'Oeil écoute*, in *Oeuvres en prose*, pp. 169-203).

47. This version appears in "Figure," p. 456. Here is the variant in "Harmonie," p. 103: "R is the butterfly net and the leg put forward, the circumflex is the Psychid butterfly, and the E below is the ladder — that is to say, the Device {*Engin*} with which we clumsily attempt to catch this airy puff. V is the arms we raise up toward it in an asymmetrical inverted gesture. And finally, the last letter is the Ladder {*Échelle*} that remains behind. The butterfly is gone." One can imagine Uncle Sigmund, or some other hermeneutist, first on and then under this ladder (Jacob's?), sent sprawling and badly bruised. The butterfly is already far away.

48. "Les Mots ont une âme" is a self-illustrative title, whose first version, for that matter, was "La Lettre M" (see *Oeuvres complètes,* 18:457).

49. Ibid., p.458.

50. Claudel, "Harmonie," p.100.

51. Claudel, "Idéogrammes," p.90. Notice the pertinence of the opposition capital/lower case, respected by the text, and also of the opposition (impossible to render here) of the handwritten/typewritten r.

52. *Trans. Note:* Claudel sees the "tail" of the donkey (*âne*) in the "bar" of a small-case *a,* whereas Genette apparently sees it better in the capital *A.*

53. Or again, the circumflex is a butterfly in *Rêve* {Dream}, the arm of a balance in *même* {same}, and a quizzical brow in *môme* {kid, or young mistress} ("*Mots,*" p.93). Claudel himself makes fun of these facile glosses in regard to the P in *Plaine* {Plain}, *Pain* {Bread}, and *Poids* {Weight} (*Conversations,* in *Oeuvres en prose,* p.799).

54. Claudel, Cahier 10 (May 1952), in *Journal,* ed. François Varillon and Jacques Petit (Paris: Gallimard, 1968-69), 2:807.

55. {Claudel, "Idéogrammes," pp.83, 86.}

56. {Ibid., p.82.}

57. Claudel, Cahier 1 (December 1904), in *Journal,* 1:19-20; cf. Coquet, "La Lettre."

58. K and W appear nowhere.

59. Coquet maintains that, for Claudel, all letters are "reducible to transformations of I and O: in other words, of the *straight line* (vertical, horizontal, or diagonal) and the *circle,* of unity and the whole. There are no elements more minimal than these" ("La Lettre," p.402). In actual fact, O is not the ultimate element here, since C and U are its differently oriented parts; for Claudel, I can be only vertical, and he does not consider neutralizing the dimensions of verticality and horizontality, which are fundamental for him. In the end, E, L, R, S, Z remain irreducible; truly, "transformation" allows quite a full scope.

60. Unless perhaps, and this is probably accidental, it is the fact that all our vowel letters have a compact, tailless form; but Claudel does not notice this.

61. See here Claudel, "Idéogrammes," pp.90-91; and see this formula, previously encountered in *Poetic Art,* p.111, which directly echoes de Brosses and Gébelin: "the letter or, more precisely, the *consonant.*"

62. Claudel, "Mots," p.91; "Harmonie," p.1420 n.20.

63. Claudel, "Harmonie," p.107. See, among other examples: "For the writer ... the consonant is the important thing. The vowel is matter; the consonant is form ... the propulsive machine of which the vowel is merely the projectile" (in Joseph Samson, *Paul Claudel, poète-musicien: Precédé d'un argument et d'un dialogue de Paul Claudel* [Paris: Milieu du Monde, 1947], p.80).

64. Claudel, "Réflexions," p.14.

65. "The color and taste of words have often been talked about. But no one has ever discussed their *tension,* the state of *tension* in the mind that utters them — of which they are the sign and the index — their *charge*" (ibid., p.6). We know that Claudel admired

the elimination of adjectives of color in Jules Renard and that he imitated this trait at least in *Connaissance de l'Est* (see Gilbert Gadoffre's edition [Paris: Mercure de France, 1973], pp.17-20). *Trans. Note:* For a translation of this work, see note 26 above.

66. "Have we not been told and retold often enough that all of Creation is like a written book? What if it is incomplete, what if it is missing one single chapter? It is done now, the whole work has been assembled and bound, for good or for ill. There is nothing we can do anymore but dive into it up to our necks, like an eager blind man rummaging through the Bible, with both hands full of Braille letters!" (*Conversations,* p.798).

67. Claudel, "La Philosophie," pp.78-79.

68. "The idea of the book, which always refers to a natural totality, is profoundly alien to the sense of writing" (Jacques Derrida, *Of Grammatology,* trans. Gayatri C. Spivak [Baltimore: Johns Hopkins University Press, 1976], p.18).

69. Claudel, *Conversations,* p.725.

70. *Trans. Note:* The French title of this chapter is "L'Écriture en jeu," which I have translated as "The Stakes of Writing" in order to capture the sense of game and daring in Claudel's enterprise—and in much of modernist poetics. Genette draws a distinction between "dreaming on writing" (*rêver sur l'écriture*) and "bringing writing into play" (*mettre l'écriture en jeu*) in order to "call writing into question," thereby "putting writing at stake," as Claudel's mimologism does. As Genette says earlier in the chapter, Claudel views his poetry and poetics as a serious game: fully aware of the facticity of his or any graphic mimologism, he nevertheless "acts as if" (*faire comme si*) the letters of words were, or at least directly referred to, things. This game (*jeu*) is fun (*ludique*), but it is also very risky (*risqué*), for it puts the meaning and purpose of writing poetry at stake (*il la met en jeu, au sens fort*). In the multiple senses of Genette's concluding pun, then, Claudel "revives" poetry (*il la réveille*) by interrogating its mimetic foundations, and at the same time "reawakens" it (*il la réveille*) from that mimological dream on writing which has kept it awake (*le rêve veille*) for so long. Hence, by phonic assimilation: *rê(ve) (ve)ille = réveille.*

CHAPTER 15

1. Michel Leiris, "Alphabet," in *Biffures,* vol.1 of *La Règle du jeu* (Paris: Gallimard, 1948), pp.11-12. *Trans. Note:* Nodier's *Dictionnaire des onomatopées,* to which Genette refers several times in this chapter, happens to include the word *biffer* (to scratch out), which is described as the "noise made by a quill pen passed rapidly over paper" (on Nodier, see chapter 8).

2. Unlike Claudel, Leiris makes no direct reference either to the *Cratylus* or to the mimologist tradition, except perhaps the rather vague remark in "Alphabet," p.52, as we shall see, and the marginal one in *Mots sans mémoire* (Paris: Gallimard, 1969), p.132. *Trans. Note:* Separate titles appearing within Leiris's major works have been added for the reader's convenience throughout chapter 15.

3. Leiris, "Dimanche," in *Biffures,* p.232.

4. {Ibid.}

5. Leiris, "Alphabet," p.76.

6. Leiris, "Tambour-trompette," in *Biffures*, pp.277–78.

7. *Biffures* was written in the main between 1940 and 1944, thus when Leiris was between thirty-nine and forty-three years old.

8. {Leiris, "Alphabet," pp.45, 76 {emphasis added}.

9. Ibid., pp.48, 69–70.

10. Ibid., pp.52, 60.

11. *Trans. Note:* Genette is working a pun on the word *départ* from the first paragraph of this chapter and from Leiris's thematization of childhood language as a beginning which is also an end: thus, *départ* (a point of departure that is also a point of return); *dé-part* (the impossible separation [Latin *de-* + *partire*] that the critic must try to make between memory and its palimpsests in Leiris's work).

12. Leiris, "Alphabet," p.52.

13. {Ibid., pp.40–41.}

14. {Ibid.}

15. This memory is confirmed in *Manhood: A Journey from Childhood into the Fierce Order of Virility*, trans. Richard Howard (1946; London: Jonathan Cape, 1968; rpt. San Francisco: North Point Press, 1984), p.73.

16. {Leiris, "Alphabet," pp.41, 49, 50.}

17. Charles Baudelaire, "Victor Hugo" (1861), in *L'Art romantique*, ed. Henri Lemaître (Paris: Garnier, 1962), p.735.

18. {Leiris, "Alphabet," p.41.}

19. {Ibid., p.40.}

20. {Ibid., p.50.}

21. {Ibid., pp.45–46.}

22. {Ibid., p.54.}

23. {Ibid., p.50.}

24. There are no colors in the repertory of the visual values of written characters, either.

25. {Leiris, "Alphabet," pp.51–52.} It is I who have added these phonetic descriptions, which are deliberately outdated and rudimentary, but not the groupings, which clearly show a tendency toward the structuring of expressive values. Unlike the letters, the phonemes are hardly ever evocative in isolation, term for term, but only when in oppositional pairs: vowels/consonants, occlusives/continuants, front vowels/back vowels, etc. We will have occasion to return to this.

26. {Leiris, "Alphabet," p.46.}

27. {Ibid., p.47.}

28. Ibid., pp.46–47.

29. As is familiar {to the Francophone reader}, these names for letters exist only phonically in French (unlike the Greek *alpha* or the Hebrew *aleph*): no one knows how to write them; their status is strange and, to my knowledge, little studied. *Trans. Note:*

The "name of a familiar part of the body" that Genette refers to is the word *cul* (ass). See n. 63, chapter 7.

30. Leiris, "Alphabet," p. 46.

31. *Trans. Note:* In French, the name of the letter *H* is pronounced like the word for axe: *hache*. The axelike shape of the letter Q {q} is jokingly connected to the "furrow" at the bottom of the body (*cul*) as cause to effect.

32. Hugo gave an interpretation of H that is more favorable to the principle of monarchy: "Words have a shape. Bossuet writes *thrône*, using that magnificent orthography of the seventeenth century which was mutilated, truncated, castrated by the eighteenth century. To remove the *h* from *throne* {modern French: *trône*} is to take away its chair. The capital H is the chair seen from the front, the small-case h is the armchair seen in profile" (excerpt from *Littérature et philosophie mêlées*, ed. Pauvret [Paris], p. 1250B).

33. {Leiris, "Alphabet," pp. 46, 51.}

34. {Ibid., p. 45.}

35. {Ibid., p. 54.} *Trans. Note:* If, as Leiris suggests, *oe* is a "visceral" digraph, it would be (mimo-)logical that *l'oesophage* (the esophagus) sounds like *les ophages*, which is like *les intestins* (the intestines), and so on …

36. {Ibid., pp. 47–48.} Also very Claudelian is the following description of language as a workbench: "tiny devices made of scrap metal that enable us to practice the metalworking profession and to join, in a seemingly logical whole, the thousand and one disparate materials stored in the warehouse of our head; the gear in a toolbox, whose attraction is perhaps analogous to that once held for me precisely by the hammer, screwdriver, pliers, cold chisel, folding rule, and so on" (p. 48).

To these interpretations of letters one might relate a fragment from *Fibrilles* (vol. 3 of *La Règle du jeu* [Paris: Gallimard, 1966], p. 218): "the man with his legs spread apart and his stomach crisscrossed by a rifle like the brutal ss, whom one imagines flung on the ground with one eye staring idiotically and with a snake ready to let out its spit or venom, at the center of the inscription o.a.s." *Trans. Note:* Leiris is playing upon historical acronyms here: ss stands for *Schutzstaffel*, Hitler's elite guard; oas refers to a right-wing political organization in France.

37. Unless otherwise indicated by page number, the reveries on nouns and names referred to here belong to first five chapters of *Biffures*. For *chemise*, see "Dimanche," p. 186.

38. Leiris, "Alphabet," p. 58.

39. *Trans. Note:* The rhyme (and hence the "gold" in the king's robe) is: *Nabuchodonosor-or*.

40. Leiris, "Il était une fois", in *Biffures*, p. 158. Another conjunction of two types of motivation appears in *Manhood*: for *suicide*, "there is the S whose shape as well as sound reminds me not only of the torsion of the body about to fall, but of the sinuosity of the blade; the UI, which echoes strangely and insinuates itself, somehow, like the tongues of the fire or the zigzags of a lightning flash; the CIDE, which concludes the word with an *acid* taste, implying something sharp and incisive" (pp. 8–9; empha-

sis added). *Trans. Note:* Howard, the translator of *Manhood,* adds: "In French, *acide* rhymes with *suicide*" (p.9).

41. *Trans. Note:* By way of encouraging the reader to join in Leiris's poetic games, basic English equivalents for French words are provided throughout this chapter. It should be remembered, however, that the *biffures* operate on French phonetic, graphic, and lexical levels, often simultaneously, so that all such English equivalents must necessarily be partial and selective.

42. *Trans. Note:* "Manon's little table" and "Des Grieux at the seminary" are allusions to Antoine-François Prévost's novel *Manon Lescaut.*

43. {Leiris, "Alphabet," p.73.}

44. Another series of lexical associations appears in *Fourbis* (vol. 2 of *La Règle du Jeu* [Paris: Gallimard, 1955], p.78): "Le Tremblay (who, I believe, was once known for his *terrains lourds* {grounds with heavy topsoil} and whose name brings to mind the noise of a small ball bounding over the wet earth [*trembler*]), Maisons-Laffitte (with the name of a great vineyard, like Château-Margaux) [*Château-Lafite*], Chantilly (a supreme aristocrat, even though his name makes one think much more of *lentilles* {lentils} than of lace *mantilles* {mantillas} or of *crème Chantilly.*" *Trans. Note:* The biblical examples discussed in the text are scattered throughout Leiris, "Alphabet," pp.55–70. *Waterloo* is a "bilingual shower" because *-loo* is pronounced in French to sound like *l'eau* (water).

45. {Leiris, "Alphabet," p.65.} *Trans. Note:* Sound and sense play upon each other on several levels here, for example in the word groups *Candaule/Aulnes/saule* and Lear/*lyre*/*pleureur.*

46. *Trans. Note:* Leiris's *frondrière* perhaps plays upon *fondrière* (rut) and *frontière* (frontier).

47. Leiris, "Tambour-trompette," pp.277–78.

48. See "Dimanche," p.189, for a very vehement tirade against the vulgarity of his father's puns and his family's jokes — a little too vehement, perhaps . . .

49. *Trans. Note:* The majority of these ludic definitions in the list are translated in the course of Genette's preceding discussion.

50. The results of this technique are called "poetic puns" {*calembours poétiques*} in *Manhood* (p.134).

51. *Glossaire* was published 1925–36 in three issues of the *Revolution Surrealiste,* then, modified, in a small volume in 1939 (this version was reprinted in 1969 in the collection *Mots sans mémoire*). But some thirty new glosses appeared in 1973 in *Michel Leiris* by Pierre Chappuis (Seghers). Thus, *Glossaire* probably extends over its author's entire literary career. *Trans. Note:* Leiris's *Glossaire: J'y serre mes gloses* appears on pp.71–116 in *Mots sans mémoire.* This title, made up of a theme word and a definition based on phonic and semantic punning, is typical of his poetic glosses: *Glossaire: [J'y] serre [mes] gloses*—"Glossary: Where I hold on tightly to my gloses," or perhaps, "Glossary: Where I write concise, condensed glosses." See Lydia Davis, trans., "Glossary: My Glosses' Ossuary (1925)" and "Glossary: My Glosses's Ossuary (1939)," both in *Brisées: Broken Branches* (San Francisco: North Point Press, 1989), pp.3–4, 61.

52. If need be, a fifth type could be considered, which is restricted to just one example: a gloss by paronymy (CAHIER — *caillé*); and a sixth type, no more frequent, by polysemy (like *sēma-sēma*): PERSONNE — *personne*. On the methods in *Glossaire*, cf. Xavier Durand, "Michel Leiris et la substance verbale," *Cahiers Dada-Surréalisme* (1970).

53. By way of a sample, the list of words starting with A includes no gloss of the first type, four of the second, and forty-eight of the fourth.

54. {Leiris, *Glossaire*, pp.78, 93, 98, 114, 102, 80, 98.} *Trans. Note:* Because Leiris's glosses operate in several different directions at once — phonetic, graphic, semantic — and because these directions depend intimately on the French language world, rendering them literally into English would not do full justice to his work. Nevertheless, in order to invite the Anglophone reader into Cratylusland, a rudimentary translation of a few of the examples Genette cites are provided here and in subsequent Notes. For instance, CHEVAL generates *C['est ac]HEV[é] À [ai]L[es]* through sound resemblance and orthographic play, which further generate the lexical identification of "horse" in general with the mythical Pegasus (a horse with wings in particular: *cheval à ailes/[a]cHEV[e] À aiLes*).

55. {Leiris, *Glossaire*, pp.80, 97, 99, 112, 84.} *Trans. Note:* MORPHINE yields *mor[t] fine* (high-quality death) because the *t* in *mort* is not pronounced in French, while *ph* is pronounced identically to *f*, so that the two words may be conflated: "*mor[t]ph[f]ine*."

56. {Leiris, *Glossaire*, pp.106, 109, 74, 94, 75, 76, 108, 76, 103, 80, 94.} *Trans. Note:* Regarding the gloss on SIGNE, see the footnote on this chapter's opening page.

57. {Leiris, *Glossaire*, pp.103, 81, 85, 77, 109, 105, 74, 88, 105, 113, 74, 93, 102, 96, 73.} The gloss on *Nord* {North} is an exception, for it is actually composed of two theme words (synonyms), the second of which is revealed *in fine*: NORD — *tu draines jusqu'à ses bords énormes la tente nocturne, ô sceptre des ténèbres que nous nions, Septentrion!*" *Trans. Note:* One example in this group, PARI — *Pa[scal] rit*, depends not only on the sound play hinted at by Genette's brackets but also on an allusion to the central metaphor in Pascal's famous argument for the existence of God in *Les Pensées:* the wager {*pari*}.

58. Paul Zumthor, *Langue, Texte, Énigme* (Paris: Seuil, 1975), p.51.

59. *Trans. Note:* The name "Rrose Sélavy" can itself be analyzed into the comment *Rose, c'est la vie* ("That's life, Rose"). Or it might be heard as *Eros Sélavy*. One of several possible readings of the first ludic statement might be: "Rrose Sélavy wonders if [Baudelaire's] *les Fleurs du mal [Flowers of Evil]* altered phallic habits." The punning involves *mal/phalle* and *Fleurs/R(r)ose*. The second statement might read: "*In extremis*, Aragon gathers up the soul of Aramis on a bed of tarragon." The word games move between *Aragon/âme/Aramis* and *Aragon/estragon*.

60. "I categorically assert that if it had not been for Desnos's wordplays, I would not have had the idea of doing *Glossaire: J'y serre mes gloses*. ... I really believe that Desnos was the inventor of lyrical wordplay. Certain of his wordplays grew into sorts of philosophical adages. The one that struck me the most was: 'Les lois de nos désirs

sont des dés sans loisir' {The laws of our desire are ceaselessly thrown dice}. That is probably what I most admired about Desnos. In *Glossaire* I wanted to take things further and make a dictionary out of wordplays" (Leiris, quoted in *Le Monde*, January 10, 1975). *Trans. Note:* Desnos's statement (literally, "The laws of our desires are dice without leisure") may be analyzed into several phonic and semantic games: *désirs/loisir, des/dés/dés[irs], lois/lois[ir], sont/sans*, and so on *ad libitum*.

61. This preface, which we will come across again, is reprinted in *Brisées* (Paris: Mercure de France, 1966), p.11. *Trans. Note:* See Leiris's preface as translated by Lydia Davis, "Glossary: My Glosses' Ossuary (1925)," in *Brisées: Broken Branches*, p.3. All subsequent references to *Brisées* cite the Davis translation.

62. Philippe Lejeune, *Lire Leiris* (Paris: Klincksieck, 1975), pp.158-59. See also the chapter on Leiris in Lejeune, *Le Pacte autobiographique* (Paris: Seuil, 1975); and in Jeffrey Mehlman, *A Structural Study of Autobiography: Proust, Leiris, Sartre, Lévi-Strauss* (Ithaca, N.Y.: Cornell University Press, 1974).

63. See chapter 1, n.39. Literally, this sentence means: "The name or noun itself alone is equivalent to an entire discourse."

64. *Trans. Note:* In the surrealist word game called *cadavre exquis*, grammatically correct sentences are generated from chance semantic choices, often with "poetic" effects. This activity is comparable to "Mad Libs," a word game organized along the same lines which was popular among American teenagers during the 1960s.

65. {Lejeune, *Leiris*, p.159.}

66. Leiris, *Manhood*, p.134, and *Brisées*, p.289 {"Author's Note," in *Brisées: Broken Branches*, n.p.} (emphasis added).

67. Leiris, "Metaphor," in *Brisées: Broken Branches*, p.18.

68. {Leiris, "Glossary," in *Brisées: Broken Branches*, pp.3-4.}

69. Plato *Cratylus* 387b-d (emphasis added).

70. To be more specific, "principle" here refers to the explicit aim of *Glossaire*, as it is established in the preface. In fact, as the reader may have noticed, certain glosses (those for *armée, clergé, église*, etc.) imply a sort of ideological consensus, roughly that of prewar anarchism in a vaguely intellectual milieu. And many other glosses meet with our agreement more easily than the preface seems to anticipate, even if the reasons for this assent are not always the same for both sides. The gloss is a bit like a BYO party: indeed, therein lies its charm.

71. Appendix to chapter 15.

Glossaire can be compared (a converse comparison has been suggested by Matyla Ghyka in *Sortilèges du verbe* [Paris: Gallimard, 1900], p.154) with another fanciful lexicon, the *Petit Dictionnaire des mots retrouvés* {Short dictionary of rediscovered words}, which was published in the *Nouvelle Revue Française* (January–February 1938) under the transparent signature of M.D., P. de L., and B. de R. This dictionary, more humorous than it is poetic (and with a sometimes strained humor at that), is presented in the preface as a parodic enterprise of "restoration," a return to the original meaning of words long since misdirected by the corruption of the French language. Under this pseudo–de Brossean cover, the dictionary in fact substitutes a fanciful definition for the everyday definition of each word.

The better to grasp the principle behind this substitution, we have to consider the other possible procedures to which it stands opposed. The substituted definition might be totally arbitrary ("suppose I ... designat{e} ... that which we now call 'man' as 'horse'"): one would merely have to select the definition of another word at random from a dictionary; this would be a Surrealist game, with the kind of meaning effects already discussed. Or, the substituted definition might be motivated by direct mimesis: taking Mallarmé literally, one might give the meaning of day {*jour*} to night {*nuit*} and vice versa; this would be a radical instance of classical secondary mimologism. In contrast, the principle behind the *Petit Dictionnaire* stems from a secondary Cratylism *based on indirect motivation;* in other words, the *Petit Dictionnaire* is to secondary mimologism what the *Glossaire* is to primary mimologism.

Each entry word is provided with a definition inspired by one (or several) other word(s) which it resembles or contains (and which must be guessed as part of the game). Thus: ACROBATE: *place publique à Corinthe. Le peuple se réunit sur l'Acrobate.* Or ESTRAGON: *Province d'Espagne.* Or CYCLAMEN: *amateurs de bicyclette. Expression anglaise en usage vers 1880.* The comparison of the entry word, whose current meaning is familiar, and the substituted definition produces a comic effect, often furthered by the "tendentious" choice, as Freud would say, of the entry word (*pédéraste, falzar, phallus* {pederast, pants, phallus}, etc.), and exploited and emphasized by an exemplary citation, as for ACROBATE. This effect is all the more intense when the example or the definition itself contains a sort of allusion to the current meaning. Thus, ASPIRINE: *épouse d'un aspirant de marine. Généralement très élégante, elle donne à la mode un cachet particulier.* Or KOULAK: *gâteau volumineux et indigeste. "Le commissaire est bien malade. Il a encore mangé du koulak."* Or again, PÉRINÉE: *chaîne de montagnes fabuleuses, couvertes de forêts, que les anciens situaient entre Lesbos et Chio.* Or finally, one that I find the most elegant: CALVINISTE: *coiffeur genevois.*

These diversions of conventional signification to the advantage of an imaginary, motivated signification offer, besides that comic function, one of the most sophisticated versions of Cratylism. For further details, the reader is referred to the two hundred or so items in the *Petit Dictionnaire,* or, failing this, one can make up new ones. Here, in anticipation, is the most laborious one: CRATYLISME: *hallucination verbale causée par l'absorption excessive d'un vin de mauvaise qualité. Chez le sujet en crise, "tout se dédouble, sans qu'il puisse distinguer où est la chose et où est le mot"* (Plato *Cratylus* 432d).

Trans. Note: Among the foregoing examples from the *Petit Dictionnaire,* the entry for ESTRAGON gives Leiris's gloss for ARAGON (cited earlier) a significant intertextual dimension. The ludic associations involving Aragon/*estragon*/*Petit Dictionnaire*/the Surrealist avant-garde provide a serious etymological tracing of Leiris's literary roots.

Genette playfully invents his own Leirisian gloss here. As a general noun, CRATYLISME is formed on the model of semantically related terms such as *alcoolisme* and *éthylisme* (synonyms for alcoholism). Etymologically, CRATYLISME can be analyzed into the Latin *cratera* (large bowl used for mixing wine with water) + *Cratylus* (the proper name and also the title of Plato's dialogue). Genette sends us to a specific passage in the latter text (432d) by way of explaining his point.

In section 432b of Plato's *Cratylus*, Socrates argues that an image perfectly congruent with its referent "would no longer be an image"; in other words, if Sr = Sd, the signifying relation itself would collapse. Of course, the double *différance* between Sr and Sd is precisely what the Cratylist tradition resists, seeking instead an unbroken continuity between sign and referent. Throughout sections 432b-e, Socrates pursues the problem of difference in relation to similarity in representation. In a famous example, he compares Cratylus the person and a painter's portrait of Cratylus, asking his interlocutor: "Would you say that this was Cratylus and the image of Cratylus, or that there were two Cratyluses?" (432c). Cratylus replies that he sees "two Cratyluses"—a position that Socrates exposes as untenable when applied to the representational status of "names" (*onomata*) or language in general. If words were to meet the Cratylian criterion of being exact "doubles" of the things to which they refer, Socrates observes, "no one would be able to determine which were the things and which were the realities" (432d).

Genette's ludic definition of CRATYLISME as a state of seeing double captures this philosophical conundrum of representation, as first set out by Plato. A Cratylist is a person who has gotten drunk on bad wine and who, in his stupor, sees everything double: for each thing, a word that looks and sounds (and even tastes) just like it.

See Jacques Derrida, "Différance" in *Margins of Philosophy,* trans. Alan Bass (Chicago: University of Chicago Press, 1982), pp.1-27; and *Of Grammatology,* trans. Gayatri C. Spivak (Baltimore: Johns Hopkins University Press, 1976), esp. chap.2 on Saussurean linguistics.

CHAPTER 16

1. *Trans. Note:* Many of Genette's quotations from Ponge refer to the collected edition published as *Grand Recueil* (Paris: Gallimard, 1961), which includes *Lyres* (vol.1), *Méthodes* (vol.2), and *Pièces* (vol.3). For the reader's convenience, I have specified also the individual titles within these three volumes as well as other works by Ponge. All translations are my own. English translations of selections from Ponge's work, however, are currently available in three books: Cid Corman, *Things* (New York: Grossman, 1971); Beth Archer, *The Voice of Things: Francis Ponge* (New York: McGraw-Hill, 1972), which offers a brief, useful introduction to Ponge's poetics; and Serge Gavronsky, *Francis Ponge: The Power of Language* (Berkeley: University of California Press, 1979). I have benefited from consulting these and encourage the reader to do likewise.

2. Francis Ponge, "My Creative Method," in *Méthodes,* p.20. Regarding the entirety of what follows, see "Mesure(s) du mot," chap.6 in Marcel Spada, *Francis Ponge: Choix de textes, biographie, bibliographie, filmographie, illustrations* (Paris: Seghers, 1974), pp.

53–65. *Trans. Note:* Ponge's capitalization and italics have been restored in citations from his work throughout the chapter.

3. {Ponge, "Creative Method," p. 20.}

4. Ponge, "Le Mimosa," in *Tome premier* (Paris: Gallimard, 1965), p. 309.

5. Spada, *Ponge,* pp. 60–61.

6. Ponge, "La Pratique de la littérature," in *Méthodes,* p. 272.

7. {Ibid., p. 273.}

8. {Ibid., p. 274.}

9. *Trans. Note:* Émile Littré, philologist and lexicographer, compiled the influential *Dictionnaire de la langue française* over a period of several years during the mid-1800s. See the new edition in seven volumes published by Jean-Jacques Pauvert (Paris, 1956), with original documents by Littré and other French mimologists of the day, including Victor Hugo and Ernest Renan.

10. {Ponge, "Creative Method," p. 272.}

11. In justification of multiple etymologies, Ponge writes: "Etymologists, do not jump to conclusions! Do we not find two plants with quite separate roots sometimes mingling their foliage as one?" ("Le Porte-Plume d'Alger," in *Méthodes,* p. 98 n. 1).

12. Ponge, "Prose à la gloire de Claudel," in *Lyres,* p. 29; "Le Peintre à l'étude" (1948), in *Tome,* p. 494.

13. Ponge, *Pour un malherbe* (Paris: Gallimard, 1965), p. 12; "Proclamation et petit four," in *Méthodes,* p. 217.

14. Ponge, "Porte-Plume," p. 98; "Mimosa," p. 307; "Les Olives," in *Pièces,* p. 110; "Escargots" and "Le Cageot," in *Tome,* pp. 57, 43. *Trans. Note:* The verb *voir* (to see) is conjugated using the form *voy-* for several tenses and persons; hence, the word *voyage* does contain *voir.* When one voyages, one sees things — especially in Cratylusland.

15. Ponge, "Réponse à une enquête," in *Méthodes,* pp. 218–19.

16. Ponge, "Le Pré," in *Nouveau Receuil* (Paris: Gallimard, 1976), p. 205. *Trans. Note: Pré* (meadow) is the starting point for numerous puns here. For example, keeping to the French language alone: *pré* (prefix) + *paré* (bedecked) = *préparé* (prepared [past participle]), but also *pré* sounds like *prêt* (ready: the *t* is silent) = *pré[t]paré; pré* + *fixe* (permanent) = *préfixe* (grammatical inflection); *préparer* (to prepare) is a synonym for *apprêter* (to prepare), and so on. The reader is invited to find or invent more homophonic etymologies: for example, the *pré* is where cattle graze (*paître*) near (*près*) the brook at the season when the farmer is prepared (*préparé*) to cut the meadow now ready (*prêt*) for mowing and bedecked (*paré*) with wildflowers. For a further exploration of Ponge's Cratylian poetics, see Lee Fahnestock's translation of "Le Pré" and *La Fabrique du Pré,* with facsimile manuscripts and illustrations, in *The Making of the Pré* (Columbia: University of Missouri Press, 1979).

17. Ponge, "Le Lézard," in *Pièces,* p. 95; "Le Gymnaste" and "L'Huître," in *Tome,* pp. 72, 48. Cf. *Entretiens de Francis Ponge avec Philippe Sollers* (Paris: Gallimard, 1970), p. 111: "Plainly, if you find words like *blanchâtre, opiniâtre, verdâtre,* or God knows what

in my text, it is also because I am motivated by the word *huître*, by the fact that it has a circumflex over the vowel (or the diphthong), and *t, r, e*."

18. Ponge, "Les Hirondelles," in *Pièces*, p.190. *Trans. Note:* Part of the ludic "analysis" of words here depends on the phonetic conflation of *horizontal* (horizontal) and *hirondelle* (swallow) into *horizondelle*. At the same time, through a semantic relay, one may picture the wings (*ailes*) of this bird (*hirondelle*) outlined against the horizon (*horizon*); hence, both *horizondelle* and *horizon d'ailes* (winged horizon). The phonetic coinage *Ahurie-donzelle* may mean something like "dizzy dame" (-*hurie*/*hori*-, *donzelle*/-*zondelle*).

19. Spada, *Ponge*, p.64; Ponge, "Le Cheval," in *Pièces*, p.147. Let us recall that the portmanteau word (see chapter 3, n.5) is a sort of factitious and reverse Socratic etymology. Instead of analyzing an existing vocable into several words that are supposed to explain and justify its signification (*alētheia* = *alē* + *theia*; "greedy" = "gripe" + "needy"; *hirondelle* = *horizon d'ailes*), several words are amalgamated into a neologism with multiple meanings: *stagnation* + *inflation* = *stagflation*; *amphibie* + *ambigu* = *amphibigu*. Once this "blending" has been accepted or imposed, all we need to do is analyze it in its turn in order to rediscover the Socratic situation. This is exactly what Humpty Dumpty does in commenting on "Jabberwocky": "Well, '*slithy*' means 'lithe and slimy'" (Lewis Carroll, *Alice through the Looking-Glass*, in *The Annotated Alice*, ed. Martin Gardner [New York: Bramhall House, 1960], p.271). Whether artificial or not, the motivating function of the portmanteau word clearly stems from the diagrammatic correspondence between the amalgam of forms and the amalgam of meanings. The motivational force of the portmanteau word is proportionate to the thoroughness of the blend: *stagflation* is still not very far from a simple compound word of the type *homme-grenouille* {frogman} or *moissonneuse-batteuse* {combine-harvester}; in *slithy* (or *smog*), the fusion is much more extensive, suggesting a genuine interpenetration of qualities.

Moreover, the feeling of "rightness" {*justesse*} is apparently that much stronger when the synthesis involves signifieds that are closer to each other and whose proximity is revealed precisely by the amalgam. *Rilchiam* in the preface to *The Hunting of the Snark* is indeed, in Deleuzean terms (*Logique du Sens*, 7th series) a "disjunctive synthesis" of *Richard* and *William* — halfway between two terms that remain heterogeneous. "If I don't know whether the King is William or Richard, I answer Rilchiam": it is merely a (cautious) compromise. In contrast, *frumious* displays a commonality of meaning between *furious* and *fuming*, which would readily suggest the proximity of signifiers — their fitness for marrying, so to speak — which is already inscribed in natural language and whose realization is only a formality. A perfect example of this form, the most economical (and hence the least *secondary*) kind of Cratylian intervention, is Michaux's *volupté*, in which a compromise formation is clearly not the point: *le viol* {rape} *is* voluptuous, *la volupté* {voluptuousness} *is* violent. This is revealed most economically and by the very fact that language knew it, and nearly said it, too. *Trans. Note:* The Cratylist travels with the linguistic baggage of the "portmanteau word," from

NOTES TO PAGES 299-301

the French, *portemanteau* (coat rack), which is mimologically related to the equally cumbersome *mot-valise* (literally, a suitcase-word).

20. Ponge, "Proclamation," pp. 214–15.

21. Ponge, "Le Lézard," in *Pièces*, p. 95; "La Rage de l'expression," in *Tome*, p. 340; "Le Peintre," p. 494; "Le Ministre," in *Lyres*, p. 18; "Proclamation," p. 217; "Rage," p. 301; "Le Gymnaste," in *Tome*, p. 72; "La Cruche," in *Pièces*, p. 105. *Trans. Note:* The French in "Le Lézard" reads: *"c'est le Z 'tortillard' du lézard." Tortillard* (local train, in the humorous or pejorative sense) has the same ending as *lézard* (lizard), and the shape of the local as it snakes along the tracks looks like the shape of the letter "Z", which wriggles, writhes, and twists (*[se] tortiller*).

22. Ponge, "Le Verre d'eau," in *Méthodes*, p. 127.

23. Ponge, "Notes pour un oiseau," in *Tome*, p. 273. *Trans. Note:* Oileau and *oiveau* are Leirisian inventions. Oileau = oiseau (bird) + *aile* (wing), with the amalgam analyzable into *oi[ai]leau*.

24. Ponge, "14 JUILLET," in *Pièces*, p. 50. Thanks to Gérard Farasse, whose unpublished commentary drew my attention to this text long ago. *Trans. Note:* This entire piece is filled with phonic, semantic, and graphic games; the French words in brackets are meant to serve as typical examples. The pun on *peuple/peuplier* (people/poplar wood) is less complicated than the phrase *Justice ça y est*, which, when pronounced in French, playfully echoes the title of the piece: *Ju-y-est = JUILLET*. Indeed, what could be more joyful (*joyeux*) than a Revolution in July (*Juillet*)? In addition, *ça y est* is a colloquial expression ("Now we've got it!") that echoes the *Ça ira*—"That's how it's going to be"—a song of the French Revolution referring to what will happen when the common people bring the aristocrats to justice (hence, Ponge's *Justice ça y est*). Another historical allusion occurs in *sans culottes* (literally, without knickers), which is what the aristocrats called the revolutionaries who wore the *pantalon* (trousers) instead of the *culotte* to mark their political allegiance. In Ponge's ludic version of the storming of the Bastille on July 14, the *sans culottes* are wearing striped trousers. (Special thanks to Jennifer Gage and Judith Radke for their suggestions regarding these wordplays.)

CHAPTER 17

1. Stendhal, *On Love* (chap. 56), trans. Vyvyan B. Holland with C. K. Scott-Moncrieff (New York: Norton, 1947), p. 236. *Trans. Note:* The French and Latin words for "church" (*église; ecclesia*) are both feminine nouns.

2. On Nodier, see Gaston Bachelard, *Water and Dreams: An Essay on the Imagination of Matter*, trans. Edith R. Farrell (Dallas, Tex.: Dallas Institute of Humanities and Culture, 1983), pp. 189–90; *Air and Dreams: An Essay on the Imagination of Movement*, trans. Edith R. Farrell and C. Frederick Farrell (Dallas, Tex.: Dallas Institute of Humanities and Culture, 1988), p. 240 ("my good mentor"); *The Poetics of Reverie*, trans. Daniel Russell (New York: Orion Press, 1969), p. 31; *The Flame of a Candle*, trans. Joni Caldwell (Dallas, Tex.: Dallas Institute of Humanities and Culture, 1988), p. 28. On Leiris, see

Bachelard, *The Poetics of Space*, trans. Maria Jolas (Boston: Beacon Press, 1969), p.147; *La Terre et les rêveries de la volonté* (Paris: Jose Corti, 1948), p.278.

3. Bachelard, *Flame*, pp.51, 15 {modified}; *Space*, p. xix; *Air*, p.253; *La Terre*, p.8.

4. Roland Barthes, *The Pleasure of the Text*, trans. Richard Howard (New York: Hill & Wang, 1974), p.37.

5. Bachelard, *Space*, p.146; *Reverie*, p.16; *Air*, p.249.

6. Bachelard, *Flame*, pp.28, 29 {modified}; *Space*, pp.196-97; *La Terre*, p.68; *Water*, p.189.

7. Jacques Damourette and Edouard Pichon, *Des mots à la pensée: Essai de grammaire de la langue française* (Paris: Collection des Linguistes Contemporains, 1911-27), 4: chap.4. However, for these authors, sexusemblance apparently was an a priori motivation of grammatical gender, a "perpetual metaphor through which things both material and immaterial all find themselves assigned a sex," and according to which the original creator-speakers of language divided objects, including the inanimate, into masculine and feminine (Pichon, "La Polarisation masculin-féminin," *L'Évolution Psychiatrique* 3 [1934]: 67). In contrast, I take "sexusemblance" to mean a metaphorical sexualization induced a posteriori from the grammatical gender of words, itself generally inherited from an entirely mechanical evolution.

8. "What a great service French does us—a passionate language which has not wanted to preserve a 'neuter' gender, that gender which does not choose when it is so *pleasant* to multiply the opportunities for choosing" (Bachelard, *Reverie*, p.39). The former choice is what Pierre Joseph Proudhon calls "giving sexes to one's words" ("Essai de grammaire générale" [1837], appendix in Nicolas Sylvestre Bergier, *Les éléments primitifs des langues* [1764; rpt. Paris, 1850]), p.46).

9. "Grammatical gender is one of the least logical and most unpredictable grammatical categories.... This distinction, which cuts across the entire language, no longer corresponds to anything in the great majority of cases: for example, certain abstract nouns are masculine, others feminine, and still others neuter without our being able to see the reason for these differences. The name of certain objects is masculine, that of others feminine, and that of still others neuter, without visible reason" (Antoine Meillet, "Le Genre grammatical et l'élimination de la flexion" (1919), in *Linguistique historique et linguistique générale* [Paris: Ancienne Honoré Champion, 1921], pp.202-3).

"The difference between the masculine and the feminine... can hardly ever be traced back to a definite signification, except in that small number of cases where it serves to mark the opposition between 'male' and 'female'" ("La Catégorie du genre et les conceptions indo-européens," in Meillet, *Linguistique*, p.228).

"This system was never coherent because, at its origin and increasingly since, arbitrariness has reigned in the designation of things and abstract ideas, while the reasons for the designations based on mythology have ceased to be recognized" (Albert Dauzet, "Le Genre en français moderne," *Le Français Moderne* 5.3 [1937]: 193). But this doctrine is not without its nuances, which we have seen in Damourette and Pichon {see note 7} and to which we will return.

10. Bachelard, *Reverie,* pp.34–35. Unless otherwise indicated, all the following citations are from this book, especially from its first chapter, "Reveries on Reverie: The Word-Dreamer."

11. I am slightly extending the sense that Bachelard proposes for this term {*génosanalyse*} on p.35: "analysis of a literary passage through the gender of the words."

12. James Harris, *Hermes; or, A Philosophical Inquiry Concerning Language and Universal Grammar* (London: H. Woodfall, 1751), p.44. This hypothesis does not seem to have been unanimously accepted in the eighteenth century. In the eighth chapter of *Lectures on Rhetoric and Belles Lettres* (London: W. Strahan & T. Cadell, 1783), Hugh Blair refers to it through examples, commenting: "This, however, appears doubtful." Natural languages seem to him "to have been more capricious, and to have proceeded less according to fixed rule" in the assignment of gender than in any other area (pp. 148–49). *Trans. Note:* Here and subsequently, I have modernized the spelling, punctuation, and typography in the English text of Harris's *Hermes.*

13. "Feminine endings have a certain delicacy"; "the feminine in a word accents the pleasure of speaking, but one must have a certain love of lingering sonorities" (Bachelard, *Reverie,* chap.1).

14. Proudhon, "Essai," p.265; Jakob Grimm, *On the Origin of Language* (1851), trans. Raymond A. Wiley (Leiden: E. J. Brill, 1984), p.17; Ernest Renan, *De l'origine du langage,* in vol.8 of *Oeuvres complètes,* ed. Henriette Psichari (Paris: Calman-Levy, 1958), p.22. The influence attributed to the *female organ* (the speech organ, I assume) in the choice of morphemes is again a slippage toward subjective mimologism, characteristic of Renan: certain phonemes are feminine through adequation not to the designated object but to the designating subject. Unless, in order to harmonize the two functions, one assumes, as Renan seems to do here, that "feminine" objects have been named by women, and masculine ones by men: the reverse of Bernardin's hypothesis, and certainly less elegant. *Trans. Note:* In this instance, I have translated from the 1859 French version of Grimm's *Origin,* because of the implications of its phrasing for Genette's argument. Wiley's English version of the passage reads as follows: "Of the vowels *a* holds the clear middle point; *i* the heights; *u* the depths. *A* is pure and fixed, *i* and *u* are liquid and capable of being restricted by a consonant. Obviously a feminine base must be ascribed to the vowels altogether; to the consonants a masculine one" (p.17).

15. *Trans. Note:* Genette here contrasts the feminine and masculine forms of "wolf" in Latin and French, respectively. His analysis of the gendering of words in linguistics and philosophy depends on the series of similar contrasts that follows — contrasts motivated by masculinist reveries on language rather than by objective data.

16. *Trans. Note:* Genette's point is that in inflected languages the phenomenon of "sexusemblance" or mimology about the gender of nouns is not necessarily dependent on morphological analysis of the nouns in question. Thus, if the femininity of the noun *eau* (water) is arguably grounded in both its morphology (the vowels *e-a-u* being mimologically considered feminine) and its grammatical entailments (the feminine article, *la* — here elided to *l'* — and the feminization of all modifiers, as in *l'eau fraîche*

et douce), the masculinity assigned to the noun *poeta* (Latin, poet), despite the association of the ending *-a* with the feminine, would seem to prove the contrary: that is, the arbitrariness or conventionality of the sign.

17. "The attribution of gender to sexless beings was a true metaphor" (Proudhon, *Essai*, p. 266). *Trans. Note:* In French, *profondeur* carries several meanings, so that Bachelard's privileging of the feminine in reverie entails the feminine as "depth" (Latin *profundus*, "deep," with a possible reversal into its opposite, "high"), hence "intimacy" and closeness to the origin of things; the feminine as "wisdom" or natural sensibility, "calmness," and "security"; and the feminine as intellectual "profoundness" or natural sagacity. Finally, the phenomenal correlate of the feminine, or water (Latin *profundere*, "to pour forth, flow"), may be in play, too.

18. {Harris, *Hermes*, pp. 44–45.}

19. Here, Harris is relying above all on Greek and Latin usage, and on the personifications in English poetics.

20. As often in this sort of analysis concerning purely hypothetical collective representations, it is impossible to distinguish between objective conjecture and unconscious projection as the point of departure. We find this ambiguity in Meillet himself regarding what he calls the "Indo-European conceptions" of gender: "The word for 'sleep,' *hypnos* in Greek, *somnus* in Latin, etc., is masculine because sleep is a powerful force that submits men to its will.... Night, whose religious character is felt in a much more lively way than that of day, because it has something more mysterious, has a feminine name everywhere.... the sky, from which fertilizing rain comes down, is masculinized, and earth, which is fertilized, is feminized; the foot is masculinized, and the hand, which receives, is feminized" ("La Catégorie du genre," pp. 222, 225, 229). It is tempting to fantasize about the masculinity of the foot, but another text by Meillet gives us an unexpected interpretation: "The foot, which is placed on the path, is conceived of as male, and the path as female" ("Essai de chronologie des langues i.-e.: La théorie du féminin," *Mémoires de la Société de Linguistique* 32.2:7).

Pichon, who cites this hypothesis and several analogous ones by the same author, speaks in this connection, in a revealing partial slip, of "that metaphorical mode of thought which we sometimes tend to *attribute* to our distant Indo-European ancestors," and which "we must really expect to encounter still existing among ourselves" ("La polarisation," p. 68). Here are several very clear instances of this metaphorization. "Language has a tendency to put into the masculine everything that is undifferentiated, and in particular everything that is compared to the young of animals, still at an age when sex does not count; everything to which we attribute an individual soul, its source of independent and unpredictable activity; everything that is fixed by a precise, methodical, and somehow material determination; and to put into the feminine material substances presented as purely abstract outside any phenomenon; everything that is in the process of undergoing an exogenous activity; everything that evokes a fecundity without variety, capable of indefinitely repeating the same type of productive activity.... These notions on the psychological signification of the distribution of gender already show us,

421

although they may still be imperfect, that we are dealing with a metaphor of *sex*. This is especially striking for the feminine: woman is passive, woman is a mother, an egg-laying creature which man fertilizes" (p.70). And Pichon also says: "Our natural language seems to tend to put in the feminine the objects, results, or residues of an exogenous activity (e.g., *la blessure* {the wound}), devices whose productive activity is always the same (e.g., *la batteuse* {the eggbeater}), and finally immaterial substances conceived of as purely abstract outside of any event (e.g.: *la bonté* {goodness}). The psychological allusion to the feminine sex is clear in all three cases: the female possessed, the egg-layer and the divine *çakti parèdre* {divine consort} of each god are still notions fully alive in the depths of our French soul" ("Genre et questions connexes: Sur les pas de Mlle Durand," *Le Français Moderne* 4.1 [1938]: 33). In those days, "sexism" had a clear conscience.

21. Not all of them: certain couples seem more conventional, such as *l'orgueil/la vanité* {pride/vanity}, or insignificant, such as *le coffret/la terrine* {vanity box/cooking terrine}, *la glace/le miroir* {looking glass/mirror}, *la feuille/le feuillet* {page/leaf}, *le bois/la forêt* {woods/forest}, *la nuée/le nuage* {stormcloud/cloud}, *la vouivre/le dragon* {serpent/dragon}, *le luth/la lyre* {lute/lyre}, *pleurs* {masc.}/*larmes* {fem.} {crying/weeping}.

22. Bachelard, *Space*, p.146.

23. The controversy over what Damourette and Pichon call the Germanic "system of distributing sexusemblance" is naturally one of the topoi of linguistic Frenchness. Here is a typical illustration from the pen of Michel Tournier, or at least from his naive pedophorous hero: "What is completely aberrant is the sex attributed by German words to things and even to people. The addition [*sic*] of a neuter gender was an interesting improvement, under the condition that it be used with discretion. Instead, we see the unleashing of a malignant will toward mispresentation in general. The moon becomes a masculine being, and the sun a feminine being. Death becomes male, life neuter. Chair is also masculinized, which is crazy; on the other hand, cat is feminized, which corresponds to the very facts. But the paradox reaches its height with the *neutralization* of woman herself, to which the German language is furiously devoted (*das Weib, das Mädel, das Mädchen, das Fräulein, das Frauenzimmer*)" (*Le Roi des aulnes* [Paris: Folio, 1970], p.425).

24. Bachelard, *Water*, p.5. On another level, the femininity of water is also opposed to the virility of wine {*le vin*}—always the *soul of the French*: "For the person who dreams substances at their deep source, water and wine are liquid enemies. They are mixed only for medicine. A wine cut with anything, a wine cut with water—the wisdom of the French language makes no mistake—is truly a wine that has lost its virility" (*La Terre*, p.327).

25. *Trans. Note:* The key terms in Bachelard's phenomenology here, *songe, rêve,* and *rêverie*, belong to a semantic field in French that does not quite correspond to the English opposition between *dream* and *daydream*. Before the Romantics, *songe* designated a sleeping dream (Latin *somnium*) and, by extension, an illusion or fancy. In

the nineteenth century, *rêve* began to be used instead to mean the imagery experienced during sleep and, again by extension, illusion or unreality. (See Sigmund Freud's theory of dreams as wish fulfillments in *The Interpretation of Dreams*.) Likewise, after Jean-Jacques Rousseau, *rêverie* took on new value as an imaginative, creative kind of daydreaming. Finally, in the context of Bachelard's phenomenology, *rêverie*—always creative and always in the feminine—takes place over an extended period of time ("unhurried" and "profound"), while *songe* (fancy) comes and goes relatively quickly and is more easily interrupted.

26. All these examples illustrate the metaphorical sexuality of inanimate objects. But the influence of gender is even more palpable in the case of certain nouns (which Pichon calls "figurative") for animal species that current parlance masculinizes or feminizes collectively: everyone knows how difficult it is to think in terms of a female version of *le renard* {fox}, *le léopard* {leopard}, *un éléphant* {elephant}, or a male version of *la panthère* {panther}, *la cigale* {cicada}, *la fourmi* {ant}; and how these purely linguistic couplings dominate children's imagination and folklore: *le rat* {rat} and *la souris* {mouse}, *le crapaud* {toad} and *la grenouille* {frog}, *le pigeon* {pigeon} and *la colombe* {dove}, and so on.

The reasons given for these arbitrary divisions by some linguists are even more revealing of a sexualizing interpretation: "If certain animals have feminine names without basis in their sex, it is only small animals, especially insects" (Meillet, *Linguistique*, p. 213). "A generic term can become feminine if the animal, by its grace, lightness, etc., evokes an idea of femininity: this is the case for *la souris* {mouse}, which was masculine in Latin {*mus*}" (Dauzat, "Le Genre," p. 205). "In the figurative group, gender takes its pattern from the comparison made between the general bearing of the animal species and that of a woman or a man: for example, the mouse, scampering about and storing up its little provisions, is considered to be feminine, like the ant; in contrast, the elephant, majestic, brave, intelligent, awesome, is masculine" (Pichon, "La polarisation," p. 75). O Ahab, was she, your whale {*la baleine*}, lacking in courage and intelligence?

27. On an analogous effect in the pair *jour/nuit* {day/night}, see Genette, *Figures II* (Paris: Seuil, 1969), pp. 102-9.

28. *Trans. Note:* As in chapter 1, where he discusses Plato's *Cratylus*, Genette plays upon the French word *propre* in several senses here. The reverie of language concerns its "own" identity with itself—an "illusion," since words are not things, and there always remains a "gap" (*défaut*) between language and the world. At the same time, the reverie of language aims at establishing the "properness" or "appropriateness" of words in relation to the things they designate. One might thus say that Bachelard takes a Cratylist position on the origin of language. In contrast, Jacques Derrida might represent the Hermogenist or conventionalist position, in, for example, his deconstruction of the "proper" through the play of identity and *différance* in *Of Grammatology* (trans. Gayatri C. Spivak [Baltimore: Johns Hopkins University Press, 1976]).

CHAPTER 18

1. André Martinet, *Éléments de linguistique générale* (Paris: Colin, 1960), p.50.
2. Paul Valéry, *Cahiers*, ed. Judith Robinson (Paris: Gallimard, 1973), 1:453.
3. Louis Aimé Victor Becq de Fouquières, *Traité général de versification française* (Paris: Charpentier, 1879), pp.222-23; Matila Ghyka, *Sortilèges du verbe* (Paris: Gallimard, 1949), p.57.
4. Albert Thibaudet, *Réflexions sur la littérature* (Paris: Gallimard, 1938), p.477.
5. Jakob Grimm, *On the Origin of Language*, trans. Raymond A. Wiley (Leiden: E. J. Brill, 1984), p.17.
6. Quoted in Gaston Bachelard, Preface to Edmond Jabès, *Je bâtis ma demeure: Poèmes 1943-1957* (Paris: Gallimard, 1959), p.16.
7. See Tzvetan Todorov, "Le sens des sons," *Poétique* 11 (1972): 446-59; Auguste W. Schlegel, *Kritische Schriften und Briefe* (Stuttgart, 1962), 1:187.
8. Jean-Jacques Rousseau, *Essay on the Origin of Languages*, trans. Victor Gourevitch (New York: Harper & Row, 1986), p.248.
9. Jacques-Henri Bernardin de Saint-Pierre, *Harmonies de la nature*, 3:234. Here, as in de Brosses, *to articulate {articuler}* is *to design {dessiner}*, and *to speak {parler}* clearly stands midway between *to sing {chanter}* and *to write {écrire}*.
10. René Chateaubriand, *Le Génie du christianisme et Défense du génie du christianisme*, rev. ed. (Paris: Garnier, 1871), 1:285-86. *Trans. Note:* Chateaubriand's book is available in English as *The Genius of Christianity; or, the Spirit and Beauty of the Christian Religion*, trans. Charles I. White (New York: H. Fertig, 1976); however, Genette quotes from a footnote to pt.2, bk.3, chap.6, that is not included in the translation.
11. Rousseau, *Essay*, esp. chap.7, "Of Modern Prosody." Cf. Ernest Renan, *Histoire générale et système comparé des langues sémitiques* (1855), in vol.7 of *Oeuvres complètes*, ed. Henriette Psichari (Paris: Calmann-Levy, 1958), p.249.
12. Victor Hugo, *Le Tas de pierres III* (1838-40) in *Oeuvres complètes*, vol.6, ed. Jean Massin (Paris: Club français du Livre, 1968), p.1160.
13. Hugo, *Le Rhin*, letter 20. We again find this idea of the primitive baroque, corroborated by the same metonymical metaphor, for example in Otto Jespersen: "Primitive language had a superabundance of irregularities and anomalies.... It was capricious and fanciful, and displayed a luxurant growth of forms, entangled one with another like the trees in a primeval forest" (*Language: Its Nature, Development, and Origin* [London: Allen & Unwin, 1922], chap.21, sec.9, p.428).
14. Clemens Brentano, *Briefe*, ed. Seebass (Nuremberg, 1951), 1:80.
15. Rousseau, *Essay*, pp.294-95.
16. Johan Gottfried Herder, *Essay on the Origin of Language*, trans. Alexander Gode in *On the Origin of Language* (New York: Frederick Ungar, 1966).
17. We have just seen, I think, why the idea of a *color of the consonants* is difficult to conceive of. For Claudel, it will be remembered, this difficulty was an obvious impossibility. Copineau and Nodier did indeed associate the color red with the consonant

r, but through the somewhat artificial go-between of the shared idea of intensity. To my knowledge, the only solid exception is in Vladimir Nabokov, who includes in the list of his synaesthesias a black *r*, steely *x*, dark indigo *z*, huckleberry *k*, brown *q*, light blue *c*, mother-of-pearl *s*, alder-leaf green *f*, unripe apple *p*, pistachio *t*, dull green and violet *w*, creamy *d*, chestnut *g*, *j*, and *h*, burnt sienna *b*, pink flannel *m*, rose-quartz *v* (*Speak, Memory: An Autobiography Revisited* [New York: Putnam 1966], pp. 34–35). But as usual with him, idiosyncracy and mystification are hard to tell apart here.

18. Victor Hugo, *Journal de ce que j'apprends chaque jour* (1846–47), ed. Journet and Robert (Paris: Flammarion, 1965), pp. 256–57; *Oeuvres complètes*, 8: 601–2. Column 2 is for words with *i*, column 1 for words with *a*, column 3 for words with both; the order is restored in the second series.

19. Notice that unlike the stars, the moon is not enough, for Hugo, to brighten up the night.

20. René Étiemble, *Le Mythe de Rimbaud*, vol. 2, *Structure du mythe* (Paris: Gallimard, 1952), pp. 84–95. The charts are reprinted in Paul Delbouille, *Poésie et sonorité: La Critique contemporaine devant le pouvoir suggestif des sons* (Paris: Les Belles Lettres, 1961), pp. 248–50.

21. The first sixteen rows in the chart reflect individual testimonies; the last six, collective surveys.

The sources for the chart are as follows: Georg Brandes, John Gould Fletcher, Legrand, X, Hugo, Rimbaud, and surveys by Grüber, Jean de Cours, and Flournoy in Étiemble, *Rimbaud*, 2: 84–95; Grimm in Benloew, *Aperçu général de la science comparative des langues* (1872), p. 105; René Ghil, *Traité du verbe* (Paris, 1887); Fechner in Delbouille, *Poésie et sonorités*, p. 84; Nabokov, *Speak, Memory*, pp. 33–35; Ghyka, *Sortilèges*; K. Langenbeck (German, 1913), S. P. (Czech), and Deichmann (German, 1889) in Roman Jakobson, *Child Language, Aphasia, and Phonological Universals* (1941; The Hague: Mouton, 1968); Franz Boas (survey of the Dakotan Indians), Elizabeth Werth (testimony of a young American of Serbian birth, 1927), and Annelies Argelander in Gladys A. Reichard, Roman Jakobson, and Elizabeth Werth, "Language and Synesthesia," *Word* 5.2 (1949): 224–33; Maxime Chastaing, "Audition colorée: Une enquête," *Vie et Langage* 105 (1960): 631–37, and "Des sons et des couleurs," *Vie et Langage* 112 (1961): 358–65.

22. Jakobson, *Child Language*.

23. Let us recall that the vocalic sounds are characterized from the acoustic viewpoint by the frequency of their two principal "formants," the high formant corresponding to the vibrations of the buccal resonator, the low formant to those of the pharyngeal resonator. The vowels become more "diffuse" as the distance between the two numbers increases (e.g., 2,500/250 units per second for *i*), and more "compact" as this distance decreases (e.g., 1,100/750 for the back vowel *a*), according to the figures advanced by Pierre Delattre in "Les attributs physiques de la parole et l'esthétique du français," *Revue d'Esthétique* 3–4 (1965): 240–54.

24. Here solely the frequencies of the high formant, as being the most clear-cut

and apparently the most perceptible, are considered—from 2,500 for *i* to 700 for *ou*— whereas the low formant ranges only from 250 (*i, ü, ou*) to 750 (*a*). Delattre's figures show that the descending range of frequencies corresponds to that of the articulatory points from front to back, and for good reason: the farther back the emission, the wider the buccal resonator is, and therefore the slower its vibration.

25. Chastaing, "Audition colorée" and "Des sons et des couleurs."

26. Jespersen, *Language*, chap. 20, sec. 6, pp. 400–401.

27. Maurice Grammont, *Traité de phonétique, avec 179 figures dans le texte* (Paris: Delagrave, 1933), p. 385. He says *a* is "blazing" {*éclatant*}.

28. Benjamin Whorf, "Language, Mind, and Reality" (1942) in *Language, Thought, and Reality*, ed. John B. Carroll (Cambridge, Mass.: MIT Press, 1956), p. 268.

29. Maxime Chastaing, "La brillance des voyelles," *Archivum Linguisticum* f. 1 (1962): 1–13.

30. Otto Jespersen, "The Symbolic Value of the Vowel *i*" (1922), reprinted in *Linguistica: Selected Papers in English, French, and German* (Copenhagen: Levin & Munksgaard, 1933).

31. In French, the vocabulary of childhood here plays upon an analogous opposition *i/a*, furnished by the Latin *pissiare* and *cacare* but exploited in pseudo-onomatopoeia.

32. Edward Sapir, "A Study in Phonetic Symbolism," *Journal of Experimental Psychology* 12 (1929): 225–39.

33. Maxime Chastaing, "Le symbolisme des voyelles, significations des *i*," *Journal de Psychologie Normale et Pathologique* July–September 1958, pp. 403–23, and October–December 1958, pp. 461–81; Chastaing, "Dernières recherches sur le symbolisme vocalique de la petitesse," *Revue Philosophique de la France et de l'Étranger*, 1965, pp. 41–42.

34. André Martinet, "Peut-on dire d'une langue qu'elle est belle?" *Revue d'Esthétique*, 1965, p. 231.

35. See Roger W. Brown, Abraham H. Black, and Arnold E. Horowitz, "Phonetic Symbolism in Natural Languages," *Journal of Abnormal and Social Psychology* (1955): 388–93; Ivan Fonagy, "Le langage poétique: Forme et fonction," *Problèmes du langage* (Paris: Gallimard, 1966), pp. 72–116. Claude Lévi-Strauss clearly (and explicitly) motivates his bilingual pair *cheese/fromage* (white/yellow cheese) {low in butterfat/high in butterfat} through the opposition light/heavy. Let us recall that he designates these sensory combinations as "a posteriori motivations," for which he gives a memorable (but extralinguistic) example in the pair *red light/green light* (*Structural Anthropology*, trans. Claire Jacobsen and Brooke Grundfest [New York: Basic Books, 1963], pp. 93–94).

36. A summary of this experiment is found in Jean-Michel Peterfalvi, *Recherches expérimentales sur le symbolisme phonétique* (Paris: CNRS, 1970), p. 36—to this day the best treatment of the whole question.

37. Chastaing, "Pop, fop, pof, fof," *Vie et Langage* 159 (1965): 311–17. Of course, a curve might be harder than a dot, but the fact that, given equal hardness, a dot makes a greater impression than a curve is enough to justify the inference.

38. Chastaing, "L'opposition des consonnes sourdes et sonores a-t-elle une valeur symbolique?" *Vie et Langage* 147 (1964): 367-70.

39. To the texts previously discussed, let us add this one: "Of the consonants, *l* will designate the soft, *r* the rough" (Grimm, *Origin*, p. 17)._

40. Fonagy, "Langage poétique," p. 79; Chastaing, "Si les *r* étaient des *l*," *Vie et Langage* 173 (1966): 468-72, 502-7.

41. See Paul Delbouille, "Recherches recentes sur la valeur suggestive des sonorités," in *Le Vers français au XXe siècle* (Paris: Klincksieck, 1967), p. 143; and Tzvetan Todorov, "Le sens des sons," p. 449.

42. Roman Jakobson, *Essais de linguistique générale* (Paris: Minuit, 1973), p. 241. E. H. Gombrich jokingly illustrates this theory (alluded to by Jakobson in the course of a conversation with him) by the pair *ping/pong:* "If these were all we had and we had to name an elephant and a cat, which would be ping and which pong? I think that the answer is clear. Or hot soup and ice cream? To me, at least, ice cream is ping and soup pong. Or Rembrandt and Watteau? Surely in that case Rembrandt would be pong and Watteau ping. I do not maintain that it always works, that two blocks are sufficient to characterize all relationships. We find people differing about day and night and male and female, but perhaps these different answers could be reduced to unanimity if the question were differently framed: pretty girls are ping and matrons pong; it may depend on which aspect of womanhood the person has in mind, just as the motherly, enveloping aspect of night is pong, but its sharp, cold, and menacing physiognomy may be ping to some" (*Art and Illusion: A Study in the Psychology of Pictorial Representation*, Bollingen Series 35, rev. 2d ed. [Princeton: Princeton University Press, 1961], pp. 370-71).

43. Grammont, "La Phonétique impressive," pt. 3 in *Traité de phonétique*, pp. 377ff.

44. This is not the opinion of T. K. Davis, who interprets the English vowel gradation sing/sang/sung in terms of a symbolism of distance: "The analogy is simple ... the present *i* is here, the past tense *a* is there, and the pluperfect ... *u* is yet more removed" (quoted in John Orr, "On Some Sound-Values in English," in *Words and Sounds in English and French* [Oxford: Basil Blackwell, 1953], p. 23) — a nice example of morphomimologism.

45. Ferdinand de Saussure, *Course in General Linguistics*, trans. Roy Harris (London: Duckworth, 1983), p. 69.

46. Jespersen, *Language*, chap. 20, sec. 12; and see all of chap. 20, "Sound Symbolism."

47. {Ibid., p. 410 n. 1.}

48. This double critique is reiterated by Jacques Derrida in *Glas* (trans. John P. Leavey, Jr., and Richard Rand [Lincoln: University of Nebraska Press, 1986], pp. 90-94).

49. Jespersen, *Language*, chap. 20, sec. 10, pp. 406-8; and "Symbolic Value," p. 301.

50. This is not entirely the case in the competition between *little* and *small*. Orr puts forward in a more convincing way the absence of posterity for the Latin *parvus*, supplanted in Romance languages by substitutes such as *petit, piccolo*, etc.

51. Jespersen, *Language*, chap. 20, sec. 11, p. 408; sec. 12, p. 411.

52. Grammont, *Traité de phonétique*, p. 400.

53. Chastaing, "La brillance des voyelles"; "Dernières recherches sur le symbolisme des voyelles"; and "Nouvelles recherches sur le symbolisme des voyelles," *Journal de Psychologie Normale et Pathologique*, January–March, 1965; pp. 75–88.

54. Gaston Bachelard, *La Formation de l'esprit scientifique* (Paris: Vrin, 1947), pp. 213ff.

55. Chastaing, "Nouvelles recherches," p. 82. {The bracketed text is Genette's.}

56. Other experiments, intended to explore a wider area of the lexicon using a different method (attempts to make subjects guess at the meaning of certain words from languages they did not know), have yielded contradictory results. See Peterfalvi, *Recherches experimentales*, pp. 129–35.

57. Saussure, *Course*, pp. 120, 116–17, 7.

58. On the prehistory and birth of phonology, and on the parallel and later convergent constitution of the concept of the *phoneme*, I refer the reader to the classics in the history of linguistics and to the invaluable historical chapters in the second volume of Jakobson's *Essais de linguistique générale*. Let us just recall that *phoneme* was originally (1873), as still for Saussure, only a synonym for *sound of language;* that Kruszowski begins to distinguish it negatively from unarticulated sound; and that Baudouin de Courtenay gives it a purely psychological definition, still accepted by Troubetskoy in 1933 ("what one thinks one is pronouncing" as opposed to "what one really pronounces"), but definitively abandoned in his *Principes de phonologie* (composed before 1938) in favor of a functional definition: "The phoneme is above all a functional concept that must be defined in relation to its function" (p. 43).

59. Karl Bühler, "*L'Onomatopée et la fonction representative du langage*," *Journal de Psychologie*, January–April 1933, pp. 101–19; rpt. in the selection published by J.-C. Pariente, *Essais sur le langage* (Paris: Minuit, 1969), pp. 111–32. See also Pariente, *Présentation*, pp. 14–15.

60. See the last paragraph and accompanying chart in Chapter 4, Master of Words."

61. Saussure, quoted in Jakobson, *Essais*, 2:277.

62. "The uttered word, the actually spoken locution, taken as a sensuous, specifically acoustic phenomenon, is something that we distinguish from the word itself or the declarative sentence itself, or the sentence-sequence itself that makes up a more extensive locution. Not without reason — in cases where we have not been understood and we reiterate — do we speak precisely of a reiteration of the *same* words and sentences. ... The word itself, the sentence itself, is an ideal unity, which is not multiplied by its thousand-fold reproductions" (Edmund Husserl, *Formal and Transcendental Logic*, trans. Dorion Cairns [The Hague: Martinus Nijhoff, 1969], pp. 19–21; note the closeness to Saussure's explanation). James M. Edie, who cites this page, rightly adds that the remark applies just as well to the phoneme, which "is not at all a sound" but an "abstract entity" ("La pertinence actuelle de la conception husserlienne de l'idéalité du langage," in *Sens et Existence* [Paris: Seuil, 1975], p. 119).

63. Michel Foucault, *The Order of Things* (New York: Random House, 1970), p. 103.

64. Jonathan Swift, *Gulliver's Travels*.

65. "Science," says Freud, "is after all the most complete renunciation of the pleasure principle of which our psychic activity is capable" ("Dostoevsky and Parricide," in *Culture and Personality*). Here again, "science" begins with language.

66. See Chapter 12, p. 236. The only example of a metonymic relation between signified and signifier encountered is Jakobson's completely hypothetical explanation of the labial "mama" by the movement of sucking in breast-feeding ("Why 'Papa' and 'Mama'?" in *Child Language*). According to this hypothesis, the mother's name would not *resemble* her but would *issue from* her through a relation of cause to effect. As for the synecdochic relation (part as symbol for the whole), dear to Coleridge and to Romantic symbolism, it does not seem to have inspired any properly linguistic speculation. A pity: the reverie of the word as member and microcosm of the thing would be pleasant.

67. Here again we have the inevitable confusion of signification attached to the term *symbol* and its derivations: sometimes (Peirce, Bühler, Lacan) the symbolic is opposed to the analogic; sometimes (Hegel, Saussure, Jespersen, and whoever discusses "phonic symbolism") it is almost equivalent to the analogic, in opposition to conventional semiosis.

68. Gaston Bachelard, *The Psychoanalysis of Fire*, trans. Alan C. M. Ross (Boston: Beacon Press, 1964), p. 2.

69. An aesthetics, one might say, whose current resurgence, passim, gives a poor idea of our critical imagination. Reading so many implicit praises of imitative harmony, one could truly say that "form" has nothing better to do than to double "content." To the contrary, Jean Renoir grumbles: "When the image says 'I love you,' music ought to say 'I don't give a damn.'" (Such was also Edgar Varèse's wish for the filmic illustration of his work.) This is a bit simplistic, but it is a little progress over simple tautology.

70. It goes without saying that for the nonspecialist the "rare" texts that as a rule make up our corpus are, for the medieval period, especially difficult of access, which suffices to explain why only one representative text from this period is discussed. But I wonder if the mimologist tradition, strictly speaking, did not suffer a veritable eclipse at that time—to the advantage of, on the one hand, etymological speculation (Isidore of Seville, etc.) and, on the other hand, those mimographic fantasies of which a few traces are found in the *ABC par équivoque* of Huon le Roi. See Paul Zumthor, *Langue, Texte, Énigme* (Paris: Seuil, 1975), pp. 44–45.

71. Ludic, but, as we have also seen, always basically serious, even when the point is, as in Proust, a serious *critique*. To my knowledge, the only example of a *parody* of mimologism (graphic, in this case) is "How the Alphabet Was Made" in Rudyard Kipling's *Just So Stories*. Unless Socrates himself . . .

Index

Abel, 357 n.63

Abelard, 216

Abrams, M. H., 370 n.76

Adelung, Johann, 179, 191

African languages, 55, 123, 192, 198, 326, 367 n.31

algebraic language, xlvii, 139, 171, 220, 222, 371 n.77

alliteration, xxxi, xxxvii, 205, 207, 218, 246

alphabet: artificial, 54, 115-20, 349 n.2, 406 n.41; hieroglyphic, xxix, xl-xlviii, 108-14, 351 n.23, 364 n.56 n.58, 403-4 n.20; history contained in, 205, 266; ideographic, 351 n.23, 364 n.58; mimetic, xxviii, 53-60; organic, xxx, 85-89, 118; and parody of mimologism, 429 n.71; plasticity of, 281-86; and poetry, 216; Roman, xxix; as test of natural language, 21; as tool kit, 273. *See also names of individual languages*

American languages, 70, 123, 186, 189, 313, 326, 353 n.21, 382 n.18

anagrams, xxv, xxxii, 218, 246

analogue versus transpositive languages, 150-51, 168, 175-76

analogy, xlii, 246, 264, 333-34

Ancient and Moderns, quarrel of, li, 143-78

Anderson, Julie, lix-lx n.25

Anglo-Saxon, 41, 202-7, 218, 351 n.23

animal names, xxviii-xxix, 122, 219, 423 n.26, 427 n.42

animal sounds: compared with human language, 277, 341 n.51, 351 n.18, 362 n.33; and onomatopoeia, xxx, lxi n.48, 127, 128, 323-24; and origins of language, xxxvii, xxxix, 123, 125, 361 n.11, 367 n.30 n.31. *See also* animal names; canine letter (*r*)

Apollinaire, Guillaume, lxiii n.63, 406 n.41

Aquien, Michel, lvix n.17

Aquinas, Saint Thomas, 344 n.24

Arabic, xliii, 121, 175, 184, 191, 195, 382 n.17, 385-86 n.24

Aramaic, 385-86 n.24

arbitrariness, xxxvi, 18, 91-92, 177, 218, 303, 333; and derivation, 77, 84; limits on, 30, 48, 82, 95, 191, 207, 209, 267, 325-26; in modern linguistics, l, 219-20; and poetic language, 216, 228, 230, 234, 242-43, 246, 262, 376 n.57, 396 n.156, 421 n.16. *See also* Hermogenism; sound and sense

Archer, Beth, 415 n.1

Argelander, 318

Aristo, 147

Aristotle, 196, 277, 386-87 n.28; and Augustine, 32, 343-44 n.19; and conventionalist thesis, 344 n.24; and definition of writing, lxii n.56, 341 n.51; and rhetoric, 34, 94, 145, 174

Armstrong, David F., lii

Arsleff, Hans, lxi n.43, 346 n.3

artificial language, 43-51; critique of, 371 n.77; English as, 204; formation of, from natural language, 62, 347 n.11; Latin as, 174; philosophical ideal of, xxv, xl, lvi, 49-50, 58-59, 118-19, 222, 349 n.26; Sanskrit as, 380 n.109. *See also* alphabet, artificial; Chinese, as artificial language

Auguste, Léopold, 264

Augustine, Saint, xxxiv-xxxv, xli, xlix, 73, 120, 148, 325, 356 n.55; and authorship of *On Dialectic*, 343 n.9; and expanded theory of imitation, lii, 30-35, 39, 48, 62, 136, 138

Aulus Gellius, 342 n.7

Averroës, 387 n.28

Babel, tower of, xxxiv-xxxv, 42, 120, 123, 124, 128, 201, 295, 367 n.26

Bachelard, Gaston, lviii n.1, lxv n.94, 422 n.25; *Air and Dreams*, 128; on gender, 419 n.8, 420 n.11, 421 n.17; mimologisms of, liii–lv, 131, 275–76, 301–8, 423 n.28; *Psychoanalysis of Fire*, 335; on vowels versus consonants, 310, 329, 333, 363 n.41; *Water and Dreams*, 99

Bacon, Roger, lxii n.56, 345 n.24

Bailly, 339 n.23

Baldensperger, 359–60 n.1

Bally, Charles, 61, 269, 397 n.177, 405 n.33

Barrès, Maurice, 245

Barthélemy, Jean Jacques, 45

Barthes, Roland, liii, lxv n.93, 251, 254–55, 258, 302, 400 n.16

Batteux, Charles, 153, 156–59, 160, 168, 170, 171–72, 174, 175, 176, 177–78, 375 n.39

Baudelaire, Charles, 76, 219, 228, 229, 245, 246, 263, 282, 314, 350 n.14

Beauzée, Nicolas, 345 n.1, 378 n.77; articles in *Encyclopédie*, 163, 353 n.25, 378 n.78; on co-existence, 33, 235; and debate on inversion, 153, 163, 159–60, 167–76, 183, 193, 377 n.64, 379 n.96, 380 n.109; *Grammaire générale*, 373 n.9; on origins of language, 148, 189, 352 n.6, 367 n.30, 373 n.17, 379 n.92

Becanus, Goropius, 347 n.18, 380 n.1

Benac, 328

Benveniste, Émile, 357 n.63

Bergier, Nicolas Sylvestre, 352 n.6, 356 n.56, 357 n.63, 361 n.11, 419 n.8

Bernadin de Saint-Pierre, Jacques-Henri, 99, 135–36, 303, 305, 311, 367 n.31, 370 n.68, 420 n.14, 424 n.9

Bettina, 313

Bible, xxxi, xxxvii, 46, 195–97, 282, 386–87 n.28

Blair, Hugh, 139, 170, 345 n.1, 389 n.26, 420 n.12

Bloch, R. Howard, xxxiv

Bloomfield, Leonard, lxii n.56, 391 n.51

Boas, Franz, 318, 425 n.21

Bochart, Samuel, 58, 350 n.12, 352 n.6

Boethius, 344 n.24

Böhme, Jacob, 47, 347 n.15

Bollack, Jean, 17, 340 n.38

Bonald, Vicomte de, 148, 189, 373 n.17

Bopp, Franz, 150, 183, 184, 193–94, 197, 380 n.4, 382–83 n.18

Borges, Jorge Luis, lvii, 365 n.2

Bos, Jean Batiste du, 154

Bouhours, Dominique, 147, 175

Bounoure, Gabriel, 310

Boussuet, 410 n.32

Bouvet, 49

Brandes, Georg, 317, 318, 425 n.21

Bréal, Michel, 34, 219–20

Brentano, Clemens, 313, 314

Brik, Osip, 397 n.163

Brisset, Jean-Pierre, 173, 187, 379–80 n.109

Bronowski, Jacob, lxiv n.87

Bruner, Jerome, xxxviii, lxi n.42

Brunschwig, Jacques, 347 n.7

Buffon, Georges Louis Leclerc, Comte de, 123

Bühler, Karl, 331–34, 429 n.67

Bullet, Jean-Baptiste, 379 n.92

Campbell, George, 390 n.51

Campos, Augustos de, xlv

canine letter (r), xxvii–xxxiii, 5, 38, 41, 47, 335, 345 n.4, 362 n.33

Capella, Martianus, 353 n.25

Carroll, Lewis, xxii, xxvii, xl, xlviii, lv, lvii, 345 n.5, 365 n.2, 417 n.19

Castel, P., 355 n.50

Cato, 80

Celtic, xl, 58–59, 125, 170, 350 n.12, 351 n.19, 351 n.23, 379 n.92

Chain of Being, xxxiv–xxxvi

Champollion, Jean François, 267, 350 n.14

Chardin, 175

Charpentier, François, 147, 377 n.64

Chastaing, Maxime, xlix, 317, 318, 319–22, 328–29, 334, 425 n.21

Chateaubriand, René, xxxvii, 311, 348 n.22, 351 n.18, 368 n.36, 370 n.65

Chaucer, Geoffrey, 203

Chavée, Honoré Joseph, 385 n.22

Chevalier, Jean-Claude, 372 n.3

childhood: as age of labials, 47, 103, 126, 127, 128, 354 n.38, 368 n.40, 429 n.66; development of language in, xxxvii–xxxix, lxi n.42, 311; mimologisms of, 277–81, 287–88, 290–91, 352 n.4, 368 n.41, 409 n.11, 426 n.31

Chinese, 202, 353 n.25, 361 n.13, 385 n.22; as artificial language, 43, 45, 46–47, 49, 346 n.5; grammar of, 184, 193, 198–99; origins of, 192; writing system, xix, xliii–xliv, xlvii,

INDEX

lxii n.61, 83–84, 108, 110, 111, 267–69, 275, 404 n.24; writing system distinguished from Egyptian, 45–46
Chompré, Pierre, 159, 171, 377 n.64
Chomsky, Noam, xxxviii, lxi n.43
chromatic values, l, 96–97, 135–37, 314–19, 322, 376 n.57
Cicero, 34, 97, 147, 152, 158, 160–61, 173
Claudel, Paul, 261–76, 396 n.156, 402 n.3, 407–8 n.65, 408 n.2; fascination with alphabet, xxx–xxxi, xliii–xliv, xlviii, 60–61, 131, 285, 403 n.20, 407 n.59, 410 n.36; graphic mimologism of, 286, 299, 356 n.53, 405 n.31 n.34, 406 n.41; ideograms of, 405 n.29 nn.31–33 n.35, 406 n.39 n.41 n.47, 407 n.53; Ponge's mimology on name "Claudel," 298; status of consonants in, 274–75, 309, 313, 314, 407 n.60 n.63, 424 n.17; and wordplay 280, 408 n.70; and "written speech," 57
climate, influence on language. See geomimology
Cohen, Gustave, 228
Cohen, Jean, 398 n.190
Cohn, Robert Greer, 391 n.54, 392 n.71
Coleridge, Samuel Taylor, 429 n.66
Collart, Jean, 30
communication, xxxiii, xxxiv–xxxv, 9, 11, 169, 190, 278, 379 n.101; poetic view of, 227, 238, 263, 396 n.144
compound words, 13, 42, 105–6, 343 n.18, 350 n.15
concrete poetry, xlv
Condillac, Étienne Bonnot de, lx n.32 n.33, lxii n.55, 62, 383 n.22; on connection of ideas in language, 154–56, 157, 162, 167, 174, 178; "An Essay on the Origin of Human Knowledge," xxxv–xxxvi, 154–56; on language acquisition, xxxviii, xxxix, lxi n.42, 160; on origins of language, 149, 170, 189, 355 n.50, 361 n.11
consonants, 41, 71, 73, 104, 185, 209; color of, 253, 265–66, 424–25 n.17; in consonantal clusters, xxvii, xxx, 37–42, 105, 180, 206; gender of, 310; graphic value ascribed to, 56–57, 60–61, 86–87, 267, 353 n.17; initial, xxxvii, 37–39, 123, 206–9, 345–46 n.6; mimetic value ascribed to, 128–30, 321–22, 362 n.30, 363 n.35 n.36 n.42, 368 n.38, 390 n.44,

427 n.39; primitive, 125; valorization of, 261, 266, 314, 382 n.17, 407 n.61 n.63. See also under vowels
conventionalist thesis. See Hermogenism
Copineau, Abbot, 355–56 n.50, 377 n.63, 381 n.6, 383 n.22, 424–25 n.17
Coppée, François, 216
Coquet, Jean-Claude, xliv, 407 n.59
Cordemoy, Gerauld de, 349 n.4
Corman, Cid, 415 n.1
correctness, mimetic, 337–38 n.7, 390 n.51, 402 n.58; and Leirisian gloss, 293; Mallarmé's illusion of, 209, 212, 213; as Socratic project, xxxiii, xlix, 7–13, 20, 26–27, 293; as test of aesthetic language, liii. See also failing (défaut), of natural language; mistakes
correspondence, xxxv–xxxvi, li; Hermogenist view of, 8, 384 n.26; diagrammatic, 143, 157; in Leiris, 280–81, 283; one-to-one, xxx, 117; rediscovery of, 141, 240, 280–81, 302, 355 n.50
countryside, language of, 112, 124, 204, 287, 288, 311–12
Cours, Jean de, 318, 425 n.21
Courtenay, Baudouin de, 428 n.58
Courturat, Louis, 346 n.4
Cratylian tradition: comparatist challenge to, xxx–xxxii, 190–91, 336, 382–83 n.18; and difference, 415 n.71; ethnocentricity of, 145, 190, 213; iconicity of writing in, xl, 353 n.13; key principles of, 209; letter r in, xxvii, 135; lexical bias of, 122, 202, 222; and magic, 261–62; in medieval period, 429 n.70; and Mimologics, lvi, 383–84 n.25; mimophony in, xlix; motivation in, 92, 208; origins of language in, xxxvii, 392 n.77; rarity of syntagmatic analysis in, 39–40; Stoicism in, 35; words and things in, xxi–xxiii, xxv, xxix–xxx, xxxiii–xlviii, li–lv, lvii, lviii, 21, 31–32, 182, 185. See also Cratylism
Cratylism: classical thesis of, xxxvi, xxxix, xlvi, lxi n.43, 24, 53, 182, 234, 258, 321; core themes of, 5–6, 12, 180–81, 334–35; ludic definition of 414–15 n.71; metamorphoses of, 29, 63, 67, 76, 83, 88, 91, 131, 144, 178, 188, 205, 382 n.18, 396 n.151; as minority position, 344 n.24; modern reappearance of, xxxiii, xlv, lvix n. 6, 208–9, 217–18,

433

Cratylism (continued)
235, 236, 257, 261, 266, 267, 276, 279, 280,
286, 293–94, 303, 327, 336, 402 n.54; and
poetry, 141, 162, 237, 263; primary, lvix n.17,
27, 219; reserved, 42; morphological, 185;
secondary, lvii, 327, 349 n.26, 402 n.58, 414
n.71, 417 n.19; subjective, 199, 336; universal
mimeticization of, xxix, 124, 188. See also
Cratylian tradition
Cratylus: affinity with Hermogenes, lvi, 90,
191, 375 n.45; versus Hermogenes, xxxv,
xxxviii–xxxix, xlvii, xli, xlix–lii, lviii, 23, 350
n.15, 356 n.59, 423 n.28; linguistic opinions
of, 130, 178, 187, 214, 245–46, 332, 335, 341
n.59; Cratylism of, distinguished from
Plato's Cratylism, 12; enthusiasm of, 75, 85;
idealism of, 48, 113, 138; Leibniz and, 43–51;
mimetic imperialism of, 62, 101; naturalist
thesis of, 6, 7; Socrates' view of, 49, 294;
and valorization of mother tongue, 146,
210, 211, 212. See also Cratylian tradition;
Cratylism; Hermogenes; Plato, Cratylus
Culler, Jonathan, lxiii n.78

d'Alembert, Jean Le Rond, 159, 162–63
d'Olivet, Fabre, 373 n.17
Dalgarno, George, 43, 44, 49, 59, 346 n.5, 349
n.26
Darmesteter, 368 n.42
Damourette, Jacques, 419 n.7 n.9, 422 n.23
Dante, Alighieri, 41
Dargaud, Marius, 371 n.83
Darwin, Charles, 326, 327
Dauzet, Albert, 419 n.9
David, Madeleine, 45, 50
Davis, T. K., 427 n.44
de Bos, 376 n.57
de Brosses, Charles, 65–90; and articulatory
mimesis, xxxii, xxxv, xxxix, lvix n.20, 48,
54, 66–68, 76, 424 n.9; and Bernadin de
Saint-Pierre, 424 n.9; and Claudel, 266,
407 n.61; contradictions of, 354 n.48; on
contrariety, 80–81, 357 n.63; on derivation,
xli–xlii, 34, 76–82, 91, 106, 353 n.53 n.55;
and Gébelin, 91, 100–108, 112–13, 360 n.4,
362 n.23, 363 n.39 n.42, 364 n.58, 369 n.45;
in history of linguistics, lx n.25 n.32, lxii
n.55, 187, 356 n.50, 382 n.18; on language as
painting, 66–67, 82–90, 352 n.8, 356 n.51,

358 n.70 n.71; and Leiris, 284, 414 n.71;
and Mallarmé, 205, 208, 215, 221, 363 n.41,
390 n.40; on mother tongue, 352 n.6; and
Nodier, xxx, xxxvi, 115–21, 124, 126, 135–
36, 138, 368 n.36, 369 n.45; on origins of
language, 66, 121, 149, 328; sound symbolism of, xxix, 70–73, 354 n.38; Traité de la
formation mécanique des langues, 65, 356
n.59; and valorization of consonant, 68–
70, 185, 309–14, 321, 407 n.61; and Voltaire,
172, 379 n.104; and Wachter, 80, 85; and
Warburton, 358–59 n.72
Deichmann, 318, 425 n.21
Delattre, Pierre, 425 n.21
Delbouille, Paul, 322, 376 n.56, 397 n.177
Deleuze, 417 n.19
Demetrius of Phalerum, 372 n.8
Democritus, 335, 341 n.53, 342 n.2
de Piis, 274, 402 n.3
Derrida, Jacques: Archeology of the Frivolous,
xxxvi; "Différance," 415 n.71; "The Double
Session," xlvi, lxiii n.71; Glas, xxvi–xxvii,
xxxii–xxxiii, xxxviii, xlvii, lvix n.7 n.12, lx
n.38, 427 n.48; Grammatology, lvix n.14, 353
n.17, 408 n.68, 415 n.71, 423 n.28
Descartes, René, lxi n.43, 174, 378 n.78
Desnos, Robert, 292, 412–13 n.60
diagrammatism, xlviii, l–lii, lxiv n.83, 177, 322,
417 n.19
Dictionnaire des synonymes, 328, 329
Diderot, Denis, li, lix, 158, 159–62, 168, 170,
173, 175, 218, 355 n.50, 375 n.45, 376 n.53 n.56
n.57, 378 n.88
Dieckmann, Liselotte, 350 n.14
différance, 415 n.71, 423 n.28
difference, 24, 114, 333; flight from, lv;
valorization of, 178
Dionysius of Halicarnassus, 29, 339 n.23, 372
n.8
Diringer, David, lxii n.56
discourse, function of, 174–75
divine, names for, 16, 17, 93, 121, 125, 129,
162–63
Domergue, Urbain, 173, 175
Donatus, Aelius Donatus, 145, 147
Dorchain, 397 n.177
Dottrens-Massarenti, 329
Douchet, 378 n.78
Du Bois-Hus, Gabriel, 376 n.57

Duclos, 384 n.2

Ducrot, Oswald, 182, 381 n.13

Du Marsais, César Chesneau, 152–53, 159, 374 n.25, 377 n.64, 378 n.76, 380 n.109; separation of rhetoric from grammar, 163–67, 170–72, 174, 377 n.67

Dumas, Alexandre, 368 n.42

Durand, Xavier, 412 n.52

Dutch, 367 n.31

Dzhugashvili, Iosif Vissarionovich, 90

Eco, Umberto, xxiv

Edie, James M., 428 n.62

Egyptian, 198. *See also* hieroglyphs

Emerson, Ralph Waldo, xli

Encyclopédie, 152, 163, 165, 373 n.17, 376 n.53, 377 n.64, 378 n.78

Encyclopédie méthodique, 378 n.177

English: "color of vowels" in, 315–17, 320; conventional qualities of, 219, 229, 331; expressive monosyllables in, xxviii, 41, 346 n.9; filiation of, 170, 351 n.23; as Indo-European tongue, 180, 184; Mallarmé's view of, xxx, 201–12, 218, 390 n.48; mimetic qualities of, 5, 37–42, 62, 329, 328–29, 350 n.13, 390 n.49, 390–91 n.51, 427 n.44; as universal natural language, 58–59, 348 n.24

Epicurus, 29, 99, 148, 190, 357 n.67

eponymy, xli, lviii n.5, 7–27, 249–60; and biblical names, xxxvii; intertextuality of, xxix, xxxi, xxxiii–xxxiv, xxxviii, 62, 287–88, 300; as game, xxii–xxvii, xxxii, 18–20; and mimophony, xliii, xlviii–xlix; reservations about, lii, liii, lviii–lvix n.6, 23–27, 258–60. *See also* Socrates, eponomies of

equivalence, 208, 229–30, 243–46, 310

error. *See* failing (*défaut*), of natural language; mistakes

Ernout, Alfred, 144–45

Estienne, 352 n.6

Etiemble, René, xlix, 317

Etruscan alphabet, 110, 111

etymology: alphabetic representation of, 87; attack on, 128, 183, 326; consonantal basis of, 69–70, 100; definition of, 339 n.22, 369–70 n.62; and derivation, 91, 389–90 n.40; distinguished from eponymy, xxiii–xxiv, 17–18, 294–95, 298, 300; "folk," 204, 287, 339 n.22; and genealogy, 401 n.44 n.54;

ludic, lviii, 264, 290, 294, 416 n.16, 417 n.18; medieval, 429 n.70; and the "mimetic gap," 29, 253, 287, 294; as motivation, 65, 344 n.23; multiple, 340 n.33, 367–68 n.32, 416 n.11; and origination, 92, 93, 94, 120; as principle of borrowing not of origination, 151. *See also* eponymy; Socrates, eponymies of

Eugenius, 147

European languages, 119, 182, 198, 311, 324

evolutionism, lii, 184, 195, 312, 326, 328, 358 n.71

exoticism, 199, 211, 212, 267

expressiveness, xxxii, 396 n.156; in mimological tradition, 5, 32, 161, 379 n.96, 409 n.25; in modern linguistics, 325–29; phonic, 29, 48, 253, 294, 331, 344 n.21, 348 n.26; and poetry, 242, 263

Fahnestock, Lee, 416 n.16

failing (*défaut*), of natural language, xxx, xlii, xlviii, 26–27, 80–82, 308, 402 n.58, 423 n.28; Mallarmé on, 82, 141, 201–47, 230, 297, 391–92 n.61, 393 n.79, 403 n.17

Fall, the, xxxiv, lx n.38, 201, 217, 277, 288

Farasse, Gérard, 418 n.24

Fauchet, Claude, 367 n.30

Fechner, 318, 425 n.21

Fenollosa, Ernest Francisco, xliii, 404 n.24

Figulus, Nigidius, 29

figures, 81, 69, 171, 174–75, 352–53 n.13, 378 n.76

Fischer, Henry George, lxii n.52

Flaubert, Gustave, 253, 406 n.41

Fletcher, John Gould, 318, 425 n.21

Flournoy, 318, 425 n.21

Fonagy, Ivan, xxxii, xxxix, lvix n.20, lxv n.89, 321–22, 397 n.178

Fontanier, Pierre, 166, 378 n.77

Fontenelle, Bernard le Bovier, de, 23

Foucault, Michel, xxxvi, lx n.32, lxiv n.86, 182, 380 n.109

Fouquières, Louis Aimé Victor Becq de, 309–10

Fourment, Gustave, 220

Fowler, H. N., 337 n.1, 337–38 n.7, 338 n.10 n.11, 340 n.37 n.43

Frain du Tremblay, Jean, 148–51, 158, 162, 169, 373 n.16

Fraser, Russell, xxxv

Frederick II, King, 66

French: alphabet, 70, 113, 116, 117–18; ambiguity of *name* in, 338 n.14 n.19; chromatic
values of, 314–20; expression of anger in,
xxxii; gender in, liv, 304–7, 419 n.8, 420
n.15, 422 n.23 n.24, 421–22 n.20; influence
on English, 42, 202–4, 214; kinship to
Greek, 352 n.6, 372 n.8; kinship to Latin,
360 n.10; mimetic failings of, 5, 26, 77, 79,
80–81, 158–59, 212–13, 219, 220, 241, 262, 390
n.51; mimetic superiority of, 120, 282, 312;
mimographic qualities of, xxxi, 267, 269,
270–71, 406 n.39; onomatopoeia in, 132–
36, 426 n.31; symbolic value of phonemes
in, xxix, 70–73, 96, 102–5; word order in,
143–78, 210, 374 n.25, 378 n.88
Freret, Nicholas, 45
Freud, Sigmund, 307, 357 n.63, 414 n.71,
422–43 n.25, 429 n.65
Fyler, John M., lx n.26

Gadoffre, Gilbert, 408 n.65
Gaède, Édouard, 216, 391 n.60
Gage, Jennifer, xix, 418 n.24
Gamaches, E. S., 154
Garot, M., 172, 379 n.106
Gavronsky, Serge, 415 n.1
Gébelin, Antoine Court de, lx n.32, lxii n.55,
91–114, 359–60 n.1, 361 n.13; and Claudel,
266, 267, 269, 274, 407 n.61; on climate,
xxxvi, 99–100, 175; Cratylism of, 48, 382
n.18, 396 n.151; hieroglyphic alphabet of,
xxix, xlii, 108–14, 364 n.56 n.58; *Histoire
naturelle de la parole*, 98–99, 362 n.33; and
Leiris, 284, 285; and national languages,
210, 350 n.13, 358 n.67; and Nodier, 115–17,
121, 122–23, 124–25, 126, 127, 129, 134–35;
and Mallarmé, 187; *Origine du langage et de
l'écriture*, 91–114, 359 n.1; on primal word,
xxxv, 91–94, 106–8, 360 n.6; principle of
harmony, 94, 99, 362 n.25; and Renan, 193;
on vowels and consonants, 94–100, 185,
310, 313, 341 n.56, 361 n.15, 362 n.30; and
Wachter, 57. *See also under* de Brosses
Gelb, I. J., lxii n.56
Gellius, Aulus, 29–30
gender, liv, 334, 419 n.7; and animal names,
423 n.26; arbitrariness of, 419 n.9, 420
n.12, 420–21 n.16; Bachelard on, 301–8, 310,
421 n.17, 422 n.24; in German, 422 n.23;

Indo-European conception of, 421–22 n.20
Genet, Jean, xxvi–xxvii, xxxii–xxxiii, xxxviii,
liv, 236, 395–96 n.144
Genette, Gérard, *Figures II*, 398 n.1; *Figures
of Literary Discourse*, lxv n.90, 309; *Introduction à l'architexte*, lv–lvi, lxv n.96 n.97;
Mimologiques, reviews of, lxv n.98; *Narrative Discourse*, lv, lxv n.96 n.97; *Palimpsestes*,
lv–lvi, lxv n.96 n.97, lxvi n.100; "Rhetoric
Restrained," lii–liii, lxv n.92, 309; *Seuils*,
lv–lvi, lxv n.96
geomimology, xxxvi–xxxvii, xlii–xliii, lvi, 99,
100, 122–23, 175, 197, 362 n.25, 385 n.24, 387
n.31
German, xxix, 5, 47, 79, 180, 194, 203, 254, 298,
312, 325; gender, 303, 306, 422 n.23
gestures, language as, xxxv–xxxvi, xxxviii–
xxxix, xliv, lii, 160
Ghil, René, 318, 425 n.21
Ghyka, Matyla, 317, 318, 413 n.71, 425 n.21
Gide, André, 219
Gil, René, 317
Girard, Abbot Gabriel, 149–50, 170, 173, 193,
387 n.32
glossogenetics, xxxix, li, lv
Godden, Richard, lxii n.59 n.60
Goldschmidt, Victor, 337 n.5, 341 n.53
Golius, Jacques, 43, 45, 46, 347 n.7
Gombrich, E. H., 427 n.42
Gomringer, Eugen, xlv
Graham, Joseph F., lxi n.43
grammar: as basis of ideal language; 222; as
basis of natural language, 203, 387 n.32;
classical, 144, 372; comparative, xxxvii,
179–88, 192–93, 262, 326, 330, 381 n.11, 382
n.16, 382–83 n.18, 383–84 n.25, 388 n.8, 389
n.24; as index to civilization, 186, 196, 198;
insignificance of, 11, 206, 264; neoclassical,
143–78, 183, 378 n.78; phonetic basis of, 57,
119. *See also* gender
Grammont, Maurice, 32, 319, 323, 328, 397
n.177
Grandval, Charles de, 379 n.92
graphic mimesis. *See* mimography
Greek, ancient, 13–27, 72–74, 81, 125, 180, 311,
339 n.24, 340–41 n.44, 357 n.67; alphabet, 55, 56, 70, 85, 110–11, 113, 116, 118, 409
n.29; ambiguity of *name* in, 338 n.14 n.19;
compared with Sanskrit, 183–85, 382 n.17;

conventional qualities of, 184, 219; and democracy, 313; gender, 303, 304; mimetic qualities of, xxvii–xxviii, 47, 102, 106, 352 n.6, 354 n.38; universality of, 66, 368 n.32; word order, 147, 150, 161, 176, 372 n.8

Green, Harriet C., 349 n.1

Greimas, A.-J., 365 n.64

Grimm, Jakob, 182, 304, 317, 318, 383 n.18, 384 n.26, 425 n.21, 427 n.39

Grüber, 318, 425 n.21

Guichard, 352 n.6

Guiraud, Pierre, 339 n.25

handwriting, 267, 405 n.34 n.36, 406 n.41, 407 n.51

Harris, James, 193, 303–4, 305, 307, 333, 376 n.57

Harris, Roy, lxii n.56, 338 n.18

Hebraicist thesis, 58, 125, 169–70, 190, 193–99, 350 n.12, 352 n.6, 379 n.92

Hebrew, 102, 304, 314, 361 n.13, 385–86 n.24; alphabet, xxix, xliii, 55, 56, 110–11, 409 n.29

Hegel, Georg Wilhelm Friedrich, xxvi, 198, 216, 391 n.60, 396 n.156, 429 n.67

Heidegger, Martin, 340 n.40

Heine, Heinrich, 306

Heraclitus, 7, 25

Herbert, George, xlv, lxiii n.63

Herder, Johann Gottfried, 139, 170, 175, 179, 186, 243, 314; on nouns versus verbs, 381 n.6; on origins of language, 181, 189, 355 n.50, 361 n.11

Hermogenes, 19–27, 85, 90, 296, 338 n.16; falseness of name, xxiii, 16; and innatist theory of language, xxxviii–xxxix; parti pris of, 187; position not purely conventionalist, xxv, 245–46. See also Cratylian tradition; Cratylus; Hermogenism (conventionalism); Plato, Cratylus

Hermogenism (conventionalism), xxiii, 7–12, 24, 26, 84, 356 n.59; arguments against, liv, 43–51, 106, 350 n.15, 393 n.89; excesses of, 327; and Formalist poetics, 238–41; intertwined with Cratylism, 88, 148, 185, 188, 215, 218, 229–30, 232, 236, 245–46, 260, 348 n.26, 375 n.45, 383 n.22; lexical demonstration of, 293, 356 n.50, 396 n.156; liberating value of, 239; logical difficulties of, 374 n.18, 373–74 n.17; in modern linguistics, xxv–xxvi,

xlix–li, 220–21, 262, 330–35; and plurality of natural languages, 213, 219, 357 n.67; rarity of pure examples of, xlvii; and Romanticism, 384 n.26; and symbolist theory, 220–22, 234, 265. See also Hermogenism, secondary

Hermogenism, secondary (secondary conventionalism), xxv, 51, 349 n.26. See also Hermogenism; Leibniz, Gottfried Wilhelm

Herodotus, 350 n.12

Hewes, Gordon, xxxix

hieroglyphs: as primeval alphabet, xxix, xxxv, xl–xliii, 91–114; versus Chinese ideogram, 45, 49, 84, 267; mimetic theory of, 53, 83, 220, 364 n.58, 376 n.53, 403–4 n.20; misunderstanding of, 350 n.14; poetry as, 161–62; rejection of, 116; as universal alphabet, 58–62, 86–87

Hippias, 341 n.53

Hjelmslev, Louis, 255, 273

Homer, 12, 17, 27, 214, 222, 336, 386–87 n.28

homonyms, 122, 266, 327

homophony, 218, 288, 294, 298, 400 n.15

Hopkins, Gerard Manley, 243

Horace, 152, 173

Horn, 11

Hugo, Victor, xxxvii, xlv, 217, 287, 312–17, 318, 319, 416 n.9, 425 n.21; on hieroglyphic alphabet, 282, 403–4 n.20, 410 n.32

Humboldt, Wilhelm von, 124, 179, 368 n.33, 384 n.26; on inflection, 183, 381 n.13, 382 n.17, 387 n.32

Huret, Jules, 216

Husserl, Edmund, 333, 428 n.62

hyperbaton, 165, 171, 373 n.11

hypertextual discourse, lv–lvi, lxvi n.100

iconicity, xlii, xliv–xlvii, l–lii, lxi n.49, lxiv n.85, lxiv–lxv n.89, 177, 235; Jakobson on, lxii n.51, 241

ideograms. See alphabet, ideographic; Chinese, writing system; Claudel; hieroglyphs; rebus

ideomimography, xxvii, xl, 53, 58, 114, 266

idioms, 124, 150, 175, 205–6, 212, 386 n.27

imitation, 5, 78, 108, 138, 237, 277. See also mimesis

Indo-European, 47, 93, 202; alphabet, xliii; conception of gender, 421 n.20; hypothesis,

Indo-European (*continued*)
66, 179–81, 187, 190, 192, 193–99, 206, 310, 348 n.18, 380 n.1, 385 n.7 n.22, 386 n.24
inflections, 164–65, 172, 179–88, 206, 378 n.84, 420–21 n.16; arbitrariness of, 383 n.22, 406 n.39; compensatory, 176; in history of Cratylism, 383–84 n.25, 387 n.32; valorization of, 352 n.6, 354 n.48, 380 n.4, 382 nn.16–18
Innocent III, Pope, xxxiv
intertextuality, xxix, xxxiii, xxxviii, lvi, lxv n.97 n.98
inversion: concept of, 156; quarrel over, li, 143–78, 184, 185, 217, 324, 334, 372 n.8, 373 n.10 n.11, 375 n.41, 377 n.63 n.64 n.67, 377 n.64 n.67, 378 n.88, 379 n.106
Irwin, John T., xli, lxiii n.63
Isidore of Seville, 29, 145, 373 n.9, 429 n.70
Italian, 120, 150, 151, 170, 173, 180, 192, 312

Jäger, Andreas, 348 n.18
Jakobson, Roman, 217, 223, 238–46, 262–63, 397 n.166 n.177; and chromatic value of vowels, 317–19; "Dialogues," lxiii n.79; *Essais de linguistique générale*, 322–23, 428 n.58; influence of Valéry on, 229–30, 242, 244–45, 395 n.127; "Linguistics and Poetics," xxxi–xxxii, lxiv n.80, 229–30; "Quest for the Essence of Language," lvi, lxiii n.77, lxiv n.83, 371 n.2; secondary mimologism of, l–liii, lxv n.92, 33, 382 n.18, 429 n.66
Japanese, xlvii
Jarrety, Michel, lxiii n.73
Jenisch, Daniel, 179
Jespersen, Otto, 15, 187, 309; on English, 40, 345 n.5, 346 n.9; and phonic symbolism, l, 346 n.9, 319–23, 326–30, 334, 391 n.51, 429 n.67; on primitive language, 424 n.13
Johnson, D. Barton, lxiv n.82
Jones, Rowland: account of, 350 n.11; and ideomimographic alphabet, xxviii–xxix, lvii, 53, 58–62, 84, 266, 269, 274; influence on Gébelin, 109, 364 n.56; on mimetic superiority of English, 58–59, 348 n.24, 350 n.13, 390 n.51; on origins of language, 350 n.15; and shift from mimophony to mimography, xl–xli, xlv; and visible speech, 117
Jones, Sir William, 380 n.1
Joubert, 301

Joyce, James, xlvii, 204, 345 n.5
Jung, Carl, 307
Jung, Hwa Yol, lxii n.61

Kant, Immanuel, 196, 295, 386 n.28
Kayser, Wolfgang, 347 n.15
Keightley, David N., lxii n.58
Kemp, J. A., 345 n.1
Keuneman, Katrine, lxv n.94
Khlebnikov, Velimir, 244
Kipling, Rudyard, 62, 429 n.71
Kircher, Athanasius, 45
Köhler, 321
Kopp, George A., 349 n.1
Koran, 195, 197
Kristeva, Julia, 398 n.190
Kruszowski, 428 n.58

Lacan, Jacques, 334, 363 n.37, 429 n.67
Lafont, R., 362 n.25
La Fontaine, Jean de, 376 n.56
Laharpian academicism, 174
Lamy, Bernard, 54, 345 n.1, 361 n.14, 367 n.30; and argument for Latin word order, 153–54, 155, 159, 178, 374 n.23; on diversity of languages, 175, 357 n.67, 380 n.111; on diversity of words, 398 n.191; *La Rhétorique*, 153, 374 n.30; on simultaneity of thought, 162, 178, 376 n.57
Landa, Diego de, lxii n.56
Landsberg, Marge E., lii, lxiv–lxv n.89
Langenbeck, K., 318, 425 n.21
language system, value and function of, xlviii, 259–60
Lanjuinais, 364 n.49
Laserstein, Paul-Gabriel, 389 n.26
Latin: alphabet, 55–56, 59, 83, 85, 116, 119, 120, 268; conventional qualities of, 219, 220, 325, 327; emancipation from, 41, 387 n.32; etymology, lviii, 29–35, 38, 80–81, 121, 128, 132, 293, 298, 357 n.67, 360 n.10, 369 n.48; gender in, 303, 304, 420 n.15; grammar, 29–35; mimetic qualities of, xxviii, 47, 61, 71–75, 77, 79, 102, 103, 106, 123, 180, 257, 285, 354 n.38; word order, 143–78, 185, 372 n.8, 374 n.23, 375 n.41, 377 n.64, 380 n.109
Lawler, James R., lxiii n.72
Legrand, 318, 425 n.21
Leibniz, Gottfried Wilhelm, xxviii, 72, 353

n.25; and Indo-European, 347-48 n.18, 380 n.1; quarrel with Locke, 43-51, 346 n.1, 350 n.15; and secondary conventionalism, xxv, 43-51, 139, 189, 222, 332, 346 n.5, 347 n.11, 348-49 n.26, 374 n.18; and unit of semantic analysis, 273

Leiris, Michel, 277-96, 365 n.63, 403 n.20; Genette's imitations of, xxxiii, lviii, 409 n.11; *Glossaire*, 290-91, 411 n.51; 413 n.70, 413-15 n.71; glossic method of, xxxi, xxxiii, 238, 334, 412 n.52 n.54 n.57; influence on Bachelard, 131, 301; influence on Ponge, 418 n.23; and mimologist tradition, 408 n.2; and "play between words," 278, 280, 284, 287, 289, 292-93, 410 n.35 n.36, 410-11 n.40, 411 n.44, 412 n.59; and Socratean eponomy, xxv-xxvi, xxxi, lviii-lvix n.6; and Surrealism, 412-13 n.60

Lejeune, Paul, 353 n.21

Lejeune, Philippe, 293-94, 413 n.62

Le Laboureur, Pierre, 146-47, 151, 154, 161, 164-65

Lessing, Gotthold Ephraim, 230, 242, 376 n.57

Lévi-Strauss, Claude, 187, 426 n.35

light, words for, xlvi, 314-15, 317-19, 328

linguistics, 143, 320-29; as counter to mimology, 141, 258, 262; eighteenth-century, 58; lexical, 66, 202-3; nineteenth-century, xliii, 193, 379-80 n.109; and psychology, liii, liv, lv, 305, 307, 317, 319, 322, 326, 331, 334; and rhetoric, 174-76; as stimulus to mimology, 336; structural, xxv, xxxii, xlviii-lv, lx n.38, 330-35

Littré, Émile, 298, 368 n.42, 416 n.9

Locke, John, xxxviii, lxii n.55, 350 n.15, 355 n.50; and controversy with Leibniz, 43-51, 346 n.1; and conventionalist tradition, li, lvii, 332, 345 n.24

Lovejoy, Arthur O., lx n.29

Lucretius, 357 n.67, 367 n.31

Lyons, John, xxxviii, lxi n.41, lxiv n.83

MacKenzie, Mary Margaret, lviii n.3

Malherbe, François de, 226, 246, 298

Mallarmé, Stéphane, 10, 80, 124, 130, 177, 201-18, 392 n.64, 388 n.5 n.18; and Claudel, 261-62, 263, 264, 403 n.17; "Crisis in Poetry," 212-17, 391 n.55; and Jakobson, 241, 242-43, 397 n.177; and Leiris, 277, 294, 414

n.71; *Les Mots anglais*, 201-12, 390 n.48 n.50, 391 n.51, 392 n.77; and Ponge, xlviii, 297, 301; and privileging of consonants, 313, 314, 363 n.41, 390 n.42; secondary mimologism of, xxxi, xlv-xlvii; and Valéry, 187, 221, 222-23, 225, 228, 230, 237, 393 n.79; on Wagner, 389 n.24. *See also* failing (*défaut*), of natural language

Martinet, André, 309, 320

Martini, 347 n.7

Martius, Galeotus, 54

Massieu, 135, 138

Mehlman, Jeffrey, 413 n.62

Meillet, Antoine, 419 n.9, 421 n.20, 423 n.26

Ménage, Gilles, 79

Mendeleev, Dmitri, 97

Méridier, Louis, 13, 17, 337 n.1 n.2 n.4, 338 n.7 n.10 n.11, 341 n.55

Merrim, Stephanie, lxv n.98

Mersenne, Marin, 348 n.26

Meschonnic, Henri, 366 n.5

metaphor: absence of, in Sanskrit, 186; as comparison between signifieds, 246; in construction of gender, 304-5, 421 n.20; as imitation of things, liv, 106, 108, 128, 237, 356 n.55; as intralinguistic mimesis, xxxii, lii, liii, 32, 84; in linguistics, 309; and motivation, 34; and poetry, 224, 264. *See also* metonymy

Metcalf, George J., 348 n.18

metonymy, lii-liii, liv, 204, 429 n.66; and derivation, 33, 80-81, 344 n.19; and metaphor, 67, 77-78, 245, 356 n.53, 424 n.13; and motivation, 12-13, 34, 235-36, 285. *See also* metaphor

Michelet, Jules, 197

Milton, John, 304

mimesis, 26, 65, 68, 75, 78, 104, 106, 121, 135, 209, 243, 355 n.48; articulatory, xxviii-xxix, xxx, xxxii, xxxix, xlii, lvix n.20, 23, 66-67, 75, 267, 321, 363 n.35 n.42, 363-64 n.45, 364 n.56, 366 n.11, 389 n.28; attacked, 239-40; contradictions of, xlvi-xlvii, 91-92, 238, 242-43, 333, 375 n.45, 396 n.156; diagrammatic, 382 n.18, 389 n.21; gestural, 20-21, 29; illusion of, in poetry, liv, 161, 237-38; indirect, xxxiv; perceptual, 356 n.54, 357 n.67; sentence level, 143, 169, 176; syntactic, 149, 167-68; vocal, 21, 76, 78, 79, 81, 88,

mimesis (*continued*)
116–17, 124, 331. *See also* mimography; mimophony; motivation; phonomimesis
mimography, xliv, l, 53–63, 261–76, 281–86, 299; absence of, 42, 119; combined with mimophony, xli–xlii, 113, 267, 286, 351 n.19; defined, xxviii; facticity of, 408 n.70; intertextuality of, xxix; in Mallarmé, 218; and mimology, 330; precariousness of, 83–84. *See also* handwriting; hieroglyphs; ideograms; ideomimography; mimotypography; phonomimesis
mimological tradition. *See* Cratylian tradition
mimologics: assessment of, 334–35; early use of term, lviii n.1; as literary genre, lvi, 335–36
mimologism. *See* mimology
mimology, xxii–xxiii, 5–6, 130, 177, 203, 265, 297, 345 n.5, 392 n.69, 414 n.71; contradictions of, 260, 261; displacements of, 50–51, 68, 187, 217, 275–76, 294, 300, 331, 384 n.26, 386 n.26; early use of term, xxxviii, lviii n.1, 126–27, 365 n.63; lexical, 15, 131, 203, 205, 211, 221, 222, 238, 282, 287, 298, 328–30, 331, 334, 389 n.21 n.30, 396 n.156; ludic, xxii–xxvii, xxxi–xxxiii, xliv, xlvi, lv, lvi, lvii, lviii, xlvii, 7, 19–20, 202, 266, 268, 299, 360 n.10, 364–65 n.63, 390 n.51, 408 n.70, 429 n.71; morpho–, 427 n.44; restrained, 330; return of, in modern writing, xxx–xxxiii, liv, 365 n.64, 403 n.15; Romantic, 10, 124, 139, 140–41, 246, 380 n.4, 384 n.26, 429 n.66; secondary, xxv–xxvi, xxx–xxxi, xxxv, xli, xlv, l, 26–27, 50–51, 54, 90, 118, 130, 177, 201, 205, 206, 214–15, 262–65, 299, 336, 345 n.5, 406 n.41, 414 n.71; sociobiological, xxxix, lii; subjective, 188, 211, 310–11, 420 n.14, syntactical, 143–44, 216–17; totalizing, 114, 124, 188, 279. *See also* Cratylism; mimological tradition
mimophony: in Cratylian tradition, xxiii, xliii, xlviii–lv, 19–20, 293, 389–90 n.40; definition of, xxiv–xxv, 53; Derrida's use of, xxvi–xxvii, xxxii; English and, 41–42; Genette's use of, xxxiii; intertextuality of, xxix; and mimography, xxviii, xl–xli, xlii, 54, 269; problems of, 24–26, 29, 31, 34–35, 109–12, 213, 323, 330; restricted, xlix, 309–36. *See*
also mimography; phonomimesis; sound symbolism
mimotypography, xxxi, xlv, xlvi, xlvii, lxiii n.63, lxiii n.76, 299–300
mistakes, xxiv, 25–26, 205, 212, 254, 277–79, 288, 290–91
Molière, Jean Baptiste Poquelin, 54, 267, 366 n.11
Monboddo, James Burnett, Lord, 367 n.31, 391 n.51
Montesquieu, Charles de Secondat, Baron de, 45, 99
Morgan, Thaïs E., lxv n.97
Morris, Charles William, 11
Most, Bernard, xxxix
mother tongue, 210–12, 352 n.6, 387 n.32, 390 n.50
motivation, xliv, xlviii–lv, 15, 24, 56–57, 188, 210, 246, 288, 296, 309, 344 n.20, 389–90 n.40; 384 n.26; by contiguity, 235–36; erasure of, 48; as gesture, xxxix; illusion of, in poetry, 161, 229–32, 295–96; and imitation, 92, 237, 396 n.151; indirect, xliii, xxvi, 251–52, 287, 293–94, 298, 299, 302, 334, 389–90 n.40, 400 n.15, 414 n.71; as instinct, 112, 365 n.63; metonymic, 12–13; morphological, 382–83 n.18; morphophonic, 18, 304–5; physical, 41, 208–9, 214; repression of, 171, 242–43, 325, 379 n.101, 397 n.178; and Romanticism, 384 n.26; semantic, 399 n.3, 400 n.12; switch between direct and indirect, lxv n.93, 19, 29–35, 39, 61, 65, 135, 144, 201, 267, 294, 389–90 n.40, 410 n.40; triggers for, 289; 384 n.26; by verbal analysis, 158, 204, 220. *See also under* etymology
Müller, Friedrich Max, xxxviii, lx n.39, 179, 339 n.25, 353 n.21, 389 n.24
Mure, Konrad von, 373 n.10
music, 57, 80, 254, 312; as imitative harmony, 130–31, 231, 261–62, 329, 348 n.26, 362 n.25; and poetry, xlvii, 140, 207, 218, 223–35, 246, 263, 274–75, 393 n.79; and speech, xlii, 21, 47, 94–100, 124–25, 213, 366 n.4; and word order, 164, 170

Nabobov, Vladimir, 317, 318, 425 n.17, 425 n.21
names, xxvi, xxxiii, lx n.32, 334, 413 n.63, 249–60, 290–91, 339 n.21, 392 n.64; biblical,

289–90; correctness of, xxiii, 288, 7–27, 261–62; diversity of, 121–22; family, 401 n.44, 401–2 n.54; ideal of language without, 222; for letters, 409–10 n.29; place, liii, 399 n.9 n.11, 400 n.12 n.15 n.16, 401 n.44, 402 n.58; and things, 9–10, 18, 44, 92, 116, 122, 211–12, 259–60, 297–98, 357 n.67, 358 n.71; truth of, xlix, 21, 131, 295. *See also* nicknames; nouns; eponymy; nomination

Nänny, Max, l, lxiii n.63, lxiv n.83

natural language, 45, 278, 369 n.44, 385 n.22; Eurocentric conception of, 66, 180, 199, 268; as foreign tongue, 211–14; gender in, 303–4; genius of, 144–78, 188, 193, 387 n.32; mimetic capacity of, 37–42, 59, 88, 323, 104–7, 326, 332, 352 n.6; mimetic inadequacy of, 25, 229–30, 329–34, 348 n.26, 381 n.11; plurality of, 202, 213, 219, 342 n.62, 357 n.67, 360 n.10, 368 n.32; and poetry, 130, 138–41, 175, 216, 263–65, 370 n.76, 371 n.19; reformation of, xxxv; shift from object to subject, 182–83, 189–90; writing as criterion of, 21, 53, 57, 119, 129. *See also* origins of language

Nelme, L. D., 351 n.23, 364 n.56

Nemours, Dupont de, 122

neologisms, 239, 244, 321, 323, 329, 345 n.5, 417 n.19

neurolinguistics, xxxviii–xxxix, li

nicknames, xxxi, 16–17

Nietzsche, Friedrich Wilhelm, 10

Nigidius, Publius, 29–30, 75

Nodier, Charles, xxxvi–xxxviii, lviii n.1, 115–41; account of, 365 n.1, 418 n.2; on consonants, 126, 209, 309, 368 n.40, 424–25 n.17; *Dictionnaire raisonnée des onomatopées françaises*, 115, 128, 131, 217, 265, 269, 301, 365 n.1 n.2, 408 n.1; on diversity of languages, xlii, 120–24, 179, 210, 358 n.67, 362 n.29, 367 n.26; etymological puns of, 369 n.48; in mimological tradition, 188, 220, 264, 301, 321, 325, 335, 336, 365 n.63, 368 n.33; and mimophonic interpretation, 285, 286, 302; and onomatopoeia, xxx, xlix, 124–36, 237, 269; and reform of language, 190, 215; on synaesthesia, 76, 135–38, 283, 355 n.50; on vowels, 124–26, 185, 300, 311, 313, 366 n.18, 368 n.36; and writing system, 54, 117–20, 370–71 n.77, 371 n.83

Norton Anthology of English Literature, xlv

nomination, xxxvi, xliv, 7–27, 67, 73–82, 288, 359 n.77

nouns, xxiii, xxxiii, xlix, 17–18, 295, 338 n.19; and negative words, 106; in Proust, 249, 399 n.3; valorization of, 65–66, 352 n.4, 413 n.63; versus verbs, 93, 182, 222, 334, 341 n.59, 361 n.11, 388 n.18. *See also* names; nomination

Novalis, 384 n.26

Nyrop, 397 n.177

Obélix, 380 n.109

Old French, 72, 135, 203, 365 n.64

Old Icelandic, 380 n.4

onomatopoeia: definition of, lviii n.1, 341 n.49, 356 n.59; fallibility of, 219, 354–55 n.48, 370 n.62; in Mallarmé, 209–11; as mimetic motivation, 31–34, 47, 72, 73–75, 237; and mimophonic motivation, 269–70, 301–2; in modern linguistics, xlix–l, 309, 321–28; in Nodier, xxx, xxxviii, 115–41, 265; and origins of language, 185–86, 190–91, 205, 369 n.44; and sibilants, 103–4. *See also* animal sounds

organic theories of language, 127, 128, 177–78, 184, 192, 197, 205

Oriental languages, xliii, 122, 125

Oriental alphabets, 100, 366 n.9

origins of language, xxviii, xxxii–xxxix, lvi, 27, 156, 201, 181, 326, 355 n.50; autochthonous, 120–27; in common primeval tongue, 92–94, 180–81, 189–99, 361 n.11; divine, 374 n.18, 384 n.2, 392 n.77; mimetic, xli, 30–33, 91–114, 124–27, 350 n.15, 391 n.51; objections to conventionalist theory of, 43–48, 373 n.17; writing and, 358 n.71. *See also* primitive language

Orphic poets, 14

Orr, John, 427 n.44 n.50

orthography, 410 n.32

overdetermination, 13, 14, 17

Pacific languages, 311, 313

painting: in mimological tradition, xxxv, xli–xlii, xlvi, 65–90, 92, 115–16, 177, 309, 364 n.56; of ideas, 101, 105, 106, 167; and speech, 331–32, 334, 356 n.51; superiority of French in, 147; and writing, xl, 108–9, 272, 358 n.70;

painting (*continued*)
and word order, 154-62. *See also under* de
Brosses
paleolinguistics. *See* origins of language
Palmer, Michael D., lviii n.2
Parain, Brice, 352 n.4
Parmenides, 25
Paronymy, 14-15, 204, 300
Parret, Herman, lx n.33
Parti pris (choosing sides), xlviii-lv, 267, 297-
300; in mimological thought, 6, 24, 183-84,
187, 333-34; national, 205, 350 n.13, 382 n.16.
See also under Hermogenes; nouns; vowels
Pascal, Blaise, 264, 330, 412 n.57
Paulhan, Jean, 199, 388 n.38
Peirce, C. S., lxi n.49, 235, 240, 396 n.156, 429
n.67
Pepin, 342 n.1
Perrault, 146
Persius, xxviii, xxix, 345 n.4, 353 n.25
Peterfalvi, 428 n.56
Petit Dictionnaire des mots retrouvés, 413-14
n.71
philology, xxiii-xxiv, lv, 191, 202, 266, 389 n.24
philosophical language. *See* artificial language
Phoenician, 77; alphabet, xxix, 85, 110, 111
phonematics, 21, 116, 130, 389 n.30
phonemes, 21, 23, 26, 97, 105, 114, 206, 216, 285,
323, 409 n.25; mimetic values ascribed to,
22, 213; redefinition of, 341 n.50, 428 n.58
n.62
phonetic evolution, 325, 328
phoneticism, lxii n.56, 97, 267, 350 n.14
phonetics, xl, xlii, l, 21, 22, 54-55, 57, 79, 117,
124, 331
phonology, lv, 31, 175, 323-32, 330-31, 333, 428
n.58. *See also* phonemes
phonomimography. *See* phonomimesis
phonomimesis, xxvii, xxx, 53-63, 67-68,
266, 269, 284-86, 349 n.2, 351 n.19. *See also*
mimophony
Phrygian, xxxvii, 350 n.12, 367 n.30
Pichon, Edouard, 419 n.7 n.9, 421-22 n.20, 422
n.23, 423 n.26
Pierce, C. S., lxiv n.83, 88, 143
Pietz, William, lxvi n.101
Plato, 353 n.25, 357 n.67, 386 n.27, 391 n.55,
402 n.59; *Cratylus*, xxi-xxvii, lxv n.93,
5, 7-27, 338 n.16; —, consonantal values

established in, 41, 71, 73, 104, 185, 209; —
as founding text, xxxiv, xxxvi, xli, xlviii,
336; —, linguistic Hellenocentrism of, 66,
124, 134, 210, 214, 390 n.50; —, theory of
imitation in, 53, 82, 105, 120, 294, 323, 326,
356 n.54; —, theory of motivation in, 29-
35, 39, 61, 65, 135, 144, 389-90 n.40; —,
sophism in, 10, 44; —, theory of names in,
74-75, 189, 190, 257, 259-60, 261, 284, 338-
39 n.21; *Euthydemus*, 337 n.4; *Parmenides*,
340 n.37; *Phaedrus*, 340 n.37; *Sophist*, 340
n.37; *Symposium*, 337 n.4; *Theaetetus*, 341
n.59. *See also* Cratylian tradition; Cratylus;
Cratylism; Hermogenes; Socrates
play. *See* mimology, ludic
Pluche, Abbot Noel Antoine, 159, 375 n.41, 377
n.64
Plutarch, 70, 370 n.76
poetic language, 212-47, 261-65; Bachelard
on, 301-8; Claudel on, 261-78, 394 n.97, 402
n.7; Diderot on, 161-62; and dream, 223-24;
idea of, absent in Batteux, 170; importance
of, in mimological tradition, xlv-xlvii, xlix,
l, lv-lviii, 141, 188, 229-31, 245-47, 331, 335-
36; Jakobson on, xxxi-xxxii, lxiv n.85, 394
n.97; 238-45, 395 n.127, 397 n.166; Leiris
on, 279, 291; Mallarmé on, xxx, 130, 201,
203, 212-18, 391-92 n.61, 392 n.73; Nodier
on, 138-41; and opposition between vowels
and consonants, 309-10; and precursors of
symbolism, 376 n.57; Sartre on, liii-liv, 232-
38, 262, 395-96 n.144, 396 n.158; Valéry on,
222-32, 394 n.119, 395 n.127 n.135. *See also
under* natural language
Poincaré, Raymond, 221
Polish, 312
Pomorska, Krystyna, lxiii n.79, lxiv n.81 n.85
Ponge, Francis, xxi, 297-300, 416 n.11 n.16;
account of, 415 n.1; and mimotypography,
xlvii-xlviii, lxiii n.76, 403 n.20
Pope, Alexander, 241-42
portmanteau words, 299, 345 n.5, 417-18 n.19
Port Royal, *General and Rational Grammar*,
146, 152, 183, 366 n.15
Portuguese, 357 n.67
Potter, Ralph K., 349 n.1
Pound, Ezra, xliii, 404 n.24
Praeconinus, Lucius Aelius Stilo, 29, 33, 343
n.8

Preckshot, Judith E., lxiii n.76
primitive language, 14, 15, 58–59, 166, 222, 310–14, 360 n.11, 383 n.22, 424 n.13. *See also* origins of language
Prince, Gerald, xix, lxv n.95
Priscianus, 145
Priscus, 145, 147
Proclus, 341 n.53
pronouns, 30, 182
Proudhon, Pierre Joseph, 304, 305, 419 n.8
Proust, Marcel, liii, lxv n.93, 131, 138, 223–24, 249–60, 280, 334; on common nouns, 12, 18, 399 n.3; and myth of Cratylist Proust, 217, 402 n.58 n.59, 429 n.71; on names of nobility, n.4, 401 n.44, 401–2 n.54; on place names, n.9 n.11, 400 n.12
Psammetichos (Psamtik I, King of Egypt), xxxvii, 123, 350 n.12, 367 n.30
puns, xxiv, xxxiii, 132, 369 n.61; Genette's, xxxiii, 338–39 n.21, 342 n.66, 390 n.50, 409 n.11; in Leiris, 290, 294, 411 n.50 n.51; in modern linguistics, 365 n.64; in Nodier, 369 n.48; in Ponge, 300, 416 n.16, 418 n.24; Surrealist, 412 n.59. *See also* wordplay
Pythagoreanism, 29, 97, 362 n.24

Quémar, Claudine, 400 n.26
Queneau, Raymond, 90
Quintilian, 34, 144, 146, 166, 372 n.4

Rabaté, Jean-Michel, xlvii, lxiii n.74 n.75
Racine, Jean Baptiste, 217
Radke, Judith, 418 n.24
Rask, Rasmus, 182, 380 n.4
reading, Cratylian view of, xlvii, 232, 302, 335
rebus, xxvi, xl, 74, 84, 116, 285, 291
referentiality, liii, lv, 11
Renan, Ernest, lxii n.57, 189–99, 380 n.109, 388 n.8, 416 n.9; ethnocentricity of, xlii, xliii, 193–99, 385 n.22, 386 n.27, 386–87 n.28; on gender, 304; *Life of Jesus*, 387 n.31; linguistic corpus of, 384 n.1, 385 n.16, 386 n.25 n.28; on origins of language, 189–91, 386 n.26; on plurality of languages, xxxvii, 191–93, 358 n.67, 385 n.22; subjective mimologism of, 420 n.14
Renard, Jules, 408 n.65
Renauld, Pierre, 389 n.24
Renoir, Jean, 429 n.69

repetition, 227, 239, 244, 246, 253–54
representation, xlvi, lviii, xlvii, 84, 331, 415 n.71
resemblance, l, lii, lxiv n.86. *See also* correspondence
reverie: in Bachelard, lv, lviii n.1, 301–8; in Claudel, 275–76; in de Brosses, 72; gender of, 301–8, 421 n.17; geomimological, xlii–xliii; in history of mimology, 178, 309, 399 n.11, 387 n.31, 408 n.70, 422 n.55, 423 n.28; in Leiris, 281, 287, 289; limitations of, 217; in Mallarmé, 202, 210, 214; mimographic, xli, 266–67; in Proust, liii, 249–60, 402 n.54; in Saussure, xxxii; in Valéry, 30, 219
rhetoric, 143–78, 264, 313, 353 n.13; and mimological tradition, xlix, lxiii n.76, 6; modern idea of, lii–liii; narrow definition of, 165, 174; and thought, 160–61, 163–64, 170–71, 174–75; tricks of, 140, 147–48, 196, 386 n.27. *See also* tropes, status of
Richard, Jean-Pierre, 206–7, 216, 348 n.22, 391 n.54, 392 n.71
Richards, I. A., liii, lxv n.92
Ricken, Ulrich, 372 n.3
Rimbaud, Arthur, xlv, lxiii n.64, 265, 274, 317, 318, 403 n.15, 425 n.21
Rivarol, Antoine, 66, 161, 172, 372 n.8
Robert, Louis, 259
Romance languages, 303, 427 n.50
Roudaut, Jean, 351 n.23, 355 n.50, 360 n.2
Rousseau, Jean-Jacques, xxxvii, 355 n.50; on natural expressiveness, 80, 139, 170, 376 n.56; on origins of language, lvix n.24, 148, 169, 311, 313, 373–74 n.17; and reverie, 423 n.25; on writing, 84, 85, 353 n.17, 358 n.71
Rousset, Jean, 376 n.57
Rudy, Stephen, lxiv n.85
Rue, Rachel, 341 n.55
Russian Formalism, liii, 238–47
Russian, 150, 311
Ruwet, Nicolas, lxv n.98
Rymer, Russ, lxi n.45

Sahlin, Gunvor, 377 n.64
Said, Edward, lxii n.57
Saint-Georges, David de, 115
Saint-Martin, Louis Claude de, 362 n.33, 373 n.17
Salignac, Mélanie de, 355 n.50

Samaritan alphabet, 110, 111, 364 n.58
Sanskrit, 176, 179, 180, 182, 183, 184, 186–87, 326, 380 n.109 n.1 n.4, 382 n.17
Sapir, Edward, xlix, 40, 196, 320, 362 n.25
Sartre, Jean-Paul, lvii, 232–38. *See also under* poetic language
Saül, 289
Saunderson, Nicholas, 76, 135, 136, 138, 355 n.50
Saussure, Ferdinand de, xxvi, xxxv, li, lxii n.56, lxiii n.78, 11, 176, 182, 233, 326, 338 n.18, 381 n.11, 396 n.156, 429 n.67; and conventionalist thesis, xxv, xxvi, xxxi, xl, xlix–l, lii, lxi n.43, 15, 18, 24, 50–51, 127, 178, 213, 220–21, 309, 332, 325–30, 335; and graphic values, 85, 117; mimologisms of, xxv, xxxii, lviii n.5, 13–14, 246, 292, 428 n.58, 428 n.62; and *parti pris*, 187; and plurality of natural languages, 92, 124, 219
Sautebin, Hippolyte, 351 n.23
Scaglione, Aldo, 372 n.3
Scaliger, Julius Caesar, 54, 378 n.76
Scandinavian languages, 219
Schlanger, Judith, 3
Schlegel, August Wilhelm von, 310, 317, 318, 384 n.26
Schlegel, Friedrich von, 150, 176, 384 n.2; influence on Renan, 189–97; on internal inflection, 177, 179–88, 380 n.4, 381 n.13, 382 n.16 n.17, 383 n.22; in mimological tradition, 178, 384 n.26; on Semitic languages, 386 n.25
Schleicher, 176, 184, 202
Schulenburg, Sigrid von der, 348 n.18
semantic analysis, changing unit of, 22–23, 26, 185, 220, 273, 298, 334
semantic values, lii, 206–7, 278, 322, 363 n.42
semiology, 50, 220, 221
semiotics, 235, 429 n.67
Semitic languages, xliii, 112, 189–99, 206, 310, 382 n.17, 385 n.7; ethnocentric view of, 69, 385–86 n.24, 386 n.27, 386–87 n.28, 387 n.31; and origins of language, 386 n.25 n.26. *See also* Hebraicist thesis; Hebrew
Senner, Wayne M., lxi n.50, lxii n.51 n.56 n.58
Servius, 145, 372–73 n.9
sexusemblance. *See* gender
Shakespeare, William, xxiii, li, 289
Shattuck, Roger, lxi n.44
sign, theory of, xxxiv–v, 114, 220, 232–38, 277–96

signifier: conventional character of, 148, 262, 330, 333; links with signified in mimological tradition, xxxv, liii, 117, 245, 246, 249–50, 252, 255, 258, 288, 300, 309, 327, 382 n.18, 399 n.11, 429 n.66
size, mimeticism of, xlix, 320–21, 324, 328–29, 427 n.50
slang, 168, 174, 347 n.11, 371 n.77, 396 n.144
Slavonian, 150
Socrates, 7–27, 31–35, 41, 338 n.16; on difference, 114, 333, 415 n.71; on elementary sounds, 20, 22–23, 344 n.21, 346 n.7, 348 n.26; eponymies of, xliii, 12–18, 24–25, 34–35, 62–63, 73, 238, 257, 259, 292–94, 298, 367–68 n.32, 417 n.19; on error, xlii, 7–12, 24–26, 107, 205, 331; on essences, 356 n.54; intertextuality of, xxxviii, 62; ironies of, xxxiii, 337 n.2, 429 n.71; Leiris's reversal of, 295–96; Mallarmé's reversal of, xxx, 209, 213–14; mimological journey of, xxvii–xxviii, liii, lvi, 48–49, 91, 260; and modern linguistics, xlix; and motivation, 16, 65, 396 n.151; secondary mimologism of, 26–27, 51, 90
sound and sense: discord between, 216, 219, 330, 397 n.177; harmony between, 180, 249–60, 328; poetic mediation between, xlvii, 229–31, 242, 245, 261–63, 266, 395 n.127
sounds, of language, 37–42, 215, 225–26, 334; conventional value of, xlvi, 331, 349 n.26; mimetic value of, xxxv, xlix, 97, 104, 324, 355 n.50. *See also* consonants; mimophony; onomatopoeia; phonetics; phoneticism; sound symbolism; vowels
sound symbolism, xxix, xxxiii, xlix, xlviii, l–liii, 31, 320–21. *See also* mimology; mimophony; synaesthesia
South American languages, 367 n.31
Spanish, 150, 151, 170, 180, 329, 357 n.67; alphabet, 110, 111, 150, 151
speech: and contradictions of conventionalist argument, 148, 169, 374 n.17; conventionalist view of, 348–49 n.26; ethnocentric view of, 196; harmony of, in primitive language, 97–98; in mimological tradition, xxxiii, xlii, 53, 76, 106–7, 115–41, 156, 167, 360 n.6; restricted role of, in modern poetics, 205, 218, 228, 230, 263, 428 n.62; Socratic idea of, 21; versus writing, 371 n.77, 404 n.24; "visible," 117, 267, 349 n.1. *See also* mimesis,

articulatory; mimophony; rhetoric; sounds, of language; writing
Spivak, Gayatri C., 423 n.28
Stam, James H., lxi n.40, lxvi n.102
Stammering, 169, 199
Stankiewicz, Edward, 381 n.6
Starobinski, Jean, lviii n.5
Steiner, Wendy, xlv
Stendhal, 251, 301
Stewart, Dugald, 179
Stoicism, 29–35, 342 n.1, 343 n.9 n.11 n.15
Strabo, 370 n.76
Structuralism, l, liii, lvi, 381 n.11
Sturrock, John, lviii–lvix n.6
stylistics, 162, 175
Surrealism, lvix n.6, 292–93, 413 n.64, 414 n.71
Sweet, Henry, 349 n.2
Swift, Jonathan, lvi–lvii, lxvi n.102, 333
symbolism, 76, 141, 234, 245, 246, 265, 376 n.57, 384 n.26, 398 n.190, 429 n.67
synaesthesia, 32, 76–77, 104, 136–37, 253, 355 n.50; modern valuation of, l, 280–81, 283, 320, 323, 425 n.17
synecdoche, lii, liv, 33, 77, 108, 278, 343 n.17, 344 n.19, 359 n.73
syntagmatic analysis, 14, 39–40, 178, 182
syntax. *See* inversion

Taylor, Talbot J., lxi n.42
Tchang Tcheng-ming, B., 267
Tel Quel, 230
Terence, 145
Thibaudet, Albert, 217, 310
Thomas, François 144–45
Thomassin, 352 n.6
Thommerel, J.-P., 203
Thoreau, Henry David, xli
Thucydides, 372 n.8
Todorov, Tzvetan, xxxiv–xxxv, 13, 322, 339 n.22, 376 n.57
Tory, Geoffroy, xxviii, xxix, 54, 345 n.4
Tournier, Michel, 422 n.23
Tracy, Destutt du, 173, 197
transcription, electronic, 54
translation, 198, 204, 222, 227, 228, 324
transposition, 150–51, 155–56, 168, 356 n.61
transtextuality. *See* intertextuality
tropes, status of, xxxvi, xlviii, lii–liii, 34, 77, 171, 230, 386 n.27

Troubetskoy, 428 n.58
Truffaut, François, xxxix
Turgot, A. R. J., 80, 187, 189, 354 n.38; conventionalism of, 345 n.24, 356 n.59, 373–74 n.17; on synaesthesia, 355 n.50
typography. *See* mimotypography

Ullmann, Stephen, 34, 397 n.178
Ulmer, Gregory L., lvix n.12
universal language. *See* artificial language; natural language
Upward, Alan, xliii
Usage, xli, 166, 169, 329
utopian fiction, lxvi n.99

Valéry, Paul, 218–32; conventionalist position of, 393 n.89; echoes of, in Sartre, 235, 237–38; influence of Mallarmé on, 217, 393 n.79; nominalism of, lxiii n.73, 30; polar axiology of, 222–23; on special status of poetic language, xlvii, 141, 262, 265, 309, 394 n.97 n.101 n.103 n.119, 395 n.125 n.135. *See also under* Jakobson
Vallot, Jacques-Nicolas, 371 n.83
Van Helmont, Franciscus Mercurius, Baron, 55
Varèse, Edgar, 429 n.69
Varro, Marcus Terentius, 29, 30, 298
Vaulchier, Henri de, lxi n.48
Vendryès, Jean, 257
verbs, 11, 65, 244, 360 n.11, 381 n.6, 392 n.64 n.76. *See also* nouns, versus verbs
Verlaine, Paul, 201
Viansson-Ponté, Pierre, 362 n.25
Vico, Giovanni Battista, 139, 170, 175, 357–58 n.67, 358 n.71, 371 n.83; influence on Gébelin, 360 n.1 n.11
Viélé-Griffin, Francis, 215, 263, 391–92 n.61
Villemain, Abel-François, 203
Virgil, li, liv, 145, 155, 173, 348 n.26, 372–73 n.9
vocables: analysis of, 11, 24, 269, 298, 417 n.19; mimological status of, 25, 33, 35, 41, 61, 204, 212, 238, 277, 278, 286, 287, 334, 399 n.9; and natural language, 105, 221, 348 n.26
Volney, Constantin-François, 367 n.30
Voltaire (François-Marie Arouet), 79–80, 172, 212, 342 n.69, 379 n.104
Vossius, 34
vowels: chromatic value of, 399 n.11; versus consonants, xlii–xliii, 79–80, 94–97, 99,

vowels (*continued*)
125–26, 195, 213, 274, 302, 309–36, 341 n.56, 351 n.21; erosion of category of, in modern period, 274–75, 283–84, 299–300; ethnocentric view of, xlii–xliii, 99, 195, 197, 206, 385–86 n.24; figured by consonants, 352 n.13; and gender, 304, 335; graphic value ascribed to, xlviii, 55–56, 59–61, 85–86, 117, 267, 352 n.13, 353 n.15, 361 n.15; mimetic value ascribed to, xlix, 265, 354 n.38, 427 n.44; sounds of, 37, 327–29, 368 n.36, 425–46 n.23; unequal to consonants 40–41, 68–73, 100–105, 362 n.33, 363 n.41
voyage, mimologics as, xxi, lv–lviii, 27, 335–36, 416 n.14, 417–18 n.19

Wachter, Johann Georg, xlvii, lvii, 70, 117, 118, 364 n.56; account of, 349 n.9; influence of phoneticism on, 274; phonomimography of, 53, 55–57, 58, 60, 85, 117, 118, 266–67. *See also under* de Brosses
Wagner, Richard, 202, 388 n.5
Wallis, John, xxviii, 37–42; account of, 345 n.1; compared with Mallarmé, 205, 206, 208, 210–11, 389 n.26, 390 n.45 n.50 n.51; on consonants, xxx, 185, 206; and mimological tradition, xxxi, xxxii, lvii, 345 n.5, 389–90 n.40; and phonetic analysis, xxxv, 59, 73, 120; and reaction against Latin, 151; valuation of English, 205, 206, 350 n.13, 346 n.10

Warburton, William, 82, 108, 358–59 n.72
Waugh, Linda R., lxiv n.81 n.85
Werth, Elizabeth, 318, 425 n.21
Wescott, Roger Williams, li, lii, lxiv n.87
West, Michael, lxii n.55, 329
Whorf, Benjamin, 196, 319, 321, 397 n.177
Wieger, Leon, 267
Whitney, 332
Wilkins, John, 43, 45, 47, 49, 59, 346 n.5, 349 n.26
Winspur, Steven, xliii
word order. *See* inversion
wordplay, 30, 183, 204, 276, 298, 335, 387 n.31, 413 n.64; and etymology, 62–63; and fictitious mimologism, 264–65. *See also under* Leiris; puns
writing system (*écriture*), xl–xlviii, 260, 261–76, 281–86, 359 n.73, 406 n.41; importance of consonants in, 313, 353 n.17; and mimography, 53–63, 78–79, 82–90, 91, 106–14, 408 n.68 n.70; and mimophony, lxii n.56, 80, 108, 115–20, 130, 132, 195, 261–76, 358 n.71, 371 n.77, 402 n.7

xenoglossia, lxvi n.99

Yaguello, Marina, lxv n.99

Zumthor, Paul, 292, 339 n.25, 429 n.70